The Church's Liturgy

AMATECA
Handbooks of Catholic Theology

AMATECA is an international series of Handbooks of Catholic Theology, initiated by Eugenio Correcco and Christoph Schönborn. To date, it comprises 22 volumes in 10 languages. As representatives of university theology and members of the Church, the authors strive to maintain a proper balance in the treatment of controversial subjects in light of the belief of the Church and its magisterium. The foundations of the series, guaranteeing the theological identity of the individual volumes, are to be found in the theologies of Hans Urs von Balthasar and Henri de Lubac.

THE CHURCH'S LITURGY

Michael Kunzler

Translated by
Placed Murray OSB, Henry O'Shea OSB, Cilian Ó Sé OSB
Monks of Glenstal Abbey, Ireland

Continuum
London New York

First published in North America and the United Kingdom 2001 by

The Continuum International Publishing Group Inc
370 Lexington Avenue, New York, NY 10017

The Continuum International Publishing Group Ltd
The Tower Building, 11 York Road, London SE1 7NX

First published in Continental Europe 2001 by
LIT VERLAG Münster – Hamburg – Berlin – London
Grevener Str. 179   D-48159 Münster

Originally published as *Die Liturgie der Kirche*
© 1995 by Bonifatius GmbH Druck – Buch – Verlag, Paderborn/Jaca Books, Milano

English translation and English language edition © 2001 by LIT VERLAG

Printed in Germany

Library of Congress Cataloging-in-Publication Data

Kunzler, Michael.
  [Liturgie der Kirche. English]
  The church's Liturgy / Michael Kunzler
    p. cm. - - (Handbook of Catholic theology)
  Includes bibliographical references and index.
  ISBN: 0-8264-1352-8 - - ISBN 0-8264-1353-6 (pbk.)
  1. Catholic Church- -Liturgy. I. Title. II. Series. BX1970.K8613 2001
  264'.02–dc21
                                              2001042150

CONTENTS

PREFACE

The AMATECA enterprise of manuals continues with the present tenth volume, which treats of the liturgy of the Church. Students of theology have to be introduced to the history, the contemporary shape and the systematic theological study of worship. They must be made familiar with the finished structures, with the spiritual demands of liturgical celebrations and also with the question of the shape of the liturgy of tomorrow.

Above and beyond all changes of time, above all cultural differences, the fact holds good that the Church's worship is only possible as the response to the service which the triune God has rendered and continues to render it. Worship is first of all God's service to the Church, his work for the many brothers and sisters of his Son; for the Church's liturgy is only possible as the response to God's action. "God needs nothing, but man needs communion with God. It is the glory of man to remain and persevere in the service of God." (Irenaeus of Lyons, Adv. haer. IV, 14, 1.)

This is why the thought of the life-giving, indeed divinizing communication between God and man forms a guide as it were through the entire work. The first part treats of God's descent to man, of the catabatic dimension of worship as an invitation to man to enter into the fullness of divine life. The second part has as its theme the follow up of this invitation, man's ascent to God, the anabatic dimension of worship.

If these two first parts constitute so to speak "general liturgy", then in parts 3 – 6 there follow the themes of special liturgy: the celebration of the Eucharist, the sacraments and sacramentals, the liturgy of the Hours and liturgy of the Word, as also the year of the Lord.

Doubtless in the present book it is a question of communicating knowledge. But still more the love of worship, of God's service to the many ("liturgy") and of the service of the many faithful to the greater glory of God ("liturgy") must be aroused and strengthened, so that in the midst of our world the presence of the heavenly liturgy can be experienced. The essential thing is to enter into it, so that people and through them the whole world can have a share in the glory of the creator and redeemer and so find their ultimate worth and beauty. Hence let the prayer from the liturgy of St Basil which opens the *Archieratikón* (Pontifical) of the Greek Church, be placed also in the front of this book, and addressed to all Christians – prior to all hierarchical differentiation- as called to the celebration of the liturgy.

Κύριε ὁ Θεὸς ἡμῶν, ὁ κτίσας ἡμᾶς καὶ ἀγαγών εἰς τὸ ζωὴν ταύτην, ὁ ὑποδείξας ἡμῖν ὁδοὺς εἰς σωτηρίαν, ὁ χαρισάμενος ἡμῖν οὐρανίων μυστηρίων ἀποκάλυψιν καὶ θέμενος ἡμᾶς εἰς τὴν διακονίαν ταύτην, ἐν τῇ δυνάμει τοῦ Πνεύματός σου τοῦ Ἁγίου, εὐδόκησον δή, Κύριε, τοῦ γενέσθαι ἡμᾶς διακόνους τῆς καινῆς σου Διαθήκης, λειτουργοὺς τῶν ἁγίων σου Μυστηρίων.

Lord our God, who created us and led us to this life, who has shown us ways to salvation, who has graced us with the revelation of heavenly mysteries and has placed us in this service, make us worthy, Lord, in the power of your Holy Spirit to become servants of your new covenant, 'liturgists' of your holy mysteries.

My heartfelt thanks to Frau Gertrud Fickinger and Herr cand. Theol. Michael Bre-deck for their valuable services in bringing this book to completion.

Paderborn, Autumn 1994

Michael Kunzler

> *Carolo Etscheid et Hermanno Helmig Trevirensibus,*
> *Gerhardo Lachmann Paderbornensi*
> *Patribus spiritualibus dedicatum*

Part I

Catabasis: God's Descent to Man

We profess in the Creed, "For us men and for our salvation, he came down from heaven." Without this descent (*'Catabasis'*) of the Son of God into the world and into the life of men, there can be no redemption and hence no salvation: this is the foundation of the Christian faith. Man can be redeemed only because God himself assumes the initiative, while "One of the Trinity, without changing himself, becomes man," as a hymn of the Byzantine Eucharist puts it. A share in the fullness of divine life for the mortal creature is conceivable only as God's gift. If the Church's liturgy claims to be powerful for the salvation of men, then this can only be so under the aspect of the divine *Catabasis*. What happened once for all in the Incarnation and redemptive work of Christ, comes to pass daily in the liturgical actions of the Church. In them there takes place God's *Catabasis*, in which the triune God assumes the initiative, and acts for the salvation of men.

1.1. A "THEOLOGICAL TURNING-POINT" IN LITURGICAL SCHOLARSHIP?

1.1.1. ON THE "ANTHROPOLOGICAL TURNING-POINT" IN THEOLOGY

To be sure, it is impossible to affix a neat label on the multifarious theological developments of the 20th century; nevertheless time and time again the "anthropological turning-point" is mentioned as the characteristic of the newer theology. At times this term is taken as marking a break in theological thinking, which separates the period of the Council and the post-conciliar time from a theology of the preceding periods, less centred on man. Whatever may be intended by the term "turning-point", the phrases "anthropological turning-point / anthropocentric turn" go back to Karl Rahner.

According to Rahner, "anthropological turning-point" means specifically that every discourse about God and divine revelation is based on a transcendental questioning of man about himself. This is not a quest for an increase of knowledge, which one could dispense with if needs be, without suffering damage to life, because "God is not an object alongside others in the *a posteriori* experiential human area, rather he is the original ground, the absolute future of all reality."[1] Theology must always speak of the salvation of man, and therefore it must start with him, with his questions and with the world in which he asks questions and which drives him to questioning. Man has always been oriented towards absolute Being; he himself is a part of the world, in which he lives, and this world accordingly drives him to ask what lies beyond the merely worldly experience of life and of the world. World history therefore is no "continuous history of apostasy from the Christian faith," rather in each of its periods it sets theology anew the task of communicating religious truths to men of various times in a human way.[2] However necessary the anthropological turning point is in theology according to Rahner, however much it seeks to establish a new theology corresponding to the "epoch-making situation of today",[3] it has not remained unopposed.

---

[1]   Rahner, Theologie und Anthropologie 50.
[2]   Cf. Fries, Theologie als Anthropologie 55.
[3]   Cf. Rahner, Theologie und Anthropologie 55f., where reference is also made to the work by Metz.

Scheffczyk warns of its closeness to existential philosophy.[4] Pannenberg sees that the danger exists of an "anthropocentric grip on theology ", a danger that "in theology man is occupied only with himself, instead of with God, and as a result misses the actual subject of theology"[5]. Finally, Häußling would not rule out the possibility that "the 'anthropological turning-point of theology' stands as a symbol of the inability to believe in God at all. "[6] In spite of the dangers, the one-sidedness and narrowing effect, Pannenberg argues persistently in favour of an anthropologically centred theology.[7]

Häußling also points out the weaknesses of Rahner's sacramental theology. "The sacrament is not experienced as coming from outside, rather it lays open inner structures of the *actus humanus* 'faith'.[8] Can Rahner really maintain the importance for salvation of the sacraments and with them of all the liturgical actions of the Church? "But it is a distinctive weakness of this thinking, to be unable to say clearly and simply enough, why the sacraments exist at all – unless of course, it be enough, that they are a "model of the revealing, definitive Word in the Church" – and how in them the Christian participates in something, which he does not otherwise already possess or even (so occasional statements suggest) possesses much better, in an absolutely different, because obviously more appropriate, way, namely in the pure decisiveness of a dedication to the faith, which grips the whole person. If this observation be true, then the conclusion must be drawn: in the sacraments man is called to a collaboration, which basically does not take him seriously, because he is bringing himself into something, where actually he is already, and from which in fact that which he is to collaborate in doing, draws its power.[9]

1.1.2. THE DOWNWARD (CATABASIS) TURNING-POINT
IN LITURGICAL THEOLOGY

A liturgical theology must also begin with man. Häußling is of opinion that a hitherto rather "*catabasis* understanding of the sacraments" is, in Rahner's case, corrected by an "*anabasis* point of view".

Two concepts are hereby named which are significant for post-Vatican liturgical theology: C*atabasis* and *Anabasis*. They describe, in complementary fashion, the essence of liturgy as dialogue between God and man. Only the divine descent (*catabasis* or salvation [redeeming] aspect) renders possible the human ascent (*anabasis* or worshipping [adoring] aspect of liturgy) in praise, petition and celebration. "The conciliar description of liturgy under both aspects in Article 7 can scarcely be rated high enough in its significance."[10] Liturgy is "an exercise of the priestly office of Jesus Christ. It involves the presentation of man's sanctification under the guise of signs perceptible by

---

4   Cf. L. Scheffczyk, Die Frage nach der Gottebenbildlichkeit in der modernen Theologie: Ibid. (ed.), Der
     Mensch als Bild Gottes. Darmstadt 1969 (Wege der Forschung CXXIV), IX-LIV. IX-XI.
5   Pannenberg, Anthropologie in theol. Perspective 15.
6   Cf. A. A. Häußling, Odo Casel – Noch von Aktualität? Eine Rückschau in eigener Sache aus Anlaß des
     hundersten Geburtstages des ersten Herausgebers, ALw 28 (1986) 357 – 387. 362.
7   Cf. Pannenberg, ib., 16.
8   Häußling, Odo Casel – Noch von Aktualität? 372. See also at the same time Rahner, Theologie und
     Anthropologie 63f.
9   Häußling, ib., 379f.
10   E. J. Lengeling, Die Konstitution des Zweiten Vatikanishes Konzils über die heilige Liturgie. Lateinisch-
     deutscher Text mit einem Kommentar von Emil Joseph Lengeling. Münster. 2nd edn., 1965 (Lebendiger
     Gottesdienst 5/6), 26.

the senses and its accomplishment in ways appropriate to each of these signs. In it full public worship is performed by the Mystical Body of Jesus Christ, that is, by the Head and his members. From this it follows that every liturgical celebration, because it is an action of Christ the Priest and of His body, which is the Church, is a sacred action surpassing all others. No other action of the Church can equal its efficacy by the same title and to the same degree" (SC 7). Liturgy is dialogue: "On God's part the gift of salvation in word and sacrament (the performance of which is ... liturgical action and event, and indeed not only in so far as it is surrounded by acts of the minister and recipient, mounting up to God) and the response of the graced man to God. Both aspects are to be found in every liturgical action." [11]

Both aspects, the *catabasis*-salvation and the *anabasis*-worshipping are only two modes of viewing the one and same reality. God does not need honour as a (worshipping) achievement by man. He is honoured when man has life, when his divine *doxa* proves its power by the fact of giving man a share in his fullness of life. Or as Irenaeus of Lyons would say: "The glory of God is man fully alive, the life of man is the vision of God." [12] The unity of *Catabasis* and *Anabasis*, of *soteria* and *latreia* consists of the communication of divine life to man and his insertion into the divine fullness of life. [13] If God's honour consists in the fact that man in dialogue with his Maker, in the participation in his fullness of life arrives at the perfection of his being, then this exchange of life can only be initiated by God. Consequently it is *Catabasis* which makes *Anabasis* possible, *soteria latreia*. Therefore according to Lengeling "the essential priority of God's 'honour' " in no way contradicts "the existential priority of the saving aspect": [14] God exists, he comes forth to man out of the inaccessible light of the divine life, in order to draw him into the fullness of life of the Trinity. This is why Christ came (John 10:10). The dialogic definition of liturgy seems at first sight to be less theocentric than a purely cultic one, which has chiefly in view the honouring of God by man in exterior acts. "In reality however the prevailing point of view in (earlier) catechisms (from the first question on: 'Why are we on earth ... '), very clearly represented in liturgists etc. and the mentality of clergy and people up to now, was rather anthropocentric: we honour God, so that we may get grace and some day come to heaven." [15] In other words, the turning from a cultic to a dialogic definition of liturgy, as it becomes unequivocally noticeable in the liturgy Constitution, is a "theocentric" or "*catabasis*" one.

1.1.3. THE ANTHROPOLOGICAL AND CATABASIS TURNING POINTS
VIEWED TOGETHER

Are the anthropological turning-point in theology and the *catabasis* oriented view of liturgy opposed to one another? An anthropologically oriented theology can no more ignore a divine initiative which precedes all human thinking and action than does the definition of liturgy which is *catabasis* oriented. Discourse about God and the divine truths is only possible, because God has turned to men in revelation. The God who

---

[11] E. J. Lengeling, Werden und Bedeutung der Konstitution über die heilige Liturgie, Die Konstitution des Zweiten Vatikanisches Konzils über die heilige Liturgie. Lateinisch-deutscher Text mit einem Kommentar von Emil Josep h Lengeling. Münster. 2ⁿᵈ edn., 1965 (Lebendiger Gottesdienst 5/6), 37*-98*. 79*.

[12] Adv. haer. IV, 20,7 – SChr 100, 648: "Gloria enim Dei vivens homo, vita autem hominis visio Dei".

[13] Cf. Lengeling, Grundvollzug 71; Werden und Bedeutung 80*.

[14] Lengeling, Grundvollzug 71.

[15] Lengeling, Werden und Bedeutung 80*.

comes to men in relationship is he who first of all makes possible the human quest for him, the speaking and thinking about him, as well as the human praying to him, praise, complaint and celebration. [16] Without the assumption of this prior downward dimension all theological discourse, indeed the whole religious disposition of man would be exposed to the suspicion that it is nothing else but the proof of a basic alienation of self or even of the psychical pathology of man as understood in Feuerbach's taunt about projection. [17] There remains only the following alternative for both – for the anthropologically centred theology of our time, just as for the definition of liturgy understood as dialogue of Vatican II – either it is accepted in faith and celebrated, that God is acting for man's salvation, that a divine descent comes about which invites to enter into the fullness of life, or religion and worship are counted among the singular phenomena of man, which is the research area of anthropology – and thereby also his strange inclination to believe, to pray and to celebrate.

From the standpoint of Eastern theology there can be no "anthropological turning point", unless theological thinking had gone astray beforehand. The whole of theology never had nor has another subject than the theandric (incarnational) basic principle of the whole economy of salvation: "for us men and for our salvation." An "anthropological turning-point" of theology, of which its opponents could say that in it there is too much talk of man and too little of God, can only be the swing of the pendulum in the opposite of another extreme, of a mere intellectual speculation about the supreme Being, withdrawn from human life and existing without reference to it. [18] Evdokimov is right in referring to the basic theandric principle of the economy of salvation and thus also of theology as the 'Principle of equilibrium'. [19] Precisely from the theandric viewpoint one cannot speak enough about man, but not about man as alienated from God, as he happens to be now – and here the 'anthropological turning-point' can in fact stand as a symbol for 'unbelief' –, nor yet about man at the cost of speaking about God, but as theological discourse about man in the relationship with God which always precedes his existence, with God who created him as a theandric being, who comes to terms with himself in deification.

There is then no other choice except for an anthropological theology which genuinely claims this title for itself, to presuppose a divine initiative, likewise for a theocentric orientated understanding of liturgy, which understands the glory of God as *catabasis*, never to lose sight of man, in whose salvation the glory of God consists. This is not reconcilable with a cultic, one-sided, *anabasis* and hence anthropocentric understanding of liturgy: 'In Christian liturgy the service which is in question in the first place is that which God does for us. God's service is what demands our service, and makes it possible.' [20]

---

[16] Cf. Wainwright, Der Gottsdienst als Locus Theologicus 250: "Liturgy is a 'unique action', in which God and man communicate with one another, to be precise, by means of verbal, material and dramatic signs which were instituted by God through Christ and are now used by the faithful in spiritual obedience".

[17] Cf. Pannenberg, Anthropologie in theol. Perspektive 15.

[18] Cf. Häußling, Odo Casel – Noch von Aktualität? 362, who says of Casel "he had in so far welcomed an anthropological turning-point, as that thereby mere speculation about the highest object of the intellect had found an end."

[19] Cf. P. Evdokimov, L'Orthodoxie, Paris 1979, 13f.

[20] Wainwright, Der Gottsdienst als Locus Theologicus 249.

Bibliography

Y. Congar, La Liturgie après Vatican II. Bilans, études, perspectives, Paris 1967.

P. Eicher, Die anthropologische Wende. Karl Rahners philosophischer Weg vom Wesen des Menschen zur personalen Existenz, Fribourg 1970.

G. Ferretti, La filosofia della religione come antropologia in un' opera di Karl Rahner, Rivista di filosofia neoscolastica 51 (1964) 95 – 106.

H. Fries, Theologie als Anthropologie, K. Rahner/H. Fries (eds.): Theologie in Freiheit und Verantwortung, München 1981.

F. Gaboriau, Le tournant théologique aujourd'hui selon K. Rahner, Tournai 1968.

B. van der Heijden, Karl Rahner. Darstellung und Kritik seiner Grundpositionen, Einsiedeln 1973.

E. J. Lengeling, Liturgie als Grundvollzug christlichen Lebens, B. Fischer / E. J. Lengeling / R. Schaeffler / F. Schulz / H. R. Müller-Schwefe, Kult in der säkularisierten Welt, Regensburg 1974, 63 – 91.

J. B. Metz, Christliche Anthropozentrik. Über die Denkform des Thomas von Aquin, München 1962.

W. Pannenberg, Anthropologie in theologischer Perspektive, Göttingen 1983.

K. Rahner, Theologie und Anthropologie, Schriften zur Theologie VIII, EinsiedelnZürich-Köln 1967, 43 – 65.

C. Vagaggini, Lo spirito della costituzione sulla Liturgia, Costituzione sulla S. Liturgia, Torino 1964, 549.

G. Wainwright, Der Gottesdienst als 'Locus Theologicus', oder: Der Gottesdienst als Quelle und Thema der Liturgie, KuD 28 (1982) 248 – 258.

1.2. THE PROBLEMATICAL CONCEPT OF 'CULT' – OR: WHAT IS THE POINT OF WORSHIP AT ALL?

When liturgy is understood dialoguewise as communication between God and man, then a one-sided cultic understanding of worship is surmounted. 'Cult' is a problematical concept. Guardini in 1964, only a year after the publication of the Liturgy Constitution, called into question in principle present-day man's 'capacity for cult', and feared that modern man may be to a large degree incapable of evolving 'an elementary awareness of the symbolic content of existence'.[21] On the other hand Corbon speaks of a 'cultic temptation', which affects particularly the faithful of fundamentalist views: the exercise of cult is the third duty of the human creature towards his Creator God, along with faith in truths which must be believed, and the keeping of commandments which have to be observed.[22]

1.2.1. THE QUESTION AT ISSUE

'Will liturgy last?' Müller asks the fundamental question and sees the survival of liturgy made uncertain by the following ways of thinking:

---

[21] Cf. R. Guardini, Der Kultakt und die gegenwärtige Aufgabe der liturgischen Bildung. Ein Brief, LJ 14 (1964) 101 – 106; also revised in R. Guardini, Liturgie und liturgische Bildung, Würzburg 1966, 9 – 18.

[22] Corbon, Liturgie aus dem Urquell, 109.

1. Liturgy consists of outward actions, which have no purpose other than to express the worship of God by men. But have these actions any proper value in view of a 'transcendental worship of God', which takes place in a Christian life following out the will of God? Is not then the practice of love of neighbour true worship, and does not the liturgical celebration serve above all for motivation and encouragement? Is liturgy perhaps only a show necessary for pedagogical reasons, aimed not at God, but rather at men?

2. This has to do with the fact that it 'seems magical' to modern man to see a divine and spiritual reality at work in material symbols and symbolic actions. Thought, discussion and the education of consciousness are in contrast with it. Liturgy is understood as a (social) pedagogical measure and a multimedia catechetical lesson, which is supposed to initiate or maintain social political processes of change.

3. Müller fears that such ways of thinking can point to a tradition reaching from Augustine to Rahner: Sacraments – and with them the whole of liturgy – are proclamations of the Word raised to a higher power through external symbolic actions, in which God's saving act and promise of salvation in Christ, which took place once and for all in the past, is now accepted into a man's concrete life situation. The exterior actions are directed to the receiving faith; the question as to how far they convey salvation remains largely unanswered. Müller sees here clear parallels to Protestant theology, which, out of concern for the purity of *sola gratia* will have nothing to do with causality of the sacraments with regard to human salvation.

Is the liturgy with its outward solemnities at all necessary for salvation? A sacramental theology – and a liturgical theology as bound up with it – which is incapable of giving a satisfactory answer to the question of the causality of the outward observances with regard to their efficacy for salvation, is readily prone to replace the outward liturgical observances with kerygma and *diakonia*.[23]

1.2.2. CRITICISM OF CULT

Every criticism of Cult – and already that in the Old Testament – starts from the fundamental question, why God should need human actions at all. In the concept of 'Divine Service' it can be easily forgotten that in the first place God serves man, and the liturgical service can be misunderstood as a necessary service of man to God. Since the Liturgy Constitution of Vatican II such a one-sided view is finally to be considered antiquated.

A typically cultic view of liturgy in modern times had a long theological and historical preparation. It prevailed generally in the 19th century, was accepted into the Code of Canon Law of 1917 (c. 1256) and was in force almost exclusively up to and including the Encyclical *Mediator Dei* of Pius XII in 1947. The cultic understanding of worship had its foundation in the classification of the worship of God by man (his acts of *latria*) in the system of virtues which was already completed in scholasticism. The powerful influence of Cicero, by whom *religio* – the virtue of cultic acts – was classed with the *ius naturae*, led the scholastic theologians to bring 'cult' into relation with the cardinal virtue of justice; man, the creature, offers to God his creator, the due cult (*cultus debitus*) of prayer and adoration. So also Thomas: *religio*, the virtue of cultic acts, is

---

[23]   Cf. Müller, Bleibt die Liturgie, 158 – 161.

the highest moral virtue, because by its exercise the creature offers to God as its creator and protector the due service of prayer in the sense of commutative justice (*iustitia
commutativa*). Since the whole man – consequently with body and soul – is obliged to
offer this thanksgiving, cult comprises especially the outward bodily side. Thus already
Thomas Aquinas says: "Quia ex duplici natura compositi sumus, intellectuali scilicet
et sensibili, duplicem adorationem Deo offerimus, scilicet spiritualem, quae consistit in
interiori mentis devotione et corporalem, quae consistit in exteriori corporis humilia-
tione." [24]

This understanding is the basis for the "Definitions" of "Liturgy" in canons 1256
and 1257 of the Code of Canon Law of 1917: liturgy is "public worship", which the
Church regulates as a public act for the fulfilling of this *adoratio debita* in its external
courses and for the performance of which she appoints suitably qualified 'cultic persons'. According to Eisenbach this cultic understanding of liturgy predominated up to
and into the encyclical *Mediator Dei* of Pius XII. Yet Roman documents maintained
this viewpoint even after the encyclical (1947); the complementarity of the *catabatic/
salvational* and *anabatic /* worshipping dimension which Pius XII, under the influence
of the liturgical movement and mystery theology, had witnessed to, no longer gets an
airing there. [25]

The concept itself of "Cult" is too ambiguous to be able to express the bodily side
of the worship of God by man as the fulfilment of a duty incumbent on the creature.
Lanczkowski, embracing its wide multiplicity of meanings, defines it as a collective
term for "fixed and organized forms of relations with the divine". But even this definition is still very general. "Cult" can also denote merely the recognition of something
greater, of a greater power, whether it be a god or even a man, on whom man knows
that he depends. Men who are possessed of a special fullness of power are able to exact
model attitudes of cult behaviour from their subordinates. [26] The ambiguity of "cult" is
based in its derivation from *"colere* – to cultivate, take care of, honour, revere, worship",
and with regard to its content of meaning it comprises a whole spectrum of "caring intercourse".

"Cult" is intercourse with the holy and the absolute, which man experiences as over-
whelming, but from which he comes to know that the security of his life depends. "Cult"
is a "caring", i.e., a "protective" intercourse with the holy and the absolute, in order on
the one hand to safeguard its holiness and on the other to shield the mortal and guilt-
laden from the all-holy and all-pure. Eliade refers to "the taboo and ambivalence of the
sacral", and the glory of God (*Kabod Yahweh)* was experienced by the Old Testament
people of the covenant as terrifying, even menacing: whoever sees God, must die (cf.
Ex 33:20). [27]

---

[24]   S. Th. 2, 2 q. 84 a.2. On the problematic nature of the concept of cult cf. Lengeling, Grundvollzug, 74;
     the article "Kult" by the same author in HThG I, 865–880; cf. Lengeling's commentary on SC 7 in E.
     J. Lengeling, Die Konstitution des Zweiten Vatikanischen Konzils über die heilige Liturgie, Lateinisch-
     deutscher Text mit einem Kommentar. Münster 2nd edn., 1965 (Lebendiger Gottesdienst 5/6) 24f, with
     special reference to Aquinas.

[25]   Cf. Eisenbach 82.

[26]   Cf. G. Lanczkowski, Art."Kult": LThK 2nd edn. VI, 659; by the same author, Art. "Gottesdienst I: Reli-
     gionsgeschichtlich": TRE XIV (Berlin – New York 1985) 1–5; C. Vogel, Das liturgische Amt im Leben
     der Kirche. Entfremdung von Kult und christlicher Gemeinschaft, Concilium 8 (1972) 76–83; A. Chollet,
     Art."Culte": DThC III, 240f.

[27]   Cf. Eliade, Die Religionen und das Heilige, §6: Das Tabu und die Ambivalenz des Sakralen, 38–43.

Worship protects as a "fixed and organized form of intercourse with the holy"; in worship man is allowed to draw near to God, because God has allowed him this approach and has given him worship for this purpose. Yahweh himself bestows on Israel worship as a way of salvation, in which he makes the giving of salvation dependent on definite symbols, rites and persons, but always reserves to himself the giving of his grace to whomsoever he wishes outside this way of salvation. Without worship man perceives every approach to God as life-threatening, a fact which the purity laws of Israel in particular point out. [28] "Separated" ("sacral") persons, places, clothes and utensils, constitute the elements of "cult" as a "caring intercourse" of man with the godhead by means of fixed binding norms established beforehand by God. This protective function of worship lives on even in secularized forms, in so far as cult practices – even when people are no longer aware of their meaning – are meant to serve to master life-threatening situations.

In Israel's faith worship is valid as ordained by God. In worship he communicates with his people, without making himself "available to manipulation", but also, as the altogether Holy and Perfect, without already in the encounter itself "slaying" limited and sinful man. Worship is the meeting place between himself and men established by God to safeguard [29] divine as well as human identity.

Nevertheless the concept of "Cult" remains dangerous, because it leads precisely to the misleading assumption of being able through human activity to prevail upon the sovereign God to perform saving acts; in a word: to be able to manipulate God by human service to him. This danger is based on the assumption of the connection between action and outcome (or respectively the connection between omission and outcome) which can find expression in the transitive verb 'colere': *colere Deum* – a work of man towards God in order to obtain a desired end.

"Cultic" is the "care" (no matter how "spiritualized"), which a man bestows upon his God in order thereby to make sure of his blessing and protection. This "anabatic one-sidedness" collides with the unavailability of God: man "cultivates" the Godhead with sacrifices and acts of worship, because he experiences himself as dependent on it. Acts of worship serve the purpose of keeping away the wrath of the Godhead and obtaining its blessing. "Cult" then serves to safeguard basic human needs or to obtain desired advantages in the sense of "*do ut des*". Schaeffler draws attention to the fact that the problematic nature of this understanding had already been seen by Plato ("For the performance of what work do the Gods need human service?"); likewise, that the concept of cult was so reinterpreted by Thomas, that "Cult" was not an action that does something, but rather points out something, an action not of intent, but rather of expression. [30]

Lengeling totally rejects the concept of "Cult" as inappropriate for understanding the nature of Christian liturgy: it moves the human act too much into the foreground, so that – as the history of the concept up to Vatican II demonstrates – the danger always exists of making the encounter between God and man dependent on human action.

---

[28] Cf. J. Scharbert, "Heilsgeschichte und Heilsordnung des Alten Testaments": MySal II, 1076–1134. 1123f.

[29] Cf. Scharbert, ib., 1123f. 1128: Reinheitsgebote. H. J. Kraus, Gottesdienst in Israel, Munich, 2nd edn. 1962, 145–148; Gerhard v. Rad, Theologie des Alten Testaments I, Munich, 9th edn. 1987, 273.

[30] Cf. R. Schaeffler, "Der Kultus als Weltauslegung" in B. Fischer / E. J. Lengeling / R. Schaeffler / F. Schulz / H. R. Müller-Schwefe, Kult in der säkularisierten Welt. Regensburg 1974, 9–62.11–13.

Eisenhofer shows clearly how the residue (reminiscent of magic) of the cult concept can still continue to have an effect: "When man draws near to God in cult, he does not merely want to render due acknowledgement to the honour of God, he wants as well *to bring about* the grace-filled condescension of God."[31] Hansens concludes in a similar way, that both tendencies, the ascending/ anabatic and the descending/catabatic, are indeed present in liturgy, but only the ascending is the essential constitutive element, a fact already expressed in the order in which both are named.[32] Lengeling remarks moreover, that the earlier liturgical scholarship had defined the salvific effects of liturgy as consequences of public worship and so had fallen into the dangerous proximity of Pelagian, if not indeed of magical, views. This is true precisely when the cult concept is seen from the angle of the scholastic doctrine of the virtues and its understanding of the cardinal virtue of justice, according to which the performance of the *cultus debitus* by man is taken as a presupposition for obtaining the divine acts of salvation.

The distorted one-sided view ignores the priority of the catabatic dimension, which alone makes the anabatic possible. "Cult" therefore remains prone to misunderstandings, which are incompatible with the revealed image of God and contain magical residua, which religious studies link with the concept of cult.[33] According to the Bible's criticism of cult also, an understanding of cult which wishes to induce by human actions in any way at all God's sovereign untouchable freedom to perform a (saving) act, cannot correspond to the revealed truth about God.[34] The Bible's criticism is meant for forms of cult, which disregard the personal freedom of the covenant God, because missing out on a personal covenant relationship they are conceived and performed as if operative of themselves. This defective form is close to what Kahlefeld describes as "autonomous cult", which – once approved by God – "works" of itself. Stendebach argues in a similar vein and sees the Old Testament criticism of cult as valid in principle for the understanding of Christian worship. Congar also declares himself against a distancing in principle of the Old Testament prophets from the liturgical performances of the Temple worship, with a side glance at the meaning of Christian liturgy, such as has been assumed above all by Protestant theologians.[35]

1.2.3. ATTEMPTED SOLUTIONS

Häußling understands "Cult" "from the anthropological aspect" – starting from man therefore – as an original human behaviour pattern. Man tries by symbolic actions to gain and safeguard the meaning of his existence within the world with its powers which cannot be manipulated and which are experienced as oppressive. That is why the phe-

---

[31] Eisenhofer I, 21.
[32] Cf. J. M. Hanssens, La liturgia nell'enciclica 'Mediator Dei et hominum', CivCatt 99(1948) I, 579–594; II, 242–255.
[33] Cf. A. Th. Khoury, "Religionswissenschaft und Kult" in K. Richter (ed.), Liturgie – ein vergessenes Thema der Theologie? (QD 107) Freiburg-Basel-Vienna, 2nd edn., 1986, 54–64.
[34] Cf. Lengeling, Liturgie-Dialog, 28; Lengeling, "Grundvollzug", 72.
[35] Cf. H. Kahlefeld, Das Problem des Kultes, LJ 17 (1967) 32–39; F. J. Stendebach, "Kult und Kultkritik im Alten Testament": N. J. Frenkle / F. J. Stendebach / P. Stockmeier / Th. Maas-Ewerd, Zum Thema Kult und Liturgie. Notwendige oder überholte Ausdrucksform des Glaubens, Stuttgart 1972, 41–64. 54f; Congar, Das Mysterium des Tempels 60.

nomenon of a cult behaviour grounded in man and the corresponding cultic behaviour models are differentiated from the essence of Christian liturgy. [36]

Schaeffler also attempts to lay an 'anthropologial foundation' for the concept of cult: "Cult" in man is a basic existential component of a religious interpretation of life, in the course of which however God's action lies at the base of all human cult. Cult is the visualization of a prototype divine action in a human model. This latter renders present in time and space the divine saving action – an action which has already taken place and will incessantly continue to take place – and so renews the celebrating cult community and the whole world beyond it. This visualization is always also an interpretation implanted by God of the reality of the world and of man within it. What is at stake therefore in cult is the interpretation of an in any case "existing" reality, to which man "gives admittance", which contains the parousia of God for him in his time and place. It is not man who brings about this presence of God and his saving action, rather he allows the real truth of God (the archetypal truth) admittance to himself and his world. Schaeffler includes the concept of cult as this kind of existential religious component in the "alphabet and grammar of religion", of which Christian preaching and liturgy also must make use.

But there are serious objections even to such new interpretations: does the 'Advent' of God not depend once again on man, who opens himself and his world for God? The persistent objections are confronted with a 'rational' image of God, according to which ethics – the active love of the neighbour – takes the place of ritual acts. "Enlightenment and Idealism drew this conclusion." [37] A religion that lays its chief stress unambiguously on ethical values, cannot accept that the presence of God in the world be brought about by ritual cultic practices. Moreover this massive calling into question was not first caused by the scientific technical conception of the world, rather it can even refer to the New Testament. The worship of God "in spirit and truth" (John 4:24) recognizes no longer any special, specifically cultic (or "sacral") times, places and rites, but takes place "through the service of all that is true and good and beautiful, and accordingly is appropriate to the spirit, and indeed in a completely everyday life. Natural law and moral law have replaced the law of cult, not because they conquered religion, but because a religious preaching itself had rendered the cultic conception of the world so very questionable, that afterwards the philosophical criticism of cult as well could achieve a widespread effect." [38] The dilemma of cult consists apparently in nothing less than in the question of the self-dissolution of religion in general.

Consequently what is worship for? It cannot be a work of man for God, nor any human completion of divine activity, as if God's action were not sufficient for itself. Man is allowed to be the image of God – i.e. the embodiment of his presence – and therefore also to bring about embodiments of presence, i.e. to perform imitative actions, in which God's sole and ever new saving work comes into this world, renewing life. Morality does not render worship superfluous, rather it is only made possible by the

---

[36] Cf. A. A. Häußling, "Liturgiereform. Materialen zu einem neuen Thema der Liturgiewissenschaft", ALw 31 (1989) 1–32. 21. 30.

[37] R. Schaeffler, Die Stellung des Kultus im Leben des Menschen und der Gesellschaft. Eine anthropologische Grundlegung: K. Baumgartner and others, Unfähig zum Gottesdienst? Liturgie als Aufgabe aller Christen, Regensburg 1991, 9–34.11f.

[38] ib., 13f.

latter: only worship constantly renews man in the image of God as the embodiment of his presence in the world. [39]

In view of the priority of *Catabasis* can one make use of the loaded and controversial concept of "cult"? Lengeling's basic scepticism towards "cult" remains justified, because with this concept one can express only with difficulty that which must precede every human activity in worship: God's saving intitiative in visible signs and outward solemnization, or the *catabatic* dimension. It alone renders the outward solemnization, the entire liturgy meaningful.

Bibliography

K. Baumgartner / F. Hahn / H. Kornemann / O. Lechner / H. B. Meyer / G. L. Müller / R. Schaeffler / H. C. Schmid-Lauber / D. Trautwein, Unfähig zum Gottesdienst? Liturgie als Aufgabe aller Christen, Regensburg 1991.

C. Colpe (ed.), Die Diskussion um das 'Heilige', Darmstadt 1977 (Wege der Forschung CCCV).

F. Eisenbach, Die Gegenwart Jesu Christi im Gottesdienst. Systematische Studien zur Liturgiekonstitution des II. Vatikanischen Konzils, Mainz 1982.

M. Eliade, Die Religionen und Das Heilige. Elemente der Religionsgeschichte, Frankfurt/M. 2nd edn. 1989.

B. Fischer / E. J. Lengeling / R. Schaeffler / F. Schulz / H. R. Müller-Schwefe, Kult in der säkularisierten Welt, Regensburg 1974.

N. J. Frenkle / F. J. Stendebach / P. Stockmeier / Th. Maas-Ewerd, Zum Thema Kult und Liturgie. Notwendige oder überholte Ausdrucksform des Glaubens? Stuttgart 1972.

A. Hahn / P. Hünermann / H. Mühlen / R Schaeffler / H. Tellenbach, Anthropologie des Kults, Freiburg-Basel-Vienna 1977 (Veröffentl. der Stiftung Oratio Dominica).

K. Forster, Der Kult und der heutige Mensch, München 1961.

E. J. Lengeling, Liturgie als Grundvollzug christlichen Lebens.In: B. Fischer / E. J. Lengeling / R. Schaeffler / F. Schulz / H. R. Müller-Schwefe, Kult in der säkularisierten Welt, Regensburg 1974, 63–91.

E. J. Lengeling: Liturgie Dialog zwischen Gott und Mensch. Ed. by K. Richter, Freiburg-Basel-Vienna 1981.

A. Müller, Bleibt die Liturgie? Überlegungen zu einem tragfähigen Liturgieverständnis angesichts heutiger Infragestellungen, LJ 39 (1989) 155–167.

K. Richter (ed.), Liturgie ein vergessenes Thema der Theologie? Freiburg-Basel-Vienna 2nd edn. 1986 (QD 107).

R. Schaeffler / P. Hünermann, Ankunft Gottes und Handeln des Menschen. Thesen über Kult und Sakrament, Freiburg-Basel-Vienna 1977 (QD 77).

R. Schaeffler: Kultisches Handeln die Frage nach Proben seiner Bewährung und nach Kriterien seiner Legitimation, R. Schaeffler / P. Hünermann, Ankunft Gottes und Handeln des Menschen. Thesen über Kult und Sakrament, Freiburg-Basel-Vienna 1977 (QD 77).

R. Schaeffler, Kultur und Kult, LJ 41 (1991) 73–87.

---

[39] Cf. Schaeffler, "Die Stellung des Kultus", 17; id., "Der Kultus als Weltauslegung": B. Fischer / E. J. Lengeling / R. Schaeffler / F. Schulz / H. R. Müller-Schwefe, Kult in der säkularisierten Welt, Regensburg, 1974, 9–62.61: Cult is "alphabet and grammar of religion"; id., "Die Stellung des Kultus" 11–14: the jeopardizing of cult by "a rational image of God" and ethical emphasis.

Schilson, Liturgie und Menschsein. Überlegungen zur Liturgiefähigkeit des Menschen am Ende des 20. Jahrhunderts, LJ 39 (1989) 206–227.

1.3. LITURGY – GOD'S WORK AND GOD'S SERVICE FOR THE MANY

1.3.1. THE CONCEPT OF "LITURGY" AND ITS PROFANE ORIGIN

"Liturgy" can also be misunderstood in a one-sided *anabatic* meaning of cult, if merely the ceremonial "exterior" of Christian worship is to be denoted thereby. [40] For Fischer "Liturgy" is a foreign word unfortunately infiltrated by the humanists; according to Brunner the concept can neither in the New Testament nor in theological reflection adequately designate the matter really in question. [41]

"Leitourgia" is of a more profane origin than "cult". Literally translated "liturgy" means "work of the people / for the people", a "matter of public concern", for instance the construction of a protecting city wall, eventually any service at all. The concept can also acquire a cultic meaning, since cult also was considered to be one of the concerns of common life. "Liturgy" then denoted a religious celebration of concern to the entire city community; all were responsible for its performance and had to take part in it in order to ensure the blessing of the "appropriate "god for the community through sacrificial offerings. At that time the religious celebration was precisely a "common concern" equally important as all other measures, which were destined to safeguard or further the people's well-being.

The Septuagint and Hellenistic Judaism understood "liturgy" above all in its general meaning as "service", in a special sense as the name for the Old Testament cult. Liturgy is the cultic service of the Covenant people to God in temple and synagogue. This is how "liturgy" is understood in the Letter to the Hebrews as well, but not however in the other passages where the New Testament adopts the concept and interprets it generally speaking as "service"; nowhere is it applied to New Testament worship or to the service of Christian office-bearers. [42]

On account of the unique character of Christian worship people at first – certainly to distinguish themselves from the pagan and Jewish environment – avoided a general concept for it. When "liturgy" was adopted for it, it was not however forgotten, that precisely it is not man who serves God in the cultic sense, but that liturgy first of all is the work of God, who brings about salvation in the world through Christ in the Holy Spirit. While in the Christian East to begin with "liturgy" was employed as a general term for all celebrations of worship – corresponding to the concept of "sacramentum'used by the Latin Fathers [43] gradually its usage narrowed down later to the celebration of

---

[40] Pius XII in Mediator Dei repudiated this inadequate interpretation, AAS 39 (1947) 532: "Quamobrem a vera ac germana Sacrae Liturgiænotione ac sententia omnino ii aberrant, qui eam utpote divini cultus partem iudicent externam solummodo ac sensibus obiectam, vel quasi decorem quemdam caerimoniarum apparatum; nec minus ii aberrant, qui eam veluti meram legum praeceptorumque summam reputent, quibus Ecclesiastica Hierachia iubeat sacros instrui ordinarique ritus."

[41] Cf. H. C. Schmidt-Lauber, Art. "Liturgiewissenschaft / Liturgik": TRE 21 (1991) 384.

[42] Cf. R. Meyer / H. Strathmann, Art. "Leitourgeo, leitourgia, leitourgos, leitourgikos": ThWNT IV. Stuttgart and elsewhere 1942, 221–238.

[43] Cf. Jungmann, "Liturgie und 'pia exercitia' 83.

the Eucharist: "liturgy" or "divine liturgy" in the East is synonymous with "Mass" in the West. There only since humanism the word group related to the concept of *"liturgia"* plays a certain role, but which is still far removed from the clarity with which the concept of "liturgy" ought to be understood by theology since Vatican II.

1.3.2. THE RANGE OF THE CONCEPT OF LITURGY IN THEOLOGICAL AND CHURCH USAGE

As dialogue and exchange of life between God and man the liturgy attains its greatest fullness in the celebration of the Eucharist. In it there is question of the participation of those celebrating in the human nature of Christ, which is the source of deification, out of which the believers receive the divine life. This originates from the Father, becomes accessible to men through the Incarnate Son, is communicated to individuals and perfected in them by the Holy Spirit, who "completes all sanctification". In this sense the Christian East designates the celebration of the Eucharist purely and simply as *the Liturgy*.

Around the centre of the celebration of the Eucharist there is wound the garland of the other sacraments. In all of them there is an inherent relation to the eucharistic centre: the complete form of Christian initiation (baptism, confirmation and First Communion) empowers a person for the Eucharist and lays the foundation in him of the exchange of life between God and man. Penance and the Anointing of the Sick are intended to bring a person back to the eucharistic community, when such a person finds himself in a crisis (a crisis of relation to God and fellow men or a critical situation of the body). Marriage as "the Church in miniature" or the "germ cell of the Church" forms the basis of the Church as a eucharistic community and provides by the new generation for the permanence of the community. The sacrament of Orders structures the eucharistic community by means of the different ministries.

This understanding of liturgy has its roots in the fundamental view of the Church and therefore concerns the universal Church beyond all regional differences and cultural particularities. Alongside this sphere of the universal Church there exist also celebrations of worship, for instance special devotions and processions, which are embodied more by regions in the local Churches. Pius XII says of them in *Mediator Dei*, "they are in a certain way inserted into the liturgical framework"[44]. In the Instruction of 1958 they were assigned as "pia exercitia" to the competence of the bishops. SC 13 distinguishes between "popular devotions of the Christian people" ("pia exercitia" like the Stations of the Cross, the Rosary) from devotions proper to individual churches, undertaken by order of the bishops according to customs or books lawfully approved. "They have a special dignity", nevertheless the pia exercitia do not count as liturgy of the Church in the strict sense. They should "accord with the sacred liturgy, in some way be derived from it and lead the people to it, since in fact the liturgy by its very nature is far superior to any of them" (SC 13).[45]

---

[44] AAS 39 (1947) 586.

[45] Cf. Jungmann, "Liturgie und 'pia exercitia' 85: "In church terminology we can no longer call these forms of worship of God liturgy, but together with the liturgy they constitute our worship (Gottesdienst), a name which which was already widely used in the same comprehensive meaning, just as in English from time immemorial "worship" and in Dutch "eredienst" are in use, meaning thereby the whole of the Church's worship.

Rennings finds this division arbitrary. "It has for example as a consequence that the Breviary prayed by an individual priest in a railway carriage is 'Liturgy', while the public Corpus Christi procession with participation of the bishop, many clergy and laity is not a 'Liturgy' but only a 'sacrum exercitium' of a local Church!"[46] Adam too resists this excessive narrowness: "Wherever a local Church under its bishop, or even an individual community or group in agreement with the teaching of the Church is assembled to hear the word of God and to pray and sing together, the High Priest Christ is present (cf. Matt 18:20). Therefore such an act of worship is shot through with the Paschal mystery, and is done for the honour of God and the salvation of the parrticipants. Why should not the definition of liturgy apply to such an event of worship ?"[47]

1.3.3. THE CATABASIS ANCHORAGE POINT OF THE CONCEPT OF LITURGY IN THE LIFE OF THE TRIUNE GOD

The concept of "Liturgy" complies with the dialogal understanding of worship as a complementary happening of the divine saving initiative (catabasis) and the human response to it (anabasis) in so far as the genitive there present can be understood in a twofold way: "work *of* the people", but also "work *for* the people". "Work for the people" is liturgy as God's action for the many, his saving action for the covenant people of the new Covenant. Looked at in this way worship is first of all God's service for men. "Liturgy" is consequently open to the prior *catabasis* dimension of all acts of worship. But the *anabasis* dimension can also be expressed in this way: worship is the work and concern of the whole people of the covenant, prior to all hierarchical differentiations. It is genuinely the service of all to God, but which only God the Father renders possible through the Son in the Holy Spirit. The *catabasis* as well as the *anabasis* dimension are contained in the concept of "Liturgy"; the subjects of the worship event are simultaneously named: God and his people. Prior to all differentiation between clergy and laity "Liturgy" implies that the work of God for the many concerns all (*catabasis* dimension) and the encounter of men with God in praise, thanksgiving, adoration and petition (*anabasis* dimension) is the affair of all.

Without misunderstanding it as the "outward, ceremonial shell" of the celebration of worship, but rather because it unites both dimensions in itself, the concept of "Liturgy" in the same way as that of "divine service" is suitable for expressing what takes place in the celebration of Christian liturgy: a life-giving communication between God and humankind. Here in the foreground is the *catabasis* dimension, which alone renders the *anabasis* possible: God takes the initiative for the divinization of man and the world, and this initiative occurs in his service, in God's service to the world; in the liturgy God's descent (*catabasis*) into the world takes place for the adoption of life-giving and divinizing communication.

It is not only now that God enters into relation with the creation, rather as the Triune he is already in himself the most intimate relationship. The God who is Trinity, who called the creation out of nothing into existence, in order to communicate with it, is none other than the three-Personed, who already communicates eternally in himself. And the way in which God communicates with creation is analogous to the communication of the three divine Persons. The ancient Church already defined this way as an order

---

[46] H. Rennings, "Über Ziele und Aufgaben der Liturgik", Concilium 5(1969) 128 – 135. 133.

[47] A. Adam, Grundriß Liturgie. Freiburg-Basel-Vienna, 5th edn. 1992, 17.

("Taxis") such as corresponds also for the relationships of the three divine Persons among themselves: from the Father through the Son in the Holy Spirit.

A. The Feast as affirming existence

Every feast has always as its theme the affirmation of life. [48] Men celebrate in order to accept ever anew their own existence, that of the others and of the world according to given situations and occasions (birthday, turning points in life such as birth, marriage, jubilees, but also death!). They observe these invitations in a festive manner, i.e. with unusual means and in an atmosphere which breaks out of everyday life since the tasks of everyday do not have this basic affirmation of existence as their theme.

On account of this basic character of affirmation of existence, every feast is of a religious nature, even should this reference to the supernatural be shrouded over by many other things: affirmation of existence is not possible if it is merely time-bound. A full affirmation of existence is only possible, if the questioning of existence by transience and death can be taken as overcome. This too emphasizes the unusual character of the feast. As against the everyday experience of transitoriness, of limitation and of death, the feast proclaims in an unusual manner the deliverance of existence from all limitation. The unusual is that which despite all repetition breaks in as the ever new and astonishing into a world whose habitual character consists in its direction towards termination and death. [49]

Becoming and passing away are usual, death is usual and the original sinful temptation of resigning oneself to the usualness of having to die is common. The genuine feast as the uncommon affirmation of life disturbs this fatal calm. It encounters man who in his everyday life has resigned himself to the finite nature of his existence, and arouses in him the yearning for the illimitable more which is inherent in every genuine affirmation of existence.

That is why in the final analysis it is God who is celebrated in every feast, he to whom everything which exists owes its being, he who loves creation and maintains it ceaselessly in existence, he from whom alone the full and therefore sole veritable affirmation of existence can come. The human feast is the retelling of this divine will for life. Therefore only such feasts can succeed and become a permanent custom, which have this basic affirmation of existence as their theme, and in this connection – independently of the fact whether the participants are aware of it – include God from whom all existence comes and in whom it attains its perfection. Every feast which is not based on the theme of the affirmation of existence wanes away after a short while, or will simply be used as free time.

B. The eternal feast of the heavenly liturgy

If it be the case that the theme of every feast is the affirmation of existence, then the triune God is celebrating an eternal feast from all eternity. The "three-personed" is the first subject of this feast, in the sense in which the Catechism answers the question "Who celebrates the heavenly liturgy?" with reference to the Anaphora of the Liturgy of St. John Chrysostom. [50]

---

[48] Cf. Pieper, Zustimmung zur Welt 46 – 64; Muße und Kult 77f.
[49] Cf. Josuttis, Der Weg in das Leben, 54f.
[50] Cf. No. 1137.

Where should the affirmation of each other's existence of one person by other persons be performed more intensively, more intimately and with the full truth of eternity, immortality and infinity than in the I-Thou-We-You relationships of the Trinity? Where else should the perfect confirmation of the goodness and beauty of a person by another person be truer than in the Trinity?

Where should the commonplace experience of transitoriness be further removed and more unthinkable than in God, who is life itself? Lengeling's remark is thus verified in a very special way that the heavenly liturgy is not only one of praise,[51] because it is not an honouring of each other by the three divine Persons – as if God himself were himself to prepare his praise –, rather it is never-ending validation of existence, in which alone the affirmation of creation's existence can find a place. A genuine affirmation of existence calls for eternity and everlastingness in the guarantor. In the Trinity the guarantor and the one guaranteed are equally eternal and unending. The implications of this for creation and for God's communication with it becomes evident from a train of thought of trinitarian theology which Staniloae develops.[52]

If God were only a single person, then he would confront everything created as the totally other and holy in such fashion that the created reality would be constantly jeopardized in its creaturely identity and limitation. Such an endangering would be the opposite of the affirmation of being. It would be the constant indication of the limits of the creature, and would necessarily involve a 'No'; here everlastingness – there transitoriness; here salvation – there woes etc. Can creation survive in its creaturely reality when such a single person God enters into relationship with it? For this reason von Balthasar says that in face of a single person God, as adored by Islam but also by the people of the Old Testament covenant, man would have no other choice but the gesture of prostration, the total submission to something which he himself is not.[53]

If God were two persons, then there would be no room for creation to be the object of this God's love. The love relations between these two divine persons would permit only a reciprocal gaze. Only in a God of three Persons is it possible to contemplate a total unification of three Persons in the identical divine nature and one and the same honour with a concurrent donation of themselves to created reality.

In the perfect love of a bipersonal God there can be no place for creation; the sole reality is the love relationship of these two Persons, whose subjective reciprocity also constitutes the only objective reality. In the triune God on the other hand, the third Person confirms in turn the love relationship between the other two, so that this is not exclusively subjective, but comes about in an objective space. It is only in the triple personality of God that there is room for objective reality; it is only in the Trinity of the divine Persons that creation finds some space distinct from God.

To use an image: while the unification of two persons leaves no 'space' for an intermediate reality, the perfect love relationship between three Persons equal in rank and identically eternal (for which there is no analogy in creation!) creates a space in which

---

[51]   Cf. E. J. Lengeling, Werden und Bedeutung der Konstitution über die heilige Liturgie: Die Konstitution des Zweiten Vatikanischen Konzils über die heilige Liturgie. Lateinisch-deutscher Text mit einem Kommentar von Emil Joseph Lengeling. Münster 2nd edn. 1965(Lebendiger Gottesdienst 5/6), 79*.

[52]   Cf. D. Staniloae, Orthodoxe Dogmatik, Zürich-Einsiedeln-Köln-Gütersloh 1985 (Ökumenische Theologie 12), 273–283.

[53]   Cf. v. Balthasar, Die Würde des Gottesdienstes 481. Israel however already differs from Islam in so far as listening to the God of the covenant who speaks in the Torah is a central focus.

created reality may have its place. Creation has in God himself the space which renders possible its own existence, or more precisely: it has it in God's inner Trinitarian relation which on account of the perfect confirmation of being of one Person by the others, on the basis of the joy of one Person in the other and the witness to them in turn by the third Person, constitutes the eternal feast of the heavenly liturgy. Already in the triple personality of God this liturgy is a'work for the others', which one Person in the God-head performs for both the other divine Persons. One person confirms the goodness and beauty of the other two and with complete joy bears witness to their reciprocal love as to a reality which goes beyond a mere relationship. The 'heavenly liturgy' as a description of the love relations within the Trinity is therefore to be characterized not only by the image of the 'eternal hymn', but includes also the concept of play; inner Trinitarian relation as 'play of perfect love', 'love-play'.

Play which is sought for its own sake detached from utility and gain, and love which is sought for its own sake belong together. 'Nowhere is there more play, more genuine play, more pristine play than in the primordial play of the Trinitarian life.' [54] What Hemmerle says about the inner Trinitarian life, Hugo Rahner applies to the relationship between the Creator and his creation: nothing in God is necessary, nothing is not free; in him there is no compulsion, but only volition alone. The Trinity is sufficient for itself in the inner divine love relations; it does not need to call any creation into being in order to be God over a reality which is not divine. That is why Rahner calls God's activity in creating and maintaining the world in existence 'play both royal and childlike', 'royal' because of the utmost significance, 'childlike' because without any constraint and in the perfect freedom of love: 'It is precisely in this dialectical paradox of "King and Child" that the metaphysical nature of creation subsists, which allows us to speak of a God at play.' [55]

The eternal love play of the triune God, in which nothing is not free, nothing necessary, in which there is nothing else but the unconditional, joyful affirmation of one Person by the other and the affirming confirmation of the relation by the third Person, in which – without analogy in creation – complete unification comes about while safeguarding the distinction of Persons (perichoresis), this love play is the nucleus of the heavenly liturgy. Or put briefly: the heavenly liturgy is the fullness of life of the triune God himself, in which the three Persons communicate with each other in a perfect manner and find their way to an absolute unity. The absolute affirmation of being of the three divine Persons is in itself already an eternal feast as the perfectly concordant Yes of one to the other, to which every usual earthly cycle of growth and decay is unaccustomed, and which is set free from every repetition conditioned by time and transience. It is the only feast that has permanence in itself, since it is not subject to the conditions of time and the void of the denial of being. It is only from this, that in the course of time and under conditions deriving from original sin, human feasts are possible as extraordinary events and deserve as well the name of 'feast'.

C. Heavenly and earthly liturgy

If the liturgy celebrated on earth is a communication between God and the creature, then it is always a participation in the eternal feast of the heavenly liturgy in the fullness of

---

[54]   K. Hemmerle, Vorspiel zur Theologie. Einübungen, Freiburg-Basel-Vienna 1976, 146.
[55]   Cf. H. Rahner, Der spielende Mensch, Einsiedeln, 9th edn., 1983, 17f.

the life of the triune God into which the heavenly Church of the angels and saints has already found an entry: "It is especially in the sacred liturgy that our union is best realized; in the liturgy, through the sacramental signs, the power of the Holy Spirit acts on us, and with community rejoicing we celebrate together the praise of the divine majesty, when all those of every tribe and tongue and people and nation (cf. Apoc. 5:9) who have been redeemed by the blood of Christ and gathered together into one Church glorify, in one common song of praise, the one and triune God. When, then, we celebrate the eucharistic sacrifice we are most closely united to the worship of the heavenly Church; when in the fellowship of communion we honour and remember the glorious Mary ever virgin... " (LG 50).

The many-faceted idea, and developed especially in the Christian East, [56] of the unity of the earthly and heavenly liturgy, has a long tradition. As its core there is always the thought that Christ himself, the bringer of salvation, is the protagonist in every liturgical action: the earthly outward appearance of the action, accessible to the senses, presents a conformity with the invisible heavenly reality. Vagaggini sees this analogy already grounded in the Letter to the Hebrews, [57] Tyciak attributes it to "the cultic interpretation of the Apocalypse", [58] an idea advocated also by Congar. [59] This unity is held especially by the Greek Fathers: Chrysostom [60] teaches this conformity just as does the "Pseudo-Dionysius" [61] and Maximus the Confessor. [62] Nevertheless Häußling has shown with regard to representatives of the École Française [63] that the idea features also in the West, and it is to be found also in the theology of Odo Casel. [64] However, even independently of the historical lines of development in theology and piety, it remains true that

---

[56]   Hence Trembelas is of opinion that a similar symbolism exists also in the Roman Catholic sphere, however it is less developed there. Cf. P. Trembelas, "Der orthodoxe christliche Gottesdienst" in P. Bratsiotis, Die orthodoxe Kirche in griechischer Sicht, Stuttgart, 2nd edn., 1970, 157–169. 164f. In effect in Jungmann a reference to the "superterrestrial altar" is found only in the context of the "Supplices te rogamus" of the Roman Canon, cf. MS II, 287–291. For the development in the East cf. K. Onasch, Art. "Gottesdienst" V, A. Der Osten. RGG 3rd edn., II, Tübingen 1958, 1766f.

[57]   Cf. C. Vagaggini, Theologie der Liturgie, Einsiedeln-Zurich-Cologne 1959, 174–176.

[58]   This is heading of the first chapter in J. Tyciak, Maranatha. Die Geheime Offenbarung und die kirchliche Liturgie, Warendorf 1947. Cf. also by the same author, Die Liturgie als Quelle östlicher Frömmigkeit, Freiburg i. Br. 1937 (Ecclesia Orans 20), esp. 23–36, "Die orientalische Meßliturgie als Mysterienfeier" as well as Wege östlicher Theologie. Geistesgeschichtliche Durchblicke, Bonn 1946, esp. 57–63.

[59]   Cf. Y. Congar, Das Mysteium des Tempels. Die Geschichte der Gegenwart Gottes von der Genesis bis zur Apokalypse, Salzburg 1960, 179f, 196–199.

[60]   Cf. H. J. Schulz, Die byzantinische Liturgie. Vom Werden ihrer Symbolgestalt, Freibu rg i. Br. 1964 (Sophia 5); G. Fittkau, Der Begriff des Mysteriums bei Johannes Chrysostomos, Bonn 1953 (Theophaneia 9).

[61]   Cf. Schulz, Byzant. Liturgie 51–55.

[62]   Cf. Schulz, Byzant. Liturgie 81–90; H. U. v. Balthasar, Kosmische Liturgie. Das Weltbild Maximus des Bekenners. Einsiedeln, 2nd edn., 1961, 313–330 "Die Synthese der drei Kulte".

[63]   A. A. Häußling, "Ist die Reform der Stundenliturgie beendet oder noch auf dem Weg?" Th. Maas-Ewerd (ed.), Lebt unser Gottesdienst?, 227–247. Note 10 on p.243 cites along with P. de Bérulle (1575–1629) and L. de Thomassin (1619–1695) "above all Ch. de Condren (1588–1641); his theology is available in the posthumously published book L'idée du sacerdoce et du sacrifice de Jésus-Christ, Paris 1677. L. de Thomassin in the Traité de l'office divin dans ses rapports avec l'oraison mentale speaks constantly of the unity of the heavenly liturgy with the earthly liturgy of the Church, in so far as the former 'would have come down' and repeatedly 'comes down' anew; however his expositions are developed within the context of the theology of the Fathers, which is frequently quoted, hence they remain less abstract."

[64]   Cf. O. Casel, Das christliche Opfermysterium. Zur Morphologie und Theologie des eucharistischen Hochgebetes, edited by Viktor Warnach, Graz-Vienna-Cologne 1968, 133–150 "Pneumatisches und himmlisches Opfer".

the liturgy which is celebrated on earth can have no other foundation than the heavenly liturgy; the worship of God on earth – and therefore God's service to man and to the world, before man raises himself to God in the liturgy – must have there its ultimate anchorage point. God communicates with his creation, offering to created reality the unconditional Yes, absolutely not necessary and totally free, of love towards the existence of the other. Such communication proceeds entirely from God, embraces man and the world, is permeated with the fullness of divine life, without however depriving them of their creaturely identity. Rather it takes care of them and leads them to perfection in the fullness of divine life, for which the Greek Fathers use the concept of "divinization".

The earthly liturgy can be effective for salvation only when it is understood as the descent into the visible world of the invisible reality of the heavenly liturgy, into which man enters. He has nothing else to do except to enter into the unceasing 'Holy' of the angels around the throne of God, and he himself becomes a visible apparition of the angels, who bear the Lord of all in the procession of the heavenly liturgy, as the *Cherubikon* of the Byzantine liturgy expresses it in the Great Entry. According to Casel the ancient world already had a vague presentiment of the fact "that all that is earthly is only the reflection and the effect of the supra-terrestrial glory"[65].

According to Congar the liturgical metaphors which the Apocalypse uses show already that the earthly reality has its own ultimate truth in the fact of being the carrier of the supra-terrestrial reality: the heavenly liturgy presents itself as the continuation or as the heavenly projection of the liturgy of the Church, which originates from the fact that what is experienced in the celebration on earth is, so to speak, a 'carrier' of a different – to be precise, a heavenly – reality, which makes itself perceptible to the senses in the earthly feast.[66] But the latter gets its true reality from that which makes itself present in it, from that which in this presence invites to communication: God's eternal, heavenly liturgy. The earthly liturgy is an icon of the heavenly; the earthly celebration belongs to the divine sphere as an essential image of the heavenly, and is as such a manifestation now of God's lordship.[67] Still more, the liturgy celebrated on earth is a rehearsal for the heavenly. According to Lang the Christian conception of the eternal life of the blessed does not fit into either the Jewish or the pagan conceptions of salvation. The new Jerusalem is neither a continuation without time limit of the earthly city with its earthly way of life nor is it an Elysium of the other world with an immeasurably heightened earthly quality of life, rather it is a "huge great temple, in which God will be present and all beings – angels and men – will worship him with songs and cultic gestures."[68] In this connection the author of the Apocalypse took as his pattern the Temple liturgy, the synagogue worship and also the official ceremonies in the pagan basilicas, whereas an image of the gr andiose worship in heaven could be obtained only with difficulty from the domestic liturgies of the early Christians.

"In the earthly liturgy we take part in a foretaste of that heavenly liturgy which is celebrated in the Holy City of Jerusalem toward which we journey as pilgrims, where Christ is sitting at the right hand of God, Minister of the holies and of the true taber-

---

[65] Casel, Kultmysterium, 16f.
[66] Cf. Congar, Mysterium des Tempels, 179f.
[67] Cf. Degenhardt, Irdische und himmlische Liturgie, 83.
[68] Lang, Das biblische Jenseits in neuer Sicht 7f. Lang adds a sketch, which takes as its model the statements of the Apocalypse and endeavours to depict the liturgical ordering of the heavenly liturgy.

nacle. With all the warriors of the heavenly army we sing a hymn of glory to the Lord; venerating the memory of the saints, we hope for some part and fellowship with them; we eagerly await the Saviour, Our Lord Jesus Christ, until he our life shall appear and we too will appear with him in glory." This statement of Article 8 of the Liturgy Constitution follows directly on the very fundamental statements of Article 7 about the liturgy as the exercise of the high priestly office of Christ and the dialogal understanding resulting from it. The mediatorship of Christ is such that it imparts to man the life-giving, divinizing participation in the heavenly liturgy, which in its inmost action is nothing other than the perfect affirmation of existence of the Trinity which is never subject to routine and hence has the character of a feast. The earthly liturgy is therefore only conceivable as the actualization in space and time of the heavenly, as it appears for instance in the cherub hymn of the Byzantine liturgy or in the reference to the heavenly liturgy at the conclusion of the preface in the western Mass.

The presence of the heavenly liturgy in the earthly makes this a feast already, because the common joy of the three divine persons for one another is extended in the events of time and space over the creation, which experiences ever anew its extraordinary i.e. its festive affirmation of existence. The Triune God enters into relationship with his creation, he celebrates with it the feast which he is constantly celebrating in himself, in order to divinize it and take it into the eternal feast of the heavenly liturgy. He does this in that order of the plan of salvation, with which especially the pre-Nicene theology contemplated the working of the Trinity in the world: from the Father through the Son in the Holy Spirit.

Through Christ the heavenly liturgy reaches the earth. Christ is the only high priestly mediator, through whom the visible action of the Church on earth is united with the invisible reality of heaven. In this sense the unity of heavenly and earthly liturgy consists in the identity of the one who performs the liturgy, "who under the veil of symbols celebrates also among us the heavenly liturgy which he solemnizes in the presence of the Father. Always and everywhere there is a return to the idea, so vivid in the ancient Church, and which Tertullian expressed magnificently when he calls Christ the *catholicus Patris sacerdos* (*Adv. Marc.* 4,9), the sole and universal priest of the Father... Seen from Christ's side our earthly liturgy consists in a constant epiphany of the priesthood, which he himself continuously exercises in the presence of the Father. Seen from the Church's side our liturgy consists in the participation in the priestly work of Christ which began at the Incarnation and is now continued in the glory of the Father."[69] Through the manhood of the Son the Holy Spirit transmits the divine life to creation and brings it to perfection within it, by inserting it into the divine love play. The way in which the triune God enters into relationship with creation is the extension of the heavenly liturgy on to the creature.[70] It is to be drawn into the inmost action of the h eavenly liturgy, into that perfect, ever-new, joyful and therefore festive affirmation of existence of one of the divine Persons by the other two.

---

[69] Vagaggini, Theologie der Liturgie, 179.

[70] Cf. Catechism No. 1136, p. 321: "Liturgy is an 'action' of the whole Christ (Christus totus). Those who even now celebrate it without signs are already in the heavenly liturgy, where celebration is wholly communion and feast." No. 1138, p.322: " 'Recapitulated in Christ,' these are the ones who take part in the service of the praise of God and the fulfilment of his plan ... " No. 1139, p. 322:"It is in this eternal liturgy that the Spirit and the Church enable us to participate whenever we celebrarte the mystery of salvation in the sacraments."

"Jesus Christ, High Priest of the New and Eternal Covenant, taking human nature, introduced into this earthly exile that hymn which is sung throughout all ages in the halls of heaven. He attaches to himself the entire community of mankind and has them join him in singing his divine song of praise. For he continues his priestly work through his Church. The Church, by celebrating the Eucharist and by other means, especially the celebration of the divine office, is ceaselessly engaged in praising the Lord and interceding for the salvation of the entire world." [71]

Perhaps in effect "the pathos of language" suggests – as Häußling assumes – that in the heavenly liturgy there is question of an otherworldly God removed from all worldly life, "whom creatures of light worship in unending hymns", of "a divine official ceremony, closed in itself", which has been sprung open by a Mediator who brings with him the "gift of the valid and great hymn so that now the liturgy of heaven may take place on the earth," namely in the Church. [72]

The concept of the "hymn" which Christ has brought to the earth, ought not to be misunderstood as an image of a one and only valid manner of divine worship given beforehand as normative in the liturgy of heaven, especially as SC 83 with this reference begins chapter 4 of the Liturgy Constitution which deals with the liturgy of the Hours.

In the comprehensive sense of the heavenly liturgy the "hymn" stands as an image of that ever new and festive "Yes" – because said from great joy and overflowing love – of one Person to the existence of the other two, which the three divine Persons in the inmost life of the Trinity have always said and are saying to each other and which through Christ in the Holy Spirit finds an extension on to created reality. The catabasis of this "hymn" of the heavenly liturgy is more than an "encounter"; heaven really remains heaven and the heavenly liturgy of the three divine Persons heavenly liturgy, but the world is taken up into it, while it lowers itself and liberates the earthly reality from out of the "exile" of its "No" far away from God into its own proper existence and invites it to the fullness of life of unending affirmation of existence. [73]

Bibliography

H. U. v. Balthasar, Die Würde des Gottesdienstes, IKaZ 7 (1978) 481 – 487.

B. Capelle, Liturgique et non liturgique, QL 15 (1930) 3 – 15.

H. J. Degenhardt, Irdische und himmlische Liturgie, P. Bormann / H. J. Degenhardt (Edd.), Liturgie in der Gemeinde (FS Lorenz Jäger), Paderborn 1965, II, 77 – 91.

E. Raitz v. Frentz, Der Weg des Wortes 'Liturgie' in der Geschichte, EL 55 (1941) 74 – 80.

Ph. Harnoncourt, Gesamtkirchliche und teilkirchliche Liturgie. Studien zum liturgischen Heiligenkalender und zum Gesang im Gottesdienst unter besonderer Berücksichtigung des deutschen Sprachgebiets, Freiburg-Basel-Vienna 1974.

---

[71] SC 83, quoted also in GILH 3 and 6 for the theological basis of the liturgy of the Hours. A statement in 'Mediator Dei' of Pius XII lies at the root of this, cf. AAS 39 (1947) 573.

[72] A. A. Häußling, "Ist die Reform der Stundenliturgie beendet oder noch auf dem Weg? Th. Maas-Ewerd (ed.), Lebt unser Gottesdienst? Die bleibende Aufgabe der Liturgiereform (FS Kleinheyer). Freiburg-Basel-Vienna 1988, 227 – 247. 227.

[73] Cf. ib. 229; "The aforementioned process is clearly defined as encounter. A plenipotentiary of heaven encounters mankind which exists outside the divine sphere. The fruit of the encounter is a new community: exchange of the spheres of life, participation in the essential service. Heaven no longer remains heaven, earth finally no longer "exile".

M. Josuttis, Der Weg in das Leben. Eine Einführung in den Gottesdienst auf verhaltenswissen-
schaftlicher Grundlage, München 1991.

J. A. Jungmann, Liturgie und 'pia exercitia', LJ 9 (1959) 79 – 86.

C. Koser, Pietà liturgica e "pia exercitia", G. Barauna: La s. Liturgia rinnovata dal concilio. Torino
1964, 229 – 277.

B. Lang / C. McDannell, Der Himmel. Eine Kulturgeschichte des ewigen Lebens, Frankfurt/M.
1990.

B. Lang, Leibliche Auferstehung und ewiges Leben. Das biblische Jenseits in neuer Sicht, Bibel
und Kirche 49 (1994) 2 – 10.

E. Peterson, Das Buch von den Engeln. Stellung und Bedeutung der heiligen Engel im Kultus,
Leipzig 1935.

J. Pieper, Muße und Kult, München 1955.

J. Pieper, Zustimmung zur Welt, Eine Theorie des Festes, München 2nd edn.1963.

H. Rahner, Der spielende Mensch, Einsiedeln 9th edn.1983.

A. Schmemann, Introduction to Liturgical Theology, Portland 1966.

1.4. THE VISIBLE WORLD AS THE PREREQUISITE FOR LITURGY

A deadly menace for liturgy came from and continues to come from spiritualizing attitudes. They are seductive, generally behave "piously" and even come up with scriptural
arguments, for example: "God is spirit, and those who worship him must worship in
spirit and truth" (John 4:24). If God is spirit, then the encounter with him demands abstraction from all that is non-spirit, consequently from the visible world which is subject
to ephemerality; in the New Testament itself the perishable "flesh" is in opposition to
the saving "spirit".

Since the Reformation and Enlightenment a periodically recurring intellectualism,
which unjustifiably quotes holy Scripture,[74] endeavours to keep the world of sense perception to a large extent out of the relationship with God. It is even suspected of disturb-
ing the spiritual relationship with God, or at least of distracting from it. Consequently
"spiritualism" can have very little use for liturgical celebration in itself, which always
has a sense dimension. It reduces it to the absolute minimum and understands the bodily and sense solemnization of worship at best as a didactic setting for the spiritual,
for the word, in which alone man is supposed to encounter God. Thus Zwingli held an
outward minimum of "ceremonies" to be necessary "so that the thing would not be handled in too meagre and raw a way, and that some concession might be made to human
stupidity."[75]

Thus "spiritualism" professes: nothing created is sacral, nothing accessible to the
senses leads to God or is a bearer of the holy. Everything is determined by the profane
nature of this world, there is no longer any sacral separated space in creation, because

---

[74] Cf. H. Schürmann, Neutestamentliche Marginalien zur Frage der 'Entsakralisierung', in: Der Seel-sorger
38 (Vienna 1968) 38 – 48.

[75] Quoted according to E. Weismann, Der Predigtgottesdienst und die verwandten Formen, Leitourgia III,
Kassel 1956, 1 – 96.37.

while "God made everything sacral, everything has become profane."[76] The aim of the present paragraph is to show that this rejection of the world of the senses puts in question nothing less than God's communication with creation itself, which the liturgy claims to be.

1.4.1. "SPACE BETWEEN" AS THE PREREQUISITE FOR ANY COMMUNICATION

In the conditions of time and space of this world, communication between persons is then only possible when there is a "space between" which makes possible a "presence" for one another for the communicating partners.[77] This "space between" is the place where their communication comes about: people communicate with each other through the corporeal reality which lies "between" them as spiritual subjects.

This "space between" is in the first place man's bodily nature, through which he must express himself, if he wishes to enter into relationship with another. This "expressing oneself" is to be understood literally as the "going out of oneself" of the spiritual kernel of the person on to the bodily "space between" of the relationship.

Every human being is a mystery in his inmost depths: the *homo ad intra* is also the *homo absconditus*. In this respect his resemblance to the *Deus absconditus* is revealed. What each one is according to his inmost person, can at most be expressed only approximately, even in a lifelong search for an individual identity. What however can be predicated of man equally as well as of God is the capacity for relationship. The person defines itself essentially from relationship, and according to Evdokimov this applies equally to God as to man.[78]

This entering into relationship by man takes place through the created reality which surrounds him, within which as present he takes up his place, and manifests himself with a view to establishing relationship with others. In the body and in his bodily actions, in his clothes, in the thing he takes up in his hand, in the dwelling in which he resides, in the homeland in which he lives, he takes his place as present, and "enters into the picture" for other people. This comes about through specific bodily activities, through the choice of special clothes and a particular object in one's hand; one also manifests oneself as the occupant of a quite definite space furnished according to one's conceptions. The surrounding created reality serves the person so much (Guardini in this connection would also speak of "soul" in order to express the spiritual kernel of the person) as the expression of itself, that everything through which man enters into relationship, can at the same time be called a "real symbol" of his person, in which as a spiritual reality he makes himself present not otherwise than as physical.[79]

To be present is then only meaningful, when it is a presence for another subject for whom the being present counts. "Presence" is therefore in itself already a concept which makes a statement about communication and relationship and must be distinguished from mere irrelevant existence. As a relationship concept "presence" always implies manifestation in the sense of the going outwards of a being which possesses life. What

---

[76] Koch, Schöpfung als Sakrament 32.
[77] Cf. Rahner, Die Gegenwart des Herrn, 395f.
[78] On this point cf. Evdokimov, L'Orthodoxie, 68.
[79] Cf. Guardini, Liturgische Bildung, 15–18, 23.

is lifeless cannot enter into relationship and hence cannot be present for something else; lifeless things coexist in the sense of a mere irrelevant existence.

The fact that living beings enter into relationship with one another by means of the "space between" of the created world, throws light on another basic dimension of communication: it always occurs under the careful safeguarding of the identity of those who are communicating with one another. The space which lies in between the I and the Thou as communication plane, but on which the I enters fully into relationship with the Thou, guarantees that neither the I is absorbed into the Thou nor the Thou into the I. Even in the most complete love relationship the persons survive in their unmistakable I, not to be transferred into the beloved. Otherwise it would not be a relationship but a dissolution of the Thou in the I or of the I in the Thou and thereby the annihilation of one person. Nevertheless both communicators are fully present in the "space between" of the relationship. Both experience themselves present for each other, for example in the body during an embrace both become "one flesh" in the bodily union, and all the same during the total presence for one another they also continue to be themselves.

In this point also man shows himself as the image of God. No communication can be thought of as more perfect than the relationship between the three divine Persons, in such a way that their relationship establishes the essence of the one Godhead. And yet each of the Persons remains itself.

1.4.2. THE "SPACE BETWEEN" IN GOD

The "space between" makes possible therefore perfect communication of persons while safeguarding their personal diversity. With every reservation about the mental transposition of a human experience on to God, such a "space between" can also be presumed for the Trinity.

According to Staniloae, Trinity implies also that one at a time of the divine Persons in turn bears witness to the perfect I-Thou-relationship and unification of the other two. The third Person – of equal dignity and nature as the other two – confirms in turn the objectivity of the love relationship between the other two and opens for them a "space" of objective truth, which transcends the mere subjectivity of a perfect relationship. Only in this "space" of the objective is there "place" for a reality that is not divine, which owes its existence completely to the inner-trinitarian relationship.

If the creation has its place in the objective triple personality "relationship space" of the Trinity [80] then, in his gift to the world, the Triune God enters into relationship with it as uncreated grace. "Uncreated grace" is not a form of relationship, nor a gracious attitude of God, but rather the relationship itself, God *ad extra* in his mode of existence turned towards creation, which differs from the mode of existence *ad intra* which is inaccessible to everything created, from "the unapproachable light" in which God "dwells, whom no man has ever seen nor can see" [1 Tim 6:16]. [81] As uncreated grace God turns himself towards created nature, without divinizing it, without robbing it of its

---

[80] On the distinction between "Ontotes" and "Metaxy" in the theology of Palamism see Kunzler, Porta Orientalis 45–48.

[81] The distinction between God's mode of existence ad intra and ad extra is the basis for the difference between Essence and Energies in Gregory Palamas as well as in the characteristically palamism theology of the Byzantine Church up to the present day. Cf. Kunzler, Porta Orientalis 6–53. Corbon too over and over again uses the concept of the "Energies" of God in a manner corresponding to the palamism theology, cf. the definition of the word in Liturgie aus dem Urquell 12.

creaturely autonomy, without however leaving the unapproachable light of the Godhead in spite of total gift and communication.

"Gratia supponit naturam": without nature there is no grace,[82] there is no communication plane for the personal relationship between God and man, and therefore no encounter. Creation itself, the world accessible to the senses, the thinking, the feelings and perception of man is the "space between" for the personal relationship of God with man. As a creature, man himself indeed belongs to creation; as an embodied spirit nature he raises himself in this respect again above it, when he uses the creation around him as a communication plane in interpersonal and personal relationship.

The dispensation of salvation has its basis in the eternal feast of the heavenly liturgy, in the loving space of the inner-trinitarian relationship; it is precisely the extension of these to the non-divine, to created reality, and is an invitation extended to men to participate. "Mankind has its place in God": what J. S. Bach proclaims in the final chorus of his Christmas Oratorio, is the final state of a process, which began with creation as the "dispensation of salvation" or "distribution of graces", in order to lead created reality to having a share in the fullness of divine life, without obliterating its creaturely identity. The continuing affirmation of being, that divine loving will for being, which is based on the perfect love play of the the three divine Persons, constitutes the festive character of this process.[83]

1.4.3. SECULARITY AS THE PRESERVATION OF CREATURELY AUTONOMY

The communication of the triune God with his creation takes place only in the "space between" of creation, in which God speaks his Yes to its being and perfection. As such a manifestation of God, creation possesses its inmost reality and beauty, as such is it drawn into the feast of a universal cosmic Eucharist, which in turn has its ultimate ground in the eternal liturgy of heaven.

Creation however is experienced as "secular" or "profane". "Secularity" first of all makes a statement about being "far from God" and consequently about a missing relationship. "Secular" is the contrary of "sacral" and "holy", and on this account is understood also as the opposite of "liturgical", because – unlike the religious celebrations of life – the secular reality of life and the world, in accordance with the human experience of reality, has nothing to do with God.

"Secularity" signifies first of all merely the proper, creaturely reality of creation vis-á-vis the divine reality of the Creator and the continuing relatedness to the holy God of the secular left in its creaturely autonomy. This distinction is no mere negative statement, rather it constitutes the prerequisite for the relationship between Ceator and creature, if it is part of a genuine relationship that the partners remain in their own identity, if an interchange not a take-over is to come about. The secularity of creation as a never-ending difference from God is precisely an expression of divine love which sets the non-divine free for what is most its own, for its own autonomy, but not that the

---

[82]   Cf. B. Stoeckle, "Gratia supponit naturam" – Geschichte und Analyse eines theologischen Axioms, Rome 1962; G. Muschalek, "Schöpfung und Bund als Natur-Gnade-Problem", in MySal II, 546–558.

[83]   Cf. Corbon, Liturgie aus dem Urquell 51, where by reference to Rev 4:8 the perpetual character of the the heavenly liturgy is given prominence.

one set free should lock itself up in its own autonomy and so perish, but rather that in a living relationship with God, the infinitely other, it should arrive at its perfection.[84]

1.4.4. THE SIN OF DESACRALIZATION OF THE SECULAR/PROFANE

That creation however is experienced by man as "secular / profane" in the sense of non-dependence on God, as abandoned by God and left to itself in its ephemerality, and precisely not as the communication partner of the infinite God, has its explanation in the Fall of man.

Man represents in this respect a special case among all created beings in that God created him as a psychosomatic nature, belonging to both visible and invisible reality. Man is, so to speak, a microcosm[85] in which God has recapitulated the entire creation in a single work. The whole of creation is gathered up in man, and he is meant as mediator to bring it into relationship with the divine life.[86] The sinless man of the origins, created good, was successful in this; for him the surrounding creation was the "space between" of God, in which the Creator's love for mankind revealed itself.

By the Fall man ended the lifegiving communication with God and thereby ran himself to death, and through himself – as microcosm – also the whole of creation. He is unfit for lifegiving relationship with the living God and hence has become a "being for death", man has become the "neighbour of nothingness"[87]. This means that for the creation surrounding him man gathers up creation in himself now as before – in this man is and remains the image of God in spite of all distance from God,– but this integration as such is no longer in view of the lifegiving relationship with God, but rather an integration for death, because creation is dragged to its own downfall along with man.

Man who is closed to communication with God and who is imprisoned in self-love without communication is the man of total desacralization. He disavows that all creation lies close to relationship with God and he completes the final profaanation of creation. He drags it with him in his separation from its Creator and renders it a "fallen creation"; he infects it as it were with his own closed self-love and makes it into the "world" which with its profane autonomy, its worldly inner meanings and with its finite joys is opposed to divine salvation.

This "world" can no longer be God's "space between", which makes his will for being and life perceptible to the senses. Man without relationship to God can only misuse creation as the "world". That an accompanying deep drift to despair is contained in this, is based on the experience of the transience of everything created, which only allows the godless man to come to terms "for a limited period" with the "world" and through its enjoyment to dismiss every thought of death. Augustine saw this very accurately and expressed it with the contrast between "using" (*uti*) and "enjoying" (*frui*) the world for the brief span of life.[88]

---

[84]   Cf. Mühlen, Entsakralisierung, 67–76.

[85]   Cf. Ch. Grawe / A Hügli, Art. "Mensch": J. Ritter, HWPh V, Darmstadt 1980, 1073, where the philosophical and historical side of the concept "microcosm" is shown.

[86]   Cf. the Pastoral Constitution "Gaudium et Spes" of Vatican II, ch. 14.

[87]   Cf. V. Lossky, La théologie mystique de l'Eglise d'Orient. Paris, 1944, 131.

[88]   Cf. G. Greshake, Gottes Heil – Glück des Menschen. Theologische Perspektiven. Freiburg-Basel-Vienna, 1983, 170f; Kunzler, Porta Orientalis 663–689.

1.4.5. SALVATION AS THE RE-SACRALIZATION OF THE SECULAR/PROFANE

The salvation of the fallen world and of man in it can only consist in restoring the lifegiving but disturbed communication with the triune God. Its completion will be the complete re-sacralization of the profane; it is still awaited as the eschatalogical realization. In it even on the bells of the horses there shall be inscribed 'Holy to the Lord'; world cooking pots will be as holy as the liturgical vessels of the Temple (Zech 14:20) and the whole earth will be filled with the glory of the Lord (Num 14:21).[89] Until then however the fallen world continues to possess its own autonomy as profane creation in the sense of "mere deprivation without the dimension of attraction"[90]. The profane world displays its separation from the living God in the boredom and tedious repetition of the selfsame and the everyday. In the world far from God there is nothing new under the sun (Eccles 1:9f), birth and death follow each other in an automatic soulless sequence.

Nevertheless the separation of original sin has indeed disturbed the communication between man and God, but not however man's aptitude for it. As a creature in the image of God man remains destined for the living relationship with God, in view of a "deprofaning" and a "devulgarizing" of the world; further, that the deadly autonomy of the world far from God will be "perforated" by the reality of the living God himself, who wishes to enter into relationship with man through the "space between" of creation.[91] Both "salvation history" as a whole and the Church's liturgy can be regarded from this point of view as a catabasis process of "perforation" of the world by God.[92]

1.4.6. THE DISTINCTION BETWEEN SACRED AND PROFANE CANNOT BE GIVEN UP

Hand in hand with the criticism of a cultic understanding of liturgy there went a radical questioning of the sacred; it manifested itself in publications especially in the revolutionary years after Vatican II.[93] Schürmann describes the desacralization ideal of that time as the sister of demythologizing. "As the programme of demythologizing wishes to purify the Christian kerygma, by interpreting existentially all 'mythical' contents of propositions, in the same way the desacralization programme wishes to make the Christian life independent of the 'sacral', perhaps even of all 'religious' elements in favour of a 'profanation' or 'secularization' of the faith in the midst of a humanized, a 'worldly world' ".[94] It was the experiences with desacralization itself which led to a "counter-movement", which Meyer associates with authors like Harvey Cox.[95] These experi-

---

[89] Cf. Kunzler, Porta Orientalis, 230–232.

[90] Mühlen, Entsakralisierung 409.

[91] Cf. Evdokimov, L'Orthodoxie, 47; Rahner, Die Gegenwart des Herrn, 395f.

[92] Cf. Evdokimov, L'Orthodoxie, 202, "De l'unique source divine 'soyez saints comme je suis saint', découle toute une graduation de consécrations ou sacres par participation. Elles opèrent une déprofanation, une dévulgarisation dans l'être même du monde. Cette action de trouer le monde appartient aux sacrements et sacramentaux qui enseignent que tout dans une vie chrétienne est en puissance sacrement ou sacré, car tout est destiné á son achèvement liturgique, á sa participation au Mystère."

[93] A good overview of the debate on desacralization, with a copious bibliography, is offered by Schürmann, especially 38–42.

[94] Schürmann 38.

[95] Cf. H. B. Meyer, "Kult – Liturgie – Sakrament. Bemerkungen zu einigen Neuerscheinungen", ZKTh 100 (1978) 122–126. 123.

ences drove men – "as a revenge of nature which remains religious" to non-Christian religions and cults. [96]

This already shows that an "anthropologically oriented" theology in no way automatically postulates desacralization. On the contrary, it is precisely with regard to man that Mühlen holds that the antithesis sacred/profane cannot be surrendered. [97] The man of original sin has the "ineradicable tendency not to interpret the "profaneness" of the profane as a reflection of the holiness of God who allows things to be and sets them free, so that we of ourselves may be god-lessly profane." The sacral nature of liturgy is based on the inability caused by original sin to value and to use created reality, without that tendency to autonomy, the renunciation of lifegiving communication with God. Man is always "in the immediate danger of confusing the *Doxa* of God which manifests itself in nature with this nature itself and thus setting it up as an absolute." Therefore in liturgy special places and times are needed for the sacred, in which in a special, precisely a sacred way, thankgiving is offered for the profaneness, for the world that is left in autonomy, but which is related to God, "so that in cult it finally comes to itself." [98] The distinction sacral/profane is to be maintained not by God but by man, and the sacral space is set up by God!

Both Schürmann and Mühlen anchor this "sacred space" in the Eucharisr. In instituting it Christ established a sacred rite of signs, "which in its effective signification in the last resort cannot be deduced from what happens within history and within the world, and therefore cannot be levelled down into ordinary everyday historical time and the profaneness of a 'worldly world'. The eucharistic event refuses from its inmost being to be integrated without distinction into a natural substantial meal, even were it ever so festive a feast!" [99] Similarly Mühlen: precisely with regard to the eucharist the "sacral" distinction is needed between ordinary and eucharistic bread. The denial of this distinction means, "that someone is merely eating and drinking at the eucharistic meal, and so 'does not discern the body'... But whoever does so eats and drinks judgment upon himself! (1 Cor 11:29). This distinction is absolutely unalterable for Christians, because it is a question here of life and death! In order to keep present the uniqueness of this bread, Christians have created a separate space, a separate time, have surrounded the meal with rites and ceremonies, which are intended to proclaim its separateness..." [100] The eucharist is therefore not only the sacrament of sacraments, rather as the centre of the whole liturgical life it is the quintessence and the festive event of the sacralization of the profane, which is all-embracing and eschatalogically already in act, carried out by Christ in the Holy Spirit. Within it sacralization takes place, the transformation of a world closed in its worldliness of lust, into one directed towards God. Sacral therefore is the authentic reality of a world in communication with the living God, and this differs radically from the profane ordinariness of the fallen world oriented towards death without a living relationship with its creator.

A difficult legacy, which needs to be overcome, is the polarity between natural and supernatural, [101] a "theology of storeys", which is based on the distinction between a

---

[96] Cf. Koch, "Schöpfung als Sakrament", 32f.
[97] Mühlen, Entsakralisierung 19, still much fuller ib., 463–467.
[98] Cf. ib. 51, 75f.
[99] Schürmann 92.
[100] Mühlen, Entsakrakisierung 19, even more exhaustively ib., 463–7.
[101] Cf. K. Rahner, Über das Verhältnis von Natur und Gnade, 324, 327f.; Zizioulas, Die Welt in eucharistis-

natura pura and the spernatural grace which is superimposed on it. At least at the level of theological thought in western theology a nature without reference to God became possible. According to Lossky, eastern liturgy has always repudiated the idea of a *natura pura* [102] and Zizioulas affirms: "What exists is simply and solely the reality of nature and of the entire creation in the unity of the heavenly and earthly world ... In such a vision of the world in the light of the eucharist it is not absolutely possible to separate natural and supernatural reality, as western theology has done in a certain fashion, placing man in face of the dilemma of having to choose between the two". [103]

But in spite of this unity, the world which finds itself in a living communicaton with God is differentiated, in so far as it is "sacral", from the world which lives far from God in non-religious profaneness. Fallen man, entangled in self-love, detaches creation from its beneficent relationship with the creator, involving it in his own separation from God. [104] That which, in the best of cases, in western theology was possible only from a theoretical point of view, has become a tangible reality (in the ecological sense): sinfully transformed into *natura pura*, the world has been rendered profane. At present it is merely a field of scientific progress, in view of technical progress and economic profit.

In the re-sacralization of the world remote from God the distinction between sacred and profane is even more emphasized: the signs, the significant actions, the gestures, the attitudes, the words, the objects of nature and of art, vestments and liturgical spaces, become "epiphany of the sacred", "they cannot emerge from earthly concepts", "they have in themselves something strange, like a cloud", [105] given the fact that they appear in the light of the transfiguration, a reality absolutely of our world, but transferred by the living God to the intermediate plane of his divinizing communication, and brought back, in so far as they are creaures, to their full reality and supreme dignity.

Bibliography

L. Bouyer, Le rite et l'homme. Sacralité naturelle et liturgie Paris 1962.

G. Greshake, Gott in allen Dingen finden. Schöpfung und Gotteserfahrung, Freiburg-Basel-Wien 1986.

R. Guardini, Liturgische Bildung. Versuche, Rothenfels am Main 1923.

K. Koch, Schöpfung als Sakrament. Christliche Schöpfungstheologie jenseits von Gottlosigkeit und Vergötterung der Welt, R. Liggenstorfer (ed.): Schöpfung und Geschichte (FS P. Mäder). Romanshorn 1991, 31–53.

H. de Lubac, Surnaturel. Études historiques, Paris 1946.

H. B. Meyer, Kult-Liturgie-Sakrament. Bemerkungen zu einigen Neuerscheinungen, ZKTh 100 (1978) 122–126.

---

cher Schau, 345; Koch, Schöpfung als Sakrament, 33–5; Greshake, Gott in allen Dingen finden, 20f; H. de Lubac, Surnaturel. Études historiques, Paris, 1946. Very critical of H. de Lubac, even in agreement on basics, is B. Hallensleben, in Die Sehnsucht der Natur nach Gott. Was bleibt von Henri de Lubacs Werk "Surnaturel"?, in ThGl 83 (1993), 131–47.

[102] Cf. Lossky, Théol. myst., 96f.

[103] Zizioulas, Die Welt in eucharistischer Schau, 345. Cf. Kunzler, Porta Orientalis, 225–34.

[104] Evdokimov, L'Orthodoxie 90, uses the image of "demoniac eucharist" for this.

[105] Cf. A. Kirchgässner, Der Mensch im Gottesdienst, in LJ 15(1965), 229–38. 231–3.

H. Mühlen, Entsakralisierung. Ein epochales Schlagwort in seiner Bedeutung für die Zukunft der christlichen Kirchen, Paderborn 2nd edn. 1970.

G. Muschalek, Schöpfung und Bund als Natur-Gnade-Problem, MySal II, 546–558.

K. Rahner, Über das Verhältnis von Natur und Gnade, Schriften zur Theologie I. Einsiedeln-Zürich-Köln 1954, 313–355.

K. Rahner, Die Gegenwart des Herrn in der christlichen Kultgemeinde: Schriften zur Theologie VIII. Einsiedeln-Zürich-Köln 1967, 395–408.

H. Schürmann, Neutestamentliche Marginalien zur Frage der 'Entsakralisierung', Der Seelsorger 38 (1968) 38–48, 89–104.

J. Splett, Sakral-Profan-Das Heilige. Philosophische Bemerkungen, Concilium 7 (1971) 130–134.

B. Stoeckle, 'Gratia supponit naturam'. Geschichte und Analyse eines theologischen Axioms, Rom 1962.

J. Zizioulas, Die Welt in eucharistischer Schau und der Mensch von heute, US 25 (1970) 342–349.

1.5. THE OLD TESTAMENT CATABASIS: THE DIVINE GIFT OF COMMUNION

The whole history of the world, in so far as it is history achieved by God, is also a "plan of salvation". Nevertheless, in the more restricted sense of Christian revelation, "salvation history" began with the choice of Israel as the people of the alliance with God. With it humanity was prepared for the coming of Christ, who was to be born in the midst of the chosen people. Here also the catabasis is in the foreground: it is God who chooses Israel, establishes an alliance of life with his people and gives it worship to enable it to enter into contact with him.

1.5.1. THE CATABASIS OF GOD IN THE HISTORY OF HIS PEOPLE

The living God, whose name is "Yahveh" (Ex 3:6), is not a "God of the philosophers", neither is he an "existence" or a "being" in the metaphysical sense. He reveals himself as the one who exists for men. "Yahveh" is a self-proclamation of God; his nature is to exist for the people of the covenant whom he has chosen for himself. [106] Ben Chorin even speaks of a "progressive revelation" of the name of Yahveh in the history of salvation of Israel, the stages of which were to announce to his people the presence of the God of the covenant and to manifest his nature of "being for" men. [107]

The doctrine of the *Shekinah* proper to the rabbis wanted to give a theological dimension to the experience of faith, according to which, God, in so far as he is the Holy One, stands inaccessible before the people, nevertheless in so far as he acts, stands absolutely close to the people. The tension has to be overcome, which, according to Congar "pious souls notice with sadness between the heavenly transcendence of God and his familiar presence in the midst of Israel, between his separateness and his nearness" [108].

---

[106] Cf. W. H. Schmidt, Alttestamentlicher Glaube und seine Umwelt, Neukirchen-Vlyn 60f.
[107] Cf. Ben Chorin, Jüdischer Glaube, 66f.
[108] Cf. Congar, Das Mysterium des Tempels, 93f.

This theology, according to which "presence and transcendence" of God "were united" gathers the glory of God (*doxa, kabod*) in a dialectical tension: it indicates not only the transcendent otherness of God, but also his dwelling (*Shekinah*) within creation. The divine glory of Yahveh expresses also his presence close to his own people; it demonstrates his own power, achieving salvation for it. Unlike the gods venerated by the pagans, the omnipresent God of the people of the covenant is not tied to a place, Yahveh acts and manifests himself everywhere. "The characteristic proper to Yahveh is to be supersensible, spiritual, independent and omnipotent, and not to be tied to any one particular place. And nevertheless, in a certain sense, his presence is localized above the cherubim in the dwelling (in the temple). In reality, Yahveh is to be found there where his people are". [109]

It is a question here of safeguarding the transcendence of God, while considering simultaneously his very real presence in creation. The Eternal stands outside the world which he has created. Because however he does not abandon it to itself, but works continuously in its encounters and maintains it in existence, "one must speak of an immanence of God, which represents the permanent force which holds the universe in motion. The opposite concepts of transcendence and immanence find their meeting place in the one eternal God, who, in his indivisible unity, is above every polarity." [110]

The clear distinction between creation and its creator, and the total presence of God in creation constitute an antithetical unity. God makes use of creation and of the history which unfolds in it, to enter into rapport with his people of the covenant and carry out the programme expressed in the name of Yahveh, in relation to his "existence-for". According to the mysticism of Franz Rosenzweig, the "existence-for" reaches to such a point, that God, so to say, "gathers himself up in himself", when the *Shekinah* which accompanies the chosen people with love and liberating force "returns to him" in the eschatological fulfilment. [111]

1.5.2. THE WORSHIP OF THE PEOPLE OF THE OLD TESTAMENT COVENANT

The presence of Yahveh is a presence of salvation, and in so far as it is such, is always a gift to men. This is particularly true of worship, which is above all of a catabatic nature. In worship too God cannot be manipulated. Israel is distinguished from its neighbouring peoples precisely by the fact that in it no anabatic human act of worship possesses any influence on the sovereign gift of divine salvation. "The Holy God offers communion, man accepts what is offered". [112] From this it follows that the relations between God and the people of his covenant go far beyond worship. In effect God meets his people in worship, in which Israel keeps alive the memory of the salvific actions of the past and in the certainty full of faith and hope that God will continue to fulfil his work of salvation with regard to his people. In worship there is proclaimed the call to a renewed

---

[109] Cf. ib. 21. 23f.

[110] Ben Chorin, Jüdischer Glaube, 70f. Cf. also A. M. Goldberg, Untersuchungen über die Vorstellungen von der Schekinah in der frühen rabbinischen Literatur, Berlin 1969; Ellen M. Umansky art. "Schekinah": M. Eliade (ed.), The Encyclopedia of Religion, New York 1987, XIII,
        236–239; Bernd Janowski, "Ich will in eurer Mitte wohnen". Struktur und Genese der exilischen Schekinah-Theologie, Jahrb. Biblische Theologie 2 (1987), 165–193.

[111] Cf. J. Moltmann, L'unitá invitante del Dio uno e trino, in "Concilium" 1 (1985) 75–87. 83.

[112] Wilms, 89.

decision of the people for the God of the covenant and the consequences derived from it. In worship therefore there is proclaimed that which is willed and indicated by the God of the covenant, who is leading his own people to a future of promises. For this reason Israel's worship is essentially orientated towards the future, and out of the memory of the past, creates the promise of what will come; the great deeds of Yahveh which are "recalled to mind", are "today" a reality which creates life. Worship, in so far as it is a communion of this nature with the God of the covenant, which in itself is liberating and alludes to the future, is characterized essentially by joy. Israel is jubilant and dances to its God present in the sanctuary. Israel feels its God present in direct proximity, and in a certain way in the temple worship; but it knows nevertheless that God cannot be imprisoned in any building made by men. Israel – and above all later Judaism – is fully aware of the intimate nearness of its God and of his absolute transcendence.[113]

Israel's worship is addressed to the God of the covenant as the Lord of history, who demonstrates his own saving power with historical acts of salvation.

To this corresponds the primacy of the sanctification of time, compared to that of place; it is in the first place sacred times and days of feasts which recall to mind the saving deeds of Yahveh. Until the conquest of the land, Israel could not have any stable holy place, but only a transportable sanctuary. God walks with his covenant people, he is not tied to any particular place. Even in the prayer of consecration of Solomon's temple there still re-echo doubts about the construction of a stable temple: "But will God indeed dwell on the earth? Behold, heaven and the highest heaven cannot contain thee; how much less this house which I have built!" (1 Kgs 8:27). For this reason Petuchowski considers the building of Solomon's temple as an assimilation of Israel to the Canaanite environment. But even after the construction of the temple, the sanctification of time remained in the first place, not tied to any place. If the spirituality of Israel had concentrated on the temple, it could not have survived its destruction.[114] The same holds true for the sacrificial cult. Petuchowski considers the sacrifices more a concession to popular piety than an urgent necessity arising from the experience of Israel in the encounters with God.[115] Grelot accepts the fact that Israel would have espoused some "traditional gestures": "the rites of worship are only of value as the expression of an interior attitude of faith; if this is present, the rites acquire their full efficacy; every physical and social aspect of human nature is brought together in relation to God, its kernel constitutes the life of faith. In this perspective Israel took up the traditional gestures with which man from earliest times has expressed his fear in face of the godhead and his efforts to enter into a living relationship with it."[116] As an expressive action, sacrificial worship was open to an ample development of spiritualization. According to Ratzinger, during the exile the idea ripened "that not any kind of rite, but the story itself of the sufferings of the people constituted the worship and the sacrifice in God's sight. Israel learns a new and more central form of sacrifice, compared to that which the temple could offer: martyrdom, in which the ritual victim is transformed into the offering which man makes of himself."[117]

---

[113] Cf. the Essentials israelitischen Gottesdienstes, in Wilms, 89f.
[114] Cf. Petuchowski, Geschichte, 13f.
[115] Cf. Petuchowski, Geschichte, 14.
[116] P. Grelot, Prezenza di Dio e comunione con Dio nell'Antico Testamento, in "Concilium" 10 (1968), 19–33.
[117] J. Ratzinger, L'eucaristia è un sacrificio? "Concilium" 4 (1967), 83–96.

To this corresponds also the passage from piety linked to cult to that linked with the *Torá*. The former is based on the idea that the violations of the orders established by God provoke misfortunes, and therefore cause threats, which can in turn be muted by rites of worship. The ambiguity could give the idea that worship worked in an "automatic" way, independently of the attitude of faith of those who celebrate it, and thence arose the Bible's criticism in the encounters with cult. It does not criticize the cult, but a certain exteriorization of it.

Like the other ancient cultures, Israel too understood the action of worship as a guarantee for existence. Worship creates a link with the cosmic divine systems, and is a guarantee of existence in face of whatever can influence it. All the same, alongside the ritual and cultic relationship with God, the biblical Jewish concept of the sacral includes also that of holiness, which is based on the election to the covenant with God. It is above all the awareness of election which makes possible the criticism of cult, in which light is shed on the ambiguity of an "automatically" efficacious cult in the presence of the lack of personal relationship with God. According to Maier, it is precisely in its biting criticism when faced with the temple worship in Jerusalem that one sees how the Qumran community would have practised a radicalization of cultic piety. [118]

Quite early the *Torá* had acquired the meaning, from a theological point of view, of a divine plan of creation or of a divine law which governs the world. In this way there was opened up the possibility of attributing to obedience to the *Torá* the same function as to worship, that is the guardianship of harmony between human and earthly relationships and the order of the world established by God. Such a transference of piety from the worship of the temple to the *Torá* and to obedience to its demands enabled the rabbinical and pharisaic Judaism to withstand the loss of the temple and the sacrificial cult practised in it. A renewed theology of the *Torá* even made possible the development of the function of worship by means of obedience to the *Torá*, at least until the coming of the new worship of the messianic age. [119] Thus in the worship of the synagogue the prayer of *musaf* took the place of sacrifice; in the orthodox communities the theme of the prayer was sacrifice, in other communities the sacrificial worship of the past was remembered, in many reformed communities it has totally disappeared. [120]

According to Petuchowski during the epoch of the second temple the nature of sacrifice contributed to the birth of the synagogue. In the countryside the priestly class was divided into 24 divisions (the so-called *mischmarot*) who in turn, for a week at a time, presided over the sacrifices in the temple. While such delegations (*ma'amadot*) were engaged in the temple, the faithful met at home during the time of the daily sacrifice, to read passages of sacred Scripture.

Whatever may have been the origins of the synagogue, the fact is important, according to Petuchowski, that through the *ma" amadot* forms of synagogical piety should have been introduced into the temple also, and alongside the sacrificial piety of the temple, there should have arisen among the priests as well a piety linked to prayer, which was in reality a characteristic of the synagogue. [121]

---

[118] Cf. J. Maier, Aspekte der Kultfrömmigkeit im Lichte der Tempelrolle von Qumran: H. H. Henrix (ed.), Jüdische Liturgie, 33–36, here 35–37.

[119] Cf. Maier, Kultfrömmigkeit, 44f.

[120] Cf. Petuchowski, Die traditionelle jüdische Liturgie, 109.

[121] Petuchowski, Geschichte, 16f.

In this regard, the synagogical worship differs in four points from the temple worship: 1) The temple worship belongs to a hereditary priestly class, the synagogical liturgy develops without any priesthood. 2) The temple is tied to a place the synagogue is not. 3) If the characteristic of the temple is the sacrificial cult, that of the synagogue is prayer and the study of the *Torá*. 4) In the temple the people are – if at all – spectators, in the synagogue on the contrary they participate actively in the worship. [122] The fact that the synagogical worship is not bound to a place, [123] the lack of sacrificial cult, the study of the *Torá* and prayer correspond thus to the original experience which Israel had of God, aware that Yahveh is the Lord of its own history – which, in so far as it is the history of a covenant, is a history of salvation – and that he journeys with it. We must praise his precepts, spell out his saving deeds in praise and to join these with a petition for new deeds of salvation. [124] As the basic impulse for the development of the Jewish liturgy, Petuchowski cites the dialectic between spontaneous prayer, the "pouring out of the human heart before God" (*kawwanah*) and the "codified community prayer" (*qäba'*). Many rabbis consider the *kawwanah* as the presupposition of every prayer: "The Lord is near to all who call upon him, to all who call upon him in truth" (Ps 145:18). But only community prayer overcomes the limits of individual life, in the perspective of history of the covenant of Israel. The individual believer places himself in the community of Israel, which is not a reality bound to a period, but embraces all the figures of the history of the faith, and thus places himself in the presence of the "God of our fathers", who has wrought salvation and will continue to save. Statutory prayer (*qäba*) establishes a means for giving the individual believer access to the prayer of the people of God. From this derives the dialectic according to which there can be no community worship without *qäba'*, yet nevertheless *kawwanah* remains the ideal of prayer. Consequently, statutory prayer ought not to fix in detail the *kawwanah* of each individual's prayer, and basically, in the *qäba'*, in the "eighteen prayers" it is a question rather of eighteen benedictions in which various thematic parameters and concluding prayer formulae are cited, without however fixed prayer texts. Thus the daily prayer includes a petition for peace but this has to be expressed always in a new form, as *kawwanah*, by the one who prays, in view of what he wishes for peace at the moment. Up to the fourteenth century the rabbis had no canonical text of common prayer in the synagogue, but a basic structure, *siddur*, an order of prayer. As a matter of fact the drafting of texts of prayers was severely forbidden among the ancient rabbis. [125]

As the first element of Hebrew worship of the beginning of the second century comes the quotation of the *Schema"*: "Hear, O Israel: The Lord our God is one Lord" (Deut 6:4–9; 11: 13–21; Num 15: 37–41) with its benedictions (*berakot*).Nevertheless the *Schema"* is not a prayer which man offers to God, but a call from God to man; therefore it is not prayed but "proclaimed" (*querija't schema"*). The proclamation is inserted into the context of three benedictions, on creation, revelation and salvation. There follow the eighteen benedictions (*schemone esre*), the central part of which was the *tephilla:* "a prayer of praise, petition and thanksgiving, each part

---

[122] Cf. Petuchowski, Geschichte, 17f.
[123] Thus Thoma, Biblisches Erbe, 49, considers the synagogue building "at most of secondary importance". The important thing would be the community of the faithful gathered together in prayer, in the midst of whom God is present in the manner of the Shekinah.
[124] Cf. Thoma, Biblisches Erbe, 60–63.
[125] Cf. Petuchowski, Geschichte, 21–31, above all 24.

of which was recited by the person leading the prayer, while the concluding doxologies were always acclaimed by the people with the *Amen (*also called the *amida*). In the doxology (*qeduscha*) of the third invocation in New Testament times it is possible that the *trishagion* was already recited". There follows the benediction attributed to Aaron, which was introduced from the temple worship into the synagogical worship, and only after the destruction of the temple was placed before the last invocation of the *tephilla.* [126] Another element is the prayer of invocation in silent recollection (*debarim* = words, *tachanunim* = supplication, *nifillat" apajim* = with face bowed to earth). On certain special days (in the morning worship of the sabbath, on feasts, on days of the new moon and on fast-days) passages of Scripture were read, a fact which, according to Elbogen, gave the first start to the liturgical assemblies. [127]

The basic component of the synagogical worship is the study of the *Torá*, given by the God of the covenant who by means of it speaks and manifests his will. For this reason the reading of the Law is more important than that of the prophets or of the other books of the Bible. It was carried out as *lectio continua* and, since the time of the Talmud, subdivided into sections (*paraschen*); in this regard there developed in Palestine a three-year cycle, in Babylon an annual. When the reading of the *Torá* was completed, they started reading it again from the beginning. In the reading of the prophets and of the other books, passages (*haftare*) were freely chosen. At the period of the Talmud great diferences arose in the choice of passages, which in some cases, persist up to today. The reading of the book of Esther is prescribed for feast of *Purim.*

Successively the custom was introduced of reading the book of Lamentations on the ninth day of the month of *ab,* the Song of Songs for the feast of Passover, the book of Ruth for the feast of Pentecost and Qoheleth on the feast of Tabernacles. [128] By *Targum* is meant a vernacular translation of the Hebrew text, from which there developed a kind of interpretative commentary, under the form of annotations to the text. This basic structure [129] expanded more and more in the course of centuries. Private forms of prayer and the recitation of the psalms, which originally were private prayers of invocation (*debarim*), after they had been written down, developed into *qäba'*, in a ritually fixed liturgical text. The oral tradition of various liturgical texts, which had been their custodian for many centuries, and the prohibition to reduce them to writing, brought it about that it was only in the ninth century that we arrive at a Hebrew prayer book, which in reality was a response from the academy of Baghdad to a Spanish community's doubts as to how a Hebrew form of worship should be properly structured. With this codification a rich formation of the rites of synagogical worship was arrived at in Hebrew orthodoxy of the various regions and countries. Subsequently this synagogical worship continued to develop constantly on the basis of the dialectic between *kawwanah* and *qäba'*. The biblical authors, the various rabbinical interpreters and commentators, the first mystics, and the successive cabbalists, all gave their contribution to the structure of the worship, in which what at one time was a *kawwanah* arising out of a given situation, quickly became fixed as *qäba'* of the community. As an example of this dialectic, Petuchowski

---

[126] Cf. Meyer, Eucharistie, 55f.
[127] Cf. Elbogen, 153.
[128] Heinemann, 557.
[129] Meyer, Eucharistie 56, holds that for the N.T. period it is not certain either that it was present as such or in the order of its various elements.

cites the popularity of a non-biblical feast of the joy of the Torá or the singing of the *hallel* psalms (Pss. 113–118) for Independence Day of the State of Israel, together with a *berakah* still forbidden by the supreme rabbinate.[130]

With the emancipation of the Jews in the nineteenth century there began the development of the reformed synagogue worship in reformed Jewry, particularly in Germany and, heavily influenced from there, in America. The aim was to adjust the the synagogue worship to the aesthetic sense of the emancipated Jews. German chorales, the use of the organ, preaching, etc., which remind one in no small way of Protestant worship, were intended to wrest the synagogue from the musty smell of the ghetto or of the East. Among the characteristics of the reformed synagogue worship, along with the possibility of varying the classic prayers and allowing new prayers, Petuchowski lists above all the abbreviation of the traditional worship, the use of the vernacular, the omission of the prayers for the return of all Jews to Israel and for the restoration of sacrificial worship, the replacement of the personal Messiah by the "messianic age" and of the resurrection of the body by the immortality of the soul.[131]

Petuchowski presents an abbreviated synagogue service for the morning of the sabbath, which comprises the elements of a traditional sabbath morning service – which with the observance of all the rabbinical prescriptions lasts from three to four hours.

It has the following structure:

1) Morning benedictions (private morning devotions, introduced only in the Middle Ages into the order of synagogical prayer); 2) scriptural verses of praise, a selection of psalms and other biblical songs of praise in a framework of benedictions; 3) invitatory to public devotions; 4) the "Hear, O Israel" and its Benedictions; 5) the principal prayer (Tephilla); 6) reading of the Torah; 7) reading from the prophets; 8) sermon; 9) concluding prayer; 10) doxology (qaddisch).[132]

1.5.3. THE PRE-LITURGICAL PERIOD

Here we have studiously avoided using the concept of "Liturgy", which ought to express more than the sum total of ritual actions. It is at most in this restricted and very dubious meaning that it can be applied to the worship of Old Testament people of the covenant, but not in the full meaning which has been pointed out of the exclusively Christian liturgy as the saving action of God for the many through his Son. Corbon is absolutely right in qualifying the period of the Old covenant as "only a pre-liturgical time".

Old Testament times "knew a worship – sacrifice and synagogue – but did not know a liturgy."[133] A detail will make this clear: investigating the corporate synagogical worship as an institution for renewal according to the model of the worship described in Neh 9, Thoma discerns in the last phrase of Neh 6 an echo of the Temple Qeduscha "the host of heaven worships thee".

At the time of Esdras and Nehemiah this was a firmly established rite of the Temple worship, marked by the idea that the festive proclamation of the "thrice Holy" by the priests took place at the same time as the acclamation "Holy Holy ... " of the angels in

---

[130] Cf. Petuchowski, Geschichte, 30.
[131] Cf. Petuchowski, Liturgiereform 119–121: Hauptmerkmal der reformierten Liturgien.
[132] J. J. Petuchowski: Le-'ovdeká be-emet – "Daß wir dir in Wahrheit dienen". Ein jüdischer Gottesdienst für den Sabbatmorgen. Mit einem Nachwort von H. H. Henrix. 2nd edn., Aachen 1988.
[133] Corbon, Liturgie aus dem Urquell 163f.

heaven, as the vision of the call of Isaiah describes it (6:3). Thus the earthly worship of the Temple corresponds to a heavenly worship at God's throne. Before the almighty God those who are praying on earth prostrate themelves like the hosts of heaven. [134]

Despite the presence of all the indisputable reminiscences already mentioned of the relationship between heavenly and earthly liturgy in Christianity, an important distinction remains to be maintained: heavenly and earthly action in worship are merely in a reciprocal relationship to one another. [135] There and here the actions take place in a parallel way. But this parallelism does not connote any communication between heaven and earth; no descent takes place of a heavenly liturgy into the visible liturgical action on earth.

Heaven ("schamajim") is the dwelling place of Yahveh, inaccessible to man, it is nothing else than "the symbol of God's aloofness". [136] In the parallel too between the heavenly and earthly praise of God, the action of the angels as well as that of men is in the strictest sense cultic; as the raisng of the heart in the expression of praise it is an anabatic movement in obedience to the Torah and loyalty to the covenant. [137]

According to Corbon such a cult does not deserve the name "liturgy": "God's saving actions, as well as the events of this world happen but once, then they belong to what is past. Certainly the heart which guards the word, remembers it in ritual actions; nevertheless they remain past events. The faithful heart which observes the law, likewise remembers it, but refers to it as to a heteronomous model (subject to different laws). One cannot avoid pointing out this twofold fatal hiatus, which still maims the religion of the old covenant: its worship does not disclose within itself the saving events, it only remembers them; its morality seeks to conform to them, but does not issue from them as from an actual flowing source. The worship of the people of the old covenant is an "expression of man's religious response". But it has not yet arrived at what is essential in liturgy, the work of God for the many: man is not yet integrated into the encounter between God and the created world,"the real encounter between gift and appropriation is reserved for the future." [138]

It is only with Christ that the heavenly liturgy descends bodily upon the earth, not as an adoring worship by the angels, but as a living exchange based on the mystery of the Triune Godhead. It is only in Christ that the dichotomy between worship and Torah piety, between human worship and obedience to the commandments is annulled, because a person who in the liturgy through the Incarnate One participates in the divine life, along with this receives even the "ethos" of loving affirmation of existence in communion, and draws the ethical consequences from it. [139]

---

[134] Cf. Thoma, "Biblisches Erbe" 57–60. 59.

[135] Cf. Heinemann 560: "A part of the liturgy is called Qeduschscha, i.e. sanctification on the basis of Isa. 6:3 and Ezek. 3:12. In these two scriptural verses one sees the daily praise which is procalimed antiphonally by the two choirs of angels." The prayer leader explains," that we (who are praying on earth) ought to sanctify God after the manner of the angels on high; following on both verses the angel inserts Israel as it were as a third choir.

[136] Cf. J. Nelis, "Gott und der Himmel im Alten Testament", Concilium 15 (1979), 150–156.151.

[137] Cf. Corbon, Liturgie aus dem Urquell 163.

[138] Cf. ib. 164.

[139] Cf. C. Yannaras, The Freedom of Morality, Crestwood – New York 1984, 82: "The eucharist unifies the life of a person in the community of Christ's theanthropic nature and thus restores the image of God's "ethos", of the fulness of trinitarian, personal communion, to man's being or mode of existence."

From this it follows that also for the Jew Jesus of Nazareth the relation to the worship of his people is determined by the dialectic of continuity and turning point. The worship of Israel was to lead up to him, but to find its fulfilment in him and to be superseded by something entirely new which began with the coming of the Son of God in our flesh. The worship of the Old Testament is" only a shadow of what is to come; but the substance belongs to Christ" (Col 2:17). But here the *Einheitsübersetzung* (German ecumencical version) unfortunately conceals the decisive point which is clearly expressed in the original text: the future reality is that of the Body of Christ. It is only in the human nature that the heavenly liturgy of the Triune God came on earth and reendered earthly liturgy possible.

Bibliography

S. Ben Chorin, Jüdischer Glaube. Strukturen einer Theologie des Judentums anhand des Maimonidischen Credo. Tübinger Vorlesungen, Tübingen 2nd edn. 1979.

H. J. Diebner: Art. 'Gottesdienst, II: Altes Testament', TRE XIV, Berlin-New York 1985, 5 – 28.

W. Eichrodt, Theologie des Alten Testaments. Teil 2/3, Göttingen, 6th edn. 1974.

I. Elbogen, Der jüdische Gottesdienst in seiner geschichtlichen Entwicklung, Frankfurt/ M. 2nd edn. 1931, Reprint Hildesheim 1962.

Heinemann: Struktur und Inhalt der jüdischen Liturgie, Concilium 10 (1974) 557 – 560.

H H. Henrix (Hg.), Jüdische Liturgie. Geschichte-Struktur-Wesen, Freiburg-Basel-Vienna 1979 (QD 86).

S. Marsili, Continuitá ebraica e novitá cristiana. Anamnesis 2, Torino 1978, 11 – 39.

J. J. Petuchowski, Zur Geschichte der jüdischen Liturgie, H. H. Henrix (ed.), Jüdische Liturgie 13 – 32.

J. J. Petuchowski, Die traditionelle jüdische Liturgie. Bemerkungen zu Aufbau und Struktur des synagogalen Gottesdienstes, H. H. Henrix (ed.): Jüdische Liturgie, 103 – 110.

J. J. Petuchowski, Liturgiereform im Judentum heute, H. H. Henrix (ed.): Jüdische Liturgie, 111 – 121.

C. Thoma, Biblisches Erbe im Gottesdienst der Synagoge, H. H. Henrix (ed.): Jüdische Liturgie 47 – 65.

P. Weimar, Kult und Fest. Aspekte eines Kultverständnisses im Pentateuch, K. Richter (ed.): Liturgie – ein vergessenes Thema der Theologie? Freiburg-Basel-Vienna 1986 (QD 107), 65 – 83.

F. E. Wilms, Freude vor Gott. Kult und Fest in Israel, Regensburg 1981.

1.6. The Liturgy of Christ the High Priest

The whole dispensation of salvation of the old covenant was directed towards the coming of Christ. It is only in Christ that God's promises come to their fulfilment. Notwithstanding the full continuity existing between the Old and New Testaments, the coming of the Incarnate Son of God portends also a break or turning point; if this be not affirmed, all specifically Christian reality would lose its meaning. [140]

---

[140] This is still to be held firmly as against attempts to rate what is specifically Christian perhaps too much in the unity of salvation history of the old and new covenants, and to speak only of a "first" and "second"

"In many and various ways God spoke of old to our fathers by the prophets; but in these last days he has spoke to us by a Son, whom he appointed the heir of all things, through whom also he created the world" (He 1:1–2).

God's speaking through the Son is not a speaking like that through the prophets in the old covenant, since "One of the Holy Trinity, without changing himself, became man"[141] while the Son of God, through whom all things were made (Jn. 1: 3) "mixed himself" with creation without becoming a part of it. Through the Son there is not handed down first of all a divine teaching, nor are merely a "new commandment" and a new promise given, rather the coming of the Son of God in our human nature establishes something absolutely new in God's communication with the world. It is only the coming of the Son of God in our flesh, his life, his passion, death and resurrection which made "liturgy" at last possible; he who ascended into heaven and who is present in the midst of his disciples is its principal celebrant until his return in glory (Matt. 18:20).[142]

1.6.1. "MAN SHALL NOT SEE ME AND LIVE" (EXOD 33:20)

This reply of God's to Moses' yearning to be allowed to behold the divine countenance is evidence of a deep lack of communication between man and God. Following the breach of original sin man has become estranged from God, and is afraid that in union with God – what the image of "sight of the divine countenance" wishes to express – he will lose himself rather than reach perfection in him. In the narrative of the Fall, Sacred Scripture of the Old Testament has a deep grasp of man's situation as of a being who has separated himself from God as from the source of all life. Between God and man there lies an impassable trench which man has dug up.[143] He has become unfit for communication with God, for receiving Uncreated grace.

As the creation of man was God's supreme act, so is the salvation of man out of the deathly lack of communication only possible as a sovereign act of God.

It took place through the incarnate, crucified and risen Son. Only through Christ could the restoration – indeed the superelevation – of the original good situation of man as creature and God's partner take place. Moses could not behold the countenance of God without dying; on the Mount of the Transfiguration the disciples were offered the vision of the godhead in a human face.

In the Transfiguration the Incarnate One showed the disciples the divine glory through the medium of a real human face. In the Person of the God-man there appears the totally new way of relationship between God and man. Without losing its identity the creature finds its fulfilment in the relationship to the Creator. On Tabor Christ showed himself as the prehistorical Logos, without obliterating the other, human truth of the genuinely Incarnate One. Rather, it is this which beams forth within the light of the godhead in a radiance never yet seen. On the Mount of the Transfiguration redemption in Christ showed itself as the counterpart to the Fall: through Christ God and man are

---

covenant, losing sight perhaps somewhat of the newness of the new, brought by Christ, cf. e.g., E. Zenger (ed.), Der Neue Bund im Alten. Zur Bundestheologie der beiden Testamente, Freiburg-Basel-Vienna 1993 (QD 146).

[141] Thus the Monogenes Hymn of the Chrysostom liturgy, cf. Kallis 56–58; Kucharek, Liturgy, 373–378.

[142] Cf. Corbon, Liturgie aus dem Urquell 163f.

[143] Cf. Lossky, Théol. myst. 131: "The infinite distance between the created and the uncreated ... becomes an impassable abyss for man, after he has fixed himself in a new state, close to non-being, a state of sin and of death."

joined together once more, through Christ man has access to divinization, through him he finds his fulfilment in the participation in the fullness of divine life, and yet remains man.

1.6.2. CHRIST'S HUMAN NATURE AS THE SOURCE OF SALVATION

The newness of God's communication with man, which beamed forth at the Transfiguration, is located in Christ's human nature itself. "Before the incarnation of the Logos the kingdom of God was as far removed from us, as heaven is far from the earth. But because the king of heaven has appeared on earth, the kingdom of God has also drawn near." [144]

It is only through Christ that human nature, which had detached itself from God, has become once again capable of communication with him, and that God's benevolence which had never ceased, can once again be received by man. [145]

With Christ the heavenly liturgy of the Trinity has appeared on earth; the work of the Son, in whose Person Godhead and Manhood are united in a unique way, is to create anew God's perfect affirmation of existence in man. The heavenly liturgy has its home on earth in the Son of God made man. His body is the temple of this liturgy (Mark 14: 58), and its gates stand open inviting to participation in the divine life.

The first decisive salvific event, to be distinguished from everything that went before it, is the incarnation of the Son. From Mary there was born not a man "endowed with grace", in whom divine grace would have been present in a special measure, but not qualitatively different from every other graced person, but rather the Logos, the second trinitarian hypostasis. It was only the unique union with human nature in his Person which opened anew for man access to the reception of uncreated grace. [146] "Nothing can come from God to man and nothing can go from man to God except through his [Christ's] body." [147] It is only since the incarnation that human nature possesses once again an "antenna" for uncreated grace, for the God who incessantly and unchangeably shows his benevolence to man and invites him to communion with himself.

This holds true first of all in a unique way for the Person of Jesus Christ.

As the truly Incarnate One he shares human nature in common with all men, just as he shares the divine nature with the Father and the Holy Spirit as the eternal Son of God. In his person godhead and manhood meet, without nullifying one another, and without mixing with each other and thus corrupting each other. In Christ they enter into a perfect union. [148] In Christ the whole fulness of deity dwells (Col 2:9); in him a real man, but who is also God from God, goes to meet man. In Christ God goes to meet man with a human face not as if he had only placed a human mask over the burning light of the godhead, but because in a manner never realized hitherto, Christ's genuine human existence is the created and already divinized "space between" in which God through the Incarnate Son enters into relationship with men. [149] Christ's human nature,

---

[144] Cf. Gregory Palamas, Hom. 31-PG 151, 392 C.

[145] Cf. Lossky, Théol. myst. 141; J. Meyendorff, Le Christ dans la théologie byzantine, Paris, 1969, 281.

[146] Cf. Gregory Palamas, Hom. 37 – PG 151, 464 A; cf. also Kunzler, Porta Orientalis 59–63 with the relevant quotations from the sources.

[147] Corbon, Liturgie aus dem Urquell 75.

[148] DH 302; cf. P. Smulders, Dogmengeschichliche und lehramtliche Entfaltung der Christologie: MySal III, 1, 424–476.

[149] Cf. Staniloae, Orthodoxe Dogmatik I, 255.

his human body, is "not a mere sign of the presence of God like the bush on Sinai, neither is it the inanimate receptacle of the godhead ... it is sacrament, it is 'anointed' with the divine nature in the personal unity of the Son."[150] And it is the work of Jesus of Nazareth, who is the Christ of God, to bless the world with the divine life, which he as the Son possesses with the Father and the Spirit from eternity.

Whosoever then participates in Christ, communicates with the Trinity through him and obtains a share in the divine life. Christ's human nature is therefore for man the "inexhaustible fountain of sanctification"[151] out of which uncreated grace flows to him. The incarnate Son of God is the communication of God in person; in him the relationship between God and man is not merely re-established, but is brought to a height which was never reached in the original good condition of man before the Fall.

1.6.3. THE SIGNIFICANCE OF DEATH AND RESURRECTION FOR REDEMPTION

If the Incarnation is thus so important for redemption, what role then do the death and resurrection of the Lord play?

The West lays a very heavy soteriological emphasis on cross and resurrection or even – especially in Protestantism – on the sufferings of the cross alone.[152] The doctrine of redemption based on vicarious satisfaction (soteriology of satisfaction) – which Anselm of Canterbury formulated in a classical manner[153] characterizes the theological tradition of the West. Today Anselm's theology of redemption is rather debated. While von Balthasar stresses its abiding value, and other theologians want Anselm's thought to subserve new insights by an "anthropological turning point", others maintain their basic criticism of satisfaction soteriology.[154]

While in Luther the theology of the cross determines greatly the doctrine of grace,[155] in the eastern theology on the contrary, the doctrine of grace, that is to say of God's communication with man in view of deification, moulds also the theology of the cross. In this way the eastern and western view of redemption through the cross and resurrection of Jesus complete one another reciprocally.

In the cross and resurrection of Christ there culminates in an unsurpassable way the loving affection of the triune God towards the world and towards man, but it "culminates" also conversely in the negative sense: the death on the cross of the Incarnate One and his descent to the dead contain the deepest depths of estrangement from God, which is the ultimate consequence of man's original sinful turning away from the life-giving relationship with God, that is death. In this total depth he who descended to the

[150] Corbon, Liturgie aus dem Urquell 76.
[151] Cf. Kunzler, Porta Orientalis 98 with the relevant quotations from the sources.
[152] Cf. Greshake, "Der Wandel der Erlösungsvorstellungen" 84f.
[153] Anselm of Canterbury, Cur Deus Homo – Warum Gott Mensch geworden. Lateinisch und deutsch. Trans. and ed. by Franciscus Salesius Schmitt. Darmstadt, 4th edn., 1986.
[154] Cf. H. U. v. Balthasar, Herrlichkeit – Eine theologische Ästhetik, Bd. II, 1.Einsiedeln, 3rd edn., 1984, 217–263. 250–257; K. Kienzler, Die Erlösungslehre Anselms von Canterbury aus der Sicht des mittelalterlichen jüdisch-christlichen Religionsgesprächs: H. P. Heinz / K. Kienzler / J. J. Petuchowski (eds.), Versöhnung in der jüdischen und christlichen Liturgie. Freiburg-Basle-Vienna 1990 (QD 124), 88–116; Kunzler, Porta Orientalis 150–175.
[155] Cf. Greshake, Der Wandel der Erlösungsvorstellungen, 92. On Luther's dialectic between God's anger and his mercy cf. Luther WA 18, 633: "Deus dum vivificat, facit illud occidendo, dum iustificat, facit illud reos faciendo, dum in coelum vehit, facit id ad infernum ducendo."

dead hell cures human nature from death and leads it back into life. In this sense one can speak of the reconciliation of man through the cross of Christ, not in the sense of a reconciliation with the angry Father, [156] but rather of man who had fallen into death with the triune God, who is life itself: man is once again capable of living, because Christ has again made possible for man seated "in darkness and the shadow of death" the relationship to the living God and opened for him the gateway to eternal life. In the cross and the descent to the dead the divine catabasis reaches its "climax" by going down to the realm of death in order to establish even there the life-giving reign of the kingdom of God.

If Christ is not only true man, but also true God, one of the Trinity, to whom then did he offer up his life on the cross, for whom is the eucharistic sacrifice intended? In a priestly prayer of the Byzantine eucharistic celebration it is said of Christ: "For you are the One who offers and who is offered, who welcomes and who is distributed." [157] Christ's work, even his sacrifice on the cross, is to be interpreted only in a Trinitarian sense: when Christ offers on the cross (and subsequently in the eucharist), then as the one who offers he performs a Trinitarian act, because as the final consequence of the incarnation he leads into the divine life and thereby gifts with life the human nature which he had assumed and which had been separated from God by original sin and exposed to death. [158]

The crucified, risen and ascended into heaven One by his high-priestly sacrificial act carries man who had fallen a prey to death up into the fullness of life of the Trinity ("carry up" as "offer", *anapherein*). [159] "He did this once for all when he offered up himself "(Heb 7:27). The crucified manhood of the eternal Son takes his seat on the throne of the Trinity and is "the source of eternal salvation to all who obey him" (Heb 5:9). "History is not concluded with the ascension; on the contrary it expands until its definitive liberation." [160]

Until the eschatological fulfilment the tension between "already" and "not yet" characterizes this interim time, during which death must still be undergone, while on the other hand every year the Easter troparion of the Byzantine Church resounds: "Christ is risen from the dead, he has conquered death by death and brought new life to those in the grave."

Resurrection is the necessary consequence for everyone who stands in communion with the living God through Christ's human nature as the fountain of grace. Cross and resurrection are not therefore isolated soteriological facts but are consistent consequences of man's renewal based on the incarnation. Here also the principle of the divine catabasis is at play: according to Evdokimov all the salvific actions of the Trinity were at all times directed to the incarnation of the Son with its inherent consequence of cross, grave, descent to the dead and resurrection. God does not merely respond to man's bondage to death, but pursues the same goal which he would have aimed at, even had the Fall not taken place: the divinization of man, his assumption into the fullness of the life of the Trinity. [161]

---

[156] Cf. Greshake, Gottes Heil 101; Müller, "Neue Ansätze" 55.
[157] Cf. Kallis 100–101.
[158] Cf. Meyendorff, Le Christ, 273. On the prayer itself: Kucharek, Liturgy, 480.
[159] Cf. Staniloae, Dogmatik II, 102–120.
[160] Corbon, Liturgie aus dem Urquell 53.
[161] Cf. P. Evdokimov, Die Frau und das Heil der Welt. Moers-Aschaffenburg, 1989, 45f.

Death as the completion of human withdrawal into the self and the ending of every relationship was shared in by the Son of God according to his human nature. His godhead however – which cannot die, as it is one with the Father and the Holy Spirit – re-creates the life-giving relationship between God and man in the dead human existence, embraces the whole mortal creation and leads it into the divine life of the Trinity, as is expressed in a prayer of the Chrysostom liturgy: "You were in the tomb with your body, in the realm of the dead with your soul as God, in paradise with the thief and on the throne Christ, with the Father and the Spirit, filling all things, O immeasurable One." [162]

Thus the life-giving relationship between God and man becomes radically new through Christ: as the dead One he unites the whole of reality together, uncreated and created, from the realm of the dead of the underworld up to the throne of the Trinity! This concentration in the dead Christ of all that exists, in the mystery of the descent to the underworld, is simultaneously the onset of Easter, as the Byzantine Easter icon portrays it: Christ stretches out his hands, even in hell he invites to the acceptance of life-giving communion, he gathers up in himself the realm of the dead which he seats on the throne together with the thief in Paradise and with the Father and the Spirit. Incarnation, death on the cross, descent to the underworld, resurrection and ascension seen from this standpoint are partial aspects of a single divine act which takes place through the Son, a single drama of salvation which has as its aim the bringing of man up to the divine life and therefore can be described as a "sacrificial offering" in the sense of "carrying up on high" (*anaphora*).

1.6.4. CHRISTOS LEITOURGOS – THE HIGH-PRIESTLY MEDIATOR

"There is one God, and there is one mediator between God and men, the man Christ Jesus" (1 Tim 2:5). This mediator is nor merely the harbinger of the Father's will or of a new commandment, nor yet the teacher of a new idea or method of man's ascent to God, rather as one of the Trinity he is the high-priestly mediator between the triune God and men.

His mediatorship consists in recapitulating in his Person the created world, separated as it is from the living God, with a view to its being carried up sacrificially on high ("*Anaphora*") through death into the fullness of life of the Trinity. This recapitulation is to be understood in the sense of that theological principle, which Irenaeus of Lyons formulated [163] and which runs through the whole of patristic theology: "*Quod non assumptum, non sanatum*". Whoever is in communion with him in his human nature as the fountain of grace, has through him communion with the triune God, from whom the fullness of life comes to him.

Through the Logos, through whom all things were made (John 1:3), and who became a real man, the triune God enters into living relationship with man. In view of the recapitulation in the Son, not only have all things been made by him, but also "in him and for him" (Col 1:16). "In him" everything has been created; he is the recapitulation,

---

[162] Cf. Kallis 104 – 105.

[163] Cf. F. Gahbauer, "O admirabile commercium". Relecture zweier Antiphoneninterpretationen, ALw 27 (1985) 70 – 90.73 where Irenaeus is treated of; cf. also N. Brox, Offenbarung. Gnosis und gnostischer Mythos bei Irenäus v. Lyon, Salzburg-München 1966, 184 – 188; P. Smulders, Dogmengeschichtliche und lehramtliche Entfaltung der Christologie: MySal III,1. Einsiedeln-Zürich-Cologne 1970, 406 – 411; W. Pannenburg, Grundzüge der Christologie, Gütersloh 1964,32 – 37.

preceding creation, of all creatures, which "through him" will be sent off to the profane status of creaturely selfhood, which however is not an end in itself, but rather the way to a goal which will be attained "through him": to arrive at glory "in him", at a participation in the heavenly liturgy of the eternal joy of the three divine Persons in one another.

Everything in heaven and on earth finds its way to a unity under Christ the Head (Eph 1: 10). [164] Christ is the new, cosmic Adam, who presents to the Father the creation which is recapitulated in him, [165] a fact which underlines once again the anaphoric point of view of sacrifice. A similar point of view has an effect in the epistle to the Romans: "From him and through him and to him are all things" (Rom 11:36).

The eschatological recapitulation of creation under Christ the Head is based, according to Rom. 6:5, on the death on the cross: "For if we have been united with him in a death like his, we shall certainly be united with him in a resurrection like his." The original Greek text however speaks of the "implanting" of man into his death and resurrection. Whoever has communion with Christ, whoever with the sisters and brothers has become "one" in Christ (Gal. 3: 28), whoever has come to unity in the new Adam, has access to the Father, "through him", in whom all the fullness of God dwells (Col. 1: 19). "Implanted" in him, whose human nature is the source of uncreated grace, there is nothing more which could separate man from communion with the living God, not even death and the underworld are an exception, ever since Christ as the source of the godhead has "embraced" into the deepest depths of human existence the whole of human nature alienated from God and fallen a prey to death. [166]

Man is redeemed while he once again, through the Son, through the incarnation and descent to the underworld,, attains the capacity to receive the uncreated grace, and hence God himself, which issues from the human nature of Christ as from a fountain. As such a visible fountain, edible in the eucharistic species, audible in his word, in short a fountain of uncreated grace accessible to the senses Christ is the primordial sacrament, which mediates divine life. Since there is no communion between God and man, which does not come about through the human nature assumed by him, he is as such the high priestly mediator, the absolute celebrant, through whom alone the divine work for the many ("*Leiturgia*") can take place of taking man – and through him the whole of creation – up into the fullness of life of the Trinity.

Christ's human nature is "sacrament" because it is united in his Person with the godhead without confusion or separation. "Because the manhood of Jesus in all the fibres of its being and in its loving acquiescence is 'sonship', it can make is own the lightest movements and the most intimate wounds of our humanity in order to infuse the Father's life into them. Henceforward the divinized energies of the body of Christ will lay hold of us in our whole being, our whole "body". Whichever of our physical realities the Lord may care to take up: water, bread, oil, man and woman, a contrite heart, he renders them suitable for himself in his growing body and makes them radiate vividly from there. What we refer to as sacraments are in reality divinized actions of the body of Christ in our humanity. These energies are sacramental with full spiritual realism,

---

[164] Cf. Josef Ernst, Pleroma und Pleroma Christi. Geschichte und Deutung eines Begriffes der paulinischen Antilegomena. Regensburg 1970 (Biblische Untersuchungen V), 154–172.

[165] Cf. Lossky, Théol. myst. 133. Lossky refers to von Balthasar, Kosmische Liturgie 267f.

[166] Cf. Corbon, Liturgie aus dem Urquell 51–55; Lossky, Théol. myst. 138.

otherwise they could not divinize us. We can only receive the Spirit of Jesus because he takes our body on himself. In a certain regard Jesus could not attain to the full maturity of his divinized power during his earthly life: he was restricted in his relationships, not through his body, but through its mortality. From the time that he conquered death, these barriers have been surmounted and laid low. In this respect Christ's body became sacramental in the fullest sense only through his cross and resurrection. "By his ascension" Ambrose says to us "Christ has entered into his mysteries", that is to say, into his sacramental energies. This transition was the Pascha. Notwithstanding the fact that from the incarnation on Christ's body was sacrament, it becomes fully and immeasurably so in his resurrection and ascension; from then on it is for evermore the sacrament of communion between God and men." [167]

This continuous action of Christ as celebrant in the liturgical rites of the Church is, according to Casel, "*mysterium*" in a third sense. "*Mysterium*" is first of all that of the living God, who dwells in unapproachable light, then the revelation of God in the incarnation of his Son. "Christ is the personal *mysterium*, because he reveals the invisible godhead in the flesh." All that Christ did and said, above all however the Lord's cross and resurrection, is "*mysterium*" in this manner. Since however Christ is not the mediator of a doctrine or a teaching, because he is no divine teacher, but rather a redeemer through a salvific act therefore he continues his salvific act in the Church in the mysteries. In this way "*mysterium*" acquires a third sense, which however is closely linked to the other two meanings, which in turn are one. Ever since Christ is no longer visible among us, 'the visible presence of our Redeemer passed over into the mysteries' as Leo the Great says. We find his Person, his salvific acts, the workings of his grace in the mysteries of cult, as Ambrose says: 'I find thee in the mysteries ... ' [168]

Bibliography

O. Casel, Das christliche Kultmysterium, Regensburg 3rd edn. 1948.

Conférences Saint-Serge, XVIIe Semaine d'études liturgiques 1970, L'économie du salut dans la liturgie, Roma 1982 (Bibliotheca EL, Subsidia 25).

I. H. Dalmais, La liturgie, célébration du mystère du salut: Martimort 1, Paris 1983, 260–282.

G. Greshake, Erlösung und Freiheit. Zur Neuinterpretation der Erlösungslehre Anselms von Canterbury, ThQ 153 (1973) 323–345.

G. Greshake, Der Wandel der Erlösungsvorstellungen in der Theologiegeschichte, L. Scheffczyk (ed.): Erlösung und Emanzipation, Freiburg-Basel-Vienna 1973 (QD 61), 69–101.

G. Greshake, Gottes Heil – Glück des Menschen. Theologische Perspektiven, Freiburg-Basel-Vienna 1983.

V. Lossky, A l'image et á la ressemblance de Dieu, Paris 1967.

S. Marsili, Verso una teologia della liturgia: Anamnesis 1, Torino 2nd edn. 1991, 47–84.

S. Marsili, La teologia della liturgia nel Vaticano II: Anamnesis 1, Torino 2nd edn. 1991, 85–105.

J. Meyendorff, Le Christ dans la théologie byzantine, Paris 1969.

G. L. Müller, Neue Ansätze zum Verständnis der Erlösung, MThZ 43 (1992) 51–73.

E. Schillebeeckx, De sacramentele Heilseconomie, Antwerpen 1952.

---

[167] Corbon, Liturgie aus dem Urquell 76.
[168] Casel, Kultmysterium 19.

1.7. THE SPIRIT, "TO BRING US THE FULLNESS OF GRACE" (EUCHARISTIC PRAYER IV)

1.7.1. "OBLIVION OF THE SPIRIT" IN THE WEST?

It is not only theologians of the East who reproach the West with giving too little consideration to the action of the Holy Spirit; theologians of the West also speak of a western "oblivion of the Spirit". Thus the Maronite archbishop of Beirut, Ziadé, declared at Vatican II, "The Latin doctrine on the Church is still in its infancy with regard to pneumatology." [169] According to Eisenbach this holds true for western liturgical theology up to Vatican II. [170] What is the salvific role of the Holy Spirit, of whom the fourth Eucharistic Prayer says he is the "first gift to those who believe", the One who will "complete [the Son's] work on earth and bring us the fullness of grace"?

Like the Son, the Holy Spirit also has his own "hypostatic function"; he assumes his own unmistakable role in the relationship of the triune God to the world. Irenaeus of Lyons wished to express this with the image of the Son and the Spirit as the "Father's two hands". [171] The distinct functions of the Son and the Spirit in the communication of the triuine God with the world are expressed in the prepositions "through" and "in": as all creation was launched into being, was redeemed and brought to the Father "through" the Son, so all sanctification is fulfilled "in" the Holy Spirit. Already the image chosen by Irenaeus implies that the salvific work of the Son and the Holy Spirit belong together.

1.7.2. FROM THE FATHER, THROUGH THE SON, IN THE HOLY SPIRIT

God enters into relationship with the world "from" the Father, "through" the Son and "in" the Holy Spirit. The anabatic return of this catabasis follows in the same order, "in" the Holy Spirit, "through" the Son, "to" the Father. Indeed the official prayer of the Church also follows the same structure. [172]

The Holy Spirit communicates with the world in no other way than "from" the Father and "through" the Son. For this purpose the Son became true man, so that he might be, according to his authentic human nature, the source "through" which the Holy Spirit imparts the divine life to man and the world. While doing so the Spirit almost foregoes the revelation of his Person and conceals himself in such a fashion behind his gift, that a confusion is possible between the Spirit and the Spirit's gift.

The Incarnate One has a visage, he is experienced as a personal *vis-à-vis,* as an I who acts and loves. The Father remains for ever the One standing over against the world, "No one has ever seen God" (John 1:18). On the other hand Jesus' witness about the Father against the background of the experience of fathers or fatherhood which is accessible to all men, none the less lends a personal "face" to the Father, even if only in the sense of a certain analogy.

---

[169] Cf. M. Garijo-Guembe, Konsequenzen des Dialogs mit der Orthodoxie für die römische Ekklesiologie: K. Richter (ed.): Das Konzil war erst der Anfang. Die Bedeutung des II. Vatikanums für Theologie und Kirche. Mainz 1991, 140–158. 143.

[170] Cf. F. Eisenbach, Die Gegenwart Jesu Christi im Gottesdienst. Systematische Studien zur Liturgie-konstitution des II. Vatikanischen Konzils, Mainz 1982. 342–348, 699–703.

[171] Cf. Adv. haer. IV,20,1 – SChr 100 (Paris 1965), 626.

[172] Cf. J. A. Jungmann, Die Stellung Christi im liturgischen Gebet, Münster 1925 (Liturgiegeschichtl. Forschungen 7/8). Neudruck mit Nachträgen des Verfassers. Münster 2nd edn. 1962 (LQF 19/20).

In contrast to Father and Son the Spirit hides his personal face, in order to express thereby something which characterizes the Trinity as a whole: to be complete communication. The personal I of the Pneuma unites itself through the gift of divine life in such a way with the personal I of the human recipient that it becomes the latter's own I, without affecting the personal identity of the Spirit or that of the man who receives the gift. The Holy Spirit is the One who stands at the frontier between uncreated and created reality, the giver and finisher humbly hiding his personal face, who so implants in the heart of man the life of the triune God – divine, therefore extraneous life – that it must become the personal life of the man so endowed and not remain something extraneous to him. [173]

"No one can say 'Jesus is Lord' except by the Holy Spirit" (1 Cor 12:3b): the confession which brings about all salvation is absolutely the confession of the believer and simultaneously absolutely a gift brought about by the Spirit. The Holy Spirit enkindles faith in man and keeps it alive, but in such a way that the believing confession none the less can become the property of the believer. The Spirit acts in such a manner that out of love he hides his face from a front view behind his gift; he is in us without replacing us; he believes, prays, hopes and loves in us in such fashion that he "demonstrates" it to us and "prompts" it to us, first of all he renders it possible for us; but at the same time it is we who believe, pray, hope and love. It is not least for this reason that the Eastern theologians distinguish between the Spirit who works in us, and the gifts of the Spirit which are given by him. [174]

The revelation of his countenance takes place in the *eschaton,* when the Spirit's work is completed, to lead creation "in him" to the fullness of God's life. The transmission of the divine life by the Spirit carries thereby so markedly the "signature" of the third Person, that the Giver remains hidden behind his gift and can be mistaken for it. But he himself stands on the frontier between created and uncreated nature as the "sanctifier" and "finisher".

1.7.3. SPIRITUS COMMUNICATOR

That the Spirit communicates with creation "through" the Son constitutes the significance of the basic christological assertion of the union "without confusion or separation" of both natures in the Incarnate One: in Christ in an absolutely unique and singular fashion human nature united itself with the divine, which in itself is trinitarian life. The Son, "through" whom all has been created and in whom the whole of creation is recapitulated, joined himself with human nature; in his Person God and man meet one another in a unique way. He is the fountain-head, from out of which the divine life – transmitted by the Spirit – streams to man. For this reason the Holy Spirit is inseparably bound up with the Son's work on earth, as with the work of the highly exalted Lord. He always comes to men through the Son and transmits to them the gift of divine life. What Vatican II afirms of the Church as the mystical Body of Christ, is based on the huuman nature of the Incarnate One united to the Godhead: "In the human nature united

---

[173] Cf. J. Meyendorff, Initiation á la théologie byzantine. Paris 1975, 228f; V. Lossky, La théologie mystique de l'Eglise d'Orient. Paris 1944, 159, 169, 243; D. Staniloae: Orthodoxe Dogmatik II. Zürich – Einsiedeln-Köln-Gütersloh 1990 (Ökumenische Theologie 15), 236f.

[174] Cf. Lossky, Théol. myst. 169; J. Meyendorff, A Study of Gregory Palamas, London 2nd edn. 1974, 230– 232; G. Richter, Ansätze und Motive für die Lehre des Gregorios Palamas von den göttlichen Energien, OstKSt 31 (1982) 281–296. 289.

to himself, the son of God, by overcoming death through his own death and resurrection redeemed man ... For by communicating his Spirit, Christ mystically constitutes as his body those brothers of his who are called together from every nation. In that body the life of Christ is communicated to those who believe and who, through the sacraments are united in a hidden and real way to Christ ... " (LG 7).

The undivided Trinity is active in the work of salvation, although not undifferentiated with regard to the divine Persons each with its different functions. Through the incarnation of the Logos the work of the Son becomes historically perceptible. According to Zizioulas however the work of the Pneuma consists precisely in this, to set free the saving work of the Son from the limitations of time and space of the Christ event. The Spirit brings about the communication between the triune God and man beyond the narrow time frame of the earthly history of Jesus. He transmits the divine life as the gift of the undivided Trinity "from" the Father "through" the Son to concrete men living in the diversity of time and place.

The Holy Spirit is therefore supremely active. He does not set up as it were a "pipeline" which would connect men with the saving work of Christ and through which the salvation won by him would come to men, rather the Spirit himself transmits the divine life as gift of the Trinity and brings it to perfection in man. The Spirit as communicator predates the saving work of Christ and completes it; he makes it possible, brings it to its ecclesial dimension and leads it to its eschatological completion. Or conversely "from below": every human response to God's invitation to enter into life-giving communion with him takes its beginning "in" the Holy Spirit, goes "through "the Son to the Father as the" Fount of Godhead", "from" whom not only the divine Persons of the Son and the Spirit have proceeded, but also he who is the fountain-head of divinization of man and the world, "out" of which the divine life streams. [175] "The unanimous patristic tradition of the East ascribes the operative power in all 'holy rites' to the hypostatic influence of the third Person of the Trinity: to the Holy Spirit, who proceeds from the Father and is sent by the Son for the all-embracing completion of the work of salvation; as creator of life, the sublime operative power of all embodiments of what is heavenly, fountain of grace and of divine energies in the bosom of the Church. As aid and heavenly fire which descends upon all flesh, he sanctifies and consecrates it. Every sacrament has its own Pentecost, its epiclesis, the prayer addressed to the Father to send the Holy Spirit. In this way the epiclesis is a liturgical confession of dogma, the worshipping application of the theology of the Holy Spirit." [176]

1.7.4. THE IMPORTANCE OF THE EPICLESIS IN THE LITURGY

The epiclesis is an official prayer of the Church which is "always answered", [177] by which she calls down from above into a situation of time and space and actualizes the uncreated grace which is always and everywhere present as the communication of the triune God with its creation. In the epicletic invocation of the Spirit as donor and finisher of this communication, the Church opens itself in a concrete historical situation

---

[175] Cf. J. D. Zizioulas, Being as Communion. Studies in Personhood and the Church. With a Foreword by John Meyendorff, Crestwood-New York 1985 (Contemporary Greek Theologians 4), 134; Ps-Dionysius, De div. nom. 2,7 – PG 3,645 B.

[176] P. Evdokimov, Das Gebet der Ostkirche, Graz-Vienna-Köln, 1986, 69f.

[177] Cf. R. Hotz, Sakramente im Wechselspiel zwischen Ost und West, Zürich-Köln-Gütersloh 1979 (Ökumen. Theol. 2), 222 – 265.

to the unchanging wooing of the Trinity, by which she allows herself to be drawn into the trinitarian communion. In the epiclesis which calls down from above the work common to all the divine Persons, "the perichoresis [being-in-one-another] communion" of the Persons of the Trinity "has its consequences" and reproduces itself in the community of Jesus', a community, "which is open to every creature." And this fellowship is "experienced in the Holy Spirit", the donor and finisher of this incorporation. [178]

The epiclesis is a concrete historical situation in so far as it admits of the wooing by the triune God (which is always there "in" the Holy Spirit), as an event in time and space in the concrete situations of life. In the eucharistic celebration, in all actions of the sacraments and sacramentals, indeed also in prayer it is the Holy Spirit who bestows the divine life on creation and brings it to completion in it, without being separated from Father and from Son in his Person or his work. Already now there radiates in creation, on which the Holy Spirit has been invoked, its eschatological beauty and dignity. Considered in this way every prayer is "epiclesis" and the epiclesis is the model for every form of Christian prayer. [179]

Once again the mutuality of the saving work of the Son and the Spirit becomes apparent: while all creatures are recapitulated through the Son as members under the one Head and brought into a unity with the human nature of Christ, from which (as Simeon of Thessalonica puts it) the grace of the Holy Spirit flows to them as "rivers", in a corresponding way the Holy Spirit brings about multiformity without eliminating that unity. The insertion of creation into the Trinitarian communion does not connote the abolition of differences, but precisely their awakening, the development of personal (charismatic) personality in the community as "jewellery" and "beauty" of diversity in unity. To the manifold working of the Spirit as donor of uncreated grace to creation there correspond the manifold epicleses according to the situation of the Chuch in time: "For wherever occurs the name and invocation of God, the most holy Trinity, who has created all, and who alone is God, there all is holy, and everything works and heals and saves through grace." [180]

Therefore the epicletic element is never lacking in any sacramental rite; in the Byzantine rite it is not lacking even in prayer since the opening prayers of each Hour of the liturgy of the Hours, as is well known, contain an invocation of the Holy Spirit. Granted that in the past there were controversies between East and West about the significance of the epiclesis in the "confection" of the sacraments, nowadays however there obtains a wide-ranging consensus on the role of the Holy Spirit in the Church's liturgy, and thence also on the significance of the epiclesis, which along with the anamnesis is a basic element of every liturgical prayer and action. [181]

It is the epiclesis which shows every liturgical act to be an entry by man into the divine fullness of life, which coming "from" the Father "through" the Son "in" the Holy Spirit, presents itself as accessible to him in time and space in the holy actions of the

[178] Cf. J. Moltmann, Die einladende Einheit des dreieinigen Gottes, Concilium 21 (1985) 35–41. 39f.
[179] Cf. R. Albertine, "Theosis" According to the Eastern Fathers, Mirrored in the Development of the Epiclesis, EL 105 (1991) 393–417. 396.
[180] Simeon of Thessalonica, Dialogos 129 – PG 155, 337 B.
[181] Cf. B. Kleinheyer, Preisung und Anrufung Gottes zur Feier der Sakramente, LJ 42 (1992) 3–24.13–24. On the controversy at the Council of Florence cf. M. Kunzler, Gnadenquellen. Symeon von Thessaloniki (+ 1429) als Beispiel für die Einfflußnahme des Palamismus auf die orthodoxe Sakramententheologie und Liturgik, Trier 1989 (TThSt 47), 338–347.

Church. This is apparent for example in the epiclesis of the Chrysostom liturgy, which simultaneously as a consecration and communion epiclesis forms a unity: "Send down your Holy Spirit on us and on these present gifts... and make this bread become the precious body of your Christ." The prayer for the descent of the Spirit for the transformation of the gifts is preceded therefore by the prayer for his descent on us. This is not a whit less a prayer for transformation. According to the Slavonic tradition the following dialogue between Priest and Deacon is inserted into the epiclesis: the priest speaks: "Lord, who sent your all-holy Spirit on the apostles at the third hour, do not take him away from us, but renew us who pray to you." The priest repeats this prayer three times, while the deacon adds verses from Psalm 50 [51] "A pure heart create for me, O God, put a steadfast spirit within me. Do not cast me away from your presence, nor deprive me of your holy Spirit." Together with the transformation of the bread and wine those who pray thus are destined to be transformed while they are incorporated into the mystery of the divinized human nature of Christ present under the species and offered as food and drink, from which men receive the Spirit who donates the divine life to them and guides it to perfection in them.

Bibliography

Y. Congar, Pneumatologie ou "Christomonisme" dans la tradition latine? Ecclesia a Spiritu Sancto. Mélanges théologiques G. Philipps. Gembloux 1970 (Bibl. Eph. Théol. Lovan. 27), 41–63.

W. Kasper / G. Sauter, Kirche – Ort des Geistes, Freiburg-Basel-Wien 1976 (Ökumenische Forschungen, Kleine ökumenische Schriften 8).

J. M. Krahe, Der Herr ist Geist. Studien zur Theologie Odo Casels. Vol. 1, Das Mysterium Christi (Pietas Liturgica 2), St. Ottilien 1986. Vol. 2, Das Mysterium vom Pneuma (Pietas Liturgica 3), St. Ottilien 1986.

L. Laham, Pneumatologie der Sakramente der christlichen Mystagogie: E. C. Suttner (ed.), Taufe und Firmung. Zweites Regensburger Ökumenisches Symposion, Regensburg 1971, 63–71.

H. Mühlen, Una Mystica Persona. Die Kirche als das Mysterium der heilsgeschichtlichen Identität des Heiligen Geistes in Christus und den Christen: Eine Person in vielen Personen, München-Paderborn-Wien 3rd edn. 1968.

H. Mühlen, Der Heilige Geist als Person. In der Trinität, bei der Inkarnation und im Gnadenbund. Ich-Du-Wir, Münster 5th edn. 1988 (Münsterische Beiträge zur Theologie 26).

G. Wagner, Der Heilige Geist als offenbar machende und vollendende Kraft. Der Beitrag der orthodoxen Theologie, C. Heitmann / H. Mühlen (eds.): Erfahrung und Theologie des Heiligen Geistes, Hamburg-München 1974, 214–222.

1.8. CHURCH I: THE CHURCH AS THE PLACE AND BESTOWAL OF GRACE

Communication presupposes partners who communicate with each other. Hence men, for whom the divine catabasis, the descent of God for a lifegiving relationship, is intended, constitute a presupposition for the realization of communication. The triune God turns towards men. In the saving work of the Son they become his brothers and sisters, people who belong to the Lord as his community ('Kyriake-Church'), who are called forth ('Ecclesia') to participation in the divine fullness of life. Associated to-gether in a new unity in Christ as their Head, the Holy Spirit bestows the divine life on them *through* Christ and brings it to perfection in them. The Church is thereby part of the divine catabasis as she constitutes the presupposition for the descent of the heavenly liturgy, which takes place only in her midst and in the time and place of her liturgy. From another – anabatic – point of view one can speak of the *Church's liturgy,* as she enters into the heavenly liturgy which is making itself present in her midst, and so accepts the invitation of the triuine God to life-giving communication with him.

Here however it is a question of the Church as a component of the divine catabasis, as something great put in place by God. As with her liturgy, she must have her ultimate basis in the inter-trinitarian life. Only so is she more than an assembly of people, and what is celebrated in her more than a human work. Therefore: God's *liturgy with respect to* the Church, which presupposes the Church, if it is to exist at all.

1.8.1. THE CHURCH AS PART OF THE DIVINE CATABASIS

God, who is in himself a most loving community of three Persons, turns to his creation inviting it to community. His catabasis too is an action in common of the three divine Persons. God – in himself already a community of persons – turns to his creation in no other way than as community forming. He turns to each one in his uniqueness and invites him to enter into a new, God-made community with him and thereby also with other people, which denotes fullness of life for all in the participation in the divine life. On this account the place of communication of God with man and the world is the human community made by him, the Church. It is the original sacrament; it is the place, the community forming event of communication between God and man with the purpose of divinizing the entire creation. [182]

As such the Church is the "salvation event". As the community of many members under the one Head Christ, who for his own is the source from which the divine life flows, the access to divine life is to be had only "in the Church by way of the sacraments; the Church is the sacramental union of the Body and Blood of Christ". [183]

For this reason one can speak of a "Paradise Church", which was given with cre-ation, of an ecclesiological dimension of the whole of creation, indeed of a Church "inherent" in the whole created world, in which and through which the life-giving com-munication with God takes place. The "Lamb slain in sacrifice ever since the world was made "points to the fact that along with creation its goal in the *communio sanctorum* was already included. The whole world is "virtually Church", it is the subject matter and the goal of history. [184]

As such, the Church is pre-existent in the divine wisdom. It was present in paradise, it revealed itself beforehand in Israel's history, and in its full form came down on earth at Pentecost. The eternal Church, to be equated with the fullness of life within the god-head, entered into the time and space of creation "through" the Son and "in" the Holy Spirit, who continues the saving work of the Son and fulfils all sanctification. [185] Simi-

[182] Cf. O. Semmelroth, Die Kirche als Ursakrament, Frankfurt/M.1953; P. Bilaniuk, The Fifth Lateran Coun-cil (1512–1517) and the Eastern Churches, Toronto 1975, 61.

[183] Cf. C. Yannaras, De l'absence et de l'inconnaissance de Dieu d'après les écrits aréopagitiques et Martin Heidegger, Paris 1971,111f. 119.

[184] Cf. Evdokimov, L'Orthodoxie 124f. with reference to Rev 13:8 and 1 Pet 1:19.

[185] Cf. Lossky, Théol. myst. 106f; Evdokimov, L'Orthodoxie 124f.

lar statements about the Church are to be found also in texts of Vatican II: the Church "already present in figure at the beginning of the world... was prepared in marvellous fashion in the history of the people of Israel and in the old Alliance. Established in this last age of the world, and made manifest in the outpouring of the Spirit, it will be brought to glorious completion at the end of time" (LG 2).

1.8.2. THE CHURCH AS THE PLACE OF THE ANAPHORA

In the Church a sacrifice is offered. This sacrifice is "Anaphora", an all-embracing lifting up of this world into the life-giving relationship with the living god; it is identical with the sacrifice of Christ on the cross, with his death and his desent into the underworld as the fulfilment of the catabasis, of the universal benevolence of God towards his creation. All the depths of creaturely existence separated from God – death itself, indeed even the distancing from God in the underworld – had to be ventured on by God himself. The Son descended into the lowest depths, to fill everything with the divine life. The body of the Incarnate One, sacrificed on the cross and exalted in the resurrection and ascension became the source of deification for all men, out of which the Holy Spirit bestows the divine life. In the cross of his Son God raises creation up to himself, and the Church is the mode of appearance of this sacrifice of God's in time and space, in reality and symbol, the "sacrificial" communication of God with the world, through which God himself raises up creation to himself.

The Church is "the place and the dramatic event of the new creation, of redemption, of transfiguration, of the deification and glorification of man, of the community of men with each other and with the entire visible and invisible cosmos." [186]

The sacrifice is to be understood as a sacrificing by God totally in accordance with the catabasis. It comes "itself already from the incarnate love of God, and so is always already from within a giving by God of himself, into which he takes man, so that he himself is the gift and as gift is once again donor". [187] In sacrifice there is a needed an "inversion of the line of vision": "the fundamental and first proposition is: God himself is acting, he sacrifices, he donates, he is the initiator of this sacrifice in which reconciliation is given, he expresses his love for us in the restless exertions of Jesus up to the complete self-sacrifice. When therefore the sacrifice on the cross or in the eucharist is spoken of, the basic point is to discern God's loving movement of surrender towards us, to welcome it and give thanks for it." [188] For this reason also there is no opposition between meal and sacrifice as the factors which shape the Mass: "eucharist" signifies "equally the gift of the *communio* in which the Lord becomes our food, just as it denotes the sacrifice of Jesus Christ who completes his trinitarian yes to the Father in the yes of the cross and in this 'sacrifice' has reconciled us all to the Father. Between 'meal' and 'sacrifice' there is no opposition; in the Lord's new sacrifice they belong inseparably together." [189]

According to von Balthasar, the incorporation of the Church into Christ's sacrifice does not consist in the oblation of a sacrifice of its own, "but rather in concurring with the Lord's sacrificial will for the sins of the world. Already in the upper chamber of

[186] Bilaniuk 61.
[187] J. Ratzinger, Das Fest des Glaubens. Versuche zur Theologie des Gottesdienstes, Einsiedeln 1981, 84.
[188] Th. Schneider, Zeichen der Nähe Gottes. Grundriß der Sakramententheologie, Mainz 6th edn., 1992, 167.
[189] Ratzinger, Das Fest des Glaubens 45f.

the Last Supper this inclusive gesture consists in the celebration of the meal, which anticipates the Lord's sacrifice of himself. Whoever wishes to let himself be "devoured" by men, needs a mouth that eats and drinks him." The community of disciples assent to Christ's sacrifice, and that which was accomplished for their own salvation they allow to happen to themselves by receiving the body offered in sacrifice. The Church accepts the sacrifice; the devouring mouth of the disciples becomes the instrument of sacrifice. The "sacrificial attitude" of Mary in her acceptance of the *fiat* serves as an example: "At the incarnation she spoke her full *fiat* and was the first to'communicate' in it; but in that same *fiat* there lay already the consent to give back fully what had been received, to release it for the Father. In her there is thus identity between communion and sacrifice, and also identity between the offering of Christ and the offering of self. It is the primal idea of the eucharistic attitude of the Church." [190]

Christ's sacrifice is anchored in the Trinity: the Son's love for the Father includes the acceptance of a sacrifice, a work of the Logos, through which the fallen world was intended to be brought up on high into the inner Trinitarian feast of perfect love. Thus Jesus' sacrifice on the cross is the total dedication of the Son to the Father expressed as an event in time and space – one should always add: in the Holy Spirit – as it takes place in the inner Trinitarian life always and ever, but now with the inclusion of the whole of creation. This sacrifice honours God, because by it man comes to the fullness of divine life.

For this there was need of a real, visible sacrifice (not only a sacrificial attitude) for which Christ's real sacrifice on the cross is the 'real symbol' which fully embodies it in the flesh. The sacrificial attitude as such can come into effect in another temporal coefficient and in another way, as in the eucharistic sacririce. For the relationship between Mass and the event of the cross the Tridentine teaching on the *sacrificium visibile* is therefore important: if in order to bring about the sacrifice, the death of Christ on the cross was the necessary visible real symbol of his inner sacrificial attitude, similarly the outward, visible shape of the Mass as a sacrificial action constitutes the equally necessary real symbol of the inner sacrificial attitude of Christ, in order that it too may be a "sacrifice". [191]

In obedience to Jesus' command of anamnesis, the Church in her liturgical action as real symbol, makes it possible for the timeless sacrificial attitude of Christ to become visible reality now, salvation reality in time and place – in her time and at a given place –, "so that Christ's sacrifice on the cross really becomes present in the place and at the time indicated by the act of worship." This "making visible" in time and space of Jesus' sacrificial attitude is the prerequisite for the Church as a reality in time and space to be able to enter into Christ's sacrificial movement. Only through her entry into Christ's sacrificial movement now made visible in the sacrifice of the Mass, will the sacrifice of the cross become the Church's sacrifice. [192] The Church shows not only her *fiat* to Christ's sacrifice, her consent to the event on the cross and in Mass, as it expresses itself especially in the communion, in the inclusion of the sacrificial gifts as well as of

---

[190] G. Bätzing, Die Eucharistie als Opfer der Kirche nach Hans Urs von Balthasar, Einsiedeln 1996 (Kriterien 74), 107–109.

[191] Cf. K. Rahner / A. A. Häußling, Die vielen Messen und das eine Opfer. Eine Untersuchung über die rechte Norm der Meßhäufigkeit, Freiburg-Basel-Vienna 1966 (QD 31), 29f.

[192] Cf. ib. 33–40.

the sacrificing priest; she admits it also in the sense that it can take place in the earthly gifts, in the liturgy in time and place.

Without the Church, for whom the sacrifice on the cross counts equally with the sacrificial action of Jesus in the Supper Room and in every celebration of the eucharist, without her consent to what took place and takes place for her salvation, there is no sacrifice! The possibility of a life-giving communication of the triune God with the fallen world and hence salvation depends on the Church and her consent! So it is literally true that outside the Church there is no salvation!

1.8.3. SACRIFICIAL COMMUNITY

The liturgical community of the participants shows that salvation never concerns persons only as individuals, but always only the individual in the community, as indeed the triune God is himself most intimate community.

It is only in community with the triune God and through him with other people that the individual personality comes to its development. The liturgical community heals the experience "of isolation, the essential loneliness of man and the incommunicability of the divided self, which J. P. Sartre, S. de Beauvoir and A. Camus as representatives of an entire generation have described, and which lies largely at the basis of the revolt against human nature, which we are experiencing." [193] A human community, which in the liturgical celebration obtains access to the community of the three divine Persons, participates in the full affirmation of existence of the one by the others. Such a community can forego fixation of roles and power structures, it is freed from the negative experiences which people cause to one another. In the measure in which the individuals have a share in the divine life, they find one another and so build up a community, which in its unconditional acceptance transcends every worldly love. "The Church is constructed out of an amorphous mass of people into a subject through him whom Paul calls its head: Christ. That means: it is only from him that it remains a compact reality." [194]

The liturgical prayer oriented to community is therefore the rule and norm also for the prayer of the individual believer. [195] The liturgical assembly is more than a sign. It is the community of those, who obtain a common share in the divine life, a visible, concretely palpable community of persons, who are in a relation to one another differing from that in any other human community.

Therefore the community itself is the basic liturgical sign, something which Lengeling insists on again and again, with reference to the post-Vatican understanding of liturgy. [196]

Still more: The Church in which the liturgy takes place as the work of God, is the "instrument for the salvation of all" (LG 9) as the "visible sacrament of saving unity". It is "sacrament", that is to say sign and instrument of the most intimate union with

---

[193] J. Ratzinger, Zur Frage nach der Struktur der liturgischen Feier, IKaZ 7 (1978) 488–497. 493f.

[194] J. Ratzinger, Wandelbares und Unwandelbares in der Kirche, IKaZ 7(1978) 182–184. 183.

[195] Cf. Evdokimov, L'Orthodoxie 240.

[196] Cf. E. J. Lengeling, Liturgie als Grundvollzug christlichen Lebens: B. Fischer / E. J. Lengeling / R. Schaeffler / F. Schulz / H.-R. Müller-Schwefe: Kult in der säkularisierten Welt. Regensburg 1974, 63–91. 76; id.,: Wort und Bild als Elemente der Liturgie: W. Heinen (ed.): Bild – Wort – Symbol in der Theologie. Würzburg 1969, 177–206; id., Wort, Bild, Symbol in der Liturgie, LJ 30(1980) 230–242.238: "The basic sign is the holy assembly of the community itself. It is the expression, the image of the Church."

God (LG 1). The Church is the "sacrament of unity" (SC 26), "the universal sacrament of salvation" through which Christ joins men to himself, and nourishes them with his Body and Blood and makes them partakers of his glorious life (LG 48). Therefore in the celebration of the liturgy which takes place in it, the Church manifests its true self. The liturgy "is the summit toward which the activity of the Church is directed; it is also the fount from which all her power flows" (SC 10 and LG 11). All other activities of the Church, its consummation in *diakonia* and martyrdom, obtain their power from the liturgy, and take place in order to unite men and women, at whom the Church's ministry is aimed, in the liturgical assembly.

1.8.4. EUCHARISTIC ECCLESIOLOGY

Such a sacramental view of the Church is the core theme of "eucharistic ecclesiology". It is derived from the liturgy which takes place in the midst of the Church community, and its roots lie in the Orthodox theology.

"Eucharistic ecclesiology" means: in the eucharistic assembly of a local community the mystery of the Church manifests itself essentially as a sacramental community. Even if ministry belongs to the local church, even if its relations to other local churches – under the primacy of the Petrine ministry – ought not to be lost sight of and therefore ministry plays a constitutive role in order to safeguard the unity of the one Church out of many churches, nevertheless the local eucharistic assembly is this one "Church" as a happening. In it is manifest what Church is in itself: the descent of the heavenly liturgy, man's entry and with him the world into the same, life-giving communication with God through Christ, whose human nature here and now in the happening of the liturgy opens the source of deification for man and the world. [197]

Zizioulas thus understands Church as the *communio* structured through the presence of the *Eschata* and he speaks of a "eucharistic view of the world and of history". [198] This is possible only by the catabasis of the divine fullness of life into which the celebrating community enters with its own relations to the world. The presentation by the faithful of offerings for the poor or for liturgical requirements made this clear in the ancient Church. The entry of men and women into the liturgy, together with the world which they bring along with them, with all their relationships to other people and to the objects of creation, all this signifies the entry into the heavenly liturgy as it lowers itself into this worldly reality.

It is first of all from the eucharist that the community of people in the Church acquires its essence: "in the eucharist prayer, faith, love, *caritas* (i.e. all that the faithful practice individually) cease to be 'mine', they become a relation between God and his people, between God and his Church. The eucharist is not only the communion of each individual with Christ, but rather it binds the faithful among themselves and unites them in the Body of Christ... Thus man ceases to be an individual. He becomes a person, i.e. a reality, which no longer represents a fragment, a part of a machine or an organization, which are equipped for their own purpose... He is no longer a means to an end, but

---

[197] Cf. J. D. Zizoulas, Being as Communion. Studies in Priesthood and the Church, with a Foreword by John Meyendorff, Crestwood-New York 1985 (Contemporary Greek Theologians 4), 148; D. Papandreou, Die ökumenische und pneumatologische Dimension der orthodoxen Liturgie. In: K. Schlemmer (ed.), Gemeinsame Liturgie in getrennten Kirchen? Freiburg-Basel-Vienna 1991 (QD 132), 35–52. 43–45.

[198] Cf. J. D. Zizioulas, Die Welt in eucharistischer Schau und der Mensch von heute, US 25 (1970) 342–349. 342.

an end in himself, an image and likeness of God, and finds his perfection only in union with God and with the others." [199]

1.8.5. ROYAL AND MINISTERIAL PRIESTHOOD

The image of man determined by the liturgical assembly determines also the view of positions, ministries and services in the Church. Before any hierarchical differentiation, all members of the Church, all the baptized and confirmed are charged with transforming the world, which consists in bringing it into the eucharistic transforming relationship to the triune God.

Every Christian is charged with co-operating in the eucharistic work of the deification of the world; Zizioulas says explicitly "ordained".

Initiation counts as "ordination": the newly baptized does not simply become "Christian", rather he is "ordained" into the eucharistic community. As soon as this "ordination character" of initiation is forgotten, the way is open for the identification of the "lay person" with the "not ordained". Either this "lay person" will be pushed aside in a clerical way out of the liturgical celebrations, or ministry will be disavowed as a sacramental reality. Zizioulas links this "Ordo character" of Christian initiation explicitly to the first reception of the eucharist, the baptismal communion. [200]

All members of the Church are "ordained" to the eucharistic meal community, to the insertion of the world into Christ's sacrificial movement, for according to v. Balthasar "the deepest sacrificial moment for the Church lies in the consummation of the meal." [201] From this point of view the laity are "anything but incompetent or only marginally competent in what concerns the properly ecclesial means of life in Christ," as Congar says, according to whom these means fall under the responsibility of the clergy. [202] All the charisms of the baptized and the confirmed are meant to serve the purpose of deification, for which reason also, according to Evdokimov there is no specific "lay spirituality", which would differentiate it from that of the monks and clergy. All Christians are inducted (initiated) into the deifying communication with the Trinity and as such are called to co-operate in the deification of the world. [203] All the baptized and confirmed are "living stones" of the Church (1 Pet 2:5) and prior to all ministerial differentiation belong to the "royal priesthood" (1 Pet 2:9). All are "spiritual persons" on whom the Holy Spirit has been poured out and in whom the promise of the prophet Joel (3:1 – 2) has been fulfilled. For those also who hold ministerial office the basic truth is primary that they are "lay", if this concept is understood of the "people of God" (Laos Theou). [204]

The true significance of clerical ministry can only be derived from the catabasis of the heavenly liturgy in the eucharistic sacrifice. The priestly office is anchored in this catabasis. Without this anchorage one would in fact have to consider renouncing

---

[199] Ib. 346f.

[200] Cf. J. D. Zizioulas, Being as Communion 216; id., Priesteramt und Priesterweihe im Licht der östlich-orthodoxen Theologie, H. Vorgrimmler (ed.), Der priesterliche Dienst V: Amt und Ordination in ökumenischer Sicht. Freiburg-Basel-Vienna 1973 (QD 50), 72 – 113. 80.

[201] H. U. v. Balthasar, Die Messe, ein Opfer der Kirche? Id., Spiritus Creator. Skizzen zur Theologie III, Einsiedeln 1967, 166 – 217.195

[202] Y. Congar, Der Laie. Entwurf einer Theologie des Laientums, Stuttgart 3rd edn., 1964, 44f.

[203] Cf. Evdokimov, L'Orthodoxie 282.

[204] Cf. K. Koch, Kirche der Laien? Plädoyer für die göttliche Würde des Laien in der Kirche, Fribourg – Konstanz 1991, 21, 37.

the concept of "priest" in connection with the office transmitted by the sacrament of Orders.[205] According to Kasper the understanding of ministry is one of the sore spots in the post-conciliar Church and "is taking on more and more the character of a serious crisis".[206] But even still in 1991 Greshake is of opinion that in theology and in the outward image of ministry "everything is tottering".[207]

According to SC 7 the liturgy is rightly seen as "an exercise of the priestly office of Jesus Christ" who "is always present in his Church". By virtue of his ordination power the priest is not substituting for an absentee. Christ is present and acts as the real celebrant. "But because in Christian worship everything takes place by means of signs perceptible to the senses, there is need of a representation, a making visible of the one who mysteriously presides over and sustains the liturgical celebration. The one who presides fulfils this task. In his person the Lord himself gets in touch with the community... The western tradition refers to this circumstance with the expressions: to act *"in"* or *"ex persona Christi", "gerere personam, gerere vicem Christi"* [PO 2, LG 10; 28]." *Repraesentatio Domini*: it is on this that the greatness of the role of president, but also its limits, are based. Christ, who acts as protagonist in the liturgy, associates to himself again and again his Church, his body and his bride. *"Una cum Ecclesia"* he accomplishes the work of our salvation. Constantly the president takes on anew symbolically the role of prayer leader and guide of the community ... He, as it were, goes ahead of the procession, which is on its way to God. With reference to this the tradition coined the expression, he acts *'Ecclesiae nomine'* [SC 33, PO 2]."[208]

Ordination in fact does not make a man the substitute for the absent Christ nor a mediator between God and man instead of him.[209] Also no socially necessary functions of leadership are delegated from below in the sacrament of Orders.[210] For the redemption of man the Christ's word in the Supper room must be spoken, if the redeeming mystery is not to become a distant past. It can be spoken in this way only from a mandate, which no one can give to himself – from a mandate which no one community or several communities transfer, but which can only be based in the "sacramental" empowering of Jesus Christ himself given to the universal Church. The word must so to speak subsist in the sacrament, in participation in the "sacrament" of the Church, in the mandate which she does not give to herself, rather in which she passes on further, what reaches beyond herself. This is precisely "priestly ordination" and "priesthood".[211]

---

[205] For example Schneider, Zeichen der Nähe Gottes 246f.; K. Rahner, Liturgiereform als Mitte einer Erneuerung der Kirche: id. (ed.) Das Konzil war erst der Anfang. Die Bedeutung des II. Vatikanums für Theologie und Kirche, Mainz 1991, 66, with particular emphasis on the royal priesthood of all the faithful as again acknowledged by the Council.
[206] W. Kasper, Neue Akzente im dogmatischen Verständnis des priesterlichen Dienstes, Concilium 5 (1969) 164–170. 164.
[207] "Everything is tottering!" With this expression of E. Troeltsch's Greshake entitles the first chapter of his book which appeared in its 5th edition in 1991: Priestersein. Zur Theologie und Spiritualität des priesterlichen Amtes. Freiburg-Basel-Vienna 5th edn., 1991, 21.
[208] J. Baumgartner, De arte celebrandi. Anmerkungen zur priesterlichen Zelebration, HID 36(1982) 1–11. Cf. Also in this connection Eisenbach, Die Gegenwart 418f.
[209] Cf. Evdokimov, L'Orthodoxie 164: "Le Christ ne transmet pas ses pouvoirs personels aux apôtres, ce qui signifierait son absence."
[210] Cf. Greshake, Priestersein 29.
[211] Ratzinger, Das Fest des Glaubens 84f. Cf. Id., Zur Frage nach der Struktur der liturgischen Feier, IKaZ 7 (1978) 488–497.489.

In the sacrament of Orders it is a question of a reality of relationships. In it there takes place the in-sertion *"ordinatio"* of a man in the midst of the Church community to which he belongs, into an iconographic function for his sisters and brothers, to reveal the Lord who is invisibly present and active as High Priest, to make him sacramentally accessible to the senses. "To be ordained" signifies consequently no personal possession of a mandate or of greater holiness, but rather – not otherwise than with respect to the community which is celebrating the liturgy – a revealing to the Church of Christ its Head, through whom in the Holy Spirit the divine life flows to all the members of his body. This revealing is neither acting a part nor a substitution, rather it happens in the sense of a really making present of the invisible in the visible. Only then is the holder of office "Typos" or "God's Place", when one has the concrete eucharistic community in view. Ordination then will be ... for the assigning of a special place in the community, and after his ordination the ordained will be defined precisely by the "place" in the community, which in its eucharistic nature reveals the reign of God here and now." [212]

That the office holder has his place precisely so in the midst of the community, a special place, which however does not stand above but rather within the assembly, that he acts *"in nomine Ecclesiae"* without opposing this to his acting *"in persona Christi"*, finds expression in the eastern view of the priest as the one empowered to pray the epiclesis. As *"typos Christi"* he calls down the Holy Spirit from above and thus represents Christ who in the promise of the Holy Spirit at the Ascension spoke the first epiclesis. [213]

To be a priest is a relational reality: in the midst of the priestly community of bearers of the royal priesthood (1 Pet 2:5,9) the holder of office represents vis-á-vis his sisters and brothers the sole priest Christ who is carrying out his liturgy, his work for the many. [214] The priest as antitype is the 'place' of Christ accessible to the senses, and priestly ordination will be for "the assigning of a special place in the community", and after his ordination the one ordained will be defined precisely by the "place" in the community, which in its eucharistic nature reveals the reign of God here and now. [215]

Relational reality is always twofold: the bishop makes Christ the Head really present in the same way that the church, over which he presides, makes the Body of Christ present. This relational reality is based on the real presence of Christ in the liturgical assembly, and as the relation of the head to the Body there is a self-evident reciprocal recall: a community cannot exist without a bishop, but the reverse also holds good: no bishop without a community! [216]

In the relational reality of the liturgy the priest indeed takes on a "role". This concept is to be ascribed to Aquinas himself: the priest *"gerit figuram Christi"*. [217] The priest says the eucharistic prayer of thanksgiving "to the Father as president of the community

---

[212] J. D. Zizioulas, Priesteramt und Priesterweihe im Licht der östlich-orthodoxen Theologie: H. Vorgrimmler (ed.): Der Priesterliche Dienst V: Amt und Ordination in ökumenischer Sicht. Freiburg-Basel-Vienna 1973 (QD 50), 72–113.93f.

[213] Cf. R. Hotz, Sakramente im Wechelspiel zwischen Ost und West, Zürich-Köln-Gütersloh 1979 (Ökumen. Theol. 2), 235–240 with reference to O. Clément, A propos de l'Esprit Saint, Contacts 85 (1974) 87.

[214] Cf. Zizioulas, Priesteramt und Priesterweihe 96; id., Being as communion 231.

[215] Ib., 93f.

[216] J. Meyendorff, Orthodoxie et Catholicité, Paris 1965, 23, 105f.

[217] Congar, Ein Mittler 129f, "Repraesentatio, gerere personam, in persona Christi. In Church life, especially in the celebration of the sacraments, the priest visibly acts the part of Christ." On "gerit figuram Christi", cf. Thomas Aquinas IV Sent. D. 24q.1 q.2a1, obj.3.

and insofar in the role of Jesus Christ as the Head of his Body." [218] Already the concept of "role" implies a capacity for relationship: the one who undertakes the role enters into communication as a "role figure" and serves this only as an evocative medium. The priestly role however is far more than a significant interpersonal interaction. There is a substantial reality to be attributed to it which scholastic theology defined with not unquestionable abstractions like "*sacra potestas*" or "*vis consecrandi*," but which nevertheless guaranteed that there is question of a reality which goes beyond interpersonal relationship.

According to Simeon of Thessalonica Christ called "*ant autou*" – which should not be misunderstood as "instead of himself", but rather in the meaning of his "living images" (*antitypoi*) – bishops as "redeemers, moulders of souls, leaders to heaven, to light and to life, fathers, shepherds and watchmen." Endowed with his strength they fulfil their office not for themselves nor by themselves, but for the flock entrusted to them. [219] This is no clerical exaggeration, but a concrete demonstration in the sacrament of Orders of what holds good for the Church with regard to redemption as a whole: a part which cannot be given up of the divine catabasis into the visible reality of this world with a view to its elevation, its "offering" into the fullness of life of the Trinity.

Bibliography

G. Bätzing, Die Eucharistie als Opfer der Kirche nach Hans Urs von Balthasar, Einsiedeln 1986 (Kriterien 74).

H. U. v. Balthasar, Die Würde der Liturgie, IKaZ 7 (1978) 481–487.

H. U. v. Balthasar, Die Messe, ein Opfer der Kirche? Spiritus Creator. Skizzen zur Theologie III, Einsiedeln 1967, 166–217.

Y. Congar, Der Laie. Entwurf einer Theologie des Laientums, Stuttgart 3rd edn. 1964.

Y. Congar, Ein Mittler, Gemeinsame Röm.-Kath./Evang.-Luth. Kommission (ed.): Das geistliche Amt in der Kirche, Paderborn/Frankfurt/M. 4th edn. 1982.

Conférences Saint-Serge, XXIIe Semaine d'études liturgiques 1975, Liturgie de l'Église particulière et liturgie de l'Église universelle, Roma 1976 (Bibliotheca EL Subsidia 7).

G. Greshake, Priestersein. Zur Theologie und Spiritualität des priesterlichen Amtes, Freiburg-Basel-Wien 5th edn. 1991.

W. Kasper / G. Sauter, Kirche – Ort des Geistes. Freiburg-Basel-Vienna, 1976 (Ökumenische Forschungen, Kleine ökumenische Schriften 8).

K. Koch, Kirchliches Leben im Zeichen des Mysteriums Gottes, A. Schilson (ed.): Gottes Weisheit im Mysterium. Vergessene Wege christlicher Spiritualität, Mainz 1989, 315–332.

H. de Lubac, Les Églises particulières dans l'Église universelle, Paris 1971.

S. Marsili, La Liturgia culto della Chiesa, Anamnesis 1, Torino 2nd edn. 1991, 107–136.

J. Ratzinger, Ist die Eucharistie ein Opfer? Concilium 3 (1967) 299–304.

---

[218] F. Eisenbach, Die Gegenwart Jesu Christi im Gottesdienst. Systematische Studien zur Liturgiekonstitution des II. Vatikanischen Konzils, Mainz 1982, 416f: "Thus it was explicitly stated and maintained against objections at the Council, that the priest in the whole of the liturgy stands "in the role of Christ at the head of the community" and that the liturgy of the Hours which he leads and celebrates is not only the Church's voice, but rather even Christ's prayer to his Father."

[219] Cf. Kunzler, Porta Orientalis 453; De Sacerdotio – PG 155, 961 B-C.

J. Ratzinger, 'Auferbaut aus lebendigen Steinen', W. Seidel (ed.): Kirche aus lebendigen Steinen, Mainz 1975, 30 – 48.

J. Ratzinger, Das Fest des Glaubens. Versuche zur Theologie des Gottesdienstes, Einsiedeln 1981.

A. Thaler, Gemeinde und Eucharistie. Grundlegung einer eucharistischen Ekklesiologie, Fribourg 1988 (Praktische Theologie im Dialog 2).

J. Zizioulas, Die Welt in eucharistischer Schau und der Mensch von heute, US 25 (1970) 342 – 349.

J. Zizioulas, Being as Communion. Studies in Personhood and the Church. With a foreword by John Meyendorff, Crestwood-New York 1985 (Contemporary Greek Theologians 4).

1.9. ANAMNESIS: GOD'S DESCENT INTO TIME

"Anamnesis" (memorial) is a key concept for liturgical theology. In worship man remembers God's saving deeds. Because it makes the claim to be of saving value for those who are commemorating, this memorial must be of a different sort than the recalling of events lying in the past, which may indeed arouse emotions, but precisely because they are human works cannot be effective for salvation. Anamnesis then must be considered under the aspect of the divine catabasis, the divine descent into time.

1.9.1. DE IMMUTABILITATE DEI

God as immutable is beyond all change. [220] He stands beyond time. But this dogma could arouse the fatal impression that the Christian doctrine about God parts company with the biblical faith experience of the living God living with his people, and turns rather to a philosophical unhistorical conception of God. In fact the philosophical doctrine about God contemplates the unchangeable God in an abstract way. Uncommitted he seems to confront with indifference the changing fortunes of men and the destiny of their lives. Well now the dogma of God's immutability in no way implies such an "absence of history".

The scriptural statements (for example Jas 1:17) about God's "immutability" need to be understood in the sense of his "unchanging fidelity to the covenant" and thus also historically as the "steadfastness of his goodness". [221] Thus the ambo prayer of the liturgy of St Chrysostom cites Jas 1:17; God's immutability is essentially the steadfast fidelity of the "Father of lights" from whom every good endowment and every perfect gift comes down. Or: the anaphora of the Chrysostom liturgy praises the triune God as the "everlasting and remaining the same", and there follows the itemizing of the mysteries of salvation from creation up to the eschatological completion. [222]

God's immutability is the steadfastness of his love and fidelity towards creatures. God's will of salvation, to allow creation to share in his life, stands immutably beyond time, but expresses itself within time as saving deeds, which in the tradition of the sacred scriptures count as epochs of salvation and entitle transient time as salvation history.

---

[220] Cf. L. Ott, Grundriß der katholischen Dogmatik, Freiburg-Basel-Vienna 10th edn. 1981, 41f.: "What is changeable passes from one state into another. Every creature is changeable on account of the finite nature of its being. God is absolutely unchangeable. De fide." For the relevant declarations of the magisterium cf. DH 197, 285, 294, 358, 416, 501, 569, 683, 800, 1330, 2901, 3001.

[221] Cf. Maas 25 – 29.

[222] Cf. Kallis 182f, 124 – 127.127

1.9.2. MAN WITHIN TIME

Subject to changeableness, man lives within time. It is for him the temporal framework of his life, to enable him to come out of himself (ex-*sistere*) to begin a relationship with God, with fellow-man and the world. It is only through relationship that man becomes a personality, which will discover itself in the measure that it experiences and realizes itself as I *vis-á-vis* the Thou. In "his" time man enters into relationship with the world around him, and even more than that, he concentrates into his person the world as he experiences it and as he lives in and with it,; he becomes a "mirror" of the world of his time, a "microcosm". The world, its daily course of events, its history, its anxieties and its hopes, stamp each individual man in the deepest way. Each one carries in himself a piece of the world predetermined by time and his own span of life and becomes hereby a "historical personality", a child of a quite specific epoch, which stamps him, which belongs to him and to which he belongs. Time as the realm of change is given to man as a task, to become himself in relationship, in order that matured in this way, he may enter into the timeless relationship with the living God, above all change: *spatium verae et fructuosae paenitentiae.*

For this reason time as a mathematical or physical dimension is something totally other than time in the existential sense. Physical time says absolutely nothing about the possibilities for man to go beyond himself, to enter into relationships and to realize himself in them or also to miss out on all this. As a mathematical abstract dimension it offers no access to a restful presence in the fullness of God's life, which bursts apart all human experience of time, which is promised in faith, which is absolute. Physical time – in any case an abstraction of our instruments of measurement as regularly recurring identical intervals of time – leads nowhere. [223] The finiteness which is given with time confronts man always with his limitations and his finitude. The linear historical time picture demonstrates this with all harshness.

The ceaseless march of time, the relentless succession of becoming and of passing away, of unique chances and opportunities never to be recovered, leaves man remaining always as fragmentary. The fleeting time never allows man to realize himself totally, to fully become himself rather it burdens him always only with fragments of his person, his relationships and his life in and with the world. "The deepest sadness of human existence comes from time: one can neither halt it nor turn it back, everything passes away, disappears, steers itself to its implacable end. Besides, time is illusory; St Augustine in his *Confessions* has brilliantly shown that none of the three divisions of time exists: the future, that which does not yet exist, passes through the present elusive moment in its fleeting swiftness, to become past and to disappear into what no longer is. [224] If not interpreted as salvation history, then the linear perception of time breathes the spirit of despair in face of an unending, absurd nothingness, from which time comes and where it goes.

The scriptural understanding of time is also linear. But according to this, time does not emerge from an endless nothingness nor does it flow into such, but it has a beginning established by God. With creation God also created time; it is his handiwork. God stands outside his work and is Lord over time. Also it has a final point settled by God. In the Christian sense time is linear as a precisely given duration, which comes from God and

---

[223] Cf. Evdokimov, L'Orthodoxie 205.

[224] P. Evdokimov, *Das Gebet der Ostkirche*, Graz-Vienna-Köln 1986, 44f.

leads back to God. It is the space of time granted by God, the Unchangeable, in which the changes of the world take place. The time which both comes from the living God and leads back to him is always salvation time, if all the vicissitudes of creation which happen within it stand under the previous aim of the participation of creation in the fullness of divine life.

History as linear unfolding salvation time is the manifestation of the divine will of salvation raised above all changes and present behind all changes.

The linear understanding of time as salvation time differentiates Israel from the neighbouring peoples who adhere to a cyclical and mystical understanding of time. Israel celebrates its worship as an encounter with the God who entered into an historical relationship with Abraham and Jacob. That is why also the historical dimension is never lacking in it. The pagan ritual however seeks to escape from an unsettled history by rituals and to find assurance in a kind of submersion into the mythical times of the gods.

"The heathens sought to escape from the historical and the secular by an initiation into the sacral. Israel's understanding by contrast brought it still deeper into history. Historicising through liturgy is therefore a secularizing or a desacralizing process. It brings man into immediate contact with created reality (the secular), but precisely insofar as this reality is permeated with the saving presence of God." [225]

God's saving will has manifested itself – unsurpassably in Jesus Christ- in historical facts, which the sacred Scriptures of the Old and New Testaments hand down and which are remembered in worship; but precisely not in the sense of an individual's thinking about it, but in the anamnetic rendering present in the presence of the celebrating community of the saving Will once revealed in a past saving deed. That is why the Old Testament yearly feasts, whose roots are pre-Yahvistic nature feasts, were historicized in Israel i.e. they were remoulded into memory feasts, in which one thinks of God's saving deeds in history. This remembering is of a special kind: Yahveh's salvation is realized afresh in ritual words and actions, and the final salvation in the future is ever promised anew.

In contrast to Israel's strictly linear understanding of time the other ancient peoples followed the cyclic, particularly the various mystery religions. The cyclic image of time is especially characteristic of mythical thinking. It is regulated to all intents and purposes by growth and decay as *the* criterions of time, and seeks to conquer both by a constant repetition of what has been. "There is nothing new under the sun" (Eccles 1:9), and the ceaseless repetitions lead to the absurd just as in the linear image of time the ultimate cut-off existence does. The given divisions of time in nature lie at the root of the cyclic image of time: day and night, month, year and the change of the seasons. The vital occupations bound to the constantly recurring periods of time of man as tied to nature (such as seed-time and harvest) furthered the cyclic understanding of time: time is the eternal return of the identical rhythm, unbroken succession of becoming and decay, and new becoming.

The change of the seasons mirrors also the decline from a golden age through various intermediate stages down to the wicked present age, marked by death and ephemerality. "By means of the cultic dramatization of the primitive myths a renewal and repe-

---

[225] E. Maly, Das Zusammenspiel von Welt und Gottesdienst in den Heiligen Schriften, Concilium 7 (1971) 89 – 94. 91f.

tition of the original act of creation takes place, by which the evil of old year just past is effaced and life is created anew. This affects not only the individual man, but rather the whole worshipping community, the entire people. Thereby it was thought possible to negate time and history." [226] This led to the deification of time from Hinduism as far as Greek culture. Its cultic veneration as God is meant to free the community from its disastrous power. In Buddhism redemption signifies emancipation from time; redeemed existence consists in Nirvana, in which time as a woebegone wheel of illusions and evil is overcome. [227] So Evdokimov's opinion that the hands of a clock lead nowhere holds good also for the cyclic image of time. [228]

1.9.3. ANAMNESIS: THE LITURGICAL PRESENCE

Evdokimov points to liturgical time as a synthesis of the linear and cyclic image of time; synthesis because of the Lord's year recurring every year as a cycle, but on whose feasts and memorials linear salvation history is remembered. This synthesis is valid in a much deeper sense.

"Liturgical time" is defined by the "now" of divine salvation, by the divine salvation presence now taking place. Liturgical time is "existential time": God's timelessness stands beyond the flow of time of creation, and pierces this in the "holy" or "liturgical" time, when God manifests himself within time. God's "eternity" is neither before nor after time, but is the penetration of the divine "now" into the course of created time. Thus the liturgy obtains its saving power from the catabatic "now", coming from God, of his redeeming presence. The *in illo tempore* in the proclamation of the goespel is no historical reminiscence of something past, it has the power "to prize open time and in that moment to place itself as the true meaning of all moments." The salvation time of a given historical moment does not repeat itself, but it is man living within the laws of time and space who repeats himself, in as much as he, again and again, enters into communication with that which remains as a lasting presence behind fugitive time: God's invitation to salvation. [229]

The Eucharist is therefore in no way a (cultic) movement of man to God, no juxtaposition of sacrifices, no reiteration of Christ's act of sacrifice by men, nor a representation bringing it to mind, but it is the presence of this sacrificial act of Christ itself. Christ is the One who offers, who is offered and who receives, as it is said in the anamnesis of the Byzantine liturgy: [230] Man offers nothing, what does not already belong to God the "cult sacrifice" in the sense of *do ut des* is here excluded. [231] Precisely in the eucharistic sacrifice Christ's surrender of himself on the cross is indeed the summit and recapitulation of the total economy of salvation as sacrificial movement through the Son towards the Father, but it does not stand exclusively in the centre as a single fact. The eucharistic celebration is the recapitulatory happening in time and space of the total economy of

---

[226] Auf der Maur, Feiern im Rhythmus der Zeit I, 23f.

[227] Cf. Auf der Maur, Feiern im Rhythmus der Zeit, I, 21f.

[228] Evdokimov, L'Orthodoxie 205.

[229] Cf. Evdokimov, L'Orthodoxie 206–208.

[230] Kallis 131ff.

[231] Cf. J. Meyendorff, Le Christ dans la théologie byzantine, Paris 1969, 275, "La notion d'échange est dépassée … "

salvation, and consequently includes also the eschatological completion in the now of the present. [232]

The liturgical memorial is no "remembrance" of something past in the sense of a linear understanding of time, but rather "anamnesis", according to Casel "memorial of mysteries", i.e. "that which was fulfilled once in an historical natural manner, is set before us again in mystery." Strictly speaking it is a question of "presence", but: "for us men in our present condition it remains a memorial, only faith sees the presence. Outwardly it is a memorial, but for the believer a presence, and moreover a presence of the *pneuma*." [233] Casel distinguishes very clearly "cult memorial" from what is usually understood by "memorial". The cult memorial is objective, "it takes place also without me. In cult something takes place which does not depend from man as subject; here a quite other, higher power is involved." [234] The "cult memorial" differs from the memorial also by the character of its act: a single non-recurring redemptive act of God becomes so present in the liturgical act that those who are celebrating can participate in the divine act. For this reason Casel speaks of a "higher presence" in the present celebration of men, of God's saving past act in history. This was true already for the Pascha feast of Israel. Jesus' Supper also establishes in the anamnesis command more than a mere remembrance of something past; Jesus is, after all, the exalted Lord present in his community and acts in it, so that there is no need of "remembrance" of him. But thereby no definitive clarification of the manner of bringing about the presence itself has been arrived at.

According to Schildenberger the Hebrew word *zikkaron* (memorial, commemorative sign) has a deeper meaning: it runs into that which the Talmud says of the "Today" in Ex 13:4: "In the *Pesachim* tractate of the Talmud the Mishnah dictates: 'In every generation man is in duty bound to look upon himself, as if he were rescued out of Egypt.' Is there question here of a merely subjective process, of an "as if", without objective basis ?" [235] The objective basis consists in the identification of each succeeding generation with that of the wandering in the desert, since God's word which issued forth to the latter affects all the descendants of Israel and thereby establishes the unity of the covenant people. The continually recurring "today" is an actualization of the enduring covenant of Sinai, and the divine act of salvation of the Exodus becomes somehow or other always new again in the celebration of the memorial in the succeeding generations. A pleasing image illustrates the "*somehow or other* always new": God's covenant on Sinai is a lasting saving work of God, continuing in existence, unique, consistent, which God does not revoke towards the people who break the covenant (Lev 26:44), even if for a time the benefits of the covenant are withdrawn from them... When God himself remembers his covenant then this "remembering" is a new revival of the ancient work of salvation: as he then led the forefathers out of Egypt, so will he free their descendants out of the exile (Lev 26:45). Both acts of salvation are particular outstanding

---

[232] Meyendorff, Le Christ 275f: The eucharist "est la réalisation, au moment où nous y participons, de l'économie du salut dans son ensemble et avec tous ses éléments rendus réellement présents: Incarnation du Logos, sa Mort, sa Résurrection et sa seconde Venue. Il est celui qui offre, mais, aussi, il 'se sanctifie soi-même' (Jean 17,19), dans son humanité, dans notre humanité réunie autour de la Table eucharistique: c'est lá le mystère de l'Eglise."

[233] Casel, Opfermysterium, ed. by V. Warnach, 487f.

[234] Ib. 492.

[235] Schildenberger, Der Gedächtnischarakter des alt – und neutestamentlichen Pascha 82f.

effects of the one activity of salvation of the God of the covenant, which could be compared with a veinstone that for the most part runs unseen underground and from time to time outcrops. [236]

What as "veinstone" runs "unseen underground" is Yahveh's "active existence": "At every moment, continuously, Yahveh puts his active existence into effect. The name Yahveh says that the God who is revealing himself with this name is the original reality, who alone is real ... to the Hebrew who thinks in a concrete fashion this original reality proves itself through the mighty works of God." [237] With the invocation of Yahveh, the God who saves, his saving deeds become present in an objective mode, not merely in the subjective recalling by the participants. That which the feast celebrates, becomes present "today" in the presence of Yahveh who at that time had saved; "today" is the Exodus from Egypt, because God saves and will save, exactly as at that time when he saved the fathers.

Basically the question at issue is not about the historical saving event through which men experienced God's saving power, but rather about this saving power itself, how "it comes to light in historical saving situations, like the generally hidden "veinstone. Since the access to this veinstone always stands open in the anamnesis, it is possible for man not only to surmount ("transcend") the monotonous flow of time moment by moment, but rather in virtue of the anamnesis in the liturgy to arrive at the intersection point of time and eternity. There he becomes a genuine contemporary of the biblical events from the creation of the world up to its eschatological completion – "we live through them as literally as did the eyewitnesses of these events" [238] – because in each of them the divinizing love of God emerges as "today", as "now" in the encounter with the living God in the liturgical celebration.

In this sense the Lord's words of the Last Supper resound across the ages. If the man of today hears them, this is not because other men repeat the happening of Holy Thursday, in order to call it to mind. "Today" the hearer of Jesus' words over bread and wine becomes "contemporary" of what happened "then", because "today" as "then" it is a question of one and the same event and which offers itself to men of other places and times only in ever varying co-ordinates of space and time. Beyond the difference of times it was and is a question of the opening of the fullness of life of the triune God for men through the incarnate Son who offers himself as food and drink in the Holy Spirit.

Thus at Christmas Christ is born before the eyes of the community which is celebrating liturgy, in Easter night he appears to it as the Risen One. Every passage of the gospel which is read makes the biblical event present. [239] Behind all the events which the scriptures narrate there exists the living tide of the stream of divine life, which knows no interruptions. Christ, through whom the Father in the Holy Spirit endows the world with his divine life, is present and comes at the same time. His presence and his coming take place in every liturgical celebration, in "moments", which are only possible, "because in them a living time freed from death breaks in on our mortal time. In other words: at the source of all our celebrations is to be found a spiritual power, from which we should drink unceasingly in the new time of the resurrection. This breaks into our

---

[236] Cf. ib. 83 – 85.
[237] Ib. 84.
[238] Cf. Evdokimov, L'Orthodoxie 241.
[239] Cf. ib., 241f.

days, weeks, years until our ancient time is absorbed by it and the mortal veil is torn. Already now, "today" we can participate in it." [240]

1.9.4. ANAMNESIS: GOD'S WORK OR MAN'S?

It is man who remembers. But the anamnesis as man's work does not transcend time, as such it cannot be sanctifying. Time after time anamneses, or at least anamnetic elements, are met with in the liturgical prayer of the Church. Anamneses are to be found at the core of the actions of the sacraments and sacramentals. The plea for the granting of salvation here and now is connected with examples (paradigms) from salvation history: as at that time you saved your people, so stand by us now. Merely to think of these saving situations experienced by the forefathers as facts lying in the past and leave them lying in the past, this is in fact simply human work, based on man's capacity to be able to remember.

But to interpret the situations experienced by men of other times and other places as salvation situations, to attach oneself to them in prayer, following their model to ask God for new salvation, presupposes the faith that what happened then, invoked in the anamnesis into the present situation, was not just an accident or lucky coincidence, but was really God's work. And the avowal that God at that time operated man's salvation, is only possible through the faith that also now and today he operates salvation. Faith does not bring about the anamnetic presence of the saving fact of yore – as if it brought it back magically over the frontiers of time and space into our present time – rather the redeeming presence of God which is behind all experiences of salvation makes itself available for the present suppliant and applicable to other situations now at hand. Without the presence of the God who stands beyond all times, active then as now, every remembrance would be a discouraged relinquishing of what has been lived and experienced, in the past which is for ever closed off and cannot be brought back again. According to Pieper it is not only exclusively the events of salvation lying in the past, through which the God who is near and saves, knocks at man's heart. Certainly also through that which preceding generations have experienced as God's saving deeds, but also through bodily cues (not least through ritual celebrations) there knocks at the heart of man "from a superhuman sphere" an awareness "about the meaning of existence, about salvation and evil, about all that which no experience and no scientific knowledge can teach or needs to learn, because as a matter of fact we already know it and have always known it", calls itself to mind and wants to be taken seriously. [241] The remembrance of this innermost knowledge is always a reminder of the salvation, which comes from God alone. He himself calls himself the only giver of salvation and life on account of man's longing for salvation and life, also on account of the example of the remembrance of his saving deeds accomplished in history, so that man would "remember" him and open himself to his action.

But faith as another name for a relationship with the living God is not first of all man's work, rather it is always first made possible by the prevenient grace of God, who thereby invites to his fullness of life, and provokes the response of faith. The faith, which alone makes the anamnesis possible, is God's work in man, is a catabatic remembrance now taking place, of other catabases which happened in history, and issuing in a

---

[240] Corbon, Liturgie aus dem Urquell 145.
[241] Cf. Pieper, Das Gedächtnis des Leibes 71.

catabatic summons to implore new salvation. "Anamnesis" is therefore the word for the life-giving and liberating relationship of God with men operative beyond the limitations of places and times and thereby of the individual remembered acts of salvation. As such a relationship it is always the work of both partners, God's prevenient catabatic work of yore and now in actively filled memorial, man's work, who accepts it as an invitation to life and lets it happen to himself. On account of this prevenient work of God the anamnesis is first of all a catabatic greatness, which yearns for the anabatic answer from man.

Anamnesis in the sense of catabasis lays the foundation for worship, the service by the God who stands beyond time for man living in time. Like the liturgy as a whole, it is neither a subjective calling to mind of biblical stories of deliverance or of other events recounted in the scriptures, nor a "memorial" of something past, organized by a community, to be celebrated in common, nor the inducing of a particular "paradigm" of whatever sort (for example moral-ethical, psychological, hortative) for the immediate present, nor a "citation" of a fact of history or rather of salvation history as the correct interpretation of a given present situation, [242] nor a playful reconstruction of past experiences of deliverance out of pedagogical or therapeutic motives.

Admittedly in the anamnesis also man stands at the focal point. He is at the centre of the divine interest in his salvation, as every good theology even without the label of "anthropological turning-point" always knows and has known, for instance as the anamnesis in the anaphora of the Chrysostom liturgy expresses it: "Mindful... of all that has happened for us: the cross, the grave, the resurrection on the third day, the ascension into heaven, the being seated at the right hand of the Father, the second, new coming in glory, we offer you what is yours from what is yours everywhere and for all." [243] The man however who stands at the focal point is he who is endowed with freedom, who is capable of relationship and who is called upon for communication with the living God. He can refuse the relationship. But he can also venture on it, he can enter into communication with God, who has indicated his interest in man's salvation also in the saving deeds transmitted in sacred scripture. Behind them all stands God's immutable will for the salvation of all men, which has revealed itself at various "junctures" within time and space. For that person, to whom the invitation to the life-giving relationship with the living God is now crucial, they mean more than facts belonging to the past; they are authenticated revelations in the past of the continuing invitation to salvation. To think of them at all, to fix one's present hope of salvation on them, is always already God's salvation and gift of grace, as it has always already proved itself efficacious.

Bibliography

HJ. Auf der Maur, Feiern im Rhythmus der Zeit I, GdK 5, Regensburg 1983, 16–25.

O. Casel, Die Liturgie als Mysterienfeier, Freiburg i. Br. 1922.

O. Casel, Zur Idee der liturgischen Festfeier, JLw 3 (1923) 93–99.

---

[242] "A prayer style of citations by means of identification of roles for the liberation of the praying subject" is a favourite thought of Häußling's, shared also by Merz. Cf. A. A. Häußling, Kosmische Dimension und gesellschaftliche Wirklichkeit. Zu einem Erfahrungswandel in der Liturgie, Alw 25 (1983) 1–8. 6–8. Id., Gedächtnis des Vergangenen 122f. M. B. Merz, Liturgisches Gebet als Geschehen. Liturgiewissenschaftlich-linguistische Studie anhand der Gebetsgattung Eucharistisches Hochgebet, Münster 1988 (LQF 70), 59f. For our critique cf. M. Kunzler, Porta Orientalis 277f., 282f., 446f., 551f.

[243] Cf. Kallis 130–133.

O. Casel, Das christliche Festmysterium, Paderborn 1941.

O. Casel, Das christliche Kultmysterium, Regensburg 3rd edn. 1948.

O. Casel, Mysterium des Kommenden, Paderborn 1952.

O. Casel, Mysterium des Kreuzes, Paderborn 1954.

O. Casel, Die große Mysteriennacht, Liturgie und Mönchtum/Laacher Hefte 36, Maria Laach 1965, 68–81.

O. Casel, Das christliche Opfermysterium. Zur Morphologie und Theologie des eucharistischen Hochgebetes, ed. V. Warnach, Graz-Wien-Köln 1968.

O. Casel, Mysterientheologie, Ansatz und Gestalt. Ed. by the Abt-Herwegen-Institut of the Abbey Maria Laach. Ausgewählt und eingeleitet von Arno Schilson, Regensburg 1986.

A. A. Häußling, Liturgie: Gedächtnis eines Vergangenen und doch Befreiung in der Gegenwart, Vom Sinn der Liturgie. Gedächtnis unserer Erlösung und Lobpreis Gottes, Düsseldorf 1991 (Schriften der Kath. Akademie in Bayern Bd. 140), 118–130.

W. Maas, Unveränderlichkeit Gottes. Zum Verhältnis von griechisch-philosophischer und christlicher Gotteslehre, Paderborn 1974 (Paderborner theol. Studien 1).

H. B. Meyer, Zeit und Gottesdienst. Anthropologische Bemerkungen zur liturgischen Zeit, LJ 31 (1981) 193–213.

J. Pieper, Das Gedächtnis des Leibes. Von der erinnernden Kraft des Geschichtlich-Konkreten, W. Seidel (ed.): Kirche aus lebendigen Steinen, Mainz 1975. 68–83.

J. Schildenberger, Der Gedächtnischarakter des alt – und neutestamentlichen Pascha, B. Neunheuser (ed.): Opfer Christi und Opfer der Kirche. Düsseldorf 1960, 75–97.

J. Tyciak, Gegenwart des Heils in den östlichen Liturgien, Freiburg i.Br. 1968 (Sophia Vol. 9).

1.10. THEOSIS-THE DEIFICATION OF MAN AND OF THE WORLD AS THE PURPOSE OF THE DIVINE CATABASIS

1.10.1. THE ESCHATA NOT TO BE QUOTED? ON THE QUESTION OF MODERN MAN'S CAPACITY FOR LITURGY

Romano Guardini's question, posed with a good measure of scepticism, about the "cult-capacity" of modern man [244] has already become a classical text of recent liturgical history. Because of it things have no longer been quiet since then. Is modern man actually still in a position to celebrate liturgy? Is its continued existence as "an anomaly of cultural behaviour" endangered, as Häußling thinks? Are radical cuts, reduction of liturgical forms necessary, so that tomorrow liturgy can still be celebrated at all? [245]

At least it would appear at present that not only do fewer people practise their faith, but that the faith itself seems to find itself in a running fight. Many people have given up the search for a meaning to life beyond this earthly existence; others seek salvation in

---

[244] R. Guardini, Der Kultakt und die gegenwärtige Aufgabe der liturgischen Bildung. Ein Brief, LJ 14 (1964) 101–106; also revised in: R. Guardini, Liturgie und liturgische Bildung. Würzburg 1966, 9–18. Guardini also maintains that modern man lacks "an elementary awareness of the symbolic content of existence", cf., Das Ende der Neuzeit. Ein Versuch zur Orientierung, Würzburg 1951, 32.

[245] Cf. A. A. Häußling, Liturgiewissenschaftliche Aufgabenfelder vor uns, LJ 38 (1988) 94–108. 104f.

the occult rites of older and newly arisen doctrines of salvation, and prove thereby that basically man after all is and remains simply religious, that his religious predisposition drives him to believe in some higher power or other and to practise his belief. [246]

For many Christians this dwindling away of faith and of the practice of the faith is a scandal, but for Häußling it constitutes a necessary component of the faith: "Is faith not also a testimony that sin and scandal exist? Does it not say that there are disasters, general and individual, that the form of this world must pass away because it is stamped with sin, that Christ became a curse and continues to be a curse, wherever he lives, even then and there when we confess him? Does he not say that the Church must be on the cross with Christ, that we cannot get off cheaply?" [247]

Is the above-mentioned however not very western and moreover very medieval? Is there not concealed behind it only one of several possibilities of speaking of the redemption by Christ, and moreover that one which people today find rather difficult? To speak today of vicarious suffering for sin, of grace bestowed through judgement and satisfaction, is that not rather a hindrance than a help? Has theology perhaps a little overlooked, that man's striving for happiness – and also that of the fallen man of original sin – in the last resort points to participation in the fullness of divine life, to deification? Perhaps not a few people in the groove of traditional views ask themselves, whether it is worth while to enter into relationship with a God, to entrust one's life to a God, whose Son "continues to be a curse" for our sake? Can the deification of *my* life be expected from him? The "crisis which has overtaken liturgical celebration", the frequently complained of "cult-incapacity" is possibly only the flight from a God, to seek whom can bring man into Christ's situation of judgement and cross. Perhaps the "cult-incapacity" is a flight from a void labelled as a "momentous sacral symbol" in face of an enigmatic God who inspires little confidence for getting something out of life. [248]

The man allegedly incapable of cult will also be scarcely moved to pray, if he, as himself, with his yearnings for happiness and fullness of life does not come up for discussion in it, but the one praying quotes only from biblical models of "situations of blessing through God's judgement", in order to protect his basic situation. This is for him – the "man ontologically far from God" – "willingness for conversion, for God freedom to confer grace and election." Häußling therefore adds to the limits of a prayer style oriented on biblical models also the biblical images of eschatological fulfilment, because they, like all statements of eschatological fulfilment, are in this sense not quotable as "prayers", because they falsify the situation of the one who prays. Only situations of conferring of grace by God's judgement are "quotable". [249]

It would seem that man is always only standing under judgement, not only under God's judgement, but also under the judgement of his fellow men. For the ancient cos-

---

[246] Cf. R. Hummel, Neue Religiosität und New Age, A. Schilson (ed.), Gottes Weisheit im Mysterium. Vergessene Wege christlicher Spiritualität, Mainz 1989, 61 – 77.

[247] Thus the criticism of the Dutch Eucharistic Prayers so fashionable in the sixties and in part theologically really so paltry, A.A. Häußling, Noch einmal: Neue Eucharistiegebete in Holland, LJ 20 (1970) 113 – 120. 119.

[248] Cf. A. A. Häußling, Die Liturgie der monastischen Kirche, Th. Bogler (ed.): Mönchtum – Ärgernis oder Botschaft. Liturgie und Mönchtum Heft 43, Maria Laach 1968, 77 – 86. 84.

[249] A. A. Häußling, Kosmische Dimension und gesellschaftliche Wirklichkeit. Zu einem Erfahrungswandel in der Liturgie, Alw 25 (1983) 1 – 8. 6 – 8.

mic symbols which have become dim in the technical world are to give way to a new symbol – reality which social relationships offer, for which modern man apparently develops a more developed feeling for amazement than for the world which surrounds him.[250] Already twelve years earlier Maldonado held the same view.[251] Relationship qualities, more precisely relationship problems and their adjustment are to be the new gateway to symbol-reality.

Man under judgement, who can only quote situations of judgement: the radical separation of nature and super-nature, for which Rahner uses the term 'extrinsecism'[252] has consequences here. If grace as 'superstructure' can only lie beyond all human experience, then nature will only be 'disturbed' by God's invitation to salvation, because the latter approaches from the outside as something foreign, and possibly does not include that for which man yearns .[253]

1.10.2. "IN THY LIGHT DO WE SEE LIGHT" (PS 36, 10B)

"If something created were in us, what would we possess that was special?" asks Simeon of Thessalonica referring to the grace which is given to man.[254] For the Christian East "grace" is never something other than "gratia increata", than God himself entering into relationship with man and abiding in life-giving communication. Love is the basis for this relationship, its purpose is the deification of the creature, man's participation in the fullness of divine life.

Man becomes "God", in the relationship he is wholly one with God, he bears him wholly in himself, and nevertheless at the same time the Trinity according to its incomprehensible essence is wholly the One confronting him and the mysterious One.[255] The eternal triune God himself is in the person who has received grace and incorporates him into the inner Trinitarian life. Therefore that which God basically places in man, and causes to grow until the eschatological completion, is something uncreated, it is he himself as communicating with his creature. Without obliterating man in his created identity, he permits him to share in his uncreated, unalterable fullness of life. Therefore man becomes "God by grace" by means of deification. He remains man, but obtains participation in God's unending fullness of life. "Deification" accordingly does

---

[250] Cf. ib. 4f.

[251] L. Maldonado, Vers une liturgie sécularisée. Traduit de l'espagnol par Lucien Nève, Paris 1971, 248: "Aujourd'hui les symboles cosmiques de la nature semblent avoir perdu leur crédit... En revanche, l'homme concret, le frère dans toute sa réalité, tout comme histoire, l'évènement, la vie quotidienne, les gestes de la vie commune, deviennent le véritable signe, le 'sacrement' le plus éloquent."

[252] Rahner speaks of an 'extrinsecism', in which "grace makes its appearance only as a mere, though indeed very beautiful superstructure, which through God's free decree is built upon nature, and to be more precise, that the relationship between both is not stronger than that of a lack of incompatibility (of a "potentia oboedientialis" understood merely negatively)." Rahner is here caricaturing a certain essentialist style of thinking: "one thinks that one knows unequivocally what this human nature exactly is and how far it reaches precisely." Rahner considers this 'extrinsecism' dangerous and in addition its ontological presuppositions as problematical. K. Rahner, Über das Verhältnis von Natur und Gnade, Schriften zur Theologie I. Einsiedeln – Zürich – Köln 1954, 323–345. 324. 327f.

[253] Cf. ib. 325. Rahner sees these difficulties still more intensified by original sin: Man "can feel God's call out of this human circle only as interference, which wants to force him to something – be this as sublime as it may – for which he is not made."

[254] Dialogos 32 – PG 155, 160A.

[255] Cf. Gregory Palamas, Défense des Saints hésychastes. Introduction, texte critique, traduction et notes par Jean Meyendorff, 2 vols., Louvain 2nd edn., 1973 (Spec. sacr. Lovan.) I, 3, 23–159.

not mean that the created reality remains as it is, that merely something is contributed to it, which it does not possess of itself, that it loses its created identity, but rather the completion of what is created as created in the participation in the divine life.

In Orthodox theology the Transfiguration of Christ on Mount Tabor occupies a key position as a "fact" of salvation history; it is the paradigm of deification. [256] The contakion of the Byzantine formulary of the feast for 6 August states the following explanation of the Tabor event: "On the mountain you were transfigured, Christ, God. The disciples gazed, as best they could, on your glory, so that when they see you crucified, will understand the suffering as voluntary, but will preach to the world that you are in truth the reflected light of the Father." [257] In Christ's Transfiguration the deification of the created, creation's sharing in the fullness of divine life began to shine. On Tabor the "overture" of perfection took place, which had still to be ratified through the death on the cross, in order to be able to encompass the deepest depths of human existence. [258]

Deification according to the paradigm of the Transfiguration is the completion of the affirmation of being, which according to Pieper is the cause and content of every feast. No assent to being can be so radical as the praise of God. Affirmation is the kernel of every liturgy; it is in fact an "unlimited statement of Yes-and-Amen". [259] Thus every genuine feast is "established by the gods" and moves "within the field of conflict between life and death" – but within the transient creation it can only just be a question of carrying out the divine affirmation of existence against finiteness. [260] The feast celebrated on earth, the liturgy as God's service to man and the world as "the constant and daily complete approval of the world for a special motive and in a non-routine manner" [261] can be nothing other than an extension upon creation of the intra-Trinitarian feast out of the overflowing love and joy of the three Persons for one another: complete affirmation of creation and joy in it, communication with it for the purpose of its deification, its participation in the divine life.

It is man's mission to bring himself forward, and through himself the whole world, into this invitation to communication and thereby into the process of deification. [262] The entry into the life-giving relationship with God implies no contempt of the world, no ascetical renunciation for its own sake, but rather the introducing of creation, of human life with all its heights and depths into the process of deification. This deification is transformation, without destruction of identity. All that we are, that we do, what interests us in this world, can and ought to be presented to God by the hands of the celebrant as an offering. Not that it ought to remain just as it is. On the other hand it should not cease to be what it basically is, but rather it should become what it really is and what sin

---

[256] Or as I. Herwegen says it in western concepts: "Transfiguration in the Christian sense is the raising of man out of the state of nature to supernature, to a share in the divine Being, in divine light and splendour." Der Verklärungsgedanke in der Liturgie, Alte Quellen neuer Kraft. Gesammelte Aufsätze. Düsseldorf 2nd edn., 1922, 22–48. 27.

[257] Edelby, Liturgikon 971.

[258] Cf. Clément 264.

[259] Cf. J. Pieper, Zustimmung zur Welt. Eine Theorie des Festes, München 2nd edn. 1964, 46–62; Muße und Kult. München 1955, 77f.

[260] Cf. M. Josuttis 54f.

[261] J. Pieper, Zustimmung zur Welt 52.

[262] Cf. D. Papandreou, Die ökumenische und pneumatologische Dimension der orthodoxen Liturgie, K. Schlemmer (ed.), Gemeinsame Liturgie in getrennten Kirchen? Freiburg-Basel-Vienna 1991 (QD 132), 35–52.41.

has disfigured. This paradox of the affirmation and denial of the world by the liturgy, i.e. the remodelling of the world, without destroying it, and its renewal without creating it anew out of nothing, reveals itself in time and space through the Eucharist as the Mysterium Christi. In it the old Adam is renewed, without being annihilated; human nature is assumed unaltered, man is deified without ceasing to be man. [263]

The person who is aware of the deification of the world and of himself, has, according to Lossky, has acquired the true gnosis. He sees the world, as it is, namely in the light of divine love, and there he discovers its true greatness and dignity: In thy light, in thy prevenient grace, we see light, the world destined for perfection in deification. [264]

He who brings the world into the process of deification, quotes the eschatological images of perfection, overcomes the rift between nature and super-nature [265], because he carries it along, in its anabasis, in its movement towards God, makes an offering of it and so leads it to its completion, when the pots will be as "holy" as the bowls before the altar, and there shall be inscribed on the bells of the horses "Holy to the Lord" (Zech 14:20f) and all the earth shall be filled with the glory of the Lord (Num 14:21).

Bibliography

M. Aghiorgoussis, Christian Existentalism of the Greek Fathers: Persons, Essence and Energies in God, Greek Orthodox Theological Review 23 (1978) 15–41.

R. Albertine, 'Theosis' according to the Easter Fathers, mirrored in the development of the Epiclesis, EL 105 (1991) 393–417.

E. Amon, Lebensaustausch zwischen Gott und Mensch. Zum Liturgieverständnis Johannes Pinsks, Regensburg 1988 (Studien zur Pastoraltheologie 6).

O. Clément, La beauté comme révélation, La Vie Spirituelle 637 (1980) 251–270.

G. Greshake, Gott in allen Dingen finden. Schöpfung und Gotteserfahrung, Freiburg-Basel-Wien 1986.

A. A. Häußling, Kosmische Dimension und gesellschaftliche Wirklichkeit. Zu einem Erfahrungswandel in der Liturgie, ALw 25 (1983) 18.

I. Herwegen, Der Verklärungsgedanke in der Liturgie, Alte Quellen neuer Kraft. Gesammelte Aufsätze, Düsseldorf 2nd edn. 1922, 22–48.

K. Koch, Schöpfung als Sakrament. Christliche Schöpfungstheologie jenseits von Gottlosigkeit und Vergötterung der Welt, R. Liggenstorfer (ed.): Schöpfung und Geschichte (FS Paul Mäder), Romanshorn 1991, 31–53.

G. Mantzaridis, The Deification of Man. St. Gregory Palamas and the Orthodox Tradition, Crestwood-New York 1984 (Contemporary Greek Theologians 2).

---

[263] J. D. Zizioulas, Die Welt in eucharistischer Schau und der Mensch von heute, US 25 (1970) 342–349. 343ff.

[264] Cf. Lossky, Théol. Myst. 215f.

[265] Cf. Evdokimov, L'Orthodoxie 90: "Pour l'ascèse occidentale, suivre la nature c'est toujours aller á l'encontre de la grâce. Pour l'Orient, l'homme á 'l'image de Dieu' définit exactement ce qui est l'homme par nature. Etre créé á l'image de Dieu comporte une grâce de cette image, et c'est pourquoi, pour l'ascèse orientale, suivre sa vraie nature c'est travailler dans le sens de la grâce. La grâce est co-naturelle, surnaturellement naturelle á la nature. La nature porte une exigence innée de la grâce, et ce don le fait initialement charismatique. Le terme 'surnaturel' dans la mystique orientale, est réservé au degré suprême de la déification. L'ordre naturel est ainsi conforme á l'ordre de la grâce, s'achève en lui et culmine dans la grâce déifiante."

J. Moltmann, Die einladende Einheit des dreieinigen Gottes, Concilium 21 (1985) 35–41.

G. Pöltner / H. Vetter (eds.), Theologie und Ästhetik, Freiburg-Basel-Wien 1985.

J. Tyciak, Wege östlicher Theologie. Geistesgeschichtliche Durchblicke, Bonn 1946.

J. Tyciak, Zwischen Morgenland und Abendland. Ein Beitrag zu einem westöstlichen Gespräch, Düsseldorf 1949.

Part II

Anabasis: Man's Ascent to God

2.1. ANABASIS AND ITS VISIBLE FORM

Man's *anabasis* is a response to the divine *katabasis*. God's descent first makes possible man's ascent to God in praise and petition, sacrifice and penance. The latreuic dimension of the liturgy, i.e. the worship of God by the human person, is indeed one aspect of *anabasis* but the latter is by no means exhausted by this worship. God has no need of human praise. If he discloses himself by *katabasis*, if he comes forth from the inaccessible light of the divinity, he does so in order to enter into a relationship with his creation. *Anabasis*, the human response to God's love of his people and of the world, is the acceptance of this invitation to communication, which means participation by the creature in the divine life. Just as God manifests himself in *katabasis*, *anabasis* happens no differently in that through it man manifests himself.

2.1.1. MAN AS A SELF-MANIFESTING BEING

God, who lives in inaccessible light, manifests himself. He enters into a relationship with his creation in order to endow it with the fullness of his life. The pre-eternal feast of the perfect mutual affirmation of the three divine persons and their joy in each other expands itself into creation.

The divine love explodes the "us" of the three persons. God comes out of the divine light proper to the three divine persons and which is inaccessible to every creature, in order to meet the human person. God steps completely out of his intrinsic way of being, without leaving the inaccessible light of the divinity. He is completely present while remaining at the same time the wholly other and the holy one. God communicates without being dissolved in this communication; he goes out from himself in order to elevate what is created to the participation in the pre-eternal feast of his love, without in any way interrupting this feast.

God wants to raise creation to himself because he loves eternally. He needs neither the human person nor the world but he desires them. Every relationship between persons presupposes the permanent distinction between an I and a Thou. The I affirms the Thou as a separate person. It is part of love that the I acknowledge the independence of the beloved Thou, indeed, that it rejoices in it. Among human beings it is the case that a love relationship is impossible without this respect for the difference between I and Thou. If this difference is abolished then there is no communication but, rather, domination in which the I shapes the Thou in its own image, does not admit its difference and with this denial destroys it.

What can already be a problem in every inner-wordly relationship between partners is even more so in the relationship between the Trinity and the human person. Here God "needs" a human Thou if genuine communication is to take place, a Thou God can ad dress as different (katabatic) and who can reply to him (anabatic) without losing his or her humanity. The reality of the human person as the image of God is the foundation on which that person's ability to communicate with God is built.

What the human person is in his or her innermost being is as much a mystery as the mystery of God. It is possible to say this much about the human person; that that person's innermost being can be described as "to have life". The human person experiences itself to the extent to which it manifests itself, to the extent to which it opens itself – that is the innermost self, the "to have life" – outwards to the establishment of relationship. [1]

In this, too, is the human person the image of God, that in all communicative manifestation of the innermost self it remains a mystery, even to itself. In the perception of itself as the image of the Deus absconditus, the human person discovers itself to be "homo ab – sconditus", as the greatest mystery after that of the three-person God. [2]

According to Karl Rahner, the human person is "Self-possession" and "Reflectivity-into-self"; this is the case with God and with the human person as the image of God: "a flowing outwards, an exposition of its own essence from its own cause – an *emanatio*, and a withdrawing into itself of this essence, which has expressed itself in terms of its specific cause – which has, as it were, revealed itself. The more interior the two phases are with regard to the emanating and returning thing which is, the more this thing is able to express itself, and in so doing, keeping itself to itself, the more the thing thus expressed can perceive itself, all the more does being display itself to itself as its own specific being-present-to-itself." [3]. Romano Guardini teaches a similar view of the human person. He describes the essence of the human person, the personal "kernel of the I", described by Gregory Palmas as "to have life", as "the soul".

The relationship between body and soul is defined in the sense of a real-symbol – nowhere else is it clearer what is meant by real-symbol than here. The human body is the preeminent real-symbol because the spiritual soul makes itself present in this body. This real-symbolism establishes the human person in its body-spirit wholeness: the human person is neither only soul nor only body. Finally, the person is even in a relationship of ownership as when he or she speaks of "my head" or "my hand" etc. The personal I, that spiritual core or soul of the individual, needs the body as the place and space of its real-symbolic manifestation: it is only thus that the spiritual I can enter into the realms of time and space. [4]

As presence-making real-symbol the body is the primary and most intimate instrument needed by the soul to exteriorize itself, to set itself outside itself and enter into communication. The body is the elemental symbol of the human person, the elemental expression of human freedom to move beyond its hidden spiritual essence in order to be there for itself and for others. [5]

While the body is the first and most intimate means of expression, it is not the only one. "The body's possibilities of expression with its surfaces, lines and movements, its members and forms are not enough to articulate the riches of the soul. The human person expands these by incorporating into its bodily sphere the things it finds in its environment." [6] These phenomena which surround the human person become part of the soul's self-expression. This person makes him or herself real-symbolically present

---

[1] Cf. Gregory Palamas, Cap. Phys. 30-PG 150, 1140 D.

[2] Cf. P. Evdokimov, Die Frau und das Heil der Welt, Moers-Aschaffenburg 1989,70.

[3] K. Rahner, Hörer des Wortes. Zur Grundlegung einer Religionsphilosophie. Neu bearbeitet von J.B. Metz, München 2nd edn. 1969, 67f. English edn.: Hearers of the Word. Revised by J. B. Metz. Translated by Ronald Wells, London & Sydney, 1969, p. 49.

[4] Cf. Guardini, Liturg. Bildung 15-18; Die Sinne und die relig. Erkenntnis 17. Compare also Gregory Palamas, PG 150, 1140 D with Guardini, Liturg. Bildung 23: The ensouled body is the soul expressing itself in the body.

[5] G. Greshake, Gott in allen Dingen finden. Schöpfung und Gotteserfahrung, Freiburg-Basel-Vienna 1986, 28f.

[6] Guardini, Liturg. Bildung 34; Die Sinne und die relig. Erkenntnis 49.

in the surrounding created realities – things with which that person enters into a personal relationship, making them places of human presence.

Guardini, though, distinguishes several levels of this emergence, which surround the I like so many "vessels" in which the soul presents itself to the outside world. "Firstly, the possibilities of expression of (bodily) form, measure, movement are enriched by clothing. Folds, colour, jewellery and the relation of the individual articles of clothing to each other, create new forms. The shape and movement of the body are emphasized and developed in various ways. Further: line and the attitude of the limbs combine with tools. Thus, the form and movement of the limb in question are accented. The expression of an offering hand is greater when that hand is carrying a dish; the force of a blow is strengthened as soon as it is made with a hammer... Form is placed in a particular surrounding, in a space which has been consciously arranged with furniture and with useful and decorative objects."

Body, clothing and tools are as it were the first three "vessels" in which the soul steps outside of itself – but they are not the only such vessels. Since, in Guardini's view, world and cosmos are too vast for human capabilities of "ensouling", a limited space of presence is required within which the individual can condense the "breadth and confusion" of the world into a manageable concept. On the basis of this "liveableness", house and space become a real-symbolic manifestations of the I. Beyond the home is the further dimension of "existence" – the home-place; but here too there are degrees: home-town, region, country: "My home-place – that is me. I cannot exist without it, but it cannot exist without me." [7]

In body, clothing, tools and objects, space, house, city, landscape, region and country, the I or the soul makes itself real-symbolically present: these form the intermediaries that make the establishment of relationships between spiritual persons at all possible. But more: the things of this world as real-symbols of the soul become part of the human person itself. A personal relationship is established between the individual and the surrounding world which affects that individual: [8] that which has found its way "from the inner depths and sense form to exterior expression" reacts in turn back "from the exterior into the sense perceiving interior." [9]

Particular bodily faculties, for example, shape man's feelings of self worth; beautiful clothes give an individual self-confidence; the experience of being at home in one's own four walls – reflected in the French expression: "il est chez-lui", "he is at home" – gives a feeling of security; the experience of belonging to a region, ethnic group or cultural community gives a particular identity. Man becomes more and more a distinctive personality the more he enters into relationship with the surrounding world, the more he is able to express himself in the world, is able to gather it to himself. The surrounding world acts on man so that he experiences himself constantly as a new and enriched person and, as such, enabled to express himself again in a new and more perfect fashion. The forms of *personare*, of the resonance of the mysterious "to have life" throughout the world which surrounds the soul become richer, the more this world is in personal

---

[7]   Cf. Guardini, Liturg. Bildung 34-37.

[8]   Cf. Karl Rahner, Die Gegenwart des Herrn in der christlichen Kultgemeinde. In Schriften zur Theologie VIII, Einsiedeln-Zurich-Köln 1967,395-408. 396.

[9]   Cf. R. Guardini, Die Bekehrung des Aurelius Augustinus. Der innere Vorgang in seinen Bekenntnissen. Reprint of the 3th edn., Mainz-Paderborn 1989, 72.

relationship to the soul. But man as a being of relationship is perfected only in communication with God. For this reason every relationship with the world and with his fellow man is perfected in *anabasis*, in the life-creating relationship of man to the living God.

2.1.2. A COMMUNICATIVE UNDERSTANDING OF SYMBOL

For communication to be effected, partners in a relationship must be present for each other. Body-spirit beings are there for each other when they meet in real-symbolic modes of presence in which the soul or the I makes itself present, for example in the body. A communicative understanding of symbol can be deduced from the body, from clothing, from tools and from the world which surrounds man as a real-symbolic making present of the soul. This understanding shows *anabasis* to be man's entry into life-creating communication with God.

Can that which is earthly and visible be the vehicle of an invisible, spiritual, reality? The answer to this question determines the understanding of symbol. If the answer to the question is negative, then a symbol is merely a sign arbitrarily set up by man as a reminder. Here there can be no talk of a real-symbol as the latter is spoken about in the context of liturgical symbolism.

Up to the beginning of the modern era the question was answered in the affirmative with the help of the (neo)platonic doctrine of participation. This teaching sought to express the notion that the finite is capable of the infinite (*finitum capax infiniti*), that, on the basis of the analogy of being, the invisible can be made present by reflection in the visible. This realistic understanding of symbol [10] conditioned not only the liturgy but gave a symbolic character to the general world-view: the ruler of the world is God the ruler of all, present in image in every worldly symbol and even more so in every liturgical symbol.

The doctrine of participation can be dangerous if it leads beyond the idea of real-symbol to a pansacramentalism. In this everything becomes capable of infinity (*capax infiniti*) on the basis of an "automatic" making present of the invisible in the visible. Corbon includes pansacramentalism along with cultism among the temptations to which liturgy is exposed: everything becomes a reality-filled sign of the presence of Christ, "one's brother is a sacrament, nature is a sacrament, art and culture, guerilla war and the maintenance of public order, psychoanalysis and group dynamics. The sacramental idea becomes a cure-all, wild liturgies abound." [11]

Hotz anchors the doctrine of participation as an "hierophanic" experience of the presence of the absolute in the finite in man, an experience which since the time of Plato has been imbued with philosophy. [12] But prior to philosophical analysis is experience and with this a relationship. Barth's replacement of the philosophical *analogia entis* with an *analogia relationis* corresponds with this: there is no analogy of being between symbol and what is symbolised, "for the being of God and that of man are and remain incomparable", but there is a an analogy of relationship: the relationship between man and God is an image of the relationship which the Trinity has within itself. [13]

---

[10] Cf. E. v. Ivanka, Plato Christianus. Übernahme und Umgestaltung des Platonismus durch die Väter, Einsiedeln 1964.

[11] Corbon, Liturgie aus dem Urquell 110.

[12] Cf. R. Hotz, Religion – Symbolhandlung – Sakrament. Die christlich-theologische Bedeutung des kultischen Symbolhandelns, LJ 31(1981) 36-54.

[13] Cf. K. Barth, Kirchliche Dogmatik III/2: Die Lehre von der Schöpfung, Zurich 2nd edn. 1959, 262.

In this it should never be forgotten that man's relationships can never take a form other than that of the "in-between" of the visible creation. The beauty and goodness of these relationships are founded on the holiness of the creator, who can be glimpsed through them, so that beauty represents a discrete source for the knowledge of God. [14] For Clément, the beauty, "which elicits all relationship (communion)", is one of the names of God. [15] The created world as a whole is a burning bush permeated by the divine light. It is an "icon" because through it the creator which permeates it is glimpsed without robbing it of its identity as creature. The world participates in God, but precisely not in the sense of a (neo)platonic participation, but in the sense of *perichoresis*. This *perichoresis* make it possible for the visible to symbolise the invisible and in "all-embracing Eucharist" to reflect the divine glory (*doxa*). [16]

According to Clément, *perichoresis*, the permeation of created reality by God, determines the Christian understanding of symbol. In this understanding, all that is earthly is viewed through a heavenly optic. The world is not subsumed into God, but becomes the place of God, the temple of the Holy Spirit, the medium of communication between God and man. The norm and model of this *perichoresis* – communicative understanding of symbol is the human nature of Christ – and with this the Eucharist, as a safeguard against pan-sacramentalism. Both the historical and the Eucharistic body of Christ remain worldly realities in their individual creaturely states. In them, however, the fullness of the godhead dwells and through them, as the same source, God enters into communion with man. It is essential that the whole of creation be drawn into the communication made possible through and in Christ, drawn into an "all-embracing Eucharist" which at the end of time flows into the heavenly liturgy.

Because this understanding of symbol in based on God's perichoretic permeating of creation, it is essentially different both from a pantheistic blending of God and the world and from any idea of a dissolution of the world in the divine. Stamped by the living relationship, this understanding of symbol does not share the impersonal (neo)Platonic doctrine of participation, according to which the exemplar makes itself present in the image. Finally this relation-based understanding of symbol corrects an Aristotelian notion, widely propagated by scholasticism, according to which a created thing is merely an effect produced by the working of the uncreated, having subsequently no further living contact with him. This notion derives the being of the world causally from a creator God but does not continue to see this God as present in the world: in the West, Deism eventually elevated this notion to a doctrine.

The Son of God made man is the quintessential model of symbol. From him alone every symbolism derives its measure of reality; from him who surpasses and thus encompasses all other understandings of symbol: Christ reconciles Plato and Aristotle, eastern and western thought. The symbol is the thing itself in its transparency for the triune God, it is the locus of the exchange of life between God and man. [17]

---

[14] Cf. Clément, La beauté comme révélation 251; cf. also H. U. von Balthasar, Wahrheit. Ein Versuch, Einsiedeln 1947, 253f.

[15] Clément, ibid., "La beauté est un nom divin et Denys l'Aréopagite, dans son traité des Noms divins, célébre 'la Beauté qui produit toute communion'. Dieu est en lui même plénitude de beauté, dans un sens inséparablement ontologique et personnel."

[16] Ibid. 253: "La périchorése, car le visible doit symboliser l'invisible, doit rendre gloire dans une immense eucharistie."

[17] Cf. ibid. 256f.

2.1.3. ANABASIS AS THE PERFECTION OF ALL HUMAN UTTERANCE AND "ANAPHORA".

The world man inhabits, the world in which he expresses himself, in which he recollects himself and which reacts to him, is God's creation. As God's creation, the world is not made to languish unrelatedly for itself or simply to be there, but is intended to serve a a medium of communication between God and man, as Lossky says, referring to Pseudo Dionysius. By performing this service, the whole of creation arrives at participation in the fullness of life of its creator. [18] Thus viewed, creation stands "between" God and man and serves both as the "go-between" of their relationship. That both God and man use the same creation as the expression of themselves is yet another illustration of the creature's being made in the image of God.

From God's point of view, what is created is "so to speak the 'continuation' of God's inner self-expression" and with that the visible self-expression of God, who in a free decision of the will left the inaccessible light of his being in order to love, in order to enter into a relationship with his creatures. [19] The visible world is "truly an expression of God, a symbol of his power and glory, a statement and promise of his salvation, in short: a sacrament of his self-revelation and with that for us a sacramental medium for experience of God". [20] "But here we are concerned not just with self-revelation but also with the self-giving of God. For it is he himself, who according to the scriptures gives life to all, who distributes food and drink, causes the rain to fall and the sun to shine on the just and the unjust, to show his love, care and concern for man." As a medium of relationship, creation is not only a means through which God is present to man, but also God's self-giving to man in order that man can partake in his fullness of life: in creation "God shows and gives himself, to the extent that he appears not simply allegorically, but expresses himself in creation and, present in this creation by means of the his life-creating Spirit, continually unites the "other" of creation to himself through this Spirit". [21]

For man, too, the world is the vehicle of self-expression and self-giving. He also steps out of the hidden depths of his "I" (or of his soul) in order to enter into relationship with what lies outside of the self. Just as the world is a "sacrament" of God's self-revelation, so it is "sacrament" for that part of man which makes itself present in her, which he impresses with his individual traits and in so doing humanises the world. This parallel between the action of God and man, reflecting man's nature as the image of God, opens up access to the mystery of the human person. [22]

---

[18]   Cf. Lossky, Théol. Myst. 92f. with reference to Pseudo Dionysius: "La création apparaît ainsi comme une hiérarchie des analogies réelles ou, selon la parole de Denys, 'chaque ordre de la disposition hiérarchique s'éléve selon sa propre analogie á la coopération avec Dieu, en accomplissant par la grâce et la vertu données par Dieu ce que Dieu posséde par nature en outre mesure.' Toutes les créatures sont donc appelés á l'union parfaite avec Dieu ... ". Ibid. 96: "Créé pour être déifié, le monde est dynamique, tendant vers son but final." From this also comes the idea of a dynamic indwelling in material creation. Cf. ibid.98f.

[19]   Cf. Greshake, Gott in allen Dingen finden 34f.; K. Koch, Schöpfung als Sakrament. Christliche Schöpfungstheologie jenseits von Gottlosigkeit und Vergötterung der Welt, R. Liggenstorfer (ed.), Schöpfung und Geschichte (FS Paul Mader), Romanshorn 1991,31-35.42.

[20]   Greshake ibid.,37.

[21]   Ibid. 38f.

[22]   Cf. Evdokimov, L'Orthodoxie 68.

In a certain sense to enter into a relationship with another person or with a thing means "to sacrifice", if one understands this word from the Greek *anapherein* as "to carry up". Persons and things are "carried up" from a state of mere detached being there to one of relationship. This being "carried up" into relationship can be concerned with material objects – for example the pursuit of riches or ideas – for example commitment to an ideology. It is at its most obvious in a human love relationship. A person who is loved is no longer simply another living being present in the world, but, through the relationship, has become a part of the personality of the lover. Without this relationship the lover is not himself. He receives his true identity from the other whom he loves.

All relationships, however, into which man enters, in which he expresses and discovers himself are, like himself, finite. Even the most intense loving relationship with another person cannot express the fullness of the lover's capacity and thirst for life. Traces of unsatisfied expectations of happiness and fulfillment always remain; death and the finitude of created things make a perfect relationship on earth completely impossible.

Every relationship, of which love is the purest and most mature form, is driven by its essence to strive for infinity. In this man has only these alternatives: either, as a creature invited to participation in the divine fullness, to lift up ("sacrifice") his expressions of his life and his relationships into the infinity of God, or, to endure in a despairing self-love, resigned to settle for meaninglessness and death. This self-love permits no genuine relationship but only the exploitation of people and things. Man is faced with the alternatives, to be a living image of God in the visible world, bringing that world into a divinising relationship, or, to be a leering demonic mask which has only destruction, death and, finally, nothingness, to offer. [23]

Thus, man's relationship to the surrounding world of his fellow men and created things, is perfected by its being taken into *anabasis*, by man carrying up his world into his relationship with God, sacrificing into God's infinity and eternity – in the actual meaning of every sacrifice. Sacrifice does not aim at the cultic destruction of life in order to obtain some reward from God, but rather, to the preservation, indeed the intensification and making eternal of life. For, "The object of every sacrifice is: to participate in the divine nature. The sacrifice does not want to annihilate us, but, on the contrary, it wants to win something for us, to obtain for us what we do not yet possess." By means of sacrifice, the offering himself is to arrive at a higher way of being. [24]

Man must sacrifice. He cannot do otherwise than raise the world that surrounds him from mere existence to a relationship with himself, in order by so doing to express himself and discover his own identity. This anaphora becomes a tragedy if it remains on the level of finite man himself, finding death along with him. It comes to perfection when the world is offered to God, when what is offered is part of the *anabasis*, is indeed its necessary expression. The full affirmation of the mortal body and its possibilities of expression is possible only in expectation of the immortal, glorified resurrected body. Joy in clothing is only more than purest vanity when it happens in the expectation and glimmer of the *indumentum salutis*. Bright, warming light has a meaning beyond technical value as illumination and heating only when it is seen as a presentiment of a light

---

[23]   Cf. ibid. 77.
[24]   O. Casel, Das christliche Opfermysterium. Zur Morphologie und Theologie des eucharistischen Hochgebetes. Ed. by V. Warnach, Graz-Wien-Köln 1968, 414, cf. too 3-19.

which knows no evening. Every loaf of bread, every cup of wine finds its fulfillment in the eucharistic gifts. Every house, the expression of human experience of security, seeks perfection in the house "not built by human hands". It is this house of which, to the extent men can make it according to their cultural yard-sticks, the human house should be a foretaste.

Bibliography

O. Clément, La beauté comme révélation, La Vie Spirituelle 637 (1980) 251-270.

G. Greshake, Gott in allen Dingen finden. Schöpfung und Gotteserfahrung, Freiburg-Basel-Vienna 1986.

R. Guardini, Liturgische Bildung. Versuche, Rothenfels am Main 1923.

R. Guardini, Liturgie und liturgische Bildung, Würzburg 2nd edn.1966

R. Guardini, Die Sinne und die religiöse Erkenntnis. Drei Versuche, Würzburg 2nd edn. 1958.

W. Hahne, De Arte Celebrandi oder: Von der Kunst, Gottesdienst zu feiern. Entwurf einer Fundalentalliturgik, Freiburg-Basel-Vienna 1990.

M. Kunzler, Porta Orientalis 265-288: Die Kritik der Diabase; 335-352: Der Mensch als Wesen, das notwending opfert.

2.2. LITURGY AND CULTURE

The liturgy is unthinkable without culture and its achievements. In the course of the history of Christian worship, the various liturgies have been stamped by many cultures and peoples. Speech, music and song, the plastic arts, including architecture, as cultural witnesses of various epochs have become interwoven with the liturgy. If *anabasis* – precisely as anaphora of the world – happens through the "in-between" of the reality which is present to man and accessible to his senses, then this *anabasis* is always already cultural event. "Nature" is the "material" open to man to discover for his self-expression; if he achieves this expression, then he also always changes what he finds by "developing" and "cultivating" (*colere*) it and in doing so turning nature into culture or civilization. Thus, the necessary drawing of nature into relationship with God always has a cultural aspect.

2.2.1. LITURGICAL STUDIES AS CULTURAL STUDIES?

Looked on purely from the point of view of scientific theory, liturgical studies could be conducted by an unbeliever. Such a scholar of liturgy would have to regard himself as a student of culture, whose primary interest is man. He would concern himself with man as a religious being, who prays and celebrates liturgy and whose religious desires also influence his culture. Liturgical studies under these circumstances would be the study of an anthropological phenomenon devoid of any theological background, a cultural investigation whose object is to increase knowledge of man seen as a being who, among other activities, prays and worships. How he prays, how he worships, when and for what reasons he does this, will provide information concerning man's understanding of himself in his particular social and cultural context. At worst, the study of liturgy could then be understood as a scientific investigation of religious symptoms, forming a special area of study in a more comprehensive (psycho)pathology of the human person.

That the possibility of an a-religious study of liturgy is at least conceivable lies in an ambivalence at the heart of culture itself.

Nature is man's living space. As an expression of himself man changes nature into culture: "Culture is the shaping of the environment by man." [25] "Culture is the universal task given by God to men; in culture man unfolds himself and completes creation." [26]

To this extent there is an inner connection between liturgy and culture, in that the man's anabatic answer to God's katabatic address to him is possible only as human self-expression within and through the medium of world in which man finds himself. [27] Man's religious expression of himself and the "cultural" manifestation of this expression can be the object of an a-religious liturgical scholarship, but this would be only one study among many of the cultural aspects of what it is to be human. But such a study would be closed to an understanding of culture as an expression of relationship with the living God. The religious value of culture depends on whether or how it succeeds in expressing man's entry into life-giving relationship with God, on whether this relationship with God and the inclusion of the world in this relationship become cultural realities.

2.2.2. LITURGY AND CULTURE – AN AMBIVALENT RELATIONSHIP

The ambivalence of culture as human self-expression is grounded in Original Sin. Culture shares man's tendency towards self-glorification and his tendency to cut himself off from God. A self-glorifying culture as the expression of a self-glorifying humanity claims the kernel of religion for itself. Such a culture serves man in imparting a peculiar, home-made, glory to his inner-worldly, godless, death-enslaved existence. This mortal glory is always a "cultural" chimera, a subtle disguising and polite labelling of a despairing surrender to finitude and death.

A self-glorifying culture strives for the negation of the existence of man as well as that of the world that surrounds him. This world must deliver self-made glory (for example riches, power) even if in doing so this world is destroyed. The world is ruthlessly exploited to provide riches – that it to produce a supposed "meaning of life". But this self-made meaning of existence can only provide a "cultural" cover-up for, at best a numbing of, the despair and sadness of a life draining into death. [28] The person who has surrendered to nothingness becomes a "demonic caricature", [29] and the world which he must use in order to make his self-glorification possible must necessarily end up in one ecological crisis after the other. [30]

Such a "culture" serves only to "refine" negativity when it tries to "render religion harmless while at the same time exploiting its power". Then this culture "includes (religion) in its repertoire, even elevates it to the level of 'culture', making religion its ultimate consecration". [31] In a self-glorifying culture there is basically no genuine rela-

---

[25] M. J. Herskovits, Les bases de l'Anthropologie Culturelle, Paris 1952, 6: "La culture est ce qui dans le milieu est dû á l'homme."

[26] Cf. Vatican II, GS 57.

[27] Every experience, including the religious, is, according to Herkovits, culturally defined, cf. op.cit., 17.

[28] Cf. Guardini, Liturgische Bildung 89f.; J. Pieper, Muße und Kult, München 1955, 51.

[29] Cf. Evdokimov, L'Orthodoxie 77.

[30] Cf. G. Greshake, Gott in allen Dingen finden. Schöpfung und Gotteserfahrung, Freiburg-Basel-Vienna 1986, 25.

[31] Guardini, op.cit. 89.

tionship, one which preserves the communicating partner in his own otherness. Instead, there is only a raid by finite man who does not "spare" but who in despairing hunger for existence and confirmation of existence absorbs other people and things into his own I, and in so doing destroys them. The spectrum of such culture is broad; it is tangible to-day in the Satan cult of a certain hard-rock scene. [32] Man's self perversion through culture is then complete when this provides the "aesthetic form" for the affirmation of rejection, when by means of this culture the practice of the aesthetic of the "beautiful corpse" becomes a matter of fun. [33]

Culture is no less perverted by Original Sin when it uses its aesthetic values to propagate doctrines of salvation – that is, fake religions – which promise man the ability to create for himself that glory he longs for as the lasting image of God. The aim of totalitarian systems such as Fascism and Communism is not the divinisation of man but his idolisation. These systems have their own rites and symbols, not infrequently reminiscent of the Church's liturgical actions, which serve as "communicative structures" to express their special profile, [34] just as art and architecture are used for self-presentation. [35] Also worthy of consideration are the cultural (i.e. advertising) values of a profit-driven consumer society which in the final analysis is no less totalitarian. Culture belongs to man. But, because of the ambivalence stemming from Original Sin, culture should be accompanied by a warning that it also presents a temptation. Is there any protection against this danger in the necessary encounter between Christianity and a given culture? Can this danger ever be totally excluded?

2.2.3. LITURGICAL INCULTURATION AS A PERMANENT TASK

Because of the body-spirit composition of man there is no relationship with God which is devoid of a cultural dimension. For this reason, the task of liturgical inculturation is one which can never be regarded as completed. In this, the danger of an absorbtion of the religious element by a self-glorifying culture should be kept in mind.

It is very dangerous to tie the expression of faith so closely to a particular culture that this cultural expression becomes mistaken for the faith. "Is faith more than the cultural garments in which it is clothed? Can it be translated into another culture? What are the criteria by which the accuracy of such a translation is measured?" The decisively new element of Christianity is precisely the *katabasis* of God in Jesus Christ. He came so that men and women would have life in full (John 10:10), in order that they might share in the fullness of the life of the Trinity. This *katabasis* must be articulated in and for

---

[32] Cf. A. Malessa, Sympathy for the Devil – Satanismus und schwarze Magie in der Rockmusik, P. Bubmann/ R. Tischer (eds.), Pop und Religion. Auf dem Weg zu einer neuen Volksfrömmigkeit? Stuttgart 1992, 101-106.

[33] The rejection of being can according to J. Pieper, Zustimmung zur Welt. Eine Theorie des Festes, München 2nd edn. 1964, 51, become so unrecognisable that it can artfully conceal itself behind the facade of a "thoroughly appealing, completely vital joy in dance, music and communal celebration", behind the mask of a "more or less forced confidence in life."

[34] Cf. K. Richter, Riten und Symbole in der Industriekultur am Beispiel der Riten im Bereich des Sozialismus, Concilium 13 (1977) 108-113; A. W. Thöne, Das Licht der Arier. Licht-, Feuer- und Dunkelsymbolik des Nationalsozialismus, München 1979; W. Reichelt, Das Braune Evangelium. Hitler und die NS-Liturgie, Wuppertal 1990.

[35] Cf. R. Wolters, Neue deutsche Baukunst, Prag 1943, 9-14; G. Troest, Das Bauen im dritten Reich I, Dresden 1938. On communist "proletarian culture" cf. C. A. Wetter, Sowjetideologie heute I, Frankfurt/M.-Hamburg 1962, 257-260; T. Grimm, Art. "Kulturrevolution", HWPh IV. Darmstadt 1976, 1342-1349.

every culture. The extent to which this articulation succeeds or fails is the criterion for inculturation of Christianity as for the Christian liturgy: "The increase in life of those addressed is the yard-stick of inculturation." [36] It is important to emphasize, though, that this increase in life must come from God and stand against the dangerous temptation to acquire, by means of culture, a high-handed self-regarding glory.

Thus, the Incarnation of the Son is "Greatest example and model of inculturation," [37] *Katabasis* already took place once before and takes place time and again as inculturation, otherwise men would not have understood it and still would not understand it. The vivifying principle of inculturation as of the incarnation of the Logos is the Holy Spirit. "But in contrast to the incarnation, inculturation is not a once-for-all historical salvation-event but, synchronically viewed, a many-sided event and, diachronically viewed, a process which continues to the end of history." This process is the dynamic aspect of tradition: "Thus, the inculturation of the liturgy remains, on the one hand, always bound up with the word of Scripture which witnesses to God's saving deeds and on the other with what Jesus established, which must preserve these saving deeds and give them a new resonance." "Tradition, as the authentic spirit-filled expression of the handing on and constantly new actualization of faith though word and sign, guarantees the continuity of the Christ-event down to the present in the Church, which in many different ways witnesses to its faith and celebrates the one Christ-event here and now." [38]

The theological basis of inculturation, and with it for all new development stemming from it, is the need, "to make man able to experience God's self-revelation in Jesus Christ so that he can receive it and respond to it." For this reason all inculturation remains bound to the Christ-event, to the Incarnation, Life and Death, Resurrection and Glorification of Christ. "Thus", this reference "has a memorial quality and creates a tradition in which loyalty to what was established by Christ finds its form as a response of faith under the impulse of the Spirit. But, again, this development of tradition may not be broken off arbitrarily but must proceed in the measure in which the Spirit directs history to its completion. Since, however, this world-historical process, in contrast to God's becoming man in Jesus Christ, unfolds not only in an historically defined and culturally contained time and place, but at all times and in all places in the world, it is possible only by taking many forms: as in the events of Pentecost, God's self-revelation is heard and answered in many languages. Thus, what is needed is not uniformity but a legitimate pluriformity." [39] In all of this it should be remembered that every inculturation of Christian faith and with it of the liturgy, must articulate undiminished for the new culture that which is specifically Christian, i.e. the increase of life of those addressed by the Son of God made man. There can be no inculturation of Christianity into an atheistic culture, but only a radical critique of that culture by Christianity!

Contemporary theology and with it the study of liturgy is faced with the task of inculturation. How can contemporary man, seemingly scarcely able to celebrate though

---

[36] Ebd. H. Weder, "Ich bin allen alles geworden ... ". Neutestamentliche Überlegungen zum Verhältnis von Glaube und Kultur, Neue Zürcher Zeitung, Fernausgabe Nr. 211 vom 13.9.1991, 37f.
[37] Meyer, Zur Inkulturation der Eucharistiefeier 8.
[38] Ibid. 9.
[39] Ibid. 15.

anxious to believe, be made able to believe and able to celebrate this belief in the liturgy?

Häußling appeals for the reduction of the liturgy for the sake of a religiously under-developed and secularized man, "but, please: a reduction not merely in the sense of a reduction of volume but as a concentration on religious and liturgical fundamentals, on basic gestures, basic formulae, basic words and structures". [40] In 1971, still in the aftermath of the reform of the liturgy, the Dutch Jesuit, H. Schmidt, proposed the total secularization of the liturgy as a necessary form of inculturation. A process of secu-larization which began at the end of the Middle Ages – and which included an "icon-oclasm and destruction of shrines," which was no less necessary, "however beneficial their income" – is judged to have been a development, historico-philosophically de-manded, which of necessity led to a non-Christian culture, "which is no way means anti-Christian". [41]

How different the picture presented by a contemporary history of ideas. Biser di-agnoses this as an arbitrary, "kaleidoscopic world-view resulting from a change of per-spectives and positions which owes more to fashion than to principle", and this along with a fatigue with search for meaning and attempts to shape the world. [42] The new barrier against belief in God is no longer a self-confident acting secular atheism, but "consists in the refusal of thought to go to the boundaries set it and to accept the trans-formation awaiting it there." Biser characterizes this attitude, "which swings between despair and pragmatism", as "an expression of post-modern arbitrariness". [43]

In the face of arbitrariness as the terminus of secularization a re-thinking is called for in which secularization is no longer seen as an historically necessary consequence of Christianity, but as an expression of man's self-concern and with it of sin, of the uncoupling of "autonomous man" from his relationship with God and with this all the necessary consequences of alienation. [44]

Perhaps it is precisely postmodern arbitrariness that make it possible to speak once more of its opposite. Perhaps the inculturation of Christianity is more than ever a faith-based critique of culture, which rents a stall in the market of possibilities and once more offers the message that liturgy possesses a "cosmic and universal character", that "liturgy is not 'done' but received and as something already existing is constantly made to live", that, as a celebration, liturgy "goes beyond the realm of what can be made and done" and "leads into the realm of the presented, the living, which gives itself to us", that "in this sense the lack of arbitrariness of the liturgy was there for the individual community and the individual celebrant", because it is a pledge and expression of the fact "that here something more and greater happens than any one community, as indeed any man could do of it – or himself". [45]

Bibliography

[40] Cf. A. A. Häußling, Liturgiewissentschaftliche Aufgabenfelder vor uns, LJ 38 (1988) 94-108.104f.

[41] Cf. H. Schmidt, Liturgie und moderne Gesellschaft. Eine Analyse der heutigen Lage, Concilium (D) 7 (1971) 82-89.

[42] Cf. Biser, Glaubensprognose 35f.

[43] Ibid. 123.

[44] Cf. ibid. 129f. Regarding the proximity of Biser to Guardini as "interpretor of the end of an epoch" cf. ibid. 23-29

[45] J. Ratzinger, Zur Frage nach der Struktur der liturgischen Feier, IKaZ 7 (1978) 488-497. 491f.

E. Biser, Glaubensprognose. Orientierung in postsäkularer Zeit, Graz-Wien-Köln 1992.

J. Gelineau, Tradition, Kreation, Kultur, Concilium 19 (1983) 91 - 98.

J. Huizinga, Homo Ludens. Von Ursprung der Kultur im Spiel, Hamburg 1956.

M. Kunzler, Porta Orientalis 690-727: Inkulturation – in eine kultlose Kultur?

H. B. Meyer, Zur Inkulturation der Eucharistiefeier im Blick auf das deutsche Sprachgebiet, LJ 41 (1991) 7 - 23.

R. Schaeffler, Kultur und Kult, LJ 41 (1991) 73 - 87.

J. Tinsley, Liturgie und Kunst, Concilium 7 (1971) 112-116.

H. Weder, "Ich bin allen alles geworden ... ". Neutestamentliche Überlegungen zum Verhältnis von Glaube und Kultur, Neue Zürcher Zeiting, Fernausgabe Nr.211 vom 3.9.1991, 37f.

2.3. THE STUDY OF LITURGY AND ITS HISTORY

2.3.1. THE DISCIPLINE OF THEOLOGY AND ITS TASK

The term "liturgiology" (*Liturgiewissenschaft*) goes back to Romano Guardini, who – like Mohlberg, Casel and Baumstark – preferred this term in order to differentiate the academic study of worship from the more pastoral and/or rubrical concerns of "liturgics". In practice, both terms are used as synonyms. "Corresponding to the state of research, the most comprehensive possible definition of liturgiology suggests itself as one in which are linked the systematic investigation of the essence of worship (grounding), of the historical and dogmatico-historical expressions of form (understanding), of the pastoral significance (experiencing) and of the actualization appropriate to content and community (shaping)."[46]

The tasks of liturgiology can be described by posing the following thematic questions: How was the worship celebrated at a given period? Why was it celebrated in the way revealed by the sources and not in another way? How did men of a particular period understand "worship" and what effect did this understanding have on the form of the liturgy? How do changed cultural conditions (intellectual, philosophical, societal as well as theological) effect the continued existence of the liturgy? How can the one faith be expressed in new liturgical forms without the substance of that faith being altered?

Despite all the ambivalence of culture as self-expression of fallen man, liturgiology is always a cultural science and "uses the various historical-critical, systematic and practical methods used by the other theological disciplines. In addition it has always used the methods of further disciplines, e.g. archaeology, hymnology and religious folklore.[47] Liturgiology is concerned with the various expressions of men from different epochs and cultures.[48] But liturgiology is primarily a theological discipline: it accepts culture not as it is, but adopts in its regard a critical position informed by faith: again, "the liturgy is self-expression of man but of man as he ought to be. Thus, liturgy becomes strict discipline ... the liturgy is man's self-expression. But, she says to him, the

---

[46] Schmidt-Lauber 384.
[47] Gerhards, Standortsbestimmung 170f.
[48] Cf. ibid. 171: Because it is concerned with the forms of man's self-expression, liturgiology must engage in dialogue with the other human sciences. These include, linguistics, communications studies, semiotics, religious studies, musicology and art history, philosophy, psychology and sociology.

expression "of a man you have not yet become. You have to attend my school. You must first become who you ought to be." [49] Thus, the task of liturgiology is, with the help of related theological disciplines and of the human sciences, to aim to investigate, to analyse and, based on the faith, to criticise, the cultural forms of human self-expression, so that these can become forms of expression of man's communication with God. Since the forms of cultural expression of "the world", because of their ambivalence which comes from Original Sin, can never completely coincide with the liturgical forms of expression of communication with God, it remains one of the tasks of liturgiology in the future, to explain the liturgy and to lead, by way of mystagogy, to the liturgy, however "transparent" the concrete from of this liturgy may appear at first sight. "The German word for strange or foreign – *fremd* – comes form the Old High German *fram*, which means 'forwards', 'distant from', 'away', the German word for pious – *fromm* – means as much as *fremd*, that is, at home in a distant world in the hereafter. This world in the hereafter crosses its borders to us in liturgical celebration, in signs that are not, cannot be, reduced to ideas stemming from this world, signs which have a strangeness about them, like a cloud." [50]

2.3.2. THE LONG ERA OF THE EXPLANATION OF THE RITE

Two sources which report on the development of the liturgy in the early Church are particularly noteworthy: one the oldest description of the liturgy by Justin Martyr (died about AD 165), [51] the other the report of the pilgrim Egeria on the liturgy in the pilgrimage city of Jerusalem, [52] whose importance for the development of the liturgy cannot be sufficiently emphasized. Above all, church ordinances provide information on the celebration of the liturgy in this period, for example the Didache [53], the "Apostolic Tradition" of Hippolytus of Rome [54] and the "Apostolic Constitutions" [55]. These formulations of ecclesiastical discipline do indeed contain models and suggestions for the celebration of the liturgy, but are not liturgical texts in the true sense. The oldest example of a liturgical book is the *Sacramentarium Veronese* [56]. Originally attributed to Pope Leo I, this sacramentary dates from the second half of the sixth century and contains the texts of certain

[49] Guardini, Liturgische Bildung 74f.
[50] A. Kirchgässner, Der Mensch im Gottesdienst, LJ 15 (1965) 229-238.233.
[51] Edition: Iustinus, Apologia: Die ältesten Apologeten. Ed. by E. J. Goodspeed, Göttingen 1984, 24-77.
[52] Editions: Itinerarium Egeriae. edd. A. Franceschini / R. Weber: Itineraria et alia geographica. Turnai 1965 (CCL 175), 35-90. Die Nonne Etheria (um 400). Peregrinatio Etheriae. Translation of the chap.1-23 by H. Donner: H. Donner (Hg.): Pilgerfahrt ins Heilige Land. Die ältesten Berichte christlicher Palästinapilger (4.-7. Jahrhundert). Stuttgart 1979, 82-137. Egerie, Journal de voyage (Itinéraire), ed. P. Maraval. Paris 1982 (SChr 296).
[53] Editions: La Didaché. Instructions des apôtres. Edited and translated by J.-P. Audet. Paris 1958. Didache (Apostellehre), Barnabasbrief, Zweiter Klemensbrief, Schrift an Diognet. Edited and translated by K. Wengst. Darmstadt 1984 (Schriften des Urchristentums 2). Didache/Zwölf-Apostel-Lehre. Translated and introduced by G. Schöllgen. Freiburg-Basel-Wien 1990 (FC 1).
[54] Editions: La Tradition apostolique de Saint Hippolyte. Essai de reconstruction. Edited by B. Botte. Münster 5th ed. (ed. by A. Gerhards with S. Felbecker) 1989 (LQF 39). Apostolike Paradosis. The Treatise on the Apostolic Tradition of S. Hippolytus of Rome, Bishop and Martyr. Ed. G. Dix. London 2nd ed. (H. Chadwick ed.) 1968. Traditio Apostolica – Apostolische Überlieferung. Edited, translated and introduced by W. Geerlings. Freiburg-Basel-Vienna 1990 (FC 1).
[55] Editions: Didascalia et Constitutiones Apostolorum 1st ed. F. X. Funk. Paderborn 1905. Les constititions apostoliques. Published and translated by M. Metzger. 3 vols., Paris 1985-1987 (SChr 320, 329, 333).
[56] Published by K. Mohlberg, Rome, 1956.

Roman celebrations in the liturgical year with the exception of the months January to April. The *Sacramentarium Gelasianum*, attributed to Pope Gelasius, actually dates from the seventh century and was intended for one of the Roman titular churches[57]. The *Sacramentarium Gregorianum* which goes back to an edition by Pope Gregory I (590-604) contains the papal stational liturgies for the course of the year. A revised copy of the Gregorianum was sent to Charlemagne. For the purposes of the standardization of the liturgy of the Frankish Church this version was provided with a postscript[58]. These Roman liturgical books contain almost exclusively liturgical texts but no descriptions of the liturgical action. What were later known as "rubrics" are contained in the *Ordines*. The *Ordines Romani*[59]. For the most part, the *Ordines Romani* were compiled north of the Alps, but also contain Roman traditions which can be reconstructed from the complementary additions. These Ordines led to further liturgical books of which the most important is "Roman-Germanic Pontifical" compiled before the turn of the century in 950 by the Benedictine monks of the monastery of St Alban at Mainz. In the second half of the tenth century – the *saeculum obscurum* in Rome during which no liturgical manuscripts were produced – the Roman-Germanic Pontifical returned to that city under the Emperor Otto I, though indeed containing additions of extra-Roman origin. This pontifical was accepted gratefully in Rome as the allegedly genuine Roman tradition[60]. The further development of liturgical books was closely bound up with the growing clericalization of the liturgy. This meant that different books for the various liturgical roles and functions were prepared in the form of handbooks for individual celebrants, as is illustrated in the development of the Missal.

The mystagogical explanations of the liturgy presented by the Church Fathers, while not to be understood as scientific studies of the liturgy in the modern sense, did nevertheless represent an explanatory theological treatment of the phenomenon that was divine worship, and as such can claim to mark the beginning of liturgics.

In the five "Mystagogical Catecheses" delivered during Easter Week, Cyril of Jerusalem (d. 386) explained the rites of Baptism, Confirmation and Eucharist to the newly-baptized who had received these sacraments on Easter night without being introduced to their theological meaning.[61] Other explanations of the liturgy were composed by John Chrysostom[62], Theodore of Mopsuestia[63] and in the east Syrian area Narses of

---

[57]   Published by K. Mohlberg, Rome 1960.
[58]   Cf. K. Mohlberg & A. Baumstark, Die älteste erreichbare Gestalt des Liber Sacramentorum anni circuli der römischen Kirche, Münster 1927 (LQ 11/12); K. Gamber, Wege zum Urgregorianum. Beuron 1956. Ibid.: Codices Liturgici Latini antiquiores, Fribourg 1963.
[59]   Edited by M. Andrieu, Les Ordines Romani du haut moyen-âge, Vols. I-IV, Louvain 1931-61.
[60]   Cf. Th. Klausner, Die liturgischen Austauschbeziehungen zwischen der römischen und der fränkisch-deutschen Kirche vom 8. bis zum 11. Jahrhundert, JAC, 3rd Ergänzungsband, Münster 1974, 139-154.
[61]   Editions: Cyrille de Jérusalem, Catéchèses mystagogiques. Ed. by A.Piédagnel, Paris 1988 (SChr 126 bis). Mystagogische Katechesen. Ed. and translated by G. Röwekamp. Freiburg-Basel-Vienna 1992 (FC 7).
[62]   Editions: Catecheses ad illuminandos 1-8: Jean Chrysostome, Huit catéchéses baptismales inédites. Ed. and translated by A. Wenger. Paris 1970 (SChr 50 bis). Johannes Chrysostomos, Catecheses baptismales – Taufkatechesen. Trnanslated and introduced by R. Kaczynski, Freiburg-Basel-Vienna 1992 (FC 6/1-6/2).
[63]   Editions: Les Homélies catéchétiques de Théodore de Mopsueste. Ed. by R. Tonneau & R. Devresse. Rome 1961 (StT 145). Commentary on Theodore of Mopsuestia on the Lord's Prayer and the Sacraments of Baptism and Eucharist. Ed. and translated by A. Mingana, Cambridge 1933.

Edessa [64]. A Western equivalent is formed in the two works *De mysteriis* and *De sacramentis* of Ambrose of Milan [65]. The *De ecclesiastica hierarchia* written in the sixth century by Dionysius the Pseudo-Areopagite had a wide influence in both West and East [66]. The homilies of the Fathers for the main feasts in the Church's year as well as their other writings contain observations on the liturgy of the patristic period [67].

The more complicated the rites became, the more they needed explanation. As Latin ceased to be the vernacular following the migrations of late Antiquity, the need for explanations of the liturgy grew even greater. Works composed in Latin were intended to equip clergy with basic liturgical knowledge needed for the celebration of worship as well as for catechetical instruction. One such work is *De libris et officiis ecclesiasticis* of Isidore of Seville (d. 636) [68].

The Carolingian era saw the appearance of a whole series of explanations of the liturgy. These tended to turn from the liturgy's own symbolic world and provide a new allegorical meaning for signs which had become foreign. Among these allegorical interpreters Amalar of Metz (d. circa 850) is of particular importance. [69] The forms of liturgical expression had become "foreign" in an unhappy manner, no longer the result of the irruption of the divine sphere into that of human actions. The meaning of these actions themselves was no longer understood. In the desire to provide some kind of meaning to rites, words, attitudes, gestures and furnishings which were not longer understood, the door was opened to an arbitrary allegorical interpretation.

There was resistance to this development. The deacon Florus (d. circa 860) compiled an explanation of the Mass based on sayings of the Fathers. [70] The *De institutione clericorum libri tres* [71] of the Archbishop of Mainz, Rhabanus Maurus (d. 856), provided a kind of encyclopaedia of instruction for clerical aspirants. Rhabanus's pupil, Walafried Strabo (d. 849), Abbot of Reichenau, in *De exordiis et incrementis ecclesiasticarum rerum* [72] described in particular the historical development of the liturgy. The period about the end of the first Millennium was rich in explanations of the liturgy: Bernard of Reichenau, Bernold of Constance, John of Avranches and Peter Damian described the liturgy itself while others, among them Guido of Arezzo (d. 1050) regarded as the perfector of Gregorian notation [73], compiled important treatises on church music.

The development of scholastic systematization led to the desire to encompass the Church's liturgy in such structure. In this attempt, the distinction between various meth-

---

[64] Also known as Narses of Nisibis, Narses the Leper or Narsai. Editions: Narsai, Doctoris Syri, Homiliae et Carmina. Primo ed. cura et studio D. A. Mingana. 2 vols., Mossul 1905. R. H. Connolly, The Liturgical Homilies of Narsai. Translated into English with an Introduction, Cambridge 1909 (Texts and Studies 8).

[65] Editions: CSEL 73, SChr. 25 bis. Most recently edited by J. Schmitz, FC 3. Freiburg-Basel-Vienna etc. 1990.

[66] PG 3, 369-584.

[67] Roetzer, for example, has gathered from the collected works all of Augustine's utterances on the liturgy, which has enabled him to draw a clear picture of the liturgy in that saint's church. Cf. W. Roetzer, Des heiligen Augustinus Schriften als liturgiegschichtliche Quelle, München 1930.

[68] PL 82,229-260.

[69] Amalarii episcopi opera liturgica omnia, ed. Joh. Michael Hanssens. Vol. 1-3. Rome 1948-1950.

[70] De expositione misssae: PL 119,15-71.

[71] PL 107,239-420.

[72] PL 114,919-966.

[73] PL 141: Micrologus Guidonis de disciplina artis musicae: 379-406. De ignoto cantu: 413-432. Quomodo der arithmetica procedit musica: 435-443. Tractatus Guidonis correctorius multorum errorum qui fiunt in cantu gregoriano in multis locis: 431-443.

ods of explaining the liturgy (allegorical-mystical interpretation, historical presentation of the verbal sense, ascetical interpretation) was not easily maintained.

Important authors of this period are the Parisian theologian John Beleth (d. circa 1165) with his *Rationale divinorum officiorum* [74], Rupert of Deutz (d.1135) with twelve volumes *De divinis officiis* [75]. The six books *De sacro altaris mysterio* [76] by Pope Innocent III became the model for a work which gained widespread importance. This was the *Rationale divinorum officiorum* of William Durandus, Bishop of Mende (d. 1296). In eight volumes, this treatise covered the whole compass of the liturgy and soon after the invention of the printing-press was printed in Mainz in 1459. [77] "The Rationale of Durandus, based totally on allegory, was to remain the handbook of liturgy for the later Middle Ages and beyond. New commentators, not insignificant in number, were to continue more or less in this well-worn path." [78] Durandus is also of great importance for his version of the Roman Pontifical. [79]

Despite the arbitrariness of an allegorical interpretation, the medieval understanding of image, showing traces of the influence platonic philosophy, is still dominant. [80] If Albert the Great's explanation of the Mass, *Opus de mysterio Missae* is totally opposed to allegorical interpretation, this has more to do with the turning of scholastic theology to Aristotelianism. Liturgical actions are not images of the world beyond but a reality in themselves. On the whole, though, scholasticism "apart from some details, has left no trace not only on the development of the liturgy of the Mass, but on the development of the understanding of the Mass". [81] Fundamentally, scholasticism is not at all interested in the liturgical actions themselves. Its concern is with what these actions effect, with the fruits of grace which they produce for mankind, with the *rite et valde* of these actions. Since liturgical signs and actions as such are of little interest they continue as heretofore to be explained allegorically. This process reaches perfection in nominalism whose incapacity for symbolic thinking, not to mention its incapacity for real-symbolic thinking [82], makes it unable to recognize any longer an inner connection between the exterior, visible, actions and the supersensible-spiritual sphere. One example from this period is Gabriel Biel's (d. 1495) [83] *Literalis et mystica canonis expositio.*

---

[74]   PL 202,13-166.

[75]   PL 170,11-332.

[76]   PL 217,773-916.

[77]   There have been many editions of Durandus' "Rationale", the most recent being that of Ch. Barthélemy, Paris, 1854.

[78]   Jungmann MS I, 152.

[79]   Durandus' pontifical was edited by M. Andrieu, Le Pontificale romain au moyen-âge, Vol.3: Le Pontificale de Guillaume Durand, Rome 1940.

[80]   Cf. W. Beierwaltes (ed.), Platonismus in der Philosophie des Mittelalters. Darmstadt 1969.

[81]   Jungmann MS I, 152.

[82]   Cf. E. Iserloh, Bildfeindlichkeit des Nominalismus und Bildersturm im 16. Jhd., W. Heinen (ed.): Bild – Wort – Symbol in der Theologie, Würzburg 1969, 119-138.

[83]   Gabrielis Biel Canonis Missae expositio, ed. Heiko A. Oberman et William J. Cortenay. Pars I-IV. Wiesbaden 1963ff. (Publications of the Institute for European History 31-34). On William of Ockham cf. G. N. Buescher, The Eucharistic Teaching of William of Ockham, Washington 1950. On Luther's eucharistic theology and practice cf. H. B. Meyer, Luther und die Messe. Paderborn 1965 (Konfessionskundliche und kontroverstheologische Studien XI).

2.3.3. SCHOLARLY INVESTIGATION OF THE LITURGY

In the Reformation period the aim of Catholic theology, stamped by humanism and its fondness for the historical, had, with the help of historical presentations, to be the defence of the Church's liturgy from the attacks of the innovators as well as its purification from excesses and false developments. Erasmus of Rotterdam (d. 1536) dealt with liturgical themes, [84] translating among other things the Liturgy of St John Chrysostom into Latin. Berthold of Chiemsee (d. 1543) in his *Rational deutsch über das Amt der heiligen Meß* and the *Keligpuchl*; the works of Georg Witzel (d. 1573), Johannes Gropper, Gerhard Lorich, Michael Helding [85] and also St Peter Canisius aimed at a more effective participation of the laity in the liturgical action through explanation of the rites. The publication of liturgical source material was intended to repel the attacks of the Reformers. So, for example, the *De divinis catholicae Ecclesiae officiis et ministeriis*, by Malchior Hittorp (d. 1584), Dean of Cologne, published there in 1568. [86]. The historical method which reached maturity through a humanistic investigation of sources led at a subsequent period to a truly scientific engagement with the Church's liturgy and its historical evolution. Scientific liturgical study is indebted to the Maurists [87] Hugh Menard (d. 1644), Jean Mabillon (d. 1707) and Edmond Marténe (d. 1739) for invaluable editions and research of sources of liturgical texts and ordines. A similar debt is owed to the Italians, Cardinal Thomasius (d. 1713) [88] and L. A. Muratori (d. 1750) [89]. The Dominican Jakob Goar (d. 1653) [90] concerned himself with Greek and Oriental liturgies as did Eusebius Renaudot (d. 1720) [91], Joseph Assemani (d. 1786) and his nephew Joseph Aloysius Assemani (d. 1782).

Liturgical scholars of the Enlightenment period were motivated not only by historical interest, but also by a desire to renew liturgical life, to adapt it to changed times. [92] While giving all due credit to the pastoral liturgical intentions of this period, one cannot ignore the general tendencies of the Enlightenment, which were antagonistic towards the Church and even towards faith. Gerhards has shown this with reference to the Synod of Pistoia, the demands of which at a first glance recall the reform achieved by the Second Vatican Council. [93] Among the authors of this period are Ignaz Heinrich Karl von Wessenberg (d. 1860) [94], der Würtembergischer Oberkirchenrat, Stuttgarter

---

[84] Cf. M. Kunzler, Die Eucharistielehre des Hadamarer Pfarrers und Humanisten Gerhard Lorich, Münster 1981 (RST 119), in particular pp. 4-56.

[85] On Catholic polemical theologians cf. the bibliography by W. Kleiber (ed.), Katholische Kontroverstheologen und Reformer des 16.Jahrhunderts, Münster 1978 (RST 116).

[86] M. Hittorp, De Divinis Catholicae Ecclesiae Officiis et Mysteriis, Köln 1568.

[87] Cf. L. Cognet, HKG 5, 104f. (Lit.), 110f., 113f.

[88] Codices Sacramentorum. Rome 1680; Responsalia et Antiphonaria. Rome 1686; Antiqui Libri Missarum. Rome 1691.

[89] Liturgia Romana vetus. Venice 1748.

[90] Euchologion sive Rituale Graecorum. Paris 1647, reprinted Graz 1960.

[91] Liturgiarum Orientalium Collectio, 2 vols., Paris 1715-1716.

[92] On the general understanding of the liturgy in the Englightenment era cf. M. Probst, Gottesdienst in Geist und Wahrheit, Regensburg 1976; J. Steiner, Liturgiereform in der Aufklärungszeit. Freiburg i. Br.1976.

[93] Cf. A. Gerhards, Von der Synode von Pistoia (1786) zum Zweiten Vatikanischen Konzil? Zur Morphologie der Liturgiereform im 20. Jhd., LJ 36 (1986) 28-45.

[94] E.g. "Ritual nach dem Geiste und Anordnungen der Katholischen Kirche, oder praktische Anleitung für den katholischen Seelsorger zur erbaulichen und lehrreichen Verwaltung des liturgischen Amtes". Tübingen-Stuttgart 1831.

Hofprediger und former Benedictine Benedikt Maria Werkmeister (d. 1823)[95], Beda Pracher (d. 1819)[96] and Vitus Winter (d. 1814)[97], whose proposals for reform were in some cases very radical. The Enlightenment was followed Romanticism, a movement whose mood was not favourably disposed to an adequate understanding of the liturgy.[98]

In the nineteenth and twentieth centuries the study if liturgy is above all an historical study. Thus, the historical discoveries of the works of Abbot Prosper Guéranger of Solesmes (d.18 75)[99] – such as the *Institutions liturgiques*, against neo-Gallican local rites, and the *Année Liturgique* – were a help to the liturgical movement. Other French-speaking historians of the liturgy were, for example, Duchesne[100], Battifol[101] and Andrieu, who rendered outstanding service as the editor of the *Ordines Romani* and other source material.[102] In Italy, clerics of the diocese of Milan, such as Mercati and Ratti, the later Pope Pius XI, were the main students of the Ambrosian liturgy. The *Liber sacramentorum* of Cardinal Ildefons Schuster of Milan contained all the Mass texts for the Church's year,[103] while the history of the complete liturgical life is presented in Righetti's *Manuale di storia liturgica*.

Many historical monographs dealing with individual topics were produced in the twentieth century. Of these only a few representative examples are mentioned: Braun concerned himself with the altar, alter-vessels and liturgical vesture,[104] J.Sauer with the "Symbolism of the Church Building and its Furnishings". Works on archeology, editions of sources, and liturgical history were produced by Franz[105], Lietzmann[106], Mohlberg[107], Probst[108] and Grisar[109]. As well as liturgical handbooks

---

[95] On Werkmeisters writings, many of which appeared anonymously, cf. A.Hagen, Die kirchliche Aufklärung in der Diözese Rottenburg, Stuttgart 1953.

[96] E.g.: "Neue Liturgie des Pfarrers M. in K. im Department L., der Nationalsynode zur Prüfung vorgelegt," composed in Tübingen in 1802.

[97] Cf. A. Vierbach, Die liturgischen Anschauungen des Vitus Anton Winter, München 1929.

[98] Cf. Anton L. Mayer, Liturgie, Romantik und Restauration, JLw 10 (1930) 77-141.

[99] Cf. L. Soltner, Solesmes et Dom Guéranger (1805-1875), Solesmes 1974.

[100] L. Duchesne, Origines du Culte chrétien. Etude sur la liturgie latine avant Charlemagne, Paris 1925.

[101] P. Battifol, Leçons sur la Messe, Paris 7th edn. 1920.

[102] M. Andrieu, Les Ordines Romani du haut Moyen-Âge, 5 vols., Louvain 1931-1974 (several printings of individual volumes); I. Le Pontifical Romain du haut Moyen-Âge. Le Pontifical Romain du XIIe siécle. Le Pontifical de la Curie Romaine au XIIIe siécle; III. Le Pontifical de Guillaume Durand; IV. Tables. Città del Vaticano 1938-1941.

[103] I. Schuster, Liber Sacramentorum. Geschichtliche und liturgische Studien über das römische Meßbuch. 4 vols., Regensburg 1929-31.

[104] J. Braun, Der christliche Altar in seiner geschichtlichen Entwicklung, 2 vols. Munich 1924; ibid., Das christliche Altargerät in seinem Sinn und in seiner Entwicklung. Munich 1932; ibid., Die liturgische Gewandung in Okzident und Orient nach Ursprung und Entwicklung, Verwendung und Symbolik, Freiburg i.Br. 1907. Reprinted Darmstadt 1964.

[105] A. Franz, Die Messe im deutschen Mittelalter, Freiburg 1902, Reprinted Darmstadt 1963; ibid., Die kirchlichen Benediktionen im Mittelalter, 2 vols., Freiburg i.Br.1909.

[106] H. Lietzmann, Messe und Herrenmahl. Eine Studie zur Geschichte der Liturgie, Berlin 3rd edn. 1955.

[107] K. Mohlberg worked on the Missale Francorum (Rome 1957), the Missale Gallicanum Vetus (Rom 1958), the Missale Gothicum (Rome 1961), the Liber Sacramentorum Romanae Ecclesiae (1960), the Sacramentarium Veronense (Rome 1956).

[108] F. Probst, Liturgie der drei ersten christlichen Jahrhunderte, Tübingen 1870; ibid., Die abendländische Messe vom 5. bis zum 8. Jahrhundert, Münster 1896.

[109] H. Grisar, Das Missale im Lichte römischer Stadtgeschichte, Freiburg i.Br. 1925.

(e.g. those by Fluck[110], Thalhofer[111], Eisenhofer[112] and immediately before the Second Vatican Council, that by Martimort[113]) there appeared constantly in the late nineteenth century and in particularly in the twentieth century valuable historical monographs. Examples of these are "genetic" explanations such as Bäumer's history of the breviary[114] or Jungmann's *"Missarum Sollemnia*, a genetic explanation of the Roman Mass", Stenzel's "Genetic explanation of the Liturgy of Baptism"[115] or Kleinheyer's study of the history of ordination rites.[116] As an academic discipline liturgy was understood as forming part of historical theology, not the least witness to this being the title Rennings gave to the *Dictionnaire d'archéologie chrétienne et de liturgie*. Side by side with this was the inclusion, up to the beginning of the twentieth century, of "liturgics" as a sub-section of Canon Law. Understood as rubrics, this concerned itself in the training of priests with the practical application of rubrical prescriptions. The most frequently quoted source were the decrees and replies of Congregation of Rites, whose *Decreta authentica*, over 4000 in number, were described by Rennings as a "jungle paradise of casuistics"[117]

The academic discipline of liturgy is more than an historical or a legal-pastoral-theological subject. It examines the "living, sacrificing, praying, Church, the Church that performs the mysteries of grace in her actual worship and, in reference to these mysteries, in their binding expressions."[118] In this, the historicity of these "binding expressions" can no more be disregarded than can their confrontation with a changed world. The works of Jungmann and others have shown clearly that reform cannot be a break with the past which ignores history but must grow out of the historical context. Along with Jungmann, the second main representative of a theological-systematic study of liturgy is Odo Casel with his theology of the divine mysteries. Neither can be understood apart from the Liturgical Movement and both share the latter's pastoral liturgical quest which is "whether and how the priestly-liturgical life of the community can be built up and preserved."[119] However different the points of departure of the individual representatives of the Liturgical Movement and however different the practical liturgical effects, for all the liturgy was the actual accomplishment in time and place of the "exchange of life between God and man" (Johannes Pinsk).[120] The common goal of all was to lead

---

[110] Katholische Liturgik, 3 vols., Regensburg 1853-1855.
[111] Handbuch der Katholischen Liturgik, 2 vols., Freiburg i.Br. 2nd edn. 1912.
[112] Handbuch der Katholischen Liturgik. 2 vols., Freiburg i.Br. 2nd edn. 1941.
[113] Handbuch der Liturgiewissenschaft. Translated by Mirjam Prager from the French original: L'Eglise en priére. Introduction á la liturgie, 2 vols., Freiburg-Basel-Vienna 1963-65.
[114] S. Bäumer, Geschichte des Breviers, Freiburg i.Br. 1895.
[115] A. Stenzel, Die Taufe. Eine genetische Erklärung der Taufliturgie, Innsbruck 1958.
[116] B. Kleinheyer, Die Priesterweihe im römischen Ritus. Eine liturgiehistorische Studie, Trier 1962 (TThSt 12).
[117] Cf. H. Rennings, Über Ziele und Aufgaben der Liturgik, Concilium 5 (1969) 128-135. 128f.
[118] Guardini, Methode 104.
[119] A. Wintersig, Pastoralliturgik. Ein Versuch über Wesen, Weg, Einteilung und Abgrenzung einer seelsorgwissenschaftlichen Behandlung der Liturgie, JLw 4 (1924) 153-167.158.
[120] On Pinsk, cf. E. Amon, Lebensaustausch zwischen Gott und Mensch. Zum Liturgieverständnis Johannes Pinsks, Regensburg 1988; ibid., Johannes Pinsk (1891-1957), LJ 43 (1993) 121-127.

the faithful to this and to make the community capable of a lively participation in it. [121]

2.3.4. REMAINING TASKS [122]

The Constitution on the Liturgy of the Second Vatican Council – a fruit of the Liturgical Movement – raised liturgy to the status one of the main theological disciplines. [123] The liturgy is "to be treated from the theological and historical perspectives as well as from the spiritual, pastoral and legal" (SC 16). According to Lengeling, the Liturgy Constitution of the Second Vatican Council marks a "Copernican revolution" and "the end of the Middle Ages": "The Constitution not only ends the post-Tridentine period but its aims take up strands which were lost or which had already been lost by the time the Church had spread into Germanic regions. The aim of the Council is not only to loosen post-Tridentine ossification: the reform ought courageously to address topics which much earlier, for various historical (cultural and also political) reasons, were missed in the Western Church." [124] For Richter, "the decisive step beyond Trent" is the fact that Vatican II for the first time since Trent officially established that "no longer the priest alone, but also the congregation as a whole is the subject and carrier of the liturgical action, because all the faithful participate in the priesthood of Christ" as the royal priesthood, "which, through Baptism, is given the right and duty to celebrate the liturgy" [125]. On this basis Häußling erects the *participatio actuosa* of all taking part into the formal criterion for the essence of liturgy at all [126] and considers that the liturgy reform of the Second Vatican Council differs fundamentally from other reforms in history and is basically unfinished: "The Council has thus left the Church a 'reform of the liturgy', as it understood it, which – despite unforeseen difficulties – is a permanent, never to be completed task. It would appear – presupposing that the Church remains true to the Council – as if liturgical reforms to date were little more than an overture." [127]

The renewal of the liturgy did not remain uncontested. Already during the work of renewal itself there was opposition from curial circles. [128] After the Council this became the aim of various traditionalist groups. [129] The most conspicuous, but not the only, opposition to the renewed liturgy came from the schismatic group founded by Marcel

---

[121] On the Liturgical Movement cf. B. Botte, Le mouvement liturgique; témoinage et souvenirs, Paris 1973; B. Ebel, Ausgansgpunkte und Anliegen der religiösen-liturgischen Erneuerung in ihren Anfängen, Liturgie und Mönchtum / Laacher Hefte 24, Maria Laach 1959, 25-40; N. Höslinger, Mit Courage und Konsequenz. Der Beitrag von Pius Parsch und des Wiener Kreises zur Liturgischen Bewegung, LJ 43 (1993) 48-61; J. A. Jungmann, Der Beitrag der Benediktiner zur Liturgiewissenschaft, Liturgie und Mönchtum / Laacher Hefte 28, Maria Laach 1961, 15-23; O. Rousseau, Histoire du mouvement liturgique, Paris 1945.

[122] Cf. A. Häußling, Liturgiewissenschaftliche Aufgabenfelder vor uns, LJ 38 (1988) 94-108.

[123] Cf. H. B. Meyer, Liturgie als Hauptfach. Erwägungen zur Stellung und Aufgabe der Liturgiewissenschaft im Ganzen des theologischen Studiums, ZKTh 88 (1966) 315-335.

[124] Lengeling, Liturgie – Dialog zwichen Gott und Mensch 13-15.

[125] K. Richter, Liturgiereform als Mitte einer Erneuerung der Kirche, ibid. (ed.): Das Konzil war erst der Anfang. Die Bedeutung des II.Vatikanums für Theologie und Kirche. Mainz 1991, 53-74. 66.

[126] Cf. Häußling, Liturgiereform 28.

[127] Häußling, Liturgiereform 30.

[128] Cf. A. Bugnini, La riforma liturgica (1948-1975), Rome 1983.

[129] Cf. on this H. B. Meyer, Una voce – Nunc et semper? Konservative Gruppen nach dem Konzil, StdZ 180 (1967) 73-90.

Lefebvre to counter the Second Vatican Council. [130] To facilitate traditionalists, the Congregation for Divine Worship on 3rd October 1984, on the basis of a papal indult, conceded to bishops the possibility of permitting supporters of the – incorrectly named – "Tridentine Rite" to celebrate Mass according to the *Missale Romanum* of 1962. This concession was not to be seen as a discrediting of liturgical renewal; the indult is an expression of concern for unity in the Church. [131]

There were, indeed, several "teething problems" during the period in which the decisions of the Second Vatican Council were implemented in the practice of the worshipping community. The origin of these is to be sought more in the spirit of the times than in the efforts at reform themselves. [132] Fischer includes in this an "anti-solemnity allergy", linked with a "Latin allergy", a "misunderstood ecumenism" which is sometimes even ashamed of of what is specifically Catholic, a "can-do mentality" linked with a "libertinism" concerning all directives and "sermonitis", the bad habit of providing a commentary on anything and everything the emphasis being on human utterance which is not always inspired. [133]

Contemporary liturgical practice and the study of the liturgy operate between the poles of traditionalist ossification in the incorrectly-named "Tridentine" liturgy and the survival, indeed the continued influence of what Fischer called "teething problems". Häußling speaks in favour of a permanent reform of the liturgy: the Second Vatican Council did not elevate the reconstruction (re-formatio) of the liturgy *secundum normam sanctorum patrum* to the level of a maxim, but, rather the full and fruitful participation of all, that is of those people who live in an environment which is, is effect, atheistic. Certain tasks emerge from all of this for the academic study of liturgy: in the change from a "numinous, cosmic dimension to a desacralised societal reality", the reform of the liturgy has to accept and do justice to a far-reaching "paradigm shift of the modern age". The criterion of *actuosa participatio* will lead to a permanent reform of the liturgy and "change the Church's liturgy in ways not yet foreseen". [134] The direction of this is described as "reduction", as "concentrating on basic religious and liturgical actions, on basic gestures, formulae, on fundamental words and structures". [135] Rennings, too, applies the principle of the *Ecclesia semper reformanda* to the Church's liturgy: the reforms of the Council did not wish to replace the rigidity of the "old" liturgy with a new liturgy frozen for several years or centuries, but to lead to a fundamentally "open"(which does not mean arbitrary) liturgy. Thus, "the search for the Church's optimal self-presentation in its practice of worship at any given time remains a constant task for the academic study of liturgy". With the following quotation from Karl Rahner, Rennings emphasizes that this task requires not only comprehensive research not only

---

[130] Cf. A. Schifferle, Marcel Lefebvre – Ärgernis und Besinnung, Kevelaer 1983; L. Kozelka, Lefebvre. Ein Erzbischof im Widerspruch zu Papst und Konzil, Aschaffenburg 1980.

[131] Cf. the commentary by O. Nußbaum, Die bedingte Wiederzulassung einer Meßfeier nach dem Missale Romanum von 1962, Pastoralblatt 37 (1985) 130-143.

[132] It is necessary to remember, for example, the debate on desacralisation, itself a product of the discussion of demythologisation of the 1960s and 1970s. For an overview of this, cf. H. Schürmann, Neutestamentliche Marginalien zur Frage der 'Entsakralisierung', Der Seelsorger 38(1968) 38-48, 89-104.38-42.

[133] Cf. B. Fischer, Zehn Jahre danach. Zur gottesdienstlichen Situation in Deutschland zehn Jahre nach Erscheinung der Liturgiekonstitution, B.Fischer et al. (eds.), Kult in der säkulasierten Welt, Regensburg 1974,117-127.

[134] Cf. Häußling, Liturgiereform 28-32.

[135] Häußling, Liturgiewissenchaftliche Aufgabenfelder 104.

in all areas of theology, but also in the human sciences: "For it is only when one knows how Christians are as humans beings of today, that one can answer the question, how the Church's liturgy must be today." [136]

"Open liturgy" can be a modish husk of words to cover attempts to elevate the "emptiness" of the distance of God or societal reality to the level of liturgical sign or to find a place in the Church for the pragmatic, "can-do" mentality of our times. But "open liturgy" can nevertheless be a necessary element in a study of liturgy which is oriented towards the human person. The continuation of the writing of works of church history and of systematic theology will continue to be necessary if individual questionable theological approaches and idiosyncratic opinions from the human sciences or art-history are not to exalted as the criteria for establishing the essence of Christian worship. And, academic liturgical studies of today, and even more so of tomorrow, cannot be understood as other than ecumenical. [137] In order to avoid the snares of a particular narrowness and of faulty approaches these studies must look beyond the borders of the pre- and post-conciliar Catholic milieu. These studies also need the balanced judgement of the human sciences, concerned as these studies are with the *humanum*, with the "in-between" of the body and its actions up to the liturgical form of space and time, which surrounds man as embodied spirit, and on which the *anabasis*, the communication with the living God, ought to find its locus. It might even be the case that this *humanum* in its relationship with God in the actuality of the liturgy and beyond the boundaries of denomination, of different eras and cultures is not so disparate after all. [138]

Bibliography

A. Baumstark, Vom geschichtlichen Werden der Liturgie, Freiburg i. Br. 1923 (Ecclesia Orans 10).

A. Bugnini, La riforma liturgica 1948-1975, Roma 1983.

B. Fischer, Wissenschaft vom christlichen Gottesdienst. Zum Verhältnis der Liturgiewissenschaft zu ihren Nachbardisziplinen, TThZ 83 (1974) 246-251.

A. Gerhards, Zur Standortbestimmung der Liturgiewissenschaft, EL 107 (1993) 169-172.

A. Gerhards / B. Osterholz-Kootz, Kommentar zur 'Standortbestimmung der Liturgiewissenschaft', LJ 42 (1992) 122-138.

R. Guardini, Über die systematische Methode in der Liturgiewissenschaft, JLw 1 (1921) 97-108.

R. Guardini, Der Kultakt und die gegenwärtige Aufgabe der liturgischen Bildung. Ein Brief, LJ 14 (1964) 101-106.

A. A. Häußling, Liturgiewissenschaft zwei Jahrzehnte nach Konzilsbeginn, ALw 24 (1982) 1-18.

A. A. Häußling, Liturgiereform. Materialien zu einem neuen Thema der Liturgiewissenschaft, ALw 31 (1989) 1-31.

---

[136] Rennings, Ziele und Aufgaben 132f.; K. Rahner, Die Praktische Theologie im Ganzen der theologischen Disziplinen: Praktische Theologie zwischen Wissenschaft und Praxis, München 1968, 63. On this cf. F. Kohlschein, Liturgiewissenschaft im Wandel? Fragmentarische Überlegungen zur Situation und Zukunft einer theologischen Disziplin, LJ 34 (1984) 32-49.

[137] Cf. K.Schlemmer (ed.), Gottesdienst – Weg zur Einheit. Impulse für die Ökumene, Freiburg-Basel-Vienna 1991 (QD 122). Cf. Gerhards, Standortbestimmung 170.

[138] Cf. for example, H. C. Schmidt-Lauber, Konvergenzen der liturgischen Bewegung und ihre Bedeutung für die Ökumene aus der Sicht eines evangelischen Theologen, LJ 43 (1993) 30-47.

A. Kavanagh, On liturgical theology, New York 1985.

S. Marsili and others, La Liturgia, Panorama storico generale, Anamnesis 2, Torino 1992.

B. Neunheuser, Liturgiewissenschaft – exakte Geschichtsforschung oder (und) Theologie der Liturgie? EcclOra 4 (1987) 87-102.

K. Richter (ed.), Liturgie, ein vergessenes Thema der Theologie? Freiburg-Basel-Wien 1987 (QD 107).

M. Righetti, Manuale di storia liturgica I. Milano 2nd edn. 1950: 43-57: La scienza liturgica; 57-85: La letteratura liturgica.

H. C. Schmidt-Lauber, Art. 'Liturgiewissenschaft/Liturgik', TRE 21, Berlin-New York 1991, 383-401.

G. Wainwright, Doxology. The Praise of God in Worship, Doctrine and Life. New York 1980.

H. A. J. Wegman, Liturgie in der Geschichte des Christentums, Regensburg 1994. Original: Riten en mythen. Liturgie in de geschiedenis van het christendom. Kampen 1991.

2.4. THE HUMAN BODY AS THE INSTRUMENT OF LITURGICAL ACTION.

2.4.1. ANIMA FORMA CORPORIS

It is part of man's mysterious nature to possess life; he is a "living soul". But he is alive only through the body. By means of the body life is exteriorized, it expresses itself and enters into relationships. "The quintessential symbolic relationship is that of body and soul. The human body is the analogy of the soul in the visible-corporeal order. If one were to wish to make bodily visible what the soul is to the spiritual, then the human body would be the result. This is the deepest meaning of the formula: *anima forma corporis*. In the body the soul translates itself into the corporeal, into its living 'symbol'." [139]

That which Guardini denotes with the term "soul", the personal kernel of the individual, is termed "the heart" by theologians of the eastern churches. [140] In a correspondence arising from of his being made in the image of God, whose divine nature is inaccessible, the heart represents man's nature; it is as hidden and inaccessible as the divine nature. As "having life" it emerges via human corporeality to the outside world in order to establish personal relationships. Thus, Evdokimov displays a direct continuity between the Orthodox vision of humanity and that of the Old Testament: man does not have a soul, rather, he is soul, to the degree to which this latter "ensouls" the body, i.e. to the degee that the "heart" manifests itself to what it outside it, through the body in order to enter into relationships. [141] It is only through relationships, and these can happen only by means of the body, that man becomes a distinctive personality. By means of the body, he becomes a face, becomes a Thou to a person addressing him. Consequently, Evdokimov attaches as great an importance to the body and to bodily actions

---

[139] Guardini, Liturgische Bildung 22.

[140] Cf. B. Zenkowsky / H. Petzold, Das Bild des Menschen im Lichte der orthodoxen Anthropologie. Marburg 1969, 72-75; P. Evdokimov, L'Orthodoxie, Paris 1979, 66-68; ibid., Die Frau und das Heil der Welt, Moers-Aschaffenburg 1989,52f.

[141] Cf. Evdokimov, L'Orthodoxie 68.63.

as does Guardini [142]: over against a dominance of the word, bodily actions in the liturgy are given the same value as that word. Blessings, Signs of the Cross, prostrations, bows etc. express the soul and as bodily actions have a reflex effect on that soul: " 'The heart is actually the master and king of the whole bodily organism, and when grace penetrates the chamber of the heart, it drives all the members and thoughts of the body', says St Gregory Palamas so felicitously." [143] Bodily actions also react on the soul by recalling in the action itself what the soul once wished to express in these actions and had later once again forgotten.

Pieper gives a literary example illustrating this: In the course of the anointing of the sick the patient who has become an unbeliever "automatically" makes the sign of the cross which he learned in the kindergarten. By means of the physical action he is "reminded" of the religious dimension of his life which is coming to an end and through it finds his way back to God: "The reminding power of the living sign", has brought it about, "that a faith in the triune God and the sacrificial death of the Lord, a faith long forgotten, neglected and almost smothered, would scarcely have become a living spiritual reality had not the hand not known the living confessing sign of this faith 'off by heart' and as it were performed it 'by itself' ". [144]

2.4.2. THE RECOVERY OF BODILY ACTION IN THE LITURGY

The regulation of the minutest detail of body-language by Catholic rubrics in the past is already an indication of the great importance of bodily actions in the liturgy. In Gerhard's view, these rubrics hindered the personal development of the celebrant, on the other hand the normative fixing of all movements guaranteed the identity of the liturgical action. [145] The focus of bodily movements in the liturgy was narrowed down to those of the priest, his actions alone were relevant and were precisely laid down. [146]

Things were different for the laity: Their role was reduced to a narrow span of communal actions in the group. "In the Middle Ages, the bodily posture of the faithful distanced itself more and more from that of the priest." [147] Where formerly all participants in the liturgy stood and prayed facing the East in the *orante* position, [148] this and other postures during prayer, was increasingly confined to the celebrating priest and his assistants. Increasingly the people stood around as passive spectators until finally, with the advent of pews, kneeling became the basic bodily attitude of the laity, at least during the less festive celebrations. [149] The exclusion of the laity from the celebration of the liturgy had an enormous effect on its physical performance; their role, according

[142] Cf. Guardini, Liturgische Bildung 15-18.
[143] P. Evdokimov, Das Gebet der Ostkirche, Graz-Vienna-Köln 1986, 42f.
[144] J. Pieper, Das Gedächtnis des Leibes. Von der erinnernden Kraft des Geschichtlich-Konkreten, W. Seidel (ed.), Kirche aus lebendigen Steinen, Mainz 1975, 68-83.76f. This refers to the death scene in Evelyn Waugh's novel Brideshead Revisited.
[145] Cf. A. Gerhards, Vorbedingungen, Dimensionen und Ausdruckgestalten der Bewegung in der Liturgie, W. Meurer (ed.): Volk Gottes auf dem Weg. Bewegungselemente im Gottesdienst, Mainz 1989,11-24.16.
[146] On the degree of obligation attached to rubrics cf. Eisenhofer I, 50f., Rubrics oblige in conscience. Regarding the prescribed raising of the eyes, cf. ibid. I, 258. For genuflection cf. p.256.
[147] Jungmann MS I,314.
[148] Cf. F.J. Dölger, Sol salutis. Gebet und Gesang im christlichen Altertum. Mit besonderer Rücksicht auf die Ostung im Gebet und Liturgie, Münster 2nd ed. 1925 (LF 4/5), Reprint Münster 1972 (LQF 16/17), 239-244.
[149] Cf. Jungmann MS I, 317.

to a sixteenth-century English source quoted by Jungmann was limited to "looking, listening and thinking" [150]. Even with regard to the renewed liturgy there is criticism of the community's participation in the physical celebration: "In the sacred actions of the altar, in prayer and psalmody, in proclaiming and preaching the word, the priest's body is far more intensively active in the cult than those of the laity who effectively are melted into a single body. The laity almost always act together and in the same space because in standing and kneeling and bowing they demonstrate an almost mimetic symmetry which is simply a function of and directed towards what is happening at the altar." [151]

The Enlightenment also contributed to the reduction of bodily involvement in worship: the Ratio hardly has need of the body. But feelings are primarily expressed through the body. [152] Jossutis's remark, "Liturgical modernity begins with the church bench" is not without foundation. If participants until then were lookers-on at a sacred ritual which unfolded independently of themselves, in the Protestant service with its lengthy sermons they became listeners. The church bench became part of an agenda – it helped to confine bodies so that souls could more easily be "worked on". If faith alone suffices, then all bodily actions other than sitting and listening to the word which alone can save, lose their meaning. [153]

Similarly, Bouyer asserts, "A seated assembly is perforce passive. Its posture is not conducive to worship but, at very best, to the reception of instruction or for most of the time to observe with more or less curiosity a play in which it does not participate." [154] Further, for polemical reasons, Protestantism abolished forms of prayer involving the body and which might have been considered "catholic". [155] On the other hand, Catholic folk piety provided para-liturgical forms of bodily prayer as an outlet for the growing exclusion of the congregation from participation in the bodily aspects of the liturgy. [156]

Baumgartner considers the almost immeasurable contemporary flood of publications about the body to be an indicator of the of the broken relationship between modern man and his corporeality. [157] He traces difficulties with bodily expression in the liturgy back to the almost complete loss of "the lightness to express itself through the body" by a technical-scientific civilization which is utilitarian and one-sidedly oriented towards

---

[150] Ibid. 319, footnote 59.

[151] Cf. H. Tellenbach, Zur Krise des Kultischen. Kulturpsychopathologische Erörterungen, A. Hahn and others (eds.): Anthropologie des Kults, Freiburg-Basel-Vienna 1976, pp. 82-97.86.

[152] Cf. Y. Congar, Mysterium des Tempels 179. For contrary movements, as for example in J.Sailer, cf. Baumgartner, Liturgie und Leiblichkeit 161 with reference to Manfred Probst, Gottesdienst in Geist und Wahrheit. Die liturgischen Ansichten und Bestrebungen Johann Michael Sailers (1751-1832), Regensburg 1976 (Studien zur Pastoralliturgie 2), 185-187.

[153] Cf. Josuttis 124. Similarly also previously in Lubienska de Lenval 78, according to whom the introduction "of pews caused this active participation of the faithful to be completely forgotten; the body no longer took part in prayer".

[154] L. Bouyer, Liturgie und Architektur, Einsiedeln-Freiburg i.Br. 1993, 92.

[155] E.G. the Sign of the Cross: There is certain comedy in the fact that Luther, referring to this practice in his verdict on the Mass in his "Buch der Winkelmessen an einen guten Freund" which appeared in 1534, remarked, "God grant to all pious Christians that when they hear the word 'Mass', they should take fright and cross themselves as they might against an attack of the Devil!" WA 38,237. Cf. Ohm 299-301.

[156] For example, the making of the Sign of the Cross with holy water on entering or leaving the church or the beating of the breast at the Consecration. More pronounced forms of prayer with the body are evident at places of pilgrimage: crawling on one's knees (cf. Ohm 357f.). carrying a cross, various kinds of circumambulations or – a popular imitation of "clericalised" poses during prayer – praying with outstretched arms.

[157] Baumgartner, Liturgie und Leiblichkeit 143.

the rational. "Whatever is not immediately profitable, whatever is not of direct use, appears suspect if not indeed meaningless to some modern individuals. Liturgy, however, becomes incomprehensible when measured with the yardstick of objective functionality. Liturgy is not geared towards efficiency ... " [158]

Precisely because liturgical reform as a child of this civilization is afflicted by its "enmity towards the body", the liturgy must "win back its character as event, as an activity expressed in gestures and symbols, in short its character a fully human act. Do we trust our liturgies any more to provide us with the ecstasy of belief?" To be wished for are: "Active participation: those who come together for worship are truly the actors in a communal deed and not mere spectators. Complete participation: not only in spirit but as complete persons, i.e. seeing, hearing, speaking, singing, standing, kneeling etc., in brief: the faithful should be present to the sacred action as doers. This even includes dance." Concrete provisions are demanded: Awareness of the bodily and affirmation of prayer with the body in the face of puritanical and rationalist prejudices; a renewed learning of basic liturgical attitudes: silence and being still, hearing and listening, looking and contemplating. The example of the priest grows accordingly in importance. [159]

The mystagogical task is defined: This is – speaking with Guardini – "clearly to highlight the content of an action in question in its most particular essence and to bring this to consciousness; further, to bring to the observer's consciousness, the gesture, bodily posture or activity being examined, in its own particular structure, its static and dynamic and specific bodily quality; to let these be performed with beauty, clarity and maturity and allow consciousness and performance to blend." [160]

2.4.3. FORMS OF BODILY EXPRESSION IN THE LITURGY

Sequeira divides gestures (and postures) as a fundamental form of liturgical body-language into expressive gestures and functional gestures. While the first (e.g. standing, walking, kneeling, sitting, blessing, crossing oneself etc.), "make an independent statement which does not need any other medium of expression than the action and/or movement of the body," functional gestures are "directed towards persons or objects" and employ complementary means of expression such as tools and materials. "These are effected when the context or the environment of the celebrants is constitutive of the language of their gestures." [161]

Functional gestures are less independent and "more strongly tied to the context of the verbal and tonal dimension of expression as well as with other elements of the dimension of movement and their expressive possibilities". Sacramental sign actions are significant examples of action gestures. [162]

Terms for movement are often used to describe the relationship between God and man: *katabasis*, *anabasis*, to enter into relationship or communication with. This spiritual reality is embodied in the movement of the body, in the focussed movement of walking as an expression of "entering" into the life-giving relationship with God. All liturgical walking is a real symbol of approach to God, of entering into relationship

---

[158] Ibid. 158
[159] Ibid. 161f.
[160] Guardini, Liturgische Bildung 33.
[161] Sequeira, Gottesdienst als menschliche Ausdruckshandlung 30f.
[162] Cf. Ibid. 36f.

with him, as is expressed in the processions and pilgrimages of all religions. [163] In his suggestions for liturgical space, Bouyer, by including provision for all participants to move from one liturgical space to another within the church, pleads for the involvement of the congregation in walking as prayer with the body. [164]

Dance is undoubtedly an outstanding act of bodily expression and for this reason is constantly mentioned in the search for new liturgical forms. [165] Not only has dance not played a great role in liturgical history, but the verdicts on it have been mixed. On the one hand the early Fathers demonized the dance that played a role in pagan cults and the worship of heretical sects as a snare of the Devil. On the other, the same Fathers speak of the dancing choirs of the blessed. Their rejection of "bodily" dance continued down through the centuries although rudimentary forms of liturgical dance survived, albeit in the face of opposition. [166]

Dance as a "fossilized relic of the living dance of earlier cultures" is used almost only for entertainment. For this reason the introduction of liturgical dance presents a culture which is "impoverished" in dance with problems which could have serious consequences. "One would at first be dependent on professional dancers who would perform at the liturgy. This would open the door to the danger of the liturgy degenerating into a 'perfectionist ballet display'. With this the aim of a revitalization of the liturgy would be frustrated – because in the final analysis the aim of whole effort can only be to enable the whole congregation to participate in the liturgical experience of a danced embodiment of Christian faith and life." [167] It is precisely dance that does not permit as many worshippers as possible to participate. According to the canons of Western dance the majority must remain spectators. There is also the remaining problem of what Baumgartner critically calls the "efficiency" of bodily actions, a problem which can never be completely avoided when a representative group dances before others. Despite this, dance as an outstanding medium of human expression should find its place in the liturgy. But many questions remain as to how this can actually be realized in liturgical practice. [168]

---

[163] Concerning movement as the preeminent expression of the bodily, cf. Sudbrack, Verherrlicht Gott in eurem Leib 89. On the procession as such in liturgical history, cf. H. Brakmann, Muster bewegter Liturgie in kirchlicher Tradition, W. Meurer (ed.) Volk Gottes auf dem Weg, Mainz 1989, 25-51; B. Jeggle-Merz, Bewegung als lebendiger Ausdruck des Glaubens. In: op. cit. infra. 52-61.

[164] Cf. All of Ch. 6 "Tradition und Erneuerung", in: Liturgie und Architektur, Einsiedeln – Freiburg i.Br. 1993, 83-112.

[165] A small selection: J. G. Davies, Towards a Theology of the Dance, ibid. (ed.) Worship and Dance, Birmingham 1975, 43-63; R. A. Sequeira, Spielende Liturgie. Bewegung neben Ton und Wort im gottesdienst am Beispiel des Vaterunsers, Freiburg i. Br. 1977; J. Baumgartner: Gefährte des Glaubens – Gespiele der Gnade. Zum Tanz im christlichen Kult: S. Walter, Tanz vor dem Herrn. Neue Wortgottesdienste mit Beiträgen von Jakob Baumgartner zum Tanz in der christlichen Liturgie, Zürich 1974; H. Lander, Tanz – sprachlose Verkündigung, KatBl 106 (1981) 63-71; T. Berger, Liturgie und Tanz. Anthropologische Aspekte – Historische Daten – theologische Perspektiven, St.Ottilien 1985.

[166] Cf. Koch, Gottesdienst und Tanz 63-66. Koch, following Heinz, counts among the relics of liturgical dance the jumping processions of Echternach in Luxemburg and Prüm in the Eifel. On the latter cf. A. Heinz, Die Prümer Springprozession. Ihr Verbot durch Erzbischof Klemens Wenzeslaus aus dem jahre 1778 und ihr Fortleben im Volk, Archiv f. Mittelrheinische Kirchengesch. 28 (1976) 83-100. Reifenberg, Fundamentalliturgie II, 130f., refers to the great significance of dance in the Ethiopian Church; despite all hindrances dance has "always been seen as a legitimate mode of expression in the Christian liturgy".

[167] Koch, Gottesdienst und Tanz 69.

[168] Cf. Sequeira, Wiederentdeckung der Bewegungsdimension 152.

Standing is also a pre-eminently expressive posture: "Let us stand with beauty, let us stand with reverence!" The introductory dialogue to the Anaphora of the Liturgy of St John Chrysostom begins with this summons from the deacon. [169] Standing is so characteristic of the liturgy that it is its "semeion". [170] Doubtless in the beginning there lay behind this summons from the deacon an exhortation to maintain a certain external discipline – as in the Clementine Liturgy in Book VIII of the Apostolic Constitutions – but this summons imparts a new quality to standing in the liturgy. Thus, there is no break with the original literal sense of the summons when in A. Schmemann's commentary on the liturgy, *stômen kalôs* is understood at an essentially deeper level and referred to the *kalón estin* of Peter in the story of the Transfiguration (Mt 17:4). [171]

As an expressive posture standing is a "standing" in salvation; man "stands" in a relationship with the God of life. Thus, for the Ukrainian liturgist Fedoriv standing is not just a symbol of the resurrection of Christ but also of the joyful lifting up of the human heart to heaven, indeed of man's spiritual resurrection which is realized in prayer. [172] Standing "is the basic liturgical posture (cf. GIRM 21) and has been understood since ancient times symbolically as the sign of the Easter existence of the redeemed (cf. Tertullian, De orat. 23; Council of Nicea can. 20)". [173] Standing as the noblest posture for prayer goes back to Christ himself who, according to the Gospel of Mark, mentions it when imparting the Our Father. [174] In Canon 20 of the Council of Nicea just mentioned, standing is prescribed for prayer during the Easter season and to this day the Byzantine Church preserves the rite of genuflection (*goniklisia*) at Vespers on Pentecost Sunday: with this rite kneeling for prayer is resumed after the end of Eastertide.

Sitting is both the posture of receptive and contemplative listening and a sign of authority. The leader of an assembly "sits before it" (pre-sides over it), the teacher has a "chair" (*cathedra*), a judge has a judgement-seat. For the listening congregation sitting is the expressive posture for its willingness to hear. For the seated preacher (the Bishop sitting on his cathedra invested with authority as teacher of his local Church) as well as the seated confessor (invested with jurisdictional power), sitting is more a functional posture. [175]

By kneeling (and even more by prostration, the laying of one's whole body on the ground during ordination and religious profession as well as at the Liturgy of the Passion on Good Friday) man expresses his nothingness before God. Kneeling is a sign of adoration and of the humility of the sinner. In the West, the genuflection became a separate gesture of reverence for the Blessed Sacrament, of the altar and of the cross (the latter particularly in the veneration of the cross on Good Friday). The Byzantines have no genuflection but, instead the "lesser" and "greater *Metania*" ("penance"), i.e. touching the ground with three fingers of the right hand followed by the Sign of the Cross

---

[169] Cf. Kallis 122f.; "kalos" is somewhat too freely translated as "dignified".

[170] Thus Ohm 326 quotes Chrysostomos, Hom. 18, I in Hebr 11 - PG 63,135

[171] Cf. K.C. Felmy, Die Deutung der göttlichen Liturgie in der russischen Theologie. Wege und Wandlungen russischer Liturgie-Auslegung, Berlin – New York 1984 (Arbeiten zur Kirchengeschichte 54), 420f. On the literal sense of the deacon's summons cf. also Kucharek, Liturgy 563-565.

[172] Cf. J.Fedoriv, Obrjadi Ukraïnskoï Tserkvi, Rome-Toronto 1970, 84.

[173] Sequeira, Gottesdienst als menschliche Ausdruckshandlung 32.

[174] Cf. Fedoriv 85; Ohm 325; Lubienska de Lenval 21; Mk 11:25: "Whenever you stand praying"

[175] Cf. Sequeira, Gottesdienst als menschliche Ausdruckshandlung 32.

or throwing one's whole body onto the ground and touching it with the forehead. [176] The new Missal mentions kneeling as the posture of the faithful during the institution narrative of the Eucharistic Prayer (GIRM 21). [177]

The various ways of holding one's hands are a notably expressive gesture of a person at prayer. According to Heiler, the *orante* posture – open hands raised to heaven – is a universal human posture for prayer widespread in all religions: [178] at one and the same time man "touches" heaven as the dwelling place of God, pleads for his gifts of grace and holds his hands open to receive them. Both the Old and New Testaments refer to the *orante* posture (e.g. Ps 28 [27]:2; Is 1:15; 1 Tim 2:8); it was the most common prayer posture of Christian. Unfortunately, this posture developed into one reserved to the priest in a liturgical context and medieval commentaries liked to employ a motif already present in the Fathers (e.g. Tertullian and Cyprian [179]) that referred the stretching out of hands to the crucified Christ and with that explained the *orante* posture of the priest at the altar in the context of the sacrifice of the Mass. There is a clericalism too in Innocent III's post-symbolic derivation of this (priestly) posture: just as Moses in Ex 17:12 had to raise his hands to heaven to make Israel's victory possible, and was helped in this by Aaron and Hur, so the Pope is assisted in this posture by his ministers. [180] Perhaps an increased recovery of prayer with the body in the liturgy could begin by the declericalizing this very ancient posture and make it available to all participants in the liturgical assembly.

The folding of hands became a very widespread prayer posture, especially among the laity. This was under the influence of symbolism employed in Germanic law. This gesture is also employed in Hinduism, Buddhism as well as in Tibetan and Japanese religion. It was an ancient Germanic prayer posture and was christianized not least by means of the oath of fealty. [181] The vassal placed his folded hands between the open hands of the liege lord, as is still the case in the promise of obedience at an ordination. Related to this, but much older, is the entwining of fingers. This is witnessed to by Pliny and Ovid and according to the Dialogues of St Gregory, St Scholastica *insertas digitis manus* with God, obtained the miracle that made it possible for her to remain with her brother Benedict. The practice of crossing the hands on the breast is of eastern origin. This was adopted by the Byzantine Church where it is still practised by communicants. It also has a certain role in the Carthusian liturgy. [182]

Laying on of hands is both an expressive and a functional gesture. The touching by one person of another is a fundamental sign of the establishment of a relationship; "it symbolizes fundamentally a turning towards and identification with the other as well as the effect of transmission of blessing and authority". [183] In the New Testament the laying on of hands is a gesture of blessing and healing, which has survived in the silent

---

[176] cf. Onasch, art. "Proskynese" 313f.

[177] On kneeling cf. Sequeira 33, Ohm 344-371, Kleinheyer, Heil erfahren 18-23.

[178] Cf. Heiler, Gebet 101f.

[179] Cf. Tertullin, De Oratione 14 – CSEL 20,189; Cyprian, De dom. orat.6 – CSEL 3,1, 269. Tertullian in addition warns that the "orante" posture should be adopted "modestly" and without rasing one's eyes brazenly to God: "ne vultu quidam in audaciam erecto": De oratione 17 – CSEL 2,190. Cf. further on this Dölger, Sol salutis 244.

[180] De sacro alt. myst II,28: De extensione manuum sacerdotis in missa – PL 217,815 B.

[181] Cf. Heiler, Gebet 103.

[182] On the whole subject of posture in prayer cf. Eisenhofer I, 266-268.

[183] Sequeira, Gottesdienst als menschliche Ausdruckhandlung 34.

laying on of hands in the Sacrament of the Sick, in which the physical touch – despite the danger of infection – is an important sign of human solidarity with the sick person. The laying on of hands is clearly a functional gesture at ordinations as is its suggestion in the raising of the hand in Confirmation and in the Sacrament of Reconciliation. At ordinations it is the sign of the transmission of the authority of office. In the Byzantine rite there is a laying on of hands in the conferring of the liturgical ministries of psalmist, lector and subdiaconate – not regarded as sacramental actions according to Western sacramental understanding. But this laying on of hands *cheirothesia* ("placing of hands") is distinguished from the *cheirotonia* ("raising of hands") in the ordination of a deacon, priest or bishop. According to Hotz the term "raising of hands" still refers to the showing of hands in a vote by an assembly of the people and with it to the participation of the people in the appointment of office-holders – although here too the "sacramental" laying on of hands by the bishop is never lacking. [184]

The Sign of the Cross is made by Christians inside and outside of the liturgy, [185] the older form of which, the "small Sign of the Cross" (on the forehead and soon after on the lips and the breast) is attested to very early on as a gesture of blessing of self. Tertullian calls it *signaculum* – corresponding to the Greek *sphragis* (seal) – and like Cyprian and Jerome refers it to those marked with the seal mentioned by Ezekiel (9:4) and in the Book of Revelation (7:-3; 9:4. The German word *Segen* – from *signare* or *se signare* – itself points to the Sign of the Cross linked with the action of blessing. The signing or sealing with the Cross on the forehead was from very early times part of the rites of the catechumenate. The "greater" Sign of the Cross on forehead, breast and shoulders can be attested with certainty only in the second millennium; Innocent III describes it as it is still practised by the Byzantines – i.e. placing the hand first on the right shoulder an then on the left as a kind of mirror-image in the one being blessed of the hand of the person blessing. Innocent is also familiar with the use of thumb, index – and middle finger of the right hand in the greater Sign of the Cross, still usual among the Byzantines, and is aware of the trinitarian reference of this. To this day among the Byzantines, the position of the fingers of a person blessing reflects the name of Christ in Greek: the straight index finger is "I", the bent middle finger stands for "C"; the cross formed by placing the thumb across the ring finger gives the "X"; the bent little finger produces the second "C":IC-XC: *Iesous Christos*. [186] Towards the end of the thirteenth century the Greeks accused the Latins of blessing and making the Sign of the Cross with five fingers, and there is evidence of this five-fingered blessing and crossing in the West. In addition, the practice in the Sign of the Cross of placing the right hand on the left shoulder first instead of on the right had become usual in the West. The words accompanying the Sign of the Cross stem from the early medieval period and – particularly when used with holy water – make the sign of the Cross a recalling of Baptism. The Sign of the Cross plays an important role in the opening and closing of liturgical actions; in rites of blessing it forms, along with the accompanying words, the centre of the celebration.

---

[184] Cf. R. Hotz, Sakrament im Wechselspiel zwischen Ost und West, Zürich-Köln-Gütersloh 1979 (Ökumenische Theol. 2), 252.

[185] Cf. Eisenhofer I, 273-281; F. J. Dölger, Beiträge zur Geschichte des Kreuzzeichens, Antike und Christentum 1 (1958) 5 -19; 2 (1959) 15-29; 3 (1960) 5-16; 4 (1961) 5-17; 5 (1962) 5-22; 6 (1963) 7-34; 7 (1964) 5-38; 8/9 (1965/66) 7-52; 10 (1967) 7 29.

[186] Cf. Fedoriv 60-64.

Beating of the breast is, according to Lk 18:9-14 a gesture of self-accusation and expresses unworthiness and guilt. Heiler traces the gesture back to ancient Egypt and links it to a Roman practice when taking an oath: whenever the word "ego" occurred in the formula, one struck one's breast. [187] This gesture is prescribed in the Confiteor, but plays a greater role in folk piety than in the liturgy itself. [188]

The kiss is also both an expressive and functional gesture [189] indicating an intimacy of relationship as, for example, at the kissing of the altar at the beginning and end of Mass, of the Book of the Gospels after the proclamation of the good news, or at the kiss of peace exchanged by Christians in ancient times. Precisely because of its intimate connotations the kiss tended already from early times to become stylized as evidenced, e.g. in the use of a pax-brede or the transformation of the kiss into – at the very most suggested – embrace. "The various forms and substitutes are to a great degree indications of how intimate gestures of touch are conditioned by time and culture. It is an important question – one indeed to be handled with discretion – how a renewed liturgy can find an appropriate expression of a human closeness (intimacy, affection) based on faith. [190]

Bibliography

J. Baumgartner, Liturgie und Leiblichkeit, HID 30 (1976) 143 – 164.

D. Forstner, Die Welt der Symbole, Innsbruck 1960.

K. Hallinger, Kultgebärde und Eucharistie, ALw 19 (1978) 29 – 41.

F. Heiler, Das Gebet. Eine religionsgeschichtliche und religionspsychologische Untersuchung, München 2nd edn. 1920.

B. Kleinheyer, Heil erfahren in Zeichen, München 1980.

K. Koch, Gottesdienst und Tanz. Marginalien zu einer noch immer problematischen Verknüpfung, LJ 42 (1992) 63-69.

H. Lubienska de Lenval, Die Liturgie der Gebärde, Klosterneuburg 1959.

W. Meurer (ed.), Volk Gottes auf dem Weg. Bewegungselemente im Gottesdienst, Mainz 1989.

Th. Ohm, Gebetsgebärden der Völker, Leiden 1948.

R. Sequeira, Die Wiederentdeckung der Bewegungsdimension in der Liturgie, Concilium 16 (1980) 149-152.

R. Sequeira, Gottesdienst als menschliche Ausdruckshandlung, R. Berger / K. H. Bieritz u.a., GdK 3: Gestalt des Gottesdienstes, Regensburg 2nd edn. 1990, 7-39.

2.5. SPEECH IN THE LITURGY

2.5.1. SPEECH AS A PART OF LIFE

Man does not "have" a body nor "is" he body, but in his body as a real-symbolic mani-festation of himself is present for others in order to enter into relationship with them. [191]

---

[187] Cf. Heiler, Gebet 102.
[188] Cf. Sequeira, Gottesdienst als menschliche Ausdruckshandlung 35. Cf. also Eisenhofer I, 281f.
[189] Cf. Heiler, Gebet 103f.
[190] Sequeira op.cit. 36.
[191] Cf. Rahner, Vom Hören und Sehen 142: "We do not only possess organs of sense; more, we are sensibility.

Man's body is really the "sacrament" of his presence towards relationship; through the body he "speaks" the in the language of the body, in the body-language in the widest sense.

The body is so refined an organ of expression that body-language can "utter" when the spoken language is silent. "Expression", the presentation of the ego outside itself in order to enter into relationship takes place most perfectly by means of the spoken word, in which the speaking person remains completely in himself while at the same time is outside of himself in his utterance. [192] By means of speech man is "not a closed entity but, rather, an existence and a self characterized by openness", which in speaking and acting fulfills and appropriates itself as "I" and "Thou", as "We" and "You" in the context of objective reality and vis-á-vis others at the remove of "he", "she", "it" and "they". According to Hünermann speech is man's "act of life". [193]

The dialectic between being completely present to oneself and to the person to whom one is speaking, corresponds to the dialectic of "internal" and "external" speech. "internal" speech "has no communicative function. It is the medium of one's own thinking and feeling." External speech transports internal speech to the person addressed. Communication is effected when, "what is alive in the internal experience of one person, begins to become present in the inner space of another through the medium of external speech". [194] Communication is an interplay: by means of external speech the listener absorbs the internal speech of the speaker – absorbs the speaker as a spiritual, thinking and feeling person. Through speech the speaker becomes present in the hearer and communicates with him. By answering the listener becomes speaker and gives himself back along with what he has previously received. Enriched now by what he has received, he becomes present in his interlocutor in a new act of communication. Every new act of address, of listening, of reception is a new becoming present of the Thou to the I, the Thou in every case enriched by the whole personality of the other.

2.5.2. "LITURGICAL SPEECH"

Accordingly, communication by speech pre-supposes understanding. It is difficult to understand how up to the reforms of the Second Vatican Council, the Church in the West, used the dead Latin language virtually exclusively in its services: "How can one ignorant of Latin celebrate the liturgy consciously and comprehendingly when a strange language prevents him from grasping the content of the texts? Here there is a fundamental breakdown in communication in the face of which all traditional arguments for Latin lose their cogency" [195].

Our corporeality (and with it our sensibility) is constituted from out of its essence by the personal subject itself, it is the permanent medium through which the spirit, that is the free subject opening and open to the totality of all possible reality, presents itself to the world."

[192] On this cf. K. Rahner: Die Gegenwart des Herrn in der christlichen Kultgemeinde: Schriften zur Theologie VIII, Einsiedeln-Zürich-Köln 1967, 395-408.396, where he speaks of man as "existence which realises itself simultaneously in its presence to itself and in its giving, entrusting, of itself in free responsibility, in personal intercommunication."

[193] Cf. P. Hünermann: Lebensvollzüge der Kirche. Reflexionen zu einer Theologie des Wortes und der Sakramente. In: P. Hünermann / R. Schaeffler (eds.): Theorie der Sprachhandlungen und heutige Ekklesiologie. Ein philiosophisch-theologisches Gespräch. Freiburg-Basel-Vienna 1987 (QD 109), 27-53.36.

[194] Louis adopts this distinction in: Das Wort des Menschen 325, by L.S.Wygotski; cf. L.S. Wygotski: Denken und Sprechen. Berlin 5th ed. 1974, 328-350.

[195] A. Adam, Grundriß Liturgie, Freiburg-Basel-Vienna 5th edn. 1992, 66.

At the beginning of the history of the Church the current languages of the region were used both inside and outside the liturgy. As well as Greek *Koiné*, the lingua franca of the whole ancient Mediterranean, these were Syrian, Coptic and Armenian. The very earliest community used Aramaic with several Hebrew acclamations inherited from the synagogue. With the spread of Christianity in the first millennium, Old Slavonic (Old Bulgarian) and Arabic were added to the repertoire. The Churches of the East were always open to the translation of the liturgy into the various vernaculars. In Rome, until the restoration of Latin under the Emperor Decius (249-251) Greek Koiné of the New Testament was the colloquial language. It was only in the third century that Latin began to encroach into the liturgy, a process that was completed under Pope Damasus around the year 380. [196] In contrast to the Arian Goths, who also celebrated the liturgy in the vernacular, the Catholic Germanic tribes adopted Latin as their liturgical language. It was believed that this would safeguard orthodoxy. But the effect was that faithful were barred from a genuine con-celebration of the liturgy. In the context of the debate surrounding the mission to the Slavs of the brothers Cyril and Methodius the ideology arose that only the three languages of Pilate's inscription on the Cross – Hebrew, Latin and Greek – were, as "sacred" languages, suitable for the liturgy. This notion was however rejected by Pope John VIII in the year 880.

Nevertheless, two hundred years later Pope Gregory VII withdrew this permission to celebrate the liturgy in the Slav language. He argued that it was God's will that as a protection from disrespect as well as misunderstanding and heresy, the Scriptures and the liturgical texts should not be generally understandable. Although Latin had long since become the medieval language of affairs and of the learned, the ordinary people remained shut out from the Latin liturgy. Thus, the participation by the "common man" in the liturgy was to become one of the motivating forces of the Reformation. Although the Council of Trent simply condemned the proposition that the Mass could be celebrated only in the vernacular [197], thus leaving the way open to further development, the Roman position against moves towards the vernacular became hardened. And so, in 1661 Pope Alexander VII put the translation of the Missal by the French priest Voisin on the Index and as late as 1857 Pope Pius IX forbade the translation of the Canon and the words of Consecration. It was only in 1897 that Pope Leo XIII opened the way for the translation of the texts of the Mass: but this did not alter the celebration of the liturgy itself. The first change came with the developments after the Second Vatican Council. While paragraph 36 of *Sacrosanctum Concilium* (SC), the council's decree on the liturgy, provided that Latin should remain as the language of the liturgy, the way was opened for the vernacular. The bishops' conferences were to decide, subject to Roman approval, the extent to which the vernacular could be used in the liturgy. [198] Further developments went far beyond what had been laid down by the constitution on the liturgy, even if these developments were not intrinsically inconsistent with this constitution whose whole drift was towards the facilitation of the *participatio actuosa* of all in the liturgical action.

---

[196] Cf. Th. Klauser, Der Übergang der römischen Kirche von der griechischen zur lateinischen Liturgiesprache: Miscellanea G.Mercati I.Cittá del Vaticano 1946, 467-482.

[197] DH 1759: "Si quis dixerit, lingua *tantum* vulgari Missam celebrari debere."

[198] On this cf. Lengeling's commentary on SC 36: Lengeling, Konstitution 83-85.

Less for considerations of respect for a venerable tradition than for the enabling of active and fruitful participation by all the faithful – as for example in the celebration of international liturgies in Rome itself or other great places of pilgrimage – the knowledge of a basic minimum of Latin liturgical texts was to be encouraged. But even in this provision the law of the functioning of verbal communication in the liturgy applies: only when those who do not know Latin are aware of what they are singing and praying in a foreign language may this also be done in Latin.

The various vernaculars also present the problem of translation. On the one hand, to translate a Latin or Greek term into a modern language without losing some of the sense is not without its problems. Literal translations are frequently unacceptable. Again, some Latin turns of phrase carry certain theological nuances from previous ages which make the whole discourse sound antiquated. As a help in overcoming these difficulties, the Roman Consilium published an Instruction in January 1969 on "The Translation of Liturgical Texts". [199] This stated that a translation was not to be slavishly literal but was to preserve, "the thought-process of the text in keeping with its literary form" (No.6). Elevated colloquial speech was given as an example. The community was to be able to make their own living prayer of the prayer texts so translated. For this reason the language of the liturgy was to be close to the language of the people without degenerating into a demotic. This language was to "condense religious experience, speak from and to God, strike the heart of man and so arrive a something close to poetry as did many psalms and hymns of the past". [200]

2.5.3. THE PROCLAIMED WORD OF GOD

The Scriptures are God's "external speech". He, "chose these to reveal himself to men, to speak to them in diverse individual and historical situations, to instruct, correct, promise comfort and hope and to lead to knowledge of God". [201] As "external speech" – as communication of God's "internal speech", that is his will for the salvation of man and the world – the Scriptures are a means of God's presence. God is as present in his word as a man makes himself present in his word to a person to whom he speaks. Just as a man's body and the spoken word, which leaves this body as sound, are "sacraments" of the presence of this man's personality, so also are the Scriptures a "sacramental" means of God's presence through the Son in the Holy Spirit: "He is present in his word, since he himself is speaking, when the Holy Scriptures are read in church" (SC 7). [202] What is said here of Christ is always also said of the Triune God, who through his eternal Word made man in the Holy Spirit enters into relationship with man and the world.

God's presence in the word is anamnetic. The anamnesis whose "clear point of emphasis lies in the reciprocal flux between the presentation of past events and their relevance for one praying today", [203] is by no means a subjective reminiscence of God's saving events lying in the past. Even less can this anamnesis be a petition for a new

---

[199] Kaczynski 1200-1242.
[200] Adam, Grundriß 67f. Cf. also the excursus: Übersetzung liturgischer Gebete in Merz, Gebetsformen 113-115.
[201] Louis, Das Wort des Menschen 331f.
[202] CF. Bieritz, Das Wort im Gottesdienst 68-71.
[203] Merz, Gebetsformen der Liturgie 106.

salvation by reminding God of his own saving deeds. "Anamnesis" is "recalling of the mystery" in Odo Casel's understanding of the term.

In the proclamation of the Israel's deliverance at the Red Sea, the unalterable will to save as evidenced then and which will save in many subsequent situations, is proclaimed anew. Today's listener to this extract from Scripture is neither being pursued by Pharao nor is he standing on the shore of the Red Sea but through the experience of others of God's saving power, the event proclaimed becomes real for the listener God's "external speech", as an expression of the abiding currency of God's approach to man. From the example of the saving deed proclaimed in the Sacred Scriptures comes God's invitation to man to open himself to God's saving power in his own particular situation in life which has hardly anything to do with that described in the Scriptures.

In anamnesis the listener hears in the biblical "words" about God's saving deeds in history God's "external voice", his invitation to relationship. To this extent anamnesis causes the past saving event to be "presented once again", as Casel says, for the "external speech" which God spoke in his saving actions in history is not distinguished from other forms of "external speech" through which he constantly invites to living relationship. The listener does not issue this invitation to himself; he hears it spoken to him through the "living sign" of God's external speech as communicated to him in the proclamation of God's word in Scripture. [204]

2.5.4. FORMS OF PROCLAMATION OF THE WORD IN THE LITURGY

A. Reading of Scripture

For the reading of Scripture in the liturgy, "pericopes" or extracts must be "cut out" from the text, a practice already employed in the liturgy of the synagogue. The custom of continuous reading, *lectio continua*, is an inheritance of the readings from the Torah which was divided for this purpose into *paraschim*, while the freer selection from the prophetic books was known as *haftarim*. Since the second century of the Christian era there have existed in parallel, a three-year Palestinian cycle and a one-year Babylonian cycle for the reading of the Torah. The choice of *haftarim* from the prophetic books is determined by the content of the preceding *paraschim* from the Torah.

The Church has taken up this inheritance from the synagogue. A peculiarity of the Old Gallican liturgy was the so-called "centonisation" or patching together of extracts of different biblical origin into one pericope. The first list of such pericopes dates from the fourth century and since the second half of the seventh century have been known as "capitularies". Lectionaries as such for the Roman Rite exist only since the second half of the eighth century while two fourth-century lectionaries from Jerusalem survive in Armenian translation. The reading of the Old Testament in the Christian liturgy underlies the principle, then as now, of *relecture*, of a "re-reading" of Israel's salvation history in the light of the saving event of Christ, to which event that salvation history was intended to lead. "The most recent revision of the lectionary for Sundays and feasts follows this practice, with an attempt to establish what is called a "contrapuntal" relationship between the re-introduced Old Testament reading and the Gospel reading." [205]

Non-biblical readings in the liturgy are found in the Liturgy of the Hours in the form of readings from the writings of the Fathers of the Church and from the lives

---

[204] On this cf. Pieper, Das Gedächtnis des Leibes 71-73.
[205] Cf. Fischer, Formen der Verkündigung 78-81.

of the saints. Readings from the latter and from the acts of the martyrs were found in the non-Roman liturgies of the Mass in the West. "Except in Milan, the development since the Middle Ages has been towards a strict monopoly by readings from Scripture, a monopoly which has not been shaken by the recent reforms." Fischer questions this strict biblical monopoly from the perspective that the continued working of the Holy Spirit in the Church might be expressed through the reading of Church documents in the liturgy – though the very form of these texts might make this appear scarcely practical. [206] It is doubtful whether, on the basis of the idea of contrapuntal reading, the proclamation of the word in the liturgy is helped by the use of a consciously anti-Church or even anti-Christian text before the reading of the gospel.

B. Addresses[207]

The address of the presider at the liturgy is also a proclamation of the word because it fulfills a mystagogical function: Justin Martyr's placing of the address between the reading of the Scriptures and the celebration of the sacrifice and as its location by Hippolytus before the communion both emphasize the function of the address to elucidate the word of God and to lead into the celebration of the mysteries. Mystagogy is also the proper theme of the homily, of the familiar spiritual discourse, while the thematic sermon – originally a mission sermon delivered outside the context of the liturgy – became dominant and ever more distinct from the liturgical action. The Second Vatican Council (SC 52) rediscovered the homily but thematic sermons are not ruled out when they are appropriate to the Church's year and/or refer to the particular liturgical celebration, thus once again fulfilling the mystagogical task.

The homily is "part of the liturgy" (SC 52) and as such is prescribed for the celebration of Mass on Sundays and feasts, and highly recommended on all other days especially in the special liturgical seasons (GIRM 42). And the homily has its place in the other liturgical celebrations. In the ancient Church the quintessential preacher was the bishop. It was only in the sixth century that the independent sermon by the priest appeared. From the time of the mendicant movement in the Middle Ages up to the Code of Canon Law of 1917 (Can.1342 §2), preaching by the laity has been generally forbidden. Canon 766 of the 1983 Code of Canon Law permits this once more but Canon 767 reserves the homily at Mass as *pars ipsius liturgiae* to the ordained minister. There are diverging positions between the Roman authorities and those of the local Churches in the matter of the so-called "dialogue homily" at small group liturgies. The dialogue homily is undoubtedly an expression of *participatio actuosa* and fulfills the increasingly important function of mutual witness to and strengthening of the faith. But here, too, it is the presider's function to "hold things together and summarize at the end is such a way that the character of the homily as proclamation – in this case by several voices – of the word of God is maintained" [208] Among addresses are also counted (ad-)monitions, introductions to prayer and the shorter introductions by the celebrant. A commentary on a liturgical celebration by a commentator can also be described as a *monitio*.

---

[206] Cf. ibid. 86-88.
[207] Cf. ibid. 89-94.
[208] Ibid. 93.

C. Accompanying – and Sacramental Formulas

These are also considered forms of the proclamation of the word.[209] Accompanying formulas – e.g. the words used when distributing Holy Communion – are intended to highlight the liturgical action and its spiritual intention. Thus these formulas have an important mystagogical function, especially when they elicit a response from the recipient – such as the "Amen" at Communion. In the case of sacramental formulas, the effect of scholastic sacramental theology has been a tendency to isolate these words by seeing them as the "essential words" (*verba essentialia*) through which the sacrament comes into being. In Fischer's opinion this tendency towards isolation is still strong in the renewed liturgy. In addition, the emphasis on the minister – the "I" formula – strengthens that formula at the expense of the epicletic element. Again, without understanding sacraments merely as proclamations of the word strengthened by external symbolic actions, the sacramental formulas are indeed in a profound sense "proclamations of the word" since they express and make effective the Lord who is acting in them, the incarnate word of God.

2.5.5. PRAYER AS A LIVING-OUT OF AND AN RESPONSE TO THE PROCLAIMED WORD

Just as *anabasis* presupposes *katabais*, man's prayer is possible only as a response to the the word spoken to him by God. Man's response to the anamnetic presence of God in his word is epicletic in the widest sense of the term: the calling down of uncreated grace upon his distinctive situation in life, a situation which is individually different from every biblical example. Listening to God's "external speech" in *anamnesis*, whose "internal speech" is his unchangeable will for man's salvation, man's *epiclesis* as "external speech". Man's "internal speech" has perceived and assessed God's external speech, heard in the anamnetic proclamation of the works of redemption, as an invitation to salvation. Man responds in the external speech of *epiclesis*.

In this *epiclesis* man – and with him the world contained in his person – consummates *anabasis*, enters into communication with the living God who spoke to him in the *anamnesis* of his saving deeds. The word of God, heard in its proclamation is meditated, upon i.e. "chewed over: "In contrast to contemporary usage, meditation at that time was understood as the recitation of Scripture passages in a low voice and usually off by heart". *Ruminare* means to chew the cud. At a first reading this term may seem strange to us but it means that just as a camel stores its feed and chews it over again and again, the word of God must be stored up inside us so that finally it becomes part of our flesh and blood and thus, coming from inside ourselves, can have concrete effect in our lives."[210] The more the word one has received from God is internalized the more clearly it is recognized as the word of the living God. The monk receives the word of God addressed to him in the passage of Scripture he recites, but he reacts as himself with his own words in prayer: "only in choosing and speaking his own words is does this insight become full realized. Man can only have as his own spiritual patrimony what he has himself grasped in words. For this reason it is right that one who is praying

---

[209] Cf. ibid. 94-96.

[210] Louis, Das Wort des Menschen 331f. Cf. H. Bacht, "Meditatio" in den ältesten Mönchsquellen, GuL 28 (1955) 366; F. Ruppert, Meditatio – Ruminatio. Zu einem Grundbegriff christlicher Meditaiton, Erbe und Auftrag 53 (1977) 85.

should constantly try to reply in his own words to what God is saying to him in the binding words of the Sacred Scriptures."[211] If prayer wants to be communication with God, internal expression must articulated in external speech. God does indeed know the thoughts of man "from afar" (Ps 139:2b) as well as all his needs (cf. Is 58:9). But in the process of translating internal into external speech the one praying opens himself to such a degree that he himself become aware for the first time of the images and ideas of the internal speech inherent in him. Thus a man's own needs, lacks and desires become his own possession which he can then bring before God as a sacrifice. God knows all needs, lacks and desires, but until they have been uttered by man in prayer God does not have them as "gifts" to be returned to man, now imbued with God himself in the economy of uncreated grace.[212]

In Byzantine Christianity this is well illustrated by the highly esteemed ideal of incessant prayer of the heart. In every situation of life ("internal speech") the Christian ought to practise prayer of the heart; it is "the uninterrupted and unceasing uttering of the divine name of Jesus with the lips, with the spirit, with the heart, conscious of his presence everywhere and it is an appeal for his mercy in every action, in every place and at all time, even in one's sleep. It is expressed in the following words: Lord Jesus Christ, have mercy on me."[213]

The psychosomatic complexity of incessant prayer finally leads to a situation in which man is no longer praying but prayer rules him completely.[214] What is determining man in his body-soul totality is communication with the triune God who more and more permeates man's whole being and permits him on earth already to participate in the divine life. According to Symeon of Thessaloniki, prayer of the heart is "epiclesis" in the real sense in that, also like the other *epicleses* in the liturgy – it invokes the Holy Spirit over created reality – in this case man himself – so that this Spirit will imbue it with uncreated grace and fill it with divine life. Symeon enumerate the fruits of prayer: communication of divine gifts, purification of the heart, liberation from sin, revelation of divine mysteries, overflowing of mercy.[215]

What happens then in prayer? God does not change himself or his actions on the strength of man's prayer, but man is opened to divinising grace; he enters into communication with God, who has never wanted or ever will want anything other than the salvation of the creature through participation in his divine life. Through prayer God is not informed of any need as if he did not already know of it, nor can there be any question of prayer effecting a change in God, who is unchangeable, from being "ungracious" to "gracious". What may appear to man as a change brought about in God by his intensive prayer, a change from not listening to listening, is the result of his entry into living communication with God. Just as in the Eucharist bread and wine are offered as gifts of creation and as an expression of man's self, in order to be transformed, so the one praying brings himself and his world to God and speaks the *epiclesis* over himself,

---

[211] Cf. Louis, Das Wort des Menschen 333: "One day Theodore [the favourite disciple of Pachomius] was sitting in his cell; making rope and meditating on passages of the Scriptures he had learned by heart; every time his heart prompted his to do so, he stood up and prayed. So, he meditated while seated and working with his hands but stood up for prayer."

[212] Cf. ibid. 329f.

[213] K. Ware / I. Jungclaussen, Hinführung zum Herzensgebet, Freiburg i. Br. 1982, 20.

[214] Cf. E. Kremer, Herzschlag und Atmung, GuL 58 (1985) 201-203.202f.

[215] Cf. Dialogos 296 – PG 155, 544 D – 545 A.

his life and everything connected with it so that they may be similarly changed by being drawn into the divine life. Only that which is offered to God, only that which is placed in relationship to him can be made holy. This is so in the case of the eucharistic gifts as much as in the case of man whose freedom to give himself is respected by God, even when he knows all man's needs and dangers.

For this reason, man who decides to communicate with God is free to open himself to God's divinising grace and its saving effects. The praying man and his world are saved through the calling down of a grace which is unceasingly at work and to which man opens himself and allows to work in himself to the extent that his prayer "succeeds": this prayer is tempered by his readiness to communicate with God, a readiness confronted and endangered by Original Sin. [216] Since the world is always contained in man – and with it his fellowmen with whom he is bound up and whose relationships with him stamp his personality – his prayer as a bringing of his life into relationship with uncreated grace is always and already intercession for his neighbour and for the world. In this sense the metaphor is valid that prayer "conquers" God, as Evdokimov asserts citing the example of St Seraphim of Sarov; similarly that God, knowing in advance of our prayer, lets it "influence" his decisions. [217]

Just as little as God "needs" petition, though he "needs" it, however, as offering, as an expression of a free man's entry into relationship with him, God needs doxology, the prayer of praise. God glory does not need man's praise, but man praises him when in his relationship with God he discovers himself. Doxology is a consequence of *epiclesis*, for which reason Evdokimov speaks of a "doxological anthropology". [218]

2.5.6. FORMS OF PRAYER IN THE LITURGY

"God's dealings with us become present in no other way than in the speech and actions of other people, more specifically in the actions of the community which in liturgical observance (in word and sacrament) praises and celebrates God's great deeds and precisely in this praising and thanksgiving commemoration makes these deeds present through proclamation. This means that God's word is uttered in, with and under the response of the community." [219]

---

[216] Here a strict scholastic definition of a sacrament fails to describe adequately the salvific effect of prayer of petition. K. Rahner, Wort und Eucharistie: Schriften zur Theologie IV, Einsiedeln-Zürich-Köln 1960, 313-355.334f. tries to find a balance: If the opus operatum, the "unfailing effect", characterizes the sacrament, but this effect, according to the teaching of the council of Trent, also depends on the disposition of the recipient, then "there are also other aspects which by God's free disposal are bound up with an unfailing working of grace and nevertheless have the character of a mere pre-condition exclusive of any element of merit; for example, pure prayer of petition as such for something that is clearly and unconditionally connected to salvation and the glory of God. Jesus's own words, which we may not dilute, have expressly promised the effectiveness of this prayer. Why is this not an opus operatum?"

[217] P. Evdokimov, Les âges de la vie spirituelle des Pères du désert á nos jours, Paris 3rd edn. 1980, 203f.: "God hears our prayer, he adjusts it and maks of it a factor which he adds to this decision. The energetic insistence of the widow in the Gospel elicits a response which highlights the power of faith. Three times Saint Paul petitions the Lord to remove the thorn from his flesh. The life of Saint Seraphim tells of the saint's prayer for the soul of a condemned sinner. Day and night the saint prayed, struggled with divine justice and although struck by lightning, his fiery prayer in its very boldness, caused divine mercy to triumph and the sinner was pardoned."

[218] Cf. Evdokimov, L'Orthodoxie 95-97

[219] Bieritz, Das Wort im Gottesdienst 62.

The forms of liturgical prayer in the Christian liturgy form a continuity with the communal forms of prayer of Israel. To these forms belong in particular the so-called *toda* and *berakah*. *Toda* is a thanksgiving – and community – sacrificial meal to offer thanks for salvation from peril. At its centre is a thanksgiving song which anamnetically makes present the rescue event and epicletically prays that Jahweh will continue to give protection and deliverance. Anamnesis, remembrance of God's saving deeds, and petition for continued salvation also play a central role in *berakah*. But while *toda* refers to a concrete situation of need, *berakah* is part of Jewish daily prayer. [220]

This fundamental structure of anamnesis and *epiclesis* is also a literary characteristic of the liturgical prayer of Christian worship. [221] This structure is broadened to include anaclesis (calling on God using names and attributes); doxology (praise of the triune God as an underlining of the basic *berakah* character of Christian prayer) and acclamation (related to doxology this formulaic proclamation of devotion or loyalty to the Lord Christ or an affirmatory response to a cue, like the acclamation after the Consecration, was adopted from the secular world of public gatherings or the entry of the Emperor. Liturgical prayer is phrased in the "we" form, to mark it as communal prayer of the liturgical assembly as distinct from the concrete speaker. Prayers in the first person are mostly formerly private prayers of the celebrant which found their way into the tight structure of the liturgy, though not without controversy.

Among the many types of liturgical prayer, the first is the "Consecratory Prayer" which is in no way confined to the Eucharistic Prayer. Under this category are included, the blessing of baptismal water, the prayer of the bishop over those being confirmed, the prayer of consecration at ordinations, the (consecratory) prayer over the oil at the anointing of the sick, the prayer at the consecration of the oils at the Chrism Mass on Holy Thursday, the prayer of consecration at the blessing of an abbot or abbess, at professions, consecrations of virgins and liturgical commissionings. The *Exsultet* at the Easter Vigil also belongs in this category. [222] A second type is the *Oratio* with the typical structure: invitation of the assembly to prayer, silence for private prayer, address to God (*anaclesis*, sometimes with relative predication to express the anamnetic dimension), petition (the epicletic dimension), formula of Christological mediatorship (which is also doxological in character) and the acclamation by the assembly (e.g. "Amen"). Related to *oratio* are prayers of blessing (in particular the "Prayers over the People") and prayers that accompany liturgical actions and comment on them, for example the *berakah*-prayers of the new Missal used at the preparation of the gifts at the Offertory. [223] If these prayers are the sphere of the one presiding over the liturgical assembly, acclamations and intercessions are the concern of the whole congregation. The intercessions in particular are open to liturgical abuses among which Merz counts subjectivism (themes considered important by individuals and often linked with moral exhortation dominate the intercessions or indeed the whole liturgy) and a complete absence of real "prayer". [224]

Bibliography

[220] Cf. Merz, Gebetsformen 99.
[221] Cf. ibid. 105-108. Cf. ibid.125; Meyer, Eucharistie 203.
[222] Cf. Merz, Gebetsformen 116-120.
[223] Cf. ibid. 120-123.
[224] Cf. ibid. 123-130.

K.-H. Bieritz, Das Wort im Gottesdienst, R. Berger / K. H. Bieritz u.a.: GdK 3: Gestalt des Gottesdienstes, Regensburg 2nd edn.1990, 47-76.

B. Fischer, Formen der Verkündigung, GdK 3, 77-96.

J. Ladrière, Die Sprache des Gottesdienstes. Die Performativität der Liturgiesprache, Concilium 9 (1973) 110-117.

B. Louis, Das Wort des Menschen an Gott – das Wort Gottes an den Menschen, GuL 55 (1982) 324-335.

Th. Maas-Ewerd, Vom Pronaus zur Homilie. Ein Stück 'Liturgie' in jüngster Geschichte und pastoraler Gegenwart, Eichstätt-Wien 1990 (Extemporalia 8).

M. B. Merz, Gebetsformen der Liturgie, GdK 3, 97-130.

J. Pieper, Das Gedächtnis des Leibes. Von der erinnernden Kraft des Geschichtlich-Konkreten: W. Seidel (ed.), Kirche aus lebendigen Steinen, Mainz 1975, 68-83.

K. Rahner, Vom Hören und Sehen. Eine theologische Überlegung: W. Heinen (ed.): Bild-Wort-Symbol in der Theologie, Würzburg 1969, 139-156.

J. Schildenberger, Der Gedächtnischarakter des alt – und neutestamentlichen Pascha: B. Neunheuser (ed.), Opfer Christi und Opfer der Kirche, Düsseldorf 1960, 75-97.

K. Ware / E. Jungclaussen, Hinführung zum Herzensgebet, Freiburg i. Br. 1982.

2.6. MUSIC AND SONG IN THE LITURGY

2.6.1. MAN AS A SINGER AND MUSIC-MAKER

"Singing" is older than speaking. Long before a person can speak he expresses the state of his soul in songlike sounds. Music, however, in the real sense is a consciously willed and produced sound-event of sounds and tones with its own laws and logic, not merely amorphous sounds. But, despite its own rationality, music is primarily grasped emotionally as reflected in the German concept of a "musical mood". This primarily emotional perception does not at all mean that music is limited in its ability to convey a message. On the contrary: beyond the logically and grammatically correct spoken utterance the content which an utterance seeks to communicate acquires its full force only through tonalities, rhythms and a graduated dynamic. The ability already possessed by an infant to express itself in sounds finds its perfection in music which has its own musical language. Combined with the spoken word, song represents for man the most comprehensive possibility of self-communication. [225]

This is the case too – though less clearly so than for the song – in the so-called "song without words", for the melody of an instrument or an orchestra. The more developed the repertoire of the musical language of a culture, the more developed and systematised the laws of harmony, the clearer the expressive content of certain sound modules, then the clearer is the expression of the non-verbal forms of music, the more a purely instrumental music can communicate a truth which is less well expressed in words.

In all ages music and song have been used as means of cultic expression. The beauty of music is believed to be particularly effective in swaying the gods or good spirits while its loudness effective in driving out demons. But the God of Israel does not allow

---

[225] Cf. Harnoncourt, Terminologische und grundsätzliche Fragen: GdK III, 134f.

himself to be beguiled or exorcised by music or noise. Nevertheless, music plays an important role in the cult of the people of the Old Covenant, primarily as song, be this purely vocal or with instrumental accompaniment. Man articulates his experience of salvation in sung praise, he proclaims this in song to his fellowman and directs his sung praise to God. Music and song also have the qualities of an eschatological sign. For this reason they play an important role in the Temple which is seen as the image of heaven. [226]

2.6.2. THE HISTORY OF MUSIC AND SONG IN THE CHRISTIAN LITURGY

The thesis, once widespread, that the earliest Churches adopted the singing of the psalms from the synagogue, which in turn had taken it from the Temple after its destruction, is increasingly called in question. "Christian psalmody would appear to have its roots not in Jewish practice but in the practice, right from the beginning in Christian liturgies of the word, of singing – in keeping with their literary character – the passages from the book of psalms that occurred in the readings from the prophets." [227] The singing of hymns, doxologies and acclamations at early Christian worship can be presumed. [228] Antiphonal singing, (between choir and congregation or between two choirs) and responsorial singing (between cantor and choir or congregation where a set verse is sung between psalm-verses sung by the cantor) are part of the early Christian patrimony. Generally, though, music had a low profile in the ancient Church. Indeed, music tended to be rejected, on the one hand for an ascetically scepticism regarding the "sensual" delight in music, [229] on the other in contradistinction to the music, especially instrumental music, of pagan cults. "Nothing is left us of the music of the early Christian liturgy. The assumption that Gregorian chant has preserved certain melodies which go back to the early Church, or indeed that by comparing Gregorian melodies with chants of the Eastern rites and the chants of the synagogues of the Jewish diaspora in the East, the song of the oldest Church in Jerusalem can be reconstructed, has shown itself to be untenable." [230]

The assumption too that Gregory the Great (d. 604) is the author or editor of Gregorian chant cannot be scientifically demonstrated. "Only the following facts can be proved: the liturgical chants of the Roman liturgy at the time of Gregory the Great were not identical with we call "Gregorian Chant" today. It is certain that an independent musical repertoire, described by modern scholarship as "old Roman", preceded Gregorian chant. This "old Roman chant" is shown to be the precursor of Gregorian chant. Even though there is no absolute certainty about when and where old Roman chant was

---

[226] Cf. Harnoncourt, Die religiöse Bedeutung von Musik and Gesang: GdK III, 138-143.

[227] Cf. Fischer, Psalmen: GdK III, 181 citing J. A. Smith, The ancient Synagogue, the Early Christian Church and Singing: Music and Letters 65 (1984) 1-16.

[228] Cf. H. Musch, Entwicklung und Entfaltung der christlichen Kultmusik des Abendlandes: ibid. (ed.), Musik im Gottesdienst I, 9-97. 11f.; H.B. Meyer: Singen und Musizieren im Neuen Testament: GdK III, 143-146.

[229] Cf. Augustine, Conf. 10,33 - CChr.SL 27,181f., in which Augustine fears that too great a care for correct singing of the psalms could lead to sin because music belongs to the "joys of the flesh".

[230] Hucke, Geschichtlicher Überblick: GdK III, 147.

transformed into Gregorian, there are good grounds to suggest that this happened in the eighth century in the region between the Seine and the Rhine (Metz?)." [231]

In the ninth century a system of musical notation, was developed to record in writing the received oral tradition for the cantor; these so-called "neumes" did not present set melodies but were more in the nature of an interpretative shorthand for the improvising singer. In contrast to these original nuemes which were not written on a line, stave notation invented by Guido of Arezzo around the year 1020 made possible for the first time both an accurate indication of musical intervals and the transmission of melodies. [232] Again, the first evidence of the system of eight Church modes or psalm-tones (to which is added the so-called *tonus peregrinus*), a system which has remained in use throughout the whole of the musical history of the West, is found in Frankish sources from the ninth century. [233]

An increasingly artistically demanding polyphony led to the separation of liturgy and music. In the thirteenth century during the "Notre Dame era", whose chief masters were Leonin and Perotin, the polyphonic motet developed out of the earlier *organum*. Departure from the plainchant melodies and the change to French, made these compositions the basis of secular motets. [234] Subsequently the *ars antiqua*, roughly between 1250 and 1310, and the "ars nova" c.1310 to 1377 became increasingly sophisticated and in the process separated itself from liturgical structure. This resulted in Pope John XXII's condemnation of excesses in his constitution, *Docta Sanctorum Patrum* of 1324 which demanded a return to a close liaison with the liturgy. But musical development could not be halted and faced with this the Church gave up the struggle and retreated to its own liturgical forms. With the *Rationale* of Durandus came the parallel reading or praying by the priest of the texts sung by the schola. In future this reading and praying by the priest was to be the only "valid" recital of the text. "Thus was established a relationship between Catholic church music and liturgy which is unique among all denominations and cultures and with it the underlying problem of Catholic church music in the history of music in the West. Music and the performance of the liturgy were separated from each other. From being one of the elements of the liturgy, music became an ornamentation." Durandus' regulation showed that the first parts of the liturgy to be affected were those that remained the same, the Ordinary of the Mass (*ordinarium Missae*) already musically stylised. The performance of the ordinary "from now on largely replaced the chants of a specific Mass, the Proper of the Mass (*proprium Missae*)". [235] The Ordinary of the Mass as a compilation of settings of the Kyrie, Gloria, Sanctus and Agnus Dei – later joined by the Credo – became one of the most important foundations of the composer's art which at this time was shifting from France to England and the Netherlands. The price of this was separation from the liturgical action and relegation of the worshippers, who once upon a time had been a singing congregation, to the role of listeners.

---

[231] L.Agustoni, Gregorianischer Choral: H. Musch (ed.), Musik und Gottesdienst. Vol.1: Historische Grundlagen, Liturgik, Liturgiegesang, Regensburg 4th ed. 1993, 199-356.212.
[232] Cf. Hucke, Geschichtlicher Überblick: GdK III,148f.
[233] Cf. Hucke, Gesangsvortrag der Psalmen: GdK III, 186.
[234] Cf. examples of notation in Musch, Entwicklung und Entfaltung 26.
[235] Hucke, Geschichtliche Überblick: GdK III, 151.

Even before the Council of Trent this divorce was criticised by Catholic humanists and reformist theologians.[236] But this separation was already so far advanced that the Council of Trent did not deal with music in the context of the liturgy but in that of the house of God, the holiness of which was to be safeguarded by the exclusion of anything "lascivum aut impurum". This was complemented in 1562 by the prohibition from March 1563 of "worldly music". More important were the standardisation, also in 1562, of liturgical texts, the radical pruning of tropes and sequences as well as the definition of the Council's understanding of church music as an "ornament of worship". There is a kernel of truth to legend that with his "Missa Papae Marcelli", Palesrtrina saved polyphony, which it was proposed to abolish completely, by successfully demonstrating that the traditional art of composition could be reconciled with comprehensibility of the text.[237]

In early Protestantism the vernacular hymn was quickly able to assert itself. Models for such hymns existed in the pre-Reformation period as in the German *Leisen*, short, four-line songs ending in *Kyrie eleison*. Many new compositions were added to those adopted from existing sources: Martin Luther is recognised today as having personally written thirty-six hymns.[238] In the 1520s alone several hymn-books appeared. While Zwingli banned music completely from the liturgy, Calvin permitted community singing in unison, but only of the biblical psalter adapted for this purpose. In 1542, *La forme des Priéres et Chants ecclésiastiques* appeared in Geneva, containing thirty-nine psalm-hymns of which thirty-two were composed by Clément Marot (1495-1544) a well-known poet at the French court. After Morot's death, Theodore Beza continued the adaptation of the psalms, so that by 1562 the Genevan singing-psalter was completed.[239] This rhyming psalter was translated into German by Ambrose Lobwasser (Leipzig 1573), who preserved the speech-rhythms and the melodies of the original. The success of the hymn in Protestantism provoked an inevitable Catholic response. There appeared as early as 1537 a hymn-book by the Dominican, Michael Vehe. This was followed in 1567 by Johann Leisentritt's "Spiritual Songs and Psalms", and in 1582 by Caspar Ulenberg's "Psalms of David", presented in the manner of the Genevan rhyming-psalter. The golden age of Baroque hymn-writing produced the Protestant pastor Paul Gerhard (1607-1676) as well as the Jesuit priest, Friedrich Spee von Langenfeldt (1591-1635) and Angelus Silesius (Johann Scheffler 1624-1677). But hymns were just as little a part of official Catholic liturgical song as were the ever-expanding and more complicated works of the Composers: all were indeed beautiful but a not absolutely necessary ornamental adjunct to a liturgy which had become the affair of the priest alone. In contrast, within Protestantism the hymn reached its apogee in the "Spiritual Concerts" of composers such as Johann Hermann Schein (1586-1630), Heinrich Schütz (1585-1672) or, finally, in the oratorios of J.S.Bach (1685-1750).

The "Roman School" originating with Palestrina continued as a "strict style" but was not the only canon. The Netherlands School produced Orlando di Lasso, the Vene-

---

[236] Erasmus already speaks about the "recitation of the text" by means of church music and urged in his tract "De amabili Ecclesiae concordia" Opera V, 503 B – that church music should not be independent of the liturgical action.

[237] Cf. Hucke, Geschichtlicher Überblick: GdK III, 154; Musch, Entwicklung und Entfaltung 34f.

[238] Cf. B. Schmidt, Deutscher Liturgiegesang: H. Musch (ed.): Musik und Gottesdienst. Vol.1: Historische Grundlagen, Liturgik, Liturgiegesang, Regensburg 4th ed. 1993, 357-474.372.

[239] Cf. Albrecht, Einführung in die Hymnologie 26f.

tian school from Ludovico Grossi da Viadana to Andrea and Giovanni Gabrieli, by the introduction of several choirs, and a sense for new sounds in the use of trumpets, trombones, violins and violas, bass- and keyboard-instruments, prepared the way for the concert type of church music of the Baroque period. This development affected all categories of church music, both those that despite the effective divorce retained some connection with the liturgy, as well as other types of "spiritual music" such as oratorios and religious concerti which had no connection at all with the liturgical structures. Even the psalms of the Liturgy of the Hours were set to this kind of music. As early as the fifteenth century polyphonic improvisations on the eight psalm modes *falsibordoni* had developed and these were sung most usually at festive Vespers. About the year 1550, Adrian Willaert, choir-master at St Mark's in Venice, composed psalm-settings for four voices which developed in the seventeenth and eighteenth centuries into polyphonic settings of Vespers and the psalms of Vespers. The Magnificat always had a special place in these settings. [240]

Church music became something which happened parallel to the liturgy, "a medium through which a static, unchangeable liturgy could be adapted to different needs and circumstances. It became a more an instrument of courtly or bourgeois show than of the Church's presentation of itself. The celebration of the liturgy largely took on the character of a musical event, becoming one of the origins of the public concert." [241] The liturgy became "a sacred spectacle, complete with all the artifice of music. The choir and the organ were for the most part transferred from the sanctuary to the west gallery at the opposite end of the church. The liturgical action and the musical programme became two separate events between which the only roles left to the congregation were those of looking and listening. Later, at the beginning of the eighteenth century, the Neapolitan School, whose most distinguishing feature is the opera, gained a profound influence on the formal structure of church music." This view corresponded with the Church's attempts to regulate matters. These were limited to the requirement that only liturgical texts, or at least texts approved by the Church, be used, to the prohibition of certain instruments associated with the theatre as well as the use of instruments at all during Lent and periods of mourning. "As pictures and statues were covered as a sign of mourning, so music was to do without the ornamentation of instruments." [242] The Vienna School of classical music and with it its style of church music developed directly form the Mannheim School. [243] The Masses of Mozart, Haydn and Beethoven were mostly commissioned by the ecclesiastical princes of the period. These continued to meet the received requirements of church music, as did the great reverberation of symphonic church music in the nineteenth century from Franz Schubert to Anton Bruckner. [244]

In reaction to Baroque excesses, the Enlightenment encouraged simplicity, reasonableness and clarity in church music. With a new emphasis on the vernacular came a renewed appreciation of the hymn. Themes were divine majesty and goodness as well as the appropriateness of creation. So-called "hymns for singing at Mass" go back to the hymn-books of the Enlightenment. Rather like a series of devotions based on the Mass

---

[240] Cf. Hucke, Gesangsvortrag der Psalmen: GdK III, 187.
[241] Hucke, Geschichtlicher Überblick: GdK III, 156.
[242] Hucke, Geschichtlicher Überblick: GdK III, 158.
[243] Musch, Entwicklung und Entfaltung 57.
[244] Musch, Entwicklung und Entfaltung 59-64.

these chants were intended to be a contemplative accompaniment to the Latin liturgy celebrated by the priest. Since efforts to introduce the vernacular into the liturgy were unsuccessful the result was a linguistic dichotomy. The priest sang his part in Latin at the altar while during the sections of the Mass which were read silently in Latin, the congregation sang German hymns. This was possible since for a long time music had been only an ornament to [245] the liturgy and not an integral part of it.

The romantic ideal of "sacred music" (*musica sacra*) understood itself as opposing the development of church music to date as represented by the Vienna classical tradition, and up to the liturgical reforms of the Second Vatican Council was to play a part in the debate concerning the correct understanding of church and/or liturgical music. The romantic ideal understood "musica sacra" to be the Italian a cappella style, more precisely Roman polyphony of the sixteenth century represented above all by Palestrina. In 1868, the Regensburg priest, F.X.Witt, exploited the blossoming middle class growth in choirs to found the "General Caecilian Society", the aim of which was the cultivation and spread of this *musica sacra*. During the First Vatican Council the society won papal approval as a kind of Church sodality. Circumventing the bishops, the society reported to Rome on the state of church music: "From then on, church music in other lands became a concern of the Roman congregations". [246]

At exactly the same time the plain chant movement was spreading from the French Abbey of Solesmes. This movement regarded Gregorian chant as quintessentially the proper music of the Roman liturgy. It was based on research on the sources of the chant which had been initiated by Abbot Guéranger himself. Gregorian palaeography as a discipline was established by the appearance in 1889 of the first volume of the *Paléographie Musicale*. [247]

Pius X's *Motu proprio, Tra le sollecitudini* of 1903 became a kind of statute book for church music. [248] Originally intended to apply only to the diocese of Rome, the efforts of the founder of the Pontifical Institute for Sacred Music in Rome, Fr Angelo de Santi SJ, led to its being addressed to the whole Church. "Sacred music" was defined according to the criteria of "holiness", "excellence of form" and "universality". The ideal is Gregorian chant, but in classical vocal polyphony, specifically that of Palestrina, these criteria are also realised to the fullest. " 'Modern' church music is permissible when it is clearly distinct from 'profane' music. Since the church choir is actually fulfilling a clerical office, women may not be members. The use of instruments other than the organ is permitted only for special reasons and with special permission." [249] "This view of sacred music as the music of the church choir explains the maxim that the choir is to be the 'humble handmaid of the liturgy'. And with this is explained the concept of sacred music as ornament and embellishment, as indeed an 'essential part' but only of the 'solemn liturgy'. The subject of Pius X's *Instructio de Musica sacra* is not singing in the

---

[245] Cf. Hucke, Geschichtlicher Überblick: GdK III, 157.
[246] Cf. Hucke, Geschichtlicher Überblick: GdK III, 159f.
[247] Cf. Agustoni, Gregorianischer Choral 221.
[248] "Tra le sollecitudini": Acta Sanctae Sedis 36 (1903-1904) 329-339.
[249] Hucke, Geschichtlicher Überblick: GdK III, 161.

liturgy but the sacred music of the church choir and the conditions under which it can be admitted in liturgical actions." [250] In 1928, Pope Pius XI expressed similar views. [251]

The caecilian movement resisted attempts by the liturgical movement to renew church music, both in the form of "German plainchant", a combination of the "liturgical" melodies of Gegorian chant with vernacular texts, as well the "popular singing" movement which, in the perceived failure of the romantic and restorationist movements to provide any new impulses in hymnody, promoted for the so-called *Betsingmesse* hymns which were "close to the liturgy" and included material from the Protestant hymn tradition. [252]

2.6.3. MUSIC AFTER THE SECOND VATICAN COUNCIL

The Constitution on the Liturgy of the Second Vatican Council devoted a special chapter to church music (SC Ch VI, 112-121 *De sacra musica*). This stated that liturgical music, above all, "liturgical song connected with the word", forms "a necessary and integrating part of the solemn liturgy". "Thus, church music is all the holier, the closer it is connected to the liturgical action" (SC 112). Gregorian chant is indeed regarded by SC 116 "as the proper song of the Roman liturgy" and it "should have the first place in liturgical actions", but other forms of church music are in no way excluded when they are appropriate to "the spirit of the liturgy". In this regard reference is made to SC 30 where the active participation of all in the liturgy is mentioned. This goal of active participation is shared by SC 118 – promotion of religious songs for the people – and SC 119 – inculturation of liturgical music with that of the liturgy in the cultures of younger Churches.

The purpose of the instruction *Musicam sacram* of 5th March 1967 was the concretisation of the general instructions of the conciliar Constitution on the Liturgy. [253] Its title alone, *Instructio de Musica in Sacra Liturgia* compared with the title of an instruction from 1958, *De Musica sacra et Sacra Liturgia*, [254] is indicative of "a fundamental change compared with preconciliar regulations regarding church music: sacred music and the liturgy are now longer viewed as two parallel entities. The term *musica sacra* is completely avoided in the title and in used the text only sparingly and in a narrower sense than hitherto." [255]

The Constitution of the Liturgy does indeed use the term *musica sacra*, but understands it completely differently from what is meant in Pius X's instruction. In the latter, church music is seen as more ecclesiastical and liturgical to the extent to which it approaches the ideal of Gregorian chant in structure, spirit and mood. In SC 112, *musica sacra* is "holier, the closer it is connected with the liturgical action". According to SC 30 singing in the liturgy is an expression of active participation. Already in the Liturgy Constitution the change in understanding has taken place: music is not a beau-

---

[250] Hucke, Instruktion 125f.

[251] Apostolic Constitution "Divini cultus sanctitatem" of 20th December 1928 – AAS 21 (1929) 33-41, Cf. Hucke, Instruktion 126.

[252] According to Hucke, Geschichtlicher Überblick, GdK III,161f., this opposition was intensified after the Second World War. It was expressed in two different journals of church music, "Musik und Altar" and "Musica Sacra", the organ of the Caecilian Society.

[253] Kaczynski 733-801.

[254] AAS 50 (1958) 630-663.

[255] Hucke, Instruktion 126.

tifying but dispensable ingredient of the solemn liturgy but, rather, a means of human expression and as such a natural medium of active participation. [256] The instruction *Musicam Sacram* confirms and strengthens this change: singing arises from the essence of the rites and from the structure of liturgical celebration – all parts which demand song ought to be sung. [257] No kind of church music is excluded when it serves the spirit of the liturgical action and does not prevent the proper active participation by the people. [258] Music and song are not longer thought of as an ornament for the solemn liturgy; genuine solemnity does not consist in extravagant song and ceremonial, but in a celebration of the liturgy which is in keeping with its nature. [259]

Not least on the basis of SC 112 (*Cantus sacer qui verbis inhaeret*) there remains a certain preference for song over purely instrumental music in the presentation of a text in the liturgy. "The value and importance of music in Christian liturgy arise form the fact that it occurs essentially in the form of song. Linked in this way with the words of the liturgy, it forms with the text a necessary and integrating part of the solemn liturgy." [260] This means that while music undoubtedly extends man's possibilities of expression, what matters essentially is utterance which can be grasped in language, in this case the presentation of the liturgical text. [261] Neither in the East nor the West have the relations of the church music tradition with instrumental music been unproblematic. The Eastern church to this day has no instruments in church and bases this on the necessary "conformity with reason" of Christian worship: "Is it not immediately obvious that these sounds – of instrumental music – are of their nature too removed from the clarity, from the 'conformity with reason' from the Logos character, from the spiritual liturgy of the Orthodox church, for their art to be appropriately usable?" [262] Organ chorales, which under J.S.Bach reached a height never to be repeated, are a special case. Even without a text, the recurring melodies of the chorale reminds the listener of the original hymn-text, whose content and linguistic peculiarities are still underlined non verbally by the appropriate musical variations and inventions and in doing so can intensify the hearer's prayerful appropriation of the text.

Despite all that has been achieved, there is much that could be wished for, for example, a greater attempt to provide liturgical music for the changeable parts of the Mass such as the Introit, Offertory and Communion – traditionally called the "Proper". Again, there is a need for new Ordinaries of the Mass which the congregation could sing in alternation with a schola or a mixed-voice choir. The constant dwindling of the knowledge of Latin, among clerics as much as among the laity, along with the growing distance from it of contemporary musical culture, makes the great esteem in which SC 116 holds Gregorian chant increasingly unrealistic and the chant itself to appear more and more as an exotic museum-piece. It is still the case that on great feast-days church

---

[256] Cf. ibid. 127.

[257] No. 7 – Kaczynski 739.

[258] No. 9 – Kaczynski 741.

[259] No. 11 – Kaczynski 743.

[260] E. Jaschinski, Musik im Gottesdienst – mehr als Textvollzug? Zu einer Formulierung im Artikel 112 der Liturgiekonsititution, HlD 45 (1991) 132-144. 136f.

[261] B. M. Huijbers also speaks of a dominace by the text in post-Vatican II church music: Liturgische Musik nach dem Zweiten Vatikanischen Konzil, Concilium 16 (1980) 143-148.

[262] P. Florenskij, Die Ikonostase. Urbild und Grenzerlebnis im revolutionären Rußland. Mit einer Einführung von U. Werner, Stuttgart 2nd edn. 1988, 109f.

choirs see themselves honour-bound to "perform" a Mass, usually from the Viennese classical repertoire, and in doing so depriving the congregation of its rights, contrary to the clear directions of the Vatican Council. In countries with a strong hymn-singing tradition the lack of convincing Ordinaries of the Mass leads to a situation where these parts of the Mass – Gloria, Creed, Sanctus, and Agnus Dei – are not sung as they are written but are replaced by hymns with similar texts or at best texts that recall these chants.

The furthering of liturgical singing of the psalms by the congregation, especially the responsorial psalm at Mass, remains a great challenge. As early as 1952 J. Gelineau presented an arrangement of the psalter dividing the psalms into metrical – and thus singable – strophes. This project was specifically intended for the responsorial singing of the psalms, a cantor singing the strophes and the congregation answering with a repeated verse. All new projects of this kind have in common that they stick to the principle of generally applicable psalm-tones and do not take the further step of providing a musical setting for each individual psalm, by which this psalm would be recognisable. [263]

As heretofore, the problem of the musical and liturgical quality of so-called "new religious songs" and of the use of contemporary popular rhythms in worship, remains unresolved. Remaining annoyances have much to do with the general crisis in bourgeois musical culture, not least with the fact that this culture, wherever it did exist, no longer exists in the way it did. "The new sounds intrude themselves into worship against the background of the youth protest movement, but, as a new type of music, have not found a place of their own. Rather, this new music has simply adapted itself to the role of the traditional hymns and chants of the Mass and, in doing so, merely stylised worship in a new musical idiom." [264] Without wishing to pay homage to an abandoned ideal of "sacred music", the fundamental question must be asked of the extent to which, in the context of the liturgy, a qualitative yard-stick can be applied to contemporary singing and listening habits, particularly when music and song are not intended to be optional ornaments, but and integral part of that liturgy.

2.6.4. INSTRUMENTS FOR LITURGICAL MUSIC

"In the Latin Church, the pipe-organ is to be held in high esteem as the traditional musical instrument." Other instruments may be permitted, "so long as they are suitable for a sacred use, or can be made suitable; are appropriate to the dignity of the house of God and truly promote the edification of the faithful". [265]

The tradition of the pipe organ in the Latin church goes back to the organ received by Charlemagne as a present from Byzantium. The organ as an instrument for use in church spread from the Imperial chapel. Since the playing of liturgical melodies on the organ was regarded as the equivalent of song, this was able to replace the second choir in antiphonal singing. [266]

---

[263] Cf. Hucke, Gesangsvortrag der Psalmen: GdK III, 188.
[264] Hucke, Geschichtlicher Überblick: GdK III, 163f.
[265] SC 120. The same Constitution mentions the necessary adaptation of the liturgy to the different cultures: SC 22 §§2,37,40.
[266] Hucke, Geschichtlicher Überbllick: GdK III, 151.

The organ achieved its first peak of technical and – e.g. in the variety of tonal colour and overtones – artistic development, in the first half of the eighteenth century: a peak, in the opinion of some, never equalled since. Among the great organ-builders were, in the North German-Danish area, Arp Schnitker and in Saxony, south Germany and Alsace, the Silbermann family. In the nineteenth century the organ was equipped not only with technical aids such as pneumatic tracker action and crescendo roller – regarded critically today – but was considered less as an instrument in its own right than as a complex apparatus for imitating other instruments or groups of instruments: e.g. the organ was equipped with a "strings" stop or a "cello" stop etc. The organ became a concert-organ for light music, an electronic organ and a synthesizer. The Organ Reform movement, mainly a German Protestant phenomenon, uncompromisingly regarded the Baroque organ as the only genuine way back to the real instrument. Against this, other well-known traditions of organ-building, such as that of the Parisian Aristide Cavaillé-Coll (1811-1899) are once more being recognised. This recognition is based not least on the principle that music of a particular period should be played on instruments of the period. [267]

At the height of the flowering of Baroque instrumental music in the Church, Benedict XIV in his encyclical *Annus qui* on 19th February 1748, emphasised that apart from the organ only those instruments were permitted that supported the voice but did not drown it. Several instruments, such as trumpets, flutes and oboes which did not meet this criterion were forbidden for use in church music. How ineffective such prohibitions were is evident not only from the fact that it was precisely these instruments that played a prominent part in the compositions of the Viennese classical school, but also that it was necessary frequently to re-iterate them, the last such being issued by Pius X. [268]

In a wider sense of the term "instruments", can be included bells and hand-bells. These were rejected along with music and musical instruments by the early Christians because of their use in pagan cults and because of apotropaic connotations – association with warding off of evil spirits. But from the fourth century, particularly in monasteries, the use of bells – and of the sounding-board or *simandron* still used in Orthodox monasteries – for giving signals and as an extra-liturgical means of summoning individuals or groups was accepted. After this it was only a small step to the use of bells as a signal for the start of the liturgy. But peals of church-bells are not attested to before the 7th century. The greater the peal, the more was developed, especially in monasteries, a fixed order for ringing the bigger and smaller bells on particular feasts and occasions. Apotropaic notions, as in the ringing of bells to ward of lightning, survived until modern time. The altar-bell or gong [269] developed in the context of Eucharistic piety as it emerged in the high Middle Ages, the focus of which was a gazing on the sacred elements. The ringing of a church bell, or, derived from this, of a smaller bell at the altar, emphasised the special moments during which the elements were displayed – the Elevation at the consecration of the Mass or at Benediction of the Blessed Sacrament. The hand-bell also drew attention to the presence of the Blessed Sacrament during the public carrying of communion to the sick or as Viaticum. [270]

---

[267] On the history of the organ and organ-bulding, particularly in the 19th and 20th centuries, cf.Klotz 159f.
[268] Cf. Eisenhofer I, 250.
[269] Cf. J. Braun, Das christliche Altargerät in seinem Sein und in seiner Entwicklung, Munich 1932, 573-580.
[270] Eisenhofer I, 394 quotes a regulation of the Synod of Exeter in 1287: "Campanella deferenda ad infirmos

2.6.5. LITURGICAL MUSIC OF THE BYZANTINE CHURCH

Apart from a few exceptions that prove the rule, musical instruments are not used in the Churches of the Byzantine Rite. This is a common inheritance from the ancient Church but otherwise the styles of singing in the individual Churches have developed in extremely different ways according to cultural circumstances. Other factors are that the East, unlike the West, did not develop a system of neumes or musical notation and that music and song, rather than being considered a cultural inheritance to be preserved, live essentially as performed. On the other hand, the tenacity of tradition permits contemporary Greek song to be traced back with some certainty to the middle – or indeed late-Byzantine song of the tenth to the fourteenth centuries. Byzantine music is based on eight Church tones which possibly originate in Syria. This music has chromatic scales which are possibly of even more ancient origin. "The octaves are not divided into twelve (semitones) but into 68 parts; thus there are intervals of 5, 7,9, 12 or 18 such parts. Singing is always in unison." [271] The spread of Greek Christianity brought with it Byzantine church music to the Balkan countries. In modern times, however, the liturgical music of these Slav-speaking peoples, the Serbs, Bulgarians and Macedonians, who worship in Church Slavonic, has been influenced by the polyphonic developments in Russian church music.

The music of the Russian Church is the one that has distanced itself most from its Byzantine origins, and although it is precisely the music that is most strongly influenced by Western music, it is regarded by many as the quintessential "Orthodox church music". The oldest Russian church music is the unison "neumatic chant" with the eight church tones and a form of neume script. Kiev led the way in musical development and it was from there that spread not only an easily-learned "Kiev chant", but polyphony too, since the middle of the seventeenth century. Kiev chant itself was sung in unison but the development of polyphony was influenced from Poland. Ukrainians had contacts via Poland with Western music and, via Cracow, learned polyphony and the use of several choirs. Finally. "they adopted the colossal Roman style and made an immeasurable impression on the faithful of Moscow with their liturgies and vigils for 24, 36 and even 48 voices". [272] The great choirs sang in the Ukrainian-Polish-Venetian style until 1736 when composers of the Italian late Baroque and Rococo came to St Petersburg as directors of the Imperial court chapel and influenced church music. One of their most important pupils was D.S.Bortnianski (1751-1825), whose successor A.Lvov (1798-1870) was also clearly influenced by German Romanticism. To Lvov is due the credit of saving Russian chant from collapse by providing it with a thorough-going harmonisation loosely based on imitation of Kiev polyphony of the seventeenth century. Towards the end of the nineteenth century two opposing schools were formed. The St Petersburg school of the "strict stylists" continued Lvov's polyphonic work. The Moscow school had a strong national accent, was freer in methods of composition and open to new discoveries. [273] In the standstill following the Revolution, it was traditional church music

---

et ad elevationem corporis Christi." On bells and altar-bells generally cf. Eisenhofer I, 387-396; H.B. Meyer, Türme und Glocken: GdK III, 383f.
[271] Totzke 214.
[272] Totzke 226.
[273] Cf. Totzke 228f.

above all that was fostered, "but there were and are signs of talents among those in exile – for example Stravinsky in America – which give grounds for hope in a continued further development". [274]

Bibliography

C. Albrecht, Einführung in die Hymnologie, Göttingen 2nd edn. 1984.

K. G. Fellerer (Hg.): Geschichte der katholischen Kirchenmusik, 2 vols., Kassel 1972/76.

Ph. Harnoncourt, Terminologie und grundsätzliche Fragen: R. Berger / K. H. Bieritz and others, GdK 3: Gestalt des Gottesdienstes, Regensburg 2nd edn. 1990, 132-138.

Ph. Harnoncourt, Die religiöse Bedeutung von Musik und Gesang: GdK 3, 138-146.

H. Hucke, Bulletin zur Instruktion über die Musik, Concilium (D) 4 (1968) 125-133.

E. Jaschinski / R. Pacik, Aussagen kirchlicher Dokumente zu Musik und Gesang im Gottesdienst: H. Musch (ed.), Musik und Gottesdienst 1, 165-198.

H. Klotz, Das Buch von der Orgel, Kassel 10th edn.1988.

H. Musch (ed.), Musik und Gottesdienst. Vol. 1: Historische Grundlagen, Liturgik, Liturgiegesang, Regensburg 4th edn. 1993.

H. Schützeichel (ed.): Die Messe. Ein kirchenmusikalisches Handbuch, Düsseldorf 1991.

I. Totzke, Die Musik der Orthodoxen Kirche: HOK II, Düsseldorf 1989, 211-235.

2.7. LITURGICAL DRESS

2.7.1. MODES OF HUMAN APPEARANCE

"The possibilities of expression of the (bodily) form, its contours, positions and movements, are enriched by clothing. Folds, colour, decoration and the relation of individual parts of a garment to each other create new forms. The shape and movement of the body are emphasized and further developed in myriad ways." [275] "From ancient times, man's clothing means more to him than a mere burdensome cover, and the attempt to explain the origin of clothing purely from the need for protection against a hostile climate or primitive feelings of shame, can be shown from closer ethnographical examination to be mistaken." [276]

In direct contradistinction to clothing as man's mode of self-presentation in general and to cultic garments in particular is the practice of cultic nakedness as an expression of penance. [277] This nakedness of the flesh contrasts with the spiritual clothing of man in Paradise, who, despite his lack of clothing, was not naked but had a wonderful garment in the form of the grace of God. Man, inheritor of Original Sin, became really naked only with the interruption of his life-giving and divinising communication with uncreated grace. Accordingly, nakedness is a theological phenomenon: man alienated from and cut off from life-giving and life-preserving communication with the living God, is

---

[274] Totzke 230.
[275] Guardini, Liturgische Bildung 34f.
[276] G. Raudszus, Die Zeichensprache der Kleidung. Untersuchung zur Symbolik des Gewandes in der deutschen Epik des Mittelalters, Hildesheim-Zurich-New York 1985, 1. On this cf. also F. Kiener, Kleidung, Mode und Mensch. Versuch einer psychologischen Deutung, München-Basel 1956, 49-67; R. König, Menschheit auf dem Laufsteg. Die Mode im Zivilisationsprozeß, München 1985, 127-147.
[277] Cf. Berger, Liturgische Gewänder und Insignien 315f.

"basar", as "corruptible flesh". [278] He is one stripped of every hope of fulfillment. This spiritual nakedness as an experience of oneself as affected by Original Sin, as "corruptible flesh", is what first causes the shame of nakedness, the shame in the face of God, of other people and even oneself.

This shame is alleviated by clothing. [279] As decoration it lends the person a self-made glory which is intended to conceal this theological nakedness but which can never be anything other than a pale reminder of the lost glory of the spiritual garment of grace. "In short, the clothes that fallen man wears are a relic of the lost garment that he wore in Paradise. This is so much a living reminder, that every alteration and renewal of fashion which we willingly accept because it promises us a new insight into our understanding of ourselves, only awakens a longing for that lost garment which alone can give meaning to what we really are, which alone can make our "dignity" visible." [280]

2.7.2. PUTTING ON CHRIST

The New Testament uses clothing as a symbol. It stands for the human under its new quality acquired through belief in Christ. It is not a "cultic garment" but an expression of the living communication with the living God which has been made possible once more by Christ.

The garment is a sign of the new gift of grace conferred by Baptism, which far surpasses the original. Christ himself is "put on" (Gal 3.27). Paul speaks of putting on an "over-garment" which signifies life, in contrast to a "stripping", which signifies a degeneration into a mere fleshly glory, a glory sentenced to death (2Cor 5.14). [281] Thus the garment, the means by which man satisfies his need to bedeck himself and to cover his body, becomes a means of expressing the new reality of faith, the draping of corruptible flesh with life, the regaining of the original garment of uncreated grace which is God himself. The phenomenon of man decorating himself and giving a fleshy glory to the body, receives its final theological intensity in the baptismal robe and in liturgical vestments. The monastic habit is also seen in terms of the baptismal robe and with it as a "putting on" of Christ. [282]

If a garment is so rich in symbolism how can it be explained that the symbolism of the baptismal garment could become peripheral? How can the development of liturgical vestments be assessed? Originally the clergy simply used festive secular clothes and it was only at a period of significant change in fashion – involving the adoption of Germanic breeches - that they retained the old Roman garments, at least in litur-

---

[278] Cf. N.P. Bratsiotis: Art. "Basar": ThWAT I, 850-867; F.Baumgärtel / E.Schweizer: Art. "Sarx", "sarkikos": ThWNT VII. Stuttgart 1964, B: Fleisch im alten Testament, 105-109.

[279] Cf. Augustine, Sermo 46,6 – CChr SL 41,553: Vestimentum bene intelligitur in honorem, quia nuditatem contegit. Est enim unusquisque homo infirmus." Cf. H. Niehr: Art. "Ärom"/'Arom": ThWAT VI, 376-380; A. Oepke: Art. "gymnos" etc.: ThWNT I. Stuttgart 1933, 773-775.774 points out the "damned are often depicted as naked."

[280] Peterson, Theologie des Kleides 352f. Of fashion as an "expression of fantasy" which attempts to make utopias real, cf. E. Wilson, In Träume gehüllt. Mode und Modernität, Hamburg 1989, 259-261.

[281] Cf. Haulotte 210-233: La formule paulinienne: "Revêtir le Christ".

[282] Cf. Ph. Oppenheim, Das Mönchskleid im christlichen Altertum, Freiburg i. Br. 1931, 248. O. Heggelbacher: Entwicklung geistlicher Kleidung in frühchristlicher Zeit und ihre treibenden Kräfte: A. Hierold and others. (eds.), Die Kraft der Hoffnung. Gemeinde und Evangelium (FS J. Schneider), Bamberg 1986, 98-107.

gical celebrations. In this way, these became for the first time specifically "liturgical vestments", complemented by civil insignia as a sign of ordination.[283]

While the ranks of white-clad newly-baptized still played a great part in the Easter liturgy of the community in the ancient Church, in the baptism of infants there came to be no longer any actual clothing of the newly-baptized but merely the placing on him of a small cloth or a bonnet, largely to justify the accompanying formula.[284] For the most part, the renewed liturgy has retained this practice. Perhaps the initiation of adults with which the congregation is involved and have an active role in accompanying the whole process of the cathechumenate, will restore to the baptismal robe the significance and dignity it once had in the ancient Church.[285]

Evidence from the Fathers of the Church[286] permit the conclusion that early on the custom had been formed of reserving festive clothes for the celebration of the liturgy – and this not just by the clergy but by all participants – thus "sacralizing" these garments, even if their style was no different from usual festive attire.[287] The extent to which this sense of the sacred last up to modern times is indicated by the terms "Holy Communion dress" or "church coat", particularly in Protestant regions: feast-day clothes were associated with the liturgy; even on a wedding-day it was never permitted to dance in one's "Holy Communion dress".[288]

2.7.3. LITURGICAL VESTURE

The retention of the clothing of late antiquity, during the changes brought about by the great migrations, led to the development of the liturgical vestments still current today.

It is likely that the new fashion of breeches, lacking as the latter did the character of a robe, was not regarded as a suitable expression of man's being wrapped around with divine glory. For this reason the retention of late antique garments was probably less a matter of chance than might appear at first sight.

The ancient undergarment, the tunic (*tunica*) became the Western alb, the name reflecting its white colour, while in the East the tunic evolved into the Byzantine *sticharion*, which like the corresponding vestment in the other Eastern rites could be coloured. Both the alb and the *sticharion* were girded, the former with a linen *cingulum* or cincture, the latter with the *zone* a cloth belt in the colour of the outer vestment. In the West, the alb developed into the ungirded *superpelliceum*, or surplice, – a shortened

---

[283] Cf. Walafried Strabo, De reb. Eccl. 24 – PL 114, 952: "Primis temporibus communi indumento vestiti missas agebant." Roetzer, 92-94, maintains that this was still the case for Augustine. P. van der Meer is more cautious: Augustinus als Seelsorger. Leben und Wirken eines Kirchenvaters, Köln 2nd edn. 1953, 250f. On clothing in the early Christian period generally, cf. J. Wilpert, Die Gewandung der Christen in den ersten Jahrhunderten, Köln 1898. On the development as a whole cf. Berger, Liturgische Gewänder und Insignien: GdK 3, 309-346.

[284] Cf. B. Kleinheyer, Die Feiern der Eingliederung in die Kirche: GdK 7,1: Sakramentliche Feiern I, Regensburg 1989, 73,120.

[285] Cf. M. Kunzler, Zur heutigen Ordnung der Eingliederung von Erwachsenen, Jugendlichen und Schulkindern in die Kirche, Klerusblatt 72 (1992) 3-7.5.

[286] E.g. Clement of Alexandria, Paidagog. 3, 11 – PG 8, 658f.: Jerome, Comm. In Ez 44 – PL 24, 436f.

[287] Cf. Heggelbacher 101; E. Dassmann, Zur Entstehung von liturgischen Geräten und Gewändern. Vorbilder und Beweggründe, Schwarz auf Weiß 16,2 (1984) 16-30.18f.

[288] Cf. M. Bringemeier, Laienkleider und kirchliches Brauchtum: ibid.: Mode und Tracht. Beiträge zur geistesgeschichtlichen und volkskundlichen Kleidungsforschung, Münster 1980, 247-252.

or "cut-off" alb, hence the term *cotta* –, which in Winter was worn over furs for heat and which, along with the cassock, forms the modern choir-dress. [289]

The outer vestment of a priest is the chasuble. In the West, since the twelfth century, because of its exclusive use at the Eucharist, this became the Mass vestment, while the cope (*cappa*) was used for other liturgical services. In the East, the equivalent of the chasuble, the *phelonion*, besides being worn at the Divine Liturgy is used at many other services. The original form of both chasuble and *phelonion* is the *paenula*, a bell-shaped garment going back to the fifth century. The material in front was folded up over the arms, which, when the material was cut away, led to the modern Byzantine *phelonion*. In the West, the increasing use of heavier materials along with the growing elaboration of embroidered and applied motifs, led to the trimming of the garment to the extent that, by the end of the sixteenth century, it had been reduced to the not very becoming "fiddle-back" chasuble. [290] The full ancient chasuble had become little more than an apron or bib, which could no longer truly express the "putting on of the vesture of Christ" mentioned in the Letter to the Galatians (Gal 3:27). The liturgical movement re-discovered the ancient form of the chasuble and returned to the so-called "gothic" chasuble and even to the bell-shaped vestment. [291]

Originally deacons also wore the chasuble. In the fourth century when the dalmatic – originating as its name suggests in Dalmatia – became the garment of honour of the Roman deacons and of the Pope, it developed into the usual official vestments of deacons in general and into a garment worn under the chasuble by bishops in the West. To this day the Byzantine bishop instead of the chasuble or *phelonion* wears the *sakkos*, a vestment similar to the dalmatic.

Insignia of office originate in the rank markings of Roman officials and judges. The question of how these came to be attributed to the clergy has not been finally answered. [292] In addition to the insignia of bishops, the so-called *pontificalia*, the stole is now the most striking symbol of office. In the West, bishops and priests today wear the stole in the same way, while the Byzantine bishop in addition to the priest's *epitrachelion* – a stole with both sides sewn together, rather like a scapular – wears the *omophorion* which resembles the *pallium* worn in the West by the Pope and archbishops. The deacon's stole in the West corresponds to the Eastern *orarion*, both of which are worn like a scarf over the left shoulder, the orarion hanging straight over breast and back and reaching to the ground. Berger, "without entering into the complicated and in many ways still impenetrable development", asserts firmly, "with the *pallium*, *orarion*, stole and their Byzantine equivalents, we are dealing with symbols of honour, analagous to the *pallium discolorum* of the Theodosian clothing regulations, adopted in the ecclesiastical sphere at the end of the fourth century with imperial permission or at least toleration" [293].

Ancient dyeing techniques using purple – from the the secretions of the porphyra or purpura snail – with the addition of various minerals were able to produce a spectrum of colours ranging from red-satinized black, through purple violet and carmine red to

---

[289]   Cf. Braun, Gewandung 139-141.
[290]   Cf. Braun, Gewandung 190-200.
[291]   Cf. A. Flüeler, Paramente, Würzburg 2nd edn. 1955; ibid., Das sakrale Gewand, Würzburg 1964.
[292]   Cf. the presentation of the various opinions on this in: Berger, Gewänder und Insignien 322f.
[293]   Ibid. 325.

shades of green. The darker a garment, the more purple was need and thus the more precious the garment. Altered sense of colour as well as improved dyeing techniques led in the later Middle Ages to different customs. One of the first colour canons, that of Pope Innocent III in the twelfth century[294], was not yet obligatory; this came with the Missal of 1570. White was prescribed for feasts of the Lord and of saints other than martyrs, red for Pentecost, feasts of the Holy Cross and of Apostles and Martyrs, violet for Advent, Lent, Ember Days and Days of Intercession, green for ferial days, black for Good Friday and Requiems. In principle this scheme is still in operation but greater freedom in the choice of colour is now permitted (cf. GIRM 307-310). The East has no binding colour canon but, at least in Byzantine churches, the custom has grown up of wearing bright and precious colours on feast-days and reddish ones at liturgies of the dead. [295]

Unfortunately, in the course of time, the symbolic character of a garment in itself and its resulting value as a sign of liturgical expression were lost. In the Christian Church, too, the liturgical garment became a prescribed cultic vestment.

Vestments were explained mostly in the sense of what Kaczynski has rightly rejected as fantasy symbolism, [296] which is characterized by a certain allegorical arbitrariness. There a numerous examples of this since Carolingian times and it lasted right up to the twentieth century – for example, the amice represents the silence during the holy sacrifice, the sleeveless chasuble the priest's renunciation of freedom. [297] The allegorical explanation of the vestments was intended to illustrate the sacrifice of the Mass. The individual vestments "recall the individual phases of the Passion of Christ and, in the person of the priest, present the suffering Saviour to view. For this reason, it was undoubtedly very practical, by explaining the vestments in terms of, for example, the chains etc of the suffering Christ, to present the priest at the altar in an almost concrete fashion as what he really is according to the teaching of the Church, i.e. as Christ's deputy. As the representative of the God-man, the priest renews the sacrifice of the Cross in an unbloody manner. In addition, this was for the faithful the most easily understood presentation of the symbolism of liturgical vesture." [298]

However much the Lutheran and Reformed traditions were agreed in their rejection of the Mass as a sacrifice, their views on liturgical vesture varied greatly. For Luther, vestments were a matter of indifference in the truest sense – *adiaphora* – which would vanish as soon as people were sufficiently mature. [299] The retention or re-introduction of Catholic vestments in various Lutheran Churches was in opposition to or as a gesture of demarcation from the Reformed traditions. [300] Nevertheless, in Protestantism for the

---

[294] De s. altaris mysterio I, 65 - PL 217, 799-802.

[295] cf. Th. Schnitzler, Vom Sinn und Geschichte der liturgischen Gewandung und Färbung, Mün. 32 (1979) 98f.; W. Schöneis, Antike Färbung und liturgische Farben, LJ 8 (1958) 140-149.

[296] Cf, R. Kaczynski, Über Sinn und Bedeutung liturgischer Gewänder, Mün 32 (1979) 94-96.94.

[297] Cf. A. Franz, Die Messe im deutschen Mittelalter, Freiburg i. Br. 1902, reprinted Darmstadt 1963, 417, 586, 646, 680, 733-735. Cf. J. Brinktrine, Die heilige Messe in ihrem Werden und Wesen, Paderborn 1931, 44-48; A. Knauer, Unser Meßopfer, Mainz 1905. 328.

[298] Braun, Gewandung 705.

[299] Cf. H.B. Meyer, Luther und die Messe. Eine liturgiewissenschaftliche Untersuchung über das Verhältnis Luthers zum Meßwesen des späten Mittelalters, Paderborn 1965, 25; Piepkorn 114f.: "Welche liturgische Gewandung trug Martin Luther?"

[300] M. Bringemeier, Tunika – Sutane - Schaube – Talar, Priester – und Gelehrtenkleidung. Ein Beitrag zur geistesgeschichtlichen Kostümforschung – Münster 1974, 47; Piepkorn 44f.: Liturgical vesture in the

greater part, the preaching-gown derived from academic dress became the dominant liturgical garment. [301] According to Josuttis, the gown and bands, the academic dress of a preacher, along with the pews of the listeners, mark the Protestant liturgy as a class or lecture. [302]

After the Second Vatican Council, criticism of a one-sided "cultic" understanding of the liturgy was also directed against "cultic dress". This was reflected in a tendency in the post-conciliar period to reduce the amount of liturgical vesture and voices were not lacking that advocated its complete abolition. [303]

A liturgical vestment, though, cannot find its full significance as a cultic garment, but only as an expression of the human being who enters – anabatically – into communication with God in the celebration of the liturgy and in doing so includes his clothing as a means of expressing his personality. Clothing is also "riddled" by grace, which leads all being to its liturgical fulfillment, its participation in the mystery" of the divine fullness of life. [304] Man who stands in relationship with the living God experiences himself as someone clothed with divine love: "Because this life is higher than that for which ordinary reality provides opportunity or form of expression, it takes over the appropriate means and forms from the only area in which they are to be found, namely from art. This life speaks in measure and melody, it moves in solemn regulated gestures, it clothes itself in colours and vestments which do not belong to everyday life." [305]

This symbolism of clothing concerns all Christians before any distinctions arising from the Sacrament of Orders. All Christians share in the royal priesthood, with their baptismal robe all express the fact of their new creation in Christ and their priestly mediating task to bring their world into the life-giving exchange with God. This is the basis of the notion that all participants in the liturgy should have a liturgical garment. It is doubtful whether this could be some kind of "Sunday best"; the whole culture of festival is evaporating and with it the idea of festive clothes. Being "clothed with Christ" demands some other type of clothing which does not originate in the civil sphere. It is all the more important that this symbolism be adopted by the ordained and by the members of the laity who have undertaken a special ministry in the liturgy. Ordained and unordained share the common royal priesthood of all believers. All Christians are entitled to the baptismal robe as the liturgical garment of the royal priesthood, but only a few, as representatives of the whole community, wear it as a basic liturgical vestment to which the ordained ministers add their particular vestments and insignia. [306]

According to no.298 of the General Instruction of the Roman Missal (GIRM), the basic vestment common to all the ordained is the alb. This need no longer be girded

---

Lutheran Churches in Scandinavia and in the New World at the turn of the seventeenth century was seen as a protest and demarcation against Calvinism.

[301] Cf. Rietschel / P. Graff: Lehrbuch der Liturgik – Göttingen 2nd edn. 1951, 124.

[302] Cf. Josuttis 124.

[303] Cf. Kunzler, Indumentum Salutis 54-58. Cf. Th Schnitzler, Versuche liturgischer Deutung, 3rd part; Das liturgische Gewand, HlD 24 (1970) 148-150. 148: "Some progessive clerics think as follows when putting on vestments in the sacristy: 'Are we still doing this?', but the average believer when he sees the curate celebrating the school Mass with only the small sick-call stole asks in bemusement, "Already? Has it already come to this?"

[304] Cf. Evdokimov, L'Orthodoxie 202f.

[305] R. Guardini, Vom Geist der Liturgie, Herder-TB 1049, Freiburg-Basel-Vienna 1983, 101.

[306] Cf. P. Parsch: Heilige Gefäße und Gewänder. Vienna-Kosterneuburg-Leipzig (Klosterneuburger Hefte Nr. 26). 28.

and, further, the amice may be dispensed with. No.301 of the GIRM permits all laypersons assisting at the altar to wear "an appropriate garment". In this context the alb as
a reminder of the baptismal robe is greatly to be preferred to imitations of episcopal
choir-dress or of monastic habits. [307] The vestments and insignia appropriate to the rank
of the ordained are worn over the alb. The Missal of 1970 presumes that these will be
the traditional chasuble and dalmatic, even if GI 304 concedes to bishops' conferences
the right to adapt liturgical vesture in accordance with local customs. The chasuble is,
as before, the Mass-vestment *per se*, but may be worn in "liturgical celebrations connected with the Mass" (GIRM 299). In many parishes, though, the practice of wearing a
light-coloured tunic-alb with a stole of the appropriate liturgical colour for all liturgical
celebrations has become usual. [308] It is doubtful whether this fashion adequately fulfils
the function of liturgical vesture to highlight the festive character of the liturgy in colour
and form, according to the liturgical season and occasion (cf. GI 297 and 307).

Bibliography

R. Berger: Liturgische Gewänder und Insignien: R. Berger / K. H. Bieritz and others, GdK 3:
    Gestalt des Gottesdienstes, Regensburg 2nd edn. 1990, 309-347.

J. Braun, Die liturgische Gewandung im Occident und Orient nach Ursprung und Entwicklung,
    Verwendung und Symbolik. Freiburg i. Br. 1907, reprint Darmstadt 1964.

E. Haulotte, Symbolique du vêtement selon la Bible, Paris 1966.

M. Kunzler, Indumentum Salutis. Überlegungen zum liturgischen Gewand, ThGl 81 (1991) 52-
    78.

M. Kunzler, Porta Orientalis 568-597.

P. Parsch, Heilige Gefäße und Gewänder, Vienna / Klosterneuburg-Leipzig o.J. (Klosterneuburger
    Hefte 26).

E. Peterson, Theologie des Kleides, Benediktinische Monatsschrift 16 (1934) 347-356.

A. C. Piepkorn, Die liturgischen Gewänder in der lutherischen Kirche seit 1555, Lüdenscheid-
    Lobetal 1987 (Ökumen. Texte und Studien 32).

E. Trenkle, Liturgische Gewänder und Geräte der Ostkirche, München 1962.

2.8. THINGS: MATERIAL OBJECTS AS VEHICLES OF ANABATIC EXPRESSION

The material objects used in the liturgy are "not externals but expression"; in them, "the
hidden divine reality expresses itself and so makes it possible for the human person to
'interiorize' this reality by means of his senses". [309]

2.8.1. THE MATERIAL OBJECT AS A MEANS OF EXPRESSION IN THE LITURGY

A material object with which a man enters into relationship by, for example, taking
it in his hand, is an expression of his personality: "line and position of the members

---

[307] Cf. R. Kaczynski, Kein "Amtsträger"- Ersatz, Gd 15 (1981) 65-68.
[308] On the history of the development of this vestment, cf. Kunzler, Indumentum Salutis 55f.
[309] Berger, Naturelemente 255.

combine with the instrument. Form and movement of the member in question are thus strengthened. The expression of the offering hand is augmented when it is carrying a bowl; the force of a blow is increased as soon as it is made with a hammer." [310] The example of a musical instrument illustrates man's use of an object for self-expression: all would say of a musician that he himself plays the piano concerto, although the sound can be heard only because the hammers of the grand piano strike the appropriate strings correctly and at the right time. Seen in this light, the material objects which play a role in liturgical celebration must give expression to man in his relationship to the living God. The object itself is affected by this, it is "riddled" by uncreated grace [311] and gives a glimpse of the eschatological culmination of this world. Of itself an object does not possess this eschatological quality, which always distances from the everyday in form and purpose. It is not an object's artistic value which give it a certain "air".

By being brought into the process of communication with God, things of this world participate in the transfiguration and are thus distinguished from what belongs to the modest unfolding of a world removed from God. The technological coldness of neon light becomes the warm light of candles; polluted air is changed to the pleasant and "sacred" smoke of incense; a purely functional vessel for the satisfaction of the body's need for liquids becomes a precious chalice. Material things by their transfiguring inclusion in the liturgy show how all of creation can become the "sacrament" of God's nearness and love. It is from God that they receive their transparency as good things of creation, as signs of God's own loving nearness.

In the material reality of the human body of the Son made man, the Holy Trinity reaches out to creation in an unparalleled fashion which once and for all remains relevant for salvation. His body is the quintessential "holy place" in which God reveals himself and from which uncreated grace reaches out to man. This applies in another sense to the Church as the mystical body of Christ. God manifests himself in the community of the faithful, the "body of Christ", and it is from this community, from the community celebrating the liturgy, that uncreated grace flows as from a spring.

But this "material", bodily, reality of the community made up of people of body and soul expands to embrace material objects used by these people. These objects also participate in the divine/human nature of the Church as Christ's mystical body. Every action of the Church is determined by the two-fold nature of Christ, by two natures, two modes of action, two wills. Just as through the human nature of Christ, the Holy Spirit functions as the "imparter" of uncreated grace, so also in the epicletic prayer of the Church in the administration of the sacraments, but also through the epicletic blessing of material objects. This insight underlies Lossky's concept of symbol and with it the theology of the icon and of symbolics: it "is the basis of the cult of sacred images, which express the invisible reality visually and make it really present, visible and active. An icon, a cross, is not simply an artistic representation intended to direct our imaginative energy while we are praying; both are material foci containing an energy, a divine power, which unites itself with human art." [312]

---

[310] Guardini, Liturgische Bildung 34f.
[311] Cf. Evdokimov, L'Orthodoxie 202f.
[312] Lossky, Théol. myst. 184: "Les sacrements et les rites sacrés accomplis dans l'Église comporteront donc les deux volontés, deux opérations s'exerçant simultanément."

Thus, everything in the liturgy, natural elements, material objects such as liturgical vessels, incense, candles, but also word and song, has an iconographic character: "all are symbols in the realistic sense of the word, material signs of the presence of the spiritual world." This symbolism is constituted by anamnesis; the symbols act not just as mere reminders to the senses, but lead one into the mystery which is present here and now, the mystery whose presence it visibly points to: "The word *anamnesis* does not simply mean 'memory', it denotes much more an initiation into the mystery, the revelation of a reality, which is at all times present in the Church." [313]

Unless the things of this world are brought into relationship with God, they remain diabolically ambivalent. "Let us deepen our grasp of the complexity of meaning that water has in the liturgy. The blessing of water expresses its demonic ambiguity. Every individual has probably experienced water in its restless flow, swirling and gurgling, at once live-giving and life-taking, gentle and fierce, transparent and inscrutable at the same time, containing in itself, magic, allure, something deeply pagan, even evil. Whoever has not felt this, does not know what nature is. In the liturgy we experience the deeply problematic character of nature, the force of the elemental powers, about which it always remains a question into whose hands they fall. If we do not give ourselves over to God, then we fall prey to evil. The purpose of the liturgy with regard to objects is, for the most part, to transfer them from the wrong hands into the right ones, from the hands of the "Lord of the World" into those of the Father. In this way, water, of which the genuinely sensitive can at times be terrified, can become the purest of elements. It cleanses and is fruitful and a living symbol of supernatural life. Similarly with other materials: fire, oil, salt, ashes, wax – it is as if we can feel the overflowing nature of things precisely at the moment when they become the expressive signs of the supernatural abundance of the spirit." [314]

2.8.2. NATURAL MATERIALS IN THE LITURGY

A. Bread and Wine [315]

Outside of the Eucharist, bread and wine also play a role if a much more modest one. (On bread and wine as gifts for the Eucharist, see Chapter 3 above.)

In Hippolytus the blessing of bread and wine form, along with the *lucernarium* at evening, the prelude to the agape. [316] In the *eulogion* at the end of Mass the faithful were given blessed bread. While this practice was discontinued in German-speaking regions in the high Middle Ages, it remained usual in parts of France right up to the beginning of the twentieth century. [317] This is still practised in the Byzantine Church as the *antidoron* and has there, from the term "gift in return", the sense of a certain substitute for Communion. The blessed bread is a physical expression of the blessing that the eucharistic celebration effects (even) for one who does not communicate. This significance becomes even more understandable when it is realized that a the preparation of the gifts (*proskomidie*) the *antidoron*, over which prayers of blessing are recited is sepa-

---

[313] Author's translation.
[314] Guardini, Liturgische Bildung 45f.
[315] Cf. Berger, Naturelemente 258-265; Forstner 640-642 (bread), 242-246 (wine).
[316] Cf. TradAp. 25, Geerlings (ed.), 274-276.
[317] Cf. P. Claudel, Die Messe, Paderborn 1939, 54f.: Das geweihte Brot. Cf. Jungmann, MS II, 564.

rated from the bread intended for eucharistic consecration.[318] The *eulogia* as a substitute for Communion was also known in the West. It was so widespread in the Middle Ages that after the change to unleavened bread for the Eucharist, this was also used for the *eulogia*, to the extent that the difference between it and sacramental Communion had to be emphasized. "Then the idea of a substitute for Communion retreated, an idea which was still emphatically prevalent towards the end of the twelfth century, and from then on blessed bread becomes a sacramental which is distributed like holy water."[319] Another possible substitute for Communion may have been the cup of blessed wine given to the bride and groom in the Byzantine liturgy of marriage. Today it is understood as a "Blessing Cup", i.e. as a physical expression of good wishes for blessings in their life together.[320] The blessing and distribution of wine on the feast of St John the Evangelist (in German *Johannesminne*) in German-speaking regions is not to be understood as a Communion-substitute but as a borrowing from Germanic customs of consecrating a drink to the gods. In the Missal of 1570 wine was drunk by the celebrant to purify his mouth.[321]

B. Water[322]

Because water makes life possible and cleanses, it is also used within and apart from the liturgy, outside the contexts of Baptism and the Eucharist (in the latter it is mixed with the wine), in the form of holy water as an apotropaic, i.e. as a protection against evil. Lustrations or purifying sprinklings took place regularly in Merovingian and Carolingian monasteries. Out of this grew, since the eighth century, a blessing of water every Sunday and a sprinkling before the main liturgy, accompanied by the singing of Psalm 51 (50) and the antiphon *Asperges me*. Parish churches adopted this practice, which was incorporated in the appendix to the Missal of 1570. According to Fischer[323] the notion of the recalling of Baptism superseded the idea of purification, an idea taken up by the Missal of 1970.[324] The blessing of water in the Byzantine rite takes place primarily on the feast of the Epiphany, i.e. the Baptism, of the Lord. This is done by immersing a cross in a river, (or barrel) as a representation of the Baptism of Jesus. Every month there is in the Greek Church a blessing of water in imitation of this Epiphany blessing.[325]

C. Oil[326]

Oil was used in the ancient culture of the Mediterranen for many beneficial purposes and was regarded as a precious gift of heaven. It gave nourishment, strength, healing (as an ointment) and provided fuel for lamps. The kings of Israel were anointed with oil. The Old Testament speaks of anointings which confer priestly power, e.g. on Aaron and his sons. Other anointings empower to prophetic service as in the case of Elisha in

---

[318] Cf. Kucharek, Liturgy 632f., 667, 734f.
[319] Jungmann MS II, 563f.
[320] Cf. Kucharek, Mysteries 313; Heitz III, 198.
[321] Cf. Berger, Naturelemente 265.
[322] Cf. Berger, Naturelemente 265-269; Forstner 89-96.
[323] Cf. B. Fischer, Formen gemeinschaftlicher Tauferinnerung im Abendland, LJ 8 (1959) 87-94.
[324] Missale Romanum, Apendix I: Ordo ad faciendum er aspergendam aquam benedictam. Cf. on this: E. Färber, Gemeinsame Tauferinnerung vor der sonntäglichen Eucharistiefeier: Th. Maas-Ewerd (ed.): Gemeinde im Herrenmahl. Einsiedeln-Zurich-Freiburg-Vienna 2nd edn. 1976, 199-208.
[325] Cf. Berger, Naturelemente 268f.
[326] Cf. Berger, Naturelemente 269-273; Forstner 230-234.

1Kings 19,16. Anointing with oil symbolizes the bond with the fullness of divine life and power. For this reason, Judaism at the time of Jesus called the expected saviour of God, the "Anointed of the Lord",- *Messias, Christos*.

The oil mentioned by Hippolytus as presented by the faithful and blessed by the celebrant [327] was not yet the oil used in later times for the anointing of the sick and which could be used only by the priest. The faithful used it for themselves and the members of their families in cases of sickness. Nevertheless the origins of the Oil of the Sick are to be found here. Distinct from this is the Oil of Catechumens, the use of which as an oil of exorcism, *oleum exorcismi* is also mentioned by Hippolytus as part of the preparation for Baptism. [328] It recalls the oiling of the body by gladiators before a fight, the intention being that an antagonist would slide off the athletes body. This explains, too, why penitents were sometimes smeared with oil. Chrism, which goes back to the anointing of the newly-baptized with the "Oil of Thanksgiving" [329] mentioned by Hippolytus, became the most sacred of the holy oils in East and West, is known in the East as *myron* and has many sweet-smelling ingredients added. [330] In the West, since the Middle Ages, balsam is added to the basic olive oil destined to be used as chrism. In addition to the continuing practice in the Rite of Baptism of post-baptismal anointing with chrism, the oil is also used at the centre of the Rite of Confirmation as well as in the explanatory rites at the ordination of priests and bishops and the consecration of a church. In Carolingian times, following the Old Testament model, an anointing with Chrism was added to the consecration or crowning of a monarch. "Many find anointing in our cultural milieu to be a strange and incomprehensible element. When one thinks, however, of the importance of rubbing with oil in contemporary bathing – and sporting activities, an understanding of the sign-value of anointing is still possible today. It is true, though, that the oil must be given the chance to speak as a sign and really flow, the aroma of the Chrism must fill the liturgical space and the senses experience some of the fullness and joy of life that God gives us through Christ in the Holy Spirit." [331]

D. Fire and Light [332]

Fire is also a precious gift of God, as is expressed in various myths, for example in that of Prometheus the bringer of fire. Fire warms, gives light and purifies – e.g. in fire gold is refined, purified of dross (1 Peter 1:17). The German word for Purgatory, *Fegefeuer* or purifying fire has its origin in refining fire. In the liturgy fire plays a role primarily as light – there is, of course, the Paschal fire at the Easter vigil from which the Paschal Candle is lighted – while the notion of purification (ashes) passed to Ash Wednesday and the blessing of ashes without fire itself any more playing a role.

Christ speaks of himself as the "Light of the World" (John 8:12) and is praised as such in the Church's liturgy, e.g. in the *Lumen Christi* of the Easter vigil. Again and again light is used as a symbol for Christ and for the Christians who belong to the Lord – "you are the light of the world", (Mt 5:14). Light is a reminder of Christ not only as the

---

[327] TradAp. 5, Geerlings (ed.) 228.

[328] TradAp. 21, Geerlings (ed.), 258: Oleum exorcismi.

[329] TradAp. 21, Geerlings (ed.), 262: Oleum gratiarum actionis.

[330] On the great significance attributed to myron by Symeon of Thessaloniki, cf. Kunzler, Porta Orientalis 599-603.

[331] Berger, Naturelemente 272f.

[332] Cf. Berger, Naturelemente 273-278; Forstner 100-104, 117-123.

"light that drives out the darkness", as in the *Exsultet* of the Easter vigil, but it is due him as an honorific similar to the ancient practice of showing honour to gods and persons of rank by the carrying of torches and candles. Hippolytus describes how every evening thanks is given for the light and it is greeted as a symbol of Christ, [333] a practice that in the form of the *lucernarium* became part of the evening liturgy. Egeria already reports the festive illumination of the house of God. [334] The use of light in the cult of the dead among pagans was transferred to Christians, but is referred to the light of Christ. The use of altar-candles goes back to the ceremonial surrounding Roman officials. Acolytes accompanied the Pope with seven lights, standing around the altar during the liturgy. The honour is paid however to Christ himself, for which reason lights were carried in the procession at the Gospel. It was not until the Middle Ages that the candles were put on the altar itself, a practice unknown in the Byzantine church to this day. It imitates the Temple at Jerusalem and places a seven-branched stand with oil-lamps behind the altar to indicate the presence of the Lord.

Present regulations (GIRM 84) allow the candles once more to be carried in the entrance-procession and placed round the altar during the celebration. The ancient practice of marking holy places with an "eternal flame" was finally confined to the place of Eucharistic reservation. A lamp is still (cf. CIC c.940) prescribed to be lit in front of the tabernacle.

E. Incense and other Perfumes [335]

Incense is made from the resin of the Arabian incense-shrub mixed with herbs or other aromatic substances derived from flowers. In ancient cultures its use for reasons of hygiene was general and widespread. From this came the attribution of atropaic effects to incense. It was supposed to banish the stench-producing demons. The use of incense to show honour to an individual stems from the cult surrounding oriental rulers. It was the custom to carry dishes of incense in front of exalted personages, including the Pope, to spare them the annoyance of evil smells on the street.

Incense in its purely religious use as a smoke-offering is found in the Old Testament (e.g. Ex 30:1-10), but also in the cult of the Roman emperor – to the extent that Christians who fell away in times of persecution were known as *thurificati*, "who had offered incense before the picture of the emperor". Since the time of persecutions Christians had an ambivalent attitude to incense, despite the fact that the Book of Revelation already mentions the cultic use of incense (Rev 5:8; 8:3-5). At first incense was used in churches for hygienic purposes. Egeria speaks of its use in the *Anastasis* in order, on account of the huge crowds, to fill the building with a pleasant smell. [336] Incense is used for the same reason at the beginning of the liturgy as described by Pseudo Dionysius [337] and still in the Byzantine rite the deacon, after the incensation of the altar, the gifts prepared for the Eucharist and the icons, walks through the church incensing the faithful – honouring the Christians who have assembled for the heavenly banquet as guests of the

---

[333] TradAp. 25, Geerlings (ed.) 274-276.
[334] Peregrinatio 24,4.9 – P. Maraval (ed.), SChr 296. Paris 1982, 240.242.
[335] Cf. Berger, Naturelemente 278-281; Forstner 298-312: Pflanzliche Duftsubstanzen.
[336] Egeria, Peregrinatio 24.10 – P. Maraval (ed.), SChr 296. Paris 1982, 244.
[337] Cf. Eccl. hier. 3.2 – PG 3.425.

Lord, just as in noble houses in the ancient East, guests were greeted on arrival with sweet-smelling incense. [338]

Despite negative experiences during the times of persecution, the practice of carrying incense in front of persons as a sign of honour made it acceptable in the liturgy. Against the background of the passage from the Book of Revelation mentioned above, incense is used in the East and the West both to honour the Lord present in his people and as a perceptible sign of the prayers of the faithful rising to the heavenly throne – or, similarly since Carolingian times at the preparation of the gifts, as a symbol of the gifts rising to heaven. Incense became part of Vespers as a dramatising interpretation of the *lucernarium* psalm 141 (142):2, but then moved to the Magnificat because Ps 141,2 was sung as a versicle before it. Parallel to this was the use of incense at the Benedictus during Lauds.

F. Further Natural Materials [339]

Because salt both conserves and purifies, it was given to cathecumens to preserve them from the foulness of sin and to maintain them in their resolve to become Christians. Salt was used, and its use is still an option in the blessing of holy water. Ashes as an end-product of purifying fire are themselves regarded as purifying, which is why the sinner puts ashes on himself (cf. Job 2:8). Ashes were and are placed on penitents (on Ash Wednesday). Certain other natural materials such as foods, and their blessing, play a role in the liturgy, for example to an elaborate extent in the Byzantine celebration of Easter. Natural materials or objects such as stone or flowers are used in worship as objects of meditation. "The danger does exist, however, that the external attraction outweighs the ultimate gain. More important than such efforts is the attempt to make the fundamental realities of the liturgy convincingly perceptible to the worshipper" [340]

2.8.3. THE LITURGICAL VESSELS

Liturgical vessels originated in the reservation of everyday objects for liturgical use. Chalice and paten were at first ordinary cups and plates which were set aside for liturgical use until finally precious vessels specifically for such use were provided. [341] This applies even to implements whose secular origin is scarcely obvious. Thus, the "sacred lance" and the communion spoon of the Byzantine rite were originally implements necessary for the preparation and consuming of food. The Greek *asteriskos* and the Latin pall were at first used only to cover the Eucharistic elements to protect them from impurities. The *hexapertygens*, icons of angels shaped like a sun-burst and usually made of metal and set on poles, were originally nothing other than fly-swatters. [342]

Berger gives five grounds for a theological explanation of this development: A. the incarnational principle – a consequence of the fact that God became man is that along with human actions everyday things which are part of man's life found their way into the liturgy. The liturgy includes eating and drinking, washing and anointing, but all in the light of the Transfiguration, "where such fundamental activities are experienced,

---

[338] Cf. Kucharek, Liturgy 328.
[339] Cf. Berger, Naturelemente 281-283; Forstner 106-108 (Ashes), 171-175 (Salt), 642-651 (Foods).
[340] Berger, Naturelemente 283.
[341] Cf. Berger, Die liturgischen Geräte 293.
[342] Cf. Onasch 114f., 237, 300; K. Kallinikos, Ho christianikos naos kai ta teloumena en auto, Athens 3rd edn. 1969, 185-187.

where they are made real, the beauty hidden in creation become luminous, making visible some of its deepest meaning"[343]. B. the principle of abundance – it is precisely in the light of the Transfiguration that there is a "drive towards exuberance" which creates the work of art. "The value is an expression of the circumstances of the celebrating community and its self-understanding as the place of God's presence and glory." C. The eschatalogical principle: "In the liturgy the future final reality already breaks through, the eschatological scenario described in the Book of Revelation is made present. Through our presence with Christ we become dwellers in God's space. We do not know what we are going to be in the future; the reality to come surpasses our powers of imagination and possibilities of expression. But because in the liturgy we already participate in this reality, man tries to express it in his worship by the exuberance of the natural means available to him."[344] D. The corrective of the Cross criticizes extravagance. "The bitterness of the Cross ought not to be obscured by the glitter of the liturgy but must remain visible and perceptible even in festive celebrations."[345] E. The influence of the spirit of the times, with its better or worse means of access to the liturgy and with them their influence on the objects used in the liturgy, requires critical reflection.[346]

The most important liturgical vessels are the chalice and the paten used for the celebration of the Eucharist.[347] The size and form of these vessels mirror the frequency of Communion in different epochs, a fact particularly reflected in the container for the Eucharistic bread. Thus the dish or bowl[348] for the bread was reduced to the size of a small plate, the paten, which could fit over the cup of the chalice and held only the "priest's host". At the same time, the container, the *capsa* or pyx, for reserving the few hosts needed for the Communion of the sick and dying, became ever bigger once the practice began of distributing hosts consecrated at previous Masses,[349] and of using the ciborium to bring the hosts intended for the laity to the altar and even to consecrate the hosts in this vessel. Provided with a foot since the high Middle Ages, this vessel in the Baroque period acquired the form of a chalice. The lid began to take the form of a tower-like superstructure, covering a round chalice-like cup. Without the typical lid, the ciborium was hardly distinguishable from a chalice. The monstrance is peculiar to Western Eucharistic piety. Originally like a reliquary it was adapted for the exposition of the Eucharistic host. A transparent cylinder for holding the host, attached to a foot, developed into the Baroque sun-burst monstrance.[350]. Another eucharistic furnishing is the drinking-tube or *fistula* which can be used for communicating with the chalice,[351] but it has never become popular. The same is true of the Eucharistic spoon,[352] which is

---

[343] Berger, Die liturgischen Geräte 295. On the incarnational principle cf. also J. M. Leniaud, Pour une théologie des objets de culte, MD 188 (191) 87-107.98f.

[344] Berger, Die liturgischen Geräte 296.

[345] Ibid. 296f.

[346] Cf. ibid. 297f.

[347] On the historical development of these cf. Braun, Altargerät 17 -196 (Chalice) and 197-246 (Paten or communion-dish).

[348] Cf. Braun, Altargerät 208-210: The form of the paten in the late antiquity and early middle ages.

[349] Cf. Braun, Altargerät 328-330. On all of this cf. P. Browe, Wann fing man an, die in einer Messe konsekrierten Hostien in einer anderen Messe auszuteilen? ThGl 30 (1938) 388-404.

[350] Cf. Braun, Altargerät 348-413.

[351] Cf. GIRM 243, 248-250.

[352] Cf. Braun, Altargerät 265-279; GIRM 243, 251.

used by the Byzantines – at least by the Slavs, though no more by the Melkites and not consistently by the Greeks – for the distribution of Communion under both kinds.

Among the "non-sacred" vessels, some of which now have only historical significance, are the containers for wine and water and for unconsecrated hosts, implements for washing of hands, the altar-cross and candle-sticks, the cup for the ablution or cleansing of the communicant's mouth after reception of the sacrament, the pax-brede for the sign of peace, the sacring bell, the container for holy water and the sprinkler or *aspergillium* as well as the thurible and incense-boat.

2.8.4. IMAGES

The icon itself, the quintessential "holy picture" is, of course, the prime example of the iconographic character discussed here. It is unquestionable a sacred object and the focus of liturgical veneration. In contrast the West, which at the Synod of Frankfurt in 794, conceded only pedagogical significance to images, the East looks on sacred images not merely as decoration or as a visual medium for the communication of a message, but as a expression of a living relationship between the observer and the person or subject depicted. Thus the icon is an organ of expression both of whom or what it depicts and also of the person venerating the icon.

According to Evdokimov every work of art entails a three-fold relationship between the artist, his work and the observer of the work. "The artist executes his work and evokes a spiritual stirring in the soul of the observer. The whole remains embraced in an aesthetic immanence." When the stirring of the soul becomes a religious experience, then this is thanks only to the subjective capacity of the observer, who could have arrived at this experience through completely different means. The icon in contrast, "breaks this three-fold relationship and its immanence by its sacramental character. Independently of the artist and of the observer it affirms its value; it effects no stirring of the soul, but adds a fourth dimension to the three-fold relationship: the entrance of the transcendent to whose presence it witnesses." [353]

The sacred icons are "Windows of the Eternal", not as visible depictions of an invisible reality in the sense of the Platonic doctrine of participation, but a genuine case of the "in-between" which is the basis of all communication between persons. By means of the material medium of the picture, the one depicted and the observer communicate with one another, because the icon makes it possible for them to be present to each other. According to John of Damascus this means that icons have something in common with the material human nature of the Son of God made man, "I saw the image of God in the form of man and my soul was saved." [354] This is in keeping with the rules of icon-painting that everything can be depicted which has appeared in the flesh – but only that.

Bibliography

R. Berger: Naturelemente und technische Mittel: R. Berger / K. H. Bieritz and others, GdK 3: Gestalt des Gottesdienstes, Regensburg 2nd edn. 1990, 249-288.

R. Berger: Die liturgischen Geräte: R. Berger / K. H. Bieritz and others, GdK 3: Gestalt des Gottesdienstes. Regensburg 2nd edn. 1990, 289-307.

---

[353] Cf. Evdokimov, L'Orthodoxie 222.
[354] Oratio I, 22 B. Kotter (ed.): Die Schriften des Johannes v. Damaskos, Berlin 1975, 111.

J. Braun, Das christliche Altargerät in seinem Sein und in seiner Entwicklung, München 1932.

R. Erni, Das Christusbild der Ostkirche, Luzern-Stuttgart 1963.

D. Forstner: Die Welt der Symbole. Innsbruck-Wien-München 1961.

L. Ouspensky / Vl. Lossky, Der Sinn der Ikonen, Bern-Olten 1952.

W. Nyssen, Zur Theologie der Ikone: HOK II, Düsseldorf 1989, 236-245.

A. Reinle, Die Ausstattung deutscher Kirchen im Mittelalter. Darmstadt 1988.

C. Schönborn, Die Christus-Ikone. Eine theologische Hinführung, Vienna 1998.

E. Trenkle, Liturgische Gewänder und Geräte der Ostkirche. München 1962.

2.9. LITURGICAL SPACE

The space which man inhabits is the immediate form of expression of his personality. The more he "invests" (Guardini) this space, the more it becomes a real symbol of the one who inhabits it.

2.9.1. A CHURCH MADE OF STONES, LIVING AND REAL.

God does not live in dwellings erected by the hands of man (Acts 7:48). The fullness of the Godhead dwells, rather, in the human nature of the Son, who is never separated from the Father and from the *Pneuma*. Through his humanity the Trinity comes to man, inviting him to participate in its life. The Logos lives among men in the flesh. Men can see his glory as Son of the Father full of grace and truth (John 1:14). Stephen's discourse in which he denies that God lives in dwellings built by the hand of man, refers not to the Old Testament polemic against the temples of the gods. "The correct parallels are to be found in the New Testament, above all the passage in which Jesus is quoted as saying the words which, like Stephen, led to his condemnation, 'I will destroy this temple which is made with hands and in three days I will build another, not made with hands' (Mk 14:58). Between the "made with hands" of Stephen and that of the Old Testament lies the life of Christ and the event of the Resurrection." [355] "The new and decisive reality which has been accomplished in Jesus Christ has replaced all other forms of God's presence among his people and with this invalidated them." [356]

Every theology of the Church as a building is based on the human body of Christ as that of the true temple in which dwells the fullness of the Godhead and through which men are to be filled with this Godhead (Col 2:9f.). "Temple" is to be understood here literally because, "the body of Christ is not invisible, is not of a purely representative, inner, order. It is sacramentally-eucharistically and communally-ecclesially tangible, extended and localized. For this reason the places which are simultaneously those where the sacramental offering of the body and of the gathering of the body of the Church take place, themselves temples or churches. These places were called by names which were applied to the sacramental body or to the communal body of the Lord: *basilike*, basilica, *kyriakon*, church, *ecclesia*." [357] The prophecy of Nathan speaks of the building of a house

---

[355] Congar, Mysterium des Tempels 53.
[356] Ibid. 129. Cf. also ibid. 131-133: Christ's body becomes the true temple through his death and resurrection.
[357] Ibid. 180f.

by God himself, "God remains one without a dwelling, one for whom every building of stone is too confined, but who, nevertheless, finds room in man, particularly in him. His living takes place in the grace which builds." He is completely present as one inviting to community in his Son become man, as in the temple in which the Godhead dwells in all its fullness. [358]

In this sense "the fundamental sign is the sacred assembly of the community itself. It is the expression, the image of the Church." [359] The community of members of the mystical body under Christ its head is *ecclesia*, the community summoned out of deadly unrelatedness. This community belongs to the Lord, who won it by his blood. It is *kyriake koinonia*, the community of the Lord, Church. The *synaxis* or gathering of men and women in Christ (*en Christo*) has to invest the liturgical space as a "corporate personality", as in Guardini's understanding, is every space inhabited by man. Since Christ has promised his presence in union with the Father and the *Pneuma*, the place in which the Church gathers is in a very real sense the "house of God", even though God is not encompassed by the heaven of heavens.

In the various epochs of its history, the Church has lived in its spaces in very different ways and with this proclaimed its own self-understanding. It did this using all the possibilities and deficits of a human community, but also of a community whose head is the glorified Lord binding it in the Spirit with the Father.

2.9.2. THE HISTORICAL DEVELOPMENT OF LITURGICAL SPACE

The first Christians gathered in private houses for the celebration of the liturgy. Bouyer, however, is certain that long before the end of the persecutions, the communities had buildings specially for worship. It is as unlikely that the layout of a Roman patrician house was adopted unaltered for worship, as was the use of the Roman catacombs of the same purpose. [360] In 1931 and 1932 a house dateable to AD 232 or 233, which had been adapted to become a church, was excavated in the ancient city of Dura-Europos on the upper Euphrates. [361] In an assembly-room measuring 13 meters by 5 meters a podium on the east end indicates the position of the bishop's cathedra or of an altar. A smaller chamber decorated with frescoes possibly served as a baptistery. The synagogue was the model for the arrangement of the space. [362]

The synagogue always more than a "teaching-house". It was always, rather, a place of ritual celebration, which remained closely bound up "with the recognition and cult of a special presence of God among his own people". [363] The synagogue had three focal points around which liturgical life concentrated. The so-called "Chair of Moses" placed in the middle of the synagogue was intended to indicate the continuity of Moses's teach-

---

[358] J. Ratzinger, "Auferbaut aus lebendigen Steinen": W. Seidel (ed.), Kirche aus lebendigen Steinen, Mainz 1975, 30-48. 33; cf. also ibid. 37, 42.

[359] E.J. Lengeling, Wort, Bild, Symbol in der Liturgie, LJ 30 (1980) 230-242. 238.

[360] Cf. Bouyer, Liturgie und Architektur 43-45. According to Adam in Wo sich Gottes Volk versammelt, p. 17, the catacombs were used for the liturgy only on the memorias of the martyrs buried there. Duval, p.7, is of the same opinion.

[361] Cf. A. v. Gerkan, Die frühchristliche Kirchenanlage von Dura, RQ 42 (1934) 219-232; C. H. Kraeling, The Christian Building: C. B. Welles: The Excavation at Dura-Europos. Final Report VIII, Part II. New Haven 1967.

[362] Cf. Adam, Wo sich Gottes Volk versammelt 15f.

[363] Bouyer, Liturgie und Architektur 17. It is true that one is always dealing here with a presence in accordance with the teachings of the Shekinah.

ing down to the present. The chair was directed towards the second focus, the Ark of the Covenant.[364] Before the Exile, the only Ark of the Covenant was in the temple at Jerusalem, its cover surmounted by the figures of two Cherubim. This was believed to be the throne on the invisibly present God of the Covenant. After the re-building of the temple the Ark of the Covenant was not replaced. The Holy of Holies remained empty, but continued to be regarded as the place of Jahweh's special presence. "The Ark in the synagogues remained as a reminder of the original Ark. Every year its cover was sprinkled with the blood of atonement as a sign of reconciliation between God and his people. The connection between these Arks and the one authentic and lost Ark consisted in the fact that the Torah-rolls were stored in them, as in the original Ark of the Covenant, as a sign of God's presence. Just as in the Holy of Holies the Ark in every synagogue was protected by a veil in front of which burned the lamps of the menorah, the seven-branched candlestick."[365] Prayer over the Ark always took place facing Jerusalem. The third focus of liturgical life was the Bema, the central platform for the reading of the Scriptures. As synagogues began to take on basilical form, they were so oriented towards Jerusalem that the Ark stood in an apse opposite the main entrance, with the Bema with the Chair of Moses, in front of it. "However the different elements may have been placed, the relationship between the assembly around the Chair of Moses, the Ark of the covenant and Jerusalem remained the same. The community gathered around the rabbi and his teaching. But the Ark from which the rolls of the law and the prophets were taken, remained for all the focus of God's permanent presence."[366]

The early Syrian churches represent a christianized form of the Jewish synagogue. The readings still take place at the Bema, the Chair of Moses has become the bishop's chair. The churches, however, are no longer oriented towards Jerusalem but towards the east from where Christ is expected as the one "mounting from on high". The altar stands in the apse in the east wall. The Ark of the Covenant in the synagogue has become the throne for the book of the Gospels.[367] Essential elements of the Christian Church building have been taken over from the Jewish tradition and represented in the early Syrian churches: the altar, the presider's seat, the place for the proclamation of the word.

Further development of the liturgical space was determined by the adoption of the plan of the secular basilica[368] in the period following the year 313. The basilica is a quadrangular building, longer than it is broad, divided by rows of columns into three or five naves.[369] On the narrow end opposite the main entrance was an apse. In the Christian basilica the bishop's cathedra stood in the apex of the apse, with seats for the presbyteral college on its right and left. In front are the altar and ambo, both part of the

---

[364] Cf. A. van den Born, Art. "Lade": H. Haag (ed.): Bibel-Lexikon. Einsiedeln-Zürich-Köln 2nd edn. 1968, 1007-1009.
[365] Bouyer, Liturgie und Architektur 21.
[366] Ibid. 23-25.
[367] Cf. ibid. 30-42: Die frühen syrischen Kirchen.
[368] "Basiliké stoá – royal hall"; it served many public purposes from market-hall, to courthouse to audience-chamber.
[369] Very early on (Tertullian, Hippolytus, the Apostolic Constitutions) the ship (nave) was used as an image of the Christian community on its journey to the harbour of heaven. The clergy are the helmsmen and sailors. Cf. Adam, Wo sich Gottes Volk versammelt 25f.

sanctuary or presbyterium, which is separated from the area occupied by the laity by low barriers (*cancelli*). In North Africa, however, the altar stood in the middle of the nave. Augustine mentions it being *in medio ecclesiae*.[370] Nor was the railing off with *cancelli* universal: they are first mentioned by Eusebius.[371] The crossing, which is not a feature of the secular basilica, may possibly have arisen form the need to provide room for the offerings of the faithful.[372] Eusebius, in his sermon preached at the dedication of the basilica at Tyre in the year 314 or 315, articulated the symbolism of the Christian basilica as the sign of the community gathered within it in its hierarchical groupings.[373]

According to Bouyer, the basilica in which the bishop's teaching-chair in the centre of the apse has become a throne reflects a profound change. The clergy had separated itself from the laity and celebrated the liturgy with elements of the state ceremonial which belonged to the secular basilica. The bishop, now become a high civic official, took the place of the altar in the apse, enthroned high above his flock. The altar itself, marked out by the *cancelli* and surmounted by a baldachin or *ciborium*, moved to the centre where once the bishop sat among his faithful. With this development the community was, at least during the celebration of the Eucharist, closer to the liturgical action. The bema had not vanished completely, but could no longer be a platform which would have obstructed the procession from the bishop's throne to the altar in the centre. Instead it took the form of an enclosure at ground level, open at both ends, in which the schola, readers, cantors and lower clergy were accommodated. Raised lecterns on the enclosure walls were used for the reading of the Scriptures.[374]

If, however, which according to Bouyer happened in St Peter's Basilica under Gregory the Great[375], the altar was moved back into the presbyterium, already separated from the community, then "the bishop and the clergy were separated from the assembly not only for the first part of the liturgy, but remained in their elevated isolation also during the Eucharist." This important change was more easily accomplished since the course of the entry of huge numbers into the Church, only a few "elite" believers received Communion and even these pious persons were, finally, replaced in the great basilicas by monastic communities. "At this time it can be established that the liturgy was no longer a public common concern of the whole Church, but had become the semi-private celebration of a community of monks and clergy in a church now seldom frequented by the laity."[376] St Peter's Basilica was a model in this for the other Roman basilicas.

---

[370] Cf. Braun, Altar I, 386: In the basilica at Carthage the altar stood in the middle of the church about 24 meters away from the apse. Cf. also J. Wagner, Locus quo ecclesia congregatur: LJ 12 (1962) 161-174.

[371] Cf. Braun, Altar I, 651-655. The Armenian rite, which preserves many peculiarities from the earliest tradition, never had any railing off of the altar, but placed it instead on a raised platform behind a curtain.

[372] This is suggested by Th. Klauser, Die konstantinischen Altäre in der Lateranbasilika, RQ 43 (1935) 179-186. According to the author, seven silver altars which Constantine had presented and which were placed in the crossing were used to receive the gifts of the faithful. Adam, op. cit. supra p. 21, mentions the distribution of Holy Communion as another possible reason for the development of the crossing.

[373] Cf. Kirchengeschichte X, 4 – H. Kraft (trans.) München 1967, 417-430.

[374] Cf. Bouyer, Liturgie und Architektur 47f.

[375] On this cf. Braun, Altar I, 570, where he speaks not about Gregory's moving of the altar to a position over the grave of St Peter but only about an instruction concerning celebration over the altar which was already placed over the grave.

[376] Cf. Bouyer, Liturgie und Architektur 50-52.

The lengthening of the crossing beyond the width of the nave walls, and the covering of the intersection of the resulting transepts and the nave with a vault, led to the development of a domed cross-shaped church. This was to become the model for the Byzantine church. Reverence for the altar led to its being surrounded with curtains or the raising of the level of the altar-rails. From the latter developed the Eastern iconostasis with its prescribed cycle of icons. [377] The extension of the apse, the addition of further apses, led to the provision of complementary spaces, *pastophoria*, which to this day fulfil a liturgical function in the Byzantine Church, in the form of the *prothesis* [378] – an apsidal space containing the table for the preparation of the Eucharistic gifts – and the *diakonikon* which corresponds to the Western sacristy. Buildings were also added to the front of the church, a closed as well as an open narthex – *exo-* and *endonarthex* – of which the inner served as the place for catechumens and penitents, for official gatherings as well other occasions at which the celebration of the liturgy played a role, as, for example, at the *litia*, a procession which was part of the celebration of a vigil. [379] With the retreat of the altar into the main apse, the dome was now enthroned over the space occupied by the laity, the *naos* or nave. The dome symbolized the heavenly Jerusalem, from which Christ in the form of a mosaic of the Pantocrator gazed down on the liturgical asssembly. [380] "Such a space is no longer a pilgrimage church but a space in which to linger under an open heaven, the apogee of the domed structure is the Emperor Justinian's Hagia Sophia at Constantinople, built between 532 and 537." [381]

North of the alps the Carolingian reform movement established its own style of church-building which borrowed from the Roman basilicas. As in these, the altar was, as much as possible, to be placed over the graves of the saint, or their relics. The apse was lengthened to form the "choir" and raised above the level of the space for the laity, so that the graves or relics became accessible in the resulting crypt. Because the west as a compass-point belonged to the Devil and the demons, the west façade was built like a fortress, a characteristic emphasized by the towers. It was the custom of the Emperor to assist at the liturgy from his own tribune in the west gallery. The majority of the Carolingian churches were basilical in ground-plan. They contained an innovation which was to have consequences for the liturgy as a whole. This was the multiplicity of altars in the west choir, in the crypt in the transepts and aisles, over the graves or relics of the saints and martyrs. Häußling associates this with the rise of the private Mass by proposing the thesis that the many altars of the Carolingian (monastic) church were intended as a representation of the many holy places in Rome. The liturgies at the different places in the holy city were imitated at the many altars. [382] A further development of the Carolingian style was the Ottonian. Peculiar to both styles was the provision of a prominent place for the secular ruler, but with the end of the controversy over Lay Investiture and with it the end of the notion of sacral monarchy, this would cease.

The Romanesque churches of the Middle Ages continued this spatial development. The notion of the "sacred fortress of God" was even more strongly emphasized, but

---

[377] Cf. Onasch, Art. "Bilderwand" 56-61.
[378] Cf. Onasch, Art. "Pastophorien" 299-300; Art. "Prothesis" 315-316.
[379] Cf. Onasch, Art. "Narthex" 279f.
[380] Cf. Onasch, Art. "Kupppel" 232f.
[381] Adam, Wo sich Gottes Volk versammelt 27f.
[382] A.A. Häußling, Mönchskonvent und Eucharistiefeier (LQF 58), Münster 1973. On Carolingian church building in general, cf. Adam, Wo sich Gottes Volk versammelt 31f.

along with it that of the sacred place, for which reason the number of altars increased even further. At the end of the first millennium, the appearance of the altar began to change. Relics, lights and a cross began to be placed on the altar. At first in the crypts, but then also at the other altars, the sarcophagi with the bodies of the saints, which were behind these altars began to be so raised up that they became visible behind the mensa of the altar. Thus developed the shrine- and retable-altars.[383] But it was not only the Mass that had become a purely clerical activity. The same was true of the Liturgy of the Hours. For this reason, since the twelfth century, many churches were divided by a rood-screed in the "clerics church" and the "people's church". The rood-screen was a stage-like construction between the crossing and the nave used for the proclamation of the readings and for preaching. Behind the screen the more complicated clerical liturgy was celebrated. In front of the screen at an altar in the crossing, the simpler liturgy for the people was celebrated.[384] "With the abolition of the offertory procession, the communion of the faithful having become an exception, the singing having for the most part been taken over by the choir, and the whole liturgy of the word, through the use of a dead language, become incomprehensible to all but the clergy, there was, in fact, nothing remaining in which the faithful could participate."[385] The Romanesque church was still in the tradition of the (neo)platonic concept of exemplar and image, as theology had received it from the Fathers: the visible is the vehicle of the invisible reality and the church reveals as God's fortress or as the Heavenly Jerusalem both the invisibly present and the one who is to come at the *eschaton*, it being the real-symbolic expression of earthly reality, of the hierarchical structure of society as the expression of the divine order.

The Gothic church also reflects an intellectual position. The Gothic era, from about 1150 with the Abbey Church of St Denis to the beginning of the sixteenth century, is almost coterminous with that of Scholasticism in theology. It is true that until the rise of Nominalism there was still a strong neo-platonic tradition, but the philosophical influence of Aristotle was to peak in the Summa of St Thomas Aquinas. Just as the theological summas aimed at final clarity in knowledge; as aristotelian thought – e.g. hylomorphism and entelechy – freeing the word from "magic", led to the development of technological thinking; so the Gothic expressed human ability and striving to raise the world to God. "The Gothic in the sense of a vertical striving means as much as power, manliness, activity, heroic passion, the will to personality and self-assertion. It is the form of creative restlessness and of the necessary suffering that results from the clash with resistance. Thus the Gothic loves and builds the tower."[386]

The Gothic took over the screen, and the many altars and chapels from the Romanesque. Participation by the people remained a mere looking-on at an action performed by the celebrant. The liturgy was seen as a dramatic representation of the life of Jesus and – in keeping with the late medieval theology of the Mass as sacrifice – as a repetition of his sacrifice on the Cross. The visible climax of the Mass was to gaze at the Host during the Consecration.[387] The heavenward striving of the Gothic cathe-

---

[383] Cf. Braun, Altar II, 555f.

[384] Cf. Adam, op. cit. supra, 38.

[385] Bouyer, Liturgie und Architektur 70.

[386] A. Hammenstede, Die Liturgie als Erlebnis (Ecclesia Orans 3), Freiburg i. Br. 6th edn. 1922, 44. For an assessment of Gothic architecture and Gothic thought cf. Kunzler, Porta Orientalis 632-637.

[387] Cf. Bouyer, Liturgie und Architektur 70-72.

dral was indeed a symbol of the Heavenly Jerusalem, [388] but the people who entered it did so as individuals or were divided into various societal groupings such as confraternities, guilds etc. They did not become a liturgical community. They practised their individualist piety while the liturgy unfolded without them and regardless of them at the various altars and in the various chapels. A community was formed at best when, under the influence of the mendicant orders and their preaching activities, vernacular liturgies of the word took place as an insertion during Mass, or as a special service in the afternoon. The pulpit, fixed on a pillar, also developed as a result of the preaching by the mendicant orders. [389] It is interesting that the German word for pulpit, *Kanzel*, is a reminder that the ambo of earlier times was part of the altar enclosure, the *cancelli*. In Meyer's opinion this separation of pulpit and altar, along with the drifting apart of clerical liturgy and folk piety, is a sign of the arrival of a new era in which the medieval world-view has been superseded. [390]

The church in the Renaissance no longer strove heavenwards but reached back to ancient models. Basilicas and domed buildings in their various combinations returned. A not purely fortuitous anthropocentrism was adopted from the ancient world and the humanism that tried to re-capture it. Even representations of Christ and the saints were determined by ancient ideals of beauty. Conversely, "the transcendence of the earthly which in the later Gothic period threatened to lead to the dissolution of all form, now returned in the measured harmony of the world of man. Sculpture, painting and ornament were integrated in and subordinated to architecture. It was as if the reform of the liturgy and of the life of the Church attempted by the Council of Trent – also itself an appeal to (ecclesiastical) antiquity, was reflected in the church building." [391] But, just as the Council of Trent did not effect comprehensive liturgical reform, so there emerged no essentially new aspects to the arrangement of liturgical space.

On the contrary, the anti-Reformation emphasis of Catholic faith led to a continuation, indeed to a reinforcement of questionable aspects such as the practice of gazing at the Eucharist, which celebrated its triumph in the Baroque church. [392] Parallel to the palaces of the absolute rules of this period, the Baroque church became a splendid throne-room of the heavenly king present in the Host. The lines of the church led to the tabernacle and the throne of exposition placed above it, leading the viewer's gaze to this as the focus of the building. With this, the most important part of the altar, the mensa, which marked it as the table of the Eucharistic sacrificial meal, almost completely disappeared in the enormously expanded reredos, itself offering its own scenario [393] with tabernacle and throne of exposition at its centre. "In these churches, the liturgy is a splendid and moving spectacle, but it is a "performance" and more the concern of the clergy, the organist, the singers and musicians than of the faithful, who 'look

---

[388] Cf. G. Jaszai: Art. "Jerusalem, Himmlisches": LCI 2, 394-399: The Cathedral as Symbol of the own city!
[389] Cf. ibid. 73; Adam, Wo sich Gottes Volk versammelt, 118-120; Reinle 40-42. The latter, p. 43, includes a representation of a moveable wooden pulpit as used by the mendicants.
[390] Cf. Meyer, Kirchenbau 55.
[391] Meyer, Kirchenbau 59.
[392] The term "Baroque" comes from the Italo-Portuguese "barocco" and was originally "a technical term usd by jewellers to describe an asymmetrical pearl. In a transferred sense Renaissance authors used it for twisted, convoluted and irregularly formed works of art, which had nothing in common with the harmony of the classical." Adam, Wo sich Gottes Volk versammelt 54.
[393] On the Baroque reredos, cf. Braun Altar II, 396-407.

on in wonder and joy'. Preaching and the – rare – reception of Communion mostly take place outside of the Mass, which particularly on Sundays and feast-days, is celebrated as a High Mass sung in polyphony (with orchestra) and practically without active participation by the people. Instead devotions blossom luxuriantly, among them Benediction, processions and pilgrimages." [394] It is certainly true that for the faithful Baroque churches were "like a piece of heaven on earth", [395] but they were nevertheless excluded from active participation in the "heavenly action", remaining on-looking and wondering "visitors".

Like the Renaissance before it, the Baroque also resorted to historical models. Classicism and to an even greater extent, Historicism, "quoted", right up into the twentieth century, "classical" building styles of a romantically idealized past. [396] The nineteenth century took over in an historicizing manner the medieval idea and structure of the church building, but falsified it to the extent that it reduced it to an "exclusive, religious island" which no longer had much to do with the rest of life. [397] Excluded was the rich life of the medieval town community in its church, which went beyond the liturgical framework and used the building as a meeting-place, as a place for lawsuits and business, in short lived-in, "invested". In the nineteenth century the Church shared with the museums, theatres and concert-halls which were arising everywhere, the maxims governing the "orientation" of the space, in this case the space for the faithful. "These are spaces which serve a purely artistic purpose, which is exercised in the "enjoyment" or absorption of the work of art being performed before his eyes." [398] The purpose is to absorb and enjoy what is presented, not to take part in it. [399]

The problem still remains after the transition to the Modern Movement. Even more, orientation becomes an almost insurmountable dilemma when it is forced to concentrate on an empty wall as a new "sacred symbol". [400] Modernism in architecture demonstrates that there is no such thing as a definitive "sacred" style of building. But a consciously desired renunciation of sacrality or the theologically problematic elevation of the profane into a "sacred symbol" led also in the building of churches – e.g. in multi-purpose buildings and spaces, used for liturgy among other things – to the same unsatisfactory results as those provoked by the post Vatican II efforts at desacralization, according to Werner, indeed to the end of the "church"-building as such. [401]

---

[394] Meyer, Kirchenbau 67.

[395] Adam, op. cit. Supra p.60.

[396] Meyer, Kirchenbau 70: "Romanticism and Restorationism discover in the Gothic a language of form which is fitting for the Christian faith, whereby Neo-gothic is to be understood as an adjunct of Neo-scholasticism."

[397] Cf. Werner 237-243. On the Protestant concept of church-building in the nineteenth century, cf. R. Volp, Liturgik. Die Kunst, Gott zu feiern, Vol. I: Einführung und Geschichte, Gütersloh 1992, 376-384.

[398] Werner 207.

[399] Cf. ibid. 228.

[400] Thus R. Schwarz's Corpus Christi church in Aachen (1928-30). On Guardini's position regarding the empty walls as an "opposite pole of the figurative" cf. Adam, Wo sich Gottes Volk versammelt 69f. On the Modern Movement, cf. ibid. 64-68.

[401] Meyer considers quite correctly, Kirchenbau 95 that: "purely functional thinking – itself a sign of a withering of spiritual competence – and the plea for a church-building which is primarily there to facilitate interpersonal contacts, must be energetically countered with the argument that the modern church, too, in its architectural form, must be understood as a 'bridge between matter and spirit'."

2.9.3. PLACES IN THE RENEWED LITURGY

There is a practice of calling locations where the liturgical action takes place, "places of function" [402] or "function-centres". [403] These are particularly the altar, the celebrant's chair, the place for the proclamation of the word as well as the places for Baptism and the Sacrament of Penance. It is primarily at these "places of function" that the liturgy happens. Since, however, in contemporary understanding of the liturgy, the whole assembly is the vehicle of the liturgical action, the area where the faithful assist is also a "place of function". With this, the whole problem of its relation to the "function-centres" remains a constant challenge.

In his encyclical *Mediator Dei*, of 1947, Pope Pius XII contradicted those who wished to restore the altar to its old form of a table. [404] The veneration of relics had led in the early Middle Ages to the placing of shrines on the altar. Since the turn of the millennium it was also usual to put candles [405] and a cross on the altar. Against the idea of the ancient Church, still observed in the Christian East, of the empty altar as a throne [406] awaiting Christ who is to come again, the character of the altar as a table was overshadowed in the West not only by the objects placed on it but also by the development of the reredos, out of which developed in the Gothic period the winged altar and in the Baroque era altarpieces of enormous dimensions.

Liturgical renewal returned to traditions of the ancient Church, according to which the ideal was to have a single altar in any church. [407] The altar should be free-standing so that one can walk around it and can celebrate Mass from either side. With this, the ancient table form has been restored. "It should be placed in a central position which draws the attention of the whole congregation" (GIRM 262). The custom of placing relics in or under the altar is retained, provided their authenticity has been proven (GIRM 266). The altar-cross can be on the altar or near it, similarly the candles. All the furnishings should be in harmony and the faithful should be able to see the altar clearly (GIRM 269-270).

With the reform of the liturgy, celebration facing the people became a trade mark of renewal. Here, an appeal to the practice of the ancient Church is as false as the suggestion from traditionalist circles that the position *versus populum* was an invention of Martin Luther. In the ancient Church the direction of the celebration was determined by the practice of facing East. This applied not only to the celebrant but also to the faithful. If the entrance was at the east end of the building, then the celebrant stood "behind" the altar, facing the congregation indeed, but facing their backs, since the community turned to the East for prayer. [408] The result of the building of increasing numbers of churches towards the East was that the direction of celebration was *versus altare*. The pastoral

---

[402] Cf. Emminghaus, Der gottesdienstliche Raum 385.

[403] Cf. Reifenberg, fundamental 358.

[404] AAS 39 (1947) 545: "is ex recto aberret itinere, qui priscam altari velit mensae formam restituere."

[405] Cf. J. Braun, Das christliche Altargerät in seinem Sein und in seiner Entwicklung, München 1932, 469-474; 492-498.

[406] Cf. Th.v. Bogyay: Art. "Thron (Hetoimasia)": LCI IV,, 304-313.

[407] GIRM 267 is not able completely to reject the long tradition of the side-altars and secondary altars. For this reason it states that there ought to be only a few other altars which, in new buildings have, if possible, each to be placed in its own side-chapel.

[408] Cf. O. Nußbaum, Der Standort des Liturgen am christlichen Altar vor dem Jahre 1000. Eine archäologische und liturgiegeschichtliche Untersuchung, 2 vols., Bonn 1965, I, 447; Jungmann, MS I, 332f,; Adam, Wo sich Gottes Volk Versammelt 104f.

advantages of celebration facing the people are certainly not to be denied. On the other hand the argument in favour of the whole assembly facing East, towards the Christ who is to come, retains its weight. It must, though, be absolutely clear that celebration *versus altare* has nothing to do with clericalist exclusivity, but, on the contrary, places the priest in the direction of the prayer of the whole community – declericalizes him. Because of traditionalist polemics, however, a restoration of this mode of celebration is unthinkable for the immediate future, although it would be perfectly possible according to the Missal of 1970.

The second place of function in the renewed Eucharistic celebration is the celebrant's chair. It is from here that the celebrant leads the assembly as "president". This chair developed from the bishop's cathedra, itself copied from the official chair of (Roman) judges and teachers. With the development of the reredos behind the altar the bishop's chair moved from the centre of the apse to the left hand side. The emergence of the private Mass and its use as the community liturgy mean that the priest remained at the altar during the whole of the celebration. At the most, during a solemn High Mass, he took his place at the sedilia until the choir had finished its part. According to the Missal of 1970, the celebrant's chair is supposed to make clear and support the presiding function of the priest. The chair may not be a throne, it must not be too far from the people and, if the layout of the building permits, it should be in the centre of the sanctuary. All who have a particular ministry in the liturgy, also have their place in the sanctuary (GIRM 271).

The third place of function is used for the proclamation of the word of God. The ambo as the "table of the word" is not a portable lectern but, in keeping with the dignity of the God's word which is proclaimed from it, should be a fixed liturgical place appropriately designed architecturally and artistically. It should be reserved for the proclamation of the word and commentators, cantors and choir directors should not use it for their particular ministries (GIRM 272).

Further places of function are those for the administration of Baptism and the Sacrament of Penance. In arranging the place of Baptism, primacy should be given to the principle of active participation. The place for the Sacrament of Penance is the now common combination of reconciliation room and confessional – the latter still required by Canon Law. [409] The place for the faithful should be so arranged "that the people may take full part in the celebration by seeing and by understanding everything" (GIRM 273). Whether this objective is best served by the use of pews – usual since the Reformation – is seriously questioned by Josuttis and Bouyer. [410] The relationship between the space for the faithful and the other "centres of function" is the subject of the next section.

2.9.4. THE REMAINING TASK OF "INVESTING" THE LITURGICAL SPACE

Epí tó autó is the oldest description of liturgical space: all came together "in once place" (Acts 2:1). *Ekklesía* and *epí tó autó* complement one another to the extent that what is meant is the community that among other things constitutes itself by coming together

---

[409] Cf. Adam, Wo sich Gottes Volk versammelt 124-129.
[410] Cf. Josuttis 126f.; Bouyer, Liturgie und Architektur 92f.

in one place.[411] This is developed in the Apostolic Fathers.[412] In the Apology of Justin (67,3) he says. "On Sunday all the inhabitants of the towns and villages gather 'in one place'."[413]

It is part of the essence of the Church as a community "summoned" to divine life, to come together "in one place", prior to all differences of office and function. This coming together for the liturgy constitutes the Church as the mystical body of Christ, the corporate personality to which is given the task to "invest", to inhabit, the space in which it gathers *epí tó autó*. The task imposed is by no means already fulfilled, even after the reforms of the Second Vatican Council, because the liturgical space is still divided into zones within which liturgical signs are "produced" and zones in which these signs are primarily received – despite all participation by means of common prayer, singing, kneeling and blessing oneself. The organization of the space confines the "visitors" in their spectator places and permits only a view from a distance. Otto H. Senn has developed an alternative: "The place of happening is the place of assembly: the differentiation of the space into an 'arena of activity' and a 'nave of the assembly' contradicts the liturgy." The place of worship is a single space - *epí tó autó* – and as such totally "centre", i.e. in itself enjoying the same rights and without prominent or less "accessible" places. The pulpit and altar are placed according to the practical demands of audibility and visibility. "In no way is the assembly 'oriented towards' these."[414]

On the basis of Catholic, Oriental and synagogal tradition, Bouyer makes fascinating suggestions for the ordering of liturgical space suitable for and making possible its investing "investing" by the liturgical assembly.[415] The celebrant and all who have special ministry stand neither above the community nor facing it, but stand in it as a "leaven". The presider gathers the assembly at sacred places such as the ambo and the altar, to which the community makes it way specially. These places thus become more than "focal points" for the fulfillment of liturgical functions, but instead, places of divine presence, -*shekinah* – as these were known in the temple and in the synagogue.

Bibliography

A. Adam, Wo sich Gottes Volk versammelt, Freiburg-Basel-Wien 1984.

J. Boguniowski, 'Epí tó autó'. Die älteste christliche Bezeichnung des liturgischen Raumes, EL 102 (1988) 446-455.

L. Bouyer, Liturgie und Architektur, Einsiedeln-Freiburg i. Br. 1993.

J. Braun, Der christliche Altar in seiner geschichtlichen Entwicklung, 2 Vols., München 1924.

J. Braun, Das christliche Altargerät in seinem Sein und in seiner Entwicklung, München 1932.

N. Duval, L'espace liturgique dans les églises paléochrétiennes, MD 193 (1993) 7-29.

J. E. Emminghaus, Das Kirchengebäude als Ort der Meßfeier. Überlegungen auf Grund der erneuerten Meßordnung: Th. Maas-Ewerd / K. Richter (eds.), Gemeinde im Herrenmahl (FS Lengeling), Münster 2nd edn. 1976, 360-369.

J. E. Emminghaus, Gestaltung des Altarraumes, Leipzig 1977.

---

[411] Cf. Boguniowski 446f.
[412] Cf. ibid. 449-451.
[413] Ibid. 453.
[414] Werner 223f.
[415] Cf. Bouyer, Liturgie und Architektur 83-112: VI. Tradition und Erneuerung.

J. E. Emminghaus, Der gottesdienstliche Raum und seine Gestaltung: R. Berger / K. H. Bieritz and others, GdK 3: Gestalt des Gottesdienstes. Regensburg 2nd edn. 1990, 347-416.

K. Gamber, Sancta Sanctorum. Studien zur liturgischen Ausstattung der Kirche, vor allem des Altarraums, Regensburg 1981 (Studia Patristica et Liturgica 10).

C. Gilardi, Le modéle Borroméen de l'espace liturgique, MD 193 (1993) 91-110.

J. E. Lenssen (ed.), Liturgie und Kirchenraum. Anstöße zu einer Neubesinnung, Würzburg 1986.

H. B. Meyer, Was Kirchenbau bedeutet, Freiburg-Basel-Vienna 1984.

V. Noé, L'espace liturgique dans l'église postconciliaire, MD 193 (1993) 129-139.

O. Nußbaum, Der Standort des Liturgen am christlichen Altar vor dem Jahre 1000. Eine archäologische und liturgiegeschichtliche Untersuchung (Theophaneia 18), 2 vols., Bonn 1965.

A. Reinle, Die Ausstattung deutscher Kirchen im Mittelalter. Eine Einführung, Darmstadt 1988.

C. M. Werner, Das Ende des 'Kirchen'-Baus. Rückblick auf die moderne Kirchenbaudiskussion, Zürich 1971.

2.10. THE CHURCH II: THE COMMUNITY AS ANABATIC REALITY

2.10.1. THE SECOND SUBJECT OF LITURGICAL ACTION: THE GATHERED COMMUNITY

The Church is once again the focus of attention. Not any more – as in the first chapter – under the katabatic, but under the anabatic aspect: the community assembled for the celebration of the liturgy is itself a primordial liturgical sign.[416] This anabatic aspect of the community assembled for the celebration of the liturgy proclaims that there is no individualistic way of salvation, no relationship of the individual person with God which avoids the community of the Church and its liturgical action. As a being capable of self-utterance, man is essentially structured towards community. *Anabasis* too, as the entry of man into life-creating communion with the triune God happens no differently than via the realities of man's life, of which communion with others is an essential element. For the relationship with the living God, this communion is not arbitrary, but (in) the Church as an integral part of the divine *katabasis*, as the work of the Son and the Holy Spirit as articulated in the first chapter.

This was already foreshadowed in the Old Testament. The community of the people of the Old Testament covenant was the locus of God's presence.[417] This was confirmed by Jesus's promise to be present in the midst of those gathered in his name (Mt 18:20). This presence is neither only a psychological nor a moral presence, but vividly real. Human community and brotherly acceptance among the faithful are the place where the life-creating communication with God happens. Thus every individual prayer of petition affects the whole community and conversely is taken up into the community's prayer.

---

[416] Cf. E. J. Lengeling, Liturgie als Grundvollzug christlichen Lebens: B. Fischer / E.J. Lengeling / R. Schaeffler / F. Schulz / H.-R. Müller-Schwefe: Kult in der säkularisierten Welt, Regensburg 1974, 63-91.76. Ibid.: Wort, Bild, Symbol in der Liturgie, LJ 30 (1980) 230-242. 238: "A primordial sign is the sacred assembly of the community itself. It is the expression, the image of the Church."

[417] Cf. Congar, Mysterium des Tempels 95.

The community of the faithful gathered for worship is, after the God who – through *katabasis* – initiates the process, the second, anabatically operating subject of liturgical action. This community activity is far more that the common action of assembled individuals. Rather, it continually establishes and renews a community of persons which transcends any inner-worldly relationship. In this community individual personalities discover one another to the extent to which they as individuals enter into a living relationship with God, who in himself is always already community.

This community is something completely different from a club or an association with a shared purpose, in which people channel their individual strengths to achieve a common goal, without having any further interest in the individual person. Greeley correctly characterizes as "naïve" the view that the purpose of liturgy is "to create community". "A significant part of the 'search for community' in the modern world is doomed to failure precisely because a close human relationship is not a goal to be aimed but rather a result." [418] In terms of the liturgy this means: close human relationships to one another cannot be manufactured but are the result of a common approach by all to God.

Every individual believer in his *anabasis* brings his world with him and with this his relationships with other people. The purer these relationships are, the more they are determined by unconditional love, by a disinterested affirmation of the being of the other for his own sake, the more they resemble the divine will to save. Here too, *anabasis* is profoundly anaphora since it means the lifting up into the relationship with God, the love for another person and joy in his being, for every true community of love desires intensity and eternity. And since in every individual there a fragment of the reality of the world is concentrated, in true love the world is also brought into the relationship with God. The whole reality of the world hovers in a mysterious relationship over the living God. [419] The faithful bring themselves and their world all together into the abundance of life opened to them by God. In this way they form the comprehensive *anabasis* of the Church as the community of those called to the common destiny of eternal life. Before any differences among the people of God effected by ordination, this mutual offering of one's fellow human beings and of the whole world by the individual believer, constitutes the dignity of the royal priesthood.

2.10.2. PARTICIPATIO ACTUOSA

"Active participation" a phrase coined by Pope Pius X [420] and elevated to a programme [421] by the liturgical movement, is often regarded as the decisively new element in the Constitution on the Liturgy of the Second Vatican Council. In several passages of this document (e.g. SC 14, 21,27,30,48) reference is made to the fact that the participation of the faithful in the liturgy should not be simply interior but "genuine", that is expressed.

---

[418] A. Greeley, Religiöse Symbolik, Liturgie und Gemeinschaft, Concilium 7 (1971) 106-111.110f.

[419] Dostoyevsky has elaborated this thought very clearly in his works. Cf. R. Lauth, Ich habe die Wahrheit gesehen. Die Philosophie Dostojewskis in systematischer Darstellung, München 1950, esp.463 – 465.

[420] In the motu proprio "Tra le sollecitudini" on church music of 22nd November 1903, the Pope asked for an "active participation in the mysteries and the public and solemn prayer of the Church", cf. AAS 36 (1903) 330.

[421] Thus Lambert Beaudoin at a Catholic congress of the archdiocese of Mechlin in Belgium demanded the "democratization" of the liturgy. On Lambert Beaudoin cf. L. Bouyer, Dom Lambert Beaudoin, un homme d'Eglise, Tournai 1964.

This is a reversal of the development since Carolingian times which had led to a clerical liturgy which relegated the community to the role of spectators, without including them in the action itself. According to SC 14, the Christian people by virtue of their Baptism has the right to participate actively in the liturgy and possesses the authority to do so.

The dignity of every Christian is based on the royal priesthood of the baptized. Every Christian is called by his relationship with God to contribute to the salvation of the world. [422] He responds to God's inviting love, as this found expression once on the cross of Christ and is now found in the bread an wine of the Eucharist, by receiving the divine love into himself, allowing Christ's sacrifice as it were to happen to himself, ratifies it and in doing this taking himself, his life and the world with him into salvation.

This is the realism with which we are concerned, which is the concern of all: if all the baptized and confirmed are ordained to participate in the mystery of the Eucharist, then conscious and active participation of the laity is a criterion of the integrity of the liturgy. And with this the death-knell of the "medieval clerical liturgy is sounded". The liturgy is not a "timeless cult" but the "Sacrament of the work of salvation". The novelty introduced by the Second Vatican Council consists in the official prescription by the Church of *"participatio plena, conscia et actuosa"*. [423]

On the other hand, *participatio actuosa* ought not to become the sole yard-stick of the liturgy. Active participation by all can be falsified into an ideology and the liturgy destroyed when the conclusion is drawn that worship is to be oriented towards a "de-sacralized societal reality" [424]. This would cast doubt not only on liturgical tradition but on the liturgy itself. For, according to Kavanagh, a liturgy which models itself on the profane, i.e. as represented, "divorced from God", reality of man and society, is in the final analysis incapable of symbol. Kavanagh prophesies its end in a radical seculariza-tion. [425] Active participation of all in the liturgy cannot mean making it busier by means of constantly new "productions" using various elements taken from secular, civic, be-haviour, thus enabling as many as possible to take part. According to Pieper, "there is a danger that constantly new "productions" of liturgical worship, whose declared in-tent is to make "active participation" possible, could actually make what is essential impossible, that is, genuine self-oblivious prayer". [426]

The key concept of *participatio actuosa* means that of its nature liturgy is a com-munity activity. "Here the Council has simply expressed with authority, what in itself is self-evident." [427] "Active participation" does not mean the extension of the action to all participants for its own sake, so that "liturgy" must be constantly re-designed to meet constantly changing expectations. In the long run that too would become bor-ing. [428] Encouragement of active participation does not mean the constant design of new

---

[422] Cf. J.D. Zizioulas, Die Welt in eucharistischer Schau und der Mensch von heute, US 25 (1970) 342-349. 345f.

[423] A.A. Häußling, Liturgiereform. Materialien zu einem neuen Thema der Liturgiewissenschaft, Alw 31 (1989) 1-32.27f.

[424] Cf. ibid. 29.

[425] Cf. A. Kavanagh, Symbol und Kunst in der Liturgie unter "politischem" Gesichtspunkt, Concilium 16 (1980) 97-105.100.104.

[426] J. Pieper, Das Gedächtnis des Leibes. Von der erinnernden Kraft des Geschichtlich-Konkreten: W.Seidel (ed.), Kirche aus lebendigen Steinen, Mainz 1975, 68-83.74.

[427] J. Ratzinger, Das Fest des Glaubens. Versuche zur Theologie des Gottesdienstes, Einsiedeln 1981, 79f.

[428] Cf. J. Ratzinger, Zur Frage nach der Struktur der liturgischen Feier, IkaZ 7 (1978) 488-497. 496; ibid., Das Fest des Glaubens 65.

structures – particularly not "reduced" structures – in order to "involve" as many people as possible and reduce the number of "spectators" and to attempt automatically to achieve a spiritual aim by external activity. "Active participation" means essentially the interiorization of the liturgical action by all who are taking part. Ratzinger believes that education for a highly active interiorization of the liturgical event to be "a matter of life or death for the liturgy as liturgy". [429] In order to prevent any misunderstanding, "interiorization" does not mean the reduction of community participation to a merely internal participation in an action performed by the priest alone. There can be absolutely no doubt that one of the greatest gains of the reforms, as an overcoming of the former clerical liturgy, has been the participation of the community in the performance of that liturgy in rite and text, through prayer and song, posture and movement. The task now is to bring the community to an active joint celebration of the liturgy, not to "produce" a liturgy according to the rubric of active participation.

Interiorization is also a precondition for liturgical community if the latter is to overflow the boundaries of inter-personal relations and find itself in God. The opening up of the "isolated egos" and their communication with one another does not happen by means of discussions and shared action, but through communal *participatio Dei*. "This means, that in the area of liturgical participation, which at its most profound must be participation in God and so in life, in freedom, interiorization must be a priority. This in turn means that this participation cannot be exhausted in the moment of the liturgical action, that liturgy cannot simply be imposed on people from outside like a "happening", but demands liturgical education and practice. Instead of constantly presenting new proposals for liturgical "productions", liturgics needs again and again to return to its original task of serving liturgical education, that is, assisting to develop in the faithful the capacity interiorly to appropriate the common liturgy of the Church." [430]

As *anabasis*, liturgy is the entrance of man in divinizing communication with the living God and expresses itself as adoration and the self-offering of the one celebrating to divine love. If a community "assembled for praise and veneration were to have something else in mind other than the act of perfect adoration and self-offering, as, for example, its own edification or some other undertaking, of which the community – as well as the Lord, who is to be adored – is the object, then that would be an alienating, if indeed a naïve, delusion". [431] According to Balthasar, "The norm and yard-stick for the shaping of our worship is the praise of the glory of his grace" (Eph 1:6). "It would be laughable and blasphemous were we to respond to the glory of God's grace with a counter-glory constructed from our own creaturely reserves, in contradistinction to the heavenly liturgies which the Book of Revelation present to us as completely overwhelmed and shaped by the glory of God. Whatever shape the response of our liturgy may display, it can only be an expression of the most selfless possible reception of the majesty of divine grace, even when reception does not imply passivity, but far more the most active reception of which the creature is capable." [432]

The "success" of a liturgical celebration does not in any way depend on the number of participants and on the extent to which they can "become active" or the degree to

---

[429] Ratzinger, Das Fest des Glaubens 65.
[430] Ratzinger, Zur Frage nach der Struktur der liturgischen Feier. 493f.
[431] H.U. v. Balthasar, Die Würde der Liturgie, IkaZ (1978) 481-487.481.
[432] Ibid. 482.

which they are emotionally "moved and edified". Balthasar considers "liveliness" as a criterion for worship, ambiguous in the extreme and criticizes false developments which were in no way desired by the Council, development which appeal to the principle of active participation but which have spawned a new clericalism, such as the joviality on the part of a celebrant and a form of currying favour with the congregation. Again, in a community a tendency to "celebrate itself and not God increases imperceptibly but necessarily to the extent to which belief in the Eucharistic event diminishes. The dignity of the liturgy increases with consciousness of one's own unworthiness. This cannot be manipulated or produced by technical means. If the Christian consciousness of (the majority) of the community and of the priest is genuine, then the celebration is dignified'." [433]

Despite all of modern man's poverty of expression in the face of the trivial and banal, the liturgy preserves its authenticity and dignity. Reduction of liturgical forms in the interest of active participation, mostly forms which resulted from a development over the course of history and not understood by most people, should not at all mean their replacement by contemporary but trivial substitutes drained of content, "but at its best, by a simplicity which does not need to be inferior in dignity to what has a worldly splendour but is no longer understood. 'Blessed are the poor in the Spirit', if they would only admit their poverty and not try to disguise it from themselves. If a generation can no longer create genuine religious images for its churches, then empty walls can concentrate the spirit more effectively on what is essential. If we have become little people we should not try to reduce the mystery we celebrate to our own dimensions. And if to a great extent we have become lacking in dignity, we ought to have retained, through the faith we profess, at least enough awareness of the majesty of God, – even if greater eras felt this more strongly – that we can feel that majesty where we meet it and behave in an authentic way towards God." [434] With this it is clear that the advancement of active participation cannot consist in, "tailoring the liturgy to suit cultural demands and creating new symbols to render the sacraments effective for modern sensibilities. The crassest experiements in this area are known to us all." It cannot be a question of a "civic re-inerpretation" of the Christian liturgy, not simply "celebration of life or of an elegant Christian ritual euphoria, an ecumenical tea-ceremony, corresponding to the well-known Chinese ritual of hospitality". [435]

It is the task of mystagogy to advance active participation, "The aim of Christian mystagogy as a spirituality of conrete intent is to lead to the experience of the mystery of God's self-giving to the world in ecclesial-liturgical and everyday-diaconal action. The fact that this primeval mystagogical character of Christian belief has been fairly thoroughly forgotten makes the present situation quite explosive. If Christianity wants to do justice to the epoch-making upheaval at the close of the twentieth century, and not simply capitulate in the face of the challenges posed, a new, comprehensive mystagogical effort is imperative." [436]

---

[433] Ibid. 483f.
[434] Ibid. 485f.
[435] A. Kavanagh, Bürgerliches Ritual und kirchliches Ritual bei der Feier von Höhepunkten im Lebenszyklus, Concilium 14 (1978) 80-86.80f.
[436] J. Schilson, Christliche Spiritualität im Zeichen der Mystagogie: ibid.: Gottes Weisheit im Mysterium. Vergessene Wege christlicher Spiritualität, Mainz 1989, 17-24.20-22: "Die Herausforderung christlicher Spiritualität", 20f.

2.10.3. STRUCTURED COMMUNITY IN CELEBRATION: PARTICULAR LITURGICAL MINISTRIES

The principle of active participation by all in the liturgy contains within it the notion that there can be various forms of participation, that individual believers assume special ministries in worship. As the active participation of all is the true communal celebration of the liturgy, so do all who undertake a special task – altar-servers, readers, choir-members, organist and others – perform "a truly liturgical ministry" (SC 29). Even shortly before the Council this was viewed differently. In an instruction from the Congregation of Rites on 3rd September 1958, there is still talk of the laity merely performing delegated tasks which properly belong to clerics. [437]

Liturgical service by the laity received a whole new importance with the abolition of tonsure and minor orders and the introduction, by the Apostolic letter *Ministeria quaedam* of 15th August 1972, [438] of the ministries of Acolyte and Lector with could be conferred on laypersons in a liturgical celebration. If minor orders had been regarded as tributaries of ordination, for which they were a preparation, the contemporary liturgical ministries are clearly distinguished from Holy Orders. A person commissioned to a liturgical ministry remains a layperson, his liturgical activity does not flow from ordination but from the dignity of the royal priesthood of all the baptized. Nevertheless in most communities, acolytes and lectors commissioned by the bishop are virtually never seen. Almost universally, without being commissioned by the bishop in a liturgical celebration, readers, Mass-servers and, "ministers of the Eucharist" operate, the latter being "extraordinary and temporary" eucharistic helpers appointed in accordance with the instruction *Immensae caritatis* of the Congregation for the Sacraments of 29th January 1973[439]. This two-track structure of liturgical ministry, both based on the dignity of the royal priesthood of all the baptized, has *de facto* had the result of re-introducing minor orders, since the obligatory commissioning of candidates for the diaconate and priesthood as lectors and acolytes along with the celebration of admission to candidacy for Orders, represent "new stages on the way to the reception of the sacrament of Holy Orders"[440]. It is to be surmised that the exclusion of women from the lay ministries conferred by the bishop for life, in contrast to the "non-commissioned" or "temporarily conferred" (Eucharistic) ministries, is to blame for this re-clericalisation. Martimort's argument for the exclusion of women from instituted ministry represents the re-introduction of minor orders, if the exclusion of women is based on the proximity of the office of acolyte to that of the ordained deacon. [441] The instituted offices are thus once more nothing other than tributaries of the sacrament of Orders, towards the reception of which they are oriented. If the liturgical ministry of laypersons, however, does not originate in Holy Orders but solely in the dignity of Baptism, then the exclusion of women is not understandable from the point of view of liturgical or sacramental theology and at best can be grounded on ecclesiastical tradition, the value of which is debatable. The same applies to the prohibition in 1980, since modified, of female

---

[437] Cf. Lengeling, Konstitution 64.
[438] Kaczynski 2877-2893.
[439] Kaczynski 2967-2982.
[440] This is the title of an article by B. Fischer in Gd 7 (1973) 19f.
[441] Cf. G.A. Martimort, La question du service des femmes á l'autel, Notitiae 162 (1980) 8-16.15, where the author speaks of a "bond" between deacon and acolyte, which excludes women from the latter ministry.

Mass-servers [442]. This prohibition is viewed by many canon-lawyers as overtaken by the provisions of Canon 230 of the code of 1983. [443] It is to be feared that the exclusion of women from instituted ministries is intended to preserve the appearance of male-only ministers in the sanctuary in order to stifle the tiresome debate over the ordination of women. Maas-Ewerd suggests that the current two-track structure of liturgical service by laypersons be overcome by the introduction of a new "lay subdiaconate", open to both sexes. [444]

2.10.4. LITURGY AND LAW – THE TENSION BETWEEN LITURGICAL ORDER AND FREEDOM

Are enforceable law and a fraternal Church founded on divine love mutually reconcilable? Not at all in the opinion of the Protestant canon lawyer Rudolf Sohm, because Canon Law contradicts the nature of the Church. [445] How much more at a first glance do liturgy and law contradict each other, the celebration of salvation and a justifiable, enforceable law with sanctions at its disposal. Does it not contradict the nature of celebration, which from general experience cannot do without spontaneity, if this celebration is subjected to legal regulation? Gerhards recalls the "euchological freedom" which was still taken for granted by Hippolytus of Rome and "which was limited only by the orthodoxy of the praying". [446]

The exchange of life between God and man takes place through the Son made man, that is in the historical tangibility of the incarnate one, who as the head of the Church throughout the ages, through this Church, which is a visible, communal reality, mediates the divine life to the individual members of the mystical body. In this sense the Church is "the sacrament, i.e. the sign and instrument of the most interior unity with God as of the unity of all of humanity" (LG 1). "The working of God's grace in the Church understood as the primordial sacrament, presupposes the natural mode of existence of a human community and makes use of this. In this way the human community as ecclesial *communio* becomes the sign and instrument of the operation of divine grace." [447] Sohm's thesis of the contradiction between Church and law can be understood on the basis of Lutheran principles, starting as it does with the *ecclesia abscondita* and speaks of Christ only as God, passing over, however, the Incarnation as a founding reality of the Church as the mystical body. [448]

---

[442] In the instruction *Inestimabile donum* of the Congregation for the Sacraments and the Liturgy of 3rd April 1980, no. 18, 9 (cf. Kaczysnski 3979) it states that women are not permitted to undertake the services of acolyte or Mass-server. On the situation following the letter of the Congregation for the Sacraments of 15th March 1994, cf. Gd 28 (1994) 66: According to this, the local bishop can permit female Mass-servers in his diocese. Cf. AAS 86 (1994) 541.

[443] Cf. e.g. K. Lüdicke: Liturgie und Recht. Beitrag zu einer Verhältnisbestimmung: K. Richter (ed.), Liturgie – ein vergessenes Thema der Theologie? Freiburg-Basel-Vienna 2nd edn. 1987 (QD 107), 172-184.

[444] Cf. Th. Maas-Ewerd: Nicht gelöste Fragen in der Reform der Weiheliturgie: Th. Maas-Ewerd (ed.): Lebt unser Gottesdienst? Die bleibende Aufgabe der Liturgiereform (FS Kleinheyer), Freiburg-Basel-Vienna 1988, 151-173.163f.

[445] Cf. the presentation of Sohm's position by P. Stevens: die rechtskonstituierende Bedeutung der gottesdienstlichen Versammlung, LJ 33 (1983) 5-29. 11-13.

[446] A. Gerhards: Liturgie und Recht. In: LJ 33 (1983) 1-4.3.

[447] Cf. Stevens, op. cit. Supra 12, quoting K. Mörsdorf: Kirchenrecht. München-Paderborn-Vienna 11th ed. 1964, I.24.

[448] ibid.

To a Church structure as a human community determined by the Incarnation belongs also a legal framework,[449] which encompasses liturgical celebration as a community activity performed by people. The essential reason for the legal ordering of the liturgy is "the legitimate and necessary clarification", which assembly has the right to appeal to Christ, "since he has bound his presence, which becomes tangible through signs, to the action of his Church. Liturgical order not only assures the possibilities of God's activity but also the connection of the visible Church with its mystical roots in liturgical celebrations, particularly that of the Eucharist."[450]

Canon law and liturgical law present two realities which are closely related. Canon Law contains only fundamental rules which are there for the protection of the liturgy, while liturgical law regulates the performance of the liturgy. Canon 2 of the Code of 1983 clearly aims at the securing of a space for the free ordering of the liturgy and liturgical law, independent of Canon law. Canon law provides the framework for this freedom; this means that a liturgical norm loses its validity if it contradicts the canons of the code.[451] Law, both canon law and liturgical law, is intended above all to protect the integrity of the faith, as it ought to be expressed in liturgical celebration. There is a reciprocity between the Church's liturgy and its teaching which is expressed in the formula of Prosper of Aquitaine, *Legem credendi lex statuat supplicandi*. On the one hand, liturgical text influence the formulation of theological statements, on the other hand liturgical formulas are concretisations of theological developments.[452]

The preservation of the principle *lex orandi lex credendi* makes necessary a limitation by law of creative liturgical spontaneity, if the liturgy is to be that of the whole Church and not that of the individual celebrant or of a group.[453] A fixed order is justified by the fact that the liturgy is not a self-created activity of the Church but an action instituted by Christ and entrusted to the Church, which "demands a basic order removed from all arbitrary interference". Other reasons are; defence against a new clericalism according to which the celebrant determines the liturgy; maintenance of the identity of the liturgy across the boundaries of time and place; the communitarian character of the liturgy which demands a clear order. The Christian community no longer holds to a "cultic law", the action of those gathered in Christ's name is holy in itself, not the ritual they follow. Such an action must be so free and flexible that in words and signs, in all cultural spheres and stages of development, it corresponds to the world of human imagination and expression and can be performed by all participants, existentially

---

[449] Cf. P. Krämer, Katholische Versuche einer theologischen Begründung des Kirchenrechts: Theologische Berichte 15: Die Kirche und ihr Recht. Ed. by J. Pfammater and F. Furger. Zürich-Einsiedeln-Köln 1986, 11-37.

[450] Rau 301.

[451] Cf. P. Krämer, Liturgie und Recht. Zuordnung und Abgrenzung nach dem Codex Iuris Canonici von 1983, LJ 34 (1984) 66-83.66f. For this reason the Congregation of the Sacraments and the Liturgy published the *Variationes in novas editiones librorum liturgicorum ad normam Codicis Iuris Canonici nuper promulgati introducendae*, Notitiae 20 (1983) 540-555. Kramer in op. cit. supra, p.67f. n.4, says about these that "in many cases they deal not with the settling of genuine contradictions between canon law and liturgical law, but rather with an adaptation to the new code and its altered legal terminology".

[452] Cf. Vagaggini, Theologie 308f, G. Wainright: Der Gottesdienst als "Locus Theologicus", or: Der Gottesdienst als Quelle und Thema der Theologie. In: KuD 28 (1982) 248-258. 253-255.

[453] Cf. G.M. Oury, Les limites nécessaires de la créativité en liturgie, Notitiae 13 (1977) 341-353.347-350. On spontaneity in the liturgy cf. also K. Richter, Spontaneität, Kreativität und liturgische Ordnung nach dem neuen Missale, BiLi 43 (1970) 7-14; B. Neunheuser, Lebendige Liturgiefeier und schöpferische Freiheit des einzelnen Liturgen, EL 89 (1975) 40-53.

and personally as their own." This requires a particular consideration of the celebrating community with regard to ability to understand and perform as well as the occasion of the celebration, e.g. the differing structures for the celebration of a feast occurring in the calendar and a family celebration. Not least, the blind observance of the rules can lead to a soporific routine, to counter which the creative freedom and awareness of all participants is required. [454]

Freedom for spontaneity in the liturgy and the observance of a pre-determined order form two poles of creative tension. [455] In the Latin Church there is clearly defined authority whose competence to demand adherence to prescribed norms not only generally limits spontaneity and confines it to conceded areas of freedom, but has a tendency to revoke the freedoms granted (by bishops and bishops' conferences).

"Church authority alone has the right to lead the liturgy (c. 838 §1). This means the right to determine the basic form of the official liturgy, the right to supervise this liturgy and the right to preside over a liturgical assembly." For the Latin Church this means that the Holy See regulates the liturgy of the whole Church by the issuing of the official liturgical books and by the promulgation of other norms. The bishop of the diocese, under the surveillance of the supreme authority, orders and supervises the liturgy in his local Church. He possesses with regard to the liturgy in his diocese (SC 13) his own juridical powers, whereby the code tolerates the persistence of a local customary law which is older than one hundred years. In order to be lawful, new liturgical practices require the bishop's consent. The bishops' conference possesses its own competence in the area of liturgical order. It has the right, by means of binding decisions, to adapt the general liturgy of the Church to the local conditions of the dioceses in its territory. This competence is subject to the consent of the Holy See. It is the function of bishops' conferences to prepare vernacular translations of the liturgical books, "which are to be suitably within the boundaries set by these texts themselves" and publish these books after their approval by the Apostolic See. More precisely there are two tasks involved here. The first is the official translation of the Latin liturgical text into the local vernacular. The second is the adaptation or alteration of all the Latin liturgical regulations in the light of and incorporation of local traditions, to the extent to which this possibility is expressly permitted in the normative Roman text. Indeed, the restrictions imposed by the CIC of 1983 on provisions of the Second Vatican Council are regrettable: "All lawmaking compentencies in the area of liturgy conceded to bishops' conferences since the Second Vatican Council, to the extent to which they are not specifically confirmed by the CIC, are withdrawn." [456]

The Orthodox Churches do not have a supreme authority responsible for a uniform ordering of the liturgy. Although the liturgy in the individual patriarchates, in the culturally diverse national, autocephalous Churches, indeed in one country, can vary greatly depending on regional custom, there is, despite all difference, a unity of liturgical performance in the individual Churches: "In the Orthodox Church it is an established fact that a norm accepted by all Orthodox churches, a norm which has been stamped with the

---

[454] Cf. Ph. Harnoncourt, Liturgie zwischen Gesetz und freier Gestaltung, Musik und Altar 21 (1969) 153-171. 166f.

[455] Cf. F. Nikolasch, Das liturgische Recht zwischen Liturgiekonstitution und neuem Kodex, LJ 43 (1993) 141-159.

[456] H. Socha, Begriff, Träger und Ordnung der Liturgie: J. Listl / H. Müller / H. Schmitz (eds.): Handbuch des katholischen Kirchenrechts. Regensburg 1983, §70, 632-641. 636. 638f.

seal of acceptance by the *pleroma* of the Church, is completely binding. This acceptance has been present with regard to the existing liturgical order from time immemorial. Such an acceptance also exists for the conviction that no single Orthodox Church can alter the order of the liturgy, because to do so would endanger the unity of all Orthodox Churches." [457]

"Acceptance from below" was essential for the growth of the order of the liturgy. Certain centres of religious life, monasteries or bishops, ordered the liturgy which became binding to the degree to which this order was adopted and followed. Reforms of the liturgy decreed "from above" were never accepted; the best known example of this were the reforms of Patriarch Nikon of Moscow which actually caused a schism. "Consciousness that liturgical order is not created by 'decrees from above' is so strong in the East that even in the Uniate Churches, which have long been living in a Western environment, it can come to rebellion among the people when the hierarchy dares to interfere with the liturgy." [458]

The *pleroma* of the Church is the guardian of liturgical order. "An order of the liturgy which was considered binding came into being without the promulgation of juridical decrees. This ordering of the liturgy is undoubtedly more complicated than that of the Roman rite. Because of the manner of its evolution it displays many variants, for no-one had the competence to harmonize or standardize these. Thus the juridical ordering of Orthodox liturgy has to be understood more as a framework within which one has to remain, rather than prescriptions which are simply applied." This permits, "a great variety in actual liturgical practice, despite the fact that the liturgical books are almost completely identical." "A liturgical ordering that is maintained by means of a living solidarity between the local Churches, but has not experienced the kind of codified uniformity of the post-Tridentine Roman Church, cannot remain so inflexible that finally, in order to escape from the consequences of a centuries-long failure to adapt, needs an almost explosive reform like that which look place in the Latin Church after the Second Vatican Council." [459]

2.10.5. LITURGY AND ECUMENISM

Drawing closer to separated Christians with a view to unity, is part of the community as an anabatic dimension of the Church. What was received as *katabasis* "from above" was unity, for Christ founded only one single Church which was to share in the unity of love of the Triune God. Men, because of error and guilt, have destroyed this unity. "They all confess themselves disciples of the Lord, but differ from each other in their thinking and go their different ways as if Christ himself were divided. Such a division clearly contradicts the will of Christ. It is a scandal to the world and damages the sacred task of preaching the Gospel to all creation; (UR 1). This statement is placed programmatically at the beginning of the decree on ecumenism of 21st November 1964. It is precisely in the area of liturgy that separation is most visible. But the most concrete efforts at rapprochement from both sides are also concentrated on the liturgy. The extent of the change which has taken place in a few years is made clear by comparing the regulations

---

[457] Suttner, Gottesdienst und Recht 34.

[458] Suttner, Gottesdienst und Recht 35.

[459] Suttner, Gottesdienst und Recht 36f.

in the canon law of 1917 with that of 1983 in the area of liturgical sharing between Catholic and non-Catholic Christians.

The Code of Canon Law of 1917 forbade as *communicatio in sacris* any active participation by a Catholic in the liturgy of another Christian denomination. Passive participation was permitted when there was no danger of scandal or of falling away from the faith (cf. Canon 1258, §1-2). A reappraisal of liturgical sharing between Catholics and non-Catholics is based on the recognition by the Second Vatican Council (LG 8,2; UR 3,2) of other Christian bodies as Churches or as ecclesial communities with which there is not yet full communion but which is shared the fact that they possess the gifts of the Spirit which are a mark the Church. Thus, in the Directory on Ecumenism[460] the earlier total prohibition of *communicatio in sacris* contrasts with *communicatio in spiritualibus*.

Along with regulations for intercommunion and intercelebration, still forbidden in principle, shared liturgical prayer and the joint use of holy things and places are recommended. "Since the Second Vatican Council, ecumenical liturgical sharing is no longer seen exclusively from the viewpoint of exclusive demarcation, but as a means towards the restoration of the unity of Christians. The Council describes as decisive principles witness to the unity of the Church and participation in the means of grace" (UR No. 8 par.4). The extent of liturgical sharing is determined by the existing similarities between the Churches. For this reason, the new regulations are not merely a softer line "but an adaptation to a changed understanding of the nature of Church."[461] Thus, Canon 844.2-5 states the limited possibilities for sacramental sharing in relation to Penance, Eucharist and the Anointing of the Sick. In situation where it is physically or morally impossible to have access to a Catholic priest, a Catholic may receive these sacraments in Churches which validly administer them. This validity depends on recognition of the validity of the Orders of the separated Church in question.

The so-called "Lima Declaration", a declaration of convergence in the areas of Baptism, Eucharist and Ministry, formulated in Peru in 1982, forms a milestone in on the ecumenical journey towards unity. On the basis of this declaration, Max Thurian of the ecumenical fraternity of Taizé composed a Eucharistic liturgy, the "Lima Liturgy",[462] which drew on the great traditions of the liturgical history of West and East and displays many similarities to the Roman Missal of 1970.

Bibliography

R. Ahlers / L. Gerosa / L. Müller (Hgg.), Ecclesia a Sacramentis. Theologische Erwägungen zum Sakramentenrecht, Paderborn 1992.

R. Civil, La liturgia e le sue leggi: B. Neunheuser / S. Marsili / M. Augé / R. Civil, Anamnesis – Introduzione storico-teologica alla Liturgia 1: La Liturgia – momento della storia della salvezza, Genova 3rd edn. 1992, 181-207.

P. Jounel, Les ministéres non ordinés dans l'Eglise, MD 149 (1982) 91-105.

---

[460] This applies to both the first directory of 14th May 1967 and to the new *Directorium oecumenicum* of 1993, AAS 85 (1993) 1093-1119, in particular Ch.4, 1087-1096.

[461] M. Kaiser: Ökumenische Gottesdienstgemeinschaft. In: J. Listl / H. Müller / H. Schmitz (eds.): Handbuch des katholischen Kirchenrechts. Regensburg 1983, §71, 641-647. 643.

[462] Cf. M. Thurian: Die eucharistische Feier von Lima, LJ 34 (1984) 21-31. On the German version with chants in the Slavic-Orthodox tradition, cf. K. Meyer zu Uptrup / M. Jung (eds.): Lima-Liturgie. Stuttgart 1990.

R. Kaczynski, Kein 'Amtsträger'-Ersatz. Der liturgische Dienst der Laien, Gd 15 (1981) 65-68.

B. Kleinheyer, Lektoren und Akolythen für die Liturgie in den Gemeinden, LJ 35 (1985) 168-177.

J. Listl / H. Müller / H. Schmitz (eds.), Handbuch des katholischen Kirchenrechts, Regensburg 1983.

K. Lüdicke, Liturgie und Recht. Beitrag zu einer Verhältnisbestimmung: K. Richter (ed.), Liturgie – ein vergessenes Thema der Liturgie? Freiburg-Basel-Wien 2nd edn. 1986 (QD 107), 172-184.

F. Nikolasch, Die Neuordnung der kirchlichen Dienste, LJ 22 (1972) 169-182.

S. Rau, Die Feiern der Gemeinden und das Recht der Kirche. Zu Aufgabe, Form und Ebenen liturgischer Gesetzgebung in der katholischen Kirche, Altenberge 1990 (MThA 12).

S. Schmid-Keiser, Aktive Teilnahme. Kriterium gottesdienstlichen Handelns und Feierns. Zu den Elementen eines Schlüsselbegriffs in Geschichte und Gegenwart des 20. Jahrhunderts, 2 vols., Bern-Frankfurt/M.- New York 1985 (Europäische Hochschulschriften, Reihe XXIII, Bd. 250).

E. C. Suttner, Gottesdienst und Recht in der orthodoxen Kirche, LJ 33 (1983) 30-42.

Part III

The Celebration of the Eucharist

Following on the basic reflections on the divine catabasis and the response to it in the human anabasis, part three is devoted to the celebration of the Eucharist. It is the centre of the entire liturgical life of the Church. All other sacraments, sacramental actions and celebrations of worship hinge on it. It is the actual consummation of the divine catabasis as well as of the human anabasis, the event which takes place in time and space of the life-giving communication between God and man.

R<small>ELATED BIBLIOGRAPHY AND OVERALL PRESENTATIONS OF THE</small> E<small>UCHARISTIC</small> C<small>ELEBRATION</small>

A. Adam, Die Eucharistiefeier – Quelle und Gipfel des Glaubens, Freiburg-Basel-Vienna 1991.

A. G. Martimort (ed.), L'Église en prière. Introduction á la liturgie, Vol. 2: R. Cabié, L'Eucharistie, Paris 1983.

Joh. H. Emminghaus, Die Messe. Wesen, Gestalt, Vollzug. Ed. by Th. Maas-Ewerd, Klosterneuburg 5<small>th</small> edn. 1962.

J. Hermans, Die Feier der Eucharistie. Erklärung und spirituelle Erschließung, Regensburg 1984.

A. Jilek, Das Brotbrechen. Eine Einführung in die Eucharistiefeier, Regensburg 1994.

J. A. Jungmann, Missarum Sollemnia. Eine genetische Erklärung der römischen Messe, 2 Vols., Vienna-Freiburg-Basel 5<small>th</small> edn. 1962.

J. A. Jungmann, Messe im Gottesvolk. Ein nachkonziliarer Durchblick durch Missarum Sollemnia. Freiburg-Basel-Vienna 1970.

J. Kucharek, The Byzantine-Slav Liturgy of St. John Chrysostom. Its Origin and Evolution, Allendale 1971.

Th. Maas-Ewerd / K. Richter (eds.), Gemeinde im Herrenmahl. Zur Praxis der Meßfeier (FS Lengeling), Einsiedeln-Zürich-Freiburg-Vienna, 2<small>nd</small> edn. 1976.

S. Marsili and others, La Liturgia: l'eucaristia: Anamnesis III, 2, Torino 1983.

H. B. Meyer, Eucharistie. Geschichte, Theologie, Pastoral. Mit einem Beitrag von I. Pahl: GdK IV, Regensburg 1989.

J. Pascher, Eucharistia. Gestalt und Vollzug, Münster-Freiburg i. Br. 1953.

3.1. T<small>HE</small> S<small>ACRAMENT OF</small> S<small>ACRAMENTS</small>

Corbon rightly thus describes the Eucharist; it is "the central liturgical celebration for us".[1] Vagaggini calls the Mass the "embodiment of the entire liturgy"[2] and refers to the theological tradition since Pseudo-Dionysius and especially to the organizing of the Church's entire liturgy on the celebration of the Eucharist as its centre.

---

[1] This is the heading for chapter XI, 119–128, which is quoted from the "Pseudo-Dionysius", De eccl. Hierarchia III, 1 – PG 3.424, where the Eucharist is described as "sacrament of sacraments"; for the status of the Eucharist in the circle of the other sacraments cf. Corbon, Liturgie aus dem Urquell 129–143.

[2] This is the heading of the 5<small>th</small> chapter, 115–131. On the other sacraments as referable to the Eucharist in Thomas Aquinas cf. C. Vagaggini: Theologie der Liturgie. Einsiedeln-Zürich-Köln 1959, 125–128.

3.1.1. PARTICIPATION IN THE SOURCE OF DEIFICATION

In the celebration of the Eucharist what is at issue is participation in the Body of Christ (1 Cor. 10:16). Through his human nature, in which the whole fullness of deity dwells bodily and from which men are to come to the fullness of life in him (Col. 2:9f.), man communicates with the living God, receives the uncreated grace.

"Nothing can go from God to man and from man to God, except through his Body." [3] Christ's human nature is the only means of communication between God and creation and the source of divine life from which deification can be bestowed on man and the world. In this way the Eucharistic celebration is the crucial moment of the exchange of life between God and man, a celebration in act of the universal Eucharist, in which the entire creation will be introduced into the fullness of life of the Trinity. Because in it there is question of the deifying communication with God through participation in Christ's human nature as the source of the gift of grace, therefore the Eucharist is the "mother of the sacraments". [4] This also accounts for the fact why the concept of "liturgy" in the linguistic usage of the Byzantines is confined to the celebration of the Eucharist: it is the work of the triune God for the many, exchange of life by means of the participation of the believers in the deified human nature of the Son in the Eucharistic gifts. What the liturgy is as a whole – God's work as inviting to participation in the divine life, and the Church's work as accepting this invitation – takes place fully in the Eucharistic celebration. It is not one among the seven sacraments, but rather the sacrament purely and simply, in which the deifying relationship between creator and creature takes place and has repercussions on the total vision of the world. [5]

In the Eucharist there takes place the elevation of the world to divine life; as such it is "the most positive active acceptance of the world and the entire creation", which shows itself particularly clearly in the gifts which the faithful brought as offerings in the Eucharistic celebration, "in order to offer them to God as Eucharist". The faithful are to present their world as an offering, and precisely so, as it is and as it will be anew when the eschatological light, the foretaste of paradise, which is made manifest in the liturgy, fades away and the faithful are called upon "to go out into the world in peace." [6] The fallen world is offered. "The liturgy precisely for this reason is a "medicine for immortality" (as St Ignatius of Antioch says), because in its acceptance and approval of the world it repudiates its corruption, it sanctifies it and offers it to the Creator: "Thy gifts, which we take from thy gifts, we offer to thee in everything and for everything." This paradox of the affirmation and denial of the world by the liturgy, i.e. the remodelling of the world, without destroying it, and its renewal without creating it anew out of nothing, reveals itself in time and space through the Eucharist as the Mysterium Christi. In it the old Adam is renewed, without being annihilated; human nature is assumed unaltered, man is deified without ceasing to be man. [7]

---

[3]   Corbon, Liturgie aus dem Urquell 75.

[4]   Evdokimov, L'Orthodoxie 265.

[5]   Cf. J. D. Zizioulas, Die Welt in eucharistischer Schau und der Mensch von heute, US 25 (1970) 242 – 249. 343.

[6]   Ib. 343f.

[7]   Ib. 344f.

3.1.2. REAL PRESENCE

The New Testament proclaims "the longer, the clearer the identity of the Eucharistic gifts with the incarnate Person of Jesus, who gives himself for us and for our salvation in the bloody atoning death on the cross – and here in the sacrament for our consumption, in order to bestow the redemption achieved in death". [8] But this does not yet say, how this presence was theologically conceived and what effects the attempts at clarification had on the liturgy.

For the Eucharistic presence also the Fathers used concepts like "image" and "symbol" (homoioma, antitypos, symbolon, similitudo, figura), but understood them nevertheless in the real-symbolical sense of platonic participation, not in the present-day understanding as "merely" symbolic. [9] The symbol reference is fully qualified by realism. [10] Other Fathers, such as Chrysostom and Ambrose, stress the complete identity of the Eucharistic with the historical Christ. Ambrose's Eucharistic doctrine holds good as "fruit of the encounter between the Latin and Greek mind": the Greek thought imagery is indeed broken through by the Latin mentality, the thought of the real symbol is however still vivid alongside a tendency, which understands the image already in the trend to a "mere" symbol. [11] On the whole however in patristic theology the question of the Eucharistic presence remained without being answered with uniformity and hence open to question.

This led to the medieval disputes in the West about the Eucharist. The decadence of symbol thinking led to a tangible objective realism. "In the foreground of interest came now the question of the somatic real presence of the Body and Blood of Christ in bread and wine, brought about by the consecratory act of the priest. The idea of the mystery presence of the saving work of Christ got lost." [12]

The monk Paschasius Radbertus in 853 unleashed the first controversy on the Lord's Supper by his capharnaite [13] Eucharistic doctrine: the Eucharist contains that flesh and blood of Christ which was born of Mary and was nailed on the cross. A static presence was asserted, the complete identity between the Eucharistic and historical Body of the Lord. Rabanus Maurus (d. 856) and Ratramnus (d. 877) on the other hand emphasized the act-presence: the Eucharist is the celebration of the redeeming act of Jesus, and participation in the sacrament, in which his Body and Blood are partaken of, is a participation in the Passion itself. The second controversy on the Lord's Supper originated with Berengar of Tours (d.1088), who opposed a merely symbolical extreme to the capharnaite extreme (represented by Lanfranc of Bec, d. 1089). Under Nicholas II (DH 690) and Gregory VII Berengar had to abjure the symbolical concept; in the form of abjuration (DH 700) there is mention of a change of substance ("substantialiter converti"). [14] The Fourth Lateran Council defined the doctrine of transsubtantiation against the denial of the Real Presence of Christ in the Eucharist by the Albigenses and the Cathari (DH 802). The definition was reinforced in 1415 by the Council of Constance against Wycliffe and Huss (DH 1198f., 1257), but above all by Trent as a reaction to the

---

[8]   Betz, Eucharistie II/1, 201. Warnach arrives at a similar conclusion, Symbolwirklichkeit 758.
[9]   Cf. Warnach 756f.
[10] Cf. A. Penna, "Eucharistie" und Messe, Concilium 4 (1968) 749–754. 755.
[11] Cf. Gerken 87f.
[12] Meyer, Eucharistie 201f.
[13] "cafarnaite" from "Cafarnaum" cf. Jn 6,22–59
[14] Cf. de Lubac, Corpus Mysticum 177–180.

questionings of the Reformation. "The objectivizing static conception, focused on the
somatic Real Presence of Body and Blood of Christ was partly overcome by the development of the doctrine of transsubstantiation. For the latter distinguished between the
invisible substance of the Eucharistic species and their visible outward appearance or
rather between the essence and the accidents of the Body of Christ and thereby avoided
the alternative between a material realism and a subjective symbolism. But it too remained immobilized on the somatic Real Presence. The dimension of the actualizing
presence of the Eucharistic celebration bound up with the memorial which renders it
present was lost and remained lost." [15] The sequence in which Trent handled the Eucharist is also evidence of this: the Real Presence occupies the first place. [16]

The liturgy Constitution of Vatican II also in this respect spells the "end of the
Middle Ages" (Lengeling) [17] when it carries through the change-over from a static to
a dynamic conception of the Eucharist. On SC 7 Lengeling remarks, the anti-heretical
emphasis of the somatic Real Presence of Christ in the species had as a result, "that
many believers no longer had an eye for the other modes of presence", and the concept of "Real Presence" in its traditional pattern had even led to the view that the other
modes of presence of Christ are less real than the somatic presence in bread and wine. [18]
Similarly on SC 7 Meyer remarks, the aspect of real-symbolical rite of signs provides
also for the Real Presence of Christ in the Eucharist: "The real-symbolical understanding of the liturgical celebrations coming from the Fathers and which got lost in the
Middle Ages was taken up again and made fruitful by the 'theology of mysteries' (O.
Casel) and the sacramental theology of the succeeding decades. The rather cosmic and
static way of thinking in terms of archetype and image derived from its platonic origin
has here been made Christian, i.e. made dynamic by the incorporation of the personal
element of salvation history and of the pneumatic dimension: the single, non-recurring
event of salvation history (archetypal event) appears as well as its repeatable celebration (image event) as relationship events achieved by the Spirit." [19] It is precisely as a
relationship event that the Eucharistic celebration calls for the active participation of all
believers: they are meant to share in Christ's Real Presence in the sense of the actual
presence of his saving work: the actual presence "first of all strictly speaking sets up
his Real Presence in the sacrament. Without the presupposition of a genuine mystery
presence, the Eucharist is indeed something holy, but fixed, an "object" of adoration,
but not a living action, which we share in acting out, in which we could actively take
part." [20]

This is not in contradiction with the firm retention of the concept of transsubstantiation in the encyclical "Mysterium fidei" of Paul VI of 1965. Starting from the diverse
modes of Christ's presence according to SC 7, it says of the Eucharistic presence in the
consecrated species, that it is real "per excellentiam, quia est substantialis, qua nimirum
totus atque integer Christus, Deus et homo, fit praesens", [21] *par excellence*, because it

---

[15] Meyer, Eucharistie 227f.
[16] Cf. ib. 257.
[17] Cf. E. J. Lengeling, Liturgie – Dialog zwischen Gott und Mensch. Edited and adapted by K. Richter,
      Freiburg-Basel-Vienna 1981, 13–15.
[18] Cf. Lengeling, Konstitution 20.
[19] Meyer, Eucharistie 447.
[20] Warnach, Symbolwirklichkeit 758.
[21] AAS 57 (1965) 753–774, here: 764.

is a substantial presence, by which indisputably Christ, God and man, makes himself wholly and entirely present. For the Pope the point at issue was to present clearly the reality of Christ's presence and to characterize other interpretations (transsignification, transfinalisation) as inadequate, because they did not comply with the understanding of reality defined at Trent. Irrespective of this would be the philosophical background, in the concrete case the Aristotelian hylomorphism, which lay in the background both in the Fourth Lateran Council and in Trent; "one would not do justice to the Eucharistic mystery, were one not to accept the wonderful conversion, defined by Trent, of the whole substance of the bread into the Body and the whole substance of the wine into the Blood". [22]

The Byzantine theology also starts out from this real understanding of Christ's presence in the Eucharistic species. It teaches the complete identity between the Eucharistic and the historical Christ, without lapsing into capharnaite naturalism, without assuming a static presence of Christ, without losing sight of the dynamic dimension of the Lord's presence – the actual presence of the mysteries of salvation. That is why the concept "Transsubstantiation" is avoided; terms of a more dynamic character are preferred, such as *metabole, metastoicheiosis* or *metarhythmisis*. The Eucharist indeed is not a thing to be contemplated from the outside, which does not concern man, it is no "symbol", but rather Christ himself. [23] For this reason the Eucharistic species offer no particular vision to human eyes, in contrast with the Western Eucharistic devotion of seeing; for the eyes the icon is the medium of revelation. The Eucharist is the "heavenly Bread", the mystery of exchange of life with God, it is "the moment and the place, in which the divinized humanity of Christ becomes ours". [24]

3.1.3. THE DIVINE LITURGY MADE ACCESSIBLE TO US – THE SACRIFICE

Again and again from the traditionalistic side the reproach is raised against the renewed liturgy that it does not portray sufficiently the sacrificial character of the Mass or that it denies it totally. [25] In view of this it must be remembered that the doctrine of the sacrifice of the Mass in the controversies of the Reformation period was criticized not without good reason, and in the post-Tridentine epoch suffered from Counter-Reformation contractions. A theologically satisfactory reply to the question of the relationship between the sacrifice of the Cross and the sacrifice of the Mass, of the bond between the biblically attested uniqueness and all-sufficiency of Christ's sacrifice on the Cross and the sacrificial character of the Mass only became possible through the theology of mysteries of our century. Therefore one must agree with Meyer when he sees the controversy about sacrifice or meal as the basic shape of the Mass as founded on the disregard of the dynamic understanding of Christ's presence in the sense of real symbol and on the limitation to the somatic static presence. [26]

---

[22] Cf. Warnach 758, note 10, and M. Schmaus, Der Glaube der Kirche V/3, St. Ottilien 2nd edn., 1982, 165.

[23] Cf. J. Meyendorff, Initiation á la théologie byzantine, Paris 1975, 271.

[24] Cf. ib. 271–273.

[25] Cf. for instance the comments of M. Lefèbvre, Der Priester und das heilige Meßopfer, Una-Voce-Korrespondenz 1 (1971) 306–313.

[26] Cf. Meyer, Eucharistie 447.

It was nominalism, incapable of (real)symbolical thinking, which in the later Middle Ages fully undid the unity between the sacrifice of the Cross and the sacrifice of the Mass. People asked about the 'worth' of the Mass for the living and the dead, about the 'fruits of the Mass' – to be applied to the donors of the stipends – and could understand a real sacrifice of the Mass only as the actual offering of a new sacrifice. The Mass was no longer seen as the real, present, one and only sacrifice of Christ, but rather as the work of the human and therefore also sinful priest, who as such can offer no sacrifice which could have infinite value. Consequently a Mass which is offered for several living and dead, has less worth for the individual than if it were celebrated for him alone. [27] This view of the sacrifice of the Mass for obtaining a limited amount of graces reinforced still more the notion widespread in the Middle Ages that one could 'buy' these fruits of grace by the contribution of the Mass stipend. [28] All told the sacrificial character of the Mass was little reflected upon, but in the explanations of the Mass for the people was popularized in a manner, which was bound to provoke the protest of the reformers. The rejection of the sacrifice of the Mass on the part of Luther and the other reformers has to be seen against the background of this development. [29]

Catholic theology was and is committed to the Tridentine definition of the Mass as "sacrificium visibile et propitiatorium" (DH 1743ff.), which however in addition compels one to express correctly the unity of the sacrificial act on the cross and in the Mass. This unity can be interpreted in a twofold way, either as the eternally actual continuation of Christ's sacrificial act in heaven, which becomes actual presence in every Mass, or as the act in the celebration of Mass, of Christ's self-offering, who as the primary agent works through his priest. [30] As Actio Christi the sacrifice of the Mass is "repraesentatio" of the sacrifice of the cross. It was only the newly rediscovered understanding of this concept of representation in the theology of mysteries which could make intelligible, how the sacrifice of the Mass can be the presence of the sacrifice of the cross and hence can itself be a sacrifice, without however being a sacrifice on its own. Without the theology of mysteries the most varied theories of the sacrifice of the Mass led into a cul-de-sac: "It seems, that devout thinking finds itself in a hopeless dilemma. Either holy Mass is a real sacrifice, but then the uniqueness of the New Testament sacrifice seems to be abandoned, or the uniqueness of the sacrifice of the new covenant is maintained, but then it seems that holy Mass cannot be referred to as sacrifice." [31]

The sacrifice of the Mass also has to be seen first of all in its catabatic dimension. That is to say, that in it "the Crucified One who has become Kyrios" is at the focal point; his sacrifice on the cross becomes present in the Mass. [32] It is in line with the precedence of the catabatic dimension if in connection with the sacrifice of the Mass an 'inversion

---

[27] Cf. E. Iserloh, Der Wert der Messe in den Diskussionen der Theologen vom Mittelalter bis zum 16. Jahrhundert, ZKTh 83 (1961) 44–79, especially 58–65.

[28] Cf. J. Merk, Abriß einer liturgiegeschichtlichen Darstellung des Meßstipendiums, Stuttgart 1928, 94f.

[29] Cf. E. Iserloh, Gnade und Eucharistie in der philosophischen Theologie des Wilhelm von Ockham. Ihre Bedeutung für die Ursachen der Reformation, Wiesbaden 1956; E. Iserloh / P. Meinhold, Abendmahl und Opfer, Stuttgart 1960; N. Halmer, Der literarische Kampf Luthers und Melanchthons gegen das Opfer der Messe, Divus Thomas 21 (1943) 63–78; H. B. Meyer, Luther und die Messe, Paderborn 1965.

[30] Cf. F. Eisenbach, Die Gegenwart Jesu Christi im Gottesdienst. Systematische Studien zur Liturgiekonstitution des II. Vatikanischen Konzils, Mainz 1982, 369f.

[31] Schmaus, Das eucharistische Opfer 19.

[32] Cf. O. Casel, Das christliche Opfermysterium. Zur Morphologie und Theologie des eucharistischen Hochgebetes, ed. by V. Warnach, Graz-Vienna-Köln 1968, 136.

of the line of vision' is required: "When we speak of sacrifice in a religious sense, we naturally think from ourselves to God. The fundamental New Testament statement on sacrifice, therefore, the sacrifice of Jesus Christ, looks precisely in the opposite direction. The fundamental and first statement is: God himself acts, he sacrifices, he gives gifts, he is the initiator of this sacrifice in which reconciliation is granted." [33] Similarly Ratzinger: "The sacrifice itself already comes from God's incarnate love, and is always already from within a giving by God of himself, into which he takes man." [34] The leading thought of the epistle to the Hebrews lies also at the basis of Luther's criticism, that Christ's sacrifice on the cross is the once for all time sufficient sacrifice, "in which God himself bestows on us the true, reconciling sacrifice in contrast to the uselessness of our cult. Christian cult can therefore no longer consist in offering its own gifts, rather in its essence it is the receiving of the once only bestowed saving act of Jesus Christ, hence thanksgiving: Eucharistia." [35] The Eucharist is the "gift of *communio*, in which the Lord becomes food for us, just as it signifies the sacrifice o f Jesus Christ, who completes his trinitarian yes to the Father in the yes of the cross and in this "sacrifice" has reconciled us all to the Father". [36]

Against the alleged opposition between the Mass as sacrifice (which formerly was to the fore) and as meal (which is presumed to be the specific mark of the renewed liturgy) one should refer to the inner unity of both aspects – already touched on in Part 1 – which according to von Balthasar consists in the acceptance by the Church of Christ's self-offering, in concurring with what Christ has accomplished for her and allowing it to take place and which expresses itself in the sacramental communion. "Whoever wishes to let himself be 'devoured' by men, needs a mouth that eats and drinks him, thus Balthasar summarizes in a unity the analogy of meal and sacrificial self-offering of Christ with the sacrificial concurrence of the Church." [37] Henrici reasons quite similarly. [38]

In the eucharistic celebration Christ offers himself as food and drink for eternal life. His death on the cross ought not to be separated from this sacrificial gift of God's Son to his disciples for their eternal life. Christ's self-offering to men for their eternal life, and the allowing this sacrifice to happen to themselves by men, constitute the Mass as sacrifice, by which mortal, sinful man is reconciled with God who is life itself, by receiving a share in the divine fullness of life. The decisive element which in addition man can and must contribute is that he allow the sacrifice to take place; first of all in himself, but after that also in the intercession for the sisters and brothers, for the living and the dead, whom he so to speak by means of himself and his concurrence draws along together with himself into this sacrifice which dispenses life.

---

[33] Th. Schneider, Zeichen der Nähe Gottes. Grundriß der Sakramententheologie, Mainz 6th edn. 1992, 167.

[34] J. Ratzinger, Das Fest des Glaubens. Versuche zur Theologie des Gottesdienstes, Einsiedeln 1981, 84.

[35] Ratzinger, Ist die Eucharistie ein Opfer? 300.

[36] Ratzinger, Das Fest des Glaubens 45f.

[37] Bätzing 107.

[38] Henrici 153: In the reception of the Eucharistic gifts the strictly speaking decisive sacramental feature is given expression: that the Eucharist is Christ's sacrifice and not in the first place a sacrifice which the faithful offer to God. It is not we who offer up Jesus to the Father, rather he offers himself, by giving himself to us. Already on the cross... the sacrifice was not fulfilled in a so to speak private relationship between two persons, between Father and Son; on the contrary his death became a sacrifice for the many, for those and through whose (sinful!) hands Jesus offered up his life.

Unworthy questions about the application and benefits of the sacrifice that can be accurately described and applied, removed far away from the whole sacrament of the Eucharist, could thus give back once again to the Mass stipend and the Mass intention connected with it, the meaning which it had in the ancient Church as the expression of co-offering. [39]

3.1.4. THE COMMUNITY WHICH CELEBRATES THE EUCHARIST

"Christ's death on the cross and resurrection constitute the genotype of the Eucharistic mystery. The essential reality and event of the Eucharistic mystery has its basis in the historical death and historical resurrection of Christ." Alongside this however there holds good: "Only as the act of the Church can the Eucharistic mystery exist." [40] Only when Christians come together to celebrate the Eucharist, can this take place; only then can Anaphora happen, the offering up of the world by man, who accepts the invitation to participation in the fullness of divine life. This is the consequence of what von Balthasar says: Only when there are people who prepare the Eucharist as celebration and make available the gifts of creation and of human work, only when people by communicating allow Christ's sacrifice to happen to themselves, can there be Eucharist. The Church as second agent of the Eucharistic celebration stands in partnership with Christ the first agent, so that the latter can succeed in working within time and space. It is already clear from the concept of Christ's sacrifice becoming accessible to us through the reception of Communion that the Eucharist never can be the "work" of the celebrating priest alone, but rather -in that partnership of agents – the work of the total community, for whom the ordained minister performs the service of the representation in time and space of the invisibly present Christ.

Both – the entry of man into the life-giving communication with God and the consequent Anaphora of creation through him – is a happening which takes place in the celebration in time and space in genuine completion with the help of reality which is accessible to the senses. In fact the community which celebrates the Eucharist, is as the mystical Body no spiritual magnitude, rather has a share in its Head, who became incarnate at a definite *kairos* in the historical reality of this world. It has "participation in the historical, not only in the mystical Christ, in so far it lives not only from the Spirit sent by the Father and Christ, but equally from the mission which Christ transmitted to his apostles, i.e. from an historical mission which established power and right in an historical form, which in turn also is present historically (not merely mystically) in the historical reality of the hierarchy, the succession of the apostles and their assistants." [41]

Within its historical limitations and cultural handicaps in the different epochs of her history, but always on the basis of the participation in the incarnate character of the Mystical Body, which persisted throughout all times and was raised above all change against all suggestions of an intellectual spiritualism – the Church makes herself and the cultural means of her respective time available, so that Eucharist can take place.

Bibliography

[39] Cf. J. A. Jungmann, Meßintention und Meßstipendium: A. Kirchgäßner (ed.), Unser Gottesdienst. Freiburg-Basel-Vienna 3rd edn. 1960, 37–43, esp. 41f.
[40] J. B. Auer, Theologie der Eucharistie in katholischer Sicht: C. Suttner (ed.), Eucharistie – Zeichen der Einheit. Erstes Regensburger Ökumenisches Symposion, Regensburg 1970, 52–66.54.
[41] Ib. 54f.

G. Bätzing, Die Eucharistie als Opfer der Kirche nach Hans Urs von Balthasar, Einsiedeln 1986.

J. Betz, Die Eucharistie in der Zeit der griechischen Väter. Vol. I/1: Die Aktualpräsenz der Person und des Heilswerkes Jesu im Abendmahl nach der vorephesinischen griechischen Patristik, Freiburg i. Br. 1955. Vol II/1: Die Realpräsenz des Leibes und Blutes Jesu im Abendmahl nach dem Neuen Testament, Freiburg i. Br. 2nd edn. 1964.

O. Casel, Das Gedächtnis des Herrn in der altchristlichen Liturgie. Die Grundgedanken des Meß-canons. (Ecclesia Orans 2), Freiburg i. Br. 8th edn. 1922

O. Casel, Das christliche Kultmysterium, Regensburg 3rd edn. 1948.

O. Casel, Das christliche Opfermysterium, ed. by V. Warnach, Graz-Köln-Vienna 1968.

A. Gerken, Theologie der Eucharistie, München 1973.

P. Henrici: "Tut dies zu meinem Gedächtnis". Das Opfer Christi und das Opfer der Gläubigen: Id., Glauben-Denken-Leben. Gesammelte Aufsätze, Köln 1993, 143–154.

A. Hermans, Die Eucharistiefeier – Gegenwart Christi. Erwägungen und Gebete zu den einzelnen Teilen der Meßfeier, Kevelaer 1987.

A. Jorissen, Die Entfaltung der Transsubstantiationslehre bis zum Beginn der Hochscholastik, Münster 1965.

H. de Lubac, Corpus Mysticum. L'Eucharistie et l'Eglise au Moyen âge, Paris 2nd edn. 1949

A. Ratzinger, Ist die Eucharistie ein Opfer? Concilium 3 (1967) 299–304.

A. Schmaus, Das eucharistische Opfer im Kosmos der Sakramente: B. Neunheuser (ed.), Opfer Christi und Opfer der Kirche. Die Lehre vom Meßopfer als Mysteriengedächtnis in der Theologie der Gegenwart, Düsseldorf 1960, 13–27.

V. Warnach, Symbolwirklichkeit der Eucharistie, Concilium 3 (1967) 755–765.

3.2. A SKETCH OF THE HISTORY OF THE EUCHARISTIC CELEBRATION

How has what has been said in the foregoing paragraphs on the significance of the Eucharist as the "Sacrament of Sacraments" affected the form of its celebration in the course of the historical development? This question must now be gone over in a broad survey.

3.2.1. FROM THE BEGINNINGS UP TO HIPPOLYTUS OF ROME

The Judæo-Christian primitive community of Jerusalem especially still lived on a litur-gical "double-track": they took part in the Temple cult and the synagogue worship, and did this without misgivings, for this worship was after all applicable to the Father of Jesus Christ, whom the Christians indeed also praised through the Son, even were al-lowed to call him their Father. How self-evident for the first Christians was participation in the synagogue worship, Ellbogen points out from the fact that among other things the adoption of prayers for the extermination of the "apostates" contributed to the definitive differentiation of Christianity from the faith of Israel, because the Judæo-Christians al-ready on their account could no longer frequent the synagogue worship, much less to appear there as cantor.[42] According to Häußling the first Christians in Jerusalem "satisfied" their desire for solemn divine services precisely in the Temple worship – their own specifically Christian liturgy at the moment was still very simple in structure.[43]

The primitive Christian Eucharistic celebration consisted of a meal in common. But already in the Jewish tradition this never lacked a religious dimension, which expressed itself especially in the 'Kiddush', in the solemn prayer of thanksgiving (Berakah) completed with a glass of wine and in the breaking of bread by the father of the house. The meal began with the breaking of bread. A solemn prayer of thanksgiving formed the conclusion, in which the father of the house spoke three prayers of blessing over a silver blessing cup (thanksgiving for the shared meal, praise for the Promised Land and a petition for Jerusalem), each time with an invitation "Praise ye Adonai our God". The blessing cup was passed to all the participants of the meal, and the meal ended with a psalm. According to the Lukan account of the Last Supper the first cup (Lk 22:17) as well as the breaking and handing of the bread stand in the tradition of the Kiddush which opened the meal, while the word over the cup "after supper"(Lk 22:20) goes back to the cup of blessing at the end of the meal. Whether then Jesus' Last Supper was a Passover meal or not, it is quite certain that it stood in the tradition of the Jewish festive meals, ritual in form and of a religious stamp, which saw themselves as religious festivals dedicated to the covenant God of Israel, far above the mere eating and experience of life together. The decisively new element is, that with the Last Supper the new covenant is established in the sacrificed Body and Blood of Christ. After the Ascension the apostles remained in the community of this breaking of bread "in the houses", but day by day were attending the temple together (cf. Acts 2:42.46).[44]

Thus the biblical expressions "breaking of bread" and "Lord's Supper" emphasize the meal character of the Eucharistic celebration. Under "breaking of bread" the relevant scriptural passages (for example Acts 20:7; 1 Cor10:16ff; 11:17–34) understand both the *agape,* the love-meal of Christians, and also the Eucharistic meal. The term "Lord's Supper" however intends to distinguish more accurately between the brotherly meal of a religious character of the faithful and the Lord's Supper strictly so called, which must differentiate itself from the *agape*, as Paul expresses it in 1 Corinthians. The problems touched on there (11,20–22.33–34), to hold separately *agape* and Lord's Supper, led to separation. According to 1 Cor 11:29 it was a question of the vitally imperative distinction between the special nature of Lord's Body and every other food.[45]

Thus Justin Martyr describes summarily the Eucharistic celebration, but does not mention the *agape* explicitly, perhaps in order not to draw too much attention to the Church's practice, on account of the prohibition of such "cult meals" by emperor Trajan.

---

[42] Cf. I. Ellbogen: Der jüd. Gottesdienst in seiner geschichtlichen Entwicklung. Frankfurt/M. 3rd edn. 1931, Reprint Hildesheim 1962, 36–38.

[43] Cf. Häußling, Liturgiereform 22.

[44] Cf. the good summary in K. Gamber: Eucharistiefeier in der Kirche der ersten Jahrhunderte: C. Suttner (ed.), Eucharistie - Zeichen der Einheit. Erstes Regensburger Ökumenisches Symposion, Regensburg 1970, 13–21 13–17.

[45] Cf. H. Mühlen, Entsakralisierung. Ein epochales Schlagwort in seiner Bedeutung für die Zukunft der christlichen Kirchen, Paderborn 2nd edn. 1970, 19: This distinction is absolutely unalterable for Christians, because it is a question here of life and death! In order to keep present the uniqueness of this bread, Christians have created for themselves a separate space, a separate time, have surrounded the meal with rites and ceremonies, which are intended to proclaim its separateness.

Tertullian indeed mentions the fraternal meal, but says that the Eucharist was celebrated in the early morning ("*antelucanis* coetibus") separately from the *agape*[46].

The separation of the Eucharist from the fraternal meal and the adoption of "cultic elements" into the Eucharistic celebration did not happen in order to satisfy an existing "need for cult" or to express the faith in contemporary thought categories, which in fact were cultic,[47] but also have to be judged according to the terms of 1 Cor 11:29.

In addition the growth of the communities had as a result that the original combination of agape and Lord's Supper for practical reasons anyway could not be maintained. Thus the tables disappeared out of the assembly room, and there remained as the origin of the Christian altar only that table on which bread and wine were laid, over which the president said the great prayer of praise. Thus according to Jungmann one can conclude from the letter written by Pliny the governor of Bithynia to the Emperor Trajan about 111–113 that there were two different meetings: a morning assembly which the Christians did not want to relinquish in contrast to an evening gathering, suggests the Eucharistic celebration, while the evening hour is interpreted as less important *agape*.[48] But something new supervened to the Eucharistic celebration separated from the fraternal meal: according to a frequently expressed opinion the early Church took over the liturgy of the word from the tradition of the synagogue and combined it with the Lord's Supper; this combination into an integrated celebration of worship is mentioned incidentally in the First Apology of Justin Martyr written about AD 150: at the Sunday Eucharistic celebration the "memoirs of the apostles" and the "writings of the prophets" were read before the president, after an address, said the great prayer of praise of the Eucharist over the gifts which had been brought to him.[49]

The distinctive nature of the Lord's Supper gained a special expression precisely in the name of "Eucharist" which prevailed more and more from the turn of the first century. By it is meant first of all the great prayer of thanksgiving: in the celebration of the Eucharist the assembled community thanks God the Father for the redemption which has taken place in Christ, of which however the saving acts are not "thought about" in the sense of an event lying in the past, but rather which the celebrating community knows is in its midst as a present salvation event. When Christ's saving acts are mentioned with praise these stand in the liturgical Now, and the celebrating community relates them to itself. In this sense the gifts of bread and wine, over which the great Thanksgiving was spoken, can also assume the designation of "Eucharist"; in the anamnetic rendering present of the Christ-event "there takes place" the same thing as in the Cenacle, because the Church does not only think about Christ, but rather knows him even as present and operative in her, and thus fulfils the anamnesis command, to do this in his memory. Remembering von Balthasar's position: the liturgical assembly, in anamnetic praise and recall, allows to happen to her, that Christ here and now offers himself for her, and becomes food and drink for her in the gifts over which the *Eucharistia* was spoken and which thereby became "Eucharist" themselves. In this way there arises a relationship of the "Eucharist" to the sacrifice.

---

[46] Cf. Gamber loc. Cit. 18f.

[47] Thus P. Stockmeier, Vom Abendmahl zum Kult: N. J. Frenkle / F. J. Stendebach / P. Stockmeier / Th. Maas-Ewerd: Zum Thema Kult und Liturgie. Notwendige oder überholte Ausdrucksform des Glaubens, Stuttgart 1972, 65–104, esp. 97f.

[48] Cf. Jungmann MS I, 23.

[49] Apol I, 67 -PE 68–73, cited according to Jungmann MS I,29f.

The praise of the Father for the redemption which has taken place in Christ does not happen without earthly gifts. The theology of Irenaeus of Lyons which was directed against the Gnostic disdain for the visible creation emphasized this particularly: the offering of the heart is decisive indeed, and God has no need of earthly offerings, but because in Christ the whole of creation is recapitulated, it too is offered in sacrifice to God the Father through Christ in the Eucharistic praise. In this way bread and wine are signs of the heart's offering, but above and beyond this, the offering of gifts of the faithful has found a place in the Eucharistic celebration which has nothing in common with cultic offering of gifts of nature. With praise the community enters into Christ's movement to the Father and brings with it the world in which it lives. Through Christ it brings to the Father and into the fullness of life of the Trinity created reality expressed by the gifts.

The most important liturgical historical source from the beginning of the 3rd century is the "Apostolic Tradition" of Hippolytus of Rome (before 170 – 235). His opposition to the Roman bishop Callistus (217 – 222) made him the ringleader of a small schismatic community. Together with Pontianus, the successor of Callistus he was banished to Sardinia, and the schism was able to be resolved. [50] The "Apostolic Tradition" composed in Rome about 215 is the first detailed description of liturgy and also offers prayer texts. After treating of Church offices and ministries there follow Ordination prayers for the ordination of the bishop, of the presbyters and the deacons, the Eucharistic Prayer, blessings for oil, cheese and olives. Regulations for the reception of new catechumens, an exposition of the catechumenate, a description of the baptism, confirmation and the first Eucharist of the newly baptized are also included. The final part of the "Apostolic Tradition" consists of separate instructions on fasting, the evening blessing of light, the common meal, the paschal fast, the duties of deacons, the careful handling of the Eucharist, cemeteries, times of prayer, and the sign of the cross. [51] In spite of the detailed description of the liturgy, in principle the freedom for spontaneous provision of liturgical texts still holds, such as meets us in Justin's Apology, where it is said, let the president, as much as he is able to, send up prayers and thanksgivings to God. Hippolytus' work is no obligatory ritual, but rather a model for liturgical action in the sense of that apostolic tradition in which the author – in contrast to his opponents – believes he stands. Hence the Eucharistic celebration described here does not portray purely and simply, the Roman Mass then customary, even if the Traditio Apostolica gives information about the liturgical life of this city. In particular the closed, strongly christologically orientated Anaphora is only one of several types in course of development, of which one expands the christological statements with Old Testament material, the other makes use of the language of Hellenistic philosophy, with which God is addressed and thanksgiving offered with concepts of cultic worship and a philosophically orientated knowledge of God ("Incomprehensible, Uncreated . . . ").But always in the Eucharistic celebration it is a question of the one, Christian thanksgiving to the Father

---

[50]   On the person and work of Hippolytus cf. B. Altaner / A. Stuiber, Patrlogie. Leben, Lehre und Schriften der Kirchenväter, Freiburg-Basel-Vienna 8th edn. 1978, 82 – 84, 164 – 169.

[51]   The latest edition of the Traditio Apostolica has been compiled by W. Geerlings and includes the edition by B. Botte: FC 1, Freiburg-Basel-Vienna 1991.

for the redemption achieved in Christ, even when the varying cultural forms already at this early stage provide for differentiation. [52]

3.2.2. FROM THE FOURTH CENTURY UP TO THE EARLY MIDDLE AGES

There are various reasons for placing a historical turning point in the fourth century: from being an oppressed minority the Church became a privileged imperial Church, it expanded greatly and became the bearer of the culture of antiquity. The communities became larger, a fact which on account of the difference between a small group and a large community, by reason of the totally differently designed spaces, at least hindered spontaneity in prayer and celebration, if not made it wholly impossible. Furthermore the fourth century was the epoch of the great disputes about the basic truths of the faith, which according to the principle established by Prosper of Aquitaine "lex orandi lex credendi" was bound to find expression also in the celebration of the liturgy. [53] Not only did it become increasingly the rule, to set down liturgical texts in writing and to re-use them on other occasions, but also to take over those of other churches, but in which the question of orthodoxy required an examination of these latter. [54] Moreover Christianity spread out from influential centres: in the East these were above all Syrian Antioch and Egyptian Alexandria. With their influence their liturgy also spread (for example the "Clementine Liturgy" ascribed to Clement I, but which first appeared about 380, and is contained in Book 8 of the Apostolic Constitutions, or the Euchologion of Bishop Serapion from Thmuis in Lower Egypt (339–362), a friend of St Athanasius. Antioch and Alexandria determined the Eucharistic liturgy of the Christian East; the Antiochene tradition turned out to be particularly fruitful: it was to reach as far as India by the various Syriac rites, and through the Slav territories evangelized from Constantinople found a wide radiation in the Byzantine rite as far as Armenia, while the influence of Alexandria limited itself essentially to Egypt and Ethiopia. [55] The singular liturgical life of Jerusalem, to all intents and purposes the pilgrim centre of Christendom, exercised a great influence on the development in East and West.

Above and beyond all differences Meyer names two characteristics of all oriental liturgies: their mystery and symbol character and the liturgy of the local community. Not least on the basis of the (neo)platonic doctrine of archetype and image there takes place in the earthly assembly by the intervention of the Holy Spirit a real symbolical imaging of the archetypal salvific action of God in Christ. The Eucharistic liturgy is a visible imaging of the heavenly liturgy and therefore above all a mystery drama with many-sided symbolism. Meyer speaks of a "present" (vertical) eschatology: in the celebration itself, "heaven opens". The realization of this mystery drama always took into consideration the varying local and cultural assumptions. In the greater autonomy of the local Churches "a continuous process of maintaining and developing of tradition" could take place, which not only produced a popular community liturgy, into which the com-

---

[52]   Cf. Jungmann, MS I, 39–42.
[53]   Cf. C. Vagaggini, Theologie der Liturgie, Einsiedeln-Zürich-Köln 1959, 309.
[54]   Thus already the synod of Hippo in the year 393 confirmed by the synod of Carthage 397, cf. Mansi III, 884 and 922: 'Et quicumque sibi preces aliunde describit, non eis utatur nisi prius eas cum instructoribus fratribus contulerit.'
[55]   Cf. Jungmann MS I, 43–57.

munity was ever more drawn than in the West, but also a pre-eminence of the liturgy over all other expressions of Church life – including theology! – which were aligned on worship as their centre.[56] Nevertheless one may not judge the Eastern special development against the background of the liturgical historical background of the West. What may appear to a westerner as a clerical liturgy (already through the division of the church into the sanctuary behind the iconostasis and the place of the faithful in front of it), is the outward scenario of a cult drama, into which the faithful were ever more actively bonded, than was the case in the western Mass of the Middle Ages. Moreover the East retained a good many things, which the post-Vatican reform still had to recover again: Theodorou rightly mentions concelebration and the ministry of (a real) deacon; in addition one could refer to the unbroken Communion under both kinds and the much less ideologically loaded question of liturgical language.[57]

The West also knew various rites up to and into the Middle Ages, all of which however possessed an important mutuality in the Latin language.

The liturgy of Gaul formed an independent important entity at least since the fifth century. It reached its highest development and widest expansion in the sixth and seventh centuries, but disappeared with the adoption of the Roman liturgy in Carolingian times. The old Gallic (an) Eucharistic celebration can be reconstituted from the sources with a certain reliability, and many elements were able to maintain themselves in the different Order liturgies and also in some localities against all unification tendencies.[58] Related to the old Gallic Mass liturgy was the "Celtic liturgy" in England, Scotland, Ireland and Brittany.[59] The Mozarabic liturgy of Spain[60] is akin in structure to the old Gallic. Its celebration – following the "Missale mixtum" which was compiled about 1500 by Cardinal Ximenes under Roman influences – is in the main confined to one chapel in Toledo Cathedral. The Mozarabic liturgy is characterized by the *Trisagion* between the Gloria and the "Oratio post Gloria", three readings (Prophecy – Apostolus – Evangelium), the kiss of peace before the Eucharistic Prayer, breaking of the host after the Eucharistic Prayer, followed by the confession of faith. The liturgy reform gave a strong impetus to efforts to revitalize the ancient Spanish liturgy.

The Milanese liturgy is celebrated in Milan up to today; it is mistakenly called "ambrosian", because there were firm liturgical traditions before Ambrose. This liturgy developed throughout many centuries by adopting also Roman, Eastern, Gallic and even Romano-Frankish elements. The Messale Ambrosiano published in 1976 is an example "of the experiment of a local Church to preserve its independence, to seek unity with the Church of Rome and in so doing to further develop its own liturgy creatively." For example formerly there was a triple Kyrie after the Gloria, today however the Milanese Eucharistic celebration follows the new Roman Missal up to the prayer of the day. Also

---

[56] Cf. Meyer, Eucharistie 148f.
[57] Cf. E. Theodorou, Die byzantinische Eucharistiefeier: C. Suttner (ed.): Eucharistie – Zeichen der Einheit. Erstes Regensburger Ökumenisches Symposion, Regensburg 1970, 22 – 30.25f.
[58] Cf. Meyer, Eucharistie 154 – 157. Like Jungmann, MS I, 61 – 63, Meyer offers 156f the reconstruction of the Gallic Mass in its final state. On the Mass of Lyons cf. D. Buenner, Die Liturgiefeier von Lyon, Liturgie und Mönchtum / Laacher Hefte 26, Maria Laach 1960, 71 – 78.
[59] Cf. Meyer, Eucharistie 160f.
[60] Cf. A. Franquesa, Die mozarabische Messe, Liturgie und Mönchtum / Laacher Hefte Heft 26, Maria Laach 1960, 58 – 70; K. Gamber, Der altgallikanische Meßritus als Abbild himmlischer Liturgie, Regensburg 1984 (Studia patristica et liturgica, 14. Beiheft), 14f.; Meyer, Eucharistie 157 – 159.

the Credo moved from its original position after the placing of the gifts (as with the Byzantines) to the usual place between the Homily and the bidding prayers. The kiss of peace can take place today either following the rite of the ancient Church before the preparation of the gifts or before the Communion. The faithful have a share in the preparation of the gifts: in addition to bread and wine they can bring other gifts to the altar and in so doing receive the priest's blessing. Apart from the four Eucharistic Prayers of the Roman Missal the Milanese Missal has two others, one for the celebration of Holy Thursday (or for Masses on a Eucharistic theme) and one for Easter night, which can also be used for the celebration of initiation. The Roman Agnus Dei is missing, in its stead the "Confractorium", a variable accompanying chant, accompanies the breaking of bread, which opens the Communion part of the Mass. The Milanese Missal contains a great number of euchological texts (prefaces, prayers); according to Meyer in contrast to the 1000 such texts in the Roman Missal there are 2500 in the Milanese. [61]

But how had the Roman liturgy developed since Hippolytus? In the second half of the third century the transition from Greek to Latin took place under Damasus (366 – 384). According to Jungmann the origins of the Latin Mass in Rome lie in 'deep darkness'; many elements of the Roman Mass can be traced back to the fifth/sixth century, but are in "sharp contrast" to that liturgy such as Hippolytus transmits to us. [62] The Roman Canon is counted among them; its transmission exhibits both Greek vestiges as well as Latin witnesses of the text in Ambrose, a fact which allows one to conclude to a link with the liturgy of Milan. The variable prefaces and the priestly prayers in the typical Roman prayer form also go back to this stage. The most important structures of the Roman Mass must have been completed at the turn of the fifth century, except for a few interventions by Gregory the Great. [63] A characteristic feature was constituted by the system of titular Churches, which were considered "filial Churches" of the single city community of Rome; the station liturgies in them were meant to emphasize the unity of the "city parish" under the leadership of the Pope. On the basis of the Ordo Romanus I Jungmann describes the station liturgy of the seventh century. [64]

The name "Mass" is connected with the dismissal formula "Ite Missa est", whence in most European languages the dependent words and word groups were formed: "Mass", "Messe", "messe", "messa" etc. The derivation from Latin "mittere – to send, dismiss" might at first set a riddle on the origin and meaning of "missa". [65] In the Reformation period the word "Mass" met with stubborn rejection, because in the Reformation view it was connected with the rejected sacrifice of the Mass. [66] In point of fact the sac-

---

[61] Cf. O. Heiming, Die Mailander Meßfeier, Liturgie und Mönctum / Laacher Hefte Heft 26, Maria Laach 1960, 48–57. Meyer, Eucharistie 161–164. Righetti also deals extensively with the history of the Milanese rite: M. Righetti, Manuale di storia liturgica III: L'Eucaristia, Milano 2nd edn. 1956. Underlying the present-day Milanese liturgy is the Messale Ambrosiano secondo il rito della Santa Chiesa di Milano. Riformato a norma dei decreti del Concilio Vaticano II, Milano 1976.

[62] Cf. Jungmann, MS I, 63.

[63] Ib. I, 75.

[64] Cf. ib. 88–98.

[65] Cf. on this: J. A. Jungmann, Zur Bedeutungsgeschichte des Wortes missa: Id., Gewordene Liturgie. Studien und Durchblicke, Innsbruck-Leipzig 1941, 34–52.

[66] On Luther's verdict against both the word and the core of the Mass cf. N. Halmer, Der literarische Kampf Luthers und Melanchtons gegen das Opfer der Messe, Divus Thomas 21 (1943) 63–78, here 70.

rifice of the Mass was defended with a reference of the name "Mass" to sacrifice. [67] It is true that the influential Peter Lombard still knew of the connection with the dismissal formula "Ite missa est", but the concept of "sending" was not understood of the dismissal of the faithful, but of the sending up of the sacrifice and the sending down from above of the Holy Spirit for the transsubstantiation. [68]

"Missa" comes from "dimissio", from the dismissal at the end of the celebration. This was no prosaic announcement of the end of the assembly, rather it was provided with a special blessing, for instance at the dismissal of the catechumens. From the solemn dismissal blessing "missa" finally acquired the meaning of "blessing" generally. Already around the year 400 there existed a renewed extension of meaning, in that the total celebration acquired the name "missa" from the closing blessing, not only the celebration of the Eucharist, but also other liturgical celebrations. "Missa vespertina" was simply vespers, just as "missa nocturna" designated the night Offices; "missa" took on the general meaning of "liturgy". The Eucharistic celebration is also such a "missa": "this linguistic usage was able all the easier to win acceptance, while the same bodily posture of bowing was demanded which one took up when the bishop or priest stretched out his hands in blessing, many times likewise also at the high points of the various functions, namely at the priestly prayers and above all at the Eucharistic Prayer of the Mass. The priestly prayer was always a kind of *missa*, it always drew down God's favour and blessing on all who bowed before God in adoration, but most of all there where the Body and Blood of Christ himself... became present." [69] Since the middle of the fifth century "missa" is unequivocally reserved as the name for the Eucharistic celebration.

3.2.3. FROM THE ADOPTION OF THE ROMAN MASS IN THE KINGDOM OF THE FRANKS UP TO THE REFORMATION

The Roman liturgy, "which up to then, apart from the Anglo-Saxon mission Church, had possessed and laid claim to recognition only for Rome and its environs, in a short time advanced to being the liturgy of a great empire." [70] In the year 754 Pippin decreed the adoption of the Roman liturgy in the kingdom of the Franks. The model was the liturgical high form, the papal station liturgy, not the simple worship of the Roman titular churches and the rural communities. This adoption had consequences for the shape of the Roman Mass and eventually retroacted in Rome. These transformations included a dramatic elaboration of the Mass liturgy (for example several incensations), the multiplication of prayers and priestly "apologies", a strong backwash of anti-Arian polemic, which obtained expression in the liturgical address to Christ or even to the Trinity, [71] as also in the maintenance of Latin as liturgical language, which excluded the greater part of the community from participation in the liturgy – especially the gap between clergy and laity with regard to the happening at the altar grew ever larger. The latter was "explained" by the allegorical explanation of the Mass in a partly quite question-

---

[67] Thus Emser, Eck, Hoffmeister and Witzel. Cf. M. Kunzler, Die Eucharistielehre des Hadamarer Pfarrers und Humanisten Gerhard Lorich, Münster 1978 (RST 119), 157f. They went back to the Hebrew text of Dt 16:10: "missat nidbat jadekah – according to what your hand is able to sacrifice".

[68] Sent. IV, D, 24, C. 19 – Ed. Quaracchi II, 904.

[69] Jungmann, MS I, 232.

[70] Ib. 98.

[71] Cf. on this the chapter "Karolingische Frömmigkeit" in J. A. Jungmann, Christliches Beten in Wandel und Bestand, 62–83.

able manner, which was practised in grand style by Amalarius of Metz. Everything without exception in the course of the Mass found interpretation as the completion of the Old Testament (typological allegory), as symbolization of the facts of New Testament salvation history (allegory of recall), as a hint of the eschatological completion (eschatological allegory) or as moral exhortation by means of the liturgical signs (moral allegory). The intrinsic value and the intended purpose of the liturgical actions themselves played as good as no further role.

The transformations of the Roman liturgy in the Frankish kingdom began already with the history of its adoption: Charlemagne received in the year 785 from Pope Hadrian I in the "Sacramentarium Hadrianum" a precious but incomplete codex, in which were contained the liturgy of the days, on which the Pope himself celebrated. In order to be able to use this sacramentary at all as the "original copy of Aachen" for the unification of the liturgy throughout the kingdom Abbot Benedict of Aniane (750–821) expanded it with an "Appendix" which drew which drew on the more recent liturgical tradition and added the feasts and rites which were customary in the Frankish kingdom. "This uniform liturgy prescribed by the central political power together with the bishops became for future time the basis of almost the whole of western liturgical usage. Diversity had found its end, but in favour of a unity, which very quickly thwarted all creative new forms and developments." [72] This transformed Roman liturgy came back to Rome from the Frankish kingdom: in the tenth century the "saeculum obscurum", in which all Church life was stagnant, there reigned in Rome a liturgical vacuum, which the Roman-Frankish liturgy refilled. [73] This took place both through the direct intervention of the Roman-German empire and by the settlement of the Cluniacs in monasteries of Rome or its neighbourhood. With Gregory VII (1073–1085) the former Cluniac monk, every worldly influencing control – for example the introduction of the Credo by a German emperor- came to an end.

Under Honorius III (1216–1227) the papal curia provided a missal adapted to its own needs, the "Missale secundum usum Romanae curiae", which the recently founded Franciscan Order also adopted. Apart from the further development of the Mass liturgy, this Missale is of importance for the arrangement of the Mass book as such. Up to then the liturgical books were role books for the various liturgical ministries. The compilation of all texts and rubrics from different books into a "full missal" gives evidence of the breaking apart of liturgical assembly, the shrinking of the liturgical ministries and the concentration on the celebrating priest alone. This development is typically western and hardly imaginable without the typically western private Mass, i.e. the Mass of a priest without participation by a community. About its origins the views of Nußbaum [74] and Häußling [75] are divergent. According to Nußbaum after the entry of Christianity into

---

[72] Emminghaus, Messe 115f. B. Neunheuser's view is more discriminating: "Without compulsion on the part of a central Roman authority, the Frankish-German Churches adopted the Roman liturgy in a free, respectful, loving decision, however they then adapted it to their circumstances likewise in respectful, sovereign freedom."

[73] Cf. Th. Klauser, Die liturgischen Austauschbeziehungen zwischen der römischen und der frankisch-deutschen Kirche vom achten bis zum elften Jahrhundert, Historisches Jahrbuch 53 (1933) 169–189.

[74] Cf. O. Nußbaum, Kloster, Priestermönch und Privatmesse. Ihr Verhältnis im Westen von den Anfängen bis zum hohen Mittelalter, Bonn 1961.

[75] Cf. A. A. Häußling, Mönchskonvent und Eucharistiefeier. Eine Studie über die Messe in der abendländischen Klosterliturgie des frühen Mittelalters und zur Geschichte der Meßhäufigkeit, Münster 1973 (LQF 58).

the Celtic and Germanic culture area a new view of the sacrifice of the Mass had arisen away from the celebration of the mystery and towards a means of salvation against man's dread about salvation. The accumulation of Masses provided for the increase of merits: series of Masses, Mass foundations and prayer fraternities provided for a share in as many celebrations of Mass as possible, which were celebrated by an ever increasing swarm of priest monks as private Masses. Häußling's view is different: according to it the great early medieval monastery regarded itself as a reproduction of the Roman city church and copied its liturgical life with the many individual celebrations at various holy places. Not individual dread about salvation, but the reconstruction of the Roman ideal lay at the origin of the private Mass, which was in no way "private", but as a blessing for the whole community carried out the necessary "cult", admittedly without participation by a congregation. But: when already through the multiplication of holy places (already through the available relics!) an increased number of Mass celebrations have to take place – and precisely as private Masses without a congregation – in order to find "appeasement and liberation in face of an overpoweringly demonized world" [76] then the leading motive for the genesis of the private Mass is all the same the dread about salvation. It shifts the point of view of the Eucharistic celebration from the celebration of redemption to an occasion for acquiring grace and for applying the grace obtained. Thus in the eighth century the daily celebration of the monk priests and soon after that of the diocesan priests became a matter of course, even when no congregation was present. Francis was still an exception, according to whom only one Mass was to be celebrated daily in the foundations of the Franciscans, even when several monk priests were present. [77] Many misunderstandings on the eve of the Reformation, the spiritual proletariat of celebrants, material and superstitious notions about the value of the Mass are somehow also connected with private Mass. [78]

The developments of the full missal and of private Mass complemented one another: all that an individual priest needed by way of text material for the celebration of "his" Mass was gathered together out of the various books of the different ministries. With the missal the private Mass also moulded the Sunday worship; only the solemn pontifical rite as well as its priestly copy – the solemn High Mass with priests in the role of deacon and subdeacon (they too had already "celebrated privately" beforehand!) remained in existence; concelebration was restricted to the ordination Mass of priests. In the full missal Low Mass is the basic form of the Eucharistic celebration. [79]

From the thirteenth century onwards the priest joined in praying also in silence the sung texts of the choir (for example Gloria, Credo etc), in order to fulfil them as it were "validly". What others prayed and performed in the Mass had become irrelevant for its validity, the priest alone celebrated "rite et valide".

The high esteem for private Mass is only one example of the trend characteristic of this epoch towards the individual and the subjective. Participants had become "present

---

[76] Thus Häußling himself in his essay: Motive für die Häufigkeit der Eucharistiefeier, Concilium 18 (1982) 96–99. 97.

[77] Cf. H. Dausend, Die Brüder dürfen in ihren Niederlassungen täglich nur eine hl. Messe lesen. Eine Weisung des hl. Franziskus nach deutschen Erklärern, Franziskanische Studien 13 (1926) 207–212.

[78] Cf. the first chapter in J. Lortz, Die Reformation in Deutschland, Freiburg i. Br. 4th edn. 1962; A. Franz, Die Messe im deutschen Mittelalter 36–72; E. Iserloh, Der Wert der Messe in den Diskussionen der Theologen vom Mittelalter bis zum 16. Jahrhundert, ZKTh 83 (1961, 0 44–79.60ff.

[79] Cf. Meyer, Eucharistie 213–215.

absentees" who pursued their private devotion and waited for the "Epiphany of God", for the "coming of God who makes his appearance among men and distributes his graces. It is above all in order to have a share in these graces that one presents oneself before the altar." [80] Everything turns on the individual blessing, the community celebration as such is almost of no account. The Mass is the occasion for "gaining" its fruits of grace, for producing the Real Presence of Christ in the Eucharistic species, from looking at which especially at the consecration one expected the same fruits as from sacramental communion. The temptation to make sure of God's grace by human activities, to "produce" it, was obvious and provoked the protest of the reformers against Mass and sacrifice of he Mass, against the priesthood and the whole Catholic conception of the Eucharist.

3.2.4. THE TRIDENTINE REFORM AND THE MISSALE ROMANUM OF PIUS V OF 1570

Trent had to counteract the worst abuses which had crept in during the course of time, but still more it was concerned with repudiating the Reformation criticism. The council took up defensive positions not only with regard to the Real Presence and the sacrificial character, but also with regard to the external course of the Mass. Thereby the development towards a clerical liturgy was fixed in writing. Many good proposals, which were put forward on the part of Catholic humanists (for example vernacular, chalice for the laity, greater participation by the congregation) were not given a chance. With the "Missale Romanum ex decreto Sacrosancti Concilii Tridentini. Pii V Pont. Max. iussu editum" of 1570 began "the period of iron uniformity in liturgy and of rubricism" which was to last until Vatican II. [81] In accordance with the introductory Bull "Quo primum" of 14 July 1570 the missal was adopted in the whole Catholic Church of the West wherever a particular tradition [82] of more than 200 years did not exist; in addition it was determined that in this missal "nothing was ever to be added, removed or altered." With the two principles of uniformity and immutability Catholic identity was to be safeguarded over and beyond all cultural differences, and the Congregation of Rites, founded in 1588, had to supervise this. That in the process much that was questionable, which one must qualify from today's perspective as faulty development, was accepted in order to preserve the status quo (for example private Mass, celebrations of Mass without communion of the faithful) [83] is evident since the reforms of Vatican II: much "remained unchanged, and indeed also unexamined, of what had lodged itself in the Frankish-German period as tasteless touching up of the austere forms of he ancient Mass of the city of Rome or what in the Gothic period had also found acceptance in the missals." [84]

The fact that Trent did not bring about any genuine renewal, that uniformity and immutability brought rubrical paralysis with them, led time and again to impulses for

---

[80]   Jungmann, MS I, 193, 155.
[81]   Cf. Klauser 117. Cf. also in this regard the judgement by B. Neunheuser, Lebendige Liturgiefeier und schöpferische Freiheit des einzelnen Liturgen, EL 89 (1975) 40–55. 49.
[82]   This affected the Orders also in addition to the few local particular traditions of ancient local Churches. For the special features of the Dominican rite cf. F. Spescha, Die Meßfeier im Ritus der Dominikaner, Liturgie und Mönchtum / Laacher Hefte 26, Maria Laach 1960, 79–88.
[83]   Cf. Meyer, Eucharistie 258f.
[84]   Jungmann, MS I, 181.

reform, admittedly no great success resulted. In France, where the bonds with Rome were always slacker there were several attempts at reform also in view of a greater congregational participation: praying aloud the Mass texts, participation of the community in the acclamations, for example, existed in several French missal of the 18th century. The Enlightenment especially reinforced these endeavours; one cannot "deny the Church spirit"[85] of much of what was realized only in the liturgy reform of Vatican II (for example increase of frequent communion, altar facing the people, kiss of peace, people's offertory procession, in general a greater participation by the congregation, above all by vernacular hymns, vernacular elements in the celebration of the sacraments, concelebration). The Synod of Pistoia of 1786 especially distinguished itself, but its condemnation was done "more out of anxiety in face of Jansenist and Febronian tendencies than of concern for the proper celebration of the liturgy."[86] But much was marked by the anticlerical, indeed anti-Christian spirit of the age of the Enlightenment and stimulated the counter-movement in the Restoration.

3.2.5. FROM THE RESTORATION UP TO THE EVE OF VATICAN II

The Restoration had its clearest influence in liturgy in the domain of Church music; especially the "Cecilian movement" pushed back the vernacular Church music in favour of Gregorian chant and Latin polyphony. Coupled with this was the fact "that the people at the celebration of Mass once again, and now more deliberately than heretofore, were forced into the role of spectators and the attempt to open up the Latin liturgy for the faithful was rejected in principle."[87] The new beginning by the abbot of Solesmes, Prosper Guéranger, was also a "restoration", although his name has a place in the history of the liturgical movement: he called for the uncompromising return to the genuine Roman liturgy, purified from all Gallic (an) admixtures, even with the acceptance of the fact that many dioceses abandoned even the most precious particular traditions. The historical studies needed for this however formed the basis in that the liturgical movement could venture on the awakening with the backing of historical findings.

The reforms of Pius X which promoted more frequent communion and children's communion preceded it, but as "communion movement" (Jungmann) at first remained still uncommitted alongside the liturgical movement. In the Motu Proprio on Church music of 1903 there was mention for the first time of the "active participation" of the faithful, although this aim was to make a break-through only in the liturgical movement itself.[88] In the Mechlin Congress on 23. 9. 1909 Lambert Beaudouin OSB gave the keynote address on the basic statement of principles of the liturgical movement. It called for the dissemination of popular missals, for participation in the parish Mass, for the abolition of private devotions during Mass, for the re-integration of communion in the celebration of Mass with the prayers of the Mass itself as preparation for communion and as thanksgiving. It was especially in Benedictine monasteries that centres of the liturgical movement were formed, particularly since Beaudouin's request for popular missals had long before been taken up by Fr. Anselm Schott's "Meßbuch der heiligen

---

[85] Ib. I, 203.
[86] Meyer, Eucharistie 277. Cf. in this connection: A. Gerhards, Von der Synode von Pistoia (1786) zum Zweiten Vatikanischen Konzil? Zur Morphologie der Liturgiereform im 20. Jhd., LJ 36 (1986) 28–45.
[87] Jungmann, MS I, 208f.
[88] Jungmann, MS I, 212f; Meyer, Eucharistie 280f.

Kirche" in its first edition of 1884 (however up to the seventh edition in 1901 without the words of consecration!). Despite all the variety among its representatives (for example I. Herwegen and O. Casel in Maria Laach; R. Guardini in the youth movement; P. Parsch in the Klosterneuburg people's liturgical apostolate, and in the Leipzig Oratory) the liturgical movement was concerned with genuine celebrating together, not with reading the Mass together. There thus emerged the "community Masses" in different forms, for instance the Latin "missa dialogata" of academic circles or of student groups, or of "Singmesse" (sung Mass) or rather "Betsingmesse" (pray/sing/Mass) with vernacular hymns, readings and prayers. Still exposed to strong opposition during World War Two, the aims of the liturgical movement found recognition in principle from Pius XII in the encyclical "Mediator Dei" of November 1947: liturgy is a reality of the whole Body of the Church, therefore the personal and active participation of the faithful is required, which expresses itself through praying and singing together. The communion of the faithful is rated as an integral component of the Mass liturgy, and to be more precise specifically with the hosts which have been consecrated in the celebration itself. In May 1948 the Pope set up a commission for the general reform of the liturgy and carried out decisive preparatory work for the liturgical reforms of Vatican II. All partial reforms were prepared and supported by the increasingly powerful liturgical movement, which since Pius XII was no longer merely the affair of "liturgically moved persons and groups', but was an aim which Pope and bishops espoused". [89]

3.2.6. VATICAN II'S REFORM OF THE MASS AND THE MISSAL OF PAUL VI

The ecclesiology of Vatican II is marked essentially by the Eucharistic mystery. According to LG 3 the Eucharistic celebration brings about the unity of the faithful in the Church as in the mystical Body of Christ. "Really sharing in the Body of the Lord in the breaking of the Eucharistic Bread, we are taken up into communion with him and with one another" (LG 7). From this and other texts the conclusion is drawn that the ecclesiology of Vatican II is "a Eucharistic ecclesiology aimed at further development." [90] The reform of the entire liturgy, especially that of the Eucharistic celebration, should accordingly not merely prune away flawed developments according to the "norms of the Fathers", rather it should satisfy the claim of the Church's Eucharistic conception of itself.

Out of the renewal of the liturgy as laid down in the liturgy Constitution of Vatican II and developed in the post-conciliar reforms, [91] there emerged Paul VI's missal, of which the Editio typica appeared in the first edition on 26 March 1970. [92] A new element contained in it is the Institutio Generalis which "offers a liturgical historical and pastoral guide to the correct understanding and carrying out of the celebration, which can hold good as an authentic "explanation of the Mass". [93] The renewed lectionary also followed the missal in the following year. The guidelines for the renewed celebration of Mass, as

[89] Meyer, Eucharistie 283.
[90] H. Riedlinger, Die Eucharistie in der Ekklesiologie des II. Vatikanums: C. Suttner (ed.), Eucharistie – Zeichen der Einheit. Erstes Regensburger Symposion, Regensburg 1970, 75–85. 81f.
[91] For a calendar of the reform as affecting the liturgical books cf. Meyer, Eucharistie 308–321.
[92] Cf. Kaczynski 2060.
[93] Meyer, Eucharistie 314.

they shall come up for treatment in the following paragraphs are, according to Meyer, given early on by the liturgy Constitution in the first two chapters (general principles): full, active and communal participation by all under the leadership of the hierarchical ministry (SC 21, 48, 22, 49f). All participants play their part in the liturgical event as in a public celebration with communal character; therefore a correct casting of roles is to be observed (SC 26 – 32, 47f). Liturgy has not only (indeed not even primarily) a character of *latreia*, rather it is first of all God's action for the believers. It is thus also "practice and expression of faith" which divine grace anticipates, and therefore should be "simple, comprehensible, transparent and along with a more ample reading from Sacred Scripture should contain appropriate elements of preaching" (SC 33 – 36. 50 – 52.54). SC 36, 37 – 40 and 44 give scope for inculturation. But tradition also is to be taken into consideration, as also the experiences made in the pre-conciliar renewal movement (SC 23. 50).[94]

Already the proviso of active participation by all entails that the renewed Mass cannot establish an "iron uniform liturgy" for the following centuries, as was the case after Trent. To a certain extent the reform of the liturgy and with it also the renewal of the celebration of Mass remains incomplete. That certainly does not mean adapting it to every all too hasty or little enlightened fashion which scarcely satisfies the demands of a genuine Eucharistic ecclesiology, and which precisely may perhaps announce itself with reference to the observance of the principle of participatio actuosa. The supreme principle of every reform in the Church, and thus also for that of the liturgy and celebration of Mass must remain that of allowing the exchange of life between God and man to take shape.

Bibliography

A. Baumstark, Vom geschichtlichen Werden der Liturgie (Ecclesia Orans X), Freiburg i. Br. 1923.

A. Baumstark, Das Gesetz der Erhaltung des Alten in liturgisch hochwertiger Zeit, JLw 7 (1927) 1 – 23.

A. Baumstark, Missale Romanum. Seine Entwicklung, ihre wichtigsten Urkunden und Probleme, Eindhoven 1929.

J. Betz, Die Eucharistie in der Zeit der griechischen Väter, 2 vols., Freiburg i. Br. 1995/1961.

B. Capelle, Travaux liturgiques de doctrine et d'histoire II: Histoire de la messe, Louvain 1962.

I.H. Dalmais, Les liturgies d'Orient, Paris 1959.

L. Duchesne, Origines du Culte Chrétien. Etude sur la liturgie latine avant Charlemagne, Paris 1925.

A. Franz, Die Messe im deutschen Mittelalter, Freiburg 1902, reprint Darmstadt 1963.

H. Grisar, Das Misale im Lichte römischer Stadtgeschichte. Stationen, Perikopen, Gebräuche, Freiburg 1925.

A. Häußling, Mönchskonvent und Eucharistiefeier, Münster 1973 (LQF 58).

E. Iserloh, Die Eucharistie in der Darstellung des Johannes Eck, Münster 1950 (RST 73/74).

J.A. Jungmann, Gewordene Liturgie, Innsbruck-Leipzig 1941.

J. A. Jungmann, Der Gottesdienst der Kirche, Innsbruck-Vienna-München 1955.

---

[94] Cf. ib. 322.

J.A. Jungmann, Liturgie der christlichen Frühzeit bis auf Gregor den Großen, Fribourg 1967.

Th. Klauser, Kleine abendländische Liturgiegeschichte. Bericht und Besinnung, Bonn 1965.

H. Lietzmann, Messe und Herrenmahl. Eine Studie zur Geschichte der Liturgie, 3rd edn. Berlin 1955.

O. Nussbaum, Kloster, Priestermönch und Privatmesse. Ihr Verhältnis im Westen von den Anfängen bis zum hohen Mittelalter, Bonn 1961.

M. Righetti, Manuale di storia liturgica III: L'Eucaristia, Milano 2nd edn. 1956.

T. Schnitzler, Eucharistie in der Geschichte. Ein kirchen-und liturgiegeschichtliches Werkbuch, Köln 1959.

H. A. Wegman, Geschichte der Liturgie im Westen und Osten, Regensburg 1979.

3.3. THE VARIETY OF FORMS OF THE CELEBRATION OF MASS

The unchangeable theological content of the celebration of Mass expresses itself in a changeable, outward shape. The specific cultural factors of the different epochs influenced the shape of the Mass. But also within an epoch and a cultural circle differing structural forms of the Mass and varying degrees of solemnity were and are determined not only by the course of the Lord's year, but also by the occasion of the celebration of Mass and hence also by the participants in the liturgical action. The "High Mass" of a major feast has a different shape to a celebration of the Eucharist in a small group on a weekday evening. However the unity of the rite must not be put in question again through the multiplicity of structural possibilities.

3.3.1. THE DIFFERENT FORMS OF CELEBRATION OF MASS BEFORE THE REFORM

"With reference to the occurring Office one distinguishes: a) the Mass of the day; b) votive and requiem Masses... The Masses which vary from the Mass of the day (extra ordinem officii) are either votive or requiem Masses." With regard to the outward solemnity there were distinguished with precise prescription of the ritual performance: "a) Low Mass (missa bassa, sine cantu), which the Celebrant reads without taking into consideration the people's singing; b) Sung Mass (missa cantata), i.e. the Mass as sung by the priest and responded to by the schola; c) solemn High Mass (Missa solemnis), which is celebrated with the assistance of deacon and subdeacon, with incensation of the altar and the giving of the Pax; d) Pontifical Mass, i.e. the solemn Mass of a prelate." With regard to the form of the celebration and the application of the fruits of the Mass the following distinctions were made: the conventual Mass in cathedral, collegiate and churches of male religious [bound to choir] and the parochial Mass in the parish church; "the remaining Holy Masses which take place in the aforesaid churches, and all which take place in the other churches are called private Masses". [95]

---

[95]   G. Kieffer, Rubrizistik oder Ritus des katholischen Gottesdienstes nach den Regeln der heiligen römischen Kirche, Paderborn 8th edn. 1935, 94.

It was above all the Roman Congregation of Rites founded in 1588[96] which took care of the uniformity of the Tridentine unified liturgy in its outward performance, also in the varying occasions and structures of the celebration of Mass.[97] As basic form of the Mass there prevailed the private Mass said silently by he priest at the altar without reference to the congregation present, and at which the server gave the responses. "High Mass differs from Low Mass chiefly by the fact that in it various parts are sung by the priest and the schola."[98] "High Mass" in which priests "acted" the roles of deacon and subdeacon was an imitation of pontifical Mass.

Before the reform the varying forms of the Mass were determined above all by the precise scale of solemnity determined beforehand for various occasions, but not by the participating faithful. Despite all the minutely prescribed details the Mass remained always the priest's work, which in its purest form was present in the private Mass with one Mass server. After the reform other criteria for the different kinds of celebration of Mass had to be laid down.

3.3.2. THE CELEBRATION OF MASS WITH A CONGREGATION AS THE BASIC FORM OF THE RENEWED EUCHARISTIC CELEBRATION

The new Missal (GIRM chap. 4) presents the various structural possibilities of the renewed Mass liturgy with the different forms of celebration of Mass. Whereas in the missal of 1570 the private Mass was the basic shape of the Eucharistic celebration, in the renewed missal it is the last of the possibilities to be named. In a "celebration of Mass without a congregation" an altar server deputizes for the latter, taking over the texts which normally are due to the congregation "a celebration without a server should not take place except for a grave necessity".[99] As basic form ("forma typica" according to GIRM 78) the rule is the celebration of Mass with the people ("missa cum populo").

With all due respect for what has been achieved: is there not hidden behind the wording "*cum* populo" a trace of that old presentation of the liturgy as the work of the celebrant? Would it not have been better to say celebration of Mass *of* the community in its hierarchical structure and in the diversity of its differing liturgical ministries? In this way it would have been said that the bearers of the ordained ministry do not stand over the community, but rather incorporated in it use their ministry. Celebration of Mass *of* the community could illustrate that the local Church (here the parish community as infrastructure of the diocesan local Church) in the celebration of the Eucharist by the holy People of God becomes a visible reality.[100] Therefore it is logical if from among all the possibilities of structuring the celebration and of community participation that Mass is given pride of place "wherein the bishop presides over his priests and other ministers with the people taking their full and active part. This is the way in which the Church is most clearly and visibly manifested" (GIRM 74).[101]

---

[96] Cf. Th. Klauser, Kleine Abendländische Liturgiegeschichte. Bericht und Besinnung, Bonn 1965, 120. 130–135: Die Ritenkongregation und ihre Arbeitsweise.

[97] So for example in a low conventual Mass two servers are allowed, and more than two candles may be lit, cf. Kieffer, Rubrizistik 97. Incense is prescribed for High Mass, ib. 223.

[98] Ib. 191.

[99] Cf. GIRM 209–211.

[100] Cf. SC 41 and 42. Cf. Meyer, Eucharistie 372.

[101] Similarly GIRM 157; in the background of both statements stands SC Art. 41.

The missal gives no regulations about the grades of solemnity of Mass with the people; where possible it should be celebrated with song and with the participation of a large number of ministers, but it can also be held without song and with only one of the faithful, who performs a special service (GIRM 77). The wish for music in the Mass refers to the ancient tradition of the missa cantata, which according to Jungmann is the "unbroken continuation of the presbyter Mass of Christian antiquity". "Of course it too was seized by the aspiration of borrowing as much as possible from the episcopal Mass." [102] Thus there developed in the high Middle Ages the "missa sollemnis" in imitation of the bishop's Mass with the assistance of ("bogus" i.e. priests in the role of) deacon and subdeacon. Nowadays after the abolition of the subdiaconate, after the retrieving of concelebration as well as of the diaconate as a proper and permanent rank of the hierarchy, and in view of the authenticity of those who carry out ministries, it is no longer possible. The Mass with one or more deacons as well with the various lay ministries is in no way inferior to it in the aspiration for solemnity.

The structure of the celebration of the Mass is determined in the first place by the course of the year of the Lord with its solemnities, feasts, obligatory and optional memorias. In addition it complies with the situation of the participants, so that today's missal offers an incomparably greater freedom than was possible before the reform. In every Mass all grades of ordination (concelebration of several priests, service of the deacon) and the holders of a lay ministry (reader, cantor, server) can function, without the number of those functioning or the style of their service being regulated.

3.3.3. CONCELEBRATION

Concelebration dates back to the directive of SC 58. Moreover a distinction is made between "sacramental or sacrificial" and "ceremonial" concelebration, according as the concelebrants join in saying the words of consecration or not. A "ceremonial" concelebration, in which only the (episcopal) chief celebrant spoke the Eucharistic prayer, and apart from that the other priests were active in the liturgy, was already normal practice in the ancient Church. The Byzantine Greeks have adhered to it until today, while the Slavs and Uniate Byzantines under Western influence changed over to the saying of the words of consecration by all concelebrants.

In the West concelebration disappeared with the rise of the private Mass. Every priest wanted to exercise his "power of consecration" and to apply the fruits of the Mass; the bonding of single Eucharistic celebration into the whole of the community and of the clerics who exercised a ministry in it had disappeared. There, where concelebration still occurred as a vestige, it was a parallel celebration, a "con-consecration", as in the rite of ordination of bishops and priests since the late Middle Ages. From the offering of the gifts onwards all the concelebrants spoke all the prayers together. The distinction between "ceremonial" and "sacramental" concelebration is intelligible only on the basis of scholastic sacramental and Eucharistic theology; it was also jointly responsible for the fact that concelebration in the West dwindled down to the particular case of the ordination liturgy. Furthermore a decree of the Holy Office of 1957 rejected in general the distinction between "sacramental" and "ceremonial" concelebration: "a valid 'concelebration' is only present, when the concelebrating priest in fact pronounces the words

---

[102] Jungmann, MS I, 277.

of consecration, because according to Christ's institution he alone 'validly' celebrates, who pronounces the words of consecration." [103] Things have remained thus up to now.

Among the merits of the present rite of concelebration are the emphasis on the unity of Christ's sacrifice and the manifestation of the unity of the college of priests (SC 57, 1). As danger there is pointed out a new clericalisation of the Mass; as wish there is expressed a desire for a greater variety of forms of concelebration, [104] which implies a fresh debate on the distinction between "sacramental" and "ceremonial" concelebration under new i.e. non-scholastic points of view. [105]

3.3.4. OTHER FORMS OF THE CELEBRATION OF MASS

Conventual and community Mass is the Eucharistic worship of a resident community. Religious communities gather together daily for a celebration of Mass in common ("conventual Mass" in monasteries, "community Mass" in seminaries and boarding schools), at which the priests concelebrate and all members of the household are expected to be present. This celebration of Mass corresponds in its structure to the celebration of Mass with a congregation and the differentiated ministries; it is the worthy successor to the private celebrations of many priests as practised formerly also in seminaries and colleges. [106] According to v. Severus monasteries today are set the task "of incorporating visitors to monastic churches into the worship of a spiritual community in such a way that active and conscious participation will be possible for them". [107] On the other hand the liturgy reform "contrary to SC 4, by the weight of settled facts, but also through the lack of understanding on the part of the central Church authorities, has in fact operated in a unifying sense, so that in the domain of the Western Church there are scarcely any Eucharistic liturgies proper to an Order any more." These took their origin when communities of the Orders stuck to the earlier usage of the local Church, in which they had taken their origin, when the latter altered their liturgy; through expansion of the Order into other local Churches the by now proper rite was exported. The Cluniacs developed special rites in the 10th century, the Cistercians in the 12th; in Germany the Benedictines of the Bursfeld Union in the 15th century, but above all the Dominicans and Carthusians. [108]

The central significance of the Eucharist is also given expression from the fact that other liturgical celebrations can be joined to the Mass (Ritual Masses): "The celebration of the sacraments, various blessings and processions as also Hours of the Liturgy of the Hours are joined on various occasions with the celebration of Mass. They substitute then for the corresponding part of the Mass (opening, liturgy of the Word, conclusion) or are inserted in or added to it." [109] The sacramental component follows after the liturgy of the

---

[103] DH 3928. Cf. K. Rahner / A. A. Häußling, Die vielen Messen und das eine Opfer. Eine Untersuchung über die rechte Norm der Meßhäufigkeit, Freiburg-Basel-Vienna 1966 (QD 31), 122–127.
[104] Cf. Meyer, Eucharistie 495–497; on the present-day structure of concelebration ib. 371f.
[105] Thus already Rahner/Häußling in 1966, loc. cit. 127: "Normal and ideal form of the celebration of Mass with the participation of several priests is rather to be sought in (ritually appropriate structured) assistance."
[106] Cf. Meyer, Eucharistie 372; E. v. Severus, Die Eucharistiefeier in den geistlichen Gemeinschaften: B. Kleinheyer, E. v. Severus, R. Kaczynski (ed.): Sakramentliche Feiern II, GdK 8, Regensburg 1984, 172–174.
[107] E. v. Severus, Die Eucharistiefeier in den geistlichen Gemeinschaften: GdK 8, 172–175. 173.
[108] Cf. ib. 175.
[109] Meyer, Eucharistie 372.

Word (for example ordinations, marriage, anointing of the sick, blessing of an abbot, various blessings); the farewell linked with funeral Mass at the end of the Mass. Meyer views the joining of individual Hours of the Liturgy of the Hours with the Mass as questionable (Hymn and psalmody substitute for the liturgy of the Word, the *Benedictus* or *Magnificat* follow the communion.)

According to Jungmann the house Mass in small groups became a living practice in antiquity and was "the precursor of a Eucharist also celebrated at a later date in a private group." [110] This practice has been revitalized in the renewed liturgy. The Roman Instruction "Actio pastoralis" of 1969 [111] puts into effect the celebration of small group Masses, which the bishops' conferences have adapted to their regions and partly amplified. In principle the celebration of community Mass holds for the structure of the celebration, nevertheless there are adaptations for the specific circumstances of the small group regarding place, time, liturgical dress, the vessels and the course of the ritual (free choice of readings, prayers and chants, cf. in this connection GIRM 313).

In Masses with special groups the following adaptations are dealt with. The adaptations of the Mass for celebration with children go back to the Roman Instruction for children's Masses "Pueros baptizatos" of 1973 [112] for which the Congregation of Divine Worship in 1974 issued three Eucharistic Prayers. The adaptations are aimed at an active introduction, corresponding to the children's understanding, into the celebration. The children ought to take on as many tasks as possible, the presidential prayers in accordance with the liturgical season may be chosen and adapted to the child's level. The Scripture reading may be limited to the Gospel; various elements of the community Mass may be omitted in the Communion part, as also in the opening rites. Referring to SC 34 (adaptation of the liturgy to the people's power of comprehension) the Directory for children's Masses itself draws attention to the fact that further adaptations are necessary for Masses with the handicapped (the mentally retarded, and the deaf). [113]

For a celebration of Mass without a congregation it is a question of the celebration of Mass with at least one altar server or one of the faithful; without these the individual celebration of a priest should take place only for a "just and reasonable motive". [114] Already in his encyclical *Mysterium fidei* of 3. 9. 1965 Paul VI ruled that such a Mass may be held "iusta de causa". [115] "The private Mass is thereby no longer as of itself justified; as a departure from the ideal structure of the celebration of Mass it must still produce a particular motive, which precisely justifies this type of celebration, or in other words: where the full possibility concretely exists of celebrating Mass in accordance with its essence in community, there is no iusta causa for the private celebration." [116] In accordance with the description of the Mass, [117] which is totally celebrated at the altar, the altar server substitutes for the congregation whose responses and acclamations

---

[110] Cf. Jungmann, MS I, 279–283.
[111] Kaczynski 1843–1857.
[112] Kaczynski 3115–3169.
[113] Cf. B. Fischer, Meßfeier mit Kindern: Th. Maas-Ewerd / K. Richter (ed.): Gemeinde im Herrenmahl 97–106.
[114] Thus c. 906 CIC/1983, similarly GIRM 211.
[115] Kaczynski 432.
[116] Rahner/Häußling 121.
[117] Richter, Meßfeier ohne Gemeinde 141, calls the description of GIRM 213–231 "almost cold"; this is be understood in view of the global conception of the new regulations.

he says. [118] Celebration of Mass without a congregation concerns primarily invalid and handicapped priests, but is "of its nature a border-line and exceptional case." [119]

In votive Masses and in Masses for various needs and occasions a particular interest of the faithful stands in the foreground. The title "votive Mass" is derived from "*votum*, vow, wish, request": the celebration of a Mass is not determined by a feast-day of the year of the Lord, but takes into consideration a wish or a special occasion of the individual believers. [120] The votive Mass therefore is no celebration of the general community and in antiquity was generally celebrated not in the church, but in houses or in private oratories. [121] A great importance among the votive Masses attached quite early to the celebration of Mass for the dead and on the days of the memorial Mass for the deceased. But other concerns of the faithful also determined the structure of the celebration of the votive Masses; private preoccupations (for example illness, travel, sterility or birthdays) are already present in the older *Gelasian* side by side with public concerns (epidemic, a threat to peace, weather conditions among other things). The Carolingian period yielded a full bloom of votive Masses, at a time when the increased number of celebrations of Mass was accompanied by the development of the private Mass. In the long run the only interest was in the offering of the sacrifice of the Mass and the application of the fruits of the Mass in favour of the "vota" of the person who gave the stipend; while there could scarcely be talk of the participation in the celebration of those who "ordered" the votive Mass. [122] In the renewed missal the meaning of the concept of "votive Mass" has changed; it comprises "a series of 15 Mass formularies for celebrating the mysteries of the faith (for example the Trinity), several mysteries of Christ (for example the Name of Jesus, the Precious Blood, the Heart of Jesus), of the angels, of the Mother of God and of other saints." [123]

The celebrations of Masses or prayers "*pro variis necessitatibus*" in the renewed missal have been newly formed and follow the sequence which holds good for the universal prayer: Church – State and Society – public concerns – other concerns. "In this section are reflected at their clearest the changes in time and the history of spirituality which since the 16th century have preceded it." [124] To these Masses also belong the "theme Masses" which have come into vogue in the wake of the post-conciliar renewal and which have never become the official liturgy of the Church. According to Häußling there is a scarcely perceived analogy between the modern attractive presentation of the Eucharistic celebration by an 'effective theme' and the spirituality of the sacrifice of the Mass of neo-scholasticism, thought of as effective of itself. [125]

---

[118] For the structure of the celebration of this Mass cf. GIRM 213–231.

[119] Meyer, Eucharistie 375.

[120] In this sense the ritual Masses as for instance for weddings, funerals and others are strictly speaking "votive Masses"; nevertheless these are to be distinguished from really particular *vota*, on the basis of an existing relationship of the occasion of the celebration to the general community (two of the congregation marry, one of the congregation has died).

[121] On the house Mass in antiquity cf. Jungmann, MS I, 279–282.

[122] Cf. ib. 285–290.

[123] Meyer, Eucharistie 380.

[124] Ib. 379f.

[125] Cf. A. A. Häußling, Meßhäufigkeit und "Motivmessen": Th. Maas-Ewerd / K. Richter (ed.): Gemeinde im Herrenmahl 143–149, esp.147.

3.3.5. A TENTATIVE EVALUATION

According to the markedly Eucharistic ecclesiology and the liturgical theology derived from it of Vatican II, the celebration of Mass of the assembled local community consequently counts as the basic form of the Eucharistic celebration. It is the full assembly of the holy people of God in a place, and in its celebration, symbolizes the Church. All other types of Mass should not come into competition with it, rather they must lead to the full and high form of the single Eucharist of the congregation. In all small group Masses and other particular groups the bond with local and universal Church must be traceable. The "theme" of a Eucharistic celebration is never anything other than the redemption of man and world. The "structuring" of a celebration of Mass according to a preconceived "theme" can run the risk of making this single basic theme forgotten behind preoccupations no matter how justified, and to use the Church's liturgy in order to motivate certain attitudes and actions. [126]

Bibliography

A. Häußling, Meßhäufigkeit und 'Motivmessen': Th. Maas-Ewerd/ K. Richter (eds.), Gemeinde im Herrenmahl, 143 – 149.

J. Hermans, Mit Kindern Eucharistie feiern. Nach dem 'Direktorium für Kindermessen', IKaZ 14(1985) 124 – 131.

Th. Maas-Ewerd, Meßfeier mit mehreren Priestern. Zur Praxis der Konzelebration: Th. Maas-Ewerd / K. Richter (ed.), Gemeinde im Herrenmahl, 126 – 135.

F. Nikolasch, Die Feier der Messe im kleinen Kreis. Arbeitspapier für die Liturgische Kommission Österreichs, LJ 20 (1970) 40 – 52.

K. Rahner / A. A. Häußling, Die vielen Messen und das eine Opfer. Eine Untersuchung über die rechte Norm der Meßhäufigkeit, Freiburg-Basel-Vienna 1966, 122 – 127 (QD 31).

K. Richter, Meßfeier ohne Gemeinde? In: Th. Maas-Ewerd / K. Richter (eds.), Gemeinde im Herrenmahl, 136 – 142.

P. Tirot, La concélébration et la tradition de l'église, EL 101 (1987) 182 – 214.

3.4. THE OPENING PARTS OF THE MASS

3.4.1. "FORECOURTS"

At one time the celebration began directly with the readings of Sacred Scripture, such as is the tradition in Justin and still the case in Augustine. [127] The principle formulated by Baumstark, that the oldest traditions maintain themselves most easily in liturgically important times, [128] is still borne out today by the Good Friday liturgy, which indeed – apart from an introductory prayer – begins directly with the Old Testament reading (Is 52:13 – 53:12). It was only in the course of time that an introductory part came to be placed before the readings; Jungmann calls it the "forecourt" [*Vorhof*]. In the Byzantine rite it is called "Enarxis" ("beginning") and is today the vestigial form of

---

[126] Cf. M. Kunzler, Themen – und zielgruppeorientierte Gottesdienste? Eine Anfrage aus der Sicht des christlichen Ostens, TThZ 96 (1987) 227 – 235; R. Schwarzenberger, Zwecksonntage – Zweckentfremdung der Feier der Heilsgeheimnisse? BiLi 52 (1979) 198 – 203.

[127] Cf. Jungmann, MS I, 29 – 33; for Augustine: De civ. Dei 22,8- CChr. SL 48, 826; Roetzer 98f.

[128] A. Baumstark, Das Gesetz der Erhaltung des Alten in liturgisch hochwertiger Zeit, JLw 7(1927) 1 – 23.

an Hour of the liturgy of the Hours which preceded the beginning of the Eucharistic celebration. The "Little Entrance" with the Gospel book still marks very clearly the original beginning of the Eucharistic celebration. [129] The questionable concept of "Fore-Mass" for the liturgy of the Word of the Eucharistic celebration can mislead in the sense also of misunderstanding this in relation to the whole, as a forecourt to the real thing, to the "Mass as sacrifice" or to the "celebration of the Meal". The opening part would then be a "fore-court to the forecourt", whose formation in the various rites took place in very different ways, if one compares for instance the preparation of the gifts of the Byzantines (the Proskomodie or Prothesis) which was fully developed only in the Middle Ages and placed before the Eucharistic liturgy, with the opening elements (for example prayers at the foot of the altar and other priestly prayers) of the Latin Mass before the reform. The concept of "forecourt" is similarly questionable as is that of "fore-Mass", because it suggests the misunderstanding of what is indeed useful but not essential. In the opening part the congregation comes together, Christ is present in its midst; it moves towards him, it invokes him as *Kyrios*, it praises him with the Father and the Holy Spirit in the Gloria, through him and in the Holy Spirit it prays to the Father. Consequently to the beginning of the renewed Mass there belong: the entry procession with the greeting of the altar, the actual opening of the Mass, the penitential act, the Kyrie, the Gloria and the Prayer of the day. Something important happens in the opening part; it is at most in so far "forecourt" as it stands on the threshold of the liturgy, but itself belongs to it completely.

3.4.2. THE ENTRY PROCESSION WITH THE INTROIT

The roots of the entry of the priest and his assistants lie in the solemn entry of the Pope to Mass in the Middle Ages: seven candles and incense were carried before him when he entered one of the basilicas with the clergy. He exchanged the kiss of peace with the clerics and venerated the altar, after he had clothed himself in the liturgical vestments in a sacristy which was situated near the entry of the church. During the solemn entry the schola sang the *antiphona ad introitum*. While in the Byzantine rite the Little Entrance belongs as a festive element of every eucharistic liturgy, the new missal (GIRM 25) mentions only briefly the entry of the priest and of All who perform special ministries. The form of the entry procession depends greatly on the spatial conditions and the occasion of the liturgical celebration. Cross, candles, incense and the Gospel book may be carried. Through the entry chant the congregation participates in the entry procession, which "must not be misunderstood in a clericalised way, but must take its meaning from its goal, which is the altar." [130] The entry procession shows to those who are already in their places the access of the whole people to God, hence it is appropriate to allow many participants – such as the lay ministers – to take part in it (GIRM 82) or also to consider an entry procession of the whole congregation after a preceding *Statio*.

3.4.3. THE VENERATION OF THE ALTAR

It is intended for Christ of whom the altar is a symbol. After the genuflection or bow (depending on whether the Blessed Sacrament is on or in the immediate vicinity of the altar) the celebrant (or if the occasion arises also the deacon and concelebrants)

---

[129] Cf. Jungmann MS I, 343f.
[130] Plock 195.

venerate the altar with a kiss. The custom lasted a long time of honouring the Gospel book and the crucifix with a kiss, as still happens today in the Byzantine rite. From the multiplicity of altar kisses in the missal of 1570 the new missal retains only those for "greeting" and for "farewell" (GIRM 85 respectively 208).

According to the occasion the altar may be incensed. As a liturgical symbol incense was already much earlier at home in Eastern Christianity and in Frankish territory than in Rome. Originally a mark of honour for important personalities, the significance of incense passed over to objects, thus also to the altar, which was given prominence as a holy place. Incense is also allowed for the cross which is on or in the vicinity of the altar (GIRM 236).

While the use of incense was formerly regulated exactly by the rubrics, its use today is optional; the range reaches from its practical abolition in many places to the possibility of its daily use. The overcoming of rubrical rigidity did not aim at the abolition of incense or of other liturgical symbols. In every Byzantine Eucharistic celebration as a rule the altar, the icons, the celebrants and the congregation are honoured by incense. For these last the model is the ancient custom in the reception of guests of administering incense against the street smells; thus the deacon imitates the house servant of antiquity and goes with the thurible through the ranks of the faithful.

3.4.4. THE OPENING: THE LITURGICAL ENTRANCE GREETING AND THE INTRODUCTION

From the celebrant's chair the priest opens the celebration with the sign of the Cross and the first liturgical greeting: "The Lord be with you" with the congregation's response "and with your spirit". The sign of the Cross at the beginning of Mass makes it clear that the community begins the sacred action in that strength which comes from the triune God through the Cross of the Lord. [131] The *Dominus vobiscum* is a quotation from Ruth 2:4, a daily form of greeting in the biblical environment. The response "*Et cum spiritu tuo*" is interpreted by Jungmann further as a Hebraism, which also could be interpreted as "and also with you". But reference is also made to the interpretation, according to which by "spirit" the ministerial grace of the celebrant is understood as gift of the Holy Spirit. According to Bernhard this interpretation clearly deserves precedence [132] and explains in addition that the liturgical greeting together with the response is reserved to the ordained celebrant. The community's response could be understood as a short intercession for its president, that he may fulfil well his role as president with the help of the Lord and in the ministerial grace bestowed by his Spirit. The introductory words are supposed to present the mystery of the Mass (GIRM 87) and not to follow in the celebration of Mass the example of secular greeting rituals.

3.4.5. THE PENITENTIAL ACT

The penitential act at the beginning of Mass stands in a long tradition, which led to the definitive shaping of the prayers at the foot of the altar in the missal of Pius V. The desire to celebrate the sacred liturgy, reconciled with God and men, led to prayers ("*Apologiæ*") for the forgiveness of sins being said. In the West on the way to the altar the priest prayed psalm 42, the prayer "*Aufer a nobis*" and finally forerunners of the

---

[131] Cf. Jungmann, MS I, 384.
[132] Cf. ib. 465f.; Bernhard especially 155f.

Confiteor. The prayers at the foot of the altar remained to a large extent reserved to the celebrant and his assistants. It was only in the liturgical movement that attempts were made to incorporate the congregation into reconciliation with God as a prerequisite for a fruitful celebration of the liturgy. So it is no surprise that in the new missal the penitential act has taken the place of the prayers at the foot of the altar. Three forms of the penitential act are provided: A: *Confiteor* of the congregation with words of absolution by the priest; B: two groups of versicles; C: Kyrie acclamations which have been expanded with invocations in the form of tropes addressed to Christ. However, whether the penitential act is suitably placed at this point of the Mass, is another question. Thus it can be omitted when another liturgical action takes place beforehand or when the celebration of Mass is marked by special solemnity. The question is discussed of relocating the penitential act in the nearby position between the liturgy of the Word and the celebration of the Eucharist:[133] after assembling for prayer and for hearing the Word of God the faithful recognize their need of forgiveness before God and one another. In line with Jesus' word (Mt 5:23f) the mutual forgiveness could be given expression here, before the gift is brought to the altar. Similarly in the Byzantine liturgy the celebrants exchange the greeting of peace immediately after the bringing of the gifts to the altar in the Great Entrance and before these are uncovered after the profession of faith.

The penitential act is omitted when at the beginning of Sunday Mass the memorial of baptism takes place.[134] In the Frankish empire monasteries and churches were walked through in procession and sprinkled with holy water; from the 9th century onwards the rural churches imitated this custom. Hincmar of Reims (806–882) is the first to mention the blessing of holy water and the sprinkling of the congregation before the Sunday Mass. Rupert of Deutz (d. 1135) interpreted the custom as a memorial of baptism, this interpretation has remained dominant since the Middle Ages.[135]

3.4.6. THE KYRIE

The acclamation "Kyrie eleison" is already known in pre-Christian antiquity as a cry of homage, with which one honoured a godhead or also the sovereign when he made his entrance in a city. The homage character of the cry for pity consists in the acknowledgement of the saving power of the one so addressed. The adoption of the Kyrie cry by the Christians witnesses to the faith in the saving presence of the Kyrios Christ in his community. In addition the Kyrios title in the background of the hymn in Philippians (2:6–11) is one of the shortest formulas of faith: in the Septuagint Kyrios is nothing less than the title "Adonai" of the Old Testament covenant God, with which the unspoken divine name Jhwh was paraphrased.

The introduction of the Kyrie into Mass goes back to the change in the practice of intercessions. In Rome about 500 the Kyrie litany was adopted from the East and replaced thereby the typically Roman types of intercession, such as we still know them from the

---

[133] Cf. Heinz, Bußritus 116–119.
[134] Cf. the appendix to MR 1970: *Ordo ad faciendam et aspergendam aquam benedictam,* the rubric in the German missal II, 325 and the appendix: *'Das sonntägliche Taufgedächtnis',* ib. II, 1207–1211.
[135] Cf. HJ. Auf der Maur, Feiern im Rhythmus der Zeit I:GdK 5, Regensburg 1983, 40f. Cf. also A. Heinz, Trinitarische und österliche Aspekte in der Sonntagsfrömigkeit des Mittelalters. Zeugnisse aus Liturgie und volksfrommen Beten: A. M. Altermatt / R. A. Schnitker / W. Heim (eds.), Der Sonntag. Anspruch-Wirklichkeit-Gestalt (FS J. Baumgartner), Würzburg-Fribourg 1986, 82–98. 88f: Die Aspersionsprozession.

Good Friday service. Furthermore the ancient Prayer of the faithful at the end of the liturgy of he Word was abandoned, so that a Kyrie litany at the beginning of the liturgy, in which the deacon spoke the petitions and the congregation answered with the "Kyrie eleison", resembled greatly the still customary Eastern usage. The most outstanding witness of such a Kyrie litany is the "Deprecatio Gelasii", whose petitions remind one of the Byzantine list of intercessions ("Ektenia"). [136] According to the Rule of Benedict also a Kyrie litany concludes the hours of the Prayer of the Hours. While the Deprecatio Gelasii still contains 18 petitions, there came about abbreviations in the course of the 6th century; under Pope Gregory I (d. 604) the naming of the petitions by the deacon was totally abandoned: there remained only the Kyrie acclamations which finally under addition of the "Christe eleison" were regulated at that ninefold, which was still in use up to the liturgy reform. A Trinitarian interpretation of the Kyrie appeared only in the 8th century. For a long time the congregation participated in the Kyrie acclamations. Their elaboration by tropes led to the oldest form of German-speaking Church songs ("Leisen" from "eleison"), but also to the new interpretation of the Kyrie into a plea for forgiveness of sins. The new missal recognizes once again the possibility of elaborating the Kyrie by tropes (GIRM 30). However the possible joining of the Kyrie with the penitential Act (Form C) which is mentioned there is only with difficulty compatible with its laudative character.

3.4.7. THE GLORIA

With the hymns "Te Deum" and "Te decet laus" the Gloria is a remnant of the rich treasury of hymns of the ancient Church which fell as victim to the prohibition of hymns by the Council of Laodicea (between 341 and 380). Already at that time the Gloria enjoyed such renown that it was not touched by this prohibition. The Council forbade all self-made hymns ("Psalmi idiotici"), because by them heretical opinions were spread among the faithful people, and substituted for them the biblical psalms and hymns. In actual fact the oldest tradition in Book 7 of the Apostolic Constitutions (about 380) [137] emphasizes the subordination of the Son to the Father. The orthodox text of the Gloria, as it exists in the Codex Alexandrinus of the New Testament from the 5th century, forms an element of the Byzantine Morning Prayer still today. The oldest Latin version is contained in the antiphonary of Bangor (about 690) and accords with the version of the Codex Alexandrinus.

The Gloria in the Mass unfolded over a long period: at first it was a component part of episcopal liturgy; the priest was allowed to intone it only on Easter night and in his own first Mass. It was only in the 12th century that these restrictions disappeared; the solution was the rule that the Gloria would be used in all festive Masses. Precisely the placing of the Gloria immediately after the Kyrie underlines the laudative character of the latter: according to the first Ordo Romanus the Pope stands at his *cathedra,* facing east, and prays in silence, while the choir of singers chant the Kyrie. After that he turns to the people and intones the Gloria, which was still a chant of the whole congregation. [138] According to GIRM 31 the Gloria is foreseen "for solemnities and

---

[136] Cf. PL 101, 560f.
[137] Apost. Const. VII, 47, 1 – SChr. 336,112.
[138] Cf. Jungmann MS I, 458f.

feasts and for specially solemn celebrations as well as on all Sundays outside Advent and Lent."

The opening words of the Gloria are quoted from the angels' song of praise in the plain of Bethlehem (Lk 2:14). Biblical textual criticism has shown that the tripartite form, such as is usual in the Eastern liturgies ("Glory to God in the highest and peace on earth to men of good will") must be replaced by a binary form: "Glory to God in the highest and peace on earth to men of his grace." The peace which has come with Christ is through and through a gift of the Father's grace and not the result of a free decision of man's will.

3.4.8. THE COLLECT

The collect closes the opening part of the Mass. Apart from the intonation of the Gloria, the presiding priest or bishop here speaks for the first time. The collect is the first of the "presidential prayers", which the priest "in whom Christ himself presides over the assembly, directs to God in the name of the entire holy people and all present", for which reason they are also called "official prayers". The two other presidential prayers are the prayer over the offerings and the concluding prayer. They all have a collective character, from which also the term "collecta" derives: the priest calls the faithful to silent prayer ("Let us pray"), followed by a brief prayerful silence GIRM 32. The priest collects the prayers of each in the prayer of the day and bears these in the Holy Spirit through the Son to the Father. The name "Oratio" derives from the spoken style of the "Oratio" with its firm structural laws and its own rhythmical art.

In an expanded form the (1.) address to God is completed by (2.) a predicative clause. There follows (3.) the naming of the petition, followed by (4.) the Trinitarian closing formula. The Latin collect for the 7th day of the Christmas octave (31st December) may serve as a typical example: 1. Omnipotens sempiterne Deus, 2. qui in Filii tui nativitate tribuisti totius religionis initium perfectionemque constare, 3. da nobis, quaesumus, in eius portione censeri, in quo totius salutis humanae summa consistit. 4. Per Dominum nostrum Jesum Christum, Filium tuum, qui tecum vivit et regnat in unitate Spiritus Sancti, Deus, per omnia saecula saeculorum.

In a simpler type the predicative clause, which includes the element of thanksgiving and praise in the prayer of petition, is dropped, and thereby also takes into account the special character of the particular liturgical day. Thus in memorias and feasts of the saints the name of the saint of the day can be included: 1. Deus, 2. qui beato Francisco paupertate et humilitate Christo configurari tribuisti, 3. concede, ut, per illius semitas gradientes, Filium tuum sequi et tibi coniungi laeta valeamus caritate. 4. Per Dominum... (Collect of 4 October).

The Collect is always orientated in the Holy Spirit through Christ to the Father, as the Council of Hippo (393) had already formulated the law for the shape of liturgical prayer: "Et cum altari assistitur, semper ad Patrem dirigatur oratio." [139] While the Roman liturgy has always observed this law, the Eastern *ekphoneses*, which sum up the diaconal intercessions and on account of their collective character could be compared to the Collect, turn to the undivided Trinity. This is accounted for by a stronger aftermath of the anti-Arian polemic. The address to Christ did not originate on Roman soil, but came

---

[139] Ib. 486; cf. Roetzer 239f.

into the Roman liturgy through influences from Gaul. In Rome in spite of the Arian disorders they held fast to the pre-Nicene mode of viewing the Trinity, even though this could be misused in the sense of the Arian denial of Christ's divinity: the triune God enters into communication with the world "from the Father through the Son in the Holy Spirit", and conversely man's prayer goes "in the Holy Spirit through the Son to the Father".

Christ is the high-priestly mediator between God and man, but this thoroughly biblical language (for example Heb 7:25, according to which Christ makes intercession for us) was open to misinterpretation in the sense of the Arian errors. The East expressed the orthodox doctrine thanks to the fact that in the so-called Little Doxology by the double "and" it was able to praise the second and third Persons in the Godhead in all clarity in the same divine dignity as the Father: Glory be to the Father *and* to the Son *and* to the Holy Spirit. In contrast to the East, which ascribes the same dignity to all three Persons also in its liturgical prayer, Rome stayed with the ancient mode of expression not least from the thought that in Christ, who as the Risen One has entered into the Father's glory, the Church has her Head in heaven, through whom her prayer reaches the Father. Rome pursued the anti-Arian preoccupation differently from the East; the second relative clause expresses clearly the divinity of the Son and that of the Holy Spirit: the Church asks the Father "through Christ, our Lord and God, who in the unity of the Holy Spirit lives and reigns with you for ever". [140] The congregation "subscribes" to the priest's prayer with their "Amen".

Until 1955 there were mostly several Collects in the Western Mass, through which in the overlapping of Sundays, feast-days and Saints' days all possible aspects of a liturgical date should be commemorated. According to GIRM 32 the rule is, that "in each Mass only one Collect is to be said"; "the same rule applies to the Prayer over the Gifts and to the Post-communion." Beyond the rich store of Roman prayers – which reach back to the time of Leo I (440–461) – there is need for the vernacular celebration of the liturgy also new creation of prayers, as was already stated in the Instruction of the Consilium on the translation of liturgical texts: "For the celebration of a radically renewed liturgy one cannot be satisfied with translations; new creations are necessary." [141] At the same time the Roman style of prayer should serve as model (SC 23). According to Baumgartner "no one indeed will think of abandoning the structure and the elements of Roman prayer. On the contrary, it will be the case of strengthening rather than dismantling specific aspects of the Jewish Berakah (for example the anamnetic factor). This leads us immediately to the biblical orientation of the official prayers, which as the liturgy Constitution explains, ought to be in line with the spirit and mode of expression of the sacred Scriptures." [142] Nevertheless the renewed liturgy, precisely with the treasure of existing Collects, knows a rich possibility of variations. For children's Masses the celebrant may select prayers from the missal, as long as the character of

---

[140] On the whole complex cf. Jungmann, Die Stellung Christi im liturgischen Gebet. Cf. also B. Fischer, Vom Beten zu Christus: Plöger, Gott feiern 94–99; it is established there that "liturgical prayer" in Jungmann means first of all the presidential prayers and not purely and simply every liturgical prayer. Gerhards completes this: Zu wem beten? Die These Josef Andreas Jungmanns (d.1975) über den Adressaten des Eucharistischen Hochgebetes im Licht der neueren Forschung, LJ 32(1982) 219–230, where it is proved that in the early period the address of liturgical prayer "ad Deum" and "ad Christum" existed side by side.

[141] Kaczynski No. 1242.

[142] Baumgartner, Neuschöpfungen 163.

the liturgical season remains safeguarded; he may even adapt the text of the prayers to the understanding of the children, yet the intrinsic meaning and the function of the prayer should likewise remain preserved. [143] Here the possibilities of choice are to be mentioned, which hold especially for weekday Masses in ordinary time, in Masses for the administration of the sacraments and in votive Masses. [144]

3.4.9. THE OPENING PART IN THE EUCHARISTIC CELEBRATION OF OTHER RITES

A. The Byzantine Liturgy

There are "forecourts" also in the Eucharistic celebrations of other Christian rites. In the Byzantine liturgy the "Little Entrance" marks clearly the original beginning of the celebration. [145] Other "forecourts" came to settle in front of this: the private preparatory prayers of the celebrant in front of the icon screen, the vesting with the liturgical garments, the *Proskomidia* (or "*prothesis*)" the preparation of the bread and wine elaborated with many rites, as well as the prayers during the carrying of these and the dialogue of the celebrants. While the congregation is not included in these parts of the liturgy, the other forecourts are "public" and count as component parts of the "liturgy of the catechumens". Among these after the priestly entrance blessing belongs the "great *Ectene*" (also called, after its opening petition the "peace *Ectene*"), a diaconal Kyrie litany, which the priest concludes with a prayer, of which the final praise is proclaimed in an audible voice (*Ecphonesis*). There follow three "Antiphons", variable psalm chants according to the liturgical season, but the Beatitudes of Matthew's Gospel may also have a place in the Antiphons. The hymn "Only-begotten Son of God", which goes back to Emperor Justinian I (527 – 565) and which was once originally an entrance chant, marks the close of the second Antiphon after the psalm. [146] The three Antiphons are subdivided by two "small *Ectene*" of the deacon's with Kyrie eleison of the congregation, consisting of the first, the penultimate and the last petitions of the peace *Ectene,* followed by a priestly concluding prayer. According to Kucharek this first part of the liturgy before the Little Entrance is the vestige of a special prayer service on Sunday morning, which finally coalesced with the Eucharistic liturgy. [147] After the Little Entrance, during which the book of the Gospels is solemnly carried, there follow chants which vary according to the liturgical day (*Troparion* and *Contakion)* and the *Trisagion,* [148] before the priest completes the "ceremony of the throne", and takes his place on the celebrant's chair near the episcopal *cathedra* in the middle of the apse to listen to the Word of God.

B. The mozarabic Liturgy

The entrance part of the mozarabic liturgy comprises the "Praelegendum", the Gloria and the prayer after the Gloria. On festive days the *Trisagion* is added between the Gloria and the prayer. [149] The Praelegendum is an entry chant analogous to the Roman introit or the Ambrosian Ingressa. Similarly as with the prayer after the Gloria and the

---

[143]   Cf. the Directorium de missis cum pueris No.s 50 – 51, Kaczynski 3164 – 3165.
[144]   Cf. J. Hermans, Die Feier der Eucharistie, Erklärung und spirituelle Erschließung, Regensburg 1984, 146f.
[145]   Cf. Kucharek, Liturgy 382f.
[146]   Cf. Kallis 56, Kucharek, Liturgy 373 – 378.
[147]   Cf. Kucharek, Liturgy 367.
[148]   On the history of the *Trisagion* cf. Kucharek, Liturgy 399 – 405.
[149]   Cf. IGMHM 25.

"Sacrificium" (analogous to the Roman Offertory) the Praelegendum is also – as are also the readings of the "Liber Comicus" – divided on a two-year cycle on the Sundays of Advent and Eastertide, as well as on the Circumcision and Epiphany of the Lord, on Ascension Day and Pentecost. [150] The Praelegendum is omitted on the Sundays of Lent, as on ferial days. While it is being sung the priest goes to the altar, venerates it with a kiss and proceeds to the celebrant's chair, where he intones the Gloria (on the Sundays outside of Lent). After the Gloria or respectively after the *Trisagion* [151] there follows the prayer, which corresponds to the Roman "Collecta" or respectively to the Ambrosian "Oratio super populum". [152] As a characteristic feature of these prayers is mentioned the fact that they take up themes from the Gloria which precede them (and provided that it is sung) from the *Trisagion*. [153] In Lent and on ferial days the whole opening part of the liturgy is omitted: after kissing the altar the priest proceeds to the celebrant's chair, and immediately the first lesson is read. [154]

C. The Ambrosian Liturgy

The opening part of the Milanese liturgy scarcely differs from that of the Roman Mass. The entry chant, the Canto d'Ingresso accompanies the entry of the priest and his assistants. After the veneration of the altar and the sign of the Cross there follows the penitential act, which the Milanese missal shapes throughout as Kyrie petitions. On special days the penitential act may be replaced by the twelvefold Kyrie. [155] There follow the Gloria and the prayer of the day, analogous to the Roman rite, but here called "orazione all'inizio dell'assemblea liturgica". [156]

Bibliography

J. Baumgartner, Neuschöpfungen sind erforderlich. Zum Problem der Alternativorationen, LJ 38 (1988) 138 – 164.

A. Baumstark, Das Gesetz der Erhaltung des Alten in liturgisch hochwertiger Zeit, JLw 7 (1927) 1 – 23.

L. Bernhard, Ursprung und Sinn der Formel 'Et cum Spiritu tuo': Anselm Rosenthal (ed.), Itinera Domini (FS E. v. Severus), Münster 1988, 133 – 156.

H. Büsse, Das 'Tagesgebet' als integrierendes Element der Eröffnung: Th. Maas-Ewerd / K. Richter (eds.), Gemeinde im Herrenmahl, 222 – 231.

---

[150]   Cf. IGMHM 156.

[151]   The *Trisagion* contains indeed all the elements, as they also occur in the Eastern liturgies, but is however expanded to an elaborate antiphony. The *Trisagion* for the Day of Pentecost may serve as an example, MHM 547f.: 'Sanctus Deus, qui sedes super Cherubim, solus invisibilis. Sanctus fortis, qui in excelsis glorificaris vocibus angelicis. Sanctus immortalis, qui solus es immaculatus Salvator, miserere nobis, alleluia, alleluia. V: Dignus es, Domine, Deus noster, accipere gloriam et honorem et virtutem. R: Sanctus immortalis, qui solus es immaculatus Salvator, miererere nobis, alleluia, alleluia. V: Quoniam omnes gentes venient et adorabunt in conspectu tuo, Domine, et dicent: R: Miserere nobis, alleluia, alleluia. V: Benedictio et honor et gloria et fortitudo tibi, Deo nostro, in saecula saeculorum. Amen. R: Miserere nobis, alleluia, alleluia.'

[152]   Cf. IGMHM 31.

[153]   IGMHM 32: "Las oraciones Post Gloriam hispánicas presentan una caracteristica especial: en el texto de la oración quedan siempre integradas lecciones extráidas del Gloria o, si se canta también el Trisago, expresiones del Gloria y del Trisagio simultáneamente."

[154]   Cf. MHM 61, Rubric No. 3.

[155]   Cf. MA, Principi e Norme No.s 25 – 29; on the multiple possibilities of choice of the Kyrie petitions cf. MA 794 – 798.

[156]   Cf. Principi e Norme No. 30 – 31.

B. Capelle, Le Kyrie de la messe et le pape Gélase, Rev. Bénéd. 46 (1934) 126–144 (= Travaux II, 116–134).

B. Capelle, Le texte du "Gloria in Excelsis", RHE 44 (1949) 439–457 (= Travaux II, 176–192).

E. Färber, Gemeinsame Tauferinnerung vor der sonntäglichen Eucharistiefeier: Th. Maas-Ewerd / K. Richter (eds.), Gemeinde im Herrenmahl, 199–208.

A. Heinz, Ein anderer Ort für den Bußritus, LJ 40 (1990) 109–119.

H. B. Meyer, Der Bußakt der Meßfeier. Möglichkeiten und Probleme: Th. Maas-Ewerd / K. Richter (eds.), Gemeinde im Herrenmahl, 209–216.

H. Plock, Die Eröffnung der Eucharistiefeier: Th. Maas-Ewerd / K. Richter (eds.), Gemeinde im Herrenmahl, 191–198.

Th. Schnitzler, Kyrielitanei am Anfang? Th. Maas-Ewerd / K. Richter (eds.), Gemeinde im Herrenmahl, 217–221.

3.5. THE LITURGY OF THE WORD

3.5.1. "MASS OF THE CATECHUMENS"

Still at the eve of Vatican II Jungmann distinguishes the liturgy of the Word as "Fore-Mass" from the "sacrifice-Mass". [157] The Byzantine liturgy distinguishes between the "liturgy of the catechumens" and the "liturgy of the faithful", which begins with the "prayer of the faithful", during which there takes place in the Great Entrance the transfer of the prepared gifts from the table of oblation to the altar. Even if the lines of demarcation are not uniform (thus for example in the 6th century the catechumens were already dismissed before the Gospel, while it was believed that on account of the *disciplina arcani* it must be withheld from them as unbaptized) still this division is preferable to that of "Fore-Mass" and "sacrifice-Mass": it can create the impression that the essential begins with the preparation of the gifts and that everything preceding this is more or less unessential, as was advocated in Moral Theology up to quite recent times. [158] If the "forecourts" of the celebration of Mass are "totally in the service of the faithful becoming one in the Christian community" [159] to which Christ has promised his presence, how much more then in focus is the encounter of the community with the Lord speaking here in his Word, before she meets him in the holy meal. Beyond all subdivisions of the celebration of Mass, and all specific characteristics of the liturgy of the Word, in which the catechumens may participate according to the new rite of the initiation of adults, before they are dismissed prior to the celebration of the "liturgy of the faithful", it must be clear that the Eucharistic celebration is an integrated whole.

As it emerges from Justin's Apology, the coalescing of the liturgy of the Word and the Eucharistic celebration in the narrower sense was already complete about the middle of the 2nd century. The separation of the Eucharist from the *agape* and its binding to a service of prayer and word constituted that unity which we know up to today. For the

---

[157] Cf. Jungmann MS I, 341.
[158] Cf. H. Jone, Kath. Moraltheologie, Paderborn 16th edn. 1953, 161, where the individual actions of the Mass up to the "Offertory" are qualified as "unimportant parts", to miss which is at most a venial sin!
[159] J. Hermans, Die Feier der Eucharistie. Erklärung und spirituelle Erschließung, Regensburg 1984, 100f.

service of prayer and reading the Jewish synagogue worship stood godparent for the primitive Church. [160]

3.5.2. THE ORDER OF READINGS [161]

According to Elbogen the public reading from the Torah and the prophets belongs to the most ancient liturgical institutions; he is of the opinion that it is likely "that the proclamation of Scripture furnished the occasion for the first assemblies of worship." [162] The reading from the law has precedence over the reading from the prophets. It takes place as lectio continua and is divided into sections (*parashoth*).

After the completion of the Torah they began again at the beginning. In the reading of the prophets passages (*haphtarah*) were chosen at will. These Scripture readings were embedded in community prayer, and the assembly closed with a blessing.

"The service of readings of the synagogical Sabbath celebration became the basis for the Mass of the catechumens", [163] as Justin's Apology witnesses. Many liturgical scholars from Baumstark to Jungmann hold this view; others call it in question. According to Meyer "a direct dependence of the Christian liturgy of the Word on the worship of the synagogue for the earliest period is neither demonstrable nor likely. It is clear however that from the 2nd to the 4th century a development took place, at the end of which the liturgy of the Word of the Eucharistic celebration in important witnesses of the East exhibits an obvious affinity with the synagogical worship as regards the order of readings but also of the prayers. Especially in the Syriac region long-standing and close contacts with the Jews had openly existed which became effective in the history of tradition, after the separation of the Church from Jewry was completed." [164]

In the 4th century in Antioch they still had a reading from the law and the prophets, supplemented with one from the letters of the apostles or respectively from the Acts of the Apostles and from one of the gospels. At the high points of the Church's year there was the tendency to limit the Old Testament readings or to omit them totally, in order to emphasize the mystery of redemption through the preaching of the New Testament alone, and so no longer through the "*relecture*" of the Old Testament, but in the fulfilment which had taken place of what was promised. So for example in the Coptic liturgy the fourfold reading remains, but all are taken from the New Testament: Pauline epistles, Catholic epistles, Acts of the Apostles, Gospel.

This tendency spread itself over the whole liturgical year, so that since the 7th century the Byzantines have only two readings, and both of them New Testament: the "Apostle" and the Gospel. The Roman liturgy experienced a similar development: at first three readings (an Old Testament, a New Testament and the Gospel) were reduced to "Epistle" and Gospel.

[160] Cf. I. Elbogen, Der jüdische Gottesdienst in seiner geschichtlichen Entwicklung, Frankfurt/M. 3rd edn. 1931, Reprint Hildesheim 1962, 36–38. Cf. in this connection also R. T. Beckwith, The Daily and Weekly Worship of the Primitive Church in Relation to its Jewish Antecedents: R. Beckwith and others, Influences juives sur le culte chrétien. Etudes présentées au Colloque scientifique organisé par l'Institut Liturgique de la Faculté de Théologie Leuven 23–25 avril 1980, Leuven (Louvain) 1981, 89–122.
[161] Cf. St. Beissel, Entstehung der Perikopen des römischen Meßbuchs. Zur Entstehung der Evangelienbücher in der 1. Hälfte des Mittelalters, Rome 1967; E. Nübold, Entstehung und Bewertung der neuen Perikopenordnung des römischen Ritus für die Meßfeier an Sonn- und Feiertagen, Paderborn 1986.
[162] Elbogen 153.
[163] A. Baumstark, Vom geschichtlichen Werden der Liturgie (Eccl. Orans X). Freiburg i. Br., 1923, 15.
[164] Meyer, Eucharistie 117.

The principle of lectio continua, acclimatized also in the ancient Church, was first of all interrupted on the greater feasts and finally also on the memorial days of martyrs. Appropriate Scripture readings were chosen for the feast, as the pilgrim account of Egeria attests for Jerusalem: the readings with the corresponding psalms and antiphons on the Epiphany and in Holy Week and Easter Week were "aptae diei".

If the principle of lectio continua in the West up to the liturgical reform of Vatican II was as good as abandoned except for vestiges in the epistles, the East remained more closely rooted in it in the sense of scriptura occurens: a sacred book would be read at least on Saturdays and Sundays, admittedly in extracts, but these extracts followed the course of the text. Thus the Byzantine Church after Pentecost has 17 Sundays with readings from Matthew's gospel, followed by 16 readings from Luke with smaller series from the gospels according to Mark and John. The order of readings of the Roman Church was almost completely constituted by the beginning of the Middle Ages. The characterization of various periods of the Church's year by certain themes in the proclamation of Scripture, the choice of proper readings for the feasts of the Lord and of the saints, the effect of the respective Roman station churches on the biblical readings caused the lectio continua in the West to disappear on a large scale. With the rise of ever more numerous saints" days this affected also the choice of passages for weekday Masses.

In line with the directive of the Constitution on the Liturgy that "the treasures of the Bible are to be opened up more lavishly so that a richer fare may be provided for the faithful at the table of God's word. In this way a more representative part of the sacred scriptures will be read to the people in the course of a prescribed number of years" (SC 51) a totally new order of readings was elaborated. In 1969 the Congregation for Divine Worship published the new "Ordo lectionum missae", of which the 2nd edition appeared in 1981.

For Sundays and feast days three readings are provided on the ancient model: Old Testament reading, New Testament reading, Gospel. The order of readings follows a three-year cycle (Years A, B, and C), in which each of the synoptic Gospels is assigned to a year, while the Gospel of John is read at certain times every year. A synthesis between thematic harmonization and lectio continua was striven for in the order of readings for Sundays and feast days. The privileged times of the Church's year (Advent, Lent, Eastertide) are more thematically determined; on the Sundays in Ordinary time lectio continua prevails. Especially between the Old Testament reading and the Gospel attention was paid to an inner correlation. This can consist in the fact that the Old Testament reading contains a passage of Scripture, which the following Gospel picks up as a quotation. Or it points out a deliberate contrast between the old and new covenant; or the continuity of salvation history is emphasized, or the Gospel appears in the full light of the Old Testament promise.

The new lectionary for weekday Masses has only two readings, which follow a one-year cycle in the privileged seasons, and outside of these, that is in the 34 weeks of Ordinary time a two-year cycle (I for odd-numbered years, II for even-numbered years). There are special orders of readings for the celebration of Mass on Saints' Days as well as for the celebration of the sacraments and sacramentals, for Masses for various occasions and also for Votive Masses. The possibilities of choice are new, this is very

restricted for Sundays and feast days, but apply all the more for weekdays, for Saints'
days and for the Masses for various occasions.

3.5.3. THE PLACE FOR THE PROCLAMATION OF SCRIPTURE

While for the opening parts of the Mass the celebrant's chair was the place that stood
out, for the liturgy of the Word it is the ambo, which takes its name from the Greek word
"to go up" (*anabeinein*) and so still points to its shape. The switching of the action to
a place proper to itself witnesses to the special character of this part of the Mass: the
presence of Christ in the celebrating community (cf. Mt 18:20) particularizes itself as
the presence of the Lord speaking in his Word, "it is he himself who speaks when
the holy Scriptures are read in the Church" (SC 7). In the past this found expression
in the division of the church – and later (in the context of the shaping of the liturgy
by the private Mass) also of the altar – into an "Epistle side" and a "Gospel side".
In the basilica of late antiquity the cathedra of the bishop standing in the middle of
the apse determined the right-hand side (therefore the left-hand side as seen from the
congregation) as the "side of honour"; on the right of the bishop, but without turning his
back on him, facing the people, the deacon read the Gospel turned towards the south or
the north, depending on whether the basilica was orientated towards the east or towards
the west. The reading facing north – usual in the older west-orientated basilicas – was
independent of the geographical situation of the church and without reference to an
original motivation for a fixed direction in which to read the Gospel. In its favour the
medieval commentators on the Mass provided explanations (powerful proclamation of
the Gospel against the north as the region of the devil and of darkness, transfer of the
preaching of the kingdom of God from the Jews to the pagans) [165] which finally were
supposed allegorically to account for the transfer of the missal from the right to the
left side of the altar. In spite of the allegories there was still a flair for a "sacramental"
character of the Lord speaking in the Gospel. The new consciousness of the dignity
of God's Word and of the Lord's presence in the preached Scripture word, which in
the anti-Reformation polemic had somewhat fallen into disregard, [166] led in the reform
to a retrieval of the ambo in close allocation to the altar and the presbyterium. This
location gives evidence symbolically of the various modes of the Lord's presence in
the gathered community according to SC 7: The altar corresponds to Christ's presence
in the Eucharistic sacrifice and in the consecrated species; the ambo to his presence in
the preached word, and the celebrant's chair to that in the gathered community under
the presidency of the celebrant. As there is only one Christ, so there ought to be in the
church only one altar and one ambo.

3.5.4. THE ACCOMPANYING RITES

The words and rites which accompany the readings are intended to underline Christ's
presence in the proclaimed word. This holds particularly for the Gospel: in East and
West the deacon asks for a special blessing for its proclamation; the priest himself also
asks for the grace of a worthy proclamation. The Gospel procession, the carrying of
candles and incense, the incensation of the Gospel book, the liturgical greeting "Domi-

---

[165] On the whole complex of Epistle and Gospel side cf. Jungmann, MS I, 529–534.

[166] Cf. J. Baumgartner, Das Wort, das in der Liturgiefeier zum Sakrament wird: J. Schreiner (ed.), Freude am
Gottesdienst. Aspekte ursprünglicher Liturgie (FS Plöger), Stuttgart 1983, 155–173.

nus vobiscum" reserved to the ordained as well as the triple small sign of the cross of the faithful on forehead, mouth and breast in the Western Mass emphasize plainly the sacramental character of the proclamation of scripture and especially that of the Gospel. The new missal emphasizes this also by the fact that the congregation answer "Deo gratias" to the readings as well as to the Gospel, after the deacon or respectively the reader, by analogy with the Old Testament prophetic formula, has announced that which is proclaimed in Mass as "Verbum Domini". [167] Long ago "Deo gratias" was used as a formula "with a religious nuance comparable to Amen to express the reception of some information." [168] Kissing the Gospel book expresses reverence and can be compared with kissing the altar. The threefold signing of the Cross by the faithful, which goes back to the 9th century, is explained by Jungmann as the desire to grasp the holy Word and to hold fast its blessing. A sign of the Cross at the end of the Gospel was meant to seal against the devil the Word of God which had been heard. The threefold signing of oneself is an expression of a courageous stand for Christ's message, for a frank confession of it, and a faithful keeping of it in the heart. [169]

3.5.5. THE RESPONSORIAL PSALM [170]

"After the first reading comes the Responsorial Psalm or Gradual, which is an integral part of the Liturgy of the Word" (GIRM 36). With the Responsorial Psalm the congregation answers to what was heard in the reading as the Word of God. It does so with the given refrain, which once again emphasizes the message of the reading. The congregation thereby responds not only to what was heard in the reading, but also to the psalm rendered by the chanter, which likewise in its content stands in a relationship to the proclaimed reading.

The responsorial response to a psalm or another biblical text was already native to the Jewish liturgy. In the Christian liturgy the responsorial psalm is attested since the 4th century and was an act of the congregation until the ever more complicated art forms of poetry and song required a special choir of singers. "We have in this responsorial rendering of psalms the earliest beginnings and the oldest form of rendering of psalmody in Christian worship; in East and West it is attested since the 4th century." But "in the course of time the Roman liturgy elaborated the responsory so richly that it could be rendered only by the chanter and choir; the psalm shrank down to a single verse." [171] Not only on account of the close relationship of the responsorial psalm with the reading, but also on account of the aim of opening up for the congregation a living access to the spirituality of the psalms, the responsorial psalm ought not to be substituted for by another chant, something which Fischer rightly emphasizes with regard to the special development in the German-speaking area. [172] It was only the retrieval of three readings

---

[167] For the Gospel the German missal gives as the special acclamation by the reader: "The Gospel of our Lord Jesus Christ" with the people's reply: "Praise to you, O Christ".

[168] Häußling, Akklamationen und Formeln 235.

[169] Cf. Jungmann, MS I, 579–581.

[170] Cf. R. Pacik, Der Antwortpsalm, LJ 30 (1980) 43–66; E. Quack, Die Gesänge zu den Lesungen: Th. Maas-Ewerd / K. Richter (eds.), Gemeinde im Herrenmahl, 232–241.

[171] Fischer, Responsa 191.

[172] There contrary to the directive for the universal Church a rubric of the German missal had unfavourable consequences, according to which the responsorial psalm "in case of necessity" may be substituted for by another suitable chant. Cf. Fischer, Responsa 191.

that restored the "intervening chants" to their proper function: in the responsorial psalm to answer what was heard in the first reading, and in the Alleluia after the second reading to greet Christ speaking in the Gospel which follows. The name "Graduale" derives from the custom that the chanter was indeed allowed to mount the ambo, but not to the highest step, which was reserved for the proclamation of the Gospel, but only as far as an intermediate level, the gradus. The name "Graduale", which occurs since the 9th century (at first as "Responsorium graduale"), implies the richly elaborated musical form of the Responsum in contrast to the original Responsorium, as was maintained in the Liturgy of the Hours. Hucke sees in the development of the Graduale a key for the development of Church music into art music. [173]

3.5.6. ALLELUIA AND SEQUENCE

The alleluia – the second "intervening chant" is totally relative to the following Gospel, it greets the Lord speaking in his word and has therefore the character of an acclamation rather than a meditation. The congregation's acclamation is always – outside Lent, GIRM 37! – the Alleluia; the verse rendered by the chanter is taken from the Gospel which follows. Alleluia derives from Jewish worship and is in the Apocalypse (19:1–7) the exultant cry of the heavenly Jerusalem and in the Western Church – in contrast to the East, which uses it all through the year and on every occasion, even in the liturgy of the dead – is given an Easter accent. On days of a penitential nature, but especially during Lent, alleluia was relinquished and substituted for by the Tractus. In addition there developed special rites of Alleluia-farewell at the beginning of Lent, and its greeting again on Easter night, which in the Middle Ages provided themes for stage plays. [174] The simpler, i.e. older melody line of the Tractus was interpreted by the medieval commentators on the Mass as "drawn-out chant" adapted to the penitential character of the season; another derivation comes from the fact that the chant is sung in one go (tractim) without responsorial interruption. In the renewed liturgy also alleluia is given up in Lent, but a responsorial chant before the Gospel has been introduced, in which the chanter's verse is preceded and followed by an acclamation to Christ (GIRM 38b).

From the Alleluia there arose the sequence. Originally it was understood as a richly elaborated wordless melody on the final -a (Jubilus) of the Alleluia. In the late Carolingian period a prose text was set to this tune, a syllable per note. In the following period by "sequence" was understood a complicated creation. The older sequence poetic compositions follow a single strophe introduction and conclusion with paired strophes in the middle part, for example the Easter sequence "Victimae paschali laudes". The newer sequence compositions of the high Middle Ages adopted rhyme and metre and made the sequence more and more like a hymn, for instance the Pentecost sequence "Veni Sancte Spiritus" from the turn of the 12th/13th century. The sequences increased to such an extent that they became a fixed component of nearly all Masses and constituted the seed-plot of popular Church hymns. The missal of 1570 took over from the many sequences only four (Easter, Pentecost, Corpus Christi and Requiem Mass), that of 1970 provides only the sequences for Easter and Pentecost (GIRM 40), while that of Corpus Christi ("Lauda Sion") and the sequence added in the early 18th century for the Seven

---

[173] Cf. Hucke, Responsa 191 – 194.193.
[174] Cf. Häußling, Akklamation und Formeln 225.

Dolours of Mary ("Stabat Mater") are optional. The sequence today is sung before the Alleluia, in order with the latter to greet Christ present in the Gospel. [175]

3.5.7. THE HOMILY

The homily "is to be highly esteemed as part of the liturgy itself" (SC 52); it is "part of the liturgy" (GIRM 41) and therefore it is prescribed for Sundays and feast days, on all other days, especially in the privileged seasons, it is highly recommended (GIRM 42). The reminder of what is an integral component of the liturgy is aimed at the feeling still prevailing in 1962 which according to Jungmann regarded the homily "as an interpolation in the course of the liturgy rather than as a step forward in its progress". [176]

In Justin's Apology (I, 67) the homily is still part of the liturgical rite. It differs from the "sermon" in so far as it is much closer bound to the liturgy, and wishes to make fruitful for a life of faith its celebrations in word and symbol and the texts proclaimed in it. The sermon is strictly speaking a mission sermon, in contrast to the homily it is aimed at the outsiders who have to be won over to the faith (or to be won back to it!), and therefore has also a much looser relation to liturgy. [177] As regards content also it differs by a wholly other range of themes. The age of the Church Fathers is also the epoch of the great homilies, nevertheless it is no longer mentioned in the descriptions of liturgy in the East as well as in the West. From Carolingian times there was a residual form, in so far as the patristic homilies were read out loud or respectively rendered more or less freely in the vernacular. A new zenith of the freely spoken, preached word came with the high Middle Ages and the mendicant Orders, but not as a renaissance of the homily, but rather of the sermon. With it there came about a further detachment of the sermon out of the liturgical process, which led finally to a vernacular block within the Latin liturgy of the Mass, which further developed into an independent preaching service. The more comprehensive this block became (vernacular repetitions of the Latin readings, announcements, prayers and songs in the vernacular), so much the more did it withdraw from the liturgy of the Mass. [178] Also the pulpit [the German word "Kanzel" reminds one still of the "cancelli", the balustrade of the choir, into which the ambo was integrated] shifted to the nave of the church, so that the preacher had to leave the altar space, which likewise made the removal of the sermon visible, all the more so that up to our own century the altar candles were extinguished during the sermon and the preacher – if he were also the celebrant of the Mass – removed the chasuble, or at least the maniple. Furthermore the sermon themes were scarcely ever orientated any more towards the liturgy or the texts proclaimed in it. So there came about a switch of the preaching service out of the Mass on to the Sunday afternoon, and this preaching service was to become the main service of the Reformed Churches. [179] That the sermon could be felt to be a "foreign body" within the celebration of Mass, is understandable also from the nature of the sermon (and of the homily) as a freely spoken word of proclamation: according to the principle "*Lex orandi – lex credendi*" the liturgy prescribed by the council of Trent was to be the same everywhere and its rubrical directives minutely

---

[175] Cf. Fischer, Sequenzen und Tropen 199f.

[176] Ib. I, 583.

[177] Cf. Maas-Ewerd, Vom Pronaus zur Homilie 74f.

[178] Cf. E. Weismann, Der Predigtgottesdienst und verwandte Formen: Leiturgia III, Kassel 1956, 1 – 96. 19 – 25: Die Ausgestaltung einer geschlossenen "Predigtliturgie" (Pronaus) im hohen Mittelalter, esp. 23f.

[179] Cf. Weismann 27 – 49: Die Übernahme des Prädikantengottesdienst durch die Reformation.

observed, in order to safeguard the identity of Catholic faith also through the liturgical celebration. The freely spoken word however is never able to be subjugated to such an iron uniformity, so that the separation of the sermon from liturgical celebration of the Mass under this aspect created the impression that in the sermon it was a question of a meritorious but free will special service of the parish priest, but not however of an integral component of the Eucharistic liturgy. That the homily in the renewed liturgy is considered an integral component of the celebration brings to an end an uncertainty of over a thousand years as regards its place in the liturgy and links up once again with the patristic tradition. The homily is directed to "insiders", to those who are assembled for the Eucharistic celebration, and is meant to give them mystagogical pointers to the practice of the Christian life. The place of the homily is the ambo, the "table of God's Word", or the celebrant's chair (GIRM 97); the sign of the Cross at the beginning or end or an opening greeting are omitted. All this underlines the fact that the homily is an organic component of the celebration of Mass. This raises not least the contested prohibition of preaching by the laity in the celebration of Mass, in which regard however the inner link between homily and Mass liturgy is then only fully safeguarded when the (chief) celebrant himself gives the homily, and its performance is seen not solely from the aspect of his ordained ministry!

3.5.8. THE PROFESSION OF FAITH

As a confessional text the profession of faith in the celebration of Mass may perhaps even still represent a foreign body, although GIRM 43 in reference to its function defines "the purpose of the Profession of Faith (or Creed) is to express the assent and response of the people to the scripture reading and homily they have just heard, and to recall to them the main truths of the faith, before they begin to celebrate the Eucharist." Already the "I" form of the Profession of Faith ("Credo") contrasts it with the liturgical "We" and points to its original place in the baptismal liturgy. The names "Symbolum" and "Apostles' Creed" derive from a text of Tyrannius Rufinus, written in 404, according to which the twelve apostles before separating to go out on mission would have "put together" (symballein) each one of the articles of faith. This legend was continued in the 8th century in a sermon attributed to St Augustine and even the individual articles were allotted the names of the Twelve. The "Apostles' Creed" is in truth a Roman baptismal creed, such as we have present in Hippolytus, and goes back possibly to the pontificate of Victor (189 – 197).[180] The Roman missal as well as the Eastern liturgies give preference to the "Niceno-Constantinopolitan" while the German missal allows also the use of the Apostles' Creed. The Profession of Faith came into the celebration of Mass through Timothy, who was patriarch of Constantinople 511 – 517, and who was said to have sympathy for the Monophysite heresy. According to the account of the historian Theodore the Lector in order to demonstrate his orthodoxy he gave orders that the Profession of Faith was to be prayed in every celebration of the Eucharist, this was soon imitated in all the East. Still in the same century the Profession of Faith came to Spain where a coastal strip was under Byzantine rule. On the occasion of the Third Council of Toledo the Visigothic king Recared with his people converted from Arianism and it was decided that the Profession of Faith was to be prayed in every Mass. A further strand of tradition reaches from the East through Ireland and the Anglo-Saxons as far

---

[180] Cf. J. N. D. Kelly

as Aachen where Charlemagne took it up into the liturgy of the imperial chapel. Not till the 11th century was it generally spread in the north, so that Henry II noticed that the Profession of Faith was missing in Rome, when he was staying there for his coronation. Benedict VIII gave into Henry's importuning and introduced the *Credo* into the Roman Mass, but soon however a restrictive regulation arose that the Profession of Faith was to be used only on Sundays and on such feast days which find mention in it. According to the present regulation (GIRM 44 and 98) the Profession of Faith is to be said or sung on Sundays and solemn feasts; it may also be said on other specially solemn occasions.

The *Credo* – perhaps contrary to the intentions of Patriarch Timothy – came into the Eucharistic celebration as the profession of the community; in the West this was firmly held on to for a long time; in the East at least a representative of the people spoke it. For this reason the sung form was mostly an ancient recitative melody. It was only with the rise of polyphony that the *Credo* intoned by the priest was continued no longer by the people but by the choir. Emminghaus recommends a widespread knowledge also of the Latin Profession of Faith, so that the unity of the Church in faith could be expressed beyond the frontiers of language – for instance at international gatherings – and thereby that the *Credo* can really be part of the gathered community and of their active participation in the liturgy. [181]

3.5.9. THE INTERCESSIONS

The reinstating of the intercessions (also called "common prayer" or "prayer of the faithful") was urged by Vatican II itself (SC 53) in line with the demand that "what had suffered loss through accidents of history" ought "to be restored according to the venerable norms of the Fathers" (SC 53). The appeal to the Fathers reaches back in the case of the intercessions to Justin Martyr, who mentions twice in his *Apology* (I, 65, 67) the intercessions "for all others everywhere", as well as prayers after the homily of the presiding celebrant. Up to today the Byzantine Eucharistic celebration, along with many other intercessory *Ektenia* after the dismissal of the catechumens and before the Great Entrance with the transfer of the prepared gifts to the altar, is familiar with a prayer of the faithful ("Only ye faithful, again and again in peace let us pray to the Lord!"), something which emphasizes and justifies the special placing of the "prayer of the faithful". It was for this reason that in the ancient Church people shrank from praying with unbelievers and the still unbaptized catechumens. The justification consists in the perception of the universal priesthood by the faithful, with which also the renewed Roman missal emphasizes the importance of the intercessions: because the congregation exercise their priestly function in the intercessions for all mankind, these should be included in every Mass (GIRM 45). Already in Justin it is said explicitly that only the newly baptized may participate in the "prayer of the faithful". The exhortation to such priestly action of the faithful (cf. 1 Pet 2:9) is given already in the New Testament (1 Tim 2: 1–4); it should take place in a sequence which GIRM 45 presents as a model: "for the needs of the Church, for civil authorities and for the salvation of the whole world, for those oppressed by any kind of need, for the local community." Accordingly the intercessions are genuine intercessions FOR, that it is to say for such as are not present in the liturgical assembly, and not OUR intercessions, which correspond to the liturgical "We" of

---

[181] Cf. Joh. Emminghaus, Die Messe. Wesen, Gestalt, Vollzug. Edd. by Th. Maas-Ewerd, Klosterneuburg 5th edn. 1992, 220.

the assembled community (as do the *Preces* in the Lauds of the renewed Liturgy of the Hours). Already the very fact that members of the community are missing in the liturgy as the assembly of God's family, is a sufficient reason to pray for them, for the sick, for the imprisoned, for those endangered in the faith. The intercessions thus express the belonging together of Christians and their fraternal responsibility for each other and for the whole world. The presiding celebrant introduces the common prayer, i.e. he invites the faithful into it and concludes it, after the individual petitions have been said by a deacon, a chanter or some other leader, and the community with a response has made them their own (cf. GIRM 49). Thus the present-day form of intercession corresponds more to the Kyrie litany which entered the Roman celebration of Mass under Gelasius than the ancient Roman form which has come down to us only on Good Friday: the designation of the need, the silent prayer of the faithful for the named need, the summing up prayer (Collect) of the presiding celebrant. That the intercessions "through accidents of history" got lost, is indeed connected with the origin of the Kyrie at the beginning of Mass. Vestiges of the common prayer survived in the French-speaking regions in the so-called "*Prières du prône*" which were very comprehensive and in their full form (in addition to an abbreviated form for every Sunday) were to be prayed at least once a month. According to Heinz this took place in the German-French frontier zone up to the eve of the liturgical renewal. However according to Heinz there was also for the German culture zone in the "General Prayer for the Needs of Christendom" of Peter Canisius a vestige of the common prayer following on to the sermon. [182] In contrast to the Byzantine *ectene*, of which the wording of the petitions is always the same, the intercessions of the renewed liturgy belong to the elements of the Mass which are freely composed. This freedom however will only then be correctly availed of, if the intercessions are composed in a fitting way: they are petitions in which the Christian community makes use of its priestly dignity for the world. The petitions must be real prayers and express genuine needs, not empty husks of words, but above all they should neither be overlaid with ideology nor contain moralizing reprimands. [183]

3.5.10. THE PROCLAMATION OF THE SCRIPTURES IN THE EUCHARISTIC CELEBRATIONS OF THE OTHER RITES

A. The Byzantine Liturgy

The reading is preceded by a priestly blessing from the celebrant's chair and by the *prokeimenon,* a "prelude" to the Scripture reading, composed of psalm verses; it corresponds also in its historical origins to the Western Graduale, which follows the reading. [184] In general the reading itself is taken from the New Testament and therefore the liturgical book also bears the name *Apostolos.* The Gospel is preceded by the chant of the Alleluia, interwoven with two verses of a psalm, during which the deacon carries out the incensation of the altar space and of the entire church. Under Western influence, in some Byzantine churches there is present once again, following an ancient tradition,

---

[182] Cf. A. Heinz, Die Oratio fidelium im deutschen Sprachraum zwischen Tridentinum und Vaticanum II, LJ 30 (1 980) 7–25.
[183] Cf. Th. Maas-Ewerd, Fürbitten. Inhalt und Form nach den Normen des II. Vatikanums, BiLi 39(1966) 140–157.
[184] Cf. C. Kucharek, The Byzantine-Slav liturgy of St. John Chrysostom. Its Origin and Evolution, Allendale 1971, 413f.

the homily after the Gospel, while other churches, in the tradition of the admonition relative to Communion present an address to the congregation during the Communion of the clergy in the altar space. The Byzantine Church has preserved, more than those of the West, the principle of *lectio continua*. [185] In the liturgy of the Word of the Byzantine Church there is to be counted also, after the Gospel or the homily, the *ectene* "of earnest prayer" as well as an *ectene* for the catechumens, after which they are dismissed by the deacon.

B. The Mozarabic Liturgy

The Mozarabic liturgy presents normally three readings: *Prophetia* (OT), *Apostolus* (NT) and *Evangelium*. In Lent there are four readings, given that the Old Testament reading is divided into a reading from the Wisdom literature (*lectio sapientialis)* and one from the historical books (*lectio historica)*. All the readings are contained in the "Liber Commicus". In Eastertide the Old Testament prophecy is substituted for by a reading from the Apocalypse. [186] The principle of *lectio continua* is rigidly adhered to. Analogously to the Roman *graduale* or the Ambrosian *psalmellus,* the prophecy (or the historical reading in Lent), is followed by the *psallendum,* which on the Wednesdays and Fridays of the five weeks of Lent is substituted for by the Lamentations, and on the feasts of martyrs by texts of the martyrology. In that case a section of the hymn of praise of the three youths in the furnace is added. [187] The liturgy of the Word ends after the Gospel, or after the homily with the *laudes,* a section of a psalm which begins and ends with alleluia, which, as in the Roman liturgy, is omitted in Lent. The Mozarabic liturgy has no chant before the Gospel. [188]

C. The Ambrosian Liturgy

The liturgy of the Word of the Milanese Mass corresponds to that of the Roman liturgy: first reading from the Old Testament, responsorial psalm, second New Testament reading, alleluia, or acclamation before the Gospel in Lent, both called "Canto al Vangelo"; after the Gospel a special chant is sung "Dopo il Vangelo". The Milanese lectionary presents itself as an "Ambrosian complement to the volumes of the Roman lectionary." [189] Accordingly many points of contact with the Roman plan of readings are given. A special feature is the blessing of the reader by the celebrant. The homily is followed immediately by the prayer of the faithful ("Preghiera universale o dei fedeli"). The intercessions are always followed by the "prayer for the conclusion of the liturgy of the Word", recited by the celebrant, before the eucharistic liturgy begins with the sign of peace. [190]

Bibliography

A. Adam, Die Meßpredigt als Teil der eucharistischen Liturgie: Th. Maas-Ewerd / K. Richter (eds.): Gemeinde im Herrenmahl, 242–250.

---

[185] For the tables of the Sunday readings and Gospels cf. Kucharek, Liturgy 443 and 422.

[186] Cf. IGMHM 34.

[187] Cf. IGMHM 35–37; MHM 64 Rubric No.10.

[188] Cf. IGMHM 38.

[189] Cf. Lezionario Ambrosiano, Milano 1976, VII: "Il presente Lezionario, che si deve più propriamente caraterrizzare come un 'Supplemento ambrosiano' ai volumi del Lezionario Romano . . . "

[190] This prayer is said even when the intercessions are omitted, cf.MA, *Principi e Norme,* No. 47 "Terminate le intenzioni della preghiera universale, il sacerdote dice l'orazione e conclusione della liturgia della parola. Essa non va mai omessa, anche quando si tralasciasse la preghiera universale."

B. Capelle, L'introduction du symbole á la messe: Ibid., Travaux liturgiques III, Louvain 1967, 60–81.

H. Denis, La prière universelle, MD 21 (1965) 140–165.

B. Fischer, Sequenzen und Tropen: R. Berger / K. H. Bieritz and others, GdK 3: Gestalt des Gottesdienstes, Regensburg 1990, 199–201.

A. A. Häußling, Akklamationen und Formeln: GdK 3, 220–239.

H. de Lubac, Credo. Gestalt und Lebendigkeit unseres Glaubensbekenntnisses, Einsiedeln 1975.

Th. Maas-Ewerd, Vom Pronaus zur Homilie. Ein Stück 'Liturgie' in jüngster Geschichte und pastoraler Gegenwart, Eichstätt-Vienna 1990.

J. B. Schneider, Die Geschichte der katholischen Predigt, Freiburg-Basel-Vienna 1969.

L. Della Torre, "Oratio fidelium". Una preghiera dell'Assemblea: Rivista liturgica 52 (1965) 46–66.

3.6. THE PREPARATION OF THE GIFTS

3.6.1. "OFFERING"?

"The word *offerimus* must not be so translated as if the sacrifice of the Mass consisted in bread and wine."[191] The terms *offerre* and *oblatio*, referring to the bread and wine, are to be understood only in the sense of presentation, while the sacrifice of the Church, which is spoken of in the eucharistic prayer means "something fundamentally other".[192] Thus the missal (GIRM 48) derives the preparation of the gifts solely from Christ's action, from his *accepit panem et calicem* at the Last Supper. Consequently there "is no doubt that in the course of the development, with the gradual growth of accompanying prayers, with the increasing meditation on the celebration of Mass from the point of view of the private Mass, with the displacement of religious interest from exultant praise of redemption to the celebration of the expiatory and saving sacrifice and its application for the needs of the moment, this original aspect of the preparation of the gifts receded sharply in awareness."[193] And nevertheless this development from a very simple bringing up of the things necessary for the celebration of the eucharist to a very developed rite of preparation and presentation of the gifts has its ultimate cause in an anti-gnostic and anti-spiritualizing emphasis on the redemption of the whole world by Christ already present in the early Fathers: "the heavenly gift had an earthly origin: it was from "the firstlings of creation" that it proceeded."[194] In Tertullian and in Cyprian, for example, the gifts which the faithful bring for the celebration of Mass – besides the bread and wine there are also gifts for the Church and for the poor – are called "offerings". The gifts also are inserted into the eucharistic sacrificial movement of Christ to the Father, who joins the Church to himself as his mystical body. Into the great prayer of thanksgiving to the Father through Christ the Head, the individual member of the

---

[191] E. J. Lengeling, Die neue Ordnung der Eucharistiefeier. Allgemeine Einführung in das römische Meßbuch. Endgültiger lateinischer und deutscher Text, Einleitung und Kommentar, Münster 2nd edn. 1971 (Lebendiger Gottesdienst 17/18), 220.

[192] Joh. H. Emminghaus, Die Messe. Wesen, Gestalt, Vollzug, ed. by Th. Maas-Ewerd. Klosterneuburg 5th edn. 1992, 240f.

[193] Berger, Gabenbereitung 264f.

[194] Jungmann, MS II, 4. (Engl. Trad. II, 2).

Church brings along with himself what he is and what he has, with the world which belongs to each individual person, which in this way finds access to the universal elevation (*anaphora*) of created nature into the triune life of God. Only in this sense can one speak of "offering", certainly not in the sense of a pagan offering of the fruits of the earth, of which the godhead would have need, but of carrying the entire world through man, through Christ the Head into the fullness of life of the Trinity. [195]

In the ritual development East and West went different ways. In the North African liturgy the offertory procession of the faithful was most closely united to the eucharistic sacrifice; the faithful themselves brought their gifts to the altar. In Rome, the Pope together with his assistants, collected the gifts from among the faithful, of these only a fraction reached the altar, while the predominant remainder was destined for the clergy and the poor. The "seven silver altars" of the Lateran basilica are interpreted as tables, on which, corresponding to the seven deacons of Rome, the gifts were placed. Klauser gives it as his opinion that the origin of the transept is connected with this fact, since space was needed for the installation of these "altars". [196] In the Roman-Frankish liturgy, after the *Credo* a procession was formed with the gifts, in which the faithful following a precise order, brought their gifts to the altar; along with many other objects – even precious objects and immovable goods in the form of deeds – bread and wine were also presented; but after the transition to unleavened *oblata* the bread was no longer destined for consecration. From the 11th century onwards money gifts moved into the foreground and thereby the people's offering lost much of its expressive power, above all when the obligatory procession of the faithful took on the character of a tax levy. In the Byzantine East the link between the people's offering and the Mass was less rigid than in the West. There the faithful gave their offerings before the liturgy of the Word, and this led to the formation of a complex rite of the preparation of the gifts (*Proskomidia*), which, with rich symbolism, is carried out still today at the "table of preparation" (*prothesis*). From there, at the beginning of the Mass of the faithful, the prepared gifts are borne to the altar during the "Great Entrance". According to the medieval Byzantine commentators on the liturgy, the *Proskomidia* is much more than a simple preparation of what is needed for the eucharistic celebration; even in the arrangement of the particles on the paten (*diskos*) the Church of the saints, of the living and of the dead finds its symbolical expression gathered around the "lamb" which symbolizes Christ. [197]

3.6.2. THE "FRUITS OF THE EARTH AND WORK OF HUMAN HANDS"

At the earliest it is since the Carolingian period that the West uses unleavened bread for the eucharist. If Jesus' Last Supper was a paschal meal, then the Lord used, in memory of the Exodus unleavened bread (*mazzen*), but during the first millennium no importance was attached to this, in the West also they used "common" i.e. leavened bread. According to Ambrose it was a question of ordinary bread (*panis usitatus*), which the

---

[195] Cf. Kunzler, Porta Orientalis, 3. Versuch, chaps. 1 – 3, 299 – 397.

[196] Cf. Jungmann, MS II, 11 (E. Tr. II, 8).

[197] Cf. M. Kunzler, Inbesondere für unsere allheilige Herrin. Der Axion-estin-Hymnus als Zugang zum Verständnis des prosferein hyper im Heiligengedächtnis der Byzantinischen Chrysostomos-Anaphora: A. Heinz / H. Rennings (eds.), Gratias agamus. Studien zum eucharistischen Hochgebet (FS Fischer), Freiburg-Basel-Vienna 1992, 227 – 240. 235f.

faithful presented during the procession of the gifts. [198] However this bread was increasingly differentiated from the ordinary type, given that only types of bread suitable for festive days were alone in question. Furthermore the bread destined for the eucharist received special names; from the fact that it was offered it was called *oblata, oblatio* (which in the East corresponds still today to *prosphora*); from Carolingian times onwards, the concept of *hostia* (sacrificial victim), wishing to allude to the Old Testament sacrifice, came more and more to displace these terms.

From the time of Gregory the Great the *corona* bread is known, the size of a hand, twisted like a braid, wound into a circlet, whose centre hole could be filled in to have the form of a disc. Very widespread also was the round loaf, divided into four parts by a cross-notch, which, following an ancient usage, could be marked with a figure or an inscription. [199] Similarly still today the *prosphora* of the Byzantines carries a stamped image, which covers that part of the sacrificial bread which in the preparation of the gifts is cut with the "holy lance" to form the "lamb": a cross, above and under whose transverse arm stand the letters IC-XC-NI-KA: Jesus Christ conquers. [200] In the 9th century there began in the West the development towards the use of unleavened bread, but which was completed only by the middle of the 11th century. For a long time East and West did not find fault with the differing usage, until the "*Azymus* question" became an aspect of reciprocal polemics. Things remained so still for a long time, in spite of the fact that the council of union of Ferrara and Florence (1439) had declared equally valid the different traditions with both types of bread. The introduction of unleavened preformed hosts is not least to be seen against the background of the further development of the celebration of Mass in the West: the preparation of the bread by the congregation ceased, the bread for the eucharist was prepared only in monasteries. Already in the 12th century, for the few days on which the people communicated, there were made along with the "host for the celebrant", "particles" the size of coins, whereby the term *hostia* – in similar fashion to the Byzantine name "lamb" – anticipating the eucharistic action, refers to Christ as the living offering. The "breaking of bread" from then on was limited to the celebrant's host alone and completely lost its former meaning. Not least, the shift in eucharistic piety towards eucharistic "seeing" needed a white form of host, easily seen at the elevation and in the monstrance, but which had almost nothing to do with real bread. The renewed missal in GIRM 282–283 while remaining faithful to the Western tradition of unleavened bread, presents a corrective: that the bread may effectively signify the meaning it is intended to convey, it must really look like bread, and ought to be made in such a way that the priest, in Mass celebrated with the people, can break it into many small pieces. In this way it will be clear once again, at least for a start, that all communicants share the one bread.

"The wine used to celebrate the eucharist must be made from the fruit of the vine (cf. Lk 22:18), natural and pure, unmixed with anything else" (GIRM 284). The adding of water, which derived not from a Jewish but from a Greek custom must, according to Jungmann [201] already have been common in Palestine in Christ's time. Against the use

---

[198] De sacramentis 4,14, ed. Schmitz 142: "Tu forte dicis: 'Meus panis est usitatus'. Sed panis iste panis est ante verba sacramentorum."

[199] Cf. Berger, Naturelemente 260f.

[200] Cf. Onasch, art."Prophore" 314–316; Kallis, 18–20.

[201] Cf. MS I, 48f (E. Tr. II, 38).

of water only in gnostic circles, Cyprian emphasizes the symbolism of the adding of water, to show the bond between Christ and his people. [202] Because the East saw in the adding of the water also a symbol for the union of the two natures in Christ, the radical Monophysites rejected it. In the East the quantity of water added was always greater than the few drops needed for the symbolism, and which in the West since the High Middle Ages, were put in with the help of a spoon.

3.6.3. THE PRAYERS WHICH ACCOMPANY THE PREPARATION OF THE GIFTS

Originally the gifts were placed on the altar in silence. It is only in the Gaul of the 9th century that we encounter a first nucleus of prayers of offering, which have an intercessory character and presuppose still the people's offering, given the fact that the intentions of the donors of the gifts are taken into account. Jungmann sees this development as analogous to the formation of the Byzantine *Proskomidia*, in which, around the "lamb" are placed in a precise order, particles of the *prosphore* in honour of the Mother of God and various saints, but also for the living and the dead. [203] In contrast to this there developed in the West a series of sacerdotal prayers of offering, which in their structure were so alike those of the Roman Canon, that they were called the "little canon": "The earlier rite of offertory contains precisely the principal characteristics of the canon; oblation (*Suscipe, Offerimus*), epiclesis (*Veni Sanctificator*), anamnesis and intercession *(Suscipe Sancta Trinitas)*." [204]

To avoid misunderstandings about the value of these prayers of offerings, in the liturgical renewal the "little canon" has been replaced by new prayers, which correspond to the model of Jewish table blessings (*berakoth*) and could almost certainly have been spoken by Jesus himself at the Last Supper. They express better and more unambiguously what was intended by the "little canon": the fruits of the earth and of the work of human hands are also at all times gifts from God, who is praised for his goodness; they are brought "into his presence", so that in the eucharistic sacrifice they may become for us "the bread of life" and "the chalice of salvation". Normally these prayers, as also the phrase which accompanies the commingling of the water should be said silently. However the German missal enlarges the active participation of all precisely in this area, that it allows that after the saying in an audible voice of the prayers over the bread and wine, the people respond with a short *berakah:* "You are blessed for eternity, Lord, our God" [the ICEL version is: Blessed be God for ever. Note by translator]. Taken over from the 1570 missal, but placed differently, is a prayer based on Dan 3:39f, for the acceptance of the offering by God, said silently by the priest, a prayer which bears a penitential character like the washing of hands which follows.

---

[202] Cyprian, Ep.,63, 13 – CSEL 3/2, 711: "Nam si vinum tantum quis offerat, sanguis Christi incipit esse sine nobis. Si vero aqua sit sola, plebs incipit esse sine Christo." In outline already in Irenaeus of Lyons, Adv. haer. V, 1, 3 – SChr 153, 26f.

[203] Cf. MS II, 53 – 56 (E. Tr. II, 44 – 46); Kallis 18 – 19.

[204] J. Hermans, Die Feier der Eucharistie. Erklärung und spirituelle Erschließung, Regensburg 1984, 218, note 19.

3.6.4. THE INCENSATION OF THE PREPARED GIFTS AND THE WASHING OF THE HANDS

Heretofore prescribed for High Mass, today the prepared gifts may be incensed in every Mass; "as a sign that the offering and prayer of the Church are to rise in God's sight like the smoke of incense. Subsequently the priest and people may be incensed by the deacon or one of the servers" (GIRM 51). In Rome, along with the custom of burning incense in fixed censers, they knew only the custom of carrying incense at the entry, at the procession for the Gospel, and at the exit, not however that which we know as incensation properly so called. The incensation of the gifts is a "fruit of the Carolingian development of the liturgy"; the special prayers for it found no inclusion in the renewed liturgy. Jungmann sees in the incensation of the gifts, but also in that of the altar, of the celebrant, of the ministers and of the people a "re-enforcement of the *Veni Sanctificator*" [205] that is to say of that prayer from the "little canon" which has a distinct epicletic character. This incensation therefore is close in spirit to the Byzantine prayer over the incense, which belongs to the *Proskomidia*, and which, not only in this part of the liturgy, confers an epicletic keynote to every other incensation in the service: "We offer you incense, Christ, our God, in the odour of spiritual perfume; accept it on your heavenly altar and send us in exchange the grace of your All-holy Spirit." [206]

"Then the priest washes his hands as a symbol of his desire for inward purification" (GIRM 52). Ablutions as the expression of the petition for inner purification are a religious phenomenon frequently met with (for example the ritual ablutions among the Jews and Muslims). A link between the washing of the hands and morning prayer is found already in the Church Order of Hippolytus. [207] Thus in the washing of hands in the liturgy the symbolical reference is always in the foreground. The explanation of the washing as a normal washing of the hands after the taking of the gifts of the faithful and after the incensation therefore is not taken into consideration; the washing of the hands remained after the people's oblation ceased to exist, and when no incense was used. Jungmann connects the hand-washing at this point of the Mass with the desire to express by an outward action the prayer for inner purity, when crossing the threshold which leads to the holiest centre of the action. For this reason in some places there were several hand-washings in the Mass. [208] Originally done in silence, the missal of 1570 prescribed as an accompanying prayer Ps 25: 6–12, which was a protestation of innocence; the new missal, puts in its place Ps 51:4, a genuine plea for pardon, which picks up the motives of washing and purification.

3.6.5. ORATE FRATRES

According to Lengeling, the invitation to prayer *Orate fratres* is "the oldest, still pre-Carolingian insertion into the Roman Ordo from Gallic sources" and "aimed above all at a silent prayer by those assisting at the altar and choir." During the course of the reform there was a plan to suppress it; but it retained its place also in the renewed celebration of

[205] Cf. MS II, 89–95 (E. Tr. II, 74).
[206] Kallis 30–32; cf. M. Kunzler, Gnadenquellen. Symeon von Thessaloniki (d. 1429) als Beispiel für die Einflußnahme des Palamismus auf die orthodoxe Sakramententheologie und Liturgik,Trier 1989 (TThSt 47) 233f, 313f
[207] TradAp 41, ed. Geerlings 298f.
[208] Cf. MS II, 97–101 (E. Tr. II, 76–82).

Mass. [209] After having added his own gifts to the gifts of the clergy and people, he asked for a silent prayer for himself. This explains the apparently clerical formulation *meum ac vestrum sacrificium*. The response *Suscipiat* comes from Italy and was adopted in the missal of 1570; while formerly it was answered only by the altar servers in a low voice, the liturgical movement made of this response an element of the people's participation and accordingly the answering of the invitation to prayer by the whole congregation in a loud voice. This call to prayer constitutes today the introduction to the prayer over the offerings, analogous to the *Oremus* which precedes the other presidential prayers, while variations are foreseen in the vernacular adaptations of the Roman liturgy. In the German missal the *Orate fratres* together with the *Suscipiat* is only one of three possible forms, while the invitation to prayer and the people's response may be totally omitted and replaced by "Let us pray".

3.6.6. THE PRAYER OVER THE OFFERINGS

"The prayer over the offerings (*oratio super oblata*) winds up the preparation of the gifts. It recapitulates the content and the meaning of the action – preparation of the gifts like that of the congregation – and leads to the solemn eucharistic prayer into which it merges – as is theologically correct – without any noticeable break." [210] The prayer over the offerings shares with the two other presidential prayers – the collect and the final prayer – the characteristic of being a synopsis or summing-up. It is all the more surprising then that in the empire of the Franks about the middle of the 8th century, they began to recite silently the *oratio super oblata* – self-evidently meant to be spoken out loud – and to make it into *secreta* –, something which was brought to an end only in the liturgical reform, which re-introduced along with the ancient name the custom of speaking it aloud. Jungmann [211] sees this as caused by the aftermath of Gallic usages as well as Eastern influences, perhaps even by reminiscences from pagan antiquity: in Gaul as in the mozarabic liturgy a sacred silence for quiet prayer reigned during the offertory procession. In the Greek liturgy of James, for example, the chanters call out "let all mortal flesh keep silence" while the priest performs silent prayer. [212] As a presidential prayer spoken aloud, the prayer over the offerings recovers its ancient function of summing up the part of the Mass dedicated to the preparation of the gifts. As "oratio" it corresponds, in its structure, to the two other presidential prayers, even if less strictly than in the collect. The conclusion of the prayer is simpler, given that the apposition of Christ as Son of God is omitted as well as the "eternity formula". In the present missal there are about a hundred prayers ove r the offerings, 60 of which were not present in the 1570 book. The greater part is taken out of ancient sacramentaries, other are new compositions out of excerpts from these sacramentaries, others again are taken from patristic literature or are totally new compositions. [213]

---

[209] Lengeling, Die neue Ordnung, 225.
[210] Emminghaus 243; cf. in this regard GIRM 53.
[211] MS II, 115f (E. Tr. II, 90–97).
[212] Cf. F. E. Brightman, Liturgies Eastern and Western, Oxford 1896, I, 41.
[213] Cf. Hermans 227f.

3.6.7. THE PREPARATION OF THE GIFTS IN THE EUCHARISTIC CELEBRATION OF OTHER CHRISTIAN RITES

The Byzantine Liturgy

It is difficult, in the context of the Byzantine eucharistic celebration, to speak in the usual sense of a part dedicated to the preparation of the gifts, because this has been held in the *Proskomidia* long before the celebration of the assembled congregation, at the "table of preparation" (*prothesis*) behind the left hand side of the iconostasis. [214] While in the Roman-western celebration of Mass the solemn eucharistic prayer follows the preparation of the gifts, in the Byzantine eucharistic celebration various prayers and actions precede the *anaphora,* which scarcely could be called "preparation of the gifts". Among them are the "prayers of the faithful", a vestigial form of the universal prayer ("intercessions") which at one time took place only after the dismissal of the catechumens. [215] There follows the "Great Entrance" during which the prepared gifts are brought solemnly from the table of preparation through the church and through the royal door of the iconostasis to the altar. The accompanying chant of the Great Entrance is the "Cherubic hymn", preceded by a long sacerdotal prayer of preparation. [216] There follow another *ectene* and a prayer for the presentation of the gifts, the kiss of peace and the profession of faith.

The Mozarabic Liturgy

The part for the preparation of the gifts begins with the *Sacrificium,* which corresponds to the Roman *Offertorium* or the Ambrosian Offerenda. The *Missale* cites explicitly the procession of the gifts which the faithful meanwhile bring to the altar. [217] After a silent prayer by the celebrant, the incensation of the altar and the washing of the hands carried out in silence, the celebrant and deacon return to the chair, from where the celebrant standing towards the congregation says the *Oratio admonitionis* whose aim is to orientate the common prayer of the faithful towards a petition in common, for which reason the missal also refers to the Good Friday intercessions as an analogy. [218] With the invitation to prayer *Oremus,* followed by an acclamation of the assembly: *Hagios, Hagios, Hagios, Domine Deus, Rex aeterne, tibi laudes et gratias,* there begins the reading of the diptychs through which the solidarity of the entire Church is meant to find expression. [219] The diptychs are interrupted by the prayer called *Alia,* which corresponds to the Roman *Oratio super oblata.* [220] The reading of the diptychs concludes with the prayer *Post Nomina.* There follows the sign of peace (*Signum pacis*), preceded by a variable prayer, a fixed transitional formula and a blessing spoken with outstretched hands over the assembly, before the deacon invites to exchange the sign of peace. The sign of peace itself is accompanied by the *Cantus ad pacem.* [221]

---

[214] On the present form of the *Proskomidia* ,of very complex structure, with the ritual preparation of the particles of bread and its many symbolical actions cf. Kallis, 18–39. On the history of the origin of the Proskomidiacf. Kucharek, Liturgy 254–324.

[215] Cf. Kucharek, *Liturgy* 473f.

[216] Cf. Kallis 96–108; Kucharek, *Liturgy* 477–484,490–503.

[217] Cf. IGMHM 39.

[218] Cf. IGMHM 43.

[219] Cf. IGMHM 46–51.

[220] Cf. IGMHM 52–53.

[221] Cf. IGMHM 55–56, MHM 69–71.

The Ambrosian Liturgy

The eucharistic liturgy begins with the sign of peace, which is followed by the preparation of the gifts. The *Missale* offers a blessing, which the celebrant imparts to the faithful who bring gifts to the altar during the offertory procession of the people: *"Ti benedica il Signore con questo tuo dono."* The *Canto all'offertorio* accompanies the procession with the gifts. The Milanese prayers for the preparation of the gifts may be replaced by those of the Roman Mass. [222] The preparation of the gifts is concluded by the prayer *"Sui doni".* There follows the Niceno-Constantinopolitan profession of faith, which in connection with the preparation for baptism is replaced by the Apostles' Creed. [223]

Bibliography

J. Baumgartner, Vom Sinn der Gabenkollekte, HlD 32 (1978) 97 – 104.

J. Baumgartner, Geldspende im Gottesdienst? Schweizerische Kirchenzeitung 153 (1985) 209 – 211.

R. Berger, Die Wendung "offerre pro" in der römischen Liturgie, Münster 1965 (LQF 41).

R. Berger, Gabenbereitung und Gabengebet: Th. Maas-Ewerd / K. Richter (eds.): Gemeinde im Herrenmahl, 264 – 271.

R. Berger, Naturelemente und technische Mittel. In: R. Berger / K. H. Bieritz and others, Gottesdienst der Kirche. Handbuch der Liturgiewissenschaft III: Gestalt des Gottesdienstes, Regensburg 2nd edn. 1990, 249 – 288.

H. Capelle, Charité et offertoire: Ibid., Travaux Liturgiques II, 222 – 235.

L. Cornet, Nouvel offertoire et Berakoth, Questions liturgiques 59 (1978) 97 – 111.

A. Härdeling, Aquae et vini Mysterium. Geheimnis der Erlösung und Geheimnis der Kirche im Spiegel der mittelalterlichen Auslegung des gemischten Kelches (LQF 57), Münster 1973.

A. Jilek, Symbolik und sinngerechte Gestaltung der Eucharistiefeier, dargelegt am Beispiel der Gabenbereitung, LJ 38 (1988) 231 – 248.

J. A. Jungmann, Die Gebete zur Gabenbereitung, LJ 23 (1973) 186 – 203.

V. Raffa, Le orazioni sulle offerte del proprio del tempo nel nuovo messale, EL 84 (1970) 299 – 322.

H. Reifenberg, Wasser im Wein? Perspektiven zum gemischten Kelch: Th. Maas-Ewerd / K. Richter (eds.): Gemeinde im Herrenmahl, 272 – 282.

3.7. THE GREAT EUCHARISTIC PRAYER

3.7.1. THE CONCEPT OF "GREAT PRAYER"

At the centre of the eucharistic celebration there stands the great eucharistic prayer. Although the concept of great prayer is used for the most part with reference to the eucharistic celebration, the category of "great prayer" is not confined to this. For ex-

---

[222] Cf. MA 807 – 809, MA, Principi e Norme 47 – 48. The Milanese prayers for the preparation of the gifts are very succinct: "O Padre clementissimo, accogli questo pane (vino), perché diventi il corpo (il sangue) di Cristo, tuo Figlio."
[223] Cf. MA Principi e Norme 53, MA 810 – 812.

ample the *Exsultet* of Easter night, the consecratory prayers in the rites of ordination, the blessing of baptismal water or the nuptial blessing are also in the category of "great prayers".[224] The essential element of the great prayer is praise, the *Berakah*[225] man praises God for the past saving deeds; in them God's redemptive love manifests itself, which is outside time and transcends all his concrete actions – and which in the naming of the past acts of salvation – is present now in the liturgical action. Out of this present man begs for new saving deeds of God from new predicaments. In the first place there is always praise, which constitutes the basis for the petition which follows from it. Both constitute the twofold basis of the great prayer out of anamnesis and epiclesis, the laudative memorial of the paschal mystery, stretched backwards as far as creation and forwards as far as the future return of the Lord (anamnesis); the invocation of the presence of Christ and of his work of salvation as well as the communion of the Church with him (epiclesis); with the acclamations[226] is expressed the common consent of the assembly with the praise and petition of the presiding celebrant. In this connection we must firmly hold that the Christian *Berakah* is always addressed to the Father, never to Christ himself – the anti-Arian emphasis on the godhead of the Son and the Spirit changed nothing of this. Through Christ, of whose sacrifice on the Cross and of whose resurrection she makes the sacramental memorial, and to whom she unites herself, the Church offers herself and with herself the whole world to the Father. This aspect stands in the Churches of the East so much in the foreground that there the eucharistic prayer is called *anaphora*. While in the East there were always many anaphoras, up to the reform of the liturgy the Western Church had known only the *Canon romanus*. It was only in the course of the reform that further eucharistic great prayers were arrived at. Alongside them the – revised – Roman Canon stands as an important witness of an ancient tradition of many centuries.

Precisely in the new eucharistic prayers the structure of the eucharistic prayer is very evident, in spite of the maintenance of the "Roman genius" as distinguished from the Eastern anaphoras which in the formulation of the prayer mention all possible saving acts of God.

3.7.2. THE STRUCTURE OF THE GREAT EUCHARISTIC PRAYER

In the basic structure the following elements are present, which characterize the great eucharistic prayer, but which are present also in other forms of prayer, to which could be applied the generic concept of "great prayer" (cf. GIRM 55).

A. *The Preface* could be misunderstood, on the basis of the term, as a "foreword" to the great prayer strictly so called. However from the late Latin meaning (*praefari*), the Preface is to be understood in the sense of proclamation, of the prayer spoken aloud "in front" of its addressees. When the custom began of speaking the great prayer silently, the preface continued to be proclaimed aloud, thereby becoming distinguished from the rest of the great prayer. This accelerated the misleading interpretation of *praefatio* in

---

[224] Cf. M. B. Merz, Gebetsformen der Liturgie: R. Berger / K. H. Bieritz and others, Gottesdienst der Kirche. Handbuch der Liturgiewissenschaft Vol. 3: Gestalt des Gottesdienstes, Regensburg 2nd edn. 1990, 116–120.

[225] Cf. the comparison between the Jewish Berakah and the elements of the Christian Berakah present in the eucharistic prayer and cited by Justin, in Kucharek, Liturgy 553f.

[226] Cf. Meyer, Eucharistie 344f.

the sense of a foreword to the "real" (and silently spoken) great prayer.[227] But that the preface is an integral component of great prayer, is already shown by the fact that it expresses with particular clarity that which makes up a great prayer on the whole, the *Eucharistia*, the great thanksgiving prayer of the Church with the anamnesis of God's great deeds (cf. GIRM 55a).

From late antiquity the prefaces multiplied in the West[228] already the oldest Roman sacramentary, the *Leonianum*, has 267 prefaces, the greater part of which were destined for the memorials of the martyrs. Jungmann speaks of "centrifugal forces" which led away from the central theme of redemption through Christ and on account of the special theme of each feast moved around in the periphery of the real theme.[229] Soon however, in the *Hadrianum,* this number was reduced to 14 prefaces and further reduced to seven in the Carolingian era; a decretal of bishop Burchard of Worms (965 – 1025) stabilized the number of eleven prefaces (the seven already mentioned and the prefaces of the Cross, of Lent, of the Trinity and of our Lady), which corroborated by the missal of Pius V remained in force until the liturgical reform. It was only in the 20th century that new prefaces were added.[230] The liturgical reform had to trace a middle way between a multiplicity of prefaces – with the danger of getting lost in the periphery – and a minimum limit, which precisely in the vernacular great prayer cannot take into account the legitimate requests for variety.[231] If the present Latin missal contains 82 prefaces, their number varies in the vernacular adaptations. The flashback to the Gospel of the Mass present in some prefaces offers the chance "of throwing a bridge from the proclamation to the eucharist, and to be more precise on the basis of a sacramental re-reading of a biblical pericope of the day, and thereby to fit both parts of the Mass more closely together."[232]

The introductory dialogue between the presiding celebrant and the congregation is of venerable antiquity. The *Gratias agamus Domino Deo nostro* can be traced back to Jewish regulations for the *Seder*, while the response *Dignum et iustum est* already expressed the approval of assembly there for the praise pronounced by the president. The precise origin of the *Sursum corda* and the assembly's response *Habemus ad Dominum* remains obscure, but already Cyprian of Carthage describes this dialogue as standard for every Christian prayer[233] and Augustine does likewise.[234] Hippolytus knows of a very similar introductory dialogue for the liturgy of light and for the agape, but keeps the

---

[227] Cf. J. Baumgartner, Die Präfationen. Das eine Mysterium Christi im Spiegel der vielen Mysterien: A. Heinz / H. Rennings (ed.), Gratias agamus 23 – 43. On the prefaces in general cf. P. Bruylants, Les préfaces du missel romain, MD 22 (1966) 11 – 133; A. Dumas, Les préfaces du nouveau missel, EL 85 (1971) 16 – 28.

[228] In the East the preface – or better: that part of the great eucharistic prayer (the *anaphora*) which corresponds most to the Western preface – remained such an integral part of the *anaphora* that it was never replaced.

[229] Cf. MS II, 148 (E. Tr. II, 118).

[230] In 1919 that for the Dead and for the feast of St Joseph, in 1925 for the feast of Christ the King and in 1928 for the feast of the Sacred Heart. On the preface of the Trinity on Sundays "through the year" of the Lord's Year cf. A. Heinz, Trinitarische und österliche Aspekte in der Sonntagsfrömmigkeit des Mittelalters: A. M. Altermat / T. Schnitker / W. Heim (eds.), Der Sonntag. Anspruch-Wirklichkeit-Gestalt (FS Baumgartner), Würzburg-Fribourg 1986, 82 – 98.

[231] Cf. Pope Paul VI in the Apostolic Constitution "Missale Romanum", Kaczynski 13 66.

[232] Baumgartner, Die Präfationen 26.

[233] Cf. De dom. Or. 31 -CSEL 3, 289.

[234] Cf. Roetzer 118f.

Sursum corda expressly for the eucharistic celebration. [235] In essence this introductory dialogue is present in all Christian liturgies. [236] The praise of the preface is addressed to God the Father through Christ, through whom and in the Holy Spirit the Father accomplishes the world's salvation. Through the incarnate mediator the earthly community joins itself to the heavenly liturgy and shares in the songs of praise of the heavenly choirs. In the Byzantine Church an analogous theme is to be understood against the background of the "Cherubic Hymn", according to which the earthly assembly is aware of the invisible presence of the heavenly liturgy, and the song of praise sung by men is a making visible and audible in the celebrating community of the heavenly liturgy invisibly present. Thereby the theme of the *Sursum corda* is present, while the heart raised up to God is freed from earthly care: "We who in this mystery represent the cherubim and sing the thrice-holy hymn to the life-giving Trinity, let us now lay aside all earthly cares... " [237]

B. *The Sanctus* is a part of the great eucharistic prayer and belongs to the congregation (GIRM 55b). [238] It goes back to the vision of Isaiah's call (6:3); in the Jewish synagogical liturgy of the 2nd century it was part of the morning prayer and is attested in the context of the eucharistic prayer in the East at the end of the 4th century, from where only at the beginning of he 5th century it came into the liturgy of the West. Almost generally *Dominus Deus Sabaoth* as the designation of God remained untranslated, it meant "hosts". On its meaning opinions are divided (for example dethroned pagan divinities, demons, or the constellations of stars understood in a religious sense), what is intended however is the universal power of Yahveh. [239] Equally universal is the glory of God, the *kabod Yahveh,* which through Christ, who is the head of creation, fills all things. Of totally Christian origin is the *Benedictus,* which was joined to the *Sanctus* in Gaul, is attested in the Roman Mass in the 7th century, not till a century later however in the East. The idea that the glory of God fills heaven and earth finds its Christian embodiment in the fact that it was only through the coming of Christ that the glory of God fills created reality unsurpassably. For the liturgy actually being celebrated this presence comes about through the coming of Christ into the celebrating community. This understanding of the *adventus Domini,* as of a present reality is expressed by the community identifying itself with the situation of the entry of Jesus into Jerusalem (Mt 21,9). On account of the rich musical elaboration of the *Sanctus,* the *Benedictus* detached itself into a chant apart which the choir sang only a fter the consecration while the priest continued to recite the eucharistic prayer in a low voice. Today however not only is the whole *Sanctus* with the *Benedictus* put in place as unity, care should be taken that this valuable part of the eucharistic prayer is due to the community, nor should it be replaced by inappropriate chants. Both the first part of the *Sanctus* as also the *Benedictus* are concluded with *Hosanna in excelsis* (cf. Ps 118:25–26a). The Aramaic *Hosanna* which signifies "Help!" is already contained in the biblical description of Jesus' entry

---

[235] Cf. TradAp 25, ed. Geerlings 276f.

[236] For the Byzantine litury cf. Kallis 122–124. On this and the preceding exhortation to the congregation "let us stand with reverence; let us attend with fear and make the holy offering in peace", cf. Kucharek, Liturgy 563–565.

[237] Cf. Kallis 96.

[238] Cf. H. Eising, Die Bedeutung des Sanctus: Th. Maas-Ewerd / K. Richter (ed.), Gemeinde im Herrenmahl 297–302.

[239] Cf. H. Groß, Art. "Heerscharen": LThK 2nd edn. Vol. V, 55; Jungmann MS II, 168f (E. Tr. II, 135f).

as an acclamation of homage, and bears out once again that the *Kyrie eleison* is not a cry for mercy, but an acclamation of homage, for in the intention of intrinsic meaning *Hosanna* corresponds exactly to what *Kyrie eleison* signifies.

C. *The Postsanctus* follows immediately on the *Sanctus* and "on the model of the Eastern and non-Roman Western eucharistic prayers continues the anamnetic part." Only the *Canon Romanus* (Eucharistic Prayer I) begins immediately with an epicletic part. [240]

D. *The Consecration epiclesis:* "This is a special petition by the Church that the power of God should intervene to consecrate the gifts offered by mankind, so that they may become the Body and Blood of Christ". The Communion epiclesis corresponds to this in which the prayer is made "that the immaculate Victim may be the source of salvation to those who share in Communion" (GIRM 55c). [241] "By epiclesis is generally meant the invocation of God on a person or an object, which are thereby sanctified. This type of prayer is carried out above all by the solemn invocation of the name of God. In this general sense the whole eucharistic prayer is an invocation upon bread and wine." [242] The epiclesis is based on the conviction of faith that every work of salvation must be implored from God. In the conception of the Trinity from the perspective of the economy of salvation the Holy Spirit gives and completes divine grace, and therefore he it is who is invoked in the epiclesis of the eucharistic prayer, but also in the epicletic elements of the other sacraments. The Communion epiclesis in which a worthy reception of Communion is prayed for, is more ancient than the consecration epiclesis. [243] Theological reflection however led to the formation of a specific epiclesis of consecration, because the consecration of earthly gifts into the Body and Blood of Christ is so clearly beyond human work, that it must be invoked as God's work. The consecration epiclesis, in the form in which still today is typical for the liturgies of the Eastern Church, is attested in all lucidity for the first time by Cyril of Jerusalem in his *Mystagogical Catecheses*: God is invoked to send down the Holy Spirit on the bread and wine, in order make the bread the Body and the wine the Blood of Christ. [244] For the Byzantine Church the salvific efficacy, not only of the eucharist, but of all the sacraments, indeed also of the sacramentals, depends on the epicletic invocation of the Holy Spirit. [245] It is true that there are also Eastern traditions which know of a consecration epiclesis before the institution narrative and a communion epiclesis after the anamnesis, yet precisely the placing of the consecration epiclesis after the institution narrative by the Byzantines led to the controversy at the council of Ferrara/Florence 1439 on the question as to what effectuates the consecration, the epicletic prayer or the words of consecration of the institution narrative. [246] In the Western tradition this view of the *forma sacramenti*

---

[240] Meyer, Eucharistie 346.
[241] Cf. B. Kleinheyer, Artikel 55 der Allgemeinen Einführung in das Römische Meßbuch zu Anamnese und Epiklese des Eucharistiegebetes: A. Heinz / H. Rennings (ed.), Gratias agamus, 167–181; R. Taft, From Logos to Spirit. On the Early History of the Epiclesis: A. Heinz / H. Rennings (ed.), Gratias agamus, 489–502.
[242] M. Probst, Das eine Hochgebet und die verschiedenen Texte: Th. Maas-Ewerd / K. Richter (ed.), Gemeinde im Herrenmahl, 283–296. 291.
[243] Thus already also in Hippolytus, TradAp 4, ed. Geerlings 226f.
[244] Myst. Cat. 5, 7- ed. G. Röwekamp, Freiburg-Basel-Vienna 1992(FC 7) 150–152.
[245] Cf. Hotz 222–265; Trembelas 24–30, 80, 141.
[246] Cf. M. Kunzler, Gnadenquellen. Symeon von Thessaloniki (d.1429) als Beispiel für die Einflußnahme des Palamismus auf die orthodoxe Sakramententheologie und Liturgik, Trier 1989 (TThSt 47), 350–356, 369–375.

can mislead into awarding to the words of institution in an isolated fashion the force of a consecratory formula, as for instance is shown in the larger print in the missals, and to more or less deny "consecratory efficacy" to the other parts of the eucharistic prayer. The controversy over the form of the eucharist will only then be brought close to a solution, if the consecratory efficacy of the eucharistic prayer as a whole is seen, to which indeed as a whole there belongs a fundamental epicletic characteristic and into which the institution narrative with the words of consecration is embedded.

E. *The institution narrative* therefore is no free standing consecratory formula, but is the central nucleus of the great eucharistic prayer, which as a consecratory prayer constitutes a unity, "in which the words of the Lord occupy the decisive position which defines the whole." [247] As part of a prayer, the mode of expression of "narrative" is misleading, since it is not a question of the narration of a past fact, but of the anamnetic making present of the institution of the Last Supper which is extolled in the "narrative". Here the embedding of the institution narrative into the ensemble of the great prayer as Eucharistia, as the great prayer of praise, which calls the saving acts of God into an anamnetic present becomes especially clear: among those acts there belongs precisely the institution on the evening before Christ's Passion. It becomes present in the celebrating community, and as at that time, the Lord takes bread and wine and changes them into his Body and Blood. The actions which accompany the institution narrative are intended as a dramatic imitation of what took place at the Last Supper and wish to express its anamnetic presence, moreover they give expression to eucharistic piety, above all the elevation of the Host. [248] This dates back to the 13th century; that of the chalice on the other hand pervaded only hesitantly and was only assimilated to that of Host by the missal of 1570. One fruit of the liturgical renewal is the anamnetic acclamation by the congregation. The non-biblical insertion *Mysterium fidei* was taken out of the words over the chalice and made into a cue for an anamnetic acclamation by the congregation. The Antiochene East also has participation by the "Amen" of the people after the words of institution over the bread and wine, but in addition to this a continuation of the anamnetic prayer addressed to Christ himself! Not least on the basis of the Eastern tradition does Fischer plead for a "freedom to invoke Christ in the middle of a prayer addressed to the Father." The anamnetic acclamation ought not of course be related in a one-sided way to the static Real Presence, but rather to the dynamic presence of Christ now working salvation. [249]

F. *The Anamnesis* carries out the command of Christ to commemorate his memorial, especially the memorial of his passion, his resurrection and his ascension (GIRM 55e). *Anamnesis* is essentially more than a subjective recalling of the past by a human being; it is the sacramental setting in place of the presence of Christ's saving deeds. Marsili [250] rightly refers to Casel's theology of mysteries: through the anamnesis of the saving deeds these themselves become present. Christ, who once in time was crucified, buried,

---

[247] B. Neunheuser, Das Eucharistische Hochgebet als Konsekrationsgebet: A. Heinz / H. Rennings (ed.), Gratias agamus, 315–326, with reference to GIRM 54.

[248] Cf. P. Browe, Die Elevation in der Messe, JLw 9 (1929) 20–66; concerning the position after Vatican II cf. A. Heinz, Schwerpunktverlagerung in der Meßfrömmigkeit: Von der Elevations – zur Kommunionfrömmigkeit, HlD 36 (1982) 69–79.

[249] Cf. A. Heinz: Anamnetische Gemeindeakklamationen im Hochgebet: A. Heinz/ H. Rennings (eds.): Gratias agamus, 129–147, 143.

[250] Cf. S. Marsili: Memoriale-Anamnesi nella Preghiera eucaristica. In: Notitiae 9 (1973) 225–227.226.

rose from death and ascended into heaven, lives in the timelessness of the eternal relationship of love of the triune God. To those who are gathered in his name, he has
promised his presence in the assembly which takes place in time. As the timeless One
present in time Christ is present as he who offered himself up out of love, vanquished
death and bore his human nature up into the glory of God. In making anamnetic mention of the mysteries of salvation the celebrating community realizes the invisible reality: Christ's love which led him to the cross, to the grave and to resurrection, is reality
now, just as it happened in the historical uniqueness of the event in Jerusalem within the
historicity of this world. Together with this love the facts of the past are also present and
prove effectual for those who celebrate the memorial. [251] Because Christ's saving deeds,
summed up in the term "offering" on the cross, become anamnetically present, this is
also the place for the community to associate itself in Christ's movement of offering to
the Father, to bring itself into his offering. For this reason the prayer of offering follows
on the anamnesis.

G. The prayer of Offering. It was the disastrous theology of the sacrifice of the Mass
of the late Middle Ages, which not without reason led to the radical rejection of the
sacrificial character of the Mass by the Reformation. The sacrifice of the Mass cannot
mean that the Church in addition to the cross of Christ offers up anew in every Mass to
God the Father his Son, in order to find grace and forgiveness. This in fact would rob
the cross of Christ of its unique salvific significance for all ages. That is why the prayers
of offering appertain to the anamnesis in closest context, both stand under the heading
of *gratias agamus,* with which the great prayer begins as the great thanksgiving in
thanksgiving – as in the gesture of the elevation of the Body and Blood of Christ during
the closing doxology – the Church brings to God the Father, what she received as a gift
from him: the Only – begotten Son and his saving deeds. Through him as the Head and
her Mediator she is united to the Father as the mystical Body of Christ. The Byzantine
liturgy says this in a nutshell: "We offer you what is yours from what is yours." [252] The
Church enters into Christ's movement of offering, in which he raised human nature to
the Father's glory, by presenting to the Father his unique sacrifice of the cross, now an
actual presence in the liturgical celebration, and so through her Head arrives at "an ever
more perfect union with God and with each other, so that finally God may be all in all."
(GIRM 55f).

H. The Communion epiclesis is the invoking of the descent of the Holy Spirit upon the
assembled community, to prepare them for a worthy reception of Communion. Its members are to become one in the Holy Spirit and so participate fruitfully in the eucharistic
gifts. Whereas in this part of the great prayer those present in the celebration are prayed
for, the intercessions break out of the confines of the celebrating congregation.

I. The Intercessions [253] are the consequence of the entry of the mystical Body into
Christ's movement of offering, even though as petitions they constitute a secondary

---

[251] Cf. the passages under "Gedächtnis, Kultgedächtnis" in O. Casel, Das christliche Opfermysterium.
    Zur morphologie und Theologie des eucharistischen Hochgebetes. V. Warnach (ed.). Graz-Wien-Köln,
    esp.496–498.

[252] Cf. Kallis 130ff; R. Kaczynski, Das Opfer Christi und die Darbringung der Kirche. Anmerkungen zur
    angeblichen Verworrenheit unserer Hochgeberstexte: A. Heinz / H. Rennings (eds.): Gratias agamus,
    149–166. 157–159.

[253] Cf. R. Kaczynski: Die Interzessionen im Hochgebet: Th. Maas-Ewerd / K. Richter (eds.), Gemeinde im
    Herrenmahl, 303–313.

element after praise and thanksgiving. The unity of the mystical Body finds expression in the "petitions" for individual members because through Christ the Head the celebrating community is in union with the Church in heaven, with the absent on earth and with the dead (GIRM 55g). [254] The intercessions therefore are not a duplication of the bidding prayers, but an expression of the fellowship of those who are celebrating the great prayer with other members of the Mystical Body. This applies indeed especially to the naming of the names of saints, to make intercession for whom in the strict sense was already qualified by Augustine as iniuria. Nevertheless the Byzantine theologians say that the saints of heaven also gain a spiritual advantage through this expression of fellowship. [255] The naming in the great prayer of the Pope, of the local bishop and of the college of bishops also serves to express ecclesial community. [256] The narrow confines of the local congregation are exploded by a universal eucharist, which the Church offers throughout the centuries until the Lord's return. Whereas the Alexandrian rites have the intercessions before the Institution narrative, the Antiochene place them after it, in the same way as do the new Roman eucharistic prayers. The subdivision of the *Mementos* in the Roman Canon into the mention of Church authorities and the *Memento* of the living before the Institution narrative and that of the dead after it, witnesses further to differing traditions of the intercessions in East and West. In the West the mention of the living was preponderant, given that the starting point here was the naming of the names during the offertory procession by the faithful. Originally part of the preparation of the gifts, already under Innocent I this naming of names came into the eucharistic prayer. The *Memento* of the dead took place at first only in funeral Masses, but not in Masses for the full community, and up to Carolingian times was even forbidden on Sundays. For the East however Cyril of Jerusalem and John Chrysostom witness to the *Memento* of the dead after the Institution narrative, and justify this location on the grounds that the memorial of the dead in the presence of the "awe-inspiring sacrifice" is particularly efficacious for their salvation. The Mass formulary of the Egyptian bishop Serapion of Thmuis knows of a *Memento* of the dead after the Institution narrative, but in line with the Alexandrian tradition moved it forward before it. According to Jungmann the close relationships between Alexandria and Rome brought the *Memento* of the dead also to Rome apart from Sunday Masses, but here it remained in its original position. [257]

J. The Concluding Doxology "is an expression of the praise of God, and is emphasized and concluded by the people's acclamation"(GIRM 55h); it is the appropriate final chord of the great eucharistic prayer, which as a prayer of praise is of a doxological character throughout. In contrast to the oriental liturgies, in which the anti-Arian polemic became rigid and led to the point in the liturgy of always praising only the undivided Trinity, in the Roman liturgy there remained the older doxology, qualified by salvation history, which is offered to the Father through the Son in the Holy Spirit. At the same time, according to Jungmann, there resonates the significance of the Church

[254] Cf. B. Kleinheyer: Heiligengedächtnis in der Eucharistiefeier: Th. Maas-Ewerd / K. Richter (eds.), Gemeinde im Herrenmahl, 150–159.

[255] Cf. M. Kunzler, Insbesondere für unsere allheilige Herrin. Der Axion-estin-Hymnus als Zugang zum Verständnis des prosferein hyper im Heiligengedächtnis der byzantinischen Chrysostomos-Anaphora: A. Heinz / H. Rennings (eds.), Gratias agamus, 227–240.

[256] Th. Maas-Ewerd, Nominari debent. Zur Nennung des Papstes, des Ortsbischofs und des Kollegium der Bischöfe im Eucharistischen Hochgebet: A. Heinz / H. Rennings (eds.): Gratias agamus,269–281.

[257] Cf. MS II, 299f (E. Tr. II, 241).

within the praise of the "Trinity of the economy of salvation": "God, Christ, Church, Church namely as the Body which is given life and held together by the Holy Spirit." [258]

3.7.3. THE FOUR EUCHARISTIC PRAYERS OF THE ROMAN MISSAL OF 1970

A. The Roman Canon

The origin of the Roman Canon lies in the period of transition from Greek to Latin in the Roman liturgy under Damasus I (366–384). There are no Roman witnesses for this eucharistic prayer, but already Ambrose of Milan (339–379) quotes fundamental passages in his work *De Sacramentis*. After about two centuries of development the *Canon Romanus* attained its present form. The Roman Canon differs from the structure of the eucharistic prayer as transmitted by Hippolytus or which characterizes the oriental anaphoras, by the fact that the flow of a great prayer of praise magnifying the *magnalia* of God is abandoned in favour of a complex order of independent units of prayer fitted together: like reflections in a mirror they stand around an anamnetic kernel consisting of the Institution narrative (*Qui pridie*) and the anamnesis (*Unde et memores*). Nearest to this kernel stand prayers of offering, joined to epicleses: before the consecration the *Hanc igitur* with an epiclesis for transsubtantiation which does not mention the Holy Spirit explicitly (*Quam oblationem*); after the consecration the *Supra quae* with a communion epiclesis (*Supplices te rogamus*): the angel stands for the unity of the earthly with the heavenly liturgy. As a second shell around the kernel are lodged intercessions in a broad sense: before the consecration the mention of ecclesiastical authorities (*in primis*), of the living (*Memento Domine*) and the expression of communion with the saints of heaven (*Communicantes*); after the consecration follows the remembrance of the dead (*Memento etiam*) and a further list of saints (*Nobis quoque*). Both lists of saints follow an internal order. [259] In the *Communicantes* after the Mother of God and saint Joseph (whom Pope John XXIII inserted into the *Canon Romanus*) the apostles are named, then early Popes (Linus, Cletus, Clement, Sixtus and Cornelius), after them martyrs in hierarchical order: the bishop and martyr Cyprian of Carthage, venerated in Rome, the deacon Laurence, the martyr bishop Chrysogonus of Aquileja, two laymen martyrs from the time of Julian the Apostate, the court officials John and Paul, as well as two beneficent doctors from the East, Cosmas and Damian, so that twelve saints follow the twelve apostles. The list of saints of the *Nobis quoque* fill in Matthias and Barnabas along with John the Baptist and Stephen the proto-martyr as the supplement to the list of apostles of the *Communicantes*, as also eleven other martyrs especially venerated in Rome. Here too there is an inner order: after John the Baptist there follow seven men and seven women, again in hierarchical order. [260] As a third shell there serve at the beginning the plea for acceptance (*Te igitur*), to which corresponds the *Per quem haec omnia* , in which at one time the blessing of natural products took place. The preface and the concluding doxology constitute the outermost shell. Despite its venerable age

---

[258] J. A. Jungmann, Die Doxolgie am Schluß der Hochgebete: Th. Maas-Ewerd/ K. Richter (eds.), Gemeinde im Herrenmahl 314–322. Cf. also A. Nocent, Les Doxologies des Prières Eucharistiques: A. Heinz / H. Rennings (eds.), Gratias agamus, 343–353.

[259] Cf. E. Hosp, Die Heiligen im Canon Missae, Graz 1926; V. L. Kennedy, The Saints of the Canon of the Mass, Rome 1938.

[260] Cf. Jungmann MS II, 217–221, 316–319 (E. Tr. II, 170–179, 248–258).

and its intricate structure Emminghaus[261] mentions also the weaknesses of the *Canon Romanus:* poor on praise, overloading of intercessions, lists of saints whose names say nothing any longer to modern man, lack of clarity in the epicletic elements and also the lack of the eschatological dimension. The necessary reform has improved much of this, but "the fact that the Roman canon was not more thoroughly revised and has remained a not very convincing succession of individual prayers, has brought it about that it now leads a sort of shadow existence and is seldom made use of". [262]

B. *The second eucharistic prayer*

Many elements of the second eucharistic prayer go back to the one which the *Traditio Apostolica* of Hippolytus transmits to us. [263] Much of it is given word for word, other parts have been introduced, for example the *Sanctus* which is lacking in Hippolytus, while others have been transposed in their sequence. The preface of the second eucharistic prayer is variable, although thereby the flow of the prayer in the text transmitted by Hippolytus is not preserved.

C. *The third eucharistic prayer*

It is the revision of a concept drawn up by the Italian liturgical scholar Cipriano Vagaggini, it is a product of our century, and in composition and content is modelled first of all on the *Canon Romanus*, although the structure of the eucharistic prayer has a far clearer effect in this new text. According to Emminghaus "one could say that here the ancient canon has been recast according to the new structural laws and has been enriched by many formulations coming from other liturgical sources." [264] The third eucharistic prayer does not claim a proper preface.

D. *The fourth eucharistic prayer*

It reminds one of Anaphoras of the Eastern church and is modelled on Antiochene traditions. In keeping with the traditions of the Eastern Church the fourth eucharistic prayer does not confine itself to a single aspect of salvation history, but refers to it in its total expanse from creation up to its eschatological completion. As Christ is the centre of history and his Pascha the loftiest height of the economy of salvation, likewise there stands in the centre of the fourth eucharistic prayer the Institution narrative with the anamnesis. Similarly the fact that the fourth eucharistic prayer offers no alternative for the preface corresponds with the Eastern Church tradition: the outline of the economy of salvation begins with the preface and continues without a break after the *Sanctus* of the assembly.

3.7.4. OTHER EUCHARISTIC PRAYERS

Other eucharistic prayers came into being in the years after the Council. In 1974 three eucharistic prayers were published for the celebration of Mass with children; on the occasion of the Holy Year of 1975 two eucharistic prayers on the theme of "reconciliation" were published that same year; after already in 1970 the eucharistic prayer for the celebration of Mass with the deaf had been composed as a first additional eucharistic

---

[261] Cf. Joh. H. Emminghaus, Die Messe. Wesen, Gestalt, Vollzug. Durchgesehen und überarbeitet von Th. Maas-Ewerd, Klosterneuburg 5th edn. 1992, 259–262.

[262] Meyer, Eucharistie 349.

[263] TradAp. 4 – ed. Geerlings 222–227.

[264] Emminghaus, Die Messe 267.

prayer for the German-speaking area.[265] Also in 1974 there was published a eucharistic prayer composed on the occasion of the Swiss synod which was borrowed in many countries, but only received Roman approbation in 1991 (for the Latin version, and 1993 for the German text) as a "eucharistic prayer for special occasions", with four different prefaces and intercessions relating to them. Alongside these official eucharistic prayers there were published, especially in Holland, from the end of the 60s, a whole series of eucharistic prayers of private origin, but which were never authorized for use in the liturgy. In a circular of 27 April 1973 of the Congregation for Divine Worship the bishops' conferences were not granted the right to compile new eucharistic prayers for their language areas, but merely the possibility of having new prefaces and inserts approved and confirmed.[266] The problems that arise from this – and precisely also after the Canon Law of 1983 – for the inculturation of liturgy in the various cultural milieux and which naturally have repercussions also on the eucharistic prayer[267] have been described by Bertsch.[268]

3.7.5. OPEN QUESTIONS AND DESIDERATA FOR THE EUCHARISTIC PRAYER

Meyer lists the following desiderata:[269] a) The eucharistic prayer is expected so to express the meaningful shape of the memorial sacrifice of praise "that it does not need many explanations. One may ask whether the composition of the elements and the literary structure of eucharistic prayers I-IV satisfy this demand." b) The intercessions in the eucharistic prayer as elements affected by the situation and subject to historical change could be "left to free choice, but precisely in such a way, that they remain in the line of the prayer for unity and do not become bidding prayers." c) The participation of the faithful is confined today to the introductory dialogue, the *Sanctus*, the anamnetic acclamation and the Amen of the concluding doxology. There could be a case for examining whether the participation could not be extended by further acclamations on the model of the eucharistic prayers for children. d) Likewise "the vocal rendering and the ritual form of the eucharistic prayer raise a series of questions" which affect gestures, the accompanying actions, etc.

3.7.6. THE EUCHARISTIC PRAYER / ANAPHORA IN THE EUCHARISTIC CELEBRATIONS OF OTHER RITES

A. The Byzantine Liturgy

---

[265] Cf. I. Pahl, Das erste Versöhnungshochgebet: A. Heinz / H. Rennings (eds.), Gratias agamus, 355–368; H Rennings: Votivhochgebet Versöhnung II: A. Heinz / H Rennings (eds.), Gratias agamus, 407–426; K. Richter: Das Hochgebet in Meßfeiern mit Kindern: A. Heinz / H. Rennings (eds.), Gratias agamus, 427–437.

[266] Cf. Kaczynzki I, 3037–3055, corroborated by *Inaestimabile Donum* No.5 of 3. 4. 1980, Kaczynski II, 3966.

[267] Cf. M. Probst, Eucharistische Hochgebete für die australischen Ureinwohner. Der Versuch der Inkulturation eines zentralen euchologischen Textes: A. Heinz / H. Rennings (eds.): Gratias agamus, 385–398.

[268] L. Bertsch, Entstehung und Entwicklung liturgischer Riten und kirchliches Leitungsamt: Der neue Meßritus in Zaire. Ein Beispiel kontextueller Liturgie. Ed. by the Missionswissenschaftlichen Institut Missio unter Leitung von L. Bertsch (Theologie der Dritten Welt 18), Freiburg-Basel-Vienna 1993, 209–256.

[269] Cf. Meyer, Eucharistie 351–353.

On most days of the year the Anaphora of Chrysostom[270] is used; the attribution of authorship to this Father of the Church is controverted.[271] The origin of the Anaphora of Basil[272] is more certain: the Byzantine Church uses it on the Sundays of Lent, on Holy Saturday, on Christmas night, on the vigil of the Epiphany and on 1 January, the day of Saint Basil the Great. After the deacon's call to attention and the introductory dialogue there follows the doxological part of the Anaphora comparable to the Western preface, which after the *Sanctus* of the assembly maintains the doxological flow and leads up to the Institution narrative. The assembly answers with the "Amen" to the words of Institution which are sung in a loud voice.[273] There follow the anamnesis with the offering, which is expressed by an elevation of the gifts with crossed hands. The consecratory effect proper is attributed to the epiclesis. There follows the memorial of the saints – culminating in the praise of the Mother of God with the appendant hymn *Axion estin* sung by the assembly – which is not to be separated from the commemoration of the dead and the further intercessions.[274]

B. The Mozarabic Liturgy

It is only for the eucharistic prayer that the priest proceeds once again from the celebrant's chair to the altar, where, analogously with the introductory dialogue of the Roman preface he invites the assembly to participate in the eucharistic prayer.[275] There follows the *Illatio*, which corresponds to the Roman preface and of which there is one for every Mass formulary.[276] Then follows the *Sanctus*, to which is appended further the acclamation: *Hagios, Hagios, Hagios, Kyrie ho Theos*. The function of the *Oratio post Sanctus* is to lead up to the Institution narrative. It is equally as rich in variants as the *Illatio* and has as its theme Christ's work of salvation.[277] There follows the immutable Institution narrative; the assembly answers after the consecration of the bread and the wine each time with "Amen". After the consecration the priest cites 1 Cor 11:26, to which the assembly answers *Sic credimus, Domine Iesu.* Equally as variable as the *Illatio* and the *Oratio post Sanctus* is the *Oratio post pridie,* which has the function of the anamnesis and the epiclesis.[278] The eucharistic prayer ends with a doxology, for which alongside a general formula for special days there are also other formulas.[279]

[270] Hänggi-Pahl PE 223–229 (Bibliography).
[271] In this connection cf. G. Wagner, Der Ursprung der Chrysostomosliturgie. Münster 1973 (LQF 59).
[272] Hänggi-Pahl PE 230–243 (Bibliography).
[273] Cf. Kucharek, Liturgy 602–605.
[274] Cf. M. Kunzler, Insbesondere für unsere allheilige Herrin. Der Axion-estin-Hymnus als Zugang zum Verständnis des prosferein hyper im Heiligengedächtnis der byzantinischen Chrysostomos-Anaphora: A. Heinz / H. Rennings (eds.): Gratias agamus,227–240; Kallis 138.
[275] This going to the altar finds its expression in the dialogue itself, cf. MHM 71: P: "Introibo ad altare Dei mei. A: Ad Deum qui laetificat iuventutem meam. D: Aures ad Dominum. A: Habemus ad Dominum. P: Sursum corda. A: Levemus ad Dominum. P: Deo ac Domino nostro Iesu Christo Filio Dei, qui est in caelis, dignas laudes dignasque gratias referamus. A: Dignum et iustum est."
[276] On the special characteristics of the Mozarabic *Illatio* cf. IGMHM 65–70.
[277] Cf. IGMHM 74–75.
[278] Cf. IGMHM 96–108.
[279] Cf. IGMHM 109–112.

C. The Ambrosian Liturgy

The new Milanese Missal has six eucharistic prayers. The first corresponds to a large extent to the *Canon Romanus,* but exhibits particular features in addition to small divergences especially in the lists of saints. [280] The second eucharistic prayer corresponds to the Roman rite, as also do the third and fourth, St Ambrose is mentioned in all. The fifth eucharistic prayer has the eucharist itself as a special theme. It is designated for the evening Mass of Holy Thursday, but can also be used in all other Masses which treat expressly of the mystery of the eucharist, of the Passion and of the priesthood. [281] The sixth eucharistic prayer has a special paschal character and is designated for the celebration of Easter night, for Sundays in Eastertide as well as for Masses which are connected with the preparation for and celebration of baptism. [282] The Milanese missal is very rich in prefaces; every Sunday and every Saint's Day is provided with a proper preface. [283]

Bibliography

A. Adam, Eucharistisches Hochgebet und Selbstopfer der Christen: A. Heinz/ H. Rennings (ed.): Gratias agamus, 5 – 10.

J. Baumgartner, Der Vollzug des Hochgebetes – eine unbewältigte Aufgabe, HlD 38 (1984) 97 – 113; 151 – 159.

B. Capelle, Innocent Ier et le canon de la messe: Travaux liturgiques II, Louvain 1962, 236 – 247.

A. Heinz / H. Rennings (eds.), Gratias agamus. Studien zum eucharistischen Hochgebet (FS Fischer), Freiburg – Basel – Vienna 1992.

J. A. Jungmann, Das eucharistische Hochgebet. Grundgedanken zum Canon Missae (Rothenfelser Hefte 1), Würzburg 1954.

B. Kleinheyer, Erneuerung des Hochgebetes, Regensburg 1969.

S. Marsili, Memoriale-Anamnesi nella Preghiera eucaristica, Notitiae 9 (1973) 225 – 227.

S. Marsili, Offerta-Sacrificio nella Preghiera eucaristica, Notitiae 9 (1973) 231 – 237.

J. H. Mckenna, Eucharistic Prayer: Epiclesis: A. Heinz / H.Rennings (eds.), Gratias agamus, 283 – 291.

O. Nussbaum, Die eucharistischen Hochgebete II-IV (Lebendiger Gottesdienst 16), Münster 1970.

H. Rennings, Zur Diskussion um die neuen Hochgebete, LJ 23 (1973) 3 – 20.

Th. Schnitzler, Die drei neuen Hochgebete und die neuen Präfationen in Verkündigung und Betrachtung, Freiburg – Basel -Wien 1968.

---

[280] Cf MA 817: diverging from the Roman rite, after the mention of the apostles there are mentioned: "Apollinare, Vitale, Nazaro e Celso, Protaso e Gervaso, Vittore, Nabore, Felice e Calimero, sant'Ambrogio e tutti i santi ... "

[281] MA 847: "Questa preghiera eucaristica si deve usare nella messa vespertina "Nella cena del Signore"; si può anche usare nelle messe che hanno come tema il mistero dell'Eucaristia e della Passione, nelle ordinazioni, negli anniversari sacerdotali e nelle riunioni sacerdotali."

[282] MA 853: "Questa preghiera eucaristica si deve usare nella veglia pasquale; si può usare anche nelle messe 'per i battezzati', nelle domeniche e nelle ferie del tempo pasquale e nelle messe rituali dell'iniziazione cristiana."

[283] Cf. MA Principi e Norme 56a.

F. Sottocornola, L'Elemento di petizione nella Preghiera eucaristica, Notitiae 9 (1973) 238–241.

C. Vagaggini, Le canon de la messe et la réforme liturgique, Paris 1967.

3.8. THE COMMUNION PART OF THE MASS

3.8.1. THE OUR FATHER

On the basis of the petition for bread Cyprian and Ambrose already relate the Our Father to the eucharist, especially as the following petition for the forgiveness of sins can be understood as a prerequisite for a worthy reception of Communion.[284] Thus the Lord's Prayer became the eucharistic table prayer, and apart from the Roman rite and among the Byzantines, in the other Eastern liturgies it was also prayed immediately before the Communion.[285] The location after the eucharistic prayer goes back to Gregory the Great; he may have been prompted by the Greeks, and defended it with the argument that the eucharistic prayer had human authors; the prayer which is said *super oblationem*, i.e. over the consecrated gifts is additional, however that prayer ought to be the first to be considered which has the Lord himself as author. In the Roman liturgy the connection with the eucharistic prayer is so close – thus there are lacking the rites which are situated before the Lord's Prayer in the Eastern rites, the formulas of blessing and the *ectenie* which close the Anaphora – that the Our Father appears almost as the continuation of the former.[286] This however had the result, that the Lord's Prayer, which as preparation for Communion is meant to be a prayer of the whole community, already according to Gregory's evidence was recited by the priest alone and became one of the prayers of his office.[287] The assembly prayed it simultaneously in a low voice: this found expression in their acclamation as the ending of the Lord's Prayer with the petition *sed libera nos a malo* and their "Amen" after the embolism. In the renewed liturgy the Our Father is once again the prayer of the whole assembly, *una cum populo*. That the priest at this same point takes up the *orante* gesture is strictly speaking inconsistent, it could be wished it were possible precisely during the Our Father to allow this ancient Christian gesture to be performed by the whole assembly. The setting also which surrounds the Our Father, the introduction and the following embolism, attests the special appraisal of its value. In line with the example of the Fathers of the Church the introductory formulas to the Our Father in East and West include the theme of boldness and freedom with which Christians may address the almighty God as "Father", to which they see themselves empowered and acknowledged by Christ himself, *divina institutione*. The Our Father is followed by a prayer to be said by the priest, the "embolism",[288] which is to be met with in all non-Byzantine oriental liturgies as well as in the Roman rite. In

---

[284] W. Dürig, Die Bedeutung der Brotbitte des Vaterunsers bei den lateinischen Vätern bis Hieronymus, LJ 18 (1968) 72–86.

[285] Cf. N. M. Denis-Boulet, La place du Notre-Père dans la liturgie, MD 22 (1966) 69–91; J. A. Jungmann, Das Pater noster im Kommunionkreis: id., Gewordene Liturgie 137–164; W. Dürig, Das Vaterunser in der Messe: Th. Maas-Ewerd / K. Richter (eds.): Gemeinde im Herrenmahl, 223–230.

[286] Cf. Jungmann, MS II, 344–346.

[287] In the East the *Our Father* always remained a prayer of the assembly, even when the choir or a leader prays it as representing the assembly.

[288] "Insertion", so called already in the second Ordo Romanus, cf. Jungmann MS II, 352. Cf. also I. H. Dalmais, L'introduction et l'embolisme de l'oraison dominicale dans la célébration eucharistique: MD 22 (1966) 92–100.

the renewed liturgy it has been maintained without the mention of the saints and today leads to the doxology which the assembly recites. This doxological acclamation "For the kingdom... " derives from the most ancient liturgy; in the *Didache* (8,2) it is found in direct connection with the Our Father, and in many biblical manuscripts it penetrated as a gloss on Mt 6:13. Its addition by the Churches of the Reformation provoked, so to speak, the impression of a "Protestant Our Father".

3.8.2. THE KISS OF PEACE

"In the Roman missal the complex of the fraction and the sign of peace had got badly confused in the course of time. The reform of the missal has especially at this point again restored good order."[289] While in the missal of Pius V the Host was still broken during the ending of the embolism, today however the fraction is taken completely out of the sign of peace. The sign of peace also is liturgical primary rock strata; it is mentioned already in Justin. The original location was at the end of the liturgy of the Word as the seal of the preceding prayer and as the expression of the fraternal attitude before the beginning of the eucharist. As has been mentioned, there are suggestions to place the penitential act in conjunction with the kiss of peace at this point as the expression of brotherly love. The Byzantines too have it approximately at this point, even if here after the placing of the gifts on the altar after the Great Entrance the theme is to the fore, according to the Lord's command to offer the gifts after having been reconciled to one another (Mt 5:23). Precisely as the seal of the preceding prayer already at the beginning of the 5th century the sign of peace was moved to follow the eucharistic prayer, in order to seal this prayer also. After the transfer of the Our Father to the immediate edge of the eucharistic prayer the sign of peace moved again to follow the Lord's Prayer as if to seal the expression *sicut et nos dimittimus debitoribus nostris*. As finally the Lord's Prayer itself was seen in close relation to Communion, so likewise the sign of peace; it passed even as a Communion substitute for the non-communicants. This view found expression also in the fact that the sign of peace started out from the altar and "and like a message or even like a gift which comes from the Sacrament, was handed on to the others and to the people."[290] The celebrant too had to receive the sign of peace as such a gift, and he did it by kissing the altar.[291] Already very early on, the intimacy of the kiss led to precise rulings: men might only give the kiss of peace to men, women to women, something that was easily practised on account of the separation of the sexes in the churches. The kiss itself changed into a merely stylized gesture, limited itself increasingly in the West and among the Byzantines to the celebrants, and experienced a further development from England by the use of the pax-brede, by means of which the laity could again be included in the kiss of peace. The celebrant first kissed the altar, then the pax-brede offered to him by an altar server, who then presented it to the others to whom the kiss of peace was permitted. As a substitute for the altar the pax-brede was often provided with the image of the Crucified; crosses also could take

---

[289] Joh. H. Emminghaus, Die Messe. Wesen, Gestalt, Vollzug. Durchgesehen und überarbeitet von Th. Maas-Ewerd, Klosterneuburg 5th edn. 1992, 274.

[290] Jungmann, MS II, 405 (E. Tr. II, 326), referring to the Ordo Romanus I.

[291] Among the Byzantines the priest and deacon, after the sign of peace to the people, kiss the covered sacred gifts and exchange the kiss of peace with the words: "Christ is in our midst" – "He is and he will be", cf. Kallis 114ff.

the place of the pax-brede. [292] The prayer for peace which precedes the sign of peace took its origin in Germany in the 11th century, based on John 14:27; it has also been adopted in the new missal. However it is no longer a silent sacerdotal prayer, but spoken aloud it includes the congregation and therefore also employs the plural "ne respicias peccata *nostra* (instead of the former 'mea')." According to the new missal the deacon (or the priest) can invite the congregation to exchange a sign of peace and love, while the celebrant gives the sign of peace to the deacon or the altar servers. "Practical details of the way this [sign of peace] is to be done are to be settled by the local Bishops' Conference in accordance with the sensibilities and conventions of the people" (GIRM 56b). While in various regions the exchange of this sign was accepted without difficulty, other cultural areas find it hard to come to terms with. [293]

3.8.3. THE FRACTION, AGNUS DEI AND COMMINGLING [294]

In the earliest times the eucharistic celebration took its name from the breaking of the bread. With reference to 1 Cor 10:16f the breaking was considered a significant expression for the entire eucharistic celebration: all who partake of the one Bread, form the one Body of Christ, because this one Bread is the communion with the Body of Christ. So long as many received Communion and leavened bread was used, the breaking of the eucharistic Bread was a significant process. It was accompanied by the chant of the *Agnus Dei,* of which it is said that Pope Sergius I (687 – 701), who was of Syrian origin, introduced it into the Mass. It was repeated for as long as required until the breaking was completed. Its provenance from Eastern Christendom is in any case very probable, because the designation of the eucharist as "lamb" was current already early in the East, in the same way as the reference of the breaking to the suffering and death of the Lord. [295] The breaking of the bread lost its practical meaning with the transition to unleavened bread and the pre-prepared small hosts for the faithful. With the disappearance of the practical meaning of the fraction the *Agnus Dei* also changed its character; in company with the kiss of peace it became a petition for peace, and correspondingly since the 11th century the third *miserere nobis* was changed into *dona nobis pacem.* The reform, in the unravelling of the accretion together of the sign of peace, fraction, commingling and *Agnus Dei,* restored to this last its original function: During the breaking of bread and the commingling the invocation "Lamb of God" is usually sung by the choir or the cantor with the people responding. If it is not sung, it should be said aloud. "The invocation may be repeated as often as is needed to cover the whole action of bread-breaking" (GIRM 56e). Account should also be taken in the liturgy of the Mass of the rich symbolism of the fraction (the Lord's death, sharing of all in the one Christ by the one bread): already in 1947 Pope Pius XII requested that the hosts to be distributed at Mass should also be consecrated during the same eucharistic celebration, a point taken up by the missal (GIRM 56h). The distribution of hosts from the tabernacle should be limited to genuinely exceptional situations, without prejudice to the doctrine

---

[292] On the history and shape of the pax-brede cf. J. Braun, Das christliche Altargerät in seinem Sein und in seiner Entwicklung, München 1932, 557 – 572 as well as the plates 116 – 120.

[293] Cf. H. O. Schierbaum, Offerte vobis pacem. Eine regionale Umfrage zur Praxis des Friedengrußes, LJ 30 (1980) 120 – 123.

[294] F. Nikolasch, Brotbrechung, Mischung und Agnus Dei: Th. Maas-Ewerd/ K. Richter (ed.): Gemeinde im Herrenmahl, 331 – 341.

[295] Cf. Jungmann, MS II, 414 – 416 (E. Tr. II, 300 – 303).

of the abiding presence of Christ in the consecrated species. Also by the use of larger hosts, which maintain more clearly the form of bread, the ideal of the participation of all (for instance in small groups – or weekday Masses) or of as many as possible, would at least be got closer to.

The *commixtio* (commingling), the dropping of a particle of the host into the conse-crated wine, has a multiform history in its origins and meaning. In the papal liturgy of the 8th century at the words *Pax Domini sit semper vobiscum* the Pope dropped a piece of the *sancta*, i.e. of that consecrated eucharistic particle, which had been kept from the previous Mass, which had been shown to the Pope on his entry and had been adored by him. "In this way the continuous unity of the eucharistic sacrifice was expressed – the same Mass yesterday and today." [296] This commingling in the papal liturgy took place by analogy to that in the non-papal liturgies in the churches of Rome and its environs: to these the Pope sent by his acolytes a eucharistic particle – the *fermentum* – as an expression of ecclesial communion, and the priest likewise at the *Pax Domini* dropped this into the chalice. This commingling "expressed the historical and vertical oneness of the unique sacrifice of Christ (*sancta*), as well as the local and horizontal oneness of the single sacrificial offering in the many Masses (*fermentum*)." [297] However in the papal liturgy there was still a second commingling: the Pope placed a piece of his Communion Bread in the chalice, while reciting the relevant commingling phrase. After the Pope's Communion the archdeacon poured the rest of the consecrated wine together with par-ticle of the host contained in it, into a chalice for the distribution, the *scyphus,* which contained non-consecrated wine. From this distribution chalice the faithful were offered communion of the chalice, into which when needed wine was added. According to an-other source this was done also with several distribution chalices. At the bottom of this there is the view still prevalent in the East today in connection with the Communion of the sick and the "liturgy of the presanctified", according to which wine by contact with the consecrated bread is consecrated and becomes the Blood of Christ. This accounts for the concept of *consecratio* in the earlier phrase which accompanied the commin-gling. From the Counter -Reformation point of view the missal of 1570 altered the text from the previous *Fiat commixtio et consecratio* into *Haec commixtio et consecratio,* which merely describes the action. [298] From Syria there originated a symbolical expla-nation of the *commixtio*: the separate consecration of bread and wine represents Christ's death, the commingling as the overcoming of the mortal separation of Body and Blood represents the Lord's resurrection. [299] The liturgical reform maintained the commingling above all for ecumenical motives: "an honest solution in line with the basic principles of the liturgical renewal would have been the relinquishment of this rite, particularly as the ecumenical motivation is only very slightly relevant", [300] given that the East Syrian liturgy practises the commingling just as little as do the Churches of the Reformation.

[296] Jungmann, MS II, 386 (E. Tr. II, 312).
[297] Cf. Emminghaus, Messe 281; O. Nautin, Le rite du "fermentum" dans les églises urbaines de Rome, EL 96 (1982) 514–522.
[298] Cf. B. Capelle, L'oraison "Haec commixtio et consecratio" de la messe romaine: Travaux liturgiques II, Louvain 1962, 332–343.
[299] Cf. Jungmann, MS II, 390–396 (E. Tr. II, 311–321).
[300] Nikolasch, Brotbrechung 339.

3.8.4. THE COMMUNION

A. The Preparation

"That he may receive the Body and Blood of Christ fruitfully the priest prepares himself in silent prayer. The people also should pray in silence" (GIRM 56f). The celebrant's prayers, provided for also in the new missal, are private prayers, and therefore not without problems in the liturgy, given that the preparation for a fruitful reception of Communion concerns the whole community. "The preparation in common for Communion acquires its concrete form in the observance of a short silent pause. This silence has the function that each person prepares himself / herself in prayer for Communion."[301] Up to the reform of the liturgy the Communion of the faithful at Mass received its characteristic features from the Communion of the sick. Up to the 11th century, the elements of the Communion part of the Mass were used, as far as possible, for the Communion of the sick. Accordingly the confession of sins was a determining element of the Communion of the sick: the *Confiteor,* the *Misereatur,* and as "absolution" the *Indulgentiam* were recited. In the *Rituale Romanum* of 1614 these elements were inserted in the order of administering Communion and retroacted on the Mass, into which the rite of Communion of the sick came in as a foreign element. This development is to be seen also against the background of the diminishing frequency of Communion and the rare obligatory Communions of the faithful, according to which there were only a few Communion days, on which so many received Communion that it was distributed outside Mass, while on the other days there was no distribution of Communion at all. This detaching of the Communion of the faithful from the Mass lasted up to our [20th] century.

B. The Invitation

"The priest shows to the faithful the eucharistic Bread which they are to receive in Communion, and invites them to the table of the Lord. Together with them he expresses, in words from the Gospel, sentiments of humility"(GIRM 56g). The reference is to the words of John the Baptist (John 1:29) and to those of the centurion of Capharnaum (Mt 8:8). In the Roman missal the invitation is completed by the quotation of Rev 19:9. Today the priest and congregation recite together, once, the response to the invitation: up to the reform priest and faithful recited it together three times.

C. The Distribution of Communion

a. The order in which it is to be received: In all rites there is an ordinal sequence, according to which the priest communicates first. Thereby it is intended to express that not the celebrant, but Christ, is the host of the meal. An adaptation to modern conventions – the host first serves his guests and then helps himself – could obscure the fact that the priest also is first of all a guest at the eucharistic table. Nevertheless such an adaptation "could be carefully considered. In smaller groups, the order followed in concelebration would certainly be possible, that the priest indeed distributes to each one by one, but that then all consume the Body of the Lord simultaneously."[302]

b. The formula of administration: The formula in use today in the Western Church "the Body of Christ" or "the Blood of Christ" goes back to the ancient Church, was already known to Ambrose and is present in the Apostolic Constitutions. Already at that time it was understood as a question about the avowal of faith of the communicant, who

---

[301] J. Hermans: Die Feier der Eucharistie. Erklärung und spirituelle Erschließung. Regensburg 1984, 303.

[302] Emminghaus, Messe 287 with reference to GIRM 197 – 199.

authenticated his faith with an "Amen". Short formulas however induce amplifications. Thus in the East reverential annexes appeared, also the fruits of reception of Communion were added. The formula of administration among the Byzantines runs thus with the addition of the name of the communicant: "The servant of God (N.) receives the precious Body and Blood of Christ for the remission of sins and for life everlasting." [303] In Frankish territory the administration formula became an optative blessing, of which the basic form in the 8th century ran:*Corpus et sanguis Domini nostri Jesu Christi custodiat te in vitam aeternam.* The phrase which accompanied the celebrant's Communion, together with a gesture of blessing with the host over the communicant, became the formula of administration. [304] Precisely the confessional character of the formula of the ancient Church at present in use again, merits precedence over the optative blessing, above all as it actively includes the communicant.

c. Communion in the Hand or in the Mouth? The manner of receiving Communion was for a time a very controversial matter, which was fought with ideological bitterness.In this regard Communion in the hand is incontestably the older practice. Already the manner of holding the hands which should form a throne is described with precision in the Mystagogical Catecheses of Cyril of Jerusalem. [305] An increasing sense of reverence, but also the fear that the eucharistic Bread could be misused for other purposes, led in the 9th century to Communion in the mouth, simultaneously therefore with the transition to unleavened bread. The Instruction of the Congregation for Divine Worship *Memoriale Domini* of May 1969 left it to the Bishops' Conferences of those regions in which it had become customary, to allow Communion in the hand as a second manner of receiving. [306] That while doing so reverence is just as much to be valued is indeed beyond doubt, likewise the avoidance of ideological trench warfare in which the protagonists of Communion in the hand or the mouth deny this reverence reciprocally to one another.

d. Communion from the Chalice: "The meaning of Communion is signified as clearly as possible when it is given under both kinds. In this form the meal-aspect of the Eucharist is more fully manifested" (GIRM 240). Only since the 12th century in the West did Communion from the chalice fall more and more into disuse. Although in the words of consecration themselves the Lord's command "bibite ex eo *omnes"* was and is maintained, there was a whole series of reasons for this serious change. First of all the fear of spilling or other profanation of the sacrament. This led to forms of Communion which were no longer a real drinking from the same chalice, for example dipping the host in the chalice or drinking with the help of a reed *(fistula).* [307] It is certain that behind the withdrawal of the chalice there stands also the medieval "viewing spirituality" which concentrated on the species of Bread.

The theological basis for the abolition of Communion from the chalice for the laity was furnished by the doctrine of concomitance, according to which the whole Christ is present in both species, and which the already existing cases of Bread Communion alone authorized, for instance Communion in the home or for the sick, or the baptismal

---

[303] Kallis 172.
[304] Cf. Jungmann, MS II, 481–486 (E. Tr. II, 389–391).
[305] Myst.Cat. V, 21 – ed. G. Röwekamp, Freiburg-Basel-Wien 1992 (FC 7), 162f.
[306] Cf. Kaczynski I, 1892–1907.
[307] Cf. Braun, Altargerät 247–265, plate 48.

Communion of small babies, to whom only the species of wine was offered. It was considered that Christ's command to receive his Blood was fulfilled by the priest's Communion alone of the chalice. Because the demand for Communion from the chalice for all was already an item in the pre-Reformation criticism of the Church (John Hus) and was taken up by the Reformers, this, among other reasons, made the abandonment of the chalice Communion for the laity a distinguishing feature of Catholicism. So things remained as regards the withdrawal of the chalice until the liturgy reform of Vatican II. [308] The Constitution on the Liturgy (SC 55b) in the beginning provided the chalice Communion only for special occasions, but which already in the new missal (GIRM 243) were considerably extended. According to the present canonical situation, regularized for particular Churches, the possibility of offering the chalice is understood in very broad terms. [309] The substitute forms for genuine drinking given in GIRM 243 are justly criticized [310].

e. The Communion Chant accompanies the Communion of the priest and of the faithful; it is meant to give expression to the spiritual fellowship of the communicants through singing together: "to show forth their joy, and to make it clear that the Communion Procession is a fraternal occasion" (GIRM 56i). Like the introit, the Communion chant is a processional chant, which is meant to accompany the communal approach of the faithful to Communion, and was already known in the 4th century as a responsorial chant between the chanter and those who were walking to Communion. By preference psalms 33 and 144 were sung; the chanter sang the psalm verses, the community answered with a refrain. In the 10th/11th centuries the psalm was dropped, only the antiphon remained, which in addition moved to after the process of communicating and finally lost its relationship to Communion. The restoration of this relationship will only in rare cases achieve the result that the designated Communion chant accompanies the faithful as they walk up to Communion; more suitable than the directive that the priest if necessary recite the Communion verse before he gives the Body of the Lord to the faithful is the suggstion made by Emminghaus to include it already in the invitation to Communion. [311]

f. The Concluding Prayer already by its Latin name *Postcommunio* (or *post communionem* in the new missal) shows that it belongs to the sphere of Communion rites. It has its roots in the communal thanksgiving after Communion. Still today in the Byzantine liturgy the deacon invites to a brief *ectene* with words which likewise are already contained in the Apostolic Constitutions: "having received the divine mysteries of Christ let us worthily give thanks to the Lord!" [312] During the *ectene* of the faithful the priest recites the thanksgiving prayer for the Communion received. In the Roman liturgy the concluding prayer is the third of the presidential prayers, shares therefore the "concen-

---

[308] Cf. the reference to Trent still contained in GIRM 241!
[309] Cf. R. Kaczynski: Die Wiedereinführung der Kelchkommunion im römischen Ritus. In: H. Spaemann (ed.): '... und trinket alle daraus.' Zur Kelchkommunion in unseren Gemeinden. Freiburg -Basel -Wien 1986, 90–92 for the German-speaking area. Cf. also H. B. Meyer: Wann ist Kelchkommunion möglich? Die kirchlichen Dokumente und ihre Interpretation. In: HD 44(1990) 27–35; K. Richter: Zur Praxis der Kelchkommunion. In: Heinrich Spaemann (ed.): '... und trinket alle daraus'. Zur Kelchkommunion in unseren Gemeinden. Freiburg – Basel -Wien 1986, 15–33.
[310] Cf. Emminghaus, Messe 290f.
[311] Cf. Emminghaus, Messe 292, this is already widely practised at least in the German-speaking area.
[312] Cf. Kallis 178; Apost. Const. VIII,14,2- scHR. 336,210–211.

trating" character of the "collect": it sums up the private thanksgivings of the faithful said silently and because of that mentions also the effects of the sacrament received. Thence there comes to the concluding prayer still another summing up: just as the blessing of the entire Mass culminates in the sacramental encounter with Christ through the reception of the eucharistic gifts, so the concluding prayer gives thanks under a eucharistic aspect for all the graces of the celebration of Mass. Considered from this point of view both indications of place in the missal for the concluding prayer are meaningful (GIRM 122): either the priest says it at the altar (special emphasis on thanksgiving for the Communion received) or at the celebrant's chair (special emphasis on the recapitulatory thanksgiving for the entire celebration of Mass).

3.8.5. THE DISMISSAL [313]

"After the concluding prayer there follow, if needs be, brief announcements to the congregation" which the deacon also can carry out (GIRM 123, 139). One may doubt whether this – as Emminghaus holds – is the most suitable moment to make announcements to the congregation. [314] Certainly this occasion is better than after the sermon/homily, when information also of a very worldly nature rather distracts from the sacred action. To make announcements with a cordial greeting to the assembly before the liturgical celebration proper, that is still before the entry, is to say the least, an alternative worthy of consideration. Nevertheless the announcements within the Communion sphere possess an ancient tradition: they reach back to when the non-communicants left the church before the distribution of Communion, and according to Roman sources of the 7th and 8th centuries, before their departure they were given information on the next stational liturgy, and the approaching feasts of martyrs, days of fasting and other church news. [315]

B. The Blessing

A blessing of the congregation before Communion had originally the meaning of preparing the faithful for a worthy Communion. This blessing, recited in solemn form by the bishop, in simpler form by the priest, was increasingly understood in the Gallic liturgies as a Communion substitute for the non-communicants, who thereupon left the church. This blessing was preceded by a call from the deacon to the faithful to bow their heads before the Lord, similarly as today the prayers in the bowed position begin in the Eastern liturgies. The Gallic pontifical blessing in imitation of Num 6:22–26 was three-membered, during which each part was answered by the congregation with "Amen"; the Church's year was also given expression in it, but never a relationship to the subsequent distribution of Communion. In spite of various objections this blessing passed from the Gallic into the Roman liturgy. [316] A stricter interpretation of the exit

---

[313] Cf. H. Rennings: Der Schlußteil der Meßfeier. In: Th. Maas-Ewerd/ K. Richter (ed.) Gemeinde im Herrenmahl, 342–350.

[314] Cf. Emminghaus, Messe 297.

[315] Cf. Jungmann, MS II, 424f (E. Tr. I, 490–492). According to Jungmann the departure of the non-communicans was almost a necessity given the Roman custom of distributing Communion in the nave of the church. "In the 6th century it was already current practice that the deacon before the Communion, called out: *Si quis non communicat, det locum*, i.e. that the non-communicants give way, which practically came to the same thing, that they had to withdraw."

[316] Cf. the prayer in the bowed position in the Byzantine liturgy following the Our Father, Kallis 152f. On the whole subject cf. Jungmann MS II, 364–367 (E. Tr. II, 439–441).

of the non-communicants came from Spain, according to which they had to be present up to the end of Mass. Consequently also the blessing moved to after the Communion. [317] Originally in the Roman rite, as a blessing, there was a prayer of blessing by the celebrant over the people at the end of Mass, the *oratio super populum*, likewise preceded by the invitation to bow the head. These prayers of blessing, which possess the strict form of the Roman *Oratio*, were originally a part of every Mass, but, at quite an early stage, became associated especially with Lent (as special prayers of blessing over the penitents). The priestly blessing common in the Gaulish liturgy could not be given up easily, however, because of popular demand. When the Roman Mass spread to the Frankish territories, resort was had to the Roman *oratio super populum* as a formula of blessing; but the latter was no longer felt to be a prayer of blessing, since in the Gregorian sacramentaries it was prescribed for the penitents. [318]

It is probable that "gestures and words of blessing were used in the form in which they were found in the Roman *Ordines* for when the celebrant left the altar. This method of blessing must habe then become generally dominant by the 11th century." We are concerned with a blessing "after mass", after the dismissal has been proclaimed, and therefore many sources from that period are silent about it. [319]

About the middle of the 12th entury, the blessing tended more and more to be given from the altar itself, and the priest's final blessing conformed more and more to the episcopal usage, though the difference between bishop and priest was expressed by small details. Thus, in the Middle Ages, the bishop blessed with the hand, while the priest did so with a consecrated object, such as a relic, a particle of the Cross, also with the paten or the corporal. Nowadays this differentiation still persists in the form of the versicle preceding the episcopal blessing. The renewed missal again provides, on certain days, the possibility of a solemn three-part blessing, to which the people respond with a threefold Amen, modelled on the Gaulish blessings, it also provides prayers of blessing for the people in the tradition of the oratio super populum and of the prayer in the bowed position. Both forms, however, are linked with the blessing in the name of the Trinity and the sign of the Cross. In the strict sense, the "Last Gospel", which used to be read, also belonged to the blessings: in the 13th century, the prologue to St. John's Gospel (John 1:1 – 14) was greatly prized as a blessing, was used as a prayer for good weather (together with the beginnings of the other Gospels) and was included in the Roman Missal of 1570.

C. The Words of Dismissal

The words of dismissal mark the end of the Mass, for even sociological reasons make necessary the clear designation of the end of an ordered assembly. [320] Thus, in pre-Christian Rome a funeral ceremony was ended with "Ilicet = ire licet, you may go". [321] The word "missa" has in this case ist original meaning of "dismissal", which, however, with the blessing connected with it, was to shape the name of the eucharistic celebration. [322] The pendant to the Roman "Ita missa est" was the Gaulish "Benedicamus Domino" and until 1960 the two formulae of dismissal had the following symbi-

---

[317] Cf. Jungmann MS II, 425f (E. Tr. 439f).
[318] Cf. Jungmann MS II, 534f.
[319] Cf. Jungmann, MS II, 547; Meyer, Eucharistie 207.
[320] Cf. Rennings, concluding section 343f.
[321] Cf. Jungmann. MS II, 537.
[322] Cf. The chapter on the development of Mass

otic relationship: "Ita missa est" was used for Masses in which the Gloria was sang, "Benedicamus Domino" for all other Masses. In the Middle Ages there were special words of dismissal for Requiem Masses: "Requiescant in pace". In the renewed liturgy there is only the "Ita missa est"; the words of dismissal are omitted, however, if another liturgical celebration immediately follows. The people's response "Deo gratias" was a widespread acclamation of agreement, or indeed of greeting, in the North African Church, also apart from church services. As a response to the Reading it meant that the hearers thus declared that they had understood the Reading; similarly, according to the Rule of Benedict, the porter should answer a knock at the door of the monastery with "Deo gratias", in order to convey that he is aware of the person desiring entry. [323] Analogously, the "Deo gratias" at the end of Mass expresses that the announcement of the end of the celebration has been understood, as well as giving thanks for the gifts of grace received. The fact that proclamation "Ite missa est" falls especially to the deacon, is derived by Jungmann from the duty of a herald, who makes his announcements in a loud voice, whereas the judge or civil servant, conscious of this dignity, speaks rather in muted tones. [324]

D. Kissing the Altar and Recession

Both are mirror images of the opening of Mass, though, as a rule, the Recession is not surrounded by as much solemnity as the Entrance Procession. The priest, "together with the altar servers, makes the required sign of reverence and returns to the sacristy" (GIRM 125).

3.8.6. THE COMMUNION SECTION IN THE EUCHARISTIC CELEBRATIONS OF OTHER RITES

A. The Byzantine Liturgy

The Communion section of the Byzantine Eucharistic celebration begins with a petitional Ektenie, which leads into the Our Father, the Embolism is unknown. There follow a prayer in the bowed position (with an acclamation by the deacon "Bow your heads before the Lord!") and a Little Elevation, with the priest proclaiming: "The holy for the holy ones!" [325] The breaking of the Eucharistic bread and the dipping of a particle in the chalice precede the rite of Zeon, that of pouring hot water into the consecrated wine. However much the historical explanations as to its origin differ, [326] the rite's mystical explanation is clear: the Zeon points to the glow of the Holy Spirit, which has produced the miracle of transubstantiation. The Communion of the clergy is followed by that of the faithful, always under both species in the form of intinction, or using the Communion spoon. The liturgy ends with a little Ektenie, the "Ambon Prayer", the blessing and the dismissal, on which often follows the distribution of the blessed bread ("Antidoron") with the individual blessing of the faithful.

B. The Mozarabic Liturgy

The Communion section begins with the recitation of the Nicene-Constaninopolitan Creed by the people. [327] Then follows the breaking of the bread, accompanied by the

---

[323] Cf. Jungmann, MS I, 537f.
[324] Cf. Jungmann, MS II, 540.
[325] Cf. Kallis 153 156; Kucharek, Liturgy 662–668.
[326] Cf. Kucharek, Liturgy 683–688.
[327] Cf. IGMHM 118–123.

"Cantus ad Confractionem". The priest beaks the consecrated bread into nine parts and lays them in the form of a cross on the paten (this is reminiscent of the Byzantine Proskomidia, in which, before the Consecration, the pieces of bread are laid on the Diskos in a definite order); each particle symbolizes one of the mysteries of Christ that are commemorated in the Year of the Lord. [328] The Our Father follows, introduced by the priest with a text that differs according to the type of Mass. The priest prays it himself, and the people respond to every separate petition with Amen, as they do after the Embolism, which continues the last petition of the Our Father. [329] As in the case of the Eastern Church, the Commixtio is accompanied by the acclamation *"Sancta sanctis"*, the particle of the host that symbolizes Christ's kingly reign (*"Regnum"*) is lowered into the chalice. [330] After a blessing in several parts, which belongs to the Proper and serves as a preparation for Communion. [331] The priests distributes the Body of the Lord with the form of words: *"Corpus Christi sit salvatio tua"*, while the deacon administers the chalice with the words: *"Sanguis Christi maneat tecum redemptio vera"*. The people got to Communion to the strains of the *"Cantus as Accedentes"*, before the choir intones the *"Antiphona post Communionem"* after Communion has been distributed. The *"Oratio Completuria"* fulfils the function of the Roman Concluding Prayer, before the people are dismissed. There ist no proper dismissal blessing, since no human ble ssing can come anywhere near the beneficent power of the Eucharist just received. [332]

C. The Ambrosian Liturgy

The Communion section of the Ambrosian liturgy corresponds largely to that of the Roman. The breaking of the Eucharistic bread and the immixtio take place, however, immediately after the closing doxology of the Eucharistic Prayer. As accompaniment, the *"Canto allo spezzare del pane"* is sung. The Agnus Dei of the Roman Mass is omitted. [333] In its place, the Milanese Missal offers a (second) Sign of Peace before the Communion; this takes place only if the first one at the beginning of the Eucharistic liturgy is omitted. [334]

Bibliography

P. Browe, Die öftere Kommunion der Laien im Mittelalter, Bonner Zeitschrift für Theologie und Seelsorge 6 (1926) 1 – 28.

P. Browe, Die Kommunonvorbereitung im Mittelalter, ZKTh 56 (1932) 375 – 415.

P. Browe, Kommunionriten früherer Zeiten, ThGl 24 (1932) 592 – 607.

P. Browe, Die häufige Kommunion im Mittelalter, Münster 1938.

P. Browe, Wann fing man an, die in einer Messe konsekrierten Hostien in einer anderen Messe auszuteilen? ThGl 30 (1938) 388 – 404.

---

[328] Cf. IGMHM 124 – 130: cf. The arrangement of the particles according to the sketch MHM 77.

[329] Cf. IGMHM 131 – 132.

[330] Cf. IGMHM 133 – 134.

[331] Cf. IGMHM 135 – 137.

[332] Cf. IGMHM 137: 'Al dar a la benediction el carácter de preparación a la comunión, se excluye la posibilidad de otra bendición al final de la misa. Se entiende que, al concluir la celebración, la mayor bendición que los fieles pueden llevarse consigo es la Eucaristia que han recibido.'

[333] Cf. MA, Principi e Norme 57 a-c.

[334] 1 Cf. MA 861: "Per giusti motivi se puó collocare a questo punto il rito della pace, omettendola prima della presentazione dei doni."

A. Heinz: Das Friedensgebet in der römischen Messe: H. Feilzer / A. Heinz / W. Lenzen-Deis: Der menschenfreundliche Gott (FS Thome), Trier 1990, 165 – 183.

O. Nußbaum, Die Handkommunion, Köln 1969.

H. Spaemann, Die kritische und pastorale Bedeutung der Kelchkommunion, LJ 15 (1965) 149 – 154.

H. Spaemann (ed.), "... und trinket alle daraus". Zur Kelchkommunion in unseren Gemeinden, Freiburg-Basel-Wien 1986.

Part IV

The Sacramental Celebrations of the Church

"Facie ad faciem te mihi, Christe, demonstrasti; in tuis te invenio sacramentis."[1] This word of Ambrose of Milan, whose sense of reality can hardly be surpassed, throws a sharp light on the essence of sacramental celebrations.They are not "symbolic actions" of the Church, by means of which she will express her faith, nor medial conveyors by means of which a truth of faith should be taught; they will rather be the believer's link with Christ, the life-giving communication though him in the Holy Spirit with the Father.

4.1. ON THE SACRAMENTS AS SUCH AND THEIR RELATIONSHIP TO THE EUCHARIST AS FUNDAMENTAL SACRAMENT.

4.1.1. THE SACRAMENTS AS MEANS OF SANCTIFICATION FOR HUMANKIND AND THE REST OF CREATION.

According to St. Thomas Aquinas the Eucharist is focus point of all the other sacraments: ordination which bestows the right to celebrate them just as baptism which gives the right to receive them. Confirmation perfects the christian so that he does not withdraw from the Eucharist. Penance and the sacrament of the sick prepare him for worthy reception. Marriage represents the union of Christ with his church as it takes place in the Eucharist.[2] The sacraments "are so strongly focussed on the Eucharist that the special grace which each one signifies is effective only in relation to the Eucharist. The Eucharist alone has power to grant grace, whereas the other sacraments are only sources of grace in so far as their recipient intends to present himself at the Lord's table."[3]

Together with the Eucharist the sacrament of baptism holds a special place in the theology of the West. Both are "sacramenta maiora", that is to say, both represent in an exceptionally effective way Christ's passage through death to life everlasting.[4] Baptism is a vivid symbol of the passage, the Eucharist is even more, it is God's sharing his own life with man. The Last Supper was unique, the Eucharist is sacramental sign of what then (once) took place. The Eucharist received after baptism forms the crowning conclusion for the sacrament of initiation. In baptism the believer is welcomed into the Son's household of salvation. To be part of him, to be member of his mystical body, to receive the uncreated grace, in other words to receive God himself in his relation to humankind and creation, the spirit which perfects all holiness, to receive all this means to become part of God's communication with the world, a reality which comes to being in the eucharist.

The Eucharist itself makes clear the necessity of other sacraments besides itself: The sacrament of sacraments founds and builds up the Church as the mystical body of Christ. This body is, however, still in the process of growth, it has not yet reached the pleroma (Eph 4:13). "And just here, in this growth-process, we experience the energies of the other sacraments; just here the dynamism of the final Parousia is expressed".[5]

---

[1]   Apol. Proph. David 12,58 – PL 14, 875.
[2]   Cf. STh III q. 65 a. 3 c.
[3]   Vagaggini 125
[4]   Cf. Y. Congar, Die Idee der sacramenta maiora, Concilium (D) 4 (1968) 9-15.
[5]   Corbon 129

The unity of Christ's body is not destroyed by the diversity of the members. On the contrary, just because the members are different, have received diverse charismas and must experience varying life-situations, can the Godhead work in a different manner in each individual member:

"Each human being is unique, because he is recognized and loved in the one and only body of the beloved Son. The sacraments reflect an all-embracing love of the Father. In the Eucharist his love for all is realized, universally, in the other sacraments then this love is shown in an individual way, according to the needs, the age, the gifts in Christ of each member. Through the mediation of the unique sacrament which is the body of Christ the other sacraments grant a gift of the Holy Spirit. For that reason each sacrament differs from another because of its own special Epiklesis."[6] The centrifugal relationship of the other sacraments to the Eucharist means, as is obvious, that they are or can be joined to the eucharist. This relationship to the main sacrament is valid not only for the six other "sacramenta maiora", so named nowdays in order to distinguish the seven sacraments from the sacramentals, the "sacramenta minora", but is also valid for all other rites, ceremonies, sacramentals, prayers which have been instituted by the church, and especially for the divine office. All these rites are meaningful insofar as they either prepare for the Eucharist or emerge therefrom as water from a spring.[7] St Thomas Aquinas explains the relation of the sacraments to the Eucharist as their centre so: three of them (baptism, confirmation and ordination) imprint an indissoluble seal and cannot be bestowed again, the believer will thus be so disposed that he either receives or gives further that which has just been celebrated.[8]

4.1.2. "ADMINISTERING" OR "CELEBRATING" THE SACRAMENTS?

God's turning to the individual member in his saving love always means that the member is incorporated into the mystical body of Christ. Even when the member is personally addressed, privately so to speak (e.g. in the sacrament of the sick or in penance) the church as the mystical body is always actively present:[9] The liturgical acts are never of a private nature, they are celebrations of the church, which is the "sacrament of unity"; she, the church, is the holy people, united and gathered together under the bishops. For that reason these celebrations concern the whole mystical body of the church, they make the body visible and affect it deeply. The individual members on the other hand are affected in another manner, the celebrations touch them in manifold ways according to their position in the world, their duties and their active participation in the celebrations. (SC 26).

It is logical and consequent to speak of "celebrating" a sacrament, not merely because the sacraments possess a public, ecclesial character, but also because the sacraments are centred about the Eucharist as their end and meaning. This is likewise the case, for example, in confession, when the sacred action is carried out between the "minister" and the "recipient" alone. The "celebration" of a feastday is a means of expressing our affirmation of existence, (acceptance of existence), this affirmation is perfectly fulfilled in the eucharistic celebration when the Lord grants us a share in his

---

[6] Ibidem 131
[7] Cf. Vagaggini, Theologie 127f.
[8] S. Th. III q. 63 a. 3 corp.
[9] Cf. Corbon 130f

godly life. In fact nothing less than "celebrating" can be fitting and apropriate for the Eucharist; we can only "celebrate" it, since it is as acceptation, full and perfect, of existence, and as complete acceptation of the mystical body into the fullness of the trinitarian life that we understand the sacrament. In anology the same is also valid for other sacraments. [10] These are also to be celebrated in a festive manner as God's acceptance of existence, by means of which the ungodly and death-pervaded world will be taken up into the perfect life of the three divine Persons, where the pettiness of everyday life falls away and all existence is feast.

When the sacraments are concerned with only one member's life situation they nevertheless make the matter a concern of the whole body, in the unity of which we all hope to attain fullness of God's own life. This is unsatisfactorily expressed when one speaks of administering the sacraments. Here we see an individualistic understanding of the redemption of the single soul and a view of the relationship between one person and "his" God which leads away from the collective dimension of church. Even when situations arise in which the community aspect is weakened, confession for example, the renewed liturgy will always, and this not only for pastoral reasons, seek to arrange the sacramental celebrations as parish services, or even to have the sacraments dispensed during and as part of the parish mass.

4.1.3. "MEANS OF GRACE" OR FUNDAMENTAL ACTS?

The sacraments are presented by the church as basic effective factors in helping members through significant situations of their lives. They are not – as anabatic, one-sided acts of worship – strengthening graces in order to help us in carrying out our duties before God, nor are they aids furthering true faith and moral behaviour. "The importance of the sacraments as the foundation for christian existence, their connection with the redeeming death and continuing activity of the risen Lord seems to have been fully forgotten. Instead we see in the background of such a theology of the sacraments a picture of the church as an institution for the protection of morality." [11]

In the celebration of a sacrament Christ turns in affection to the believer and pours out on him ever again the grace which takes him into the life of the one Godhead in three Persons. His turning to us is always a sharing of himself, the Incarnate God, we become members of his mystical body and as members receive through the head the life of the Divine. The link with the head is always a link with the other members, that is to say with the church, we all share the same life. Therefore every sacramental act serves to build up the church and is hence an act which belongs to the very ground-work of the church: In the church's nature "we can perceive the nature of the sacraments, and likewise in the nature of the sacraments the nature of the church is manifested." The church is the fundamental sacrament of salvation, "the ever-remaining presence of God's self-giving to mankind in Jesus Christ, the presence of truth and love giving themselves to us." [12]

The sacraments as self-realisation of the church share in the Incarnation of the Logos, and as a consequence share in the incarnational structure of the church. The fact

---

[10] Cf. SC 27
[11] Cf. Th. Schneider, Zeichen der Nähe Gottes. Grundriß der Sakramententheologie, Mainz 6th edn. 1992, 53.
[12] So Rahner quoted according to Schneider, Zeichen 53.

of divine grace being bound to visible things and actions is therefore not arbitrary, the bond is rather the necessary inclusion of creation into the communication between God and man, the connecting link underlying every relationship. Christ, source of the sacraments, makes his redeeming will effective throughout all time in the one universal sacrament, the church, by means of visible signs. [13] They are "sacraments of the church" in a twofold way: they are "by means of the church", "for she is the sign of Christ's activity, who thanks to the sending of the Holy Spirit, is at work in her. And they 'exist for the church'; they are the 'sacraments by means of which the church is built' (Augustine. civ. 22,17), for they proclaim to us and give to us, above all in the eucharist, the mystery of our community with the God, who is love, the one in three persons." [14]

4.1.4. WORD AND SIGN

"Take the word away and what will water be other than mere water? When the word comes to the element however, then the sacrament comes to being." [15] In this sentence Augustine himself qualifies the sacraments as communicative acts. [16] The scholastics also say the same in other concepts. [17] Is the sacrament however more than, as Augustine says, a "visible word"? Is it more than a "word-proclamation made potent by sign and symbolic action, a "potentiated" word, which "for now and for all time, proclaims Christ's redeeming act and redemptive will for all mankind", so that all which is needed is the recipient's acceptance in faith, forgetting any further mote points on questions of causality? In short: to what measure can one think of the effect of grace being really dependent on the carrying out of outward, material signs? [18] Is this word-proclamation, pregnant as it is with significant actions, merely a concession to the "weak", something which the "strong", for whom the word alone is enough, do not need? So our question.

The word which must be added to the sign is not descriptive, it is performative, that is to say, a word setting out, establishing reality. [19] If it were merely descriptive, "describing", then that would imply understanding the sacraments as "proclamation by means of potentiated word", this would be a dangerous questioning of the sacraments, indeed of the whole liturgical life. The word however which is added to the sign establishes a divine reality. This affects the material sign just as it does the recipient. Word, sign and the carrying out of the sign, each complementing the other, become a rite or action which gives the unchanging, divine Love a place where man can find it, bound as he is to place and time. [20] From this the meaning of epiklesis in each sacrament and sacramental action can be deduced: The performative word undermines and defeats the

---

[13]   Cf. Schneider, Zeichen 41, espec. Note 21 with ref. to O. Semmelroth.
[14]   Catechism 1118.
[15]   Hom. 80, 3 in Joh. – PL 35, 1840. This word of Augustin was even taken into the Decretum Gratiani: c. 54 C 1 q 1 – E. Richter / E. Friedberg (eds.): Corpus Iuris Canonici, Editio Lipsiensis secunda, 2 vols., Leipzig 1879-81, I, 379.
[16]   As Hünermann does today. Comp. P. Hünermann, Sakrament – Figur des Lebens: R. Schaeffler / P. Hünermann: Ankunft Gottes und Handeln des Menschen. Thesen über Kult und Sakrament – Freiburg – Basel-Vienna 1977, 51 87.
[17]   Cf. Schneider, Zeichen 58 about the theology of the sacraments of Petrus Lombardus. For Thomas Aquinas comp. ibid. 59.
[18]   Cf. A. Müller, Bleibt die Liturgie? Überlegungen zu einem tragfähigen Liturgieverständnis angesichts heutiger Infragestellungen, LJ 39 (1989) 156-176, 160.
[19]   Cf. Schneider, Zeichen 60.
[20]   So Müller, Bleibt die Liturgie? 163

irreverence of a godless world by means of uncreated grace. Christ himself "acts in his sacraments in order to bestow the grace, which the sacrament signifies. The Father is ever ready to listen to the prayer of his Son's church, while the church in the epiklesis of each sacrament expresses her faith in the power of the Holy Spirit. As fire changes everything it takes possession of into itself, so does the Holy Spirit change that placed under his power into the life of God." [21]

4.1.5. THE RITUAL

The history of the Ritual, the book setting down the rules for the celebration of the sacraments and sacramentals can be traced back to the "Apostolic Tradition" of Hippolytus. The 'Apostolic Tradition' also hands down how sacraments were celebrated, but was 'pattern ritual' in the truest meaning of the word. It was a standard example in the hands of a celebrant showing him how to proceed, either in this or in like manner. The books setting down the rites, usually called sacramentals, had already quite another degree of obligation: they contained the order for the celebration of the Eucharist, indeed also for the sacraments, in case they were celebrated in connection with the Mass. The sacramental-books determined the structure of the Year of the Lord. A Ritual of a quite special type is the Pontifical, it first appeared in Metz in 950, a new form of church-book, which laid down the rubics for rites carried out by the Bishop. In the period following imitations for use in monasteries appeared, which were then taken over by the diocesan clergy and received various names, such as Sacerdotale, Agenda, Manuale, Pastorale or Obsequiale. Since it was an age in which copying was general all these books were more or less private in character. It was only when printing became possible that a wider circulation followed, and then as a result the unification of liturgical rites in the bishoprics.

On the 17th of June 1614 the Rituale Romanum appeared, the last of those liturgical books which had been decided upon in a decree issued during the last session of the Council of Trent on the 4th of December 1563. [22] The Rituale Romanum differs from the other liturgical books, which were brought out during the post-tridentine renewal period, in one essential point: Pope Paul the fifth's introductory letter declares the new ritual to be a uniform world-ritual, binding for all, but, and this is important, it is offered and recommended rather as a pattern or model ritual, one which does not annul any special diocesan traditions. In spite of ever-arising, repeated, tendencies to a worldwide unification of the sacramental rites there remained well into the 19th century a certain amount of freedom and choice. Then however (from Gregory XVI until the 1st Vatican Council) the Rituale Romanum became increasingly regarded as binding for the whole world, a ritual to which a diocesan bishop might only add an appendix when it was approved by Rome. Fischer sees in this development the restoration, which, "as a result of the writings of the Benedictine abbot, Prosper Guéranger, had led everywhere in France to a tempestuous casting out of local liturgical traditions, both those estimable as well those as less so, in favour of the Roman liturgical books. ... By the end of the century the thesis that the Rituale Romanum was obligatory and that only appendices

---

[21] Catechism 1127.
[22] In 1568 the Breviarium Romanum appeared, in 1570 the Missale Romanum, 1596 the Pontificale Romanum and in 1600 the Caeremoniale Episcoporum.

approved by Rome could be allowed had become sententia communis." [23] . In 1925 a revised Editio typica of the Rituale Romanum appeared, made necessary by the Codex Iuris Canonici of 1917. "The Codex and the new standard edition of the Rituale Romanum had for their part made necessary a revision of diocesan rituals, which as we have seen and in accordance with liturgical law were merely appendices to the Rituale Romanum. Hence the year 1925 marked the beginning of an intensive reform of rituals on a diocesan and also even on a national level." [24]. Not least thanks to the influence of the Liturgical Movement a unified ritual for the German dioceses came gradually into being, the "Collectio Rituum", which was published in 1950. This became a model for further two language rituals in other countries; its articles (stipulations) also influenced a renewal of the rites for the sacraments. [25]

In spite of all efforts of the Curia to forge a Roman centralism [26], the Second Vatican Council decided upon a "co-existence" between the Rituale Romanum and the particular diocesan rituals: "The competent ecclesiastical superior of each particular region should as soon as possible create special rituals which are suited to the needs of the individual areas, also as regards language; after approbation by the Apostolic See these should be used in the areas concerned" (SC 63b). Thus the new Rituale Romanum becomes a prototype. This means the bishops' conferences not only have the right, but also the duty to accomodate it according to the needs of their areas. The Rituale Romanum is therefore so conceived that it should be adapted, especially regarding the use of the mother tongue in a particular region. The original intention of leaving the Latin sacramental formulae as binding was opposed by the missonary bishops and the Council with overpowering majority agreed to their wish. Decisive was the effect of SC 59, according to which the sacraments not only presuppose faith, but also nourish and strengthen it, manifesting in word and material thing why they are also named "Sacraments of Faith". It would hardly have befitted this declaration if one had in the same breath proclaimed officially the exclusive use of Latin for the sacramental formulae, and then proceeded to forget these decisive words on sacraments nourishing the faith of the "recipient". [27] In 1969 the "Ordo baptismi parvulorum" was published, the first of the Roman prototype rituals, which laid and still lay the responsibility of adapting the rituals according to the different languages and cultures of a particular region on the local authorities. Meanwhile the publishing of the new liturgical books is almost concluded; in fact as regards many of them a second edition of the Editio typica has already been brought out. This shows that – unlike the situation after Trent – the liturgical reform has not ended, it is rather a task which must ever be taken up afresh.

The ritual of the Western Church corresponds to the Euchologion of the Byzantine rite for rites exercised by a priest. When a bishop is celebrant then the Archieratikon is used. The earliest manuscript of a Greek Euchologion stems from the 8th/9th century

---

[23]   Cf. Fischer, Rituale, 262f., 266f.

[24]   A. Heinz, Die Feier der Sakramente in der Sprache des Volkes 260f.

[25]   Cf. ibidem. 269f.

[26]   These endeavours were expressed in the "Codex rubricarum" published in 1960, in an Editio typica of the Brevriary 1961 and in the Roman Mass Book 1962, despite the fact that Pope John XXIII had on January the 25th promulgated the Council!

[27]   Fischer, Rituale 269

(Codex Barberinus graecus 336), the earliest church Slavonic manuscript from the 11th century (Euchologion sinaiticum). [28]

Bibliography

B. Fischer, Das Rituale Romanum (1614-1964). Die Schicksale eines liturgischen Buches, TThZ 73 (1964) 257-271.

A. Ganoczy, Einführung in die katholische Sakramentenlehre, Darmstadt 1979.

A. Heinz, Die Feier der Sakramente in der Sprache des Volkes. Zur Ritualereform vor dem Zweiten Vaticanum, TThZ 102 (1993) 258-270.

R. Hotz, Sakramente im Wechselspiel zwischen Ost und West, Zürich-Köln-Gütersloh 1979.

P. Jounel, Le Pontifical et le Rituel: Martimort III, Paris 1984, 11-20.

C. Kucharek, The Sacramental Mysteries. A byzantine approach, Allendale 1976.

H. Leclercq, Art. "Livres liturgiques": DACL IX, 1882-1891.

S. Marsili and others, La Liturgia: i Sacramenti. Anamnesis III/1, Torino 1986.

Th. Schneider, Zeichen der Nähe Gottes. Grundriß der Sakramententheologie, Mainz 6th edn. 1992.

Th. Schnitzler, Was die Sakramente bedeuten. Hilfen zu einer neuen Erfahrung, Freiburg-Basel-Vienna 1981.

4.2. THE SACRAMENTS OF INITIATION

4.2.1. THE MEANING OF INITIATION.

Specialists in the study of religions speak of "initiation", they mean the reception of a person by ritual into a community of believers or being raised to a higher order or category in the same community [29]. "Christian Initiation" means that a person is incorporated by baptism, confirmation and first communion into the mystical body of Christ, so that he may for the first time be present with others at the celebration of the Eucharist. A person can receive the grace which raises him to the divine only when he has been initiated into the mystical body. God acts directly on the soul; he lays the foundation for the synergy [30] between himself and man which leads to divinisation, man can now again receive uncreated grace [31]. All analogies for baptism as "being born" or "new creation" stem from this concept.

Initiation takes place in three stages: baptism, confirmation and the communion received at baptism. Baptism incorporates into the mystical body of Christ – and thus into the redemptive work of the Son – the soul can then receive the giver and fulfiller of all

---

[28]   Cf. N. Cappuyns, L'histoire des livres liturgiques grecs, Studi byzantini 6 (1940) 470-473; E.G. Pantelakis, Les livres ecclésiastiques de l'Orthodoxie. Étude historique, Irénikon 13 (1936) 521-557; A. Raes, Livres Liturgiques des Eglises Orientales: DDC VI (1957) 606-610; K. Onasch, Kunst und Liturgie der Ostkirche in Stichworten, unter Berücksichtigung der Alten Kirche, Vienna-Köln-Graz 1981, Art. "Euchologion" 109f.

[29]   Cf. M. Eliade, Birth and Rebirth. The Religious Meanings of Initiation in Humane Culture, New York 1958

[30]   The concept of "Synergy" is fundamental for the theology of the East, comp. Corbon, Liturgie aus dem Urquell 30, Anm. 3, 79-80, Anm. 1.

[31]   Cf. J. Meyendorff, Initiation á la théologie byzantine, Paris 1975, 181

holiness, the Holy Spirit, the divine life, proceeding from the Father. Confirmation then leads into the Spirit's redemptive work. And the Eucharist which is taken at baptism becomes the bond which links the believer with the holy mystery of the church. He receives as bearer of the royal priesthood his place at the eucharistic table. The sacraments of initiation are as "mystagogical sacraments" a combination of the whole economy of salvation and they lead us into its saving grace [32].

4.2.2. CHRISTIAN INITIATION IN THE EARLY CHURCH

In scripture there are accounts of spontaneous baptisms of those who have come to believe. (E.g. the baptism of the Ethiopian courtier in Acts 8:26-40). The legitimacy of child baptisms can be presumed from the "Oikos-formulae" of the New Testament, – for example, Acts 16:15 the purple seller, Lydia, was baptised with all in her "house" ("Oikos"), there is, nevertheless, no conclusive certainty about child baptism in New Testament times [33]. At the end of the 2nd century however traces of a catechumenate can be found. It is only in Hippolytus's "Apostolic Tradition" that we first receive a clearer insight into how the catechumenate and the final initiation ceremony were conducted.

The decision to lead a christian life must already have been taken before asking for baptism, since at the petition questions about one's position in life and the work carried out are put; quite a number of pursuits were considered incompatible with being a Christian. An early form of the idea of godparents can be perceived in TradAp. 15 [34]. The catechumenate lasted about three years, it could however be shortened (TradAp. 17). The catechumens did not pray together with the faithful, nor did they exchange the kiss of peace with them. At the agape they had a special place apart from the faithful and were wholly excluded from the Eucharist (TradAp. 18, 26-27). The immediate preparation for baptism began with hearing the testimony of witnesses and garantors. From now on those preparing were allowed to listen to the Gospel reading. A characteristic of the last phase of preparation was a series of daily exorcisms, the last of which was performed by the bishop himself. A day of fasting was held on the Friday before baptism, (Good Friday) and on Holy Saturday the bishop performed the last exorcism, the laying on of hands, then followed the breathing on the catechumen and the signing of forehead, ears and nose with the sign of the cross (TradAp. 20). The christening itself (TradAp. 21) began after the vigil "at cockcrow" with the prayer over the baptismal water. Then the bishop consecrated the oils needed for the anointing. The candidate for baptism spoke the rejection of Satan after which he was anointed with the oil of exorcism. His baptism then followed: A deacon stepped into the baptismal font with the candidate, the celebrant standing at the edge. The baptiser laid his hand on the candidate and questioned him in a three-part formula, reminiscent of the Apostolicum, about the faith. After each answer "I believe" the celebrant laid his hand on the candidate's head and immersed him in the baptismal water. Baptism took place in a special place, since after dressing the newly baptised betook themselves to the church, where the bishop laid hands on them and anointed them on the head with the "oil of thanksgiving". He

---

[32]   Cf. L. Laham, Pneumatologie der Sakramente der christlichen Mystagogie: E. C. Suttner (ed.): Taufe und Firmung. Zweites Regensburger Ökumenisches Symposium, Regensburg 1971, 69.

[33]   On this discussion and the doubts of the Church of the Reform about the legitimacy of child baptism comp. Kleinheyer, Eingliederung 33-35.

[34]   Cf TradAp. 15, ed. Geerlings 182.

made the sign of the cross on the foreheads of the newly baptised and gave them the kiss as sign of reception into the church. During the eucharist which followed baptism a chalice containing a mixture of milk und honey was offered as sign, that the baptised had reached the Promised Land. (Ex 3:8).

The "catechumenate as institution in the church of the Roman Empire had fallen into disuse long before the time when Ambrose was bishop in Milan".[35] While Ambrose was bishop at the end of the 4th century the admission to the catechumenate took place with a special rite, in which the candidate received the sign of the cross on his forehead. No account of rites during the catechumenate are extant for Milan, neither is there a set length of time.[36] The time when one was accepted as suitable began with the enrolling ("Nomendatio") at the beginning of Lent. A confession of sins is mentioned, which seems to have replaced the "examination of the candidate's way of life until then, an examination of which also took place, according to other records." The time of preparation was a time of instruction, but even more so a time of penance: The canditates fasted, except on Saturdays and Sundays, and led a life of heartfelt prayer. As well as that, scrutinies were held, i.e. examinations and exorcisms. On the Saturday before Easter the "Traditio Symboli" took place: the bishop preached, during the sermon the text of the creed was repeated several times. "The concluding part of the traditio symboli was the admonition not to write down the creed, rather to learn it by heart or to repeat it often, but not aloud, in order that it might not become known to catechumens or to heretics."[37] The candidates had some days time in order to become acquainted with the words of the creed, before they had to repeat it by heart during the "Redditio Symboli". According to Schmitz this was the last liturgical act of candidatship[38]. Neither a handing over nor repetion of the "Our Father" text, as was custom in Rome and elsewhere,[39] were known to Ambrose. The initiation took place only during the night before Easter; it began on Holy Saturday with the "Mystery of the Opening" – the Effata-Rite –, The bishop touched the ears and nose of those about to be christened, as the Lord had once done. (Mk 7:32-35).[40]. Then followed the blessing of the baptismal water, the fore-baptismal anointing for the struggle against evil, the renunciation of satan (Abrenuntiatio) when one faced towards the West, followed by a vow of fellowship with Christ, turned towards the East,[41] then the climax: Baptism itself. In the Ambrosian church the baptiser also put the three questions about belief in the Trinity, and after each "credo" the candidate was immersed in the water by the deacon standing beside him.[42] The passage through the baptismal font was a memorial reminding all

---

[35] So Schmitz in his introduction to "De Sacramentis" and "De Mysteriis", Freiburg-Basel-Vienna 1990 (FC 3) 16.

[36] Schmitz, loc. cit. 17, assumes, "that in Milan there was no special instruction for the candidate besides the introductory catechesis. When reading Ambrose we can understand that the catechumens were allowed to take part in the liturgy of the word at Mass, including listening to the sermon, and so heard the usual instruction for the faithful in matters of faith and morals."

[37] ibidem. 25.

[38] Cf. ibidem. 28

[39] Cf. J. A. Jungmann, Gewordene Liturgie. Studien und Durchblicke, Innsbruck-Leipzig 1941, 168f.

[40] According to Schmitz, loc. cit. 29, the Effata-rite is first mentioned by Ambrose; it is probable that he took it over.

[41] Facing East or West is a rite already known to Cyril of Jerusalem (Myst. Cat. 1, 2 – SChr 126bis, 84); the rite is part of the byzantine baptismal ritual even today.

[42] Comp. Schmitz, loc. cit., 34-39. Schmitz is convinced that baptism took place by immersion, against

of the passage of the Israelites through the Red Sea. The anointing after baptism was for Ambrose "an act with greatest effect, it fulfilled the act of baptism itself"[43]; it is however to be distinguished from the "sealing with the Holy Spirit". Before this took place there was a reading from the Gospel (John 13:4-14), a foot washing, which the Church father understands as a freeing from original sin, in the light of John 13:8, and the bestowal of the white baptismal garment. The sealing with the Holy Spirit is to be understood as "nothing less than sign of the cross on the forehead... There is no indication in the writings of Ambrose, neither expressly nor is it hinted at, that the signing with the cross was given with an anointing".[44] The baptismal eucharist was then given the newly baptised who received Communion at the Atlar.

The decline of the catechumenate and the fact that child baptism was becoming the more usual form had a deep-going effect on the rite of initiation. The elements of the catechumenal preparation and of the celebration of baptism itself grew together into a single rite, everything concentrated together. We must also call to mind that the separating of the other two initiation sacraments, confirmation and baptismal eucharist, at a later point and in other chronological order likewise effected the rite. As well as that, those rites which once took adult applicants for granted were now used for minors. The baptismal formula itself was also affected by the change over to child baptism as the norm: since as long as one might reckon with adults the three-fold confession of faith in the form of question and answer combined with the three-fold immersion could remain. With child baptism however the confession of faith became a recitation, the indicative baptismal formula, to use a grammar term.[45] Another point was that children were now being christened as soon as possible after birth, this became more and more frequent, so that the church's times for baptism lost importance. A ritual for child baptism was developed which hastened through the rites of the ancient initiation period in a kind of time-lapse photography; this ritual was in principle to remain until the liturgy reform of the Second Vatican Council.

4.2.3. CHILD BAPTISM: DEVELOPMENT AND PRESENT FORM.

In the Rituale Romanum of 1614 child baptism (II,2) was the rule. The question regarding the name of the child was not put, the rite began straight away with a "catechetical instruction" for the newly born. Then followed the exorcisms (with the breathing on the child) and the sign of the cross on forehead and breast. Salt was given after having been blessed. The placing of salt on the tongue was a rite stemming from North Africa which had once been taken into the Roman Ritual. The preserving quality of salt was to be sign that the catechumen's decision to receive baptism would be lasting.[46]. Another interpretation was Stenzel's understanding of salt as "sal sapientiae" – salt was given a guest at his reception before a meal. An allusion to the real food of life, the Eucharist, which was taken after Baptism.[47]

Kleinheyer, who by reason of archaeological findings, believes that although the candidate was standing in the water, he was christened by water being poured over him.

[43] Ibidem. 41
[44] Ibidem. 49f.
[45] Cf. Kleinmeyer, Eingliederung 119.
[46] Cf. Ebd. 109.
[47] Cf. Stenzel 171-175.

Further rites out of the catechumenal preparation were added, more exorcisms, the sign of the cross on the forehead, the traditio of the creed and of the Lord's prayer, the Effata-rite. Before baptism there were the renunciation of satan, the anointing with catechumen oil and the three questions on the faith. The symbolic rites remained the same: anointing with chrism, handing over of the baptismal garment and of the burning candle. The reform of the rite of baptism got rid of various elements, which in spite of venerable age were no longer understood by present day Christians, for example, the giving of salt, exorcism by breathing (Exsufflatio) and the use of saliva during the Effata-rite. "It is really time to stop considering the infant about to be christened as small grown-up, who in one short half-hour must undergo whole process from the Ordo ad catechumenum faciendum, through the electio, until he at last reaches the rites of Holy Saturday and the Easter Night. Instead of a 'parody' a fitting order for infant baptism has now emerged".[48]

The renewal of the baptismal rite is laid down in SC 67: "The rite for child baptism shall be revised and adapted to the actual situation of children; moreover the role of parents and godparents with their respective duties shall clearly come to the foreground". On Ascension Day 1969 the new Rituale for child baptism in the universal church appeared as prototype for rituals in local churches, the "Ordo Baptismi parvulorum".[49] According to SC 27 (Precedence of celebrations in community) the order of baptism for several children takes precedence before that of one child.

The structure of the new christening rite:

1. Greeting, words to the parents,

    Word to the godparents   (Church entrance area)

2. Service of the Word and catechumenal rites.   (Body of church)

    Reading (s) and homily

    Signing with cross

    Bidding prayers

    Calling on the saints (especially the patron saints)

    Prayer for befreeing from evil (Exorcism)

    Anointing with oil of catechumens.

3. Baptism   (Baptistry, or baptismal font)

    Prayer over the water/consecration of baptismal water

    Renunciation; confession of faith

    Baptism by three-fold immersion or three-fold pouring.

4. Symbolic rites:

    Anointing with chrism

    Clothing with baptismal garment

    Handing over of baptismal candle

---

[48] B. Fischer, Die Intentionen bei der Reform des Erwachsenen – und des Kindertaufritus, LJ 21 (1971) 65-75 (= Redemptionis mysterium 210-219). 66.

[49] Cf. Kaczynski 1774-1842.

Effata-rite

5. Conclusion of ceremony   (Altar)

Our Father

Blessing of parents and dismissal.

Instead of a meaningless conversation with the infant the parents and godparents are asked about the faith in which the child will be baptised. This gives the parents for the first time a constitutive part in the baptismal rite. In former times the child was christened as soon as possible after birth [50], the high death rate among infants made this a real necessity, but it also meant that the mother could not be present at her child's christening. Even the father was seldom present at the baptismal ceremony – this varied according to region; from the Age of Enlightenment onwards the congregation at a baptism was reduced "to an indispensable triad (threesome) of midwife, godfather and godmother". [51]

In the renewed rite the parents are given a far higher importance than the godparents, for that reason the Praenotanda place the date for the christening in the first weeks after birth. [52] In the dialogue at the beginning of the baptismal ceremony it is the parents who are asked about their decision to have their child christened; they testify to the faith into which the newborn will be baptised. In the initiation for adults the sponsors certainly play an important role, but in the baptism of children it is natural that the parents bear the main responsibility for the belief and growth in faith of their children. [53]

The service of the word is a "renovation", a winning back of something which was formerly an integral part. [54] After the reading from Scripture and homily in the body of the church there follow the bidding prayers and a litany of invocations of saints. This leads over to the catechumenal rite of the exorcism (no longer a forswearing of the devil, but a humble prayer begging freedom from the power of evil) and to catechumenal anointing. (According to the decision of the bishops' conferences this may be facultative). After proceeding to the baptistry or to the font [55], the essential parts of the sacrament begin with the hymn of praise over the water and the blessing of the baptismal water (outside Eastertide). In accordance with SC 67 the parents stand in the middle, in front of the godparents, also during the renunciation of satan and the confession of faith.

The Rituale Romanum (II,2,20) also knew of a baptism by immersion besides the long customary threefold pouring of water. Baptism by threefold immersion is named in our present Rituale first, that is, even before Baptism by pouring water; Fischer sees this as a winning back again of something which a former misunderstanding of rites had long forgotten (SC 50) [56]. Immersion in water certainly corresponds more clearly to burial with Christ in Baptism (Rom 6:3ff.) than baptism by pouring. Nevertheless

---

[50] Cf. The stipulation of Can. 770/CIC 1917, which determined the time of baptism "quam primum".

[51] Cf. A. Heinz, Eine neue Chance für das Taufbrauchtum: M. Klöckener / W. Glade (eds.), Die Feier der Sakramente in der Gemeinde, 169-178, here 171.

[52] Praenotanda 8, 3 – Kaczynski 1819.

[53] Cf. Praenotanda generalia 8 – 10 – Kaczynski 1784-1786.

[54] Kleinheyer, Engliederung 177, points to the service of readings during Easter Night as model.

[55] If no change of place can follow, then the parents come forward with the child, while all others stay in their places.

[56] Cf. Fischer, Intentionen 72f.

the ancient church also recognized baptism by pouring of water (Infusio) or sprinkling (Aspersio) as a special case for the sick ("Hospital baptism").

Probably the oldest witness for baptism by immersion is the Didache, which also takes it for granted that immersion in "living water" is the usual form of baptism: "If you have no living water, baptize in other water; if you cannot baptize in cold water, then in warm! If you have neither then pour water thrice over the head in the name of the Father and the Son and the Holy Spirit!" [57] Stenzel is of the opinion that both immersion and infusion were practised. He bases his opinion on archeological findings which show a lack of depth in baptismal "pools" ("piscinae"), making a total immersion of an adult impossible. Pictorial representations which reflect baptismal procedures of the time strengthen his opinion: "The person being baptized stands in water which reaches only half way up his body and water is poured from above. If the flow of water is sufficient then he is wholly covered at least for an instant with water and so 'buried', 'immersed' as the Fathers say." [58]

Baptism by immersion was practised with children (up to the child's head) well into the late Middle Ages; from the turn of the 15th to the 16th centuries rituals show that more and more often a change over to pouring of water was taking place. [59] Much as we might like to have baptism by immersion again allowed, total immersion in water, even if it is as symbol clearer, is hardly suitable to achieve our end. A combination of immersion and pouring might however find a positive resonance, that is, a baptism in "living water" with the whole body covered in a stream of water.

The symbolic rites, that is, anointing with chrism, the handing over of the white garment, giving of the burning candle (which the father lights from the Easter Candle) and the Effata rite, taken over from catechumenal liturgy, all these have been retained. At the conclusion of the ceremony there is again a change of place: all taking part proceed to the altar and say the Lord's Prayer. In the solemn concluding blessing the newly baptized's parents are especially mentioned.

4.2.4. THE PRESENT DAY RITE FOR THE RECEPTION OF ADULTS INTO THE CHURCH [60]

A. The Initiation Ceremony for Adults

One of the most valuable achievements of the liturgical renewal has been the bringing back of the rite of initiation of adults, as was once the usage in the ancient church. It is true that the Rituale Romanum of 1614 recognized besides a rite of baptism of children (II,2) a rite of initiation for adults in the form of a celebration of all three initiation sacraments together (II,4), this remained however mostly theory [61]. Because

---

[57] Didache 7, 2-3 – ed. G. Schöllgen Freiburg-Basel-Vienna etc. 1991 (FC 1), 118f.
[58] Cf. Stenzel 108 – 110.
[59] Cf. ibidem. 278f.
[60] Cf. In this connection: B. Fischer, Das amerikanische Beispiel. Die Rezeption des Ritus der Erwachseneninitiation von 1972 in den Vereinigten Staaten, LJ 37 (1987) 68 – 74 (= Redemptionis mysterium 241 – 246). B. Fischer, Zur endgültigen Gestalt des Ritus der Erwachseneninitiation in den USA ab 1. 9. 1988, LJ 38 (1988) 223 – 230 (= Redemptionis mysterium 258 – 265).
[61] Cf. Kleinheyer, Eingliederung 246.

of the experience of the church in mission countries[62] the reformers of the liturgy re-introduced an initiation rite for adults with a catechumenate in different stages.[63]

In 1972 there appeared the "Ordo Initiationis Christianae Adultorum" (short form: OICA)[64] as basis or model for the different vernacular rituals.[65] The rite of adult initiation has been given the following form:

a. The reception: this is the beginning of the catechumenate. The reception takes for granted that a basic introduction to the christian faith has been given; the candidate's reasons will also be examined, and under certain circumstances emended (OICA 68 and 69). After presentation of the candidate and the expression of his wish to receive baptism he makes a confession of faith. This is in the form of questions put by the celebrant, the candidate confirms his belief in the form of an answer. It is now that the sponsors, or guarantors, first appear; they must accompany and encourage the candidates during the time of preparation, and are now asked about their readiness "to help our candidates to find Christ and follow him" (OICA 77). An exorcism is now offered, the candidate is free to accept or refuse, and, when it is meaningful, there is a renunciation of heathen rites. The sign of the cross is then made by the celebrant on the candidate's forehead, and if wished for, on the ears, eyes, mouth, breast and the shoulders. The sponsors and catechumens may also take part in this rite, it is the celebrant however who says the accompanying words. In order to make the ceremony more impressive for the candidate a cross can now be presented to him (OICA 83 – 85). If the opening part of the ceremony has taken place at the church door, or in another part of the building, all now enter the church itself for the service of the word, in order to hear the Lord's Word. After the readings and the homily the celebrant solemnly presents the candidates a Gospel-Book (OICA 93). Before the eucharistic service begins the candidates, in accordance with the custom of the ancient church, are asked to leave the gathering (that is, before the preparation of the offerings).

b. The elementary preparation, which can last several years, is liturgically characterized by "lesser exorcisms", these are performed either at the beginning or end of a catechetical instruction by laying on of hands. If the bishops allows it, a lay catechist can also perform this ceremony (OICA 109 -110). Evidence of this is given by Hippolytus: "After the prayer the teacher lays hands on the cathecumens, prays and dismisses them. This should always be done, no matter whether the teacher is cleric or layman"[66]. If

---

[62] Of all the other Council Documents it was especially Art. 14 of the Mission Decree "Ad gentes" which spoke out in favour of the rite of adult baptism, and also made recommendations for the liturgical celebration, so that Kleinheyer, Eingliederung 251, names this article the "Magna Charta" of the catechumenate. For the relationship between AG 14 and SC 64 and 66 see B. Fischer, Die Fortschreibung der Liturgiekonstitution in den nachfolgenden Konzilsdokumenten, LJ 36 (1986) 211 – 221, here espec. 217f.

[63] Cf. SC 64; SC 66 demands the working out of a Mass formula ' Baptism taking place during Mass'; this can be taken as an indication on how all initiation sacraments are to be celebrated at the end of the catechumenate.

[64] Cf. Kaczynski 2639 – 2800.

[65] For example there appeared in 1975 as a study edition for German speaking areas "Die Feier der Eingliederung Erwachsener in die Kirche", later editions appeared in 1986 and 1991 now brought into accordance with the new Codex of 1983. There appeared likewise in 1986 as an independent appendix the ritual: "Die Eingliederung von Kindern im Schulalter in die Kirche", a version of chapter 5 of the "Ordo Initiationis Christianae adultorum", which had been revised on the basis of pastoral experience.

[66] Hippolytus TrAp 19, ed. Geerlings, 253.

there are good grounds (shortness of time available, the candidate's maturity) the rites belonging to the latter part of the preparation may be brought forward, for example, the rites of presentation and the anointing with catechumen oil.

c. The last part of the preparation begins with the "Enrolment ceremony". "In this ceremony the sponsors and the catechists give testimony about the candidates, while the latter confirm their wish to be baptized. The celebrant acting in the name of the church ascertains the degree of their preparation and decides whether they may receive the Easter sacraments" (OICA 133). The heart of the ceremony is the enrolment: After the testimony of the sponsors (guarantors) and the candidates' declaration of readiness their names are "given". This can be done by merely saying their names, or by actually writing the names in a register. The catechumens thus become "Chosen Ones" (Electi), who will receive the initiation sacraments during the Easter Night to come. The sponsor are now called upon again; above all in the latter phase of the preparations it will be their task to uphold and strengthen the candidates on their way. Generally speaking this will correspond with the penitential time before Easter (OICA 152), so that the enrolment ceremony should if possible take place during Mass on the first Sunday of Lent (OICA 140).

d. The last phase of preparation as a time of purification and enlightenment has a liturgical structure of its own. The penitential acts have their place in the Masses on the third, fourth and fifth Sundays of Lent, in this respect the readings of Year A are meaningful (OICA159). After the homily the candidates come forward with godfather and godmother and stand before the celebrant. The congregation prays in silence for the candidates, then follow the bidding prayers, and a prayer for freedom from all evil, the celebrant laying his hands on each candidate in silence. The Celebration of the Eucharist begins only after the candidates have been asked to leave. In the week after the first penitential act, that is in the third week of Lent the solemn giving of the articles of the creed takes place: the celebrant together with the whole congregation recite the creed, the candidate must impress it on his memory, so that he is able to repeat it on Holy Saturday. Through baptism one becomes a child of God. Hence there is also a solemn giving of the Our Father: this takes place in the fifth week of Lent, and means the newly baptized will now be allowed to recite the Our Father with the congregation when they assist at all the Mass and before they receive the Eucharist for the first time.

e. Finally on Holy Saturday the "celebration of the immediate preparation" can be held. In it the candidates must show that they know the creed and do so by reciting it; this is the repetition of the articles of faith which they had been given some weeks before. Then follows the Effata-Rite; candidates may also choose a new name, if they feel the name they bear does not befit a Christian. The candidates are now anointed with the oil of catechumens: "This may be performed separately or together with the repetition of the creed, either just before it or afterwards as a strengthening symbol" (OICA 206).

f. The "Celebration of being taken into the Church" as the climax and conclusion of the catechumenate should in principle take place during the night before Easter; "the sacraments are performed after the consecration of the baptismal water, as the rite of Baptism during the Easter vigil provides for" (OICA 208). After the candidate has renounced satan and has said the Creed aloud he is baptized, then follow the giving of the baptismal garment and the burning candle, symbols eloquent and profound. If confimation is conferred straight after baptism then the anointing with chrism is omitted. The newly baptized will be mentioned by name during the Canon of the Mass and will take communion under both species, as also do the godparents, the catechists and members of the family.

g. Eastertide is for the new Christians "the time of reflection and deepening" (Mystagogy): "during it they have a special place among the faithful at Sunday Mass. They should endeavour to participate with their godparents at the Masses. The conclusion of a more intensive introduction at the end of Easter time, that is about Whitsunday, should be celebrated in a special manner" (OICA 236-237). "On the anniversary of their christening it is desirable that the new Christians come together again, in order to thank God, to talk about spiritual experiences and to gather fresh strength" (OICA 238).

B. The Christening of Children of School Age
In the fifth chapter of the "Ordo Initiationis Christianae Adultorum" there is a special initiation procedure for children who are capable of understanding catechetical instruction: "Ordo Initiationis puerorum qui aetatem catecheticam adepti sunt". An adapted version of this fifth chapter designed to help in gaining pastoral experience was published in 1986 for German speaking regions. It appeared first as independent appendix for study purposes with the title "Die Eingliederung von Kindern im Schulalter in die Kirche" (Children of school age becoming members of the Church).[67] The preparation for and celebration of baptism were adapted to suit the very different standards and ages of the children. Keeping such in mind the rites were arranged in analogy with the baptismal rites for adults: Solemn reception into the catechumenate, permission to receive baptism and finally the celebration of baptism itself. There were several distinct stages: initiation before the child begins school; initiation at first communion age; and initiation for those between the ages of 10 and 14. The principle was made however that all three initiation sacraments should be performed in one ceremony.

C. An Attempt at a theological assessment.
Kavanagh describes the Rite of Initiation for Adults as the "most essential and also the clearest result of the Roman reforms".[68] Five years before this Fischer had thought himself obliged to defend the proposed initiation rite against the objection that it was an article taken out of a museum and polished up.[69] According Kavanagh however it is just the return to the practice of the early Church which makes the baptismal rite for adults the "maturest document of the liturgy reform of the 2nd Vatican Council". The rite represents an important model both for future theological reflection as well as for future pastoral work in liturgy[70], indeed even beyond the area of the initiation sacraments.[71] Kavanagh believes that among other things the problematic splitting asunder of baptism as infant and confirmation as youth is now clearly seen in the light of the newly won rite of adult baptism as a mistaken development.[72]

---

[67] Einsiedeln-Zürich-Freiburg-Vienna 1986.
[68] A. Kavanagh, Christliche Initiation in der nachkonziliaren katholischen Kirche, LJ 28 (1978) 1-10. 1.
[69] Cf. B. Fischer, Österliche Eingliederung, Gd 7 (1973) 65 – 67. 66.
[70] Cf. Kavanagh, Christliche Initiation 8
[71] Cf. ibidem. 5f.: "The new order breaks the shackles of conventional forms of church life."
[72] Cf. ibidem. 4.

4.2.5. CONFIRMATION IN THE PAST AND PRESENT: INJUDICIOUS ADOPTION OF AN OLD TRADITION?

A. Confirmation misunderstood.

The two sacraments Baptism and Confirmation form a unity and belong together. They were given at the same ceremony in the ancient church and this is still so in the Eastern churches. The reason for their being separated can be found in the thoughtless adoption of a custom in the city of Rome. Confirmation has become separated, and the throwing overboard of the former unity of the initiation sacraments (baptism-confirmation-eucharist), from an ecumenical standpoint a most regretable development, could only happen because of the pious, not to say thoughtless, adoption of a special Roman custom in regions outside the city where distances were far greater. The tradition which Hippolytus has handed on to us was quite impossible in these areas. [73] Confirming was strictly reserved to the (auxiliary-) bishop, baptism on the other hand was given by the priest. The time between baptism and confirmation became ever greater according to the size of the diocese. It took the bishop sometimes even weeks before he could simply reach the parish and confirm the newly baptized. The older tradition had therefore to be dropped and the new usuage given a theological support.

A Whitsunday sermon preached by the southern Gallic and Semipelagian bishop Faustus of Riez [74] bears witness to this new interpretation of confirmation, now customary in the West: The baptized person "is like a soldier who has enlisted, but who has not yet been given his weapons. In baptism the Holy Spirit grants the grace of innocence, but in confirmation an increase of grace, the spiritual weapons for moral struggle. Until the present day no basis for such a theology has been found in the New Testament, there is nothing either in the liturgical texts for confirmation, and only few elements in the theology of the Fathers, who do not stress this aspect as Faustus does." [75] Thomas himself holds confirmation to be a useful sacrament for strengthening, but as an element of christian initiation, not so meaningful for salvation. [76]

The change of meaning was continued as confirmation came to be seen as a sacrament of decision; for this reason efforts were made to put the age for confirmation at end of school time and to make a thorough-going catechetical preparation part of admission to the sacrament. "So without any foundation in tradition confirmation came to be understood as a kind of liturgical 'coming of age for a young Christian' ". [77] This concept often corresponds today to a hankering after a transition from a popular, or "traditional" church to a church of decision, in which membership follows upon a definite decision. [78] Thus confirmation is interpreted as the sacrament of decision: of the decision to ratify one's baptism, of commitment to the church and to parish, of life according to chris-

---

[73]   Cf. A. Heinz, Die Firmung nach römischer Tradition. Etappen in der Geschichte eines abendländischen Sonderwegs, LJ 39 (1989) 67 – 88. 71f.

[74]   Regarding this homily (based on anonymous tradition) of Faustus see: L. A. van Buchem, L'Homélie pseudoeusébiene de Pentecôte. L'origine de la confirmation en Gaule méridionale et l'interprétation de ce rite par Fauste de Riez, Nijmegen 1967.

[75]   Lengeling, Firmalter und Firmspendung 110.

[76]   Cf. S. Th. III, 65, 4; III, 72, 1-3.

[77]   Heinz, Die Firmung nach röm. Tradition 85.

[78]   Cf. A. Jilek, Die Diskussion um das rechte Firmalter. Eine Übersicht über die deutschprachige Literatur der letzten Jahrzehnte, LJ 24 (1974) 31-51. 40-44.

tian ideals and way of thinking. [79] This view of confirmation as "decision sacrament" [80], means we understand life as a spiritual combat in which we freely accept the gifts of the Spirit as help, well and good, but it is a falsification of the sacrament and it stems from Faustus: The last decades have been confronted with a series of "confirmation theologies" all of which are based on Faustus and other likewise unreliable elements. They understand confirmation in a one-sided manner: Sacrament of psychical maturity, of responsibility, of the apostolate, of Catholic Action, of membership of the universal Church and like theories;" [81] Kleinheyer is in full agreement. [82] One result of confirmation at a later age is according to Richter a considerable number of "half-initiated". [83]

B. The Eastern Church's Theology and Practice of Confirmation as a Corrective Element.

"To take over the eastern ritual unity of initiation seems to me the theologically ideal solution: Who is being baptized, will at the same time also be confirmed, independent of age!" [84] Lengeling speaks of a "desirable taking over of the logical practice of the Eastern church." [85] The retention of unity of the three initiation sacraments in the Christian east is more than faithful adherence to the tradition of the ancient church, it shows an understanding of initiation, well grounded in the economy of salvation, which sheds a very critical light on the theology and practice of confirmation in the West. [86] Only that person who has been fully initiated through baptism, confirmation and baptismal communion can share in redemption, which is a complementary working of the Son and the Spirit as the hands of the Father, an insight which Symeon of Thessaloniki [87] takes over from Irenaeus [88]. To break up the unity of the initiation sacraments means therefore nothing less than to underestimate and disregard the (trinitarian saving-) order of redemption.

The theology of the modern Eastern church teaches likewise, for example, B. Meyendorff [89], and Zizioulas, who stresses the bond between baptism and confirmation as expression of that between Christology and Pneumatology. This bond had in the east Syrian area the effect of recognizing the *pre*-baptismal anointing as an imparting of the Holy Spirit. Something which was later accepted uniformly in all the church ("groß-kirchlich") [90]. The awareness of the complementary unity of Pneumatology and

---

[79] Cf. M. Kunzler, Die Firmung – Sakrament der Entscheidung? Klerusblatt 70 (1990) 273-276.

[80] Cf. Apart from Jilek, Die Diskussion um das rechte Firmalter, P. Nordhues, Das Sakrament der Firmung und die mündige Gemeinde, Diakonia 4 1973

[81] E. J. Lengeling, Firmalter und Firmspender, Gd 5 (1971) 108-110. 108.

[82] See his letter in: Pastoralblatt 26 (1974) 346-350.

[83] K. Richter, Fragen um die Firmung. Die gegenwärtige Praxis und ihre Kritik, BiLi 48 (1975) 159-172. 165.

[84] K. Richter, Firmung zwischen Taufe und Eucharistie, Diakonia 4 (1973) 52-53. 53.

[85] E. J. Lengeling, Die Einheit der dreigestuften Initiation, Diakonia 4 (1973) 46-49. 48.

[86] Cf. M. Kunzler, Ist die Praxis der Spätfirmung ein Irrweg? Anmerkungen zum Firmsakrament aus ostkirchlicher Sicht, LJ 40 (1990) 90-108.

[87] Cf. PG 155, 344 A

[88] Adv. Haereses IV, 20, 1 – SChr 100, 626f.

[89] Cf. J. Meyendorff, Initiation á la théologie byzantine, Paris 1975, 255-258.

[90] Cf. Kleinheyer, Eingliederung 91-95.

Christology as the twofold access to the mystery of Redemption must be just as much stressed as the unity of the initiation sacraments of baptism and confirmation.[91]

C. The renewed Rite of Confirmation

On the 22nd of August 1971 the revised rite for confirmation com-missioned by the 2nd Vatican Council[92] appeared as an appendix to the Roman Pontifical[93]. The rite has the following form:

1. Presentation of those to be confirmed and the celebrant's homily.
2. Renunciation of satan and confession of baptismal faith.
3. The congregation is asked to pray in silence.
4. The celebrant's prayer for God's Spirit and his stretching out of hands over those to be confirmed.
5. Anointing on the forehead.
6. Bidding Prayers, continuation of the service.

Those to be confirmed are presented to the bishop – according to c. 882/CIC 1983 "minister ordinarius" of confirmation. After that the homily and the confession of baptismal faith of those being confirmed. The heart of the ceremony is a prayer of the celebrant, during which he stretches out his hands over the candidates and begs God for the seven gifts of the Holy Spirit.[94] The relationship between the laying on of hands and the anointing with chrism has still to be clarified. Since the 18th century editions of the Pontificale Romanum have appeared which designate a combination of laying on of hands (with four fingers of the right hand) together with an anointing of the forehead. In the Ordo Confirmationis 9 confirmation is given "per unctionem chrismatis in fronte, quae fit manus impositione, atque per verba: Accipe signaculum Doni Spiritus Sancti."[95] According to Kleinheyer the laying on of hands is represented ("repräsentiert") by the anointing with chrism: "The laying on of hands has been taken into the chrism-anointing, is blended into it. One can understand the misgivings of the authors. In view of tradition and the practice of the Ecumene the laying on of hands is still crucial, even of central importance. Moreover there appears to be an insoluble conflict between the statement that the laying on of hands is performed in the chrism-anointing and the fact that the stretching out of hands (referring to the biblical gesture) has certainly been kept and is characterized as being of great importance for the integrity of the rite."[96]

---

[91] Cf. J. D. Zizioulas, Being as Communion. Studies in Personhood and the Church. Crestwood-New York 1985 (Contemporary Greek Theologians 4), 128.

[92] SC 71 demanded that the renewed rite for confirmation 'should show more clearly the deep connection of this sacrament with the whole process of christian initiation'; for this reason a renewal of the baptismal promises should be made before confirmation. Confirmation should be celebrated within Mass, otherwise during a Service of the Word.

[93] Kaczynski 2602-2621.

[94] Concerning this stretching out of hands, or laying on of hands, see Kleinheyer, Eingliederung 227f.

[95] Kaczynski 2611. The impositio manuum quae fit super confirmandos is distinquished from that performed with the celebrant's prayer just before. We are told that it is not necessary for the validity of the sacrament, but that it has great importance for the integrity of the rite. There has been a lively discussion among theologians on the meaning of the relative clause 'quae fit manus impositione', see, for example, H. Auf der Maur, Unctio quae fit manus impositione: H. Auf der Maur / B. Kleinheyer (eds.), Zeichen des Glaubens. Studien zu Taufe und Firmung (FS Fischer), Einsiedeln – Freiburg u. a. 1972.

[96] Kleinheyer, Eingliederung 228f.

The former confirmation formula "Signo te signo crucis et confirmo te chrismate salutis in nomine Patris… " has been replaced by the words: "Sphragís doreás pneúmatos hagíou – N., accipe signaculum Doni Spiritus Sancti". This is the formula used to the present day in the Byzantine rite and first witnessed towards the end of the 4th century. The new formula makes it clear 'that God's redeeming work achieves it completion, is made perfect, here in the sacramental action of the Church – and that this is its sign; the formula will therefore say: God has given thee his Holy Spirit in the redemptive signs of baptism and confirmation.[97] The alapa, the stroke on the cheek after anointing with chrism, has been dropped. Durandus suggests among possible meanings for the stroke on the cheek the function of reminder, of memento. The person confirmed should impress firmly on his memory that he has received the sacrament. This stroke was a custom taken over from germanic legal symbolism. Further symbolic interpretations of the stroke were influenced by the idea of knighthood, a knight was touched on his shoulder with a sword. This brought in the meaning, quite foreign to the whole initiation ceremony, that confirmation was to give strength and courage for service in the army of the Lord. Some authors are of the opinion that Durandus himself introduced the alapa into the rite of confirmation.[98] In spite of the progress achieved by the renewed confirmation rite the fundamental questions concerning the form of confirmation as part of christian initiation, which are essentially dependant on the questions what age the candidate should be and who should be the celebrant, have not yet been solved.

4.2.6. FROM BAPTISMAL COMMUNION TO FIRST COMMUNION: THE EUCHARIST AS PART OF THE INITIATION RITE

All those who have been baptized and confirmed are called upon to take an active part in the divination of the world through partaking in the celebration of the Eucharist. Zizioulas says expressly that they are "ordained" for this: The newly baptized do not simply become Christians, rather they are "ordained" into the eucharistic community. As soon however as this "ordination character" of the initiation is overlooked, then the way is free for the identification of "layfolk" as the "not ordained" and thus for clericalism; and then as a reaction against clericalism for the complete rejection of any special vocation to consecrate. Zizioulas expressly connects the "ordo-character" of the initiation sacraments with the communion at baptism.[99] The "ordination" to the royal priesthood of all Christians is perfected in the communion at baptism, during which the new Christian is shown to his rightful place and rank at the eucharistic table of the community as God's family. The Christian through his baptism and confirmation now has the right to receive the eucharist; his allocation to a place at the altar is the consequent perfection of his initiation, while at the same time in celebrating with the eucharist with others he is entrusted with the task of making this world more godlike.

---

97 Ibidem. 230.
98 See: A. Adam, Firmung und Seelsorge. Pastoraltheologische und religionspädagogische Untersuchungen zum Sakrament der Firmung, Düsseldorf 1959, 218-236; Kleinheyer, Eingliederung 207f.
99 Cf. J. D. Zizioulas, Priesteramt und Priesterweihe im Licht der östlich-orthodoxen Theologie: H. Vorgrimmler (ed.): Der priesterliche Dienst V: Amt und Ordination in ökumenischer Sicht, Freiburg-Basel-Vienna 1973 (QD 50), 72-113. 80.

It was only in the second millenium that communion for children at baptism was fully lost to the Western Church,[100] in the East the practice differed greatly according to region. By the time of the Pontificale of Durandus the unity of baptism and communion is no longer mentioned. Moreover the fact that confirmation had been separated from the initiation ceremony had led to a breaking up of the classical sequence: baptism – confirmation – eucharist, a sequence which is of importance for the ecumenical dialogue with the Eastern Churches. In the 12th century children were given communion at baptism under the form of wine; in the 13th the practice was given up completely. The 4th Lateran Council (1215) made the yearly Easter communion obligatory for all "postquam ad annos discretionis pervenerit". "Indirectly this meant that there was no such obligation for infants and small children. Stipulations which both before and after 1200 forbid communion for infants at baptism are, like the the decree of the Lateran, an expression of a change in the theological stand-point. Furthermore in the 13th century the age of confirmation was ever more often advanced, thus since confirmation was not given before the age of discretion, and since on the other hand nobody was allowed to receive the eucharist who had not been confirmed, then the question of baptismal communion for those under the age of reason had already been shelved."[101] The communion at baptism was changed to first communion, which was finally put at 13 or 14 years of age. Set forms of a catechetical instruction came only during the 17th and 18th centuries, under the influence of Jesuits. As a result of preparation common for all children the Sunday after Easter was then decided upon as the day for solemn first communion. Only later was the age for first communion again put back to a child's 7th year, this was under Pope Pius X.[102] In spite of the lowering of the age, and in spite of many a reference to baptism in the preparation for and celebration of first communion (For example: renewal of the renunciation of satan and of the confession of faith, white dresses, first communion candle, among others) people no longer look upon first communion and confirmation as an integral part of christian initiation, nor are the two sacraments understood or experienced as "ordination" in the meaning which Zizioulas has suggested. In this context – and also for confirmation – a correction might be achieved only by bringing back the complete initiation ceremony as when adults are being received into the Church.

4.2.7. INITIATION AMONG BYZANTINE CHRISTIANS

It also holds true for the Byzantine Church that rites really belonging to the catechumenal preparation for adult baptismal candidates have evolved into a single church ceremony now used for the christening of newly born and small children. To this day the candidate is spoken to as an adult, and the role of godparent is just as important as in the baptismal ceremony of the Roman rite before the reform.

---

[100] Cf. Stenzel, 279-282: Communion at baptism was the general practice until the 12th cent. After that wine from the ablutions was given.

[101] Kleinheyer, Eingliederung 243. See also Meyer, Eucharistie 561-565.

[102] The Decree "Quam singulari" of the Congregation for Sacraments from 8th Aug. 1910 (AAS 2 (1910) 577-583) brought according to Meyer, Eucharistie 563, a clarification of the long disputed question on the age for first communion, but regarded communion not as an integral part of the celebration of the Eucharist, but as an instrument used in pastoral care. Concerning the whole question see: P. Hellbernd, Die Erstkommunion der Kinder in Geschichte und Gegenwart, Vechta 1954.

The four exorcisms ("Aphorkismoi") call to mind those of the catechumenate, the first part of the baptismal ceremony is at the same time the conclusion of the catechumenate. Then follows the renunciation of satan, spoken towards the West and accompanied by a symbolic act of spitting; the wish to follow Christ is spoken towards the East, then there is the confession of faith which is repeated three times by the candidate and reminds us of the Redditio Symboli. [103] Even in our times the Euchologien set an unmistakable caesura at the beginning of the essential parts of baptism. [104] A special, new heading as well as the opening by the deacon's ektenie make clear that this is the beginning of a new part. Then come the blessings of the baptismal water and of the oil of catechumens, some of which is poured into the water by the priest. The candidate is then anointed "with the oil of joy", the ears are anointed ("so that faith may be heard") and this reminds us Romans of the Effata rite. The candidate is then baptized with a threefold immersion and the speaking of the passive form of the baptismal formula; the clothing follows. [105] Imperceptibly, and suddenly, the Euchologion changes the chapter heading within the initiation ritual, we see that the title "Akolouthía tou Chrísmatos" is placed before the texts and rites of confirmation, whereas the concluding rites appear again under "Baptism". [106] After an introductory prayer "the priest anoints the baptized person with the holy myron (chrism), making the sign of the cross on forehead, eyes, nostrils, mouth, both ears, breast, hands and feet, saying at each anointing: The sealing of the gifts of the Holy Spirit. Amen". [107] After the anointing there is a dance-like movement around the baptismal font, repeated three times, (movements of this kind are also found in the wedding and ordination liturgies), a reading (Rom 6: 3b-12), alleluja, Gospel (Mt 28:16-20) as well as the deaconal ektenie. [108] "Normally speaking the baptized infant is now given communion (Initiatio christiana)." [109] According to the liturgical books the ritual washing away of the oils and the cutting of hair follow on the eighth day, in practice however this takes place immediately in the same service.

Bibliography

A. Adam, Erwägungen zum Patenamt bei Taufe und Firmung: H. Auf der Maur / B. Kleinheyer (eds.), Zeichen des Glaubens. Studien zu Taufe und Firmung (FS Fischer), Freiburg-Basel-Vienna 1972, 415- 428.

R. Cabié, L'initiation chrétienne: Martimort III, Paris 1984, 21-114.

B. Fischer, Redemptionis Mysterium. Studien zur Osterfeier und zur christlichen Initiation, ed. by A. Gerhards and A. Heinz, Paderborn-München-Vienna-Zürich 1992.

P. M. Gy, Histoire liturgique du sacrement de confirmation, MD 58 (1959) 135-145.

---

[103] Cf. Heitz III, 21-38.

[104] Cf. ibidem 39, Hagiasmatarion, Rome 1954, 25: The heading before this break is: "Táxis ginoméne pro tou hagíou baptismatos", after that: "Akolouthía tou hagíou baptismatos".

[105] Cf: Heitz III, 39-47. For the history of the different development of the baptismal formula in East and West see: Trembelas 104.

[106] Cf. Hagiasmatarion 34-39. Heitz III, 49, makes a full caesura: "Order of the mystery of the holy anointing with myron or of the sacrament of confirmation".

[107] Heitz III, 50.

[108] According to Kucharek, Mysteries 151f. this service of the word calls to mind the Eucharistic service in which the newly baptized took Communion for the first time.

[109] Heitz III, 52. The rubric is missing in the Roman Hagiasmatarion of 1954. Concerning baptismal communion see: K. Kallinikos, Ho christianikós naós kai ta teloúmena en autô, Athens 3th edn. 1969, 400.

A. Kavanagh, The shape of baptism. The rite of Christian initiation, New York 1978.

B. Kleinheyer, Die Feiern der Eingliederung in die Kirche: GdK 7,1, Regensburg 1989.

M. Probst / H. Plock / K. Richter (Hgg.), Katechumenat heute. Werkbuch zur Eingliederung von Kindern und Erwachsenen in die Kirche, Einsiedeln-Zürich-Freiburg-Vienna 1976.

M. Righetti, Manuale di storia liturgica IV: I sacramenti, i sacramentali, Milano 1953, 1-87: Il Battesimo – 88-104: La Confermazione.

A. Stenzel, Die Taufe. Eine genetische Erklärung der Taufliturgie, Innsbruck 1958.

4.3. THE EUCHARIST AS SACRAMENT OUTSIDE OF MASS.

The "static" and not the "dynamic" eucharistic presence of Christ is in the foreground here. The presence of the Lord is 'dynamic' in the congregation which is celebrating the eucharist; he is present where two or three are gathered together in his name (Mt 18, 20); he is present in the Word which is being preached, in the celebrant who is presiding and finally in the consecrated species, through which he gives himself to his own, in order that they may through him share in the life of God (SC 7). The faithful become part of his sacrifice, enter into the all-embracing Anaphora of the world to the Father and participate in the mysteries of redemption being consumated at the altar. The presence of Christ in the eucharistic species however is according to Catholic (and Orthodox) belief is not bound to the time during which the liturgy is being celebrated.[110] It does not end when the liturgy is over, the presence remains on in a 'static' manner, so to say, even after the Mass: Christ offers us his Body and Blood under the signs of bread and wine as a healing remedy to strengthen and nourish our souls on the way to everlasting life, he is always present even when the eucharist itself is not being celebrated. The nourishment is there to be partaken of, and when we honour him as present under the eucharistic signs it should always be with the intention of going forward later to receive the heavenly gifts.

4.3.1. RECEIVING COMMUNION OUTSIDE MASS

The first historical traces of communion being received outside Mass are found in the ancient church. The wish to receive communion daily or more often, that is on days when the liturgy was not celebrated, led to the custom, attested in the 2nd century, of taking the eucharist home, so that one could receive it there.[111] Later the eucharist was celebrated oftener, this custom together with concern about misuse and the lack of reverence led in the 5th and 6th centuries to the dropping of the custom of house communion altogether. It continued on however in monasteries where there was no priest for the liturgy.[112]

The custom of giving communion in the church, but outside of Mass, arose during the Middle Ages when the faithful began receiving the eucharist less and less often. Finally the 4th Lateran Council (1215) decreed that every Christian must receive the

[110] Cf. Paul VI's Encyclical "Mysterium fidei" of 3. 9. 1965, DH 4411 referring to Council of Trent: DH 1642.
[111] Cf. Nußbaum, Aufbewahrung 266-291.
[112] Cf. Meyer, Eucharistie 550f.

sacrament at least once a year, that is during Eastertide. [113] The days for receiving communion became gradually fewer, on those days so many of the faithful came forward to take the sacrament that the Mass lasted far too long; for practical reasons then the church began giving communion apart from Mass.

The custom of taking of communion outside the celebration of Mass had two far-reaching consequences: the early church had problems with particles left over from Mass [114] and the eucharist was kept only for communion of the sick or for the dying, but now priests began consecrating in order to have "a reserve supply". [115] This however was not the only reason that the inner unity between the celebration of Mass and communion was lost to sight, but also the fact itself that one could communicate outside of Mass led to an individualistic Holy Communion piety ("Jesus as the guest of my soul"). The Mass itself had now become that necessary sacrificial act which brought about the real presence, so that one could receive Christ in "private" communion. It is true that the Council of Trent had already recommended reception of communion during Mass [116], but communion outside it remained widely accepted until the Liturgical Movement of our times. Then in 1947 Pope Pius XII expressly praised the communion of the faithful during Mass and the taking of the Host which had just been consecrated, [117] he did this without in any way questioning the practice of giving hosts which had beforehand been consecrated (something dogmatically, at least, quite correct), nor without questioning the custom of giving communion outside the celebration of Mass. Taking communion at Mass with hosts consecrated at the same Mass is also recommended by the Constitution of the Liturgy (SC 55) as the "better way of assisting at Mass". Nevertheless communion apart from Mass was a quite acceptable usage in many places. After the appearance of the appendix to the Rituale on 21st June 1973 "De sacra communione et cultu mysterii eucharistici extra Missam" [118] communion during Mass has become the rule, [119] likewise set down in c. 918/CIC 1983. Communion may however be given outside Mass to those who "justa de causa" ask for it, "servatis liturgicis ritibus".

What can be said about these rites? The appendix just mentioned offers two forms, one with a lengthier service of the word and one with a shorter. The first one includes greeting, confession of faults, reading (s), bidding prayers, the Lord's Prayer, invitation to and giving of communion, concluding prayer, blessing (intercessory form if the celebrant is layman) and dismissal. The second form offers only a short word from Scripture instead of a reading.

The conjunction of communion together with a service of the word has become the rule in many places for the Sunday parish service without a priest. The question whether communion should be given during such a service or not is still being discussed. Those against communion argue with SC 7: Christ is also present in his word, he is present when Christians come together for a liturgical celebration. If communion is always part of a service without a priest, then the old individualistic Holy Communion piety,

---

[113] DH 812.
[114] Cf. Jungmann MS, 504-506.
[115] Cf. on this: P. Browe, Wann fing man an, die in einer Messe konsekrierten Hostien in einer anderen Messe auszuteilen? ThGl 30 (1938) 388-404.
[116] DH 1747: "*in* singulis missis."
[117] Cf. Mediator Dei: AAS 39 (1947) 521-599, here 565.
[118] Kaczynski 3060-3108.
[119] Kaczynski 3075

detached from the Mass could return, and with it other questionable forms of eucharistic piety which had been considered overcome (e.g., exposition piety). [120] For pastoral reasons others prefer communion in such services, among them a directory in 1988 from the Congregation for Divine Service. [121] According to Meyer there are tensions in the ongoing discussion between pastoral considerations on the one hand and liturgical-theological reasons on the other. On the question whether communion should be given or not Meyer himself thinks that an attitude of reserve is to be recommended. [122]

4.3.2. COMMUNION FOR THE SICK AND THE LAST RITES.

Justin expressly mentions that the deacons took the eucharist to those who had been absent from the liturgy, no doubt also to the sick. As early as the year 416 Innocent I stresses in his letter to bishop Decentius of Gubbio that no penitent should die without having received communion beforehand. Until the early Middle Ages there was no set ritual form for communion of the sick. It was taken to them immediately after Mass. [123] Since in those days serious illness nearly always led to death communion for the sick became part of the last rites and was given, following confession, after the anointing with holy oil, (the "last sacraments", "extreme unction"). In the Middle Ages and at the beginning of modern times communion of the sick was given a form of its own which consisted of elements from the Mass (Our Father, kiss of peace, invitation to and reception of communion) and other parts (e.g. sprinkling with holy water at first, then confession of faith, or questions regarding the faith, confession of sins). In the Rituale Romanum of 1614 (V,4) communion for the sick differed from the communion of the last rites (viaticum) merely through another formula of administration. [124]

The renewed rite for communion of the sick consists of the following: Greeting, sprinkling with holy water, confession of faults, reading from scripture, the Lord's prayer, invitation to communicate "behold the Lamb of God", preparation "Lord, I am not worthy", word before communion, giving of the host with the formula, prayer, blessing. Ministri ordinarii are priests and deacons, but acolyths and ministers of communion could help in order that the sick receive communion as often as possible. [125]

Strictly speaking the sacrament of the dying is communion, viaticum. In case of lack of time it may be given before the confirmation "in danger of death" and the anointing with holy oil. Viaticum may also be given during Mass, its rite of administration is based the rite for communion of the sick, modified however by the following elements: Introductory words, granting of the indulgence for the dying, confession of faith, special texts for the bidding prayers, special formula of administration ("Christ keep thee and lead thee to everlasting life") and concluding prayer with kiss of peace. Even when anointing (and confirmation) are administered with viaticum "the service remains in principle the same as for the celebration of the viaticum, shortened only by the scripture reading; the other sacraments are given between the bidding prayers and the Lord's prayer." [126] According to CIC/1983 c. 911,1 the ordinary minister of viaticum is, except

---

[120] Cf. for example, Nußbaum, Gemeindegottesdienst 72-74.
[121] Directorium de celebrationibus dominicalibus absente presbytero: Notitiae 24 (1988) 366-378.
[122] Cf. Meyer, Eucharistie 559, to the whole matter 556-559.
[123] Cf. Nußbaum, Aufbewahrung 94-96.
[124] Rituale Romanum Tit. V, 4, 19-20.
[125] Cf. Meyer, Eucharistie 552f.
[126] Cf. R. Kaczynski, Wegzehrung: GdK 8, section 432. Regensburg 1984, 220f.

in case of need, the parish priest, or the house superior in a monastery or religious institute.

4.3.3. VENERATION OF THE EUCHARIST

The veneration of Christ's presence in the eucharist is a special aspect of Catholic spirituality and liturgy, an aspect which was strengthened by the Church's defence of her eucharistic beliefs during the Reformation. During the Counter Reformation and the Barock period "the veneration and glorification of the sacrament, which people thought the reformers had sinfully doubted, was placed so much in the foreground that one is inclined to consider the Mass itself from this standpoint above all others." [127]

The keeping of the eucharistic species has a varied history. In the East there was a tendency, to leave nothing of the eucharistic offerings over. [128] Well into the Middle Ages care was taken to consecrate only so many hosts as were necessary for communion at Mass and viaticum. [129] Eucharistic species were reserved principally to give communion on days on which no liturgical celebration took place, or to enable priests to give the sacrament to the sick or to the dying, they were not reserved in order to venerate them. Receptacles for keeping the hosts ("Capsa, Pyxis") were used, which after the custom of house communion was no longer practised, had their place in a side chapel in the church. From the early Middle Ages on a connection between the place where the hosts were reserved and the altar was developed (altar tabernacle, artophorion – a small tower-like box among the Byzantines –, hanging tabernacles in the shape of a "eucharistic dove" in East and West [130]), until finally during the Counter Reformation the tabernacle was placed on the High Altar and became the middle-point of church planning [131], a period when the real and continual presence of Christ in the species was a matter which bore no discussion. Another alternative, which disappeared in the post tridentine period, was the little house for the sacrament in Gothic churches. The central position of the tabernacle made clear that a change had come about in the reasons for reserving the sacrament: the sacrament was reserved in order to venerate it, and gradually the faithful came to understand that the presence of the Lord depended on the presence of the eucharistic species, acts of veneration changed accordingly, for example, a genuflection instead of a bow towards the altar. [132]

The veneration of the eucharist took on diferent forms, for example, the eucharistic procession, exposition, devotions in honour of the sacrament and Benediction. In this respect the introduction of the feast of Corpus Christi with the eucharistic procession played a decisive role. [133] At Corpus Christi the unveiled host was venerated, unveiled

---

[127] Jungmann MS I, 199.

[128] Concerning usage with left-over hosts in East and West see: Browe, Wann fing man an ... 388-396.

[129] This is still true even for the 13th cent. See Browe a.a. O., 395: Remaining hosts as well as those for viaticum were consumed by the priest, if he consecrated new particles for viaticum. As regards the thesis that pilgrimages to Jerusalem (Latin rite) had led to the custom of giving hosts which had been consecrated at an earlier Mass, a custom then taken to Europe by monks of Cluny, see: loc. cit., 397f.

[130] Regarding the eucharistic dove cf: J. Braun, Der christliche Altar in seiner gesch. Entwicklung, 2 vols., München 1924, II, 608-616.

[131] As regards the tabernacle: Cf. Loc. cit. 623-647. The first ritual instructions about the altar tabernacle stem from St. Charles Borromeo and are to be found in his "Instructio fabricae ecclesiae" (Acta Eccl. Mediol. 568), see Braun, loc. cit. 645.

[132] Cf. Meyer, Eucharistie 582-585.

[133] Cf. Browe, Verehrung 91-115: Die Prozession am Sakramentsfeste.

exposition became more and more common also outside the Corpus Christi octave, until even Mass was celebrated before the exposed host, liturgically and theologically a problematic custom. It became a custom in German-speaking countries in the 14th cent. to expose the host at the end of the Little Hours, there was then adoration and as climax a blessing with the host in a monstrance. This form of devotion was first officially authorized in the Caeremoniale Episcoporum of 1600 and was then taken into the Rituale Romanum of 1614 (Tit. X, 5, 5-7), a blessing with the host so became the normal conclusion for every public exposition [134] of the Blessed Sacrament. Special forms of eucharistic devotion from the 16th cent. on were the forty hours prayer and "perpetual adoration". The forty hours prayer had its beginnings in the custom of laying Christ's body to rest on Good Friday. Instead of using a cross or a figure of the dead Redeemer a host – sometimes veiled – was put into the grave and a time of adoration was held until the Resurrection was celebrated. A further development was "perpetual adoration" which was introduced by the Capuchin Joseph de Ferno in Milan in 1537. The adoration began in the cathedral and was continued throughout the whole year in other churches. [135]

"A decisive change in the understanding of the eucharist and in the question of eucharistic veneration began with the Liturgical Movement and its influence on Vatican II. Witness to this radical change in thinking is the Instruction 'Eucharisticum mysterium' of 25th of May 1967." [136] It reminds us of the main purpose for the reservation of the sacrament namely, viaticum, only then are reception of the sacrament outside of Mass and veneration of the real presence named. [137] Background and inspiration for the appendix to the Rituale "De sacra communione et cultu mysterii eucharistici extra Missam" from 21st June 1973 is the already mentioned Part III of the Instruction. Here also details are regulated by the 3rd chapter: "De variis formis cultus sanctissimae Eucharistiae tribuendi". The Celebration of the Eucharist, the Mass, is source and high point of all eucharistic piety. All other forms of piety derive from here and should lead the faithful back to the Mass. [138]

When exposition and eucharistic blessing follow Mass a host consecrated at that Mass should be used; consciousness that the eucharist is for our spiritual welfare will thus be enlivened. Exposition during Mass is not allowed. Every exposition should include a short prayer as well as adoration in silence; prayers and hymns during exposition should be chosen so that the holy mystery of the eucharist is brought to mind. If there is a eucharistic procession, then a host consecrated in the Mass just before shall be used. [139]

All forms of eucharistic veneration [140] are directed to the Lord, who gave himself up for us and continues to offer himself for us so that we may receive the healing power of everlasting life. When we pray or meditate in the eucharistic presence of the Lord we are helped to grasp and understand his redeeming love; this love will awaken in us the desire to be united with him in communion. His sacrifice which is for all mankind unites

---

[134] In contrast to "private exposition" in which the Blessed Sacrament remained in a closed ciborium.
[135] Cf. Meyer, Eucharistie 591f.
[136] Ibidem. 588. Regarding the Instruction itself: Kaczynski 899-965, for special consideration see Part III: De cultu sanctissimae Eucharistiae prout est sacramentum permanens, Kaczynski 947-965.
[137] Kaczynski 947.
[138] Kaczynski 3087.
[139] Cf. Meyer, Eucharistie 594f.; Kaczynski 3090-3104, CIC/1983 can. 941 §2.
[140] Cf. Meyer, Eucharistie 601f. In this connection also Catechism 1378-1381.

the individual soul with him and through him with the eternal God in three Persons, in this intimate bond with Christ we cannot forget to pray also for our brothers and sisters.

Bibliography

P. Browe, Die öftere Kommunion der Laien im Mittelalter, Bonner Zeitschrift für Theologie und Seelsorge 6 (1926) 1-28.

P. Browe, Wann fing man an, die Kommunion außerhalb der Messe auszuteilen? ThGl 23 (1931) 755-762.

P. Browe, Die Verehrung der Eucharistie im Mittelalter, München 1933, Reprint Sinzig 1990.

P. Browe, Die Sterbekommunion im Altertum und Mittelalter, ZKTh 60 (1936) 1-54, 211-240.

O. Nußbaum, Die Aufbewahrung der Eucharistie, Bonn 1979 (Theophaneia 29).

O. Nußbaum, Sonntäglicher Gemeindegottesdienst ohne Priester. Liturgische und pastorale Überlegungen, Würzburg 1985.

4.4. THE SACRAMENT OF PENANCE

4.4.1. THE LITURGICAL ETHOS

We understand a culpable turning away from God and the wish to reconcile oneself again with him under the aspect of a "liturgical ethos", that is to say we understand this reconciliation in its relationship to the eucharist. Evdokimov draws up a plan for a "liturgical or doxological anthropology" in which the nature of man as God's image is realised in its profoundest way through its vital, creative relationship with God; a realisation which is most perfectly achieved in the divine liturgy, performed in the time-space dimension of human existence. [141] The acceptation, and respectively, refusal of this life-giving communication is according to Yannaras a question of the "liturgical ethos". Good and evil, virtue and vice, all are founded on the openness of the soul to God or its sullen reticence before him. Good and evil are not merely abstract axioms, but good, respectively evil, deeds and are the logical consequences of readiness, or, as the case may be, refusal, to enter into that life-giving relationship with God which takes place in the church, and above all in the eucharistic liturgy. Correspondingly "penance" is to be put on the same footing as turning away from refusal to communicate and instead willingness to enter into a relationship, which reaches its highest point in sharing the eucharist. [142] Zizioulas has a like standpoint: Morality is not a system of behaviour, it is not an autonomous area of Theology. It arises out of a re-forming and renewal of creation and mankind in Christ, and in such a way that every moral commandment should only be understood as a result of this sacramental re-forming. The liturgy, for that reason, accepts only one single moral terminology: the sanctification of soul and body, in order that in community with "the Blessed Virgin and all the saints we entrust ourselves, each other and our whole life to Christ, our God." To put that in other words, the liturgy does not offer the world a moral behaviour system, as it were, instead it offers

---

[141] Cf. P. Evdokimov, Die Frau und das Heil der Welt, Moers-Aschaffenburg 1989, 88 – 90; the same: L'Orthodoxie, Paris 1979, 202-204.

[142] Cf. C. Yannaras, The Freedom of Morality, Crestwood-New York 1984, espec. 29-48. 81-89.

a re-formed and sanctified community, a leaven, which radically changes all creation with the power of its sanctifying presence.' [143]

The sacrament of penance brings a soul which has turned away from God back into the holy unity of Christ's body, to the eucharist as his body and to his body as the church. The sacrament of penance is God himself acting, it is on no account identical with a change of heart in the sinner. The soul separated from God by original sin cannot join the stream of divine life just by changing its way of thinking, the Son of God must descend and redeem it, in the same way a person cut away by sin from God and the divine fullness of life can only be saved by God's redeeming hand in the sacrament. God alone forgives sin, [144] but he does this in the church and through the ministry of the church, which as community of the mystical body is included in the reconciliation of her separated members. [145]

4.4.2. THE SACRAMENT OF PENANCE IN HISTORY AND IN THE PRESENT.

The early church was confronted by the following problem: In baptism all sinful faults were radically wiped out, but how was the church to treat persons who after baptism again fell into serious sin. Early Christian rigorism, which also knew "unforgivable sins", testifies to the difficult question about the possibility of a "second penance", that is, after baptism and the complete forgivenness of sin. Even in the 3rd cent. after the question had received a positive solution and the form for a canonical penance had been worked out and laid down, the relationship of the "second penance" with baptism was firmly adhered to. The second penance "is certainly not something to strive after, it is to be used only in extreme necessity. Its effect is, as is the case in baptism, a sharing in the community of the church as the Body of Christ (present in the celebration of the eucharist). The second penance is not however a repetition of baptism, it is rather a new promise or pledge of that which had been promised once and for all in baptism, namely: freedom from sin and a new life." [146] The view that the renewed promise was possible only once during a life-time was propagated in the early church by the "Shepherd of Hermas", a second century document which reckoned with the imminent return of Christ and exhorted to works of penance. Whoever sinned in face of the expected Parousia manifested an unwillingness to do penance. For the Church Fathers penance is "the rescuing plank after shipwreck." [147]

By the end of the 3rd century the view that all sinners without exception could be reconciled once in their lifetime by undergoing eccesiastical penance was generally accepted in the whole church. Rigorism became more and more a characteristic of esoteric groups cut away from the universal church (Montanists, Novatianists). The oldest witness for a procedure of canonical penance as "paenitentia secunda" after baptism stems from Tertullian. The canonical penance restricted itself to "capital sins" (falling away from the faith, murder and adultery); for everyday sins it was accepted that prayer,

---

[143] J. D. Zizioulas, Die Welt in eucharistischer Schau und der Mensch von heute, US 25 (1970) 342-349. 347.
[144] Cf. Cathechism 1441-1442.
[145] Cf. ibid. 143-145.
[146] Meßner 53.
[147] Cf. Poschmann, Buße und Letzte Ölung 14-18. 54.

fasting, alms and the reconciling power of the eucharist would bring forgiveness. [148] The penitential procedure, allowed only once in lifetime, began with a secret confession of sins before the bishop, reception into the status of penitent, the laying-down of the form of penance and excommunication from eucharistic celebration, or under circumstances, from communion. In contrast to the West the Church of the East accepted different degrees of penance: the "weepers" were obliged to stand at the narthex and beg those going in for their intercession; the "listeners" were allowed to stand at the church door, but had to leave with the catechumens before the celebration of the eucharist. The "kneelers" had their place inside the church door, but likewise had to leave with the catechumens, the "standers", however, were allowed to assist at the whole celebration with the faithful, but without receiving communion. [149] Acceptance into the group of penitents took place from the 5th century at the beginning of Lent; reconciliation was performed in Rome on Holy Thursday by the bishop through laying on of hands and prayer.

As Christians became more numerous and the Church embraced an ever greater number of opinions and degrees of fervour the decline of the canonical penance procedure set in. For many Christians it was just too much. A penance which caused discrimination in society [150] or represented an unbearable burden for the penitent, and above all the fear of falling into sin again meant that many put off doing penance until the end of their lives. [151] A new aspect had now come into consideration, namely that this penance for those ill was expected not only from those in mortal sin, but also from all Christians as a act of piety. It "was an integral part of christian life as preparation for a holy death. A change in the understanding of redemption had come about among Christians: Whereas in the Early Church a baptized person knew he was already redeemed by being a member of the holy Church, it was now held that one prepared oneself for redemption in the next life by a life led in accordance with the commandments (the ten commandments and the precepts of the Church), together with good works and acts of piety." [152] During the Carolingian reform efforts were made, in spite of all signs of decline, to reintroduce public penance. Even the High Middle Ages recognized a public penance: the "poenitentia sollemnis", or "poenitentia publica", one form of this was a pilgrimage undertaken as penance, and then the "poenitentia privata", the private confession of sins. [153] And as late as 1596 the Pontificale still contains the "Expulsio publice poenitentium ab Ecclesia" for Ash Wednesday and the "Reconciliatio poenitentium", which took place on Holy Thursday.

---

[148] Cf. Comp. Meßner 70-83: "Paenitentia quotidiana".

[149] Cf. Meßner 97f. There were in fact attempts in the West to introduce a readmittance of sinners by various degrees, but the specially formed groups of penitents remainded typical for the East.

[150] Cf. Poschmann, Buße und Letzte Ölung 55: The "penance once and for all" was a counterpart to the "one baptism" and as such set a kind of stamp on a soul, which remained even when the official time of penance had ended. Whoever had taken on the penance was for ever a Christian of the second class.

[151] The Council of Nicea had already laid down in c. 13 the disciplinary decree that the Eucharist should never be refused the dying, even when they could no longer do penance. Cf. I. Ortiz de Urbina, Nizäa und Konstantinopel, Mainz 1964 (Geschichte der ökumen. Konzilien 1) 125f.

[152] Meßner 117. A further aspect must also be referred to, that is, monasticism, which among early Christians claimed for itself the consciousness of being an elite. Whoever wanted to take Christian life seriously became a monk, and the monks' profession became a "second baptism".

[153] C f. Meßner 121f

Confession however had now become generally accepted as the new form of penance. Confession can be traced back to monastic sources, to be more exact, to the spiritual guidance customary in monastic circles. Clement of Alexandria and Origenes saw in the spiritual guide a healer, both stress the therapeutic method of talking openly together, "still not forgotten in the Greek Church. In this healing process the sinner needs the corrections and prayer of the spiritual guide, a healer, skilled in guidance, above all one who comes from the circle of those called to be shepherds, leaders in the church. He wins forgiveness for the sinner from God not because of his function in the church, but though his prayer and mortification". [154] This spiritual guide need not be a priest. Even at the beginning of the 15. cent. Symeon speaks of spiritual guidance and a confession of sins to a charismatically gifted layman (monk). If however the penitent wants sacramental absolution he must go to a priest. [155] Private confession to a cleric had its beginnings in the Celtic Church in Ireland and brought with it a change in the understanding of penance. It was now the duty of the priest to judge the gravity of transgressions and to impose a fitting atonement for offences against God, before giving absolution. The canonical, ecclesiastical forms of penance with a given ritual existed no more, instead there were lists of penances for various sins were drawn up to help the priests in deciding what form of penance was fitting (penance lists). Penances were secret and could be repeated, they no longer had the reputation of being something extraordinary and a sinner did not incur any public discrimination. As a result they could be inflicted for transgressions which might never come under canonical censure. [156] Under the Iroscottish monastic mission in France confession replaced canonical, ecclesiastical penance which had now fallen out of practice. There was nevertheless even in the 9th cent. some difficulty in asking a penitent, who had fulfilled his penance, to come back again a second time in order to receive absolution. For this reason reconciliation, that is absolution, could in cases of exception follow immediately after confession, [157] something which became the general rule soon after the turn of the millenium. [158] The ecclesiastic and canonical penitential custom regarding capital offences was also deemed necessary in regard to confesion, that is to say, mortal sins had to be confessed. Another point: quite independent of individual guilt it was laid down by the 4th Lateran Council 1215 that every believer must go to confession once a year. [159]

If one seeks a generally accepted set formula of absolution, one seeks in vain: "the sacramental power of absolution lay in the act of reconciliation with the church as

---

[154] H. Tüchle, Kirche und Buße. Aus der geschichtlichen Entwicklung der Bußpraxis. In: Buße und Bußsakrament. Studientagung des Klerusverbandes in St. Ottilien vom 17. Bis 19. April 1972, 22-38. 24f.

[155] Cf. M. Kunzler, Gnadenquellen. Symeon von Thessaloniki (+ 1429) as example for the Palamismus influence on Orthodox theology of the sacraments and theology of the liturgy, Trier 1989 (TThSt 47), 285.

[156] Cf. B. Poschmann, Die abendländische Kirchenbuße im frühen Mittelalter, Breslau 1930 (Breslauer Studien zur historischen Theologie 16), 8-10.

[157] Jungmann 272 names such an exception: "Si vero simplicem vel brutum eum intellexeris, statim reconcilia eum."

[158] For example in a confession rituale from Arezzo dating the beginnng of the 11th cent. we read the following: "Tunc dicat ei sacerdos surgere, et statim per stolam, qua indutus es, in dextera manu paenitenti facit remissionem." Jungmann 193, Note 104.

[159] DH 812.

such"[160] The discussion among the Scholastics regarding the role of the priest in the sacrament of Penance led to replacing the deprecative formula ("Misereatur") by the indicative ("Ego te absolvo"). In the Decretum pro Armenis of the Council of Florence 1439 the indicative absolution fomula is attested as the forma sacramenti and since the Council of Trent is the only formula allowed.[161] The Rituale Romanum of 1614 (Tit. IV, 2) links the deprecative elements ("Misereatur" and "Indulgentiam") with an indicative formula of absolution of emphatic juridical character: "Dominus noster Jesus Christus te absolvat: et ego auctoritate ipsius te absolvo ab omni vinculo excommunicationis, suspensionis, et interdicti, in quantum possum, et tu indiges. Deinde ego te absolvo a peccatis tuis, in nomine Patris … " The new absolution formula on the other hand corresponds to the amamnetic-epicletic root structure of liturgical prayer: the trinitarian directed order of salvation is mentioned first (Anamnesis: "God, the allmerciful Father, has reconciled the world with himself through the death and resurrection of his Son and has sent the Holy Spirit for the forgiveness of sins.") only then are pardon and peace requested in epiclesis form and by inclusion of the church ("Through the service of the church may he grant thee forgiveness and peace.") The indicative mood is kept for the concluding formula ("I absolve thee … ") which for psychological reasons (confirmation that sins have been forgiven independent of the penitent's emotional mood) is of greater advantage.

Steinruck mentions three possible sources for general absolution: 1. The monastic chapter of faults with the concluding absolution given by the abbot, which had to do with violations against the Rule, it was not an absolution from sin. 2. The inclusion of all the faithful on Holy Thursday when absolution was imparted to sinners after their public penance. 3. Confessions in emergency situations, e.g., in time of war.

Among the Scholastics there was disagreement on the question whether general absolution was a sacrament or not. Another form of "general absolution" which was in fact very popular, but never understood as sacrament, was a general confession after the sermon and an absolution following thereon, the congregation simply said the Confiteor as a preparation for the eucharist and the priest gave a general form of absolution.[162] "The gradual development of the ecclesiastical institution of penance came to an end about 1250. The practice and application of penance has hardly changed in the Church to the present time. … The Council of Trent rigidly kept to the traditional, fixed form handed down practically unaltered since the 13th cent., the Council had not realized however that this form was not the original form of the Early Church."[163]

4.4.3. THE RENEWED ORDER FOR THE SACRAMENT OF PENANCE[164]

---

[160] Steinruck 62 with reference to Poschmann, Buße und Extreme Unction 77-79.

[161] Cf. DH 1323, 1673.

[162] Cf. Steinruck 63f

[163] Ibidem 64f.

[164] Cf. B. Fischer, Zum neuen römischen Ordo Paenitentiae vom 2. Dezember 1973, Theologische Fakultät Trier (ed.): Dienst der Versöhnung. Umkehr, Buße und Beichte. Beiträge zu ihrer Theologie und Praxis, Trier 1974 (TThSt 31), 109-120. Kaczynski 3170-3216 Cf. R. Kaczynski, Erneuerte Bußliturgie, ThPQ 122 (1974) 209-221. 209f. Nr. 12 - Kaczynski 3184. According to c. 964,2 the penitent has the right to confession in a confessional, for that reason there must one in the church, Cf. Meßner 224, Note 286. Meßner 225. Cf. Kaczynski 3203.

The 2nd Vatican Council decided: "Rites and formulae of the sacrament of penance shall be so revised that the nature and effect of the sacrament are clearer expressed" (SC 72). The "Ordo Penitentiae"[165] appeared on 2nd Dec. 1973, its very name makes it clear that besides the sacramental penance there are other non-sacramental forms. The new Ordo recognizes accordingly three models *with* sacramental absolution (Form A: private confession; Form B: the general Service of Reconciliation, followed by private confession and absolution; Form C: the community Service with general acknowledgement of sin and general absolution); and then services of reconciliation *without* absolution. (De celebrationibus paenitentialibus).

The place for private confession is the confessional or a special room for confessions. Meßner describes the present rite of private confession as "a trimming up of the traditional post-tridentine form". As regards Form B he considers adding private confession on to a parish Service of Reconciliation, after the Service is over, to be an external appendix, after all, so his opinion, private confession takes place between a single penitent and the priest, it is a private matter, independent of the parish. Form C, the general absolution after a confiteor recited in common, is designed for emergency or exceptional cases only, the Ordo (Nr. 31) also mentions, apart from danger of death, the situation which might arise when there is a great number of persons wishing to confess with only few confessors. The Ordo (Nr.34) in accordance with the teaching tradition of the Church on full and complete confession, stipulates that even after having received general absolution a penitent shall confess any possible mortal sins during a later private confession. The Swiss[166] and French bishops allow a general absolution which is sacramental when there is great number of penitents waiting for confession before the greater feastdays, the German and Austrian bishops' conferences do not. They refuse to accept the presence of a great numbers of penitents as a sufficient reason for granting a sacramental general absolution. In any case there is seldom a great number of penitents in our time. Besides these three sacramental forms of the Sacrament of Penance the new Ordo contains a non-sacramental Service of Reconciliation. In this form there is, instead of a prayer for sacramental absolution, "only" a prayer for the forgiveness of sin. This follows after prayer, hymns, readings from Scripture and homily, all of which should move the soul to to "sorrow for sin and readiness to amend one's life." The Ordo stresses that these Services of Reconciliation should not be confused with the celebration of Sacrament of Penance.[167] Meßner however holds that this distinction stems from the scholastic-tridentine theology of the Sacrament of Penance and regards it as questionable considering the historical development of this sacrament[168]

Coming now to forms B and C: There is no doubt that in forms B and C as well as in the Services of Reconciliation the relationship of the Church both to penance and to

---

[165] The Council of Trent deems an all-embracing confession of sins by the penitent to be essential to the sacrament of penance, Cf. K. J. Becker, Die Notwendigkeit des vollständigen Sündenbekentnisses in der Beichte nach dem Konzil von Trient, ZThPh 47 (1972) 161-228; F. Nikolasch, Das Konzil von Trient und die Notwendigkeit der Einzelbeichte, LJ 21 (1971) 150-192. The "Normae pastorales" of the Congregation of the Faith on the imparting of general absolution took this question up as early as 1972, Cf. Kaczynski 2825. Kaczynski 3206

[166] Cf. J. Baumgartner, Neuordnung der Bußpraxis in der Schweiz, Gd 8 (1974) 169-172.

[167] E.g. Nr. 37. - Kaczynski 3209: "Caveat ne hae celebrationes, in opinione fidelium, cum ipsa sacramenti Paenitentiae celebratione confundantur." Indentical in Appendix II, Nr. 1 – Kaczynski 3213.

[168] Cf. Meßner 226

the Sacrament of Penance are clearer presented than in private confession. Even in private confession, however, the importance of the Church for salvation is expressed in the new formula of absolution, together with the decisive facts of God's order of redemption. [169] Meßner raises an objection to the new formula and also to the second trinomial formula, which was specially composed for General Absolution, [170] he is critical of the scholastic-tridentine understanding of the sacraments, and deems the stressing of the "verba essentialia" to be a matter worthy of re-consideration. He argues that the concept of "essential words" represents a temptation to a minimalising, validity-thinking, which is in opposition the the anamnetic-epicletical character of prayer in our Christian tradition of praying. [171]

4.4.4. THE BYZANTINE RITE OF RECONCILIATION

"The Roman Catholic confession box in which the penitent is separated from the priest is unknown in the Orthodox Church, and this is something characteristic for both... We confess in the church, there is nothing dividing priest from penitent. The connection with the church is confirmed through the modus that in the Orthodox Church there is a special liturgical service for confession... So the Sacrament of Penance is in this manner firmly built into the liturgical life of the Church." The celebration of the sacrament of Penance among the Byzantines corresponds in fact to the present form B in the Roman liturgy, that is, the service of Reconciliation celebrated in common followed by private confession and absolution imparted for the individual. The Byzantine rite is as follows: after the liturgy of the word celebrated together the penitents go forward to the priest who is waiting beside the Blessed Virgin ikon in the Ikonostasis in front of the Analogion. They confess their sins to him and receive absolution. The absolution is imparted by laying on of hands and stole. Greek and Slav traditions as well as local customs differ not only in the structure of liturgy of the word celebrated together, but above all in the absolution formula. The Slav Churches, influenced by Petrus Mogila's latinising Euchologion, that introduced the questions on consent into the marriage liturgy,

---

[169] Cf. Nr. 19 – Kaczynski 3191: "Formula absolution indicat reconciliationem paenitentis a misericordia Patris procedere; nexum ostendit inter reconciliationem peccatoris et mysterium paschale Christi; Spiritus Sancti munus in remissione peccatorum extollit; demum aspectum ecclesialem sacramenti in luce ponit eo quod reconciliatio cum Deo petitur et datur per ministerium Ecclesiae."

[170] Zweck 125 expresses the wish that this "festive" absolution formula should be possible in individual confession of sins. Cf. H. Zweck, Reformschritte in der Bußliturgie: Th. Maas-Ewerd (ed.), Lebt unser Gottesdienst? Die bleibende Aufgabe in der Liturgiereform (FS Kleinheyer), Freiburg-Basel-Vienna 1988, 107-133. 125. Cf. Meßner 223. A. Alevisopoulos, Buße und Beichte in Pastoral und Katechese der Kirche von Griechenland, E.C. Suttner (ed.), Buße und Beichte. Drittes Regensburger Ökumenisches Symposium. Regensburg 1972, 1972, 61-75. 64f.

[171] Concerning the Slav usage Cf. Heitz III, 114-119, regarding the Greek rite ibidem 120-129. The Euchologies contain a great choice of prayers, psalms, portions of the penance canons (E.g. that of Andreas of Crete) and the priest may choose according to desire and the time at his disposal whatever he thinks fitting for the occasion., Cf. E. Theodorou, Bußvollzug und Beichtpraxis in der byzantinischen Kirche, E. C. Suttner (ed.): Buße und Beichte. Drittes Regensburger Ökumenisches Symposium. Regensburg 1972, 55-60. 58.

use a mixed deprecative-indicative formula of absolution;[172] the Greeks recognize only a deprecative form.

4.4.5. PENANCE IN THE CHURCHES OF THE REFORMATION

Luther understood absolution in private confession as a form of the preaching of the Gospel. "It (preaching the Gospel) alone determines the nature of confession; the penitent must turn away from himself and his repentance and put all his trust in God's word, which does not lie. Since Christ himself is present in the preaching of the Gospel, it is he who absolves; the confessor has the task of preaching the word, a task to which no special sacramental competence (potestas) has been given." Preaching is placed in the foreground, the full and complete confession of sins loses importance. In the Pietistic period private confession was replaced by "general confession". Attempts to reintroduce private confession have not achieved the desired effect. It is mainly practised in movements which in any case attach a greater importance to the liturgical life of the church, for example, in the Lutheran Michael's Brotherhood.[173]

Calvin holds "confession before God" (A heartfelt prayer for forgiveness of sin) as something laid down in Holy Writ, but confession before another human being as also in conformity with Scripture. Absolution pronounced by a bearer of an office in the church serves to assure the believer of the sin-forgiving power of faith; in Calvin's understanding the pastor wields the power of the keys by preaching the Gospel. In this sense the pronouncing of the absolution by the pastor is simply serving the Gospel, it is "personal application of God's promises to all and witness of forgiveness", it must be borne in mind however that the exercise of the power of the keys is put on the same level as preaching the Gospel.

Bibliography

P. M. Gy, La pénitence et la réconciliation: Martimort III, Paris 1984, 115-131.

P. Jounel, La liturgie de la réconciliation, MD 117 (1974) 7-37.

J. A. Jungmann, Die lateinischen Bußriten in ihrer geschichtlichen Entwicklung, Innsbruck 1932.

R. Meßner, Feiern der Umkehr und Versöhnung. Mit einem Beitrag von R. Oberforcher: GdK 7,2, Sakramentliche Feiern I/2, Regensburg 1992, 9-240.

B. Poschmann, Die abendländische Kirchenbuße im Ausgang des christlichen Altertums, München 1928 (Münchener Studien zur historischen Theologie 7).

B. Poschmann, Buße und letzte Ölung: Handbuch der Dogmengeschichte, ed. by M. Schmaus and others, vol. IV/3, Freiburg i.Br. 1951.

M. Righetti, Manuale di storia liturgica IV: I sacramenti, i sacramentali, Milano 1953, 106-227: La Penitenza.

---

[172] Heitz does not mention them in Mysterium der Anbetung III anymore, but does so in: Der Orthodoxe Gottesdienst I: Göttliche Liturgie und Sakramente, Mainz (1965), 501, which he brought out in 1965. It is as follows: "May Our Lord and God Jesus Christ forgive you, my child N., all your sins through the grace and mercy of his love of mankind; and through the power given me, an unworthy priest, I also forgive you and absolve from all your sins, in the name of the Father ... " Cf. Kucharek, Sacramental Mysteries 240.

[173] Cf. Meßner 195-199. Cf. H. Schützeichel, Die Beichte vor dem Priester in der Sicht Calvins: Theologische Fakultät Trier (ed.), Dienst der Versöhnung. Umkehr, Buße und Beichte. Beiträge zu ihrer Theologie und Praxis. Trier 1974 (TThSt 31), 67-89, here 76.

J. Steinruck, Buße und Beichte in ihrer geschichtlichen Entwicklung: Theologische Fakultät Trier
(ed.), Dienst der Versöhnung. Umkehr, Buße und Beichte. Beiträge zu ihrer Theologie und
Praxis, Trier 1974, 45-66 (TThSt 31).

4.5. THE ANOINTING OF THE SICK

4.5.1. AFFIRMATION OF LIFE FOR BODY AND SOUL

Sickness is not a punishment from God, it does however show a person his limitations
and reminds him of his mortality. Many sick persons experience illness as being cut off
from those possibilities of life which they had hitherto taken for granted; relations with
other persons are also affected by it. Every harm-ridden situation has been caused by
separation from the living God, who is the source of all good. This separation is the real
sickness which leads to death, not only of the body, but also of the soul.

God's redeeming work in the sacraments intends to overcome this separation and
join man to the vital stream of divine life. Since man is a being of body and soul the
body, that "living symbol of the soul",[174] is always included in the salvation which
comes from God. The body as the material symbol of the soul is the first and most
intimate instrument by means of which the soul expresses itself and establishes contact
with the material world.[175] It is an old theological didactic principle, over and above
the findings of the humanistic sciences on the psychosomatic contexts of sickness, that
the body's corrupt condition cannot be separated from the religious dimension. The
separation of the human being from God, source of all life, is also the reason for the
sinful condition of the body.

Symeon of Thessalonica wrote with biting scorn of an understanding of the Sacrament of the Sick, coming from the West, which tended to overlook the promise of solace
and redemption for body and soul in the sacrament and instead stressed the aspect of
forgiveness of sin in face of oncoming death. He taught that, according to Luke 7:36ff.,
Christ himself received an "anointing of the sick", and that from the hands of a sinful
woman, an anointing which must strictly be distinguished from the anointing of Jesus by
Mary, Lazarus' sister (John 12:1-11): this anointing took place in view of Jesus' burial,
that of the sinful woman refers to the Anointing of the Sick, since Jesus received the oil
from the hands of person who through the forgiveness of her guilt experienced support
and comfort.[176] The fact that a sinful woman administered this "anointing" makes it
clear that the sacrament not only serves a sick person in strengthening and supporting
his body, but also purifies the soul, that is, it bridges over its remoteness from God,
and that of course has a retroactive effect on the body. Symeon thus defines the effects
of the Holy Oil as overcoming of sicknesses, as restoration of the sick person and as
forgiveness of sins.[177] As regards the integral healing of persons the Euchelaion ("the
beneficial anointing") is in a special way image of the divine mercy which brings about
all salvation.[178]

---

[174] Cf. Guardini, Liturgische Bildung 22
[175] Cf. Guardini, Liturg. Bildung 15-18; The same author: Die Sinne und die relig. Erkenntnis 17.
[176] Cf. Dialogos 56 – PG 155, 204 B – 205 A.
[177] Cf. Ibid. 205 A, Dialogos 284 – PG 155, 317 C.
[178] Cf. Dialogos 57 – PG 155, 205 C.

The Byzantine prayer at an anointing praises God the Father as "Healer of our souls and bodies", who sent his only-begotten Son in order to heal sicknesses and redeem from death. "Jesus healed the sick during his earthly life; he gave them back their mortal lives. When the Holy Spirit however penetrates our body destined for death he transfers it beyond death: death is no more, for Christ our God has risen." [179]

4.5.2. HISTORICAL DEVELOPMENT OF THE ANOINTING OF THE SICK TO "EXTREME UNCTION"

Apart from the mandate of Mark 6,13 for the church to care for the sick the locus classicus for the sacrament of anointing is Jas. 5,13-16. [180] The next reference thereto is found only in the tradition of the consecration of oil in Hippolytus. After the Eucharistic Canon had been prayed fruits of the earth were blessed, among them oil. The oil, made holy by the Thanksgiving, (Eucharist), was intended after the blessing to give those who tasted it strength and those who needed it health. [181] The Euchologion attributed to the Egyptian bishop Serapion of Thmuis (d. after 362) contains a prayer of blessing for oil and water as well as for oil or bread or water, whereby the texts expressly mention only that oil which serves for anointing and for which healing power is invoked; it is then clearly named "oil of the sick" ("elaion nosounton"). In Rome also there was a blessing of fruits of the earth at the end of the eucharistic canon, the conclusion of the Roman Canon bears witness to this: "Per quem haec omnia, Domine, semper bona creas, sanctificas, vivificas, benedicis et praestas nobis." [182] The liturgical place for the blessing of the oil for the sick has remained the same to the present day and shows that in ancient times oil for the anointing of the sick was among these fruits of the earth. Kaczynski recapitulates the first epoch in the history of the anointing of the sick as follows: "At first the faithful took the oil themselves to the church, there it was blessed by the bishop or presbyter. In the Roman rite this blessing took place at the end of the canon of the Mass, since the 5th century the blessing is by the bishop alone and only on Holy Thursday; in other Western rites the oil was blessed during the anointing as part of the ceremony, this held until the Roman custom was taken over. Nothing is known about the Eastern usage. When the faithful gave up taking oil to the church they could there receive blessed oil in order to take it home with them and use it according to necessity. This was a custom similar to that of taking home the Eucharist for communion in the house. The blessing spoken in the church could be considered as the 'prayer of faith' over the sick person demanded by St James in 5:15: Well into the 8th century layfolk were allowed in principle to apply the blessed oil to themselves or to members of their families. Which part of the body was anointed is not clear from the prayer-texts. The use of the oil by layfolk did not exclude the use of it by priests, a fact which is clearly testified in the 5th century in Rome. The sick person was considered in his totality, as full human being, when he was anointed. In the prayers of blessing it was certainly the anointing's effect on the body that was mainly in the foreground, whereas the effects on soul and psyche are mentioned in a more reserved manner. The forgiveness of sins

---

[179] Cf. Heitz III, 158; Corbon 138f.
[180] Regarding the argument for anointing of the sick in the Letter of St. James Cf. Kacyznski, Krankensalbung 253-257.
[181] TradAp 5, ed. Geerlings 228f.
[182] Cf. Jungmann MS II, 322-324.

"as an effect of the anointing came only gradually to be mentioned in the prayers." [183] It appears from the letter of Innocent I to Decentius of Gubbio in the year 416 that the pope qualifies the oil itself, and not the anointing, as "sacrament". The sick were anointed without mention of the degree of illness; "Since danger of death is necessary for lifting excommunication an excommunicated penitent could not be considered for anointing, it can here be a question only of the sick and not of the dying". [184]

Caesarius of Arles (d. 542) alludes to anointing by laymen, apart from anointing by priests. The anointing of the sick brought about – contrary to pagan magic healing – forgiveness of sin and healing. Statements similar to this were made by Eligius of Noyon. (d. 660). Bede the Venerable (d. 735) in his commentary on the Letter of James refers to anointing by lay persons; here too the sacrament is concerned with healing the recipient, and not at all with his death. [185]

In the 8th century the Church was surprisingly concerning itself with re-introducing the anointing of the sick, for it had fallen out of practice. Admonitions to receive it "were being made more and more often in conjunction with directions regarding penance on the deathbed and on viaticum", with the aim that the faithful might ask for the sacrament. With this however began another development, namely towards "limiting the anointing to serious illness and danger of death and thus to understanding the sacrament of the sick as the sacrament for the dying, all the more so when it was only to be administered after Viaticum". [186]

Scholastic theology cemented this interpretation. The trio of the sacraments of initiation at life's beginning: (Baptism – Eucharist – Confirmation; note this already altered sequence!) were echoed by the complementary trio: Penance – Eucharist (Viaticum) – Anointing of the Sick as sacrament of departure at life's end, "sacramentum exeuntium" (Albert the Great.) [187] The effects of the anointing of the sick were understood as cleansing from sin in preparation for the heavenly glory. For this reason its "principalis effectus" was seen in the cancelling of any venial sins of which the soul might be guilty (Bonaventure, Duns Scotus) [188] or in the healing of any weakness resulting from moral corruption which would hinder entrance into heaven. (Thomas). Together with the replacement of canonical penance by confession and the understanding of the Sacrament of the Sick as the sacrament for the dying there arose another development: the consequences of the penance performed by a sick person in receiving this sacrament were linked in the case of a cure to the Sacrament of the Sick. That is to say, the cured person was taken, by reason of his receiving the sacrament, into the canonical state of penitent, something which might bring considerable effects with it, for example, dancing with "consecrated feet" was no longer allowed. The anointing which according to the Roman Pontifical of the 12th cent. was performed on those parts of the body which represented

---

[183] Cf. Kaczynski, Krankensalbung 272f.

[184] Ibid. 270.

[185] Cf. Ibid. 270-272.

[186] Cf. Ibid. 276 Cf. ibid. 283.

[187] The administration is therefore valid only 'when death must be presumed (Bonaventure)', or the sacrament is only fully effective when the patient can sin no more (Scotus)', thus E. J. Lengeling: Todesweihe oder Krankensalbung? In: M. Probst / K. Richter (eds.), Heilssorge 39-54. 44 unter Berufung auf Poschmann 134-138. Lengeling's article is also printed in: LJ 21 (1971) 193-213. As to this and other impositions Cf. Lengeling, Krankensalbung oder Todesweihe (in: Probst / Richter) 43.

[188] Cf. Kaczynski, Krankensalbung 274-285, regarding the name of the sacrament ibid. 247f. DH 1324.

the five senses, in order to free them from sins, imparted an indelible "character" on the recipient, just as Confirmation and the Sacrament of Orders. The Anointing of the Sick had become "Extreme Unction", the last anointing. This was not in the sense of the anointings received during life-time (Baptism, Confirmation, Ordination), but as a consecration for death, an idea which was brought up again towards the end of the 19th cent.

The Western Church remained steadfast in this view of the sacrament as "Extreme Unction", the last anointing. The Decretum pro Armenis demanded from the faithful of that rite that they should give up their correct understanding of the sacrament and replace it by an acknowledgement that the Anointing of the Sick, as a sacrament, could only be administered to those in danger of death. The Council of Trent did not define the Anointing of the Sick as sacrament for the dying, kept however to the customary understanding. An understanding which came increasingly under criticism in the course of the Liturgical Movement. It was due to the Movement that even before the Council the name "Extreme Unction" was dropped in favour of the term "Anointing of the Sick", as, for example, in the Catechism for the German Bishoprics (1955), and in quite a number of diocesan hymnals.

4.5.3. THE REFORM: FROM "EXTREME UNCTION" BACK TO ANOINTING OF THE SICK

The Constitution on the Liturgy does not decide that the name "Extreme Unction" should be changed to "Anointing of the Sick", but it clearly prefers the second term, in order to indicate that it is not the sacrament for those who are in extreme danger of death, but for the seriously ill. Serious illness does not of itself exclude recovery (SC 73). Regulations were made (apart from the creation of a unified rite for Penance, for taking the Eucharist and for Anointing the Christian who has come to the end of his life [189]) as to the number of anointings and prayers, which should be so revised that "that they are befitting the various circumstances of the person receiving the sacrament" (SC 75). On the 7th of Dec. 1972 the new "Ordo Unctionis infirmorum eorumque pastoralis curae" appeared as part of the Apostolic Consitution of Paul VI 'Sacram Unctionem infirmorum' of 30th November of the same year. [190] The basic form of the celebration consists of four structural elements:

1. Opening (Greeting, Sprinkling with holy water as remembrance of baptism and the hope of salvation founded thereupon, Introduction to the celebration, General Confession of sins or Sacrament of Penance).
2. Liturgy of the Word (Reading, short Homily as an explanation of the texts, Bidding Prayers).
3. Essential Rites:

---

[189]   SC 74. Lengeling says in his commentary that the Anointing of the Sick is not exclusively for the dying, but can also be administered to them. Cf. E. J. Lengeling, Die Konstitution des Zweiten Vatikanischen Konzils ueber die heilige Liturgie. Lateinisch-deutscher Text mit einem Kommentar. Münster 2nd edn. 1965 (Lebendiger Gottesdienst 5/6), 157.

[190]   Cf. Kaczynski 2925-2966, 2918-2023.

a. Laying on of hands in silence. This takes its inspiration from the biblical gesture and intends being a gesture of healing and solace as well as token of loving nearness in a time of increasing "fear of coming too near to others" (danger of infection!), a gesture of great importance even when no words are uttered.

b. Consecration of the oils, or thanksgiving prayer for the oil. As a rule the oil of the sick consecrated by the bishop is used, this is done in order to make clear that the ceremony (there are perhaps few persons taking part) is related to the whole Church, and also to stress the importance of the bishop for all liturgical services in his diocese. (Cf. SC 41). Only when oil consecrated by the bishop is not available does the priest consecrate the oil himself, otherwise he says the Prayer of Thanksgiving in the form of the Jewish Berakah.

c. The anointing itself was given a completely new form. In the old rite there was a six-fold anointing, that is on eyes, ears, nose, mouth, hands, and feet (this last anointing might be omitted), in which the accompanying words spoke, not of recuperation and comfort, but of the forgiveness of sins which might have been committed by those members of the body.[191] In the new rite on the other hand only the forehead and the palms of the hands are anointed, parts of the body which represent the thinking and bodily active human being. The sacrament is celebrated, as distinct from administered, the distinction is clear in that the recipient and all those present confirm the words accompanying the anointing by their "Amen". The words used at anointing have clearly been inspired by Jas 5:14f. The three verbs "to save" and "to strengthen" – in the main clause – as well as "to free" (from sin) in the subordinate clause have been used. St James makes it clear by his choice of words that the Anointing of the Sick effects both body and soul. 'The sacrament is not administered solely with regard to the future fate of a person's soul, but also with regard to his body, beset by weakness and frailty, for sickness concerns the whole person whom the Lord will help and save in the manner which is best fitting for the individual.'[192]

d. The prayer following belongs to the very heart of the sacred action, since the "Prayer of Faith" is according to Jas: 5,14f. a constituent element of the liturgy. The new Rite offers as well as this prayer a choice of other prayers which are adapted to the personal situation of recipient (prospect of recovery, danger of death, viaticum accompanying the anointing, death struggle).

4. Concluding rites: Our Father, if occasion rises Communion, Blessing.

This sacrament ought to be celebrated during a service held in common, and that for several reasons: to remove the fear of the Anointing of the Sick considered as the sacrament for the dying, above all to include the service in the liturgical life of the parish, so that its celebration truly becomes a sacrament of comfort and promise of redemption in the heart of the community for those members who are ill. According to von Arx the pastoral care of the sick has as its wellspring the French pilgrim town of Lourdes. In 1969 Bishop Théas together with eleven other French dioceses received permission to hold a communal service of Anointing of the Sick "ad experimentum". The experi-

---

[191] Rituale Romanum Tit. VI,2: "Per istam sanctam unctionem, et suam piissimam misericordiam, indulgeat tibi Dominus quidquid per visum (auditum, odoratum, gustum et locutionem, tactum, gressum) deliquisti."

[192] Kaczynski, Krankensalbung 312.

ence [193] with this service was so favourable that Pope Paul VI himself administered the sacrament to fifty sick persons during a service for the sick on the 5th October 1975. During the following years the communal form of the service for the sick was adopted into the vernacular rituals, at the same time the possibility of incorporating it into the celebration of the Eucharist was also allowed, according to the pattern of other Masses of the ritual. The CIC/1983 also alludes to the communal service of Anointing of the Sick (c. 1002). [194]

4.5.4. OPEN QUESTIONS

After the renewal of the rites in the sacrament of Anointing of the Sick the question concerning the minister arose. In order to prevent the sacrament becoming a forgotten sacrament, as its history until the 8th century shows had actually happened, the suggestion was made, and still continues being put forward, to allow not only a priest to administer the sacrament, the "minister ordinarius", but also to allow deacons and designated lay persons (acolytes and ministers of the Eucharist) to do so, as such they would be considered "ministri extraordinarii". According to Kaczynski there is no objection to this from the standpoint of dogma: the word "presbyteroi" in Jas 5:4 does not mean priests by office. It should be remembered that the Council of Trent names the priest as the proper minister, a definition which does not exclude an extra-ordinary minister. The weightiest argument is the historical one, that is to say, until the carolingian reform of the liturgy all Christians, not only the official ministers, performed the sacrament of Anointing for themselves and those belonging to them with the oil which had been consecrated by the bishop. [195] The argument is analogous to the giving of communion by non-priests (deacons and lay persons): that which has been consecrated by the priest is given to all who come.

Difficult questions arise here: does the consecration of the oil by the bishop and with it the oil itself receive a quality of consecration similar to that of the Eucharist and in such wise a manner of "real presence" of the healing Saviour? How can the Anointing of the Sick be incorporated into the liturgical life of the whole Church if the presence of the official representative of the Church is dispensed with. How can one prevent it becoming – in the extreme case – a purely private affair which can no longer claim the connotation "Service of the Church?" In fact it is precisely the development of the Anointing of the Sick so that it became a sacrament administered by a priest which can be held to its favour, since in this manner the bond with the whole Church is established even in a service with the smallest group of participants.

The question concerning the recipient is also one of the open ones, e.g., when is an illness serious, what is the criterion? it is difficult to determine exactly when. One would like to see a sick person who is going through a serious spiritual crisis as a recipient of the Anointing. A crisis which makes it difficult for him to foster faith and hope and to lead a life worthy of a human being with resolution and dignity. Whenever the weakness

---

[193] P. M. Théas, Rapport sur la célébration communautaire de l'onction des malades dans les sanctuaires de Notre-Dame de Lourdes, Notitiae 6 (1970) 24-33.

[194] Cf. von Arx 264f.

[195] Cf. Kaczynski, Krankensalbung 314f. In the letter from Innocent I to Decentius of Gubbio of March 416 there is a reference to Jas. 5,14f.: The faithful who are sick and can be anointed with the holy oil of chrism, consecrated by the bishop, must grasp and understand that not only the priests, but also all Christians may use it to anoint themselves according to their own needs or the needs of their kinsfolk.

which endangers the patient's life is not simply bodily, but psychosomatic, then it is the recipient's personal disposition which is the decisive factor. That means: that which is valid for all the sacraments holds also here, the initiative for celebrating the anointing of the sick must be taken by the recipient himself. The sick person, him – or herself, must judge whether the sacrament is wholesome for his or her wellbeing as a fully developed person or not. [196]

Notwithstanding the rejection of the term "Extreme Unction" in the reform of the liturgy for the Anointing of the Sick in the sense of sacrament for the dying, there are theologians who still defend theses which relate the Anointing of the Sick to life's end. Zerfaß criticises the reformed Anointing of the Sick from a pastoral-theological stand-point. He claims that it is a typical example "for the downright distressing repression of the fear of death', which together with other examples (e.g. The removal of the lamentations from the liturgy or the leaving out of those perikopes in the readings which 'cast shadows') portray the liturgy in a rather triumphalist manner". [197] Greshake pleads for an understanding of the Anointing of the Sick as "sacrament of baptismal renewal in face of death." [198] The Anointing of the Sick is the distinct expression, celebration and redemptive presence of the eschatological centre of the Christian faith. It is the mediator of "Christian hope." [199] It is certainly correct to say the following: the manifold uses of holy oil in the ancient Church, [200] together with the lack of a straightened out concept of "sacrament" until the zenith of scholastic theology, as well as the anchoring of all the sacraments in the fundamental sacrament, which is Christ himself, as the "unchanging incarnate redemptive gift of God to mankind", all this allowed a broader interpretation of the Sacrament of the Sick.

In face of the Eastern Church's tradition it is quite justifiable to ask if the Western understanding of the Sacrament of the Sick as the "final anointing" before death was "legitimate". It is unnecessary to demand a return to the "apostolic tradition" in order to defend an understanding of "Extreme Unction", as "Sacrament of baptismal renewal in face of death", against the Anointing of the Sick understood as spiritual uplift, consolation and comfort. There is no need for this, all that is needed is a glance at the continuity in teaching and practice of the Eastern Church, contrasting strongly with the irregular developments in the West. [201] That is also valid for Gerosa's suggestion that the sacrament could be taken as the "group sacrament" of the sick. The sick are "consecrated" by it and at the same time show the whole Church in their progressive assimilation into the death of Christ that they are making a pilgrimage, which they have set out upon in order to follow Christ existentially in renouncing the world. [202]

---

[196] D. N. Power, Das Sakrament der Krankensalbung. Offene Fragen, Concilium 27 (1991) 154-163. 159.

[197] Cf. R. Zerfaß, Gottesdienst als Handlungsfeld der Kirche. Liturgiewissenschaft als Praktische Theologie? LJ 38 (1988) 30-59, here 55, especially note 55.

[198] Greshake, Letzte Ölung oder Krankensalbung 128.

[199] Ibid. 134.

[200] Ibid. 122f: "Fundamentally it represented something like the 'holy water' of ancient times, that is to say, something analogous to our present day use of holy water or Lourdes water."

[201] Kaczynski, Krankensalbung 313, objects that not only do the liturgical texts themselves deliver no proof for such an understanding of the Anointing of the Sick, but also "it is difficult to understand why only the sick can receive it and not also Christians, who without being ill, face certain death."

[202] Cf. L. Gerosa: Krankensalbung, R. Ahlers / L. Gerosa / L. Müller (Hgg.), Ecclesia a Sacramentis. Theologische Erwägungen zum Sakramentenrecht, Paderborn 1992, 71-82, especially 76-80: Die verfassungsrechtliche Bedeutung der Krankensalbung

4.5.5. THE BYZANTINE EUCHELAION

Even among the Byzantines the development of the sacrament was not without problems, it went however in the opposite direction. If in the West "Extreme Unction" became the sacrament of the dying, in the East the Anointing of the Sick became the sacrament for every sick person, that is to say, even for the only slightly ill, who were not in any way going through a crisis in body and soul, also for the spiritually ill, that is, for every sinner. The result was that in the Byzantine Church the aspect of forgiveness of sin was just as much monopolised as in the West, it even entered into competition with the Sacrament of Penance. Correspondingly all the faithful can receive the Anointing of the Sick, especially during an annual service usually held on Wednesday of Holy Week. [203]

The complete, unabridged form of the service is performed by seven priests. This because of the plural "presbyteroi" in Jas 5:14. The rite consists of three principal parts: 1. The "Paraklisis" is moulded after the Orthros, the morning prayer of the little hours and comprises after the Opening Ps 143 (142) small Ektenie, Troparia with Ps 51 (50), the "Canon", the psalms from Lauds 148-150 with Troparia, Trishagion and Our Father. [204] 2. The Blessing of the holy oil: the Peace Ektenie, Prayer of Blessing and Troparia. [205] 3. The anointings proper: Each of the seven priests performs a separate anointing, which is preceded each time, that is seven times, by a liturgy of the word, consisting of Prokimenon, Lesson, Alleluia, Gospel, small Ektenie and Priest's Prayer. The anointings are performed on the forehead, side of the nose, cheek, mouth, breast and on the palms and uppers of both hands. The prayer which accompanies each speaks of healing and support. [206] After the seventh anointing the open Gospel-book is laid on the head of the sick person, at the same time a prayer begging forgiveness for sin is spoken; after various Troparia the dismissal follows. [207] This complete form is in fact printed in the Euchologia, but in practice hardly ever used (Except perhaps in monasteries). In a normal case even in the Byzantine rite one priest presides over an anointing of the sick and he can choose from a great variety whatever texts he thinks fitting for the situation. "It is probably due to Roman influence that in the liturgical books of the Greeks united with Rome the shortening of the formula has been laid down exactly." [208]

Bibliography

W. von Arx, Das Sakrament der Krankensalbung, Fribourg 1976.

W. von Arx, Die gemeinsame Feier der Krankensalbung: M. Klöckener / W. Glade (eds.): Die Feier der Sakramente in der Gemeinde 263-271.

G. Greshake, Letzte Ölung oder Krankensalbung? Plädoyer für eine differenziertere sakramentale Theorie und Praxis, GuL 56 (1983) 119-136.

R. Kaczynski, Feier der Krankensalbung: GdK 7,2: Sakramentliche Feiern I/2, Regensburg 1992, 241-343.

---

[203] Cf. the description of such services in B. Groen, Die Krankensalbung in der griechisch-orthodoxen Kirche, Concilium (D) 27 (1991) 125-131, especially 126-128.

[204] Cf. Heitz III, 136-149; Kucharek Mysteries 255.

[205] Cf. Ibid. 150-153, loc. cit., 255f.

[206] Cf. Heitz III, 158 the prayer: "Holy Father, Healer of our souls and bodies"

[207] Cf. Ibid. 154-177; Kucharek, loc. cit. 256f.

[208] Kaczynski, Krankensalbung 318. Concerning the whole Cf. 317-321, concerning the Anointing of the Sick in the other oriental Churches ibid. 315-323

A. G. Martimort, Priéres pour les malades et onction sacramentelle: Martimort III, Paris 1984, 132-153.

B. Poschmann, Buße und Letzte Ölung: Handbuch der Dogmengeschichte, ed. by M. Schmaus and others, Bd. IV/3, Freiburg i.Br. 1951.

M. Probst / K. Richter (eds.), Heilssorge für die Kranken und Hilfen zur Erneuerung eines mißverstandenen Sakraments, Freiburg-Vienna-Einsiedeln-Zurich 2nd edn. 1975.

M. Righetti: Manuale di storia liturgica IV: I sacramenti, i sacramentali, Milano 1953, 228-251: L'estrema Unzione.

4.6. THE SACRAMENT OF HOLY ORDERS

4.6.1. THE RENEWAL OF THE LITURGICAL RITE OF ORDINATION

The former rite for ordination of priests contained the words: "Accipe potestatem offerre sacrificium." We have great difficulty today in understanding the Sacrament of Ordination as first and foremost a bestowal or conferring of fullness of power. It is of course true that in this sacrament something is imparted on the receiver which must be considered as bestowal of fullness sacerdotal authority, that is, a priestly power which must be related to the universal priesthood of all baptised, but which is not of the same nature. [209] The aspect of conferring of the fullness of power can however then become dangerous for the image of the priest when it is severed from its place in the community of the church, to which it of necessity belongs, and narrowed down to personal power given to the recipient. [210] The renewal brought about by the council stressed the communal aspect of orders: [211] The ordained person does not receive a power of consecration and absolution which is independent of the community to which he belongs, rather "the Church itself is effective token of grace in her whole nature, whole structure and in the ecclesiastical office which is established in her." [212]

Even the rite itself called for renewal. According to Kleinheyer many elements of the old rite of ordination were decidedly more questionable than, for example, elements of the Mass rite before its reform and have indeed obscured the real meaning of the ordination rite. Historical knowledge must help to show the "way to a future fruitful for both for pastoral work and liturgical celebration." [213] The Council laid open this way, which has not come an end with the second edition of the section on Orders in the Roman Pontifical. [214]

---

[209] Cf. LG 10,2: "The common priesthood of the faithful, however, and the priesthood of service, i.e., the hierarchical priesthood differ not only according to nature but also according to degree (licet essentia et non gradu tantum different). Nevertheless they stand in relation to each other" Cf. also Catechism 1538.

[210] On the "one-sided interpretation" of the office of ordination "in the past". Cf. Lengeling, Theologie des Weihesakramentes 157f.

[211] Cf. Lengeling, Theologie des Weihesakramentes 158-160: Die Rückkehr zum Neuen Testament im Vaticanum II

[212] L. Müller, Weihe, R. Ahlers / L. Gerosa / L. Müller (eds.): Ecclesia a Sacramentis. Theologische Erwägungen zum Sakramentenrecht, Paderborn 1992, 103-124, here 120.

[213] B. Kleinheyer, Überlegungen zu einer Reform des Priesterweiheritus, LJ 14 (1994) 201-210, here 202

[214] Pontificale Romanum: De Ordinatione Episcopi, Presbyterorum et Diaconorum. Editio typica altera, Rome 1990

4.6.2. THE RITE OF ORDINATION IN HISTORY AND PRESENT DAY

The imposition of hands and prayer formed already in New Testament times the central elements of ordination (Cf. Acts 6:6). [215] The same is true even in Hippolytus's Church Order in which the bishops present at the consecration of a bishop and the priests at the ordination of a priest all took part in the laying on of hands, [216] – a characteristic difference, apart from the ordination of a deacon. The imposition of hands is an epicletic gesture, [217] Kleinheyer differentiates nonetheless quite correctly between the assisting bishops' imposition of hands on the candidate and the laying on of hands among priests, this is more the gesture of confrères. At the ordination of a deacon the bishop alone lays on hands, since the deacon "non in sacerdotio ordinatur, sed in ministerio episcopi, ut faciat quae iubet ei". [218] The ordination prayer contained in the Traditio Apostolica [219] is the oldest attested prayer and served as model for the prayer at the consecration of a bishop in the Roman Pontifical of 1968. Hippolytus names Sunday as consecration day. The newly consecrated bishop presides over the Eucharist following his consecration. [220] It is attested for the first time in chapter eight of the Apostolic Constitutions which originated in Syria about 380 and were influenced by Hippolytus that at the consecration of a bishop two deacons laid a Gospel book upon the candidate's head during the prayer of consecration. [221] A hundred years later the Statuta Ecclesiae antiqua [222] testify that in South Gaul the same custom also held, and a similar usage is authenticated for Rome in the 6th century. "Just as for priests and deacons the bishop who laid hands on them remains the enduring sign of their ordination to office, so the Gospel book is for bishops, whose consecrators do not remain, the ever present reminder that they received the Holy Spirit during the ceremony of their consecration." [223]

In Rome the Ordines Romani as well as the sacramentaries of the city itself formed the sources for the rite of ordination. This remained the case until the Pontificale Romano-Germanicum which originated in Mainz about 950 was also accepted in Rome for use in the city. The day for consecration of a bishop was as before Sunday. The preparations for the consecration of a bishop (from elsewhere) in Rome have been described in detail: On Friday the candidate took the oath that he was free of all impediments for consecration. On Saturday the Pope had the validity of the election held by the clergy and people of the local church confirmed and held the "examination": he asked the candidate about his curriculum vitae, about family circumstances, likewise concerning the canon of the biblical books read in his local church. The candidate was

---

[215] The discussion continues whether the laying on of hands might have been inspired by the Jewish ordination of scholars. The prayer on the other hand does not seem to have originated in Jewish customs, Cf. Kleinheyer, Ordinationen 25.

[216] Cf. TradAp. 2, edn. Geerlings 214-217; 7 (Geerlings 230f.), 8 (Geerlings 232f.).

[217] Hippolytus mentions expressly the congregation's silence during the laying on of hands "propter discensionem spiritus", Geerlings 216.

[218] TradAp. 8,ed. Geerlings 232, Cf. Kleinheyer, Ordinationen 26f.

[219] TradAp. 3, ed. Geerlings 216-221.

[220] Cf. TradAp. 2, ed. Geerlings 214f.; TradAp. 4, ed. Geerlings 220-223.

[221] Apostolic Constitutions VIII, 4,6 – SChr 336, 142f.

[222] The author of the Statuta Ecclesiae antiqua from the second half of the 5th cent. was probably the Provence Presbyter Gennadius. They have been edited by Ch. Munier, Les Statuta Ecclesiae antiqua. Edition-Etudes critiques, Paris 1960 (Bibliothèque de l'Institut de droit canonique de l'Université de Strasbourg 5). Cf. Kleinheyer, Priesterweihe 89-93.

[223] Cf. Kleinheyer, Ordinationen 29 with a reference to the Ordo Romanus 40A,5.

instructed about his future duties of office. From the time of Gelasius I (492-496) the ordination of priests and deacons did not take place any more on Sunday, but during the vigil service of Ember Saturday, [224] after the candidates on Monday of Ember Week had sworn under oath that they were free from all impediments which might hinder the consecration, and after on Wednesday and Friday the consecration had been made public with the call that any known impediments were to be revealed; any persons making false accusations were threatened with excommunication. [225] From the time of Gelasius there was a stipulation in the liturgy of consecration that the newly consecrated should at once preside over the Eucharist. The consecration was so placed that the newly consecrated bishop could preside as soon as possible. For that reason – in contrast to the Traditio Apostolica – the consecration of the Roman bishop took place immediately after the opening part, whereas candidates from outside the city were consecrated between the Gradual and the Alleluia of the Mass. The ordination of priests and deacons followed after the last Reading and before the Gospel.

The actual Ordination service began with the bishop's call to prayers for the candidates, the prayer of the congregation is a Kyrie litany. Meanwhile the consecrator, the candidates and all the clergy had cast themselves on the ground in front of the altar. The essential part of the ceremony followed, that is, the imposition of hands and the consecrating prayer. The stipulation made by the Council of Nice which laid down that at least three bishops had to take part in the imposition of hands (chap. 4) shows that at a consecration of a bishop not all the bishops present were doing so. In Rome the Nicean rule was valid only for the case in which the pope was not consecrating; if he undertook the consecration then he alone laid on hands on the candidates. Otherwise the rule was a maximum and a minimum of three bishops. In analogy to a consecration of a bishop by the pope, only the pope laid on hands at the ordination of priests, after three cardinal priests had performed the rite before him. [226] Other rites at a Mass of consecration were the Pax after the consecrating prayer, the proclamation of the Gospel by one of the newly ordained deacons, whereas the new priest himself only took part in giving communion, at the most. In order to make up for that the newly ordained priests who were natives of Rome went in solemn procession to their title church, where they celebrated their first Mass. [227] The sources show that there was no unity of rite as regards the presenting of vestments and insignia, this was not so important in Rome since the Archdeacon performed these rites before the ordination. [228]

It cannot be denied that the Roman rite of ordination was influenced by non-Roman ordination liturgies issuing from the West. The Frankish Church enriched the Roman rite with further elements. The anointings came from the Irish-Celtic or the old Spanish ordination liturgies of the 6th and 7th centuries. More importance was given the presentation of vestments, which the bishop performed saying the accompanying prayer; the handing over of the insignia of office ("Traditio instrumentorum") is also attested for Spain. The imposition of hands and the consecrating prayer and they alone as the

---

[224] Cf. Kleinheyer, Priesterweihe 36-38, concerning the consecration day in Spring as well as the preferred Ember Day in December Cf. 38-47.

[225] Cf. ibid. 47-52: Der Eid der quattuor capitula und die Befragung der Gemeinde. Cf. Kleinheyer, Ordinationen 30f.

[226] Cf. Kleinheyer, Priesterweihe 58-67. Same author: Ordinationen 32f.

[227] Cf. Kleinheyer, Priesterweihe 71-74.

[228] Cf. Kleinheyer, Priesterweihe 74-82; the same author: Ordinationen 35f.

essential action did not seem expressive enough for the Middle Ages, hence new elements were added in order to heighten expressiveness, but which in fact forced the essentials into the background. [229] The same new elements came to Rome through the Pontificale Romano-Germanicum and determined further developments. The influence of the Mainz Pontifical was far-reaching indeed and through the pontificals of the 12th cent., the Pontifical of the Roman Curiae, through that of William Durandus, and finally the Roman Pontifical of 1596 came to influence the reform of the Second Vatican Council. According to the judgement of Cardinal Tommasius (d. 1713), the historian of the liturgy, the Pontificale Romano-Germanicum really a "farrago diversorum rituum", an disordered hoard of the most diverse rites. It was really more a collection of material gathered together from Roman and other traditions than a book suited to liturgical practice, according to Kleinheyer the same statement could indeed be made concerning the rites of Ordination. [230]

This rather untidy collection of ritual actions, which into the bargain were given very different grades importance led to the result that the importance of the essential acts, i. e., imposition of hands and the prayer of consecration, in themselves quite simple, was no longer perceivable, there were indeed submerged in a quagmire of rubrics. The imposition of hands in the Consecration of a bishop had as signifying word ("Accipe Spiritum Sanctum"), and the prayer of consecration was interrupted by the Whitsunday hymn and the main anointing following thereon. [231] In the ordination of a priest there was also a specifying word accompanying the imposition of hands: "Accipe Spiritum Sanctum, quorum remiseris peccata, remittuntur eis, et quorum retinueris, retenta sunt" (John 20:23). These words were no longer spoken at the imposition of hands (formerly the only one), the central point of the ceremony, but accompanied another imposition of hands during a second series of rites after communion. These rites were as follows: until this part of the ceremony the priest's chasuble remained folded on his shoulders, it was now unfolded together with this second laying on of hands. This rite was to signify the "completion" of the priestly ordination with the conferring of power to forgive sins. Only at the end of the second series of rites did the newly ordained declare his promise of obedience by placing his hands between those of the bishops, the rite of "clasping of hands". This was a symbolic gesture borrowed from Germanic law and the feudal system. The idea could thus arise that the power of consecration and absolution were in this manner given ecclesiastical sanction. We can perhaps realise how the essential acts, that is, the (silent) imposition of hands and the prayer of ordination, were almost overlooked when we read that the handing over of chalice and the paten with the prepared offerings (Traditio instrumentorum) were considered to be the essential elements (forma sacramenti) of the ordination rite. This misunderstanding, which was reinforced by the accompanying words, [232] was made obligatory by the Council of Florence 1439 for the Armenians (DH 1326). It was a misunderstanding which remained in force un-

---

[229] Cf. Kleinheyer, Ordinationen 36-43.

[230] Cf. Kleinheyer, Priesterweihe 143-146.

[231] Cf. Roman Pontifical 109-117. Analogously the consecrating prayer in the ordination of deacon was also interrupted, here however at the laying on of hands itself, this was performed with only one hand and accompanied by the signifying words: "Accipe Spiritum sanctum, ad robur, et ad resistendum diabolo, et tentationibus eius. In nomine Domini." Cf. Roman Pontifical 84.

[232] "Accipe potestatem offere sacrificium Deo, Missasque celebrare, tam pro vivis, quam pro defunctis. In nomine Domine." Pont. Rom. 93.

til the correction made under Pius XII. A correction which made it again quite clear that the imposition of hands and the consecratory prayer were the essential rites, while the Traditio instrumentorum belonged to the explanatory rites. [233] "This clarifying correction of Pius XII established the guiding lines for the post conciliar renewal of the ordination rite." [234]

In the revised Ordination liturgy of the Roman Pontifical of 1968, [235] demanded by the Council (SC 76), the imposition of hands and the consecratory prayer constitute the essentials in all three ordinations. [236]

Consecration of Bishop	Ordination of Priest	Ordination of Deacon
After the Gospel:	After the Gospel:	After the Gospel:
Presentation of candidate	Presentation of candidate	Presentation of candidate
Reading of papal letter	Bishop calls candidates	Bishop calls candidates
Consecrator's homily	Consecrator's homily	Consecrator's homily
Candidate's vow of loyalty	Candidates" vows of loyalty	Candidates" vows of loyalty
–	Imposition of hands	Imposition of hands
–	after vows	after vows
Invitation to prayer.	Invitation to prayer.	Invitation to prayer.
Litany.	Litany.	Litany.
Imposition of hands by	Imposition of hands	Imposition of hands
all bishops present.	by bishop and priests.	by bishop.
Placing of Gospel Book.	–	–
Consecratory prayer.	Consecratory prayer.	Consecratory prayer.
–	Vesting with sacerdotal	Vesting with deacon's
	stole and chasuble.	stole and dalmatic.
Principal anointing.	Anointing of hands.	–
Presentation of	Presentation of	Presentation of
Gospel Book.	Bread and Wine.	Gospel Book.
Bishop receives ring.	–	–
Mitre placed on bishop's head.	–	–
Presentation of crozier.	–	–
Inthronation of bishop.	–	–
Kiss of peace.	Kiss of peace.	Kiss of peace.

The liturgy of the consecratory Mass leads us forward to the essential actions after the Gospel has been proclaimed. At the consecration of a bishop the papal letter (mandatum apostolicum) is read out after the presentation of the candidate, or candidates. [237] At an ordination the names of the priests, or as the case may be, deacons, are called out. This is a confirmation of the request for ordination; the people also contribute to its realization hence a question is put to the congregation, a minute remembrance of

---

[233] By analogy there was also in the ordination of deacons a rite in which a "potestas" was imparted by the handing over of the Gospel Book: "Accipe potestatem legendi Evangelium in Ecclesia Die, tam pro vivis, quam pro defunctis. In nomine Domini." Pontificale Romanum 85.

[234] Cf. The Apostolic Constitution "Sacramentum Ordinis" of 30. 11. 1947, DH 3857-3861; Kleinheyer, Ordinationen 47.

[235] Cf. The Apostolic Constitution "Pontificalis Romani" of 18th June 1968, Kaczynski 1080-1088.

[236] See Kleinheyer, Ordinationen 48.

[237] CIC/1917 c. 953 is confirmed by CIC/1983 c. 1013: A bishop must not consecrate anyone until he has received the apostolic mandate.

the canonical election of clerics, and the whole congregation also answers: Thanks be to God. There is a model form of address inspired by Scripture and the statements of the 2nd Vatican Council for each of the three rites. The former calling on the congregation to give its opinion regarding the choice of candidates has been dropped. When the sermon or address has been given the candidate, or candidates pronounce their vows, in the ordination of deacons and priests there is a promise of obedience with the gesture "clasping of hands". In the consecration of a bishop the former "examination" has been integrated into the vow taken; an examination has now been introduced into the ordination of a deacon, in view of the fact that the diaconate is an ordination in its own right. It is only logical that the promise of obedience follows directly on the vows: the exercise of priestly or diaconal duties is only possible in a specific local Church, which the bishop represents. [238] The three petitions for the candidates in the litany preparatory to the central rites have now been better blended into the whole ceremony. Before the liturgical reform the bishop himself sang them and at the same time blessed the candidates, this has been changed in the new handbook to the Pontifical "thus the temptation to allow the former practice to stand and have the bishop sing the petitions has been quite emphatically checked". [239]

The consecratory prayer is now no longer interrupted by other actions, whether it be an essential rite (as, for example, the imposition of hands in the former rite of ordination of deacons) or explanatory signs or gestures (as the principal anointing at the consecration of bishops). No explanatory words are spoken during the imposition of hands, the consecratory prayer itself is "explanation". Likewise at the ordination of priests the second imposition of hands has been dropped during the second series of rites after communion. At the consecration of a bishop all the bishops present take part in the laying on of hands, the number is no longer limited to three. As at the time of Hippolytus the three distinct degrees of ordination are distinguished in that there is a distinction regarding those taking part in the laying on of hands. The placing of the Gospel book has been kept for the consecration of bishops, now however the book is clearly placed on the candidate's head, and the epicletical character of the essential action is emphasized. Kleinheyer thinks it problematic that in the consecratory prayers "verba essentialia" are still especially stressed. [240] In the second edition of the handbook to the Pontifical "De Ordinatione" of 1990 the revision of the rite of ordination of priests is more extensive than that for the ordination of deacons. [241]

The explanatory rites were so structured that the essential part of the ceremony stands out clearly and is not overshadowed by details of secondary importance. For example, it was deemed more meaningful that the newly ordained should appear before bishop and congregation in the appropriate vestments as visible signs of the degree of their ordination than that they should receive the vestments from the hands of the bishop. The anointings and presentations are now also clearly apparent as explanatory symbolic actions. (The rectifying of "rubical accident" was necessary as regards the anointing: until the reform the rubrics prescribed oil of catechumens, now chrism is

---

[238] Cf. In this regard L. Müller's explanation, Weihe, R. Ahlers / L. Gerosa / L. Müller (eds.), Ecclesia a Sacramentis, 103-123: Das Sakrament der Weihe in der kirchlichen Communio.
[239] Kleinheyer, Ordinationsfeiern 94.
[240] Cf. Kleinheyer, Ordinationen 50, espec. Note 42.
[241] Cf. Kleinheyer, Ordinationsfeiern 104-106, 115f.

of course prescribed, since the anointing has to do with the whole person and does not impart a "special skill to hands in order to benedicere, sanctificare, consecrare" [242]; nowhere in the renewed liturgy are text and symbolic action allowed to give the impression that here the essentials of the ordination liturgy are performed. That which Kleinheyer terms "Kiss of Peace" might more properly be named "Kiss of admission". For example, in the ordination of deacons there was a regulation, not obligatory, which allowed deacons who were present also to give the kiss of peace after the bishop had done so. In the second edition of the revised Ordination ritual of 1990 this regulation is taken for granted: "Similiter faciunt omnes vel saltem nonnulli diaconi praesentes." [243] Accordingly this kiss is clearly understood as a kiss welcoming the brother in office to the new ordination status. [244]

Kleinheyer asks whether the rite of ordination of deacons, which presumes that the deacon will now exercise his office for life, or at least over a lengthy period, and which is thus a rite concerning first and foremost only deacons as such, [245] should also be used unchanged for candidates to the priesthood, who in fact exercise this office of deacon only for a short time. [246]

4.6.3. THE RITES OF APPOINTMENT TO THE MINISTERIES [247]

These rites do not really belong to ordination ceremonies, a fact which is already confirmed by the oldest source for the rites followed in appointment to office: When one reads Hippolytus it becomes clear that the appointment to office of subdeacon and lector was distinct from the consecration of bishop and from the ordination to priesthood and diaconate. [248] An imposition of hands does not take place, and as regards the lectorship there is the first description of a lector being introduced to his office by the presentation of a characteristic object, in this case a book. [249] Indeed the traditio instrumentorum becomes the central rite in the appointment to these services (lectionary, book with the exorcisms for exorcists, processional candle holders for acolytes as well as chalice and paten for subdeacons). In the Roman-Germanic Pontifical from the middle of the tenth century the elevation of the subdiaconate to the "higher" orders is already hinted at (suggested); in the Pontifical of the 12th century the elevation has become a fact. Some ritual elements of the ordination rite have been taken up into the "ordination" of subdeacons (e.g. litany prayer, rite of presentation of vestments). [250] "One thing however is absolutely definite: non imponetur manus, there is no imposition of hands." [251] The development of such ritual elements, which can also be observed in the other "minor

---

[242] Kleinheyer, Ordinationen 56.

[243] Roman Pontifical ... De Ordinatione Episcopi, Presbyterorum et Diaconorum. Editio typica altera. Romae 1990, 125.

[244] Cf. Kleinheyers Commentary to the second edition: Ordinationsfeiern 95.

[245] Cf. N. Trippen, Die Erneuerung des Ständigen Diakonats im Gefolge des II. Vatikanischen Konzils, J. G. Plöger / H. J. Weber (eds.), Der Diakon. Wiederentdeckung und Erneuerung seines Dienstes, Freiburg-Basel-Vienna 1980, 83-103.

[246] Cf. Kleinheyer, Ordinationen 58.

[247] Cf. Chap. 2.10.3. Various celebrations in Church life: the special liturgical appointments.

[248] According to the Statuta Ecclesiae antiqua it is even the Archdeacon, who introduces the acolyte into his office, Cf. Kleinheyer, Ordinationen 63.

[249] Cf. TradAp. 13 and 11, ed. Geerlings 242-243.

[250] Cf. Jounel, Ordinations: Martimort III, 186-187

[251] Kleinheyer, Ordinationen 62

orders" can be explained by the fact that they were considered as preliminary steps in the preparation for the sacrament of Holy Orders, one might perhaps understand them as "side-products". [252]

According to the Motu proprio of Pope Paul 6th "Ministeria quaedam" of 15th August 1972 [253] the "minor orders" as well as the tonsure, [254] understood as entrance into clerical state, have been abolished in favour of the newly established offices of lector and acolyte. Only those who have received one or more of the three sacramental ordinations now belong to the clerical state. The persons appointed to these newly established offices are therefore laypersons who perform them in the dignity of the royal priesthood. [255] The inner contradictions of this Motu proprio and the practices following thereupon (De facto re-establishing of the "minor orders" for candidates to the priesthood, exclusion of women) have already been treated elsewhere. [256] In accordance with the latest reform the rite for assignment to the new tasks of lector and acolyte together with that for the reception of candidates to the priesthood and diaconate, and also that for the promise of celibacy, all make up part of the revised Roman Pontifical. [257] The bishop makes the appointment while the introduction to the office is performed as before by the "Traditio instrumentorum" (lectionary, or as the case may be, ciborium and wine cruet). The appointment to these permanent offices by the bishop reminds one all the more of the minor orders when one compares it with the installing of ministers of the Eucharist [258] by the parish priest.

The reception as candidate for the priesthood or deaconship cannot be considered an ordination. Until the revision of the liturgy one became a cleric by receiving the tonsure, and hence a candidate for the reception of holy orders. [259] After the reform of the (instituted) offices "it seemed meaningful instead of the rite 'De clerico faciendo' to introduce a service of reception when candidates were being received for office." [260] The service of "Admissio", which may not be joined to an ordination or appointment, is conducted by the bishop. The candidates proclaim before him their decision to serve "God and the Church in Holy Orders". In accordance with the second edition of the fascicle

---

[252] Cf. Maas-Ewerd, Nicht gelöste Fragen 152f. Th. Schnitzler, starting from the understanding that the minor orders were products of the major orders, argued with logic, and that before the reform of the liturgy, that even the office of altar-server was really a clerical office, and the Mass-server a delegate of the priest, Cf. art. "Ministranten": LThK 2nd edn. VII,429: "Ideally clerics should take over the duties of Mass-servers."

[253] Cf. Kaczynski 2877-2893.

[254] Concerning the ritual cutting of hair Cf. Ph. Gobillot, Sur la tonsure chrétienne et ses prétendues origines paiennes, Revue d'histoire ecclésiastique 21 (1925) 399-454.

[255] Cf. Kaczynski 2880, 2883.

[256] Cf. Maas-Ewerd, Nicht gelöste Fragen 160-164. On the exclusion of women from the instituted service as acolytes Cf. Nußbaum, Lektorat und Akolythat 23; A. G. Martimort's explanation is interesting, which however does not make it more comprehensible, La question du service des femmes á l'autel, Notitiae 162 (1980) 8-16, especially 15.

[257] Pontificale Romanum..., De institutione Lectorum et Acolythorum, de admissione inter candidatos ad Diaconatum et Presbyteratum, de sacro caelibato amplectendo, Rome 1972. On the adoption by the various local churches Cf. Kaczynski, 2924.

[258] Ministers of the Eucharist according to the Instruction "Immensae caritatis" of 29th Jan. 1973, Cf. Kaczynski, 2967-2982.

[259] By the Motu proprio "Ad pascendum" of 15th August 1972, Kaczynski 2894-2912, and the fascicle "De institutione Lectorum" of the Roman Pontifical of 3rd Dec. 1972. The Motu proprio lays down clearly: "Ingressus in statum clericalem et incardinatio alicui dioecesi ipsa ordinatione Diaconali habentur", Kaczynski 2910.

[260] Kleinheyer, Ordinationen 59.

to the Pontifical "De ordinatione" of 1990 the vow of celibacy for presbyterandi and unmarried diaconate candidates is from now on part of the vows taken at the ordination of deacons. [261]

4.6.4. THE BYZANTINE LITURGY OF ORDINATION

In the Byzantine rite there is even at the consecration of "candle-bearer" (acolyte), of chanter, lector and subdeacon an imposition of hands. In contrast to the sacrament of Ordination the imposition is not described as "Cheirotonia", but as "Cheirothesia". [262] The "major orders" are also distinguished from the "minor" by the part of the church where they are given, the former are held at the altar, while the latter are received in the nave. At an ordination there is always only one candidate, while for the other offices there may be several candidates. [263]

The ordination liturgies are all characterized by a structure of the "uttermost simplicity" [264]: 1. The "Bidding Forth" call marks the beginning of the ordination ceremony proper, together with the presentation of the candidate for ordination. 2. The candidate walks three times around the altar. 3. The candidate's genuflection before the altar and the touching of it with his forehead. 4. The imposition of hands by the bishop with the "Theia-Charis" formula. 5. First epiclectical silent prayer of the bishop, while the clergy and congregation sing the Kyries. 6. The second epiclectical silent prayer of the bishop, while the deacon sings the Peace-ektenia with the congregation. 7. Vesting of the newly ordained with garments of office, together with the "Axios" exclamations of the bishop, the clergy and the congregation.

All three major ordinations (Cheirotoniai) take place during the eucharistic celebration. The ordination to the diaconate is performed after the eucharistic anaphora, the ordination to priesthood after the solemn entrance and the consecration of a bishop after the Trishagion: [265] The newly ordained should already exercise his new official functions during the ordination liturgy. [266] A vestigial remainder of the canonical election of an office-holder are the "bidding exclamations" of the deacons to the clergy and assembled people in which they are called upon to undertake the holy ordination. [267] The bishop's imposition of hands is accompanied by the "Theia-Charis" formula, differing in the naming of the degree of ordination. In the ordination of a deacon it is as follows: "The divine grace, which always healeth and maketh up for what is lacking, doth promote N. N., the most pious Hypodeacon, to be deacon; let us therefore pray for him in order that the grace of the all-holy Spirit come upon him!" [268]

Some hold the "Theia-Charis" formula to be the same consecratory prayer for all degrees of ordination. In other oriental Churches however it is only the announcement of

---

[261] Cf. Kleinheyer Ordinationsfeiern 111.

[262] Cf. A. v. Maltzew, Die Sacramente der Orthodox-Katholischen Kirche des Morgenlandes. Deutsch und slawisch unter Berücksichtigung des griechischen Urtextes, Berlin 1898, 304 und 314. According to Hotz – Sakramente 252 – the notion "cheirotonia" still indicates a vote with with raised hand at a meeting, that is, an electing procedure on the part of the people.

[263] Cf. Maltzew, Sacramente 301f.

[264] See: J. M. Hanssens, La forme sacramentelle dans les ordinations sacerdotales de rite grec, Gregorianum 5 (1924) 208-277, 6 (1925) 41-80; here 218f.

[265] Cf. Heitz III, 217, 221, 229. Maltzew, Sacramente 319, 333, 442; Kucharek, Mysteries 297f.

[266] Cf. Hotz, Sakramente 253.

[267] Cf. Kucharek, Mysteries 298.

[268] Maltzew, Sacramente 322f.

the act of ordination by the Archdeacon and the ascertaining of a legitimately carried out election. [269] Trembelas however holds the wish to establish the "verba essentialia" of the ordination ritual to be an illegitimate latinization; "the consecratory epiclesis is spread throughout the whole ceremony and above all throughout the prayers." [270] According to Hanssens the two silent prayers of the bishop following upon the imposition of hands, he still continues imposing hands, constitute the form of the ordination sacrament; they are accompanied by a diaconal ektenia, which is as follows: "For the servant of God N., who now *will* be ordained deacon and for his salvation let us pray to the Lord." [271] The claim to perceive the forma sacramenti in the "Theia-Charis" formula alone can indeed be questioned, although it has been so defined for the Ukrainian Church in union with Rome. It might be better to consider the formula with the two silent prayers of the bishop as a unity, with the formula seen as a prelude to both deprecative prayers of the bishop. [272]

The "interpretative rites", the handing over of the vestments of office now follow, together with the "Axios" exclamations, which the clergy and congregation repeat after the bishop; Heiler perceives this as an active partaking of all present by reason of the royal priesthood. [273] In the Greek tradition the presentation of the newly ordained and the admission kiss of the bishop on his forehead now follow. Among the Slav Churches "traces of the false theory of Latin scholastics can be detected, according to which the matter of the sacrament of ordination consists of the handing over of the instruments, see, for example, Gabriel Severus and Petrus Mogilas." [274] The newly ordained deacon is given the Rhipidia, and a priest the Euchologion (Sacramental), or even liturgical vessels. [275]

Bibliography

I. H. Dalmais: Die Mysterien (Sakramente) im orthodoxen und altorientalischen Christentum: W. Nyssen / H. J. Schulz / P. Wiertz (eds.), Handbuch der Ostkirchenkunde II, Düsseldorf 2nd edn.1989, 141-181.

I. Doens, Der Weiheritus in der Ostkirche des byzantinischen Ritus: K. Rahner / H. Vorgrimler, Diakonia in Christo. Über die Erneuerung des Diakonates, Freiburg-Basel-Vienna 1962 (QD 15/16), 57-61.

P. Jounel, Les ordinations: Martimort III, Paris 1984, 154-196.

P. Jounel, Les institutions aux ministères: Martimort III, Paris 1984, 197-200.

B. Kleinheyer, Die Priesterweihe im römischen Ritus. Eine liturgiehistorische Studie, Trier 1962 (TThSt 12).

B. Kleinheyer, Weiheliturgie in neuer Gestalt. In: LJ 18 (1968) 210-229.

---

[269] Thus F. Heiler, Urkirche und Ostkirche München 1937, 276, contrary to Hotz, Sakramente, 252f

[270] Trembelas 327f.

[271] Heitz III, 219

[272] Cf. J. M. Hanssens, La forme sacramentelle 75f.

[273] Maltzew, Sacramente 329f. Cf. Heiler 277: "At the ordination of priest and deacon the laity co-operate by reason of their universal priesthood, in that they confirm the 'Axios exclamation of the bishop, which is repeated by the clergy, with their own 'Axios' (he is worthy)."

[274] F. Heiler: Urkirche und Ostkirche. München 1937, 275.

[275] Cf. Maltzew 330 and 342; Heitz in Mysterium III, 220 also mentions the presenting of the Rhipidion. Cf. also Kucharek, Mysteries 299: "The priest is given a service book to guide him in the holy ministry. In some churches, he is also handed a chalice and diskos (paten)."

B. Kleinheyer, Ordinationen und Beauftragungen: Sakramentliche Feiern II, GdK 8, Regensburg 1984, 6-65.

B. Kleinheyer, Ordinationsfeiern. Zur zweiten Auflage des Pontificale-Faszikels 'De Ordinatione Episcopi, presbyterorum et diaconorum': LJ 41 (1991) 88-118.

E. J. Lengeling, Die Theologie des Weihesakramentes nach dem Zeugnis des neuen Ritus, LJ 19 (1969) 142-166.

Th. Maas-Ewerd, Nicht gelöste Fragen in der Reform der 'Weiheliturgie': Ibid. (ed.), Lebt unser Gottesdienst? 151-173.

O. Nußbaum, Lektorat und Akolythat. Zur Neuordnung der liturgischen Laienämter, Köln 1974 (Kölner Beiträge 17).

O. Nußbaum, Theologie und Ritus der Diakonenweihe: J. G. Plöger / H. J. Weber (eds.): Der Diakon. Wiederentdeckung und Erneuerung seines Dienstes, Freiburg-Basel-Vienna 1980, 122-146.

M. Righetti, Manuale di storia liturgica IV: I sacramenti, i sacramentali, Milano 1953, 252-333: L'Ordine.

K. Ware, Man, Woman and the Priesthood of Christ: Th. Hopko (ed.), Women and the priesthood, Crestwood-New York 1983, 9-37.

4.7. THE SACRAMENT OF MARRIAGE

4.7.1. ON THE HISTORY OF THE MARRIAGE LITURGY

No other sacramental rite has been so influenced by pre-christian and non-christian practices as the wedding rite. Jewish and heathen marriage customs left their mark on the initial stages of Christian marriage. According to the letter of Diognet "Christians marry just as all others do". However, this view must not hinder the other: The followers of Jesus endeavour to live in harmony with the new order of their master, they seek ways and means to help them grasp the ecclesial and christological dimension of wedded life in signs and words of prayer, it is their intent to understand, confess and live marriage as a sign of faith." [276]

We learn from Ignatius of Antioch that Christians marry as all others do, but they do this "with the assent of the bishop", so that "their marriage comes from the Lord and not from lust". [277] Ignatius does not however provide us with any further information concerning the (liturgically composed?) form of this assent. There is a disputed passage among Tertullian's writings which is concerned with matrimony "quod ecclesia conciliat et confirmat oblatio et obsignat benedictio, angeli renuntiant, pater rato habet". [278] Some authors, for example Ritzer, [279] refuse to accept that marriage liturgy existed, others Crouzel, [280] for example, see here an indication that such did exist, for

---

[276] Diognet-Brief 5,6 – ed. K. Wengst, Schriften des Urchristentums II, Darmstadt 1984, 318; Cf. Kleinheyer, Riten 82. On late Jewish, Greek and Roman wedding ritual Cf. ibid. 77- 80.

[277] Ad Polycarpum 5,2 – PG 5, 868 A.

[278] Ad uxorem II, 8,6 – CChr SL 1, 393.

[279] Cf. Ritzer 58-67.

[280] Cf. H. Crouzel, Deux textes de Tertullien concernant la procédure et les rites du mariage chrétien, BLE 74 (1973) 3-13.

the majority, however, e.g., Martimort,[281] the question, was there indeed a marriage ritual, remains unanswered. Kleinheyer, referring to Vogel[282], maintains that the wedding blessing in the nuptial chamber, described by the Apostel Thomas, is an indication that there was an early Christian form of marriage ritual (even if this evolved earlier in Gnostic circles than in the universal Church).[283]

In the universal Church two different viewpoints emerged; the Western Church follows the principle "consensus facit nuptias" and the husband and wife administer the sacrament. This viewpoint dates from the time of Hippolytus' quarrel with Callixtus concerning the ecclesiastical recognition of a marriage not recognized by the state; such a recognition created a special ecclesiastical code of law for marriage, (the liturgical rite is to this day almost secondary, hence the possibilty of the unliturgical "sanatio in radice", or the dispensation from every form of liturgical ritual of marriage). In the Eastern Church the standpoint is as follows: the priest is considered the minister of the sacrament, in a liturgical rite in which the couple pronounce their consent and which may not be omitted, he raises a natural marriage by virtue of an epicletical blessing (or consecration) to the dignity of a sacrament. When studying all phases of the liturgical development of the marriage rite in West and East this difference must be taken into consideration.

The oldest Roman Sacramentals attest a blessing for the bride and a celebration of the Eucharist at a marriage ceremony. The relationship between the bridal blessing, going together with the velatio nuptialis, the veiling, something taken over from Roman customs, and the bridal Mass is a disputed point. Typical for this further stage of development – regionally in quite different forms – is according to Kleinheyer: a) The transference of the blessing from the father of the family to the bishop, or under circumstances, to the presbyter, b) the combination of velatio and benedictio is no longer for the bride alone, but for the bridal couple and c) the taking of this ceremony out of a house-liturgy and making it part of a parish liturgy and a eucharistic celebration.

Moreover a marked difference between the Greeks and Latins now ensued: for the Greeks the marriage ceremony in the church is essential, this was still held to be valid civil law in an instruction of Pope Nicholas to the Bulgarians from the year 866. In the Western tradition on the other hand the publicly announced will to marry established a marriage.[284] A characteristic feature of the Old-Gallic liturgy is the blessing in the nuptial chamber ("Benedictio in thalamo"), after the bride has been taken to the bridegroom's house, this was imparted instead of a benedictio nuptialis in the domestic area or in the church.[285]

The ecclesiastical blessing had been regarded not only as civil law, but even as "civic duty" – at least for the first marriage – in the Eastern patriarchates since the fourth century.[286] The civic official took over the "Ekdosis", from the father, that is: the handing over of the bride to the bridegroom by giving of hands. The bishop, or the presbyter, had the duty of saying the blessing prayer, and, at least conceivable, the

[281] Cf. Martimort, Contribution de l'histoire liturgique á la théologie du mariage, Notitiae 14 (1978) 513-533.
[282] C. Vogel, Le rôle du liturgie dans la formation du lien conjugal, RDC 30 (1980) 7-27.
[283] Cf. Kleinheyer, Riten 82.
[284] Cf. Kleinheyer, Riten 89-91.
[285] Cf. Kleinheyer, Riten 92f.
[286] Cf. Ritzer 82.

crowning[287] of the bridal couple. Gregory of Nazianzus protested against this, he wanted to have the crowning performed by the bride's father.

In the Western Church the ratifying of a Christian marriage was taken completely out of the area of home and kinsfolk during the Middle Ages, marriage had now become a matter of public interest and the cermony took place in the parish. The conclusion of a marriage "in facie ecclesiae" is taken literally: the wedding ceremony was performed in front of the church, at the bridal-door. The roots of this development are to be found in the changes brought about in society by the migration of the peoples, there was now a demand for greater legal security and for validly ratified marriage: in accordance with the principle "consensus facit nuptias" the freely taken decision to wed must be expressed before the greatest possible number of witnesses. The origins of the wedding ceremony at the bridal-door of the church are to be found in the Anglo-Saxon and Norman areas. South of a line drawn from Bordeaux to Grenoble the "benedictio in thalamo", the blessing of the ring and the bridal offerings determine the church's part in the ratifying of marriage, north of this line, however, the by then more familiar ceremony at the bridal-door was ratified by the priest's questions regarding mutual consent. He finally took over from the bride's father the giving of hands, or he confirmed the couple's giving each other the hand on their own initiative. Then followed the handing over of the marriage contract, the blessing of the ring (worn by the bride alone on her left hand) and the bridal offerings, after which blessing prayers completed the ceremony and gave the signal for the entry into the church. In Germany there was only slow acceptation of the ceremony at the bridal-door; it was finally accepted by the Bavarian dioceses towards the end of the 15th cent. The older Benedictio nuptialis was made an integral part of the Mass which followed on the ceremony at the bridal-door. Its place within the liturgy of the Mass was different according to region, and even the velatio, which was joined to it had various forms. If a priest omitted the Benedictio nuptialis he was threatened with suspension; according to Kleinheyer this sanction indicated that a sacramental rite was indeed being here performed.[288]

The Council of Trent confirmed the doctrine that marriage is a sacrament[289], this against the Reformers' denial of the teaching. The Council also still continued holding fast to the principle that the consent of the bridal couple constitutes a marriage, and, as had been expressed in the decree "Tametsi",[290] the consent is the obligatory form.[291] The questions regarding the will to marry and the declaration of consent take place from now on in the church. The blessing and the giving, or exchange, of rings were performed differently according to region, likewise the blessing of the bridal offering, an offering in the form of a gift of coins which lasted in some regions of France well into the 20th cent. The velatio was still quite common in France in the 18th cent. In 1850 it was forbidden by the Roman Congregation of Rites, but was allowed again a little later by indult for the bishopric of Nancy in Lorraine. Concerning the history of

---

[287] This was originally a heathen wedding custom. It was rejected by Tertullian and only became "acceptable" when Chrysostomos gave it a Christian interpretation in the Christian marriage liturgy. Cf. Kleinheyer, Riten 95.

[288] Cf. Kleinheyer, Riten 100-110.

[289] DH 1801.

[290] DH 1813.

[291] Kleinheyer, Riten 113, remarks in this respect: "The course, which had been begun in the development to the bridal-door marriage, is continued logically to its conclusion with 'Tametsi' ".

the wedding ceremony until the Second Vatican Council it can be said in summing up that the regional difference, allowed by the Roman Ritual of 1614, preserved many variants of the marriage rite. A unification on an over-diocesan level was brought about for German speaking countries by rituals like the "Collectio rituum" only in 1950. Unfortunately the marriage rite within the Eucharistic Service, as is customary today, was not introduced; this was however usual in the bishopric of Metz due to an older tradition, everywhere else the marriage ceremony was performed first and was followed by the wedding Mass, which began with the prayers at the foot of the altar.

4.7.2. THE REVISED RITE OF MARRIAGE

The Council asked for a renewal of the marriage rite. According to SC 77 the marriage rite should be so revised and enriched "that it indicates more clearly the grace of the sacrament and urgently stresses the duties of married people." It is expressly laid down that local usages and special customs should be kept. Under SC 78 it is stipulated that a marriage ceremony within the bridal Mass (after the Gospel and homily) should be the rule. A marriage ceremony not celebrated with Mass should take place during a Service of the Word, in which the reading and Gospel of the Wedding Mass are proclaimed; the wedding blessing must always be given. [292] The revised marriage liturgy contains the "Ordo celebrandi matrimonium" of 19th March 1969, [293] in the second edition (Editio typica altera) which appeared on 19th March 1990.

A. Structure of Marriage Ceremony

After the Gospel and homily of the Wedding Mass, or Service of the Word follow:

1. Questions on the readiness to enter into the married state
2. Blessing of the Rings
3. Declaration of Consent (with different forms)
4. Confirmation by Celebrant
5. Blessing of the wedding couple
6. Bidding Prayers

The Mass, or Service of the Word, is then continued, with special final blessing.

The questions on the will to marry correspond in content to the Collectio rituum. The pronouncing of consent by the bridal couple themselves is the usual case, for which a formula of consent taken from the Anglo-Saxon-Norman tradition is used. If need be the celebrant may also inquire about consent. The confirmation of the consent is a quotation from Mt. 19,6b and in the form of a petition for blessing. It takes the place of the formula in the Roman Ritual of 1614: "Ego vos coniungo in matrimonium," a formula which, contrary to the Western understanding that the bridal couple administered the sacrament, endeavoured to foist upon the priest the role of minister. Today the putting of the ring on the partner's finger is part of the expression of consent, and this action is accompanied by a word of explanation. The blessing of the bride has become a blessing of the bridal couple. The liturgy of the Nuptial Mass forms the guiding lines for the Service of the Word at a Wedding. The blessing of the bridal couple follows immediately after main rite as a high light, so to speak, of the ceremony. In German speaking

---

[292] Before the reform of the liturgy the benedictio nuptiarum was given only: 1. at a following wedding Mass, 2. outside the "forbidden times", otherwise only with dispensation, 3. at the bride's first wedding.

[293] Cf. Kaczynski 1249-1267.

countries "the rite for celebration of Marriage" also follows this usage in the nuptial Mass, whereas the Roman Missel in the desire to follow tradition places the blessing after the Our Father of the Mass. [294]

4.7.3. THE BYZANTINE "CELEBRATION OF CROWNING"

In the present rite the betrothal and the actual celebration of the crowning have been woven together into one single liturgical act. It is also part of the betrothal that the priest puts the rings on; the place where the ceremony takes place is the nave, but not yet the analogion, a table with the Gospel-book, which is placed in front of the royal door of the Ikonostasis. [295] In the ceremony of crowning the deacon first sings the peace ektenia, then the priest recites three long epicletical prayers in which God's sanctifying grace is called down upon the bridal couple. Then follows the actual crowning:

The priest takes the crowns or the specially made bridal wreaths, makes with them a cross on the Gospel-book, makes the sign of the cross with them over bride and bride-groom and holds them over the couple with the words: "The servant of God N. N. (the handmaid of God N. N.) is crowned by the handmaid of God N. N. (by the servant of God N. N.) in the name of the Father... ". He who has conducted the bride and is now standing behind the couple exchanges the crowns and places them on their heads. The "Synaxis for those who have been crowned and for those belonging to them" now follows, that is: Reading, Gospel, Ektenia. The ceremony ends with the giving of a chalice with blessed wine and a round-dance about the analogium which is led by the priest and to which the choir sings troparia. [296] It strikes one at once that in the marriage rite all the activity is left to the priest, he is responsible for the epicletical prayers, the performing of the crowning and even putting the rings on; in the Greek ritual the bridegroom and bride say nothing. In the nuptial rite of the Russian-Orthodox Church, however, questions regarding consent are put, which as regards the theology and canon-ical understanding of marriage, are fully in harmony with the understanding of the Latin Church. [297] This inquiry regarding consent has its origins in the euchologion of Petrus Mogila (Ukrainish: Petro Mohyla) from the year 1646, which was strongly influenced by the Latins. Latin thinking finally left its mark on the liturgy reform of the Moscow Patriarch Nikon (1652-58) through Mogila's influential Euchologion. [298] The Serbian ritual also contains the question on consent. Raes explains this by the fact that the Serbs possessed no printing press of their own because of the occupation by the Turks and had to use Russian books. [299]

---

[294] Concerning the revised rite of marriage, and also the different European marriage rites Cf. Kleinheyer, Riten 125-137.

[295] Cf. Heitz III, 184-187.

[296] Cf. ibidem 188-201.

[297] Cf. in this respect the Motu proprio of Pius XII from the year 1949 "De disciplina sacramenti matrimonii pro Ecclesia orientali", AAS 41 (1949) 89-117, in which many canons are fully in harmony with the CIC of 1917. Cf. Trebnik (= Euchologion) v dvuch castjach, cast a, published by the Patriarchat of Moscow, Moskva 1979, 100-101. For the Ukrainian Euchologion Cf. Malej Trebnik, Rome 1973, 60-61.

[298] Cf. A. Raes, Le consentement matrimonial dans les rites orientaux, EL 47 (1933) 34-47, 126-146, 244-259, 431-445; 48 (1934) 80-94, 310-318; A. A. Wenger, Les influences du Rituel de Paul V sur le Trebnik der Pierre Moghila, Mélanges en l'honneur de Msgr. Andrieu, Straßburg 1956, 477-499.

[299] Cf. Raes, Consentement 440.

4.7.4. WHO ADMINISTERS THE SACRAMENT OF MARRIAGE?

There are differences between the Western-Catholic and the Eastern-Orthodox under-standing of the sacrament of marriage, there are also differences regarding the minister of the sacrament, these differences then in their turn influence the form of the marriage liturgy.

According to Catholic teaching when two baptized persons live together as wedded couple, their marriage is always a sacrament since Christ has raised the marriage bond to the dignity of a sacrament. [300] Consequently the husband and wife are themselves ministers of the sacrament for each other. According to the Decretum pro Armenis the couple's declaration of consent concerning the triplex bonorum of matrimony con-stitutes the "Causa efficiens" of the sacrament. [301] The official ecclesiastical act at the concluding of a marriage is thus limited to the acceptance of the consent by the re-sponsible priest and the blessing of the couple now considered as already married by reason of their consent. The acceptance of this consent by the priest is obligatory since the introduction of the obligation of form by the Council of Trent. Endeavours to make the priest's activity in the liturgy of marriage the basis of its sacramental character have not won acceptance in the Catholic Church. [302] The importance Catholic theology at-taches to consent as the basis for the sacramental character of marriage becomes clear precisely in the provisions for exceptional cases and dispensations (in extreme cases, dispensation from canonical form, as a dispensation from every prescribed liturgical celebration of marriage).

The theology of the Orthodox Church accepts a gradual realisation of the sacramen-tal marriage on the basis of an existing consent to marry on the part of the couple. [303] The celebrant asks for this marriage consent as a requirement for every sacramental-liturgical action *before* the beginning of the betrothal rite, the intertwining of which with the "ceremony of crowning" has a long tradition. [304] According to Trembelas the fact that the consent is no longer pronounced in a liturgical form reveals the natural wed-lock itself, which must be raised to the dignity of sacrament by the ceremony of crown-ing. [305] The natural bond of marriage, which belongs to the reality of creation, but which was corrupted by the fall into sin, receives in the ceremony of crowning a transforma-

---

[300] Cf. c. 1012 CIC 1917: "§1 Christus Dominus ad sacramenti dignitatem evexit ipsum contractum matri-monialem inter baptizatos. §2 Quare inter baptizatos nequit matrimonialis contractus validus consistere, quin sit eo ipso sacramentum." This definition of the sacrament of marriage is to be found in c. 1055; §2 / CIC 1983, which was taken word for word from the CIC of 1917, the definition has indeed been broadened, but the original wording has been kept almost unchanged

[301] DH 1327: Causa efficiens matrimonii regulariter est mutuus consensus per verba de praesenti expressus. Asignatur autem triplex bonorum matrimonii.'

[302] Cf. L. Ott, Grundriß der Dogmatik. Freiburg-Basel-Vienna 10th edn. 1981, 557 and J. Ratzinger / J. Auer, Kleine kath. Dogmatik VII, Regensburg 1972, 276f.

[303] Cf. A. Kallis, "Kröne sie mit Herrlichkeit und Ehre". Zur Ekklesiologie der orthodoxen Trauung, K. Richter (ed.), Eheschließung 133-140; M. Kunzler, Das Zustandekommen des Ehesakraments in der russisch-orthodoxen und der ukrainisch-katholischen Trauliturgie, K. Richter (ed.): Eheschließung – mehr als ein rechtlich Ding? Freiburg-Basel-Vienna 1989 (QD 120), 141-151.

[304] Cf. A. Raes, Le Rituel Ruthène depuis l'union de Brest, OrChrP 1 (1935) 361-392; 386: "Chez les Byzantins, existait depuis plusieurs siècles la coutume de faire suivre immédiatement le jour même du mariage, l'office des fiancailles par l'office du couronnement … " Likewise: A. Raes, Le mariage dans les Eglises d'Orient, Chevetogne 1958, 56f.

[305] Cf. Trembelas 364: Le consentement naturel des époux constitue une condition préalable indispensable á la célébration du sacrement de mariage et il est le mariage en tant que lien naturel béni par le Créateur.'

tion into a sacrament. The minister of this sacrament can only be the priest. [306] Hotz has stressed the importance of the epiclesis for the oriental understanding of sacraments [307] and only the bishop or priest can validly invoke the epiclesis.

In spite of historical objections – according to Vogt Hippolytus would hardly have remained silent if he had known of a liturgically celebrated marriage [308] – Trembelas holds the later promulgated legal requirements not to be sufficient evidence that in the Byzantine Church an (epikletical) blessing of the bridal couple as basis for a sacrament did not exist; [309] he also considers this present teaching on marriage as generally valid for the Orthodox Churches and certainly not the theologoumenon of one or two theologians. The basis for this teaching (now finding increasing interest) is the insight into the sacramental nature of the Church and her acts of worship, whose structural elements are, in fact, anamnesis and epiclesis. Even among Western theologians a lively discussion is in progress concerning the idea that the sacrament of marriage is validly completed through the priest's blessing. [310]

Jilek seeks access to the problem from his own angle. He likens the marriage liturgy to the liturgy at the consecration of a bishop, as it is described in the Apostolic Tradition of Hippolytus, from where the constitutive elements of the sacramental celebrations should as a general rule be taken. Jilek's argurment could be formulated so: the liturgy of consecration is "significant co-operation between the official Church and the Church which is actually present and assembled". To administer a sacrament means: "a concrete life-situation is explained in the light of faith, and as an act which both praises God's redemptive work and begs his help, that is to say, proclaimed in an anamnetic and epicletic prayer." [311] The Benedictio nuptialis, or benedictio in thalamo corresponds in analogy to the prayer of consecration of a bishop. The following comparisons are made: "1. Just as the choice of candidate precedes the episcopal consecration (including his acceptation of the election), so also the agreement and decision on the part of the couple precedes the church service. The legal form... can be left aside. 2. The fact that the Church has found a suitable candidate is cause for intoning a solemn anamnetic-epicletical, that is doxological, prayer. The same is valid for a marriage. 3. The content and intention of this solemn prayer: the actual occasion – in the first case the Church has found a suitable candidate for the office of bishop; in the second a man and a woman have discovered in mutual love the wish to marry. This actual occasion is explained and

---

[306] Trembelas 364: "... le mariage posséde la bénédiction comme aspect extérieur principal et le prêtre en est le seul ministre compétent."

[307] Cf. Hotz 222-265.

[308] H. J. Vogt, Die Eheschließung in der frühen Kirche, K. Richter (ed.): Eheschließung, 119-132. 132.

[309] Trembelas 365: "... on ne peut déduire qu'à l'origine du christianisme cette bénédiction n' était pas en vigeur chez les chrétiens."

[310] Cf. for example, H. Vorgrimmler, Zur dogmatischen Einschätzung und Neueinschätzung der kirchlichen Trauung: K. Richter (ed.): Eheschließung 62-83. R. Puza, Kirchenrecht-Theologie-Liturgie. Kanonistische Überlegungen zur Identität von Ehevertrag und Ehesakrament sowie zum 'Spender' des Ehesakramentes: K. Richter (ed.): Eheschließung 62-83. A. M. Triacca is studying the epicletical aspect of the blessing over the bridal couple and speaks of the sacrament of marriage as a "azione trasformatrice dello Spirito Santo", Cf. the essay: Spiritus Sancti virtutis infusio, Notitiae 26 (1990) 365-390. Cf. also A. Schilson: Die liturgische Feier der Eheschließung als Sakrament. Anstöße zu einer sakramententheologischen Neubesinnung aus zwei neueren Publikationen, Alw 32 (1990) 365-381.

[311] A. Jilek, Das Große Segensgebet über Braut und Bräutigam als Konstitutivum der Trauungsliturgie. Ein Plädoyer für die Rezeption der Liturgiereform in Theologie und Verkündigung, K. Richter (ed.): Eheschließung, 18-41. 23.

proclaimed as the working of God himself; at the same time the continuation of his redemptive activity hic et nunc and for the future is prayed for. 4. A candidate is certainly
not already a bishop by his election, even less so do the two persons form a married
couple in the eyes of Christian faith just by making their decision. Just as these two
events are necessary requirements for the two liturgical services, the following is also
valid, that is: the chosen candidate will only become bishop and the wedding couple will
only become man and wife, ... when and in so far that the Solemn Prayer over them
proclaims God's working in an anamnetic-epicletical manner. 5. This Solemn Prayer
is central point and kernal act in a liturgical service... 6. The congregation gathered
together in divine worship offers up this prayer. He who is presiding over the liturgy
offers up this prayer in the name of all assembled. 7. The offering up of this prayer by
the president takes the form of word and symbolic action." [312]

Jilek's stressing of the complemenary aspect of nuptial consent and priestly blessing
in order that the sacrament of marriage is administered was already discussed in 1969
by Corecco. He, Corecco, points out that Melchior Cano (+ 1560) had already supported this theory at the Council of Trent, but did not succeed in getting it accepted. [313]
According to Corecco it is important that what was correct in Cano's ecclesiological
and sacramental-theological position must be discovered again. "The doctrine of solus
consensus and the inseparability of marriage contract and sacrament is not contradicted
by saying that, as well as the marriage contract, the priest has constitutive power to establish a marriage"; all the more so since the questions concerning the minister of the
sacrament cannot be solved alone by interpreting canon law in positivistic manner, or
solely in the sense of the principle solus consensus, a principle which stems from Roman law". [314] The 2nd Vatican Council's view of the family as "ecclesia domestica" and
place in which the Church is realized "forces one better to express the sacramental and
ecclesiological symbolism also in regard to marriage. This can only be properly done in
that the priest's blessing in the marriage liturgy is also recognized by the Latin Church
as an essential component in the ordinary legal form for contracting marriage." [315] This
desideratus has not yet been fulfilled, as Jilek also announced in 1988. [316]

4.7.5. THE SO-CALLED "ECUMENICAL WEDDING SERVICE"

One point must be made clear: in the strict sense of Church law there is no such thing.
There is merely a Catholic wedding service in which an official non-Catholic minister
may co-operate, and there is correspondingly a non-Catholic marriage ceremony for
which a dispensation from the Catholic ritual has been granted to a Catholic and in
which a Catholic cleric may co-operate. That such has developed is only due to the
ecumenical openess which is justifiably connected with 2nd Vatican Council.

---

[312] Ibidem 33f.
[313] Cf. Corecco, Der Priester als Spender des Ehesakramentes 528f.
[314] Ibid. 554.
[315] Ibid. 556. Cf. also: E. Corecco, Die Lehre der Untrennbarkeit des Ehevertrages vom Sakrament im Lichte
des scholastischen Prinzips "Gratia perficit, non destruit naturam", Archiv für kath. Kirchenrecht 143
(1974) 379-442. The same, Das Sakrament der Ehe: Eckstein der Kirchenverfassung, Archiv für kath.
Kirchenrecht 148 (1979) 353-379.
[316] Cf. A. Jilek, Fragen zur heutigen Feier der Trauung, Th. Maas-Ewerd (ed.), Lebt unser Gottesdienst?
Die bleibende Aufgabe der Liturgiereform (FS Kleinheyer), Freibur-Basel-Vienna 1988, 174-212, espec.
200f.

According to the instruction "Matrimonii Sacramentum" of the Congregation for the Faith of 18th March 1966 a non-Catholic cleric was allowed offer the bridal couple his best wishes for their happiness and to say prayers together with the non-Catholics who were present. In Germany there appeared added to the regulations for implementing the Roman Motu proprio "Matrimonia mixta" of 31st March 1970 the "Common Church Marriage Service", that is, a Catholic, or as the case may be, Protestant marriage Service, in which the cleric of the other Church may co-operate. Further rituals appeared in 1973 for Switzerland (also named "Ecumenical Marriage"[317]), in 1974 for the Archdiocesis of Freiburg/Baden and in 1979 for Austria. The Freiburg ritual entrusts the Catholic cleric with the acceptation of consent, both in Catholic as well as Protestant churches, so that, according to the preface of the ritual, there is no need to apply for a dispensation from the obligatory rite, strictly speaking this is in any case a "Catholic" marriage.[318]

4.7.6. THE LITURGICAL CELEBRATION OF WEDDING JUBILEES

There were indeed in the early Middle Ages Mass formulas for the 30th day after a wedding and for each anniversary, but "the practice is testified first in diocesan rituals, only very late in the Roman Ritual, with the rubrics for celebrating marriage jubilees in church".[319] First evidence is according to Kleinheyer a Constance ritual from the year 1776. A ritual from Mainz from 1889 sets down the following rite: after a sermon, but before the Mass, the married couple may renew the marital promises, they then give each other the hand, the priests winds his stole around both hands and says a prayer of blessing. The Roman Ritual offered a corresponding rite only in 1952 (Tit. VIII 7). Included in this rite is the admonition that the celebration of wedding jubilees should not give the impression that the marriage "is again being blessed". The following is suggested: a short address before the votive Mass "In Thanksgiving"; after which psalm 128(127) with versicle and prayer is said, the Te Deum is sung and the priest sprinkles holy water on the couple. The Missal of 1970 also offers the votive Mass 'In Thanksgiving', whereas according to the German Benedictionale for the celebration of 25 and 50 year jubilees the priest invites the jubilee couple after the homily to give each other the hand, around which he then winds his stole and says a prayer of blessing.[320]

Bibliography

E. Corecco, Der Priester als Spender des Ehesakramentes im Lichte der Lehre über die Untrennbarkeit von Ehevertrag und Ehesakrament: A. Scheuermann / G. May (eds.), Ius sacrum (FS Mörsdorf), München 1969, 521-557.

P. Evdokimov, Sacrement de l'amour. Le mystère conjugal á la lumière de la tradition orthodoxe. Paris 1962.

---

[317] A revised edition appeared in the year 1993: "Ecumenical Celebration of Marriage. Published by the Board of the Swiss Evang. Confederation of Churches, the Swiss Bishops' Conference, the Bishop and Synodal Council of the Christ-Catholic Church of Switzerland, on the basis of the preparatory work of the Ecumenical Committee for the pastoral care of mixed marriages in German-speaking Switzerland". Fribourg-Zürich 1993.

[318] Cf. Kleinheyer, Riten 141-145.

[319] Kleinheyer, Riten 149. Cf. also K. Küppers, "... bis der Tod euch scheidet." Ehejubiläen als Zeugnis christlich gelebter Ehe, M. Klöckner / W. Glade (eds.), Die Feier der Sakramente in der Gemeinde, 307-317.

[320] Cf. Kleinheyer, Riten 149f.

J. Évenou, Le mariage, Martimort III, Paris 1984, 201-224.

B. Kleinheyer, Riten um Ehe und Familie, GdK 8, Regensburg 1984, 67-156.

A. Raes, Le mariage dans les Églises d'Orient, Chevetogne 1958.

K. Richter (ed.), Eheschließung – mehr als ein rechtlich Ding? Freiburg-Basel-Vienna 1989 (QD 120).

M. Righetti, Manuale di storia liturgica IV: I sacramenti, i sacramentali. Milano 1953, 334-350: Il Matrimonio.

K. Ritzer, Formen, Riten und religiöses Brauchtum der Eheschließung in den christlichen Kirchen des ersten Jahrtausends, Münster 2nd edn. 1981 (LQF 38).

4.8. FURTHER SACRAMENTAL CELEBRATIONS OF THE CHURCH

4.8.1. SACRAMENTAL ACTIONS APART FROM THE SEVEN SACRAMENTS

The seven sacraments do not by any means make up the whole sacramental life of the Church. These are "indeed essential, indispensable and irreplaceable vital actions of the Church", apart from these, however, "the Church also celebrates and brings the mystery of Christ into our present life by means of ritual signs and can thus act sacramentally".[321] These sacramental actions are separate from the sacramental seven and have been instituted by the Church, they achieve their effectivity "through the operation of the ever-living activity of the Church, insofar as she is holy and acts in conjunction with her head".[322] These signs are modelled on the sacraments and bring about grace through the intercessory power of the Church; they prepare for the sacraments and sanctify our lives at various times and on various occasions (cf. SC 60). Sacramentals are also to be seen at the celebration of the sacraments themselves, when they prepare us for the kernal action and interpret it. Others accompany us throughout the Liturgical Year (e.g. the sprinkling of ashes on Ash Wednesday, the blessing of palms), others then accompany the lives of individuals (e.g. the blessing of married couples at their wedding jubilees), or the parish life (e.g. consecration of church) or the life of a religious community (e.g. profession, blessing of an abbot.).

Byzantine theology also recognizes the seven sacraments. Meyendorff asserts however that the number seven is of purely Western origin and was taken over by the East merely out of enthusiasm for playing with symbolic numbers, and only in the 13th century.[323] Thus Byzantine theology hardly differentiates between the seven sacraments regarding their effectivity for redemption and that which the West terms "sacramentals". This is justified by the importance given to the epiclesis: "Where then the name and the invocation of God, of the most holy Trinity, that has created all things and that alone is God, takes place, there everthing is holy, and everything acts, heals and redeems through grace."[324]

---

[321] Kaczynski, Benediktionen 238.
[322] Pius XII, Mediator Dei, DH 3844.
[323] Cf. J. Meyendorff, Initiation á la théologie byzantine, Paris 1975, 253-255.
[324] Symeon of Thessaloniki, Dialogos 128 – PG 155, 336 D. Cf. Kunzler, Porta Orientalis 259f.

The theology of the West distinguishes between sacraments and sacramentals in that the former are believed to act "ex opere operato". The sacraments are effective in the power of Christ, and this is by virtue of a sacramental sign, which must be made in the sense which the Church intends it, when a sacrament is to be administered. [325] The sacramentals on the other hand are effective "ex opere operantis ecclesiae", that is effective by virtue of the praying Church. When she prays she always does so in turning to the Father in the Holy Spirit, through the Son. She establishes a relationship with God, in that she praises the Father, commemorates anamnetically the redemption brought by the Son, and calls down in epiclesis the Holy Spirit, who achieves all sanctification. That is why the sacramentals also receive a redemptive effectivity, which is without doubt catabatically justified, even if it is the Church herself which sets up signs of redemption in the sacramentals. [326]

4.8.2. BLESSINGS

The Codex of 1917 differentiated – objectively speaking this is still valid - between the "benedictiones constitutivae" and "benedictiones invocativae". The former are blessings and consecrations of persons and objects, which constitute a permanent and also legal effect (c. 1148). The latter blessings are such that neither do they affect the normal life of persons nor do they change the manner objects are normally put to use (e.g. blessing of sick persons, blessing of food). The constitutive blessings on the other hand bring about a change in the way of life (e.g. consecration of virgin), or they reserve an object for use in divine service (e.g. consecration of a church, consecration of liturgical vessels). For that reason these are referred to as consecrations, rather than blessings.

The Church is here concerned with taking a specific part of the secular-profane world (a human being, or indeed any other part of creation) out of the deadly godlessness of a world which original sin has turned against the living God, in order to lead it back to a relationship with the God of Life. In the blessings the anaphora of the world are made tangible and definite by the Christian: the world, summed up in man, his relationships with other persons, with those parts of creation which have life as well as with those which have not, succeed in him and through him into a vital-creative communication with the living God.

This thought was very much alive in the ancient Church, we see this in the fact that the blessings were part of those anaphora of the eucharistic Canon which praised and thanked God for the elevation of the whole world through Christ. As early as Hippolytus [327] this was the case and the idea continued well into the late Middle Ages when, for example, at the "Per quem haec omnia" of the Roman Canon gifts of nature were blessed. [328] For a person of faith "almost every happening in life is sanctified by the di-

---

[325] According to Schneider, Zeichen 67, the Opus operatum means binding God's immutably guaranteed commitment within a special sphere. His working in the Church is so incarnated in the Church's decisive performing of holy rituals, so deeply, so inextricably woven into the historical situation, that then, and always then, when a sacrament is correctly administered the recipient can be certain, that God now turns to him in Jesus with love and affection, even if the administering priest were an utterly unworthy instrument for the celebration.

[326] Cf. A. Gerhards / H. J. Becker, Mit allem Segen seines Geistes. Zur theologischen Bestimmung der Benediktionen, A. Heinz / H. Rennings (eds.), Heute segnen, 15-32, hier 26-28.

[327] For example the blessing of milk, honey and water during the baptismal Eucharist in TradAp 21, ed Geerlings 266.

[328] Cf. Jungmann MS II, 322-324.

vine grace which streams forth from the Paschal Mystery... of Christ", and because there is hardly a correct use of material things which has not as its end and aim the sanctification of mankind and the praise of God (SC 61). For that reason then all expressions of life in a Christian, together with all his human relationships, embrace the whole world about him (fellow human beings and created nature). Indeed these expressions and relationships can hardly become reality in any other way than by means of "the go-between" and mediation of the world of nature.

Since every Christian has been "ordained" to the royal priesthood by his Baptism and Confirmation (and Eucharist!), and since every Christian has been entrusted with the anaphora of the world, the Christian has therefore the duty of blessing "his world". According to the ecclesiastical order of Hippolytus lay persons blessed as teachers the catechumens. The Constitution of the Liturgy (SC 79) opened up new possibilities for blessings at the hands of lay persons, something which was further developed by the 1984 edition of the Roman Benedictional ("De Benedictionibus"). [329] Certain blessings in the public life of the Church have been reserved to those holding an office, this was done in order to make clear that both the praise of God for creation and the renewed immersion of creation into the realm of divine grace are matters which go beyond the limited temporal possibility of the individual Christian. The Church as the organic community of all those who make up the mystical body embraces far greater dimensions of reality, hence the person holding an office represents the whole Church when he praises God or begs his blessing for this greater sphere of existence. Bishops and priests bless therefore in those areas of public life where the diocese or the parish are involved, and when the Church should be presented as an organic community. [330]

It has been said that the blessings as sacramentals "imitate" to some extent the sacraments. It is true that in the blessings there is the twofold aspect of the anamnesis as praise, the realising of the presence of divine love, [331] and the pleading of the epiclesis, the calling down of God's saving power on the persons or things which are to be blessed. Therefore praise and intercessory prayer are constitutive elements of blessings.

The blessings considered as the lifting up of creation into a vital relationship with the Divine have nothing in common with human endeavours to win control over God's healing power by means of magic. On the contrary they are unthinkable without a living relationship to God, for "not only do they presuppose faith, they also nourish the same faith by word and object, they strengthen it and are a witness to it" (SC 59). The blessings possess an anamnetic-epicletic structure; the kernal action of the blessings are the anamnetic-epicletic blessing prayer with the corresponding symbolic act (e.g. sprinkling with holy water, making the sign of the cross), this structure is part of a service of the word, a service which is also characterized by the same twofold structure: the anamnetic reading from Scripture makes present again the redemptive acts of God, while the bidding prayers are epicletic and carry the petition for further grace beyond the actual service into the future.

---

[329] Cf. W. v. Arx, Christen segnen einander. Laien als Leiter von Segensfeiern: A. Heinz / H. Rennings (eds.), Heute segnen 106-115.

[330] Cf. B. Kleinheyer, Zum Segnen bestellt. Bischof, Priester und Diakon als Leiter von Segensfeiern: A. Heinz / H. Rennings (eds.), Heute segnen 94-105.

[331] Kaczynski in his book Benediktionen 240 quite correctly points out the twofold meaning of "benedicere", which can be understood in the Greek sense of eulogein, or in the Hebrew brk as praise of God

A personal blessing of special importance and with its own problematic history is the blessing of a mother and her child after birth. It came through the Christian East from Jewish purifications rites into the Western (non-Roman) Churches. According to this custom a mother was not allowed to visit a church during the 40 or even 80 days after the birth of her child. The liturgy in the non-Roman areas added to the blessing a character of purification and absolution which was to enable a mother to take part in liturgical services again. [332] This notion of absolution and purification remained long in popular piety, although the Roman Ritual of 1614 placed the notion of thanksgiving in the foreground. The liturgical form however (e.g. the mother had to wait at the church door until she was called) shows that the blessing was still understood as absolution and purification. The renewed rite of Baptism takes it for granted that a mother is present at the christening of her child and has changed this blessing into a blessing for parents at the end of the ceremony, the notion of purification and such like has been fully dropped. [333] Further blessings during lifetime are the blessing at the celebration of an engagement, the blessing of a mother before a birth, blessings on the occasion of wedding jubilees, a priest's blessing after his ordination, blessing of the sick and the blessing of pilgrims. [334]

There is a great number of blessings for objects, and Kaczynski has divided them according to the different liturgical books. The Mass book contains those blessings which come up in the course of the liturgical year and are imparted during a celebration of Mass on special days (Blessing of candles on Candlemas Day, blessing of ashes on Ash Wednesday, of palm branches on Palm Sunday and so on). The Ritual also contains blessings, these are part of other celebrations of sacraments or of sacramentals, e.g., the blessing of rings at a wedding, or of a grave at a burial service. The formulae for the blessing of objects which we find in the Pontifical are the consecration of the holy oils, as well as the consecration of a church, of an altar, or of liturgical vessels. [335] There are further blessings for persons or objects in the Roman Benedictional, which appeared as part of the renewed Roman Ritual only in 1984, six years after the German "Benedictionale" of 1978. A blessing which plays an outstanding part in the life of a parish is the consecration of a church or of an altar. [336] From the 4th century on there arose a richly developed ceremonial for the consecration of a church, in which the placing of relics under the altar played an important part, so important indeed that the anniversary of the consecration of the church could become as "Depositio" a feast celebrating those saints whose relics lay under the altar. In the non-Roman West there

---

[332] Cf. Kleinheyer, Segnungen anläßlich der Geburt 152f., F. Kohlschein, Die Vorstellung von der kultischen Unreinheit der Frau. Das weiterwirkende Motiv für eine zwiespältige Situation? In: T. Berger / A. Gerhards (eds.): Liturgie und Frauenfrage. Ein Beitrag zur Frauenforschung aus liturgiewissenschaftlicher Sicht, St. Ottilien 1990 (Pietas Liturgica 7), 269-288.

[333] For the history of the blessing of mothers from the Roman Ritual of 1614 until the present day cf. Kleinheyer, Segnungen anläßlich der Geburt 154-156. Cf. also: R. Schwarzenberger, Der Muttersegen nach der Geburt: A. Heinz / H. Rennings (eds.), Heute segnen 279-284.

[334] Cf. in this respect the individual headings in A. Heinz / H. Rennings (eds.), Heute segnen: K. Küppers: Die Feier der Verlobung, 259-264; A. Jilek, Segensfeier vor der Geburt, 265-271; M. Probst, Segnungen aus Anlaß von Ehejubiläen, 285-290; H. B. Meyer, Der Primizsegen, 291-299; G. Duffrer, Der Krankensegen, 300-307; D. Eissing, Der Pilgersegen, 308-316.

[335] Cf. Kaczynski, Benediktionen 261-270.

[336] Cf. as regards what follows: A. Adam, Wo sich Gottes Volk versammelt. Gestalt und Symbolik des Kirchenbaus, Freiburg-Basel-Vienna 1984, 144-156.

were richly developed rites for the consecration of churches, many of these rites show signs of influence from Eastern christianity, the Roman-German Pontifical which was brought out in Mainz in 950 achieved in this regard a certain amount of unity. The rite for the consecration of a church was further embellished in the Pontifical of Durandus and in general this remained the norm until the Reform of the liturgy during the 2nd Vatican Council. This rite had many repetitions, exaggerated allegorical tendencies and elements which overstressed the material side of things and was certainly in need of reform. Then in 1977 there appeared as complement to the renewed Roman Pontifical the "Ordo dedicationis ecclesiae et altaris". [337] This dedication ritual opens with a rite of taking possession, which was taken from the old rite into the German Ritual, the Roman Ritual omits it: the bishop draws letters of the Greek and Latin alphabet with his crozier on a cross on the ground made of ashes; this is a custom which has been explained in various ways, it may take its origin from Roman land surveying methods, or the signing of the forehead at a christening, or even from a symbolic defence against evil spirits. [338] The "washing" of the altar and the church wall with holy water reminds one of baptism. After the homily, the creed and the litany of the saints the relics are placed under the altar (no longer in the altar table). After the prayer of consecration and the anointing of the altar with chrism incense is burnt on the altar and the whole church is incensed. Adam offers various interpretations for the ceremony with incense: it symbolizes Christ's sacrifice ascending from the altar, taking with it the prayers of the faithful; the fragrant perfume of Christ fills the newly consecrated church; incense is also a symbol for the presence of the Holy Spirit. [339] The ceremony reaches its climax in the first Eucharistic service held in the now consecrated church, after the altar has been decorated and the candles have been lit.

4.8.3. THE RITE OF EXORCISM

Jesus gave the command: "Cast out devils!" (Mt 10:8). Neither the Old nor the New Testament deny the existence of Satan or of devils, those spirits of "continual negation" (cf. Goethe's Faust) who can drive a soul into a death-filled: No, I will not, to God's affirmation of its existence. "The Church has in every age accepted its duty to cast out devils. Even today she accepts it as her task. One must understand however that there are no clear criteria for deciding whether a certain sickness is due to demoniac influences, or whether a person who believes himself or herself to be in the power of the evil one, is really possessed. An exorcism should therefore not be undertaken too readily or without weighing up the matter at great extent." [340]

  In Hippolytus's time the exorcism prayer over the catechumen was already part of the preparation for baptism. [341] In addition he mentions an exorcism for objects, here the exorcism oil. [342] By calling upon God it should receive the power to exorcise. Later, another standpoint became generally accepted, namely that created things which were used for a ceremony should beforehand be wrested from the power of Satan by an ex-

---

[337] Kaczynski 3534-3619.

[338] Cf. Adam, Wo sich Gottes Volk versammelt 147f.

[339] Cf. loc. cit. 150f.

[340] R. Kaczynski: Der Exorzismus: GdK 8. Regensburg 1984, 275-291. 281

[341] TradAp 20, ed. Geerlings 245

[342] TradAp 21, ed. Geerlings 258: "Et sumit quoque aliud oleum quod exorcizet et vocat illum oleum exorcismi."

orcism. [343] Further exorcisms were meant for the energumen (a possessed person). Texts which had become more and more extensive found their way into the Roman Ritual of 1614 (Tit. XII,2: The "Greater Exorcism, De exorcizandis obsessis a daemonio"). In 1925 a shorter form of exorcism was added to the Ritual (Tit. XII, 3: "Exorcismus in satanam et angelos apostaticos"), a form which had been brought out in 1890 under Leo XIII. [344] In the liturgical renewal the exorcism of things has been completely dropped. The exorcism which went together with the preparation for Baptism has become a prayer for freedom from the power of evil, in the ceremony of adult Baptism the strengthening of the spiritual life has been placed in the foreground, stressing this aspect more than liberation from the power of satan.

Christ or the Father is always addressed in the prayers, the devil is now never directly addressed. The reform of the liturgy had great difficulty in view of modern medical knowledge with the renewal of the exorcism prayers, prayers which the Roman Ritual had used from 1614 until the Council. [345] The German Bishops' Conference set up a commission in 1979 made up of theologians, medical experts and psychologists to study the matter; "it was hoped that decisions might be taken as a result of the studies concerning the future form of the greater exorcism and that corresponding suggestions from the German Bishops might be drawn up and sent to the Roman Congregation responsible for such matters." [346] The Codex of 1983 c. 1172 speaks of "the legitimate exorcism over possessed persons" which may only be spoken with special permission from the Ordinary, and the Catechism of the Catholic Church (Number 1673) even mentions 'the greater exorcism'. Meanwhile the Roman Congregation for Divine Worship has drawn up a form for the greater exorcism which may be used "ad experimentum" by priests who have been appointed for such tasks by the local Ordinary.

4.8.4. SACRAMENTALS IN THE LIFE OF RELIGIOUS COMMUNITIES

Sacramentals which are celebrated in monastic communities are the religious profession and the blessing of an abbot, or of an abbess. The oldest form of profession is the "professio super altare": after all the community had assembled for the clothing in the monastic habit the vows were pronounced in public. This took place in the monastic chapel in front of the altar with the relics, on which the document of profession was placed. Besides this ritual two other forms appear during the Middle Ages, first, the "professio in manus", the person making profession made public his devotion to Christ by placing his hands between the hands of the superior, this form had its origin in Frankish legal customs and was similar to the rite at the ordination of a priest. A second and more recent ritual was a profession in the form of an oath taken before Christ present in the Eucharist: the formula of profession is spoken, when a Mass is being celebrated, immediately before Communion in front of the host; if the profession is

---

[343] Cf. E. Bartsch, Die Sachbeschwörungen in der römischen Liturgie, Münster 1967 (LQF 46).

[344] According to E. J. Lengeling, "Der Exorzismus in der katholischen Kirche". Zu einer verwunderlichen Ausgabe, LJ 32 (1982) 249-257, 250 under Pius XII the Ritual was enlarged by the section on Confirmation (new Tit. III) so that in the latest edition of the Ritual the exorcism part is XII, and no longer Tit. XI.

[345] Cf. regarding the whole material: Kaczynski, Exorzismus 279-291.

[346] Lengeling, "Der Exorzismus in der katholischen Kirche" 256f.

made outside Mass the profession is spoken in front of a monstrance. This form was practised by the Jesuits and by many modern religious congregations.[347]

According to SC 80 "a rite for profession and renewal of vows should be created which is characterized by greater unity, simplicity and dignity". In addition it was stressed that profession and renewal of vows should take place during Mass. The new "Ordo professionis religiosae" appeared on the 2nd of February 1970.[348] The reception into the noviceship does not take place publicly nor during the celebration of the Eucharist. For simple and perpetual profession however eucharistic celebration should be normal. Especially the latter profession ritual shows certain parallels to the ordination rite. After the Gospel has been read the candidates who seek permanent membership in the monastic community are called forward. Then follows a sermon after which the candidates are questioned (Scrutinium), the litany (of the saints) is recited, followed by the pronouncing of perpetual vows, the document of profession is then placed on the altar, this may be signed on the altar itself, a rite which originates in Germanic liking for symbolism. In the Benedictine tradition psalm 119 (118), verse 116 is sung: "If you uphold me by your promise I shall live; let my hopes not be in vain". The sollemn blessing is then prayed over the newly professed and the symbolic rites are performed, i.e., the handing over of the signs of profession (for example, ring, choir-garment, breviary). The ceremony ends with the kiss of reception into the community.[349]

In the blessing of an abbot there were analogies with the liturgy of ordination, especially since the 9th cent. after abbots had been given the right to use episcopal pontificals. This raising of abbots to the stand of prelates remained to the present day despite the requirements of SC 130.[350] Hence analogies to the consecration liturgies are still very clear: after the Gospel the candidate is presented, there then follows a sermon, after which the candidate is questioned concerning his intention. The litany is recited and the prayer of consecration spoken, the signifying rites follow, i.e., the handing over of the book with the Rule of the Order in question, the giving of the ring and the crozier, in special cases, the mitre. The consecration of an abbess is similar, in the Roman rite however a crozier is not presented.

Only with reservation can the consecration of a virgin be counted among the sacramentals of religious communities, since after the promulgation of the "Ordo Consecratio Virginum" of 1970 even virgins living in the world are allowed to receive it.[351] Even in the early Church there were consecrated virgins living not only in communities, but also active in the world; they placed themselves especially at the disposal of the local Church. The adoption of symbols from the marriage liturgy into the rite for the conse-

---

[347] Cf. v. Severus, Feiern geistlicher Gemeinschaften 177.
[348] Kaczynski 2029-2049.
[349] Cf. v. Severus, Feiern geistlicher Gemeinschaften 178-180.
[350] SC 130 wishes to restrict the use of pontificals to bishops and those who exercise special jurisdiction. Cf. R. Reinhardt: Die Abtsweihe – eine "kleine Bishofsweihe"? In: ZKG 91 (1980) 83-88.
[351] Cf. Kaczynski 2082-2092, here 2085: "Ad consecrationem virginalem admitti possunt sive moniales sive mulieres vitam saecularem agentes." E. v. Severus 183 comments: "The importance of this reform does not lie in reverting to ideal and historically vouched for conditions of the early Church, but in its relation to present time. This renewal not only rescinds the with authority stressed reservation of the consecration of virgins to cloistered nuns made under Pius XII (1939-1958), but also acknowledges the manifold service of unmarried women in the Church of our time: pastoral assistants, social workers, and assistants in the care of souls."

cration of virgins in order to express the union with Christ also stems from antiquity.[352] The rite of consecration of virgins can be joined to the perpetual profession of women in congregations or orders. The rite, which is presided over by the local bishop, begins with the calling forward of the candidates. After the homily they are questioned, the litany is then recited, after which the candidates make their vows to follow Christ as virgins, the symbolic rites in which they are presented with the veil, ring and breviary come at the end.[353]

4.8.5. THE LITURGY OF THE FUNERAL RITES.

The liturgy for funerals is also a sacramental. The (necessary) setting of a dead body in a grave should be an action which signifies and expresses the Christian hope of resurrection and everlasting life. The body of a Christian was during the time of his or her earthly life the material symbol of his very self. Our faith tells us that the person who has died is now in the hands of the merciful God, and the placing of the mortal remains into the earth becomes a significant expression for the rising again of that which cannot die into the world of the living God. The first Christians took over for burials of the faithful the customs of the culture in which they lived, just as they had done for wedding ceremonies; however faith in the risen Christ and in the eternal life of the deceased corrected and amplified the usual rites of the time. Above all anything which might be brought into connection with belief in heathen gods was to be avoided, on the other hand the hope of resurrection was to be clearly expressed. Thus the lamentation for the dead was replaced by the singing of psalms, by readings from Scripture and prayers, something which Jerome in his day characterized as Christian tradition.[354] Augustine confirms moreover that the Church keeps the customs of each people when it is honouring the dead in its services.[355] Repasts taken at the graveside on the third, seventh, thirtieth or fortieth day after death was a custom which was also adopted. Already by the 2nd cent. however, these ceremonies in memory of the dead, which were held to express union with the deceased, were joined to a celebration of the Eucharist in the family circle.[356] The more prominent or better known the dead person had been, the more public was the celebration of the Eucharist; those celebrated at the grave of a martyr became the divine service of the community, for which then a basilica was built over the grave.

Rites for the dying and rites for burial became in the 7th/8th centuries[357] a single service, a service which could be held mainly in monastic communities. This included the giving of Viaticum at the approach of death and the reading of the Passion by a priest or deacon until the moment of passing. The moment itself of death was accompanied by the actual prayers for the dying. The last of these was the "Commendatio

---

[352] Cf. Konetzny 479.

[353] Cf. v. Severus 182-184, Konetzny 481-487.

[354] Vita S. Pauli 16, PL 23,27. Also something very striking is the differentiation between heathen despair and Christian hope in a the writings of Chrysostomos, Sermo de S. Bernice et Prosdoce – PG 50, 634.

[355] Referring to Jewish burial customs at Jesus's burial according to John 19,40, Cf. In Io tract. 120,4 CChr SL 36, 662.

[356] Cf. Jungmann, MS I, 285-287.

[357] This is described in the 49th Ordo Romanus. Cf. B. Bürki: Die Feier des Todes in den Liturgien des Westens. Beispiele aus dem 7. und 20. Jahrhundert. In Becker / Einig / Ullrich (eds.): Im Angesicht des Todes II, 1135-1164, bes. 1136-1141.

animae", the first intercessory prayer for the deceased. Afterwards psalms were sung with responsorium and antiphon "Requiem aeternam". The deceased was then taken on a bier to the church while psalms were sung, where after more psalms (this developed later into the Office for the dead) Mass was celebrated. The procession to the grave was also accompanied by the singing of psalms, as likewise the placing in the coffin and the burial itself.[358] According to Sicard "Mass was celebrated on the day of death itself only for monks, 'for good Christians' on the third day after death, for 'penitents' on the thirtieth or seventh day, after a seven day fast, which was demanded of the next of kin of the deceased". The tradition in Gaul was quite different, here the Mass was a regular part of the liturgy of burial.[359]

That which presented a unified liturgy in the monasteries of the early Middle Ages, from the giving of viaticum immediately before death until the actual burial itself, was later divided into several different rites. In the Roman Ritual of 1614 the Viaticum had become a special form of Communion for the Sick (Tit. V, 4,20). The Viaticum was given some time beforehand, since one understood the "Last Anointing" as the sacrament of the dying, when one also said the prayers for the dying (Tit. VI,5: "Modus iuvandi morientes"; VI,6: Apostolic Blessing and complete absolution in "articulo mortis"; VI,7: "Ordo commendationis animae"; VI,8: "De exspiratione"). Burial is treated in Titulus VII. The preparation of the dead body and the period until the time of the burial rites themselves are no longer considered part of the liturgy. The funeral liturgy itself begins with the taking of the deceased from the former dwelling place in procession to the church, then follow if circumstances allow a part of the Office for the Dead (Tit. VII,4), the Requiem, Absolution, the Procession to the graveyard and finally Burial. The Christian message of hope and redemption had become in the course of time so clouded over by the fear and dread of God's judgement, that the change to a liturgy determined by Easter and the risen life could only gradually affect a change in the attitude of the faithful. Black vestments, the absolution,[360] the penitential psalms and the sequence "Dies irae" surrounded the the funeral liturgy with an atmosphere of darkness and gloom. "The stressing of atonement and begging of forgiveness had as consequence neglect of the eschatological character of the Eucharist, so much so that the Eucharist was no longer celebrated as part of the funeral rites for children."[361]

The 2nd Vatican Council requested a revision of the funeral liturgy. It "must more clearly set out resurrection as the meaning of Christian death" (SC 81). All the pomp which in the late modern era encompassed funerals and even led to different "grades" of funerals was banned in SC 82, according to which there was to be no sign of rank or person either in the rites or outer cirmcumstances. Finally SC 82 decided that the rite for the funeral of children should be revised and receive a special Mass form.

On the 15th of August 1969 the "Ordo exsequiarum"[362] appeared as model for rituals in the vernacular. It is the intention of the renewed funeral liturgy "to set out clearly the Easter aspect of Christian death in the texts and rituals, in accordance with the

---

[358] Cf. Kacynski, Sterbe – und Begräbnisliturgie 209-213 with more exact references to the psalms.
[359] Sicard, Begräbnismesse 93.
[360] According to Kaczynski, Sterbe- und Begräbnisliturgie 216, the absolution, which had originally been part of a rite taking farewell of the dead, gradually became an ever more important element of the rites, in it prayers were offered that the dead person be freed from all punishment for sins committed.
[361] Ibid.
[362] Kaczynski 1921-1947.

wish of the Council." Kaczynski regrets, and rightly so, that the Halleluja as witness to Christ's victory over death at Easter finds no place in the renewed liturgy for funerals. However the psalms as well as the retention of the early medieval antiphon "Subvenite", the "In paradisum" and the "Chorus angelorum" impart an Easter character, the "Libera" and the "Dies irae" have been deleted. [363]

The revised Ritual does not prescribe any standard rite, instead it offers three basic forms, they are so drawn up that they take local conditions into consideration and differ according to the stations: the first basic type begins with the opening rite in the house of the deceased, or in the graveyard chapel, the funeral Mass in the church follows, the burial rites form then the third station. The second type considers only the stations in the chapel and at the graveside; the third takes into account only the assembly at the graveside or in the chapel, under circumstances in the crematorium, where after the opening rite and service of the word the burial or leave-taking (in case of cremation) take place. The ancient Church rejected cremation of the dead and practised burial in the earth in memory of Christ's burial. [364] When the practice of cremation began again in the 2nd half of the 19th cent. anti-Church arguments were put forward in its favour, for which reason the Church forbade all religious rites at cremations. This prohibition was lifted during the Council [365] provided that cremation was not chosen as an expression of the deceased person's hostile attitude to the faith or the Church. Kaczynski draws attention to two noteworthy renovations in the new liturgy for funerals: farewell ceremonies have taken the place of absolution: the symbolic actions (Sprinkling of holy water, incensing, casting of earth and the setting up of a cross, or making the sign of the cross) are performed in order to express a temporary leave-taking from the dead person, since the faithful are joined in Christ with the departed, and ought not to be understood as prayers on the part of the mourners for the departed now facing God's judgement. A burial prayer from the Anglican and Reformed tradition was adopted for the letting down of the coffin into the earth which "interprets the procedure in a Christian manner and expresses the hope of resurrection." [366]

Something which is typical of the Byzantine funeral liturgy is the use of different prayer formulae for layfolk, clerics, monks and nuns, men and women, boys and girls. The Easter Week has its own formulae, modelled on those of the Easter Vigil. The body of the deceased person is in fact taken into the church where a somewhat longer service of the word is held, but no Eucharist, at the end the farewell kiss is given. The burial ritual itself is very short; blessed oil and the ashes taken from the remains of incense in the thurible are often put into the grave. In Protestant traditions the funeral liturgy is celebrated as proclamation of the glad tidings of the Gospel, since the reformers were very sceptical as regards intercessory prayer for the dead. [367]

Bibliography

---

[363] Kaczynski, Sterbe – und Begräbnisliturgie 223.
[364] Cf. Kaczynski, Sterbe – und Begräbnisliturgie 206 with the example of Minucius Felix.
[365] Cf. The instruction of the Holy Office of the 8th May 1963: AAS 56 (1964) 822f.
[366] Kaczynski, Sterbe – und Begräbnisliturgie 224.
[367] Cf. ibid. 226f. Cf. also K. C. Felmy, Die Verwandlung des Schmerzes. Sterbebegleitung und Totengedächtnis in der östlich-orthodoxen Kirchen: Becker / Einig / Ullrich: Im Angesicht des Todes II, 1087-1133.

H. J. Becker / B. Einig / P. O. Ullrich (eds.), Im Angesicht des Todes. Ein interdisziplinäres Kompendium, 2 Vols., St. Ottilien 1987 (Pietas Liturgica 3-4).

Y. Congar, Die Idee der 'sacramenta maiora': Concilium 4 (1968) 9-15.

A. Franz, Die kirchlichen Benediktionen im Mittelalter, 2 vols., Freiburg i. B. 1909, Reprint Graz 1960.

A. Heinz / H. Rennings (eds.), Heute segnen. Werkbuch zum Benediktionale, Freiburg-Basel-Vienna 1987.

P. Jounel: Les bénédictions: Martimort III, Paris 1984, 282-305.

R. Kaczynski, Sterbe – und Begräbnisliturgie: GdK 8. Regensburg 1984, 191-232.

R. Kaczynski, Die Benediktionen: GdK 8. Regensburg 1984, 233-274.

B. Kleinheyer, Segnungen anläßlich der Geburt: GdK 8. Regensburg 1984, 151-156.

G. Konetzny, Die Jungfrauenweihe: T. Berger / A. Gerhards (eds.): Liturgie und Frauenfrage. Ein Beitrag zur Frauenforschung aus liturgiewissenschaftlicher Sicht, St. Ottilien 1990 (Pietas Liturgica 7), 475-492.

A. Nocent, La consécration des viérges: Martimort III, Paris 1984, 225-237.

A. Nocent, Rites monastiques et profession religieuse: Martimort III, Paris 1984, 306-331.

K. Richter (ed.), Der Umgang mit Toten. Tod und Bestattung in der christlichen Gemeinde. Freiburg-Basel-Vienna 1990 (QD 123).

M. Righetti, Manuale di storia liturgica IV: I sacramenti, i sacramentali. Milano 1953, 351-420: I Sacramentali.

I. Scicolone / A. Nocent / M. Augé / L. Chengalikavil / A. M. Triacca / P. Rouillard / D. Sartore / A. J. Chupungco, I Sacramentali e le benedizioni: Anamnesis VII, Torino 1989.

E. v. Severus, Feiern geistlicher Gemeinschaften: GdK 8. Regensburg 1984, 157-189.

D. Sicard, La liturgie de la mort dans l'église latine des origines á la réforme carolingienne, Münster 1978 (LQF 63).

D. Sicard, La mort du chrétien: Martimort III, Paris 1984, 238-258.

Part V

The Hallowing of Time, 1:
Liturgia Verbi –
Liturgy of the Hours and
Liturgy of the Word

5.1. THE HALLOWING OF TIME

All created things must be brought into the worshipping communication with God, including time. This communication takes place during the time for prayer. Through his eternal Word and in the Holy Spirit, God expresses his invitation to the world. On behalf of the whole of creation, and exercising its royal priesthood, the community of the brothers and sisters of his Son replies in praise to his love, as it has shown itself in the acts of Redemption. The community commemorates them anamnetically, when it performs for the world the service of intercession, through which Christians exercise their priestly office of mediation, which is to include all creation in the divine work of salvation.

The custom of Christians coming together for common prayer in the morning and in the evening goes back to the beginnings of the Christian faith. In the case of the people of the Covenant in the Old Testament, the daily meeting can be "traced back to the Mosaic legislation, in which it was interpreted as the daily renewal of God's redemptive will. The evening sacrifice is based on the fundamental, expiatory idea that Yahveh repeatedly grants liberation and redemption, whereas in the morning inexhaustible love is expressed, as promised in the Covenant." [1]

5.1.1. BASIC FEATURES OF A THEOLOGY OF PRAYER

Prayer presupposes that God turns towards man and thus enables the latter in the first place to respond to him. In the first instance, prayer is completely the work of God the Father through Christ in the Holy Spirit: "For we do not know how to pray as we ought, but the Spirit himself intercedes for us with sighs too deep for words" (Rom 8:26). And: "No one can say 'Jesus is Lord' except by the Holy Spirit" (1 Cor 12:3). Praise and intercession are no merely human work, neither solely the fulfilment of the creature's duty to thank nor a "winning over" of God on the part of the person praying, but "Opus Dei", God's communication with man, effecting salvation and creating life. Prayer – apparently a merely human activity – comes down, as it were, from heaven, before it returns to God through man, not without accomplishing that for which God has sent it out (cf. Is 55:10f.).

The Christian's prayer is "a relationship under the covenant between God and man in Christ. It is action on the part of God and on the part of man. It proceeds from the Holy Spirit and from us." [2] Prayer is "blessing": "Blessing represents the fundamental event of Christian prayer: the encounter between God and man. In the blessing God's gift and and its acceptance by man are combined in a reciprocal invocation. The prayer of blessing is man's response to God's gifts. Because God gives blessings, the heart of man can praise God, who is the source of all blessing." [3]

Thus, the most eminent form of prayer is the praise of God, which encloses the other forms of prayer: God himself, who wishes his creatures to have life in full, makes it possible for man to pray. That already shows the person who prays to be someone blessed by God and engaged with him in a life-giving communication. In that praise, God is

---

[1]   G. Winkler, Über die Kathedralvesper in den verschiedenen Riten des Ostens und des Westens, ALw 16 (1974) 53-102.101

[2]   Cf. Catechism No. 2564.

[3]   Cf. Catechism No. 2626.

acknowledged, "because he is" – not in the philosophical sense, but as the all-merciful, in the sense of the name Yahveh.[4] His honour consists in the life of men;[5] so that they might have life, he sent his Son and the Spirit into the world as his "hands", bringing about salvation in created things.[6] Taken by the Son and the Spirit into the worshipping service of God, "it is man's glory to remain in God's service and to persevere in it".[7] The thanksgiving that culminates in the Eucharist therefore characterises the prayer of the Church, which perseveres in that thanksgiving, in the lifegiving service of God. As the mystical body of Christ, she participates in the thanksgiving of her Head, who has freed her – and through her also the whole of creation – from sin and death, and leads them back to the Father, to give honour to him who exists in the life of creation.[8]

This praise receives concrete form in adoration. That "is the first attitude of the person who recognises himself as a creature before his Creator. It glorifies the greatness of the Lord, who has created us, and the omnipotence of the Saviour, who delivers us from evil. The spirit casts itself down in adoration before the 'King of glory' (Ps 24:9-10) and keeps reverent silence before the 'ever greater God' (Augustine, Ps 62:16). The adoration of the thrice holy God, who is to be loved above all, fills us with humility and allows us to petition him with confidence."[9]

The prayer of petition, the "first movement" of which is the asking of forgiveness,[10] is always a return to God, to whom the person addresses himself in his petition;[11] after all, separation from God, the source of all life, is the origin of all misery. Whoever asks for something reveals a need; as a finite being, needy in every way, man stands before the unlimited and infinite God and asks him to overcome his misery, to allow him to have a part in God's unlimited fullness of life. Participation in the divine life is the "Kingdom of God", in which he reigns who is the source of life and who deifies his creation. "According to Christ's teaching, desiring and seeking the Kingdom of God" are regarded as the core of the Christian's prayer of petition. Through this desire, the Church, in its prayer of petition, in which the individual joins, co-operates in the work of salvation carried out by the Son and the Spirit, who come into the world, to lead it into the divine fullness of life, which is the Kingdom of God.[12] The shape of that Kingdom in its eschatological perfection transcends all earthly experiences and notions. The petitioner can only depend on his belief that everything will turn out for the best and all misery come to an end. The Christian's prayer for the coming of salvation is thus more a "sighing in the heart" for the revealing of the children of God than a petition for the granting of concrete requests; indeed, he does not know what he should pray for in the right way, but in the midst of our sighs the Spirit helps us in our weakness (cf. Rom 8:22-26).[13] Thus considered, the prayer of petition is "anaphora": joined to the sacrifice of Christ, it is the one who prays sacrificing himself, and his world, his relationships

---

[4]   C. Catechism No. 2639.
[5]   Cf. Irenaeus of Lyon, Adv. haer. IV,20.7 - SChr. 100,648.
[6]   Cf. Irenaeus of Lyon, Adv. haer. IV,20,1 – SChr. 100,626.
[7]   Irenaeus of Lyon, Adv.haer.IV,14,1 – SChr.100,540.
[8]   Cf. Catechism No. 2637.
[9]   Cf. Catechism No. 2628.
[10]   Cf. Catechism No. 2631.
[11]   Cf. Catechism No.2629.
[12]   Cf. Catechism No.2632.
[13]   Cf. Catechism No.2630.

and his life history being drawn up into the fullness of God's life, in which one day everything will have come to perfection. For that reason, we always find, linked to the prayer of petition, intercession for others and for the whole world; this intercession makes the petitioner the imitator and follower of the interceding Christ. [14] In the Holy Spirit, the Church turns in prayer through Christ to the Father, after it has received the Holy Spirit through Christ, that Spirit which proceeds from the Father and the Son. [15] Made possible in this way by the triune God himself, "every happening and every need can become a sacrifice of thanks, as they can also become the subject of a prayer of petition. The letters of St. Paul often begin and end with an expression of thanks, in which Jesus is always referred to. 'Give thanks in all circumstances; for this is the will of God in Christ Jesus for you' (1 Thess 5:18). 'Continue steadfastly in prayer, being watchful in it with thanksgiving' (Col 4:2)." [16] "Whoever thus participates in God's saving love, grasps that every need can be the subject of a prayer. Christ, who has taken everything to himself, in order to redeem everything, is glorified through the petitions we present in his name to the Father. Confident of this, James and Paul admonish us to pray always." [17]

According to Symeon of Thessalonica, perpetual prayer is for all Christians in every state of life, the precondition for obtaining the blessings of salvation and for receiving grace. "This, then: to possess Christ, to carry him about in one's heart and in one's thoughts, to remember him continually, to meditate on him, to burn with longing for him like the seraphim, to see him always like the cherubim, to have him rest in one's heart like the Thrones – that is the work of prayer." The Jesus prayer, "Lord Jesus Christ, Son of God, have mercy on me" is an "epiclesis", which embraces all types of prayer: petition and adoration, confession of faith, but also the gift of the Holy Spirit, the transmission of divine gifts, cleansing of the heart and casting out of demons. Prayer is not the fulfilment of the obligation to give God the honour due to him, but the establishment of communication with the uncreated grace; through this communication, the person praying makes room in himself for the divine fullness of life. As a joining in the service of the angels before the throne of God, it is, even for the person still living on earth, participation in the heavenly liturgy. [18]

5.1.2. BASIC STATEMENTS OF THE GENERAL INTRODUCTION TO THE LITURGY OF THE HOURS

The General Introduction to the Liturgy of the Hours not only regulates the external performance, but also offers a theological foundation for an appropriate internal fulfilment. Bugnini describes the General Introduction as "one of the most remarkable products of

---

[14] Cf. Catechism No. 2634-2636.
[15] Cf. Catechism No.2627
[16] Catechism No. 2638
[17] Catechism No. 2633. On the principle "Quod non assumptum, non sanatum" in Irenaeus of Lyon (Adv. haer. V,14,1) and the history of its effect, Cf. F. Gahbauer, " 'O admirabile commercium.' Relecture zweier Antiphoneninterpretationen", ALw 27 (1985) 70-90.
[18] Cf. Dialogos 293,296 - PG155, 545 D – 548 A, 537 D – 540 A, 544 D – 545 A; Resp. ad q 79 – PG 155,937 B -C.

post-conciliar, liturgical literature". [19] The first chapter devotes itself to laying this theological foundation. [20]

The theme of the heavenly liturgy is taken up in a quotation from the Constitution on the Liturgy of Vatican II: "As the high priest of the new and eternal covenant, Christ Jesus, assumed human nature, he brought with him into the exile of this world that hymn which resounds for ever in the heavenly dwellings" (GILH 3, SC 83). Reference is made again to SC 83: "Prayer to God must take place in conjunction with Christ, the Lord over all men and the only mediator, through whom alone we have access to God. He gathers the whole human community about him, so that the prayer of Christ and the prayer of the whole of humanity are bound together through an innate necessity. For it is in Christ, and in him alone, that the whole human worship of God attains its saving power and its highest purpose." [21] The title of the foregoing, "The Church continues the prayer of Christ", [22] is hardly appropriate, for it could give rise to the misunderstanding that the Church was acting independently from its head, whose action it was continuing, while he himself had terminated it.

The theological emphasis is concentrated on two aspects: The Liturgy of the Hours is, as a prayer of praise and petition, prayer of the Church with and to Christ. And: "According to ancient Christian tradition it hallows the whole course of the day and night; therein lies its special character as opposed to the other liturgical acts." [23]

The Liturgy of the Hours is indeed liturgy, and thus a dialogic happening; God speaks to his people, the people answers with song and prayer (SC 33). Therefore, the dialogue between God and man is the "essential structure" of the Liturgy of the Hours. [24] This addressing of God is first thought of in association with the psalms, and for that reason a distinction is made between praying the psalms and the intercessions and prayers composed by the Church (GILH 105). "Prayer must not always mean addressing. Thus, in the psalms we are concerned with a meditative listening, speaking and singing, which seeks the explicit response of the person praying." [25] It is logical, then, that Haunerland prefers the term "Stundenliturgie", which more clearly expresses this basic dialogic structure. [26] [Translator's Note: The normal German version of "The Liturgy of the Hours" is "Das Stundengebet", literally, "The Prayer of the Hours".]

As prayer with Christ and to Christ, the Liturgy of the Hours is the prayer of the Church, which is his mystical body, and all the members of which, before any distinction is made through the sacrament of Holy Orders, participate in the priesthood of Christ, which also comes into action in the Liturgy of the Hours (cf. SC 7). Only the royal priesthood of the whole people of God makes prayer a priestly activity, which has recourse in the Holy Spirit through the Son to the Father, thus mediating salvation.

---

[19]   Cf. Haunerland, Schwerpunkte 123; Bugnini, Liturgiereform 543.
[20]   GILH 1-33 under the title: The significance of the Liturgy of the Hours in the life of the Church.
[21]   GILH 6; Cf. SC 83: "He gathers the whole human community about him to sing together with it this divine song of praise. This priestly task he continues through his Church; it praises its Lord without ceasing and intercedes with him for the salvation of the whole world, not only in the celebration of the Eucharist, but also in other forms, especially in the performance of the Liturgy of the Hours."
[22]   GILH 6; Title: Orationem Christi Ecclesia continuat.
[23]   GILH 2 and 10; Cf. Haunerland, Schwerpunkte 123.
[24]   GILH 33: "Essentialis structura huius Liturgiae colloquium inter Deum et hominem."
[25]   Cf. Haunerland, Schwerpunkte 125 with reference to GILH 104.
[26]   Cf. Haunerland, Schwerpunkte 125f.

Logically, catechumens cannot validly perform the Liturgy of the Hours.[27] As opposed to remnants of its erroneous development into the prayer of the clerical class, which are found even in the Constitution on the Liturgy,[28] the laity are invited in the General Introduction "to fulfil the duty of the Church and celebrate a part of the Liturgy of the Hours".[29] The special mention of clerics and religious as people particularly charged to perform the Liturgy of the Hours, is justified on ecclesiological grounds: the Liturgy of the Hours is really the concern of the whole Church, which commits the charge to those people in a special way, "so that this task of the whole community will be reliably and constantly performed at least by them, and in order that thus the prayer of Christ will continue unceasingly in the Church" (GILH 28).

The special, distinguishing feature of the Liturgy of the Hours is the hallowing of time: "According to ancient Christian tradition, it hallows the whole course of day and night; in that consists its special feature as opposed to the other liturgical acts."[30] This hallowing is catabatically established in the anamnetic representation of the event of salvation, and is anabatically completed in the Church's prayer through and to Christ, for, "as prayer at the different times of the day, the prayer of the Church is also influenced by it and intended to experience the passing time as a time of salvation, and to integrate it into the proclamation of the Faith".[31]

Since the dialogue between God and man culminates in the celebration of the Eucharist, there is an intrinsic connection between the Liturgy of the Hours and the Eucharist. The Liturgy of the Hours leads to the Eucharist and even forms a necessary precondition of fruitful participation in the celebration of the latter; in common with the Mass, the Liturgy of the Hours has "praise and thanksgiving, the commemoration of the saving mysteries, prayers of petition and a foretaste of heavenly glory, but, in the latter, those are "extended to the various hours of the day".[32] Therefore, various aspects of the event of salvation are associated with the different Hours: Lauds are a commemoration of Christ's resurrection, Vespers a commemoration of the redeeming self-giving of Jesus at the Last Supper and on the cross, and the Small Hours commemorate various happenings in the Passion of Christ or the spreading of the Gospel.[33] Especially from the point of view of the hallowing of the day, the veritas horarum, the holding of the individual Hours at the proper time, which was previously sometimes forgotten, is more than just a disciplinary matter.

---

[27] Cf. Haunerland, Schwerpunkte 128, GILH 7.

[28] Cf. SC 84, in which priests and "those charged in accordance with Church regulations" are mentioned first, and then the "Christian faithful" appear, "who, together with the priest, in an approved form", perform the Liturgy of the Hours.

[29] GILH 27. The laity "must know that they, through public worship and through their prayer, come into close contact with all humanity and are able to contribute not a little to the salvation of the whole world.

[30] GILH 10. The first sentence of GILH 11 continues this: "Quoniam ergo sanctificatio diei totiusque operositatis humanae..."

[31] Harnoncourt, Theologische Grundlagen 10.

[32] Cf. GILH 12.

[33] Cf. GILH 38, 39, 75.

5.1.3. AN EXALTED THEOLOGY OF PRAYER – AND A PROFOUND DIFFICULTY IN PRAYING

In contrast to that exalted theology of prayer, many people today experience profound difficulty in praying. Häußling connects this serious paradox to the idea of the eternal hymn, contained in the Constitution on the Liturgy and quoted in the General Introduction to the Liturgy of the Hours, the hymn that he who became Man brought with him from the heavenly heights, in order to sing it with the whole human community gathered around him.

This idea expressed in SC 83 is to be found not only in the "Mediator Dei" of Pius XII,[34] but is rooted more deeply in theological tradition. Thus, Guéranger stood for a "catabatic-spiritual derivation of liturgy"; according to him, however, it is the Holy Spirit that transmits liturgy to the Church:[35] the Spirit puts "into the mouth (of the Church) her longing, her petitions, her songs of praise, it stirs up her enthusiasm, awakens her desire. That has led her to be silent neither by day nor by night, eighteen centuries long; and her voice always has a loving ring, her word always penetrates to her bridegroom's heart."[36] However, Guéranger, too, adopts from tradition the idea of the heavenly liturgy coming down to us; it is contained both in the decree "Divinam psalmodiam" of Urban VIII, through which a new editio typica of the post-Tridentine breviary was promulgated, and in the representatives of the École Française; in the final analysis, it is based on patristic theology.[37]

Häußling, however, is of the opinion that the theme of the heavenly liturgy coming down to us became transformed, first at the hands of Guéranger, then at those of Pius XII and similarly in Vatican II, from a theologically profound idea into a "popular Church ideology", through whose claim to exclusiveness, not previously made in that form, the "withdrawal of the Church out of the world into the still surviving sanctuary of the liturgy" is propagated.[38]

If the eternal hymn brought to us by Christ, and sung together with him, is devoted to the Father, is any prayer at all possible to Christ himself? According to the tradition of the Church stretching back to the earliest days, indeed there is, but Guéranger and his successors ignore the bipolarity of Christian prayer in the addressing of the Father through Christ and of Christ himself "for the sake of the purity and exclusiveness of the recognised, eternal truth", and distinguish the "liturgical" prayer of the Church, directed to the Father, from the "private" prayer of the Christian to the Lord Jesus. Correcting this tradition, SC 84 does indeed also speak of prayer as the voice of the bride speaking to the bridegroom, but, according to Häußling, this statement gives the impression of being "an interspersion generated by perplexity".[39] The performance of the "exalted, eternal hymn" remains, as it were, "bloodless" and removed from the earthly reality, which is mostly full of need and suffering; the brother and friend of man, who himself became man, seems more "open" to this reality, and it is to him that the people turns

---

[34] A.A. Häußling: Ist die Reform der Stundenliturgie beendet oder noch auf dem Weg? Th. Maas-Ewerd (ed.): Lebt unser Gottesdienst? 228; on "Mediator Dei", Cf. AAS 39 (1947) 573.

[35] Cf. Häußling, loc. cit. 230.

[36] P. Guéranger: Das Kirchenjahr I, Mainz 1874, 1f.

[37] Cf. Häußling, loc. cit. 230. Cf. what we have written in 1.3.3. C on the heavenly liturgy.

[38] Cf. Häußling, loc. cit. 230.

[39] Cf. Häußling, loc. cit. 231-233.

in subjective forms of piety and devotional practices, to which, however, the quality of "liturgy" is denied. Singing the eternal hymn with Christ to the Father becomes an imposed cult performance, so that even for those obliged to observe the Hours, a radical separation between the "liturgical" performance of prayer as the fulfilling of a duty and "private" prayer as the expression of the personal relationship with God is created, indeed could even be propagated. Thus, Pascher was of the opinion that the prayer of the breviary, which was culturally over ordinary people's heads, did not suffice "to keep the Christian's spirit at the high level of divine life". He thought that it did not exhaust all the necessities and possibilities of spiritual life, and that, if it were the sole form of prayer life, it would truly represent an unbearable impoverishment.[40]

Häußling sees a second problem organically connected with this: the "tiresome question" as to "who then may, in fact, say this lofty prayer 'in the Church's name', what proof of authenticity those praying with Christ must be able to show". Vatican II still names the clergy and the members of religious orders in the first place, thus still "insisting on the special, canonically based authorization": "It does not seem to be baptism that qualifies a Christian to pray thus and to act with Christ in such a way; beyond that, or as well as the fundamental sacrament of the Faith, an authority is needed that is at least canonically, if not sacramentally guaranteed. The Christian living in a world bearing an atheistic stamp... will have to come to the logical conclusion that such a liturgy is only for the perfect, not for the Christian who, whether he likes it or not, must live in these confused times, though not without God's all-powerful providence... The Liturgy of the Hours is out of the question for the vast majority of Christians."[41]

Indeed, it is not just in the matter of the Liturgy of the Hours – in which nowadays more of the laity than ever take part (by the "laity" we mean here the baptised and confirmed who do not have a particular role canonically, but who are considered here simply as members of the people of God, the laos theou), since the Liturgy of the Hours ceased to be a parish service – but also in the question of prayer itself that misery and perplexity have become general[42] to such a degree that it can no longer be associated just with the eternal hymn brought by Christ from heaven and with an ideological misunderstanding of that statement in SC 83.

It may well be that this narrowed-down view that the hymn was directed to the Father alone, consolidated itself in the minds of Guéranger and his school. However, there is just as little on the theme in SC 83 as there is in the encyclical "Mediator Dei" of Pius XII.[43] Under consideration is the hymn which rings out in the heavenly dwellings through all eternity. This hymn, as the core action of the heavenly, more exactly the intertrinatarian liturgy, is nothing other than the "yes" of one Person in the Trinity to the existence of the other two, spoken in overflowing love, and ever newly expressed; it is hymnic rejoicing by the one at the existence and the beauty of the other two; it is perfect affirmation of being. Christ brought this hymn to earth. In it there rings out –

---

[40] Cf. J. Pascher, Sinngerechtes Brevierbeten, München 1962, 67f. Kohlschein's post-conciliar view is more differentiated; Cf. F. Kohlschein, Die Tagzeitenliturgie als Gebetsauftrag des einzelnen: M. Klöckener / H. Rennings (ed.), Lebendiges Stundengebet 525-542, 528f.: Die Qualität des Persönlichen.

[41] Häußling, loc. cit. 233f.

[42] Cf. F.J. Steinmetz: Not und neue Erfahrung des Gebetes. In: Beten mit der Kirche, 9-17.

[43] AAS 39 (1947) 573: "Dei Verbum, humanam naturam assumens, terrestri huic exsilio hymnum illum invexit, qui in supernis sedibus per omne aevum canitur. Universam hominum communitatem ipse sibi coagmentat, eamdemque in divino hoc concinendo laudis carmine secum consociat."

leading the way catabatically! – the divine "yes" to the existence of the world and of each individual human being. Christ collects humanity about him, teaches it with this divine hymn the "yes" of the Trinity to existence, and invites it to join in the song, to express a human assent to the divine, ever solemn "assent to the world" [44] and, in the final analysis, to nothing other than participation in the fullness of life of the triune God in "inviting unity". [45]

It may be for some that also this reference to the eternal hymn of the heavenly liturgy, in view of the profound and widespread problems with prayer, represents a too lofty theology of prayer, which is incapable of giving direct answers to perplexed questioners. But what else is a person looking for, even if he is very far from God, but an unreserved "yes" to his being, a "yes" that accepts him and that only the threefold God can give, in whom there is only that "yes" that appeared with Christ as eternal hymn on earth (2 Cor 1:19f.)! The problem of prayer, which also affects the Liturgy of the Hours, cannot be solved by new structures, models and reforms alone, but by the attempt to make this endless "yes" of God to humanity and the world, which is be solemnly celebrated and which affects body and soul, capable of being credibly experienced – this attempt is behind all further innovations of both the Liturgy of the Hours and of prayer life in general.

5.1.4. CONCLUSIONS TO BE DRAWN CONCERNING THE DESIGNATION OF THE SUBJECT UNDER CONSIDERATION

Before the reform of the liturgy, when people spoke of "praying the breviary", they meant praying the "horae canonicae", which were to be recited by those obliged to do so. [46] From practical experience, the expression "praying the breviary" impressed itself so much on people's minds that even Eisenhofer puts the title "Praying the Breviary" on the historical development of the Liturgy of the Hours. Through the use of this concept, a certain stage of development is given normative status: a stage which involved the private recitation of a private, "short form" of a former parish service, which was to continue until the reform of the liturgy. The terms "Opus dei" and "Officium divinum" are found in the Rule of St. Benedict, but "Officium divinum" established itself as the most generally recognised description. [47]

The Constitution on the Liturgy itself, as well as the General Introduction, , use the term "Officium (divinum)", but are quite clear that the Liturgy of the Hours is to be regarded as real liturgy. The term "Liturgia horarum" "gives the 'Officium' the status of liturgy. In that way, the Liturgy of the Hours is, like all other liturgical actions, 'the exercise of the priestly office of Jesus Christ' (SC 7)." As in the Constitution on the Liturgy, so must the complementing of the anabatic-latrial view by the pre-eminent catabatic-soteriological, which is also found in other places, be clearly expressed. "Liturgy is a dialogic happening"; that is also valid for the Liturgy of the Hours. [48] The term "officium" could be misunderstood in two ways: on the one hand it describes the Liturgy of the Hours as an "official" activity ("officium") of the person obliged to carry it out,

---

[44]   Allusion to J. Pieper, Zustimmung zur Welt. Eine Theorie des Festes. München 2nd edn. 1964.
[45]   Allusion to J. Moltmann, Die einladende Einheit des dreieinigen Gottes, Concilium 21 (1985) 35-41.
[46]   Cf. CIC/1917 cc. 135, 610 1,3,1475.
[47]   Cf. Eisenhofer II, 418f.
[48]   Haunerland, Schwerpunkte 124.

the neglect of which is viewed in the category of guilt for sin; then, the concept of "officium" can also infer having to pray the whole "officium", as it is prescribed in the rubrics for the corresponding day, in order to fulfil one's duty. [49]

The term "Liturgy of the Word", which brings together all the non-sacramental and sacramental services other than the Liturgy of the Hours, deserves, for reasons similar to those which are valid for the "Liturgy of the Hours", to have priority before "Devotions", "pia exercitia", "Meditation", or other descriptions that express only the human activity.

In the term "Liturgy of the Word" ("liturgia verbi") the catabatic-soteriological line is also expressed, since "Word" means not only the word of prayer spoken by human beings, but also God's word, which the liturgical assembly takes in by hearing Scripture and answers in the words of human prayer, in praise and petition.

Bibliography

German Bishops' Conference (ed.), Beten mit der Kirche. Hilfen zum neuen Stundengebet. Published by the Secretariat of the German Bishops' Conference, Regensburg 1978.

B. Fischer, Dienst des Lobes – Dienst der Fürbitte. Zur Spiritualität des Stundengebetes. Köln 1977 (Kölner Beiträge 23).

Ph. Harnoncourt, Theologische Grundlagen des Stundengebetes, HID 41 (1987) 2-11.

W. Haunerland: Theologische Schwerpunkte der "Allgemeinen Einführung in das Stundengebet": M. Klöckener / H. Rennings (eds.): Lebendiges Stundengebet. Vertiefung und Hilfe (FS Brinkhoff), Freiburg-Basel-Vienna 1989, 123-139.

A. H. M. Scheer, "Tota Ecclesia orans". Anmerkungen zum Subjekt der Stundenliturgie: M. Klöckener / H. Rennings (eds.): Lebendiges Stundengebet, 70-97.

J. A. Jungmann, Christliches Beten in Wandel und Bestand. New edition with a foreword by K. Richter, Freiburg-Basel-Vienna 1991.

5.2. THE HISTORICAL DEVELOPMENT OF THE LITURGY OF THE HOURS

5.2.1. THE JEWISH LEGACY AND EARLY DEVELOPMENTS

Set times for prayer are a legacy from Israel. The obligation already existed to say the "Shmah Israel" every morning and evening (Deut 6:7; 11:19). As well as that, there were three further prayer times, spread over the day (Dan 6:11, 19). During the Exile, there were added to the Jerusalem Temple worship the services in the local synagogues, which were linked to the Temple worship insofar as prayer services were held in the synagogues at the times of the daily sacrifice in the Temple, particularly as far as the recurrent evening sacrifice was concerned. Outside Jerusalem, the devout came together at this hour for a service in the synagogue, or prayed in private, at least. Morning and

---

[49] Cf. H. Jone: Katholische Moraltheologie. Unter besonderer Berücksichtigung des Codex Iuris Canonici sowie des deutschen, österreichischen und schweizerischen Rechtes. Paderborn, 16th ed. 1953, 128f., according to which the possibility is not excluded of omitting Nones without committing a sin, provided that Sext is prayed twice, "since the obligation to say the breviary refers more to quantity than to quality; the quantity, however, is more or less the same". Whoever does not fulfil the duty of saying the breviary, loses the income from his benefice, according to the provisions of can. 1475 CIC/1917; Cf. ibid. 131.

evening prayer were already the pivotal points of a Jewish Liturgy of the Hours, which included five such Hours. The three Hours spread over the day were probably held about the times of Sext, Terce and Nones: the event of Pentecost can be regarded as beginning in the morning with the Apostles assembled in prayer (Acts 2:15); Peter was at prayer when he had his midday vision in Joppa (Acts 10:9); and the man lame from birth was healed at "Nones", as Peter and John entered the Temple for the daily prayer (Acts 3:1). [50]

After the destruction of the Temple, the whole life of divine service was transferred to the synagogue. While the evening service put the emphasis on praise and petition, there were catechetical elements and preaching in the morning service. The Christian Liturgy of the Hours took over the existing tradition and continued it, or changed it for its own purposes.

While the Christian morning service was characterised by praise (laudes matutinae), "which is expressed primarily by the regular recitation of the 'Hallel' psalms, Ps 148-150", the evening service was given a sacrificial emphasis: the recitation of Ps 141 (140),2: ("Let my prayer be counted as incense before thee, and the lifting up of my hands as an evening sacrifice!") gave "occasion to ritual development"; another sacrificial element (in the sense of a sacrifice of praise) was added by a service of light (lucernarius). We refer to the possible influence of a service of light in the domestic sabbath ritual and to that of the blessings on the Christian hymns and prayers on the theme of light. In the evening – but also in the morning – this symbolism of light was transferred to Christ as the rising Sun of Justice, or as the light that knows no evening. "Besides this institution of prayer assemblies at the turning-points of the day, the practice of praying thrice a day has been taken over from Judaism to Christianity. The Didache, at the beginning of the 3rd century, prescribes the following after it has given the Our Father: 'Pray thus three times a day!' The Lord's Prayer here takes the place of the Jewish Prayer of Eighteen Intercessions." [51] Still, Gerhards thinks, after referring to Taft, that "the relationship of the Christian compared to the Jewish prayer traditions is less close than is often assumed. Though the Christians continue Jewish usages, the content of their prayer has been given a definitive, new form by the Christ happening." [52] For the shaping of the Liturgy of the Hours in practice, the Apostle Paul's exhortation – "Pray constantly" (1 Thess 5:17) – was to be a motivation of no little power. [53] [54]

Tertullian (died after 220) recommends the third, sixth and ninth hours as times of private prayer; here, in the background, there are salvation mysteries from the Acts of the Apostles, which are mentioned in connection with the prayer: the third hour is that of the descent of the Spirit (Acts 2:15), the sixth that of Peter's vision (Acts 10:9-16), the ninth that of the healing of the paralytic (Acts 3:1). In addition, Tertullian mentions the prayer at the beginning of the day and of the night as a self-evident duty of the Christian, as well as the prayer during the night itself. [55]

---

[50] Cf. Martimort 173-176: La prière juive au temps du Christ.
[51] Cf. A.Gerhards, "Benedicam Dominum in omni tempore". Geschichtlicher Überblick zum Stundengebet: M. Klöckener / H. Rennings (eds.), Lebendiges Stundengebet 3-33.6-8.
[52] A.Gerhards, Das Stundengebet in Ost und West. Neue Erkenntnisse der vergleichenden Liturgiewissenschaft, LJ 38 (1988) 164-172.165.
[53] De oratione 25 – CSEL 20, 197f.
[54] De oratione 25 CSEL 20, 198.
[55] Ad uxorem II,5 – CSEL 70, 118.

Hippolytus mentions a number of prayer times, which correspond only in part to the hours of the later Liturgy of the Hours. "If one may assume a uniform system behind the various items given, the following custom forms the basis: private prayer on rising, at the third, sixth and ninth hour, on going to bed, at midnight and at cockcrow. General assemblies take place in the morning for instruction and in the evening at the Agape." The prayer times at the third, sixth and ninth hour are based on the chronology of the Passion in Mark's gospel "and thus possibly constitute evidence of a very early Roman prayer cycle". [56] The chronology embraces the Crucifixion (third hour), the eclipse of the sun (sixth hour), the death of Christ and the piercing with the lance (ninth hour). [57] In Pascher's opinion, however, Hippolytus has codified the Christian tradition that gives the following order of prayer at the beginning of the third century: Morning prayer – Terce – Sext – Nones – Evening Prayer – Night Prayer. [58]

The morning and evening assemblies are particularly important. The morning service in the church has a catechetical character: "You will hear something you do not know, and you will profit from what the Holy Spirit will give you through the one who teaches. ... You will also be told there what you must do at home. Therefore, each one should endeavour to go to the church, the place where the spirit flowers. If there is no instruction on a particular day, and everyone stays at home, then each should take the holy Scripture and read in it as much as he can and as seems useful to him." [59] The evening assembly for the Agape is characterized by the thanksgiving for light. The deacon [60] carries in the lamp as darkness falls, and the bishp intones the praise of the light as symbol of Christ, the everlasting light, without, however, saying the "Sursum corda" in the introductory response – that remains reserved for the eucharistic celebration. [61] Gerhards traces the thanksgiving for the light back to the evening Berakah in the synagogue, not to the light Berakah in the family on the sabbath: "The Christian at prayer experiences the continuing presence of the risen Christ, the everlasting light, in contrast to the dying light of day as darkness falls. The later evening light rituals of the Christians cannot be explained completely with reference to the Jewish light ritual on the eve of the sabbath. Pagan influences seem to be involved here." [62]

5.2.2. "CATHEDRAL" AND "MONASTIC" LITURGY OF THE HOURS

In the following period the Liturgy of the Hours develops a dualism, dividing into the "cathedral" and "monastic" types. The "cathedral type" – the Liturgy of the Hours celebrated by the faithful gathered about their bishop and his presbyters – developed in the course of the 4th century especially in the urban communities of the Orient; it was characterized by regular assemblies in the morning and in the evening, occasionally supplemented by vigils. The "monastic type" strives for the ideal of perpetual prayer.

---

[56] Gerhards, Benedicam 9.
[57] Cf. TradAp. 41, ed. Geerlings 300-302.
[58] Pascher, Stundengebet 23.
[59] TradAp. 41, ed. Geerlings 300-301.
[60] According to a theory of Plank's, the deacon takes on the function of the housewife in the Jewish evening ritual of the sabbath evening, which also includes a light ritual: the lighting of the sabbath candles; the place of the household, even in Jewish practice, could be taken by the community of disciples about a rabbi. Cf. Gerhards, Benedicam 30, Anm. 33.
[61] Cf. TradAp. 25, ed. Geerlings 275-277.
[62] Gerhards, Benedicam 11.

In it, the recital of psalms currente psalterio is central, i.e., the choice of psalms is independent of the time of day, and "generally the Liturgy of the Hours of monastic stamp lacks any ceremonial action. In contrast, the morning and evening offices in diocesan churches possessed a central guiding thought, which expressed itself in the psalms chosen for morning and evening, and in a clearly visible ceremony." [63]

The "cathedral type" consists of psalms, hymns and ritual acts. In all cases, the thanksgiving for the light plays a meaningful role in the evening. Among the various and also differing data, Gerhards regards the following elements as characteristic: for the morning service, morning psalms and canticles – among them Ps 62(63) –, Gloria in excelsis, intercessions, blessing and dismissal. Besides that, the Resurrection Vigil on Sunday is structured as follows: three antiphons with prayers, intercessions, incensing, Gospel, blessing and dismissal. [64]

The cathedral Liturgy of the Hours in Jerusalem, which already shows influences of monastic spirituality, is described by the pilgrim Egeria. [65] Before cockcrow, monks, virgins and lay people go into the Church of the Holy Sepulchre in order to keep early vigil. Until sunrise, hymns and psalms are sung alternately, as well as antiphons; every hymn is concluded with an oration; to say that is the task of the clerics, who are also present. As day breaks, the "matutini hymni" are sung. On every occasion the bishop appears, proclaims the intercessions, in which names are mentioned, blesses the catechumens and, after a prayer, the believers. [66] At the tenth hour, the Lucernarium is celebrated in Jerusalem. The people foregather in the Anastasis, and so many torches and candles are lit from the Eternal Light of the Grotto of the Holy Sepulchre, that "fit lumen infinitum". The "psalmi lucernares, sed et antiphonae diutius" are sung. In the presence of the bishop "hymni et antiphonae" are sung. The deacon leads a Kyrie litany, followed by a prayer of the bishop. Then follow prayers spoken with bowed head for catechumens and believers, before the bishop blesses the congregation and is accompanied by it to the relic of the Cross. [67] The Sunday vigil includes an incense ceremony and the proclaiming of the Gospel of the Resurrection by the bishop. [68] Besides the selection of psalms suitable to Sundays and feastdays, "so that their contents suited the theme of the other texts of the particular day", the Jerusalem Liturgy of the Hours described by Egeria includes: "1. Morning (cum luce, matutini) and evening service (licinicon, lucernare) are celebrated together by clergy, ascetics and faithful (with catechumens). 2. The common prayer of the aputacticae (= monks) consists of the Hours of Terce (in Lent), Sext and Nones (throughout the year). Pilgrims and the faithful also participate, on a voluntary basis. 4. The content of those services consists of psalms with antiphons, an oration, responsories (psalmi responsorii), hymns and readings from the Old and New Testaments. The reading of the Gospel, above all the Resurrection readings of Sunday, mostly fall to the bishop, who usually appears only at the end of the Hours and gives the blessing. 5. Here, for the first time, the particular slant of the Hours becomes

[63] G. Winkler, Über die Kathedralvesper in den verschiedenen Riten des Ostens und des Westens: ALw 16 (1974) 53-102.53f.
[64] Cf. Gerhards, Benedicam 14.
[65] Egeria, Peregrinatio – Égérie, Journal de Voyage. Introduction, texte et traduction par P. Maraval, Paris 1982 (Schr 296).
[66] Egeria, Peregrinatio 24,1,2-4 – SChr 296, 234-237.
[67] Ibid. 24,4-7 – SChr 296, 234-237.
[68] Cf. ibid. 24,10 – SChr 296, 244f.

clear: the selection of the psalms, antiphons, prayers, reading and hymns according to the theme of the feast. The pilgrim noticed that as different to her western custom. Thus, in Jerusalem, in the episcopate of Cyril, for the first time, the complete liturgical cele-bration of the whole day is taken over from the practice of the ascetics into the service for the public, which takes place under the leadership of the bishop and clergy and in the celebration of which the people participate." [69]

The "monastic type" of the Liturgy of the Hours is based on the peculiar spirituality of monasticism, which wants to approach the ideal of perpetual prayer as closely as possible. Thus, Pachomius makes perpetual prayer a duty for monks, no matter where they are or what they are doing. Besides that, there are common prayer times in the morning, in the evening and in the night, for which there is a fixed quota: in the "Vita S. Pachomii" we are told an angel ordered that twelve psalms were to be prayed in every Hour. Goltzen considers that "the understanding of the service of prayer as a quota" was "one of the most influential thoughts for the whole development of the Liturgy of the Hours". [70] The Egyptian monasticism of the Thebais und the monastic tradition of Cappadocia developed the two prototypes of the monastic Liturgy of the Hours: "The Egyptian monks assembled only in the morning and the evening for the meditation in common on two consecutive psalms, which were followed by two readings. The urban monasticism of Cappadocia, on the other hand, had adopted the selected psalms for morning and evening from the cathedral office, and in addition the Liturgy of the Hours that had been simply recommended to all Christians from the 2nd to the 4th century, namely, Terce, Sext, Nones, Compline and the prayer at midnight. Those Hours now form the permanent component of the monastic cursus. In addition, the midnight office of the Basilean monastic communities can be traced back in its structure to the usage of Egypt. The Psalmodia currens usual in the morning and evening in Egypt was here shifted in time to the night office. The Syro-Palestinian monastic office takes up a middle position between the anachoretic type in the south and the urban form in the north." [71]

The Liturgy of the Hours in Greek monasticism was formed by the Rule of Basil the Great (d. 379). Its ideal, too, is perpetual prayer: "Since giving thanks is always commanded even by a law (Eph 5:20) and is evidently necessary for our life according to both nature and reason, so the prayer times laid down in the brotherhoods must not be missed." [72] Mentioned are morning prayer (orthros), Terce, Sext and Nones, an Hour when the day draws to an end, a further one as darkness falls, as well as an Hour at midnight, and, besides, a prayer time before dawn breaks. [73] Goltzen interprets this as a new Hour, which has separated itself from the night Hour. "One must question whether the prayer at midnight and that before dawn originally came from the full Vigil, which naturally could not regularly be held in full, and was replaced by a symbolic visitation of the stages of the night. [74] Before 390 John Cassian [75], who died about 435 as Abbot in

---

[69] Goltzen 140f. Cf. also Winkler 58f.
[70] Cf. Goltzen 136.
[71] Winkler 57.
[72] Cf. Rule of Basil 37, edited by H.U. v. Balthasar. In: Id. (ed), Die großen Ordensregeln, Einsiedeln 3rd edn. 1974, 97.
[73] Cf. ib. 98f.
[74] Goltzen 137
[75] Schnitzler, Stundengebet 77, describes him as "Forerunner of Benedict and Father of Monasticism, and –

Marseille, lived in a monastery in Bethlehem; he then stayed about seven years with the
Egyptian monks in the desert of Skete and, between 417 and 425, put his experiences in
writing in his work "De institutis coenobiorum" [76]; he wished to use those experiences to
reform Gaulish monasticism. The Egyptian monks did not have Terce, Sext and Nones,
but joined their prayers to their work. Lauds were not distinguished as a separate Hour.

"The heart of the prayer times consists of twelve psalms, which are recited by an
individual currente psalterio, i.e. continually. Between the psalms there are phases of
silent prayer, during which the monk stands with arms raised, and which are punctuated
by a prostration and concluded by a collect from the superior. The twelfth psalm, a Hallel psalm, ends with the Gloria Patri. The psalmody is followed by a service of readings
with two readings ... " The typical features of the monastic Liturgy of the Hours were
already present: the psalms are not selected thematically, but are prayed consecutively;
neither are they interrupted by antiphons; "set forms of prayer are less an end in themselves than the frame for personal prayer", which the monk practises unceasingly, also
during work. [77] "However, Cassian reports that the Egyptians, too, 'at certain times also
rose before cockcrow and extended the night vigils after the celebration of the canonical
Hour until it became light, so that the rising early light might find them in this fire of
the spirit' (Institutions III,5)." [78]

In Palestine the day Hours were also kept; Cassian reports from his time in Bethlehem about the introduction of Matins, so that the number seven mentioned in the psalm
(Ps 118:164) was reached. "This morning Hour competed with the prayer at cockcrow.
But Cassian emphasizes that the old order of the psalms is not interfered with by this
new introduction. At the end of the Vigils, which are usually finished after cockcrow
and before dawn, psalms 148-150 should be sung, and in the new Hour Pss 50, 62 and
89. In Terce, Sext and Nones, too, three psalms and orations are prayed." [79]

Compline is rooted in the fact that only on Saturdays and Sundays was there a special evening meal after Vespers, and that a special prayer time occurred before bedtime
only on those days, without already carrying that name. "The older Matins (= Prime)
and the prayer before going to bed (= later Compline), in contrast to the other Hours,
arose from the circumstances of monastic community life, whereas a biblical source was
ascribed to the older Hours. Thus, this order, now fitted to monastic life, only needed to
be summarized and laid down for western monasticism – and that was to be done in the
Rule of St. Benedict." [80]

In the west it was Benedict of Nursia (d. 547) "who wrote down for the monasteries
founded by him the first ordering of the Liturgy of the Hours that went into detail". [81]

---

more than a father of western piety – a bridge between the Church in the east and the Church in the west,
the intersection point of the lines which run from Anthony the Great, from the legacy of Origen, from
Augustine and Leo".

[76]   Exact title: "De institutis coenobiorum et de octo principalium vitiorum remediis", ed. J. C. Guy, SChr
109, Paris 1965.

[77]   Gerhards, Benedicam 16.

[78]   Pascher, Stundengebet 35.

[79]   Pascher, Stundengebet 36.

[80]   Goltzen 143f.

[81]   Pascher, Stundengebet 44. At the same time, Benedict, however, in the 18th chapter of his Rule permits
a surprising degree of freedom: "Vor allem indes liegt es uns daran festzuhalten: sollte dem einen oder
anderen diese Verteilung der Psalmen nicht entsprechen, so möge er sie ändern, wie es ihm besser zu
sein scheint. Er muß aber in allen Fällen darauf achten, daß jede Woche das ganze Psalter mit seinen

This was not new; it took up that already existing in the Roman church. [82] "Even before him, Prime and Compline had been integrated into the old system. Vespers are a day Hour. Thus, the day Hours were Prime, Sext, Nones and Vespers. The following were foreseen for the night: Compline, Nocturns and Matins (= Lauds). ... For the first time one finds an ordering of the psalms for the whole weekly office. Still, Benedict leaves some space for freedom in that he does not insist unconditionally on his way of dividing the psalms, as long as the whole psalter is prayed every week." [83] "The following can be regarded as the basic quota for the whole office: 'Psalterium per hebdomadam, scriptura per annum'." [84] This division, which respects the balance between the individual Hours, also, according to Goltzen, bears witness as much to "moderation" as Benedict's basic virtue as does the moderate allocation of the monks' work. It ends with Vespers, which should be held so early in the afternoon that lamplight is not yet necessary. Compline closes the monastic day. [85]

When the Lombards destroyed the monastery of Monte Cassino about 580, the fleeing monks found refuge in Rome. Gelasius II assigned them accommodation near the Lateran, where soon several of their monasteries flourished. In the succeeding centuries, Benedictine monasteries also appeared near the other principal churches of Rome; these monasteries assumed responsibility for the Liturgy of the Hours in the basilicas. Benedict had probably composed his order under the influence of Roman customs. Now these returned in the Benedictine form and from there they could set out on their triumph over the whole western Church. [86] Through the collapse of the ancient urban culture in the Dark Ages, the monasteries took on an enormous significance. Many bishops who came from the monasteries introduced Benedict's Liturgy of the Hours into their churches. The Benedictine missionary monks carried the Roman Liturgy of the Hours to northern Europe and Britain. According to Gerhards, Gregory VII "possibly introduced it in the Iberian peninsula, so that in the Middle Ages the Roman office was in use practically everywhere, after it had squeezed out most local traditions". [87]

However, these extra-Roman traditions should not be disregarded. For instance, according to Martimort, until into the 11th century the Spanish church distinguished between the cathedral ordo ("Quod est Matutini et Vespertini sive Completi officium") and that which the monks contributed as prayer times ("Officium sollicite exsolvendum monacis"). [88] The Milanese church was also able to preserve its own traditions in the Liturgy of the Hours, and those even experienced a renewal in the spirit of Vatican II. [89] As typical for the Milanese Liturgy of the Hours – the small Hours of which correspond to their Roman counterparts - Martimort mentions the lucernarium of Vespers, the

150 Psalmen gebetet werde, und da man stets am Sonntag bei Nachtgottesdienst neu beginne." H. U. v. Balthasar (ed.), Die großen Ordensregeln, Einsiedeln 3rd edn. 1974, 214f.
[82] Cf. Bäumer 170-172.
[83] Pascher, Stundengebet 35.
[84] Goltzen 154.
[85] Cf. Goltzen 155-157.
[86] Pascher, Stundengebet 44f.
[87] Gerhards, Benedicam 23.
[88] Martimort 263.
[89] Martimort 266: "La réforme de l'office ambrosien dans l'esprit de Vatican II a reçu un commencement de mise en pratique avec la publication en 1981 d'un diurnal, Diurna laus. Il s'agit surtout d'alléger l'office par une meilleure répartition des psaumes, de mieux mettre en valeur la commémoration baptismale et les intercessions, de réviser le répertoire euchologique."

memorial of baptism in the evening and morning services, which was connected with a procession to the baptistry, an "antiphona ad crucem" reminiscent of the Jerusalem Liturgy of the Hours, and the profusion of euchological texts on feastdays. [90]

5.2.3. FROM THE LITURGY OF THE HOURS TO THE PRAYER OF THE BREVIARY

The transformation of the Liturgy of the Hours, a service that is celebrated, into the private recitation of the breviary, is connected, according to Martimort, with a new practice with regard to ordination: until the 11th century a priest was ordained for a certain church. This involved the obligation to celebrate the Liturgy of the Hours there. As priests began to be ordained without being bound to a certain church, the obligation to celebrate the Liturgy of the Hours was no longer attached to the place, but became the personal obligation of the ordained. The more ordination became disconnected from the attachment to a church, the more the private recitation of the Liturgy of the Hours outside choir became widespread. Thus, the Hours also began to be detached from their proper starting times; "now the night prayer could be said by day, indeed even on the day before". [91] The praying of the Hours outside choir gave birth to the "breviary"; the textbooks distributed to the bearers of various roles could hardly be considered for the purpose of private recitation. With the abridgements of the readings, hymns and prayers taken into consideration, everything necessary for private recitation was brought together in one book, the "breviary". It proved to be decisive that the Papal court prayed the Liturgy of the Hours according to the "Breviarium secundum consuetudinem curiae Romanae", and that this was adopted by the new Franciscan order. [92]

It was especially the secular clergy that was affected by this new Liturgy of the Hours. Gerhards sees the reason for this in the changes in the structure of the Church; in the first millennium the episcopal churches were liturgical centres in the cities. In the countryside there were also centres of clerics or monks living in community. In these centres a division of labour between prayer in choir and pastoral work could take place. With the development of the parish in its present sense since the 12th century and the individualisation of the clergy brought about by that, the common celebration of the daily liturgy became impossible. "Rather than the liturgy being reduced to the original cathedral elements, the trend towards the private recitation of the whole office was encouraged." Chrodegang of Metz (d. 766) already prescribed that the canons regular should recite the office privately when they were absent from choir; by the "canonici", however, in the Carolingian period, all clerics were understood. [93]

Through this development the secular priest was practically done away with: "With ordination the monastic status is conferred also, not only as far as the way of life is concerned, but also with reference to spirituality. Up to the most recent reform of the liturgy, as far as praying the breviary was concerned, the priest was a kind of "monk on a journey" with the obligation to privately go through the Liturgy of the Hours, which

---

[90] Cf. Martimort 264-266.
[91] Pascher, Stundengebet 56.
[92] Cf. ibid. 57f.
[93] Cf. P. Salmon, Die Verpflichtung zum kirchlichen Stundengebet: J. A. Jungmann (ed.), Brevierstudien. Referate aus der Studientaguung von Assisi 14.-17. September 1956; Trier 1958, 85-116. 94f.

no longer existed as such."[94] Travelling did indeed provide many occasions for private meditation; the mendicant monks, living without "stabilitas loci", could not participate in the Liturgy of the Hours outside their communities, and prayed the Hours privately. Also, the clerical students at the mediaeval universities, who were obliged as benefici- aries to perform the Liturgy of the Hours, "relying on the advice of the moralists, were eager as far as possible through private recitation" to compensate for their absence from their churches.[95] This was all the more valid since the "performance" of the Liturgy of the hours (whether privately or in choir) was reckoned against the income (benefices) of the clerics.

The subjectivist piety of the high and late Middle Ages also encouraged the trend towards a prayer attached to the clerical state.[96] The Jesuit order, founded in the 16th century, managed without any Liturgy of the Hours; its members confined themselves to the obligatory recitation of the breviary. Since the 10th century there developed from the official Liturgy of the Hours the Officium parvum, a small supplementary office in honour of the Trinity, the Mother of God or a saint. Separated from the main office, it developed into an independent Liturgy of the Hours, which was above all practised by educated lay people. But in their case too it took place in the form of individual prayer from a "Book of Hours", of which many gained fame because of their artistic decoration.[97] Many cloistered communities in modern times adopted the Little Office of Mary as daily, obligatory prayer for their members.[98]

Commissioned by Clement VII, the Spanish Franciscan Cardinal Francisco de Quiñones published in 1535 a breviary for purely private use. Quiñones gave three rea- sons for the priest's obligation to say the breviary: the priest must pray for the people, who are otherwise occupied; he must give example to others; and he must learn from the daily reading of the breviary for his catechetical activities. The Liturgy of the Hours had been completely transformed into the prayer of the clerical state.[99] Initially very successful, the history of theis breviary was at an end only after half a century. Jung- mann explains the reasons why Quiñones" reformed breviary was opposed, but also points out its after-effects even after the publication of the Roman breviary of 1568, as, for example, in the English Book of Common Prayer, in neo-Gallican breviaries of the 18th and 19th centuries, in breviaries for non-clerical communities of religious and in special breviaries for different dioceses.[100] Quiñones" breviary, which had been developed specially for individual recitation, was, in the end, too great a break with tra- dition: "This consequence was not drawn by the highest authority, which did not wish to surrender the theoretical claim that the prayer of the Church was the Liturgy of the Hours."[101]

[94]   Gerhards, Benedicam 24. Winkler (54) reaches a similar conclusion.
[95]   Salmon, Verpflichtung 101.
[96]   Cf. Salmon, Verpflichtung 111.
[97]   On breviaries for the laity or "Livres d'heures" cf. H. Bacht; Art. "Laienbrevier": LThK 2nd edn. VI, 743.
[98]   Cf. Art. Officium parvum: Adam-Berger 370.
[99]   Cf. Pascher, Stundengebet 59; Quiñones' breviary was also called "The Breviary of the Cross" because its author was Cardinal Priest of S. Croce in Gerusalemme.
[100]   Cf. J.A. Jungmann, Warum ist das Reformbrevier des Kardinals Quiñonez gescheitert: Id., Liturgisches Erbe und pastorale Gegenwart. Studien und Vorträge, Innsbruck-Wien-München 1960, 265-282.
[101]   Gerhards, Benedicam 25.

Things went otherwise with the breviary that was commissioned by the Council of Trent and appeared in 1568; it was to remain valid for over 400 years. As in the case of the missal, only those churches that had a two-hundred-year-old particular tradition could retain the latter. The new breviary was approved for public as well as private recitation [102], and spread very quickly. It was revised already under Urban VIII (d. 1644); the hymns were revised in classical style and the asterisk was inserted in the psalms. [103] Nevertheless, there remained the serious shortcomings of the breviary, those of a prayer-book for the clergy; "in its community dimension" it represented "nothing more than a continuation of the status quo". [104] There were efforts at reform in the Germany of the Enlightenment, when it was attempted to introduce "German Vespers" as a service for the people. [105] "The elements of the Latin Liturgy of the Hours still remaining in the parishes were adapted for the use of the faithful through German translations and the insertion of German hymns." [106] For the priest, however, nothing had changed; at public Vespers on a Sunday afternoon he was still obliged to pray "his" breviary while the faithful prayed, if he had not recited the corresponding hour long "in advance".

There was a reform under Pius X, who, on the 1st November 1911, organized the psalter anew by the Bull "Divino afflatu spiritu", according to which the psalter was to be prayed once a week. Through the motu proprio "In cotidianis precibus" of the 24th March 1945 Pius XII permitted the use of a new Latin translation of the psalms, based on the original Hebrew text. Still, there was as yet no sign of a comprehensive reform of the breviary. [107] The decree of the Congregation of Rites of 23th March 1955 simplified the rubrics, but still this did not bring much as far as a return to the communal celebration of the Liturgy of the Hours was concerned.

The active participation of the faithful in the holy mysteries, as the programme of the liturgical movement, was also to include the Liturgy of the Hours. In his publication "La piété liturgique", which appeared in 1914, Lambert Beaudouin called for Vespers and Compline on Sundays to be maintained or reinstated, as the case might be. The same demand was made in 1925 by a Benedictine of the Abbey of Maria Laach, A. Wintersig. In 1923 Romano Guardini made a beginning with explanatory translations of the Liturgy of the Hours for the laity; of these were published Prime, Vespers, Compline and the Matins of Holy Week for communal celebration in Burg Rothenfels. The common celebration of Hours from the Liturgy was also practised by the circle about Pius Parsch. [108]

---

[102] Cf. Salmon, Verpflichtung 108: "In den Dekreten des Konzils von Trient wurde man vergebens nach einem Text suchen, der die Privatrezitation rechtfertigt, oder gar nach einem solchen, der sie als obligat hinstellt. Dagegen fehlt es nicht an Kanones, die die Verpflichtung zum Chorgebet, sogar in den Pfarreien, wieder ins Gedächtnis rufen."

[103] Cf. Pascher, Stundengebet 61-63.

[104] Gerhards, Benedicam 25.

[105] Cf. L. Brinkhoff, Art "Vesperdienst (en avondoefening)": LW II, 2796f.

[106] F. Kohlschein, Die Tagzeitenliturgie als "Gebet der Gemeinde" in der Geschichte, HID 41 (1987) 12-40. 29.

[107] Cf. Th. Klauser, De ratione reformandi Breviarium romanum, EL 63 (1949) 406-411; B. Fischer, Brevierreform. Ein Vorschlag, Trier 1950.

[108] Concerning the liturgy of the day hours in the liturgical movement Cf. Kohlschein, Tagzeitenliturgie 30-37.

5.2.4. THE RENEWED LITURGY OF THE HOURS

At the Council there was no doubt about the need to reform the Liturgy of the Hours: "In almost all speeches by the Fathers a lively anxiety was expressed about whether in these times praying the breviary had become, for the continually active pastor, rather a crushing burden than an effective cultivation of the spiritual man." A dualism between the personal piety of the one praying the breviary and the spirituality of the Liturgy of the Hours, a lack of spiritual quality in the breviary in general, as well as a "quota attitude", according to which the obligatory amount of prayer was gone through by not a few independently from the starting-point in time of the actual Hours (i.e., it was "anticipated") – all those were deplored. [109]

Vatican II devoted a special chapter (SC 83-101) to the reform of the Liturgy of the Hours. SC 89 lays down the following guide-lines for the reform: "a) Lauds as morning prayer and Vespers as evening prayer, according to the revered tradition of the whole Church the two points on which the daily Liturgy of Hours hinges, should be regarded as the most important prayer times and should be celebrated as such. b) Compline shall be arranged in such a way that it corresponds fully to the end of the day. c) Matins, so called, should of course retain in choir its character of nocturnal praise of God, but it should be so arranged that it can be meaningfully prayed at any time of the day. It should consist of fewer psalms and lengthier readings. d) Prime should be dispensed with. e) In choir the little Hours Terce, Sext and Nones should be retained. Outside choir one of them may be selected that best suits the particular time of day." SC 88 defines the "veritas temporis": the reform should make it possible for "the Hours to be given back their correct starting times as far as possible. At the same time, the conditions of modern life should be taken into consideration, because especially those who are apostolically active live under these conditions."

For seven years work continued on the renewed Liturgy of the Hours in a working group of the "Roman Liturgical Council"; on All Saints' Day in 1970 it was approved by the Apostolic Constitution "Laudis canticum" of Paul VI, [110] and in Easter 1971 the first volume of the Editio typica of the "Liturgia horarum" appeared. [111] It was followed immediately by the different vernacular editions. [112]

SC 95-98 deal with the obligation to pray the Liturgy of the Hours. Clerics in higher orders who are not obliged to appear in choir have the duty to pray it together or alone every day (SC 96); here the common is mentioned before the private performance. According to SC 99, clear preference is given to the Liturgy of the Hours performed in common. Despite all weighting in favour of prayer in common, according to Richter there are in the Constitution on the Liturgy still some traces remaining of a clericalist understanding of the Liturgy of the Hours. He says it is symptomatic that after all those obliged to perform it are named, the Liturgy of the Hours is also recommended to the laity (SC 100), but there is no longer any question here of anybody being commissioned by the Church. Richter agrees with Taft's assessment that even Vatican II still regarded

---

[109] E. J. Lengeling, Die Konstitution des Zweiten Vatikanischen Konzils über die heilige Liturgie. Lateinisch-deutscher Text mit einem Kommentar. Münster 2ⁿᵈ edn. 1965 (Lebendiger Gottesdienst 5/6), 176.

[110] Kaczynski 2196-2214.

[111] Kaczynski 2538.

[112] As, for instance, a preliminary edition of a French Liturgy of the Hours in 1969, a German preliminary edition with the title "Neues Stundenbuch"; the authentic edition for German-speaking areas was published in 1978/79 in three volumes.

the Liturgy of the Hours as a prayer for priests and religious, and that it is presupposed that it is usually performed in private, and only exceptionally celebrated in public. Anyway, in his opinion, the historical basis for the reform was largely incomplete, because it was built almost exclusively on the post-mediaeval Latin tradition. [113] Thus, he concludes, the principle "Liturgia semper reformanda" is especially valid for the Liturgy of the Hours. Following on that, it should be considered whether a collection of material, offering no hard and fast Ordo, but only a kind of framework omitting all detailed development, "would not be a further practical step towards removing from these liturgical celebrations, so neglected in our parishes up to now, but yet so necessary, any remaining appearance of a prayer reform only of concern to the clergy". [114] According to Häußling, too, the Liturgia Horarum and the vernacular editions derived from it have not yet succeeded in accommodating to the difficulty individual Christians and congregations have in praying, and in leading them to prayer. The "goal of the Council 'to deepen more and more the Christian life among the faithful', and, as a way towards that goal, to get 'a general renewal of the liturgy' under way, has not been reached yet by a long chalk in the area of the Liturgy of the Hours, despite some admirable works." [115]

Bibliography

S. Bäumer, Geschichte des Breviers, Freiburg i. Br. 1895.

R. Biron, Histoire du Bréviaire, 2 vols., Paris 1905, reprinted Rome 1967.

H. Goltzen, Der tägliche Gottesdienst. Die Geschichte des Tagzeitengebets, seine Ordnung und seine Erneuerung in der Gegenwart: Leitourgia III Kassel, 1956, 99-294.

J.A. Jungmann (ed.), Brevierstudien. Referate aus der Studientagung von Assisi 14.-17. September 1956, Trier 1958.

R. Kaczynski, Schwerpunkte der Allgemeinen Einführung in das Stundengebet, LJ 27 (1977) 65-91.

A. G. Martimort, La priére des heures: L'Église en priére IV, Paris 1983, 169-293.

J. Pascher, Das Stundengebet der römischen Kirche, München 1954.

J. Pinell, Litugia delle ore: Anamnesis – Introduzione storico-teologica alla Liturgia 5, Genova 2nd edn. 1991.

M. Righetti, Manuale de storia liturgica II: L'Anno Liturgico – Il Breviario, Milano 1955, 469-558: La Storia dell'Ufficio.

Th. Schnitzler, Was das Stundengebet bedeutet. Hilfe zum geistlichen Neubeginn, Freiburg-Basel-Wien 1980.

R. Taft, The Liturgy of the Hours in East and West. The Origins of the Divine Office and its Meaning for Today, The Liturgical Press, Collegeville 1986.

---

[113] Cf. K. Richter, Die Reform des Stundengebetes nach dem Zweiten Vatikanischen Konzil: M. Klöckener / H. Rennings (Hgg.), Lebendiges Stundengebet. Vertiefung und Hilfe (FS Brinkhoff), Freiburg -- Basel-Wien 1989, 48-69.54.

[114] Ibid. 65.

[115] A. Häußling, Ist die Reform der Stundenliturgie beendet oder noch auf dem Weg? Th. Maas-Ewerd (ed.), Lebt unser Gottesdienst, 227-247. 242.

5.3. THE RENEWED LITURGY OF THE HOURS AND ITS ELEMENTS

5.3.1. THE RENEWED LITURGY OF THE HOURS AS SUCH

The renewed Liturgy of the Hours returns to the sacred number of seven for the divine praise of each day. As a "symbolic expression of perpetual prayer"[116] it had a certain meaning in tradition, following Ps 119 (118):164. The daily Liturgy of the Hours is divided up after the Invitatory (Invitatorium) into Lauds (Morning Prayer), the Little Hours of Terce, Sext and Nones, Vespers (Evening Prayer) and Compline (Night Prayer). While the Office of Readings (Officium Lectionis) – outside choir – can take place at any time,[117] in the case of the other Hours great value is put on the "veritas horarum".[118]

A. The Office of Readings

1. Opening versicle: "O God, come to my aid" – "Glory be to the Father... "
2. Hymn
3. Psalmody (three psalms, each with antiphon)
4. Versicle leading on to the readings
5. First reading (from Holy Scripture) with responsory
6. Second reading (from works of the Church Fathers or ecclesiastic writers, or a hagiographical reading) with responsory
7. Hymn "Te Deum" on Sundays outside Lent, on the days of the Easter and Christmas Octaves, on Solemnities and Feasts
8. Prayer of the day and closing rites: Blessing/Prayer for Blessing (in community) or versicle (GILH 60-69).

The Office of Readings "should familiarise the people of God, especially those who are consecrated to God in a special way, with the meditations from the most beautiful parts of Holy Scripture and from the works of spiritual writers". This Scripture reading "must, however, be accompanied by prayer, 'so that it may become a dialogue between God and man; then it is he we address when we pray, he we hear when we read the divine words' ".[119] The quotation from Ambrose recalls the understanding, already described, of "meditation" in the sense of a "ruminating perception" of God speaking in his word, to which man must give an answer.[120]

The Office of Readings can be expanded into the Vigil. "First, the Office of Readings is celebrated, exactly according to the book, up to and including the readings. The Canticles, which can be found in the Appendix to the Liturgy of the Hours, are then inserted before the Te Deum; after that is read the Gospel, which may also be followed by a homily. Then come the hymn Te Deum and the prayer. The Gospel is

---

[116] Thus F. Kohlschein, Die Tagzeitenliturgie als Gebetsauftrag des einzelnen: M.Klöckener / H. Rennings (eds.): Lebendiges Stundengebet, 525-542. 534.

[117] GILH 57, citing SC 89c. Cf. also GILH 59, according to which it can also be held after Vespers in the evening of the previous day.

[118] Cf., in agreement with SC 88, GILH 29: as far as possible, the correct starting times of the Hours are to be preserved; c. 1175 of the CIC/1983 has almost the same wording.

[119] GILH 55-56; the quotation is from Ambrose, De officiis ministrorum I, 20, 88 - PL 16, 50.

[120] Cf. H. Bacht: "Meditatio" in den ältesten Mönchsquellen, GuL 28 (1955) 366; F. Ruppert: Meditatio – Ruminatio. Zu einem Grundbegriff christlicher Meditation, Erbe und Auftrag 53 (1977) 85.

taken on Feasts and Solemnities from the Mass Lectionary, on Sundays from the series of Easter Gospels in the Appendix to the Liturgy of the Hours" (GILH 73). In this
way, the long tradition of Vigils before major Feasts is taken up again; the common
"mother" of these is the vigil on Easter Night, which Augustine described as "mother
of all Vigils". [121] Vigil was kept through the night with readings, prayers and hymns,
until the Eucharist was celebrated at daybreak. The Vigils were originally services for
the people in preparation for Solemnities, while the Office of Readings can be traced
back through Matins to the monastic custom concerned with combining private prayer
and Scripture in a communal framework at night. This nocturnal "Office of Readings"
served to consecrate the night hours, whereas the purpose of the Vigil was the preparation for the following feast-day. In the course of time, the Vigils were brought further
and further forward into the day before, until the Vigil Mass in the morning of the latter
had completely lost sight of the nocturnal preparation for the Feast. This also led to the
"Celebration of Easter Night" being placed in the morning of Holy Saturday; this lasted
until the reforms under Pius XII. When the Vigil was revived, it was not the renewed
celebration of Easter Night which was used as a model, but the Matins for Sundays and
feast-days, which are more richly provided with readings. [122]

From "Matutin" – the "Office of Readings" of the monastic choir office – is derived
the term "Mette", which still appears in German as the "Christmette" of Christmas Eve
and recalls the Matins celebrated before Midnight Mass. The name "Trauermetten" was
given to a celebration of Matins and Lauds on Good Friday and Holy Saturday, distinctive features of which were the Lamentations (Lamentationes Ieremiae Prophetae) and a
special ritual of light: on a triangular candlestick carrying 15 candles, after every psalm
one candle was extinguished, and this was interpreted allegorically as the flight of Jesus'
disciples. Fuchs suggests restoring both "Metten" as services for the people. [123]

B. Lauds and Vespers

Lauds are subdivided into:

1. Opening Versicle
2. Hymn
3. Psalmody: first psalm – Canticle from the Old Testament – second psalm, each with
   antiphon
4. Short reading
5. Responsorium breve
6. Canticum de Evangelio
7. Preces: petitions, in which the day and its work are consecrated to God
8. Our Father
9. Concluding prayer and concluding rites.

Vespers are similarly constructed. They differ from Lauds in the following respects:

3. Psalmody: first psalm – second psalm – Canticle from the New Testament, each with
   antiphon
6. Canticum de Evamgelio: Magnificat, Lk 1:46-55, with antiphon
7. Intercessions (GILH 41-54)

---

[121] Sermo 219 – PL 38, 1088.
[122] Cf. Fuchs 99
[123] Cf. Fuchs 108-114

"The purpose of Lauds is to consecrate the morning." As a prayer hour in the light of the dawning day it recalls the resurrection of Jesus. The rising light of day reminds us of Christ, the true light that enlightens every man (Jn 1:9), of the "sun of justice" (Mal 4:2), of the "day dawning from on high" (Lk 1:78), as it stands in the Benedictus of this Hour (cf GILH 38). The Vespers, celebrated at the hour of the evening sacrifice of the Old Testament, remind us of Christ's evening sacrifice on the cross, but also of the "evening sacrifice" in the institution of the Eucharist. However, in Vespers, too, there is the theme of light: those praying turn their hopes to Christ, the light that knows no evening or setting (cf GILH 39). Lauds and Vespers have a special dignity; both hours are "cardinal points" (cardo) of the Liturgy of the Hours and may be omitted only for serious reasons. [124] Lauds and Vespers are entitled to "great respect as the prayer of the Christian community"; for that reason, their public and common celebration is strongly recommended (GILH 40).

C. The "Little" or "Middle" Hours: Terce, Sext, Nones

1. Opening Versicle
2. Hymn
3. Psalms: 3 psalms (sections of psalm), each with antiphon
4. short reading
5. Versicle
6. Concluding prayer and concluding rites.

With Terce, Sext and Nones is associated "the remembrance of certain events in the Lord's Passion and in the initial spread of the Gospel" (GILH 75). The "Passion sequence" (crucifixion, darkness, hour of death) is based on the timings given in the synoptic account of the Passion; these timings are not to be understood as accurate records, but as statements "that Jesus endured the decisive phases of his dying at the prayer times of his people, the faith community he stemmed from". [125] Hippolytus recognizes the "Passion sequence" alone as the motive for the Little Hours. [126] Tertullian mentions the events in the Acts of the Apostles (that of Pentecost at the third hour, Peter's vision at the sixth, and, at the ninth, the healing by Peter and John at the Beautiful Gate of the man paralyzed from birth), while Cyprian combines both sequences of argument. Since, according to Arens, in Nones and Terce services live on that in Israel were celebrated at certain times of the day, and in which the evening and morning sacrifices were combined with the evening commemoration of the Pasch and the morning commemoration with the making of the Covenant at Sinai, it is not hard to understand "why the Church continues to commemorate the saving death of Christ at the ninth hour and the sending of the Spirit, the Sinai event of the New Testament, in the third: evening came, and morning: the one day of salvation in Jesus Christ." [127]

[124] GILH 29. Similarly in GILH 27, as a quotation from SC 89a. With regard to the degree of obligation obtaining in the GILH and in the CIC of 1983 for Lauds and Vespers on the one hand, and for the other Hours on the other hand, Cf. B. Fischer, Das Stundengebet im Codex Iuris Canonici von 1983 M. Klöckener / H. Rennings (Hgg.), Lebendiges Stundengebet, 98-197. 101.
[125] B. Kleinheyer, Das Gedächtnis des Heilswerkes Christi im Gebet der kleinen Tagzeiten: M. Klöckener / H. Rennings (Hgg.), Lebendiges Stundengebet, 409-430. 423.
[126] Cf. TradAp. 41, ed. Geerlings, 300-303.
[127] Kleinheyer, Gedächtnis des Heilswerkes 424f.

D. Compline

This is the "last prayer of the day and should be held immediately before retiring, if necessary also after midnight". It is subdivided into:

1. Opening Versicle
2. Examination of conscience, confession of guilt, request for forgiveness
3. Hymn
4. Psalmody (except in the 1 Compline of Sunday and on Wednesday, a psalm with antiphon)
5. Short reading with invariable responsory
6. Canticum de Evangelio: Nunc dimittis, Lk 2:29-32, with invariable antiphon
7. Blessing for the night
8. Marian antiphon (GILH 84-92)

Compline is rooted in the monastic custom of saying a prayer in private before retiring. That developed not only into a liturgical Hour, but, in more recent history [128], also into a time of prayer well known to the public. Two themes dominate: a look back on the day, linked with examination of conscience and act of penance (cf GILH 86); and contemplating the end of the day as analogous to the end of life: the thought of the "commendatio", surrendering oneself into the hands of God, is already dominant in the New Testament Canticle "Nunc dimittis". [129]

E. The combination of individual Hours with the Mass or with each other

The rules governing the combination of individual Hours with the celebration of the Mass are rather restrictive. [130] Although there is a profound inner connection between the celebration of the Mass and the Liturgy of the Hours, in that each is a memorial of the one, saving mystery of Christ, they still constitute two independent quantities, the respective, individual characters of which should not be confused; the corresponding Hour is neither an appendix of the Mass nor a broader development of its opening section. When Hour and Mass are combined, the opening rites of the latter are omitted. As far as combining the Hours among themselves is concerned, only the Office of Readings is changed in such a case; if it precedes another Hour, "the hymn appropriate to the latter can open the Office of Readings. At the end of the Office of Readings the concluding prayer and rite are omitted; the opening versicle of the following Hour is also left out" (GILH 99).

5.3.2. THE SEPARATE ELEMENTS OF THE LITURGY OF THE HOURS

A. The Invitatory [131]

---

[128] Cf. Th. Maas-Ewerd, Zur Bedeutung der Komplet in der Jugendseelsorge der dreißiger Jahre: Klerusblatt 68 (1988) 317-321; A. Heinz, Die Komplet der Jugend in den vierziger Jahren. Ein Bericht aus Trier: E. Renhart / A. Schnider (eds.): Sursum corda. Variationen zu einem liturgischen Motiv (FS Harnoncourt), Graz 1981, 185-194.

[129] So also Th. Maas-Ewerd, Pastorale Erwägungen zur Komplet: M. Klöckener / H. Rennings (eds.): Lebendiges Stundengebet, 431-441, 438f.: "Die Commendatio der Komplet bereitet die Commendatio morientis vor."

[130] Cf. GILH 93: "When circumstances permit, in special cases ... but no harm should be caused in the pastoral area." On the whole area, Cf. GILH 93-99.

[131] Cf. H. Rennings: Zum Invitatorium der täglichen Stundenliturgie und seinem Psalm 95 (94): M. Klöckener / H. Rennings (Hgg.), Lebendiges Stundengebet, 241-251.

In the celebration of the Liturgy of the Hours, too, an "outer court" has developed: the Invitatory. Its classic form, Ps 50 (51):17, followed by Ps 94 (95), is already to be found in the Rule of Benedict. [132] As in the celebration of the Mass, so also in the Liturgy of the Hours the "outer courts" have with time increased in number and magnitude. In the Cluniac monasteries the opening rite was preceded by "a preparation, that, little by little, assumed a length that sometimes exceeded that of present-day Matins". Eisenhofer counts 30 psalms that were to be prayed before the actual beginning of the Liturgy of the Hours. "According to the statutes of Benedict of Aniane (d. 821), the brethren had to visit the separate altars of the church before the beginning of Matins – a custom that also penetrated into the churches controlled by the secular clergy. Durandus hints at that when he describes it as the object of the Inivitatory, to summon those praying in front of the separate altars to make their way into choir." [133]

Today, the Invitatory precedes the first Hour of the day, i.e., Lauds or the Office of Readings. Normally, Ps 95 (94) functions as Invitatory Psalm, through the words of which "the believers are daily invited to sing God's praise, to hear his voice; they are stimulated to look out for the 'Lord's rest'. Instead of Ps 95 (94) the psalms 100 (99), 67 (66), or 24 (23) can also be used" (GILH 34).

B. The Hymns

Besides the psalms, hymns also belonged to the prayer material on which early Christians drew; numerous hymns are found in the New Testament itself. As "self-made psalms" ("Psalmi idiotici", in contrast to those of the biblical psalter) they enjoyed great popularity, so that heretical groups sought to spread their teachings especially through hymns. This led to a prohibition of hymns at the Council of Laodicea, which cannot be exactly dated; the result of this prohibition was that out of the great number of early and ancient Christian hymns almost the only one handed down to us is the Gloria of the Mass. [134] Fischer sees in this the cause of the "long-lasting reserve which the Liturgy of the Hours in the city of Rome displayed towards the hymn, a reserve, the after-effects of which, up to the most recent reform, have meant that hymns were missing for more than a thousand years in the Roman Liturgy of the Hours in Holy and Easter Weeks". [135] However, this rigorism did not last; in east and west, hymnographers like, for instance, Ephraim the Syrian (d. 373) and Ambrose of Milan (d. 397), saw to it that the hymn regained its significance and, indeed, experienced a revival. In this process, the influence of Ambrose was so strong, that the term "Ambrosian" became synonomous with "hymn", even though the genuine authorship of the Milanese bishop was not being asserted. The Middle Ages produced a great number of hymns of very varying quality; this number was dramatically cut back in the Roman Breviary of Pius V. Under Urban VIII there occurred in 1631 a somewhat questionable correction of the hymn texts, according to the standards of classical Latin; this correction, expressing humanistic taste,

---

[132] Cap. 9. Cf. F. Faeßler / L. Hunkeler, Die Regel des hl. Benedictus: H. U. v. Balthasar (ed.): Die grossen Ordensregeln, Einsiedeln 3rd edn. 1974, 207f.

[133] Cf. Eisenhofer II, 504.

[134] Cf. Martimort IV, 229: Les débuts de l'hymnographie. As well as the Gloria, the "Phos hilaron" ("Bright light") and the "Soi prépei ainos" ("Te decet laus"). Le Te Deum latin est beacoup plus tardif.

[135] B. Fischer, Poetische Formen: GdK III, Regensburg 2nd edn. 1990, 210.

sometimes produced curiously pagan echoes (e.g. oblique references to the world of the Olympian gods). [136]

According to the Constitution on the Liturgy, the hymns "should be restored in their old form; in that process, whatever possesses mythological features or corresponds less to Christian piety, should be removed. When it seems advisable, other hymns found in the treasury of tradition should also be adopted" (SC 93). The translation of the hymnal into the vernacular proved an especially difficult task. [137]

A special position is occupied by the hymn "Te Deum", which follows the responsory after the second reading in the Office of Readings on Sundays outside Lent, on the days of the Easter and Christmas Octaves and on Solemnities and Feasts (GILH 68). Under Cesarius of Arles, the "Te Deum" followed the Gospel of the Resurrection at the end of the Morning Office on Sundays, while the Rule of Benedict was placed before the reading of the Gospel; this gave the hymn a paschal connotation. [138] In the Middle Ages it was taken over from the monastic Liturgy of the Hours and inserted into the breviary; in the renewed Liturgy of the Hours, it kept its place in the Office of Readings. [139]

C. The Psalmody

In accordance with the instruction of the Council (SC 91) that the psalms were to be no longer spread over a week, but over a longer period of time, a four-week cycle is laid down. "This means that a few are left out, and that others, which have a special place in tradition, recur frequently. Lauds, Vespers and Compline are provided with particularly appropriate psalms" (GILH 126). Psalms 58 (57), 83 (82) and 109 (108) were omitted because of their predominantly cursing character. Further, Gerhards shows how the "Te Deum" took on a life of its own as a "fixed expression of a community's thanksgiving", and how, especially since the Baroque period, richly orchestrated and performed by a choir, it was performed as a hymn of thanks on major state and social occasions.Similarly, individual cursing verses in other psalms are left out. [140] Longer psalms are subdivided into sense units, in order to indicate the three-part structure of the psalmody of each Hour. Each psalm is concluded with the minor doxology, in order to give the Old Testament prayer not only the character of praise, but also a trinitarian and christological sense (cf GILH 123-124). The antiphons framing each psalm are to be understood as aids to the personal prayer of the psalm, in that they take up a weighty saying from it, or put the psalm in a particular context (e.g. that of a special liturgical day) (cf GILH 113). In addition to the psalms, the biblical canticles – "psalms" outside the biblical psalter – find their place in Lauds and Vespers; the canticles from the Old Testament were extended to such a degree that every day of the four-week cycle has its own canticle, placed between the two psalms at Lauds. Vespers have, following the psalms, a canticle from the New Testament. Thus, the principle of the sequence Old

---

[136] Cf. Fischer loc. cit., 210f.

[137] Cf. W. Dürig: Von den Hymnen: J. G. Plöger (ed.): Gott feiern, 436-443, 437.

[138] Cf. A. Gerhards, Te Deum Laudamus – Die Marseillaise der Kirche? LJ 40 (1990) 65-79. 70.

[139] Gerhards mentions also the high solemn "Te-Deum-Services" as special form of thanksgiving-liturgy esp. in baroque time.

[140] GILH 31: "These omissions from the text were made because of certain psychological difficulties, although cursing psalms occur even in the devotional world of the New Testament (e.g. Rev 6:10) and are not in any way intended to lead people to curse."

Testament – reading from the Apostles – Gospel (in this case the Cantica de Evangelio) is observed in the Liturgy of the Hours also (cf. GILH 139).

Praying the psalms was indeed a constituent part of the Jewish service, but, according to Martimort, the Christian use of the psalms went far beyond the Jewish. That, he says, also applied to the content: the first Christians saw in the psalms the prayer of Christ and, at the same time, the expression of the prayer directed to Christ. [141] Especially in the psalms it was proved true that what had been prophesied in the Old Testament was fulfilled in Christ. According to Tertullian, the voice of Christ himself is heard in the psalms, "as he speaks to the Father, as Christ speaks to God". [142] But the voice of the Father speaking to his Son ist also heard in the psalms; equally, they speak with the voice of the Church, "which, for its part, makes its own the history of Israel, in order to express its sufferings under persecution, its hope of deliverance and its trust." [143] Augustine offers the most comprehensive interpretation of the psalms: "It is God's will that, when we pray to him, we should not shut out his Son from him, and that, when the body of the Son prays, it should not separate itself from its head. Our Lord Jesus Christ, the Son of God, must be the only Saviour of his body; he prays for us and in us, and we pray to him as our God. Let us therefore recognize our voices in him, but also his voice in us." [144]

Right from the beginning the biblical psalter formed a part of the Liturgy of the Hours. Whereas the psalms were selected for morning and evening prayer in the "cathedral" type of the Liturgy of the Hours, in the "monastic" type the psalter was recited in full within a set period of time. This distribution over a certain period of time must not distract us from the fact that in reality the psalms were the subject of meditation; this is pointed up by the psalm collects. Either the praying community contemplated the psalm in silence after reciting it, or it was already provided with a definite direction of contemplation through an antiphon or heading. The prayerful and meditative silence after the recitation was then ended by a prayer said by the person presiding, [145] which, as a collect summarized the silent prayers of the different individuals. The psalm collects did not become an official part of the Liturgy of the Hours, however; they found admittance neither to the Rule of Benedict, nor to Pius V's breviary of 1568, nor to the new official liturgical books. [146]

D. The Readings in the Liturgy of the Hours

Scripture readings form a part of every single Hour. It was the ideal of Egyptian monasticism to have every psalmody followed by a reading from the Old and New Testa-

---

[141] Cf. A. G. Martimort, Vom Beten der Psalmen: J. G. Plöger (ed.): Gott feiern, 384-394. 348ff., with reference to B. Fischer, Die Psalmenfrömmigkeit der Märtyrerkirche, Feiburg i.Br. 1949; id., Le Christ dans les psaumes, la dévotion aux psaumes dans l'Église des martyrs, MD 27 (1951) 86-113; id.: Christliches Psalmenverständnis im 2. Jahrhundert. Düsseldorf 1962; id.: La christologisation des psaumes: Martimort IV, 209-211.

[142] Adv. Praxeam 11,7 – CChr SL 2, 1172.

[143] Martimort, Vom Beten der Psalmen 386.

[144] Enarr. In Ps 85:1 – CChr SL 39, 1176.

[145] Cf. Martimort, Vom Beten der Psalmen 387: id., Les collectes psalmiques: Martimort IV. 22f.

[146] The following have published psalm collects: H. Rohr / G. Duffrer, Sing-Psalter. Alle 150 Psalmen zum Singen eingerichtet, mit Einführungen und Psalmenorationen. Freiburg-Basel-Vienna 1982; B. Fischer, Dich will ich suchen von Tag zu Tag. Meditationen zu den Morgen – und Abendpsalmen des Stundenbuches. Freiburg-Basel-Vienna 3rd edn. 1990.

ments. [147] The short reading provided for in Lauds and Vespers is a "genuine proclamation of God's word", "which vividly presents a religious thought". Especially in the key Hours it is possible to use longer readings and to interpret them in a short homily. The responsory that follows the reading "is the answer to God's word". The short readings change daily in the four-week cycle; there are weekly series for Advent, Christmastide, Lent and Eastertide. [148]

The Office of Readings in the renewed Liturgy of the Hours has its origins, according to Kaczynski, in the midnight, private prayer of the faithful, which was later performed in common by the monastic communities and called "Vigil"; the scripture reading, which was originally performed in private too, became joined with this common night prayer. While Chrysostom mentions only the scripture reading, [149] according to the Rule of Benedict readings from the Church Fathers, as well as those from Holy Scripture, also form part of the divine service at night. [150] Hugo Rahner sees the readings from the Fathers in the Liturgy of the Hours as rooted in the homily of the bishop in the vigil ceremony, interpreting the scripture. In the 5th/6th century, however, he maintains, a slow transition took place from the homily given to fit the particular occasion to a fixed series of model homilies from the Fathers, which followed a fixed order of prescribed scripture readings. [151] In the 8th century these homilies from the Fathers were collected in a "homiliarium / sermonarium". Significance was attached to that of Paul the Deacon, which he produced between 786 and 792 at the direction of Charlemagne; however, it could not suppress the many different books of homilies then in use. The cutting down process which led to the "breviary" brought with it a reduction in the number of the biblical and patristic readings, in some cases even a mutilation of them; this was not corrected until the reform of the Liturgy of the Hours in the 2nd Vatican Council. [152] The "Accounts of the Sufferings of the Martyrs and of the Lives of the Catholic Fathers" are of Gaulish origin; hagiographical readings are attested there since the end of the 7th century, in Rom since Hadrian I (d. 795). [153]

For the scripture reading, the Council directed that it should be ordered in such a way "that the treasures of God's word become easily and more fully accessible" (SC 92a). Two cycles are offered, in which the Gospels do not appear, as they are read in full in the Mass every year. [154] As well as a one-year cycle, there ist also a two-year cycle, which contains "in each year almost all books of scripture and especially those longer and more difficult texts that hardly fit into the Mass". The New Testament is read in full every year, divided between Mass and the Liturgy of the Hours; from the

[147] Cf. Martimort IV, 238.
[148] Cf. GILH 44-49, 156-158.
[149] Cf. R. Kaczynski, Vom Lesen der Väter: J. Plöger (ed.), Gott feiern 423-435, 426.
[150] RegBen. 9, ed. F. Faeßler / L. Hunkeler, Die Benediktsregel: H. U. v. Balthasar (ed.), Die großen Ordensregeln. Einsiedeln 3rd edn. 1974, 208: "Beim Nachtgottesdienst werden die von Gott beglaubigten Bücher des Alten und Neuen Testaments gelesen, wie auch die Erklärungen dazu, die von namhaften und rechtgläubigen katholischen Vätern stammen."
[151] Rahner, Väterlesungen 43: "Daß eine solche Sammlung, und zwar doch eine stadtrömische, im 9. Kapitel der Regula Benedicti vorauszusetzen ist, dürfte unbestritten sein."
[152] Cf. M. Klöckener, Die Lesungen aus den Vätern und Kirchenschriftstellern in der erneuerten Stundenliturgie: M. Klöckener / H. Rennings (eds.), Lebendiges Stundengebet, 267-300, 269f.
[153] Thus quoted in Kaczynski, Vom Lesen der Väter, 426f. about the gaulish recension of Ordo Romanus XIV 10 – Andrieu OR 3,41.
[154] GILH 144, if one disregards the Vigil according to GILH 73.

Old Testament texts are picked out "that are imprtant for understanding salvation history and for encouraging piety". [155]

The Council (SC 92b) directed that "the readings from the works of the Fathers, the Doctors of the Curch and ecclesiastical writers should be more carefully chosen". [156] Kaczynski differentiates the patristic readings first under the aspect of the homily, through which a passage of scripture (from the Liturgy of the Hours of the Mass) is to be interpreted liberally, then also authors from periods that no longer belong to the patristic epoch should be read, as well as those of modern times. [157] As for the hagiographical readings - by these is understood the reading of a text "that speaks of the saint whose feast is being celebrated, or that can be related to him; or an extract from his own writings or his vita" (GILH 166) – it is required that they should be historically true (SC 92c). [158]

E. The Cantica de Evangelio: Benedictus – Magnificat – Nunc dimittis
Songs of praise from the New Testament, to which "the same honour and ceremony should be shown as to the Gospel" (GILH 138), form the "dramatic" high point of Lauds, Vespers and Compline. [159] Benedictus and Magnificat are attested for the first time for Lauds and Vespers in the Rule of Benedict; [160] both the Rule of the Master (beginning of the 6th century) and the order of divine service in the Roman basilicas of the 6th century were possibly acquainted with both canticles in the Liturgy of the Hours, even though they may have been in different places. The allocation of the canticles to the three Hours mentioned has been decided by their content, even though the Magnificat belongs to the morning Hour in the Byzantine rite: the mention of "the day (dawning) upon us from on high" confers on the Benedictus a "proximity to Lauds and with the remembrance of the Resurrection, which is connected with the former since early times, while Mary's grateful praise is related to the thanks at evening for the past day and for redemption. Still clearer is the proximity of the content of "Simeon's evening hymn" to the close of day. However, it is not yet Benedict, but Amalar of Metz (d. about 850) who first mentions the "Nunc dimittis" as a constituent part of Compline." [161] The special status of the canticles is emphasised by significant features in their performance. They are sung standing, are preceded by the sign of the cross, and at the Benedictus and the

---

[155] GILH 146.

[156] For the criteria to be enployed, cf. Klöckener, Die Lesungen aus den Vätern und Kirchenschriftstellern 272-278. Klöckener gives (288-293) a table showing the authors and anoymous works of the readings from the Fathers an ecclesiastical writers in the Liturgia Horarum and in the German Book of Hours.

[157] Cf. Kaczynski, Vom Lesen der Väter 428-431.

[158] This requirement is taken up in GILH 167. On the problem as a whole, cf. H. J. Limburg, Die Wahrheit der Heiligen. Ihre Lebensbeschreibungen in den Lesehoren des deutschen Stundenbuches: M. Klöckener / H. Rennings (eds.), Lebendiges Stundengebet, 301-315.

[159] Cf. F. Schneider, Die Lobgesänge aus dem Evangelium. "Benedictus" – "Magnificat" – "Nunc dimittis": M. Klöckener / H. Rennings (eds.), Lebendiges Stundengebet, 252-266.252. Schneider (206f.) is even of the opinion, that it is permissible before the background of the Berakah to speak of the canticles even as of the Eucharistic Prayers of the Liturgy of three Hours, in analogy to the celebration of the Mass.

[160] Cf. F. Faeßler / L. Hunkeler, Die Benediktsregel: H. U. v. Balthasar (ed.), Die großen Ordensregeln. Einsiedeln 3rd edn. 1974. RB 12,4 – p. 210; 13,11 - p. 211; 17,8 – p. 213.

[161] Schneider, Lobgesänge 254.

Magnificat the altar can be incensed as a symbol for the ascending movement of the prayer of praise. [162]

F. Prayers and Intercessions

The first clear evidence of an intercessional prayer at the end of Lauds and Vespers in the form of a Kyrie litany comes from the Christian East of the 4th century. [163] This Kyrie litany spread out from the pilgrimage centre of Jerusalem not only in the Mass, [164] but also in the morning and evening divine services. [165] Baumgartner accepts this for Rome also "with considerable certainty". A change came when, from the 7 century on, in Rome and north of the Alps the individual prayer intentions were responded to with psalm versicles, instead of with the unvarying Kyrie. Three different prayer types, "the Eastern (litany of intentions with Kyrie response), the Irish (litany of intentions with responses in the form of psalm verses), and the Gallic (prayers composed simply of psalm versicles), all influenced each other, so that an unsatisfactory mixture was produced, which later got into the Roman breviary and survived right down to the most recent reform of the Liturgy of the Hours, under the name "Preces feriales ad Laudes et Vesperas". [166] The fact that these prayers had definite penitential associations is based on a misunderstanding: the Kyrie litany was performed in a kneeling position, perhaps remembering the ancient Roman fashion of intercession, with the deacon's summons, "Flectamus genua – levate". Since the Council of Nicaea had forbidden prayer in the kneeling position during Eastertide, this type of prayer was identified with the penitential periods, so that the prayers appeared only at those times, i.e. Lent, Quarter Tense, Advent and Vigils, but also on the old days of penance in ordinary time (Wednesday and Friday). [167] The "preces" (prayers) became the "preces flebiles", which bore practically no resemblence to the old litany of intercessions.

---

[162] Cf. GILH 261 and 263. According to Schneider (Lobgesänge 261), the incense was originally linked to the Vespers psalm 142:2, and moved with this verse as versicle before the Magnificat, until it was joined to it; later analogically the Benedictus.

[163] Cf. B. Fischer, Die Anliegen des Volkes im kirchlichen Stundengebet: J. A. Jungmann (ed.): Brevierstudien. Referate aus der Studientagung von Assisi 14.-17. September 1956. Trier 1958, 57-70.59, where Egeria's report is referred to, 24,2.5 – SChr 296, 236, 240.

[164] In the form of the Deprecatio Gelasii, cf Jungmann MS I, 433.

[165] Cf. Chrysostomos, Hom. 6,1 – PG 62,530. Cf. to that J. Baumgartner, Die "Preces" in Laudes und Vesper. Ein zurückgewonnenes Element christlichen Gebetsgutes: M. Klöckener / H. Rennings (eds.), Lebendiges Stundengebet, 368-397. 370f.

[166] Baumgartner 373.

[167] Cf. Fischer, Anliegen des Volkes 62-66, Jungmann, Die Liturgische Feier 92-93.

The reinstatement of prayers and intercessions in Lauds and Vespers is part of the process instituted by the reform of the liturgy to restore what had been lost "by the ravages of time" (SC 50). It was Pope Paul VI who wished to introduce into Lauds elements offering and sanctifying the day's work. The prayers of the morning office thus continue the theme of sanctifying the day, which was associated with the discontinued Hour of Prime, while Vespers actually contains an intercessional prayer in the strict sense – its last intercession is always for the dead. [168]

G. The Our Father and the concluding rites

The praying of the Our Father at Lauds and Vespers was already a requirement of the Rule of Benedict. [169] The requirement that the superior, departing from the practice at the other celebrations, should say it aloud, was new, according to Häußling: for reasons connected with the already outmoded arcane discipline, the Lord's Prayer had, up to then, been said only in a low voice, but from that time on saying of the prayer aloud was intended to remind the brethren of their duty to forgive each other. Benedict could build on a venerable tradition: the Didache [170] already admonished every Christian to say the Lord's Prayer three times a day, this constituting, as it were, "the minimum of a Christian's prayer obligation". [171] According to Jungmann, the Our Father at the end of the Hours had the function of a collect, but gradually disappeared as the Liturgy of the Hours developed into the breviary; [172] through the ending of the Hours on feast days with a proper concluding prayer, through the multiplication of the versicles originally having a concluding function after the Lord's Prayer, and through the penitential character that became wrongly associated with the preces, the Our Father was maintained with them only on penitential days.

The reform reintroduced the Our Father at the end of the principal Hours Lauds and Vespers with the argument that these were the most likely to be celebrated with the people (GILH 194). A connection is also made with the tradition of saying the Our Father three times daily – the third occasion besides the principal Hours being that of the Mass. [173] "The Our Father is said by all together. It can be preceded by a short, transitional passage." [174] The Hours conclude with a prayer; in the Office of Readings it is the same as the concluding prayer in the Mass. [175] It is the task of an ordained president to bless and dismiss the assembly (cf GILH 256 and 258).

---

[168] Cf. Baumgartner 375; GILH 179-193.

[169] Cf. F. Faeßler / L. Hunkeler, Die Benediktsregel: H. U. v. Balthasar (ed.), Die großen Ordensregeln. Einsiedeln 3rd edn. 1974. RegBen. 13 – S. 211.

[170] Didache 8,3 – ed. G. Schölgen. Freiburg – Basel – Wien u.a. 1991 (FC 1), 120f.

[171] A. A. Häußling: Vom Gebet des Herrn: J. Plöger (ed.), Gott feiern, 444-450.446. Didache 8,3 – SChr 248, 174.

[172] Cf. J. A. Jungmann, Das Gebet des Herrn im römischen Brevier: id., Liturgisches Erbe und pastorale Gegenwart. Studien und Vorträge, Innsbruck-Vienna-Zürich 1960, 252-264. Cf also id.: Das Kyrie eleison in den Preces. In: loc. cit., 239-252. 240f.: The Our Father serves as the final collect of a Kyrie litany.

[173] GILH 195; Häußling, however, criticises this because of "undifferenzierter Zusammenstellung von Horenoffizium und Eucharistiefeier"; the association with the celebration of the Mass is already found with Ildefons Herwegen, cf. Häußling, Vom Gebet des Herrn 449f. Anm. 5 und 12.

[174] GILH 196. The transitional passage reminds one still of the old Kyrie litany.

[175] On the prayer, cf GILH 197-200.

H. The concluding Marian antiphons at Compline

They are a fruit of the "Marian spring" of the High Middle Ages, the piety of which is marked less by the Easter event than by Christ's becoming man and by his solidarity with the destiny of humanity. Thus, his mother Mary moves into the foreground, especially in the spirituality of the orders which were founded in the Middle Ages. In the 13th century, Cistercians, Dominicans and Camaldolese ended Compline with a Marian antiphon. A decision of the Chapter General of the Franciscans, made in 1249, was very influential; "it prescribed the use in turn of the four Marian antiphons that were usual up to the liturgy reform after the 2 Vatican Council, 'post Completorium decantandis' ". [176] The timing in the evening before the beginning of the night's rest was supported by the then usual evening timing given for the Annunciation, arising from theological symbolism (for the unredeemed world nearing its end). For this reason, the antiphons themselves refer to the event of the Annunciation, or remind us of it by their "salutatory" wording. [177]

The "Alma Redemptoris Mater", conventionally associated with Advent and Christmastide, is of anonymous origin, just as the "Ave, Regina caelorum", usually linked with Lent. Both are first attested in an antiphonary of the Abbey St. Maur-des-Fossés in Paris. [178] The "Regina caeli laetare" of Eastertide is found for the first time in a Roman antiphonary from St. Peter's at the beginning of the 13 century, according to the liturgical historian, the Theatine Cardinal Giuseppe Tomasi di Lampedusa (d. 1713). It was modelled on a Christmas hymn of the 11th century. The "Salve Regina" is the oldest of the Marian antiphons; for a long time it was ascribed to the monk Hermannus Contractus of Reichenau. Heinz, however, thinks that Bernard of Clairvaux is the author, and that he passed it on to his friend Abbot Peter of Cluny. [179] As well as those four classical Marian concluding antiphons, the Liturgy of the Hours also offers the "Sub tuum praesidium". It comes from the Christian East and "can, according to the present state of research, be regarded as the oldest Marian prayer outside the bible"; its Greek text was discovered in 1917 in Egypt on a papyrus from the end of the 3rd century. "In order to fully understand the oldest Marian prayer of Christendom, it is advisable to take note of the Greek original behind the Latin text. In the original Greek version it begins thus: We flee to thy compassion (eusplangchnia). Eusplangchnia means literally 'entrails, body, womb'. The transferred meaning of the expression is a feeling of heartfelt compassion, of sympathetic mercy. The Ambrosian variant of our antiphon thus translates: 'Sub tuam misericordiam confugimus'." [180]

---

[176] A. Heinz, Die marianischen Schlußantiphonen im Stundengebet: M. Klöckener / H. Rennings: Lebendiges Stundengebet, 342-367.344.

[177] Cf. Heinz, Schlußantiphonren 345f. Heinz points to the 3rd verse of the Advent hymn "Conditor alme siderum", where it says: "Vergente mundi vespere / uti sponsus de thalamo / egressus honestissima / Virginis matris clausula".

[178] Cf. Heinz, Schlußantiphonen 347-351.

[179] Cf. Heinz, Schlußantiphonen 355.

[180] Heinz, Schlußantiphonen 358-361.

5.3.3. SUGGESTIONS FOR NEW ELEMENTS IN THE LITURGY OF THE HOURS, OR FOR ELEMENTS TO BE RESTORED TO IT

Many suggestions are made for reviving the Liturgy of the Hours as a service for the people. [181] If one wishes to retain the traditional form of the Hours which has grown up through the years, thus keeping to the renewed Liturgy of the Hours, and if one wants to avoid again alienating the faithful through (new) parallel and special forms of that Liturgy, then it is principally non-verbal elements, as well as the possibilities of changing various elements and of adaptation to local circumstances, which could liven up the celebration of the Hours. [182] From among Fuchs's suggestions we present three here, which relate to the principal Hours Lauds and Vespers, which, in turn, are especially suitable for celebration with the people.

A. Evening light ritual / Lucernarium

Despite the significance of light as a symbol in divine service, no light ritual has developed in the evening prayer of the Roman rite, in contrast to other Christian rites, although Hippolytus specially mentions a thanksgiving for light, admittedly in connection with the evening Agape. Although use is made of metaphors concerning light in order to introduce people to the theological significance of Vespers – mentioning the hymn "Phos hilaron" (cf GILH 39) of the ancient Church, still used by the Eastern Church in the Lucernarium – no further suggestion for structuring a light ritual is made. Fuchs suggests that on the opening verse of Vespers the light be carried in by a deacon or another member of the faithful; then there could be a thanksgiving in the form of the Berakah, to which the people could reply with an acclamation or also with a hymn, upon which all candles are lit and the light is distributed to the people. [183] By "Lucernarium" Fuchs understands – quite independently from his other uses for the ritual of light – an evening service oriented towards the Vespers of the ancient Church (i.e., thanksgiving for the light, incense rite with Ps 141 and prayer, but without continual psalmody). [184] In this connection, Fuchs makes the critical remark that, when one goes back to formulae of the ancient Church for structuring the Lucernarium, one should not be tempted, "so to speak, to ransack history and the individual rites. A combination of old Spanish, Cappadocian and Roman prayer formulae, enriched by tunes of the Eastern Church and rounded off by a shot of Taizé: the liturgical menu must not look like that." [185]

B. Sacrifice of incense

Incense came into the Liturgy of the Hours as a dramatic mise en scéne of verse 2 of the evening psalm 141. As the latter lost its significance in view of the continual psalmody of the monastic Liturgy of the Hours, it was sung – reduced to verse 2 – first as a versicle at the end of the psalmody, and then before the Magnificat: "Let my prayer be counted as incense before thee, and the lifting up of my hands as an evening sacrifice!" When this

---

[181] R. Berger offers an encouraging report based on experience: Eine Gemeinde betet das Abendlob: M. Klöckener / H. Rennings (eds.), Lebendiges Stundengebet 495-505.

[182] Cf. Berger loc. cit. 503.

[183] Cf. Fuchs 77-83, also 70, where, in tabular form, the non-verbal elements light ritual and water ritual are compared.

[184] Fuchs 83. Reference is made to H.J. Becker / A. Gerhards, Den Abend segnen? In: A. Heinz / H. Rennings: Heute segnen. Werkbuch zum Benediktionale. Freiburg-Basel-Vienna 1987, 322-333; H. Becker, Luzernarium: W. Meurer (ed.), Volk Gottes auf dem Weg. Mainz 1989, 169-174.

[185] Fuchs 84f.

versicle finally disappeared in the renewed Liturgy of the Hours, the incense became an accompaniment to the New Testament Canticle of the principal Hours, thus also to the Benedictus (cf GILH 261), although that has no relationship to the evening sacrifice. "Incense in a prayer service can really be only a symbol of prayer – and nowhere more emphatically as here. The form of the rite should correspond to its meaning." Fuchs suggests dispensing with the thurible and putting in its place an incense bowl before or on the altar. Incense can be offered when Ps 141:2 is put as a versicle before the Canticle (Magnificat / Benedictus) without reference to the evening sacrifice; alternatively, the offering of incense can be regarded as a "sacrifice of incense" expressing a "sacrifice of the lips", while the faithful place incense grains in the bowl as the intentions of the prayers (in the morning) and the intercessions (in the evening) are mentioned. [186]

C. Baptismal Vespers / Commemoration of Baptism in Lauds

By the term "Baptismal Vespers" we understand Vespers in which baptism is commemorated by a procession with hymns and prayers to the place where baptisms take place (baptismal font / baptistry). Already in Jerusalem processions were part of the Liturgy of the Hours, such as the procession "before and behind the Cross", in which prayers were said and the faithful and the catechumens were blessed. [187] According to Jounel the baptismal Vespers are descended from another Jerusalem procession described by Egeria, which took place in the Easter Octave, and in which the newly baptised also took part, but it had no relationship to the places themselves where baptisms were carried out. [188] The Ordo Romanus 27 describes the baptismal Vespers in the Rome of the early 7th century, as they were celebrated until the 13th century during the Easter Octave. The first part of the Vespers ended after the third psalm, Magnificat and Easter prayer, and the participants processed to the baptistry and to the Consignatorium (Confirmation chapel), at each of which the last two psalms were sung, followed each time by the (second and third) Magnificat with corresponding prayer. [189] Spreading out from Rome, these baptismal Vespers established themselves in the Frankish empire and maintained themselves there even after they had been given up in Rome because of the changeover to the curial liturgy; they persisted in France and in the cathedral of Trier far into the 19th century. They have also been preserved in the Ambrosian liturgy of Milan. [190] As well as for the revival of baptismal Vespers [191] , Fuchs also pleads for the introduction of a new element: a memorial of baptism in Lauds, since that Hour lacks – except for the possible use of incense at the Benedictus – a non-verbal form of expression corresponding to the evening Lucernarium. [192] In this connection, people proceed from the Asperges rite as a Sunday memorial of baptism; after all, the rite originally took place

---

[186] Cf. Fuchs 59f.

[187] Egeria, Peregrinatio 24,7 – SChr 296, 240. "Crux" and "post crucem" are, according to Maraval, technical terms for the hill of Golgotha and a chapel situated behind it, cf p.284, Note 2.

[188] Cf P. Jounel, Les Vêpres de Pâques, MD 49 (1957) 96-111. 97f. Cf. Egeria, Peregrinatio 39 – SChr 296, 292-294.

[189] Thus the description of the rite according to Ordo Romanus XXVII from the 7th century. Cf. B. Fischer: Formen gemeinschaftlicher Tauferinnerung im Abendland: B. Fischer, Redemptionis Mysterium. Studien zur Osterfeier und zur christlichen Initiation, ed. by A. Gerhards / A. Heinz, Paderborn – München – Vienna - Zürich 1992, 141-150. 143.

[190] Cf. Fischer loc. cit. 144.

[191] Cf. Fuchs 114-116.

[192] Cf. Fuchs 68-71.

before Mass. Lauds could begin after the opening verse with the preparation of the water, over which a prayer of thanks or blessing is said before it is distributed to the faithful; the Lauds hymn then follows. Fuchs would like to suggest this non-verbal performance only for Lauds on Sunday, which are connected with the celebration of Mass; in that case, however, it could no longer be considered generally as the desired pendant to the Lucernarium of Vespers, if one considers the connection between Lauds and the celebration of Mass as an exception.

Bibliography

R. Berger, Stundengebet nach dem II. Vaticanum, HID 47 (1993) 108-115.

G. Fuchs, Singet Lob und Preis. Stundengebet mit der Gemeinde feiern, Regensburg 1993.

A. Gerhards, Das Stundengebet in Ost und West, LJ 38 (1988) 165-172.

M. Klöckener / H. Rennings (eds.), Lebendiges Stundengebet. Vertiefung und Hilfe (FS Brinkhoff), Freiburg-Basel-Vienna 1989.

A.-G. Martimort, La priére des heures: Martimort IV, Paris 1983, 167-293.

J. Pinell, Liturgia delle Ore: Anamnesis. Introduzione storico-teologica alla Liturgia V, Torino 1991.

J. Plöger (ed.), Gott feiern. Theologische Anregungen und geistliche Vertiefung zur Feier von Messe und Stundengebet (FS Schnitzler), Freiburg-Basel-Vienna 1980.

H. Rahner, Zur Reform der Väterlesungen des Breviers: J. A. Jungmann (ed.), Brevierstudien. Referate aus der Studientagung von Assisi 14.-17. September 1956. Trier 1958, 42-56.

M. Righetti, Manuale di storia liturgica II: L'Anno Liturgico – Il Breviario. Milano 1955, 559-632. Gli elementi costitutivi dell'Ufficio; 633-715: Le singole ore.

P. Ringseisen, Morgen – und Abendlob mit der Gemeinde. Geistliche Erschließung, Erfahrungen und Modelle. Mit einem Beitrag von M. Klöckener. Freiburg-Basel-Vienna 1994.

5.4. THE LITURGY OF THE HOURS IN THE CHURCHES OF THE EAST AND THE REFORMATION

5.4.1. THE LITURGY OF THE HOURS IN THE BYZANTINE CHURCH

The Liturgy of the Hours in the Byzantine Church is regarded as having a far more monastic mould than that of the West; this is put down to the greater difference between the secular clergy, many of whom are married, and the monks. The Liturgy of the Hours is thus the concern of the monks; they have "given the Hours their definitive form and regulated their performance, e.g. through the Typikon. It was their Office that, in the end, in the cathedrals and parishes, ousted an office that was more popular because it was largely sung." [193]

According to Simeon of Thessaloniki, the Liturgy of the Hours is only a minimal form, designed for the weak, of the ideal put before every Christian - that of perpetual prayer; [194] for the sake of the weak the Church introduced special prayer times, according to the model of the Old Testament. [195] The midnight Hour calls this to mind, because it also obeys the command to be on the watch – a command imposed on all. [196] This monastic understanding, which, on theological grounds, knows that it is committed to the ideal of perpetual prayer, regarded the people's Liturgy of the Hours as far too weak, and made it complicated, since even the monks' Liturgy of the Hours was considered as a "concession" to human weakness.

Schulz describes the form of the Byzantine Liturgy of the Hours as "the result of complex processes of change and fusion between the patriarchal traditions of Rome and Jerusalem, as well as between the old celebration of times of day by the people and the monastic Office". In this symbiosis, he maintains, the monks "overlaid" the people's prayer times in morning and evening (Orthros and Hesperinos) with their cursory praying of the psalms, and, in addition to these and the three old Day Hours of the third, sixth and ninth hour, had also created, impelled by their own need, the prayer at midnight (Mesoknytikon), the First Hour (Proteé) and the late evening prayer (Apodeipnon), as well as the intermediate Hours of the Typika". [197] This process of monastic overlaying was pursued during the iconoclastic controversy by the Studion monastery in Constantinople, which, in turn, observed the order of the Saba monastery in Jerusalem. Because of the complicated construction of the Byzantine Liturgy of the Hours, we shall concern ourselves here only with the morning and evening Hours.

The Hesperinos (Vjetschernaya, Vespers) begins after the doxology with the Creation psalm 103 (104). All the while, the priest prays silently the "light prayers", old prayers of the people. Then follows, as in the Eucharist, a great Ektenie (Kyrie litany); following that, the psalms are sung. In parish churches, however, the psalter is often

---

[193] Raes, Streiflichter 119.

[194] Cf. Dialogos 297 – PG 155, 549 B – C.

[195] Cf Resp. ad q 79 – PG 155, 937 D.

[196] Cf Dialogos 299 – PG 155, 549 D – 552 A. Cf also: H. A. J. Wegman, "Schau, der Bräutigam! Geht aus, ihm zu begegnen!" Die Theologie der Vigil: M. Klöckener / H. Rennings (eds.), Lebendiges Stundengebet, 442-461. See also Heitz I, 237-241.

[197] Schulz, Liturgie 48f.

shortened beyond recognition, or even omitted completely. The second part of Vespers still contains elements of the cathedral evening service. There are sung verses from the psalms 140 (141), 141 (142), 128 (129) and 116 (117), the last eight to ten verses of which alternate with poetic strophes ("Stichera" to "I call upon thee, O Lord", Ps 140:1). then follow the Lucernarium (in the form of lighting all the lights in the church) and the sacrifice of incense (in the form of an incensation of the church, the celebrants of the liturgy and the faithful by the deacon). After that comes the evening hymn "Phos hilarón". Then the responsory (Prokeimenon) is sung, whereas the scripture reading nowadays occurs only in Lent and on the eve of major Feasts. The last part of Vespers consists essentially of petitionary prayers: "urgent Ektenie", the reader's evening prayer ("Kataxion himas – Acknowledge us, O Lord"), petitionary Ektenie, prayer spoken inclined, Lite ("petitional procession" into the portico, narthex, with fortyfold Kyrie). Vespers end with the Aposticha (poetic verses to selected psalm verses), the "Nunc dimittis", Trishagion, Our Father, Troparion of the day and Marian Troparion (Theotokion). [198]

The Orthros (Utrenja, Lauds) begins after the introductory doxology with the reading of the six psalms (Hexapsalmos) 3, 37 (38), 62 (63), 87 (88), 102 (103) and 142 (143). During that time, the priest silently prays the twelve morning prayers. Then follow the Great or Peace Ektenie, a responsory ("The Lord is God, and he has given us light", Ps 117:27a as response to verses 1, 10, 17, 22f.), the Troparion of the day and the Theotokion. In the Orthros, too, the psalmody provided for (three Kathismata, i.e. subdivisions of the psalter, with small Ektenies between them) is greatly shortened or is omitted completely. The second part of the Orthros has no counterpart in the Hesperinos and constitutes a short service of proclamation: the psalms of praise 134 (135) and 135 (136) (called "Polyeleos – much mercy" after Ps 135 [136]) are sung, while all lights are lit, the doors of the ikonostase opened and incensation takes place. On Sundays songs praising the Resurrection ("Eulogetaria of the Resurrection") follow, on major feasts the song praising the mystery of the feast (Megalynarion). The Resurrection is praised also in the Songs of Ascents (Anabathmos), originally antiphons to the psalms of ascents 119-132. The morning Gospel is preceded by a double responsory (a first depending on the tone of the church, followed by a second, invariable Prokeimenon). The Gospel itself is always an Easter Gospel, and is taken from a series of eleven passages on the theme of Christ's Resurrection or the appearances of the Risen One. [199] The Resurrection hymn ("We have seen Christ's Resurrection") meditates on the Gospel just heard, while the Gospel book is presented for the faithful to kiss. The third part of the Orthros is dominated by hymnic elements, and begins with Ps 50 (51) and an intercessional prayer ("Save thy people, Lord, and bless thine inheritance"). The "canon" with its complicated structure comes next, "a 'series' of normally eight poetic odes (consisting of Odes 1 and 3 to 9), which were originally designed to follow the performance of biblical Canticles as poetic paraphrases of the same, whereas today only in the case of the 9th ode (based on the New Testament Canticles Magnificat and Benedictus) is at

---

[198] Cf. Schulz, Liturgie 57-60.
[199] On the passages themselves, cf Schulz, Liturgie 62, Note 131. Schulz maintains that a Jerusalem tradition going back as far as Egeria is still observed, according to which the bishop himself (or the priest) proclaims the Gospel, not the deacon.

least the biblical text of the Magnificat heard." [200] The Magnificat as 9th ode is accompanied by an incensation, and is followed on Sundays by the Prokeimenon "Holy is the Lord, our God" and, corresponding to the eleven Gospels of the Resurrection, one of the eleven Exaposteilria (an invocation requesting light to be sent out by Christ, the Light). It is only at this point that the psalms of praise (148-150) appear, properly speaking: "in their performance, too, the dominant element nowadays is the poetic element of the Sticherá, which are inserted between the verses of the psalms; the second last one (connected with the 'Glory be to the Father' of the 150 psalm), performed on Sundays, corresponds exactly to content of the Gospel of the Resurrection proclaimed". [201] On the Great Doxology, which contains the "Gloria in excelsis Deo", as well as other textual elements, there follow the Troparion of the Resurrection (Apolytikion) and the prayer section corresponding to the Hesperinos. [202]

The complicated character of this evolved rite has led to the textual elements being radically shortened, at least when it is celebrated with the public. In addition, they are contained in a whole series of different books: the Liturgikon for the priest's use, the psalter, the Menologion (a twelve-volume work [one volume for each month] with the Proper of each day), the Gospel book, the Kanonikon etc.; "books of Hours", i.e. Horologies or Anthologies from those different books, were made up more according to the model of the Western breviary. [203] In contrast to the West, where great store was set by performing the Liturgy of the Hours in full and exactly in correspondence with the liturgical day, with the Byzantines parts of the Office can be shortened or left out completely, according to local usage. [204]

A peculiarity is represented by the "Liturgy of the Presanctified", Vespers with distribution of Communion, in which also other elements of the Eucharistic Liturgy are present, which do not belong to the Communion section of the same. The Liturgy of the Presanctified is celebrated nowadays on the Mondays and Fridays of Lent, on the first three days of Holy Week and on the Feast days of Lent. Here we have the reason for the emergence of the Liturgy of the Presanctified: it is to permit the reception of Communion on the "aliturgical" days of Lent. [205]

5.4.2. THE LITURGY OF THE HOURS IN THE CHURCHES OF THE REFORMATION

Luther felt that the obligation to perform the Liturgy of the Hours was a piece of "donkey work", which ran counter to justification by faith alone. In addition, "the Liturgy of the Hours in its complete form had become to such a large degree a monastic and priestly service that the thought of a comprehensive adoption, examination and Ger-

[200] Schulz, Liturgie 63f.

[201] Schulz, Liturgie 64.

[202] Cf. Schulz 60-65. The texts of the Byzantine Litutrgy of the Hours are also presented by S. Heitz, Das Gebet der orthodoxen Kirche (Horologion und Oktoich), Köln 1981; idem: Mysterium der Anbetung I: Göttliche Liturgie und Stundengebet der Orthodoxen Kirche. Köln 1986. The French translation was provided by the monks of Chevetogne in their series: La prière des églises de rite byzantin 1: La prière des heures. Chevetogne 1975.

[203] Cf. M. Kunzler, Art. "Anthologion": LThK 3rd edn. I, 720 (Bibliography).

[204] Cf. Raes, Streiflichter 120.

[205] Cf. K. Onasch, Kunst und Liturgie der Ostkirche in Stichworten, unter Berücksichtigung der Alten Kirche, Vienna-Köln-Graz 1981, Art. "Liturgie der vorgeweihten Gaben", 252-254 (Bibliography).

manization of the whole Office for the people could not suggest itself to him. But his criticism of the canonical Hours is the same as that of the Roman priesthood and the monastic state generally: that "much law and work" was "taught", and that this legalism led to desperation." [206] As well as the fact that the Liturgy of the Hours accorded with scripture, it was also the teaching of the priesthood of all the baptised that moved Luther to pray the principal hours in the morning (Matins) and evening (Vespers) with the people – or at least with the pupils of the grammar-school; in both Hours scripture reading and interpretation are central. Besides that, prayers at midday and at night are recommended, but remain optional. [207] That Luther's plans never got further than the drawing-board [208] is due to the fact that they were too demanding: three sermons were required on Sundays, two on weekdays: "Where, apart from larger towns with several clergymen, could all those sermons, instructions and exhortations have been provided? And where could a congregation be found that can assimilate so many sermons per week?" The marked orientation of the Liturgy of the Hours to pedagogic aims did not remain without effect: "The strong emphasis of the pedagogic purpose has turned the prayer to be said into a school task. Those external motives have a ruinous effect on the spontaneous execution of the divine service! … Only rarely does a vague realisation dawn that the daily services, beyond their pedagogic aim of instructing young people at school and teaching the public, could also have a value for the spiritual formation of a life-long relationship." [209] From the Liturgy of the Hours (also called "secondary services" in relation to the "principal service", the preaching service that succeeded the parish Mass on Sunday) emerged the bible service for the people: "When Luther's aim, which was generally directed towards bible reading and psalm singing, was no longer understood (because bible reading had generally become private), these 'secondary services' sometimes took the form of short preaching services, at other times that of 'liturgical' singing, musical or occasional services." [210] Thus, the various "Vespers" and "Matins" in Protestant parish churches (especially at Christmas) have hardly anything to do with Vespers or Lauds in the traditional Liturgy of the Hours, but basically constitute just a preaching service with special musical arrangements.

"Other forms of piety now moved of necessity to fill up the space which had become free through the decline of the Liturgy of the Hours, or which had never been properly filled from the point of view of popular piety": the prayer of the Church at different times of the day was replaced by edifying literature for the individual's private prayer in the morning and evening. Luther himself had already produced such works, such as the "Simple way of praying for a good friend", which appeared in 1535, which saw itself as a substitute both for the rosary of the laity and for the canonical Hours for "priestlings and monks". Pietism encouraged this development, the final stage of

---

[206] Goltzen 188.
[207] Goltzen 194: "With this evaluation Luther showed his sure glance for what could be expected from his flock, its pastors and particular groups (at that time the grammar-schools) as far as daily divine service was concerned."
[208] Hertzsch also mentions exceptions, however: In the north German Hansa towns and in Nürnberg the system of the Roman Hours was retained for a long time; in Nürnberg there were daily Matins until well into the 18th century, cf E. Hertzsch, Art. "Stundengebet I. Liturgisch 3": RGG 3rd edn. VI. Tübingen 1962, 435f.
[209] Goltzen 196f.
[210] L. Fendt, Einführung in die Litugiewissenschaft, Brerlin 1958, 210-212: Das Stundengebet bei Luther, 211.

which Goltzen sees constituted by the "Mottoes" of the (Bohemian) Brethren, which have appeared in book form since 1731: "For each day, from a heap of several thousand sayings, a saying from the Old Testament is drawn by lot, and, in addition, a "teaching text", i.e. a saying from the New Testament, chosen at random. To those are added 2 verses of a hymn, mostly from the Brethren's hymn-book ... The bible is reduced to the level of a dictionary of quotations and a book of oracles." [211] It was only in the 20 century that the attempt was made to take up again the reforming efforts to achieve a people's liturgy for the various times of the day; the stimuli came principally from the High Church movements, but there was too much of a tendency to link up with Catholic traditions. [212] Albrecht proposes the following structure for the organization of the Hours ("Mette" = Lauds, Vespers and Compline) of a Protestant Liturgy of the Hours: Ingressus (opening versicle), hymn of the Hour (if applicable), psalm with antiphon, reading with brief sermon (if applicable), hymn, Canticle (Benedictus, Magnificat, Nunc dimittis [the last can alternate in Vespers with the Magnificat if Compline is not held]), Kyrie, Our Father, prayers, silent prayer, final prayer, blessing. [213]

The ecumenical community of Taizé has played a significant role in finding new ways to bring the Liturgy of the Hours closer to young people. [214] The Rule of Taizé links the thrice daily prayer with the New Testament exhortation always to pray and to persevere in prayer (e.g. Eph 6:18). [215] The Rule says nothing about the structure of the community's daily prayer, which does not dispense the individual monk from personal prayer. The founder and Prior of Taizé, Roger Schutz, himself admits that the prayer in community seems "to some like a beautiful mosaic, to others to lack form and shape." "What remains meaningless for some, wakes an echo in others. One loves the psalms, the long periods of silence after the scripture readings, or the litanies." [216] Here, elements of the Liturgy of the Hours are mentioned, which, however, are not embedded in the structure of the traditional Liturgy of the Hours. Many of those elements are imitated in parish churches and youth groups on an international scale. [217]

5.4.3. THE LITURGY OF THE HOURS IN THE ANGLICAN CHURCH

However successfully the "Breviarium secundum consuetudinem Romanae curiae" was able to impose itself with the help of the Franciscan Order, it had "in the 14th century by no means as yet effected a complete conquest. In those places where the old cathedrals had preserved a healthy self-confidence und their ancient pride at possessing the true Roman tradition, even the influence of the new Curia was ineffectual." This is especially valid for England: "An example of tradition in the best sense is the Ordinale of Exeter, which Bishop John Grandisson issued for use in the Cathedral and Diocese of Exeter in 1337." [218] Guiver, too, considers it certain that the great significance of the

---

[211] Goltzen 214f.

[212] Thus, Heiler published an "Evangelisches-katholisches Brevier", Munich 1932. For other suggestions with regard to structuring, cf Fendt 211f.

[213] C. Albrecht, Einführung in die Liturgik, Göttingen 3rd edn. 1983, 76f.

[214] Cf. M. Entrich, Ein einschneidender Rhythmus – Das Stundengebet in Taizé: Beten mit der Kirche, 117-120.

[215] Régle de Taizé – Die Regel von Taizé. Gütersloh 4. Aufl. 1967, 14f.

[216] Thus Schutz in a quotation from A. Stökl, Taizé. Geschichte und Leben der Brüder von Taizé, Hamburg 1975, 123.

[217] E.g. the prayers and songs of the community, brought out by its own publishers "Les Presses de Taizé".

[218] J. Pascher: Das Stundengebet der römischen Kirche. München 1954, 58f.

daily Liturgy of the Hours in the Anglican Church "is to be traced back in part to the conservative attitude peculiar to the English". Guiver traces this conservatism back to times long before the Reformation; now as then, he maintains, the Benedictine legacy is tangibly present in the Church of England, and has "exercised a greater influence on ecclesiastical life in general than presumably is the case in any other European country. The peculiarly Anglican tradition of the daily performance of the Liturgy of the Hours is deeply indebted to that legacy."[219]

The Book of Common Prayer, which appeared first in 1549 and has been handed down practically unchanged to the present day, contains the two traditional cathedral Offices: "Mattins" (Lauds) and Evensong (Vespers). Thomas Cranmer, Archbishop of Canterbury and author of the Book of Common Prayer, took his inspiration inter alia from the Breviary of Cardinal Quiñones, "but his main source was the Roman Liturgy of the Hours according to the mediaeval usage of Sarum (Salisbury), which at the end of the Middle Ages became the most-used book of the Roman liturgy in Britain". Guiver gives the following layout of Cranmer's Liturgy of the Hours, as it has been celebrated, with few changes, right up to the present day: [220]

MATTINS (LAUDS)	EVENSONG (VESPERS)
Exhortation	Exhortation
General confession	General confession
Absolution	Absolution
Our Father	Our Father

The above parts are often omitted. From the following parts, these come from the

Vigil:	Vespers:
O Lord, open thou our lips … ,	O Lord, open thou our lips … ,
O Lord, make haste …	O Lord, make haste ...
Gloria Patri, versicle, Venite (Ps 95)	Gloria Patri, versicle
Psalms of the day	Psalms of the day
Reading (O.T.)	Reading (O.T.)
Te Deum	Magnificat
Reading (N.T.)	Reading (N.T.)
Benedictus (from Lauds)	Nunc dimittis (from Compline)
Apostles' Creed (Prime)	Apostles' Creed (Compline)
Kyrie (from Lauds)	Kyrie (from Vespers)
Our Father, intercessions	Our Father, intercessions
Prayer of the day (Lauds)	Prayer of the day (Vespers)
Two morning collects	Two evening collects
(from Lauds and Prime)	(fom Vespers and Compline)
Anthem	Anthem
(choir piece from the Marian antiphon)	(choir piece from the Marian antiphon)
Further prayers and thanksgiving	Further prayers and thanksgiving

"The psalms are said monthly (in numerical order), the whole bible is recited yearly. The anthem is a musical element that is only activated when a choir is present, and

---

[219] Guiver, 108
[220] Cf Guiver 109f.; cf: The Book of Common Prayer, Cambridge and elsewhere 1968, 1-26

which can take on any suitable form." The priest is obliged to celebrate the Liturgy of the Hours daily in the church, so that a celebration with the people is always possible. In many churches the daily Liturgy of the Hours is taken for granted. [221] The Liturgy of the Hours in the Alternative Prayer Book of 1980 does not find much favour with Guiver. "A surprisingly high number of priests and parishes has therefore abandoned the Anglican Liturgy of the Hours in favour of the Roman, or that of Taizé etc. Now, however, people are giving the matter their attention, and it is to be expected that further developments will follow in the next few years." [222]

Bibliography

H. Goltzen, Der tägliche Gottesdienst. Die Geschichte des Tagzeitengebets, seine Ordnung und seine Erneuerung in der Gegenwart: Leiturgia III, Kassel 1956, 99-294.

G. Guiver, Das Stundengebet in der Anglikanischen Kirche: H. Rennings / M. Klöckener (eds.), Lebendiges Stundengebet, 108-120.

A. Raes, Streiflichter auf das Brevier in den orientalischen Kirchen: J. A. Jungmann (ed.), Brevierstudien. Referate aus der Studientagung von Assisi 14.-17. September 1956, Trier 1958, 117-126.

H. J. Schulz, Liturgie, Tagzeiten und Kirchenjahr des byzantinischen Ritus: HOK II, Düsseldorf 1989, 30-100.

5.5. POPULAR DEVOTIONS

5.5.1. SERVICES OF THE WORD AND THE LITURGY OF THE HOURS

Guardini once said that the objective prayer of the Liturgy stood over against the subjective prayer of popular devotions. Casel, for his part, held that from the 16th cent. onwards the Liturgy had become such an established and fixed official prayer, that all inward piety had retreated into other forms of devotion; he thought however that with the awakening of the Liturgy to new life both liturgical and private prayer would come nearer to each other, and would finally shed all differences and become one. Guardini later took up a middle position, according to which a popular devotion might as it were mediate between objective and subjective prayer. [223] The distinction between "objective" and "subjective" prayer is something which stems from an understanding of prayer of the Church as something fixed and rigid, a purely clerical form of the Divine Office which excluded any lay participation, the Divine Office being the priests" obligation, and the laity's "wish to partake in the prayer of the Church in the form of sequences, hymns, antiphons and prayers", these were added to the "objective" Liturgy of the Church, and finally took the place of the Divine Office. [224]

Schnitzler rightly remarks that "the popular devotional service has its origins in the Office understood in a broader sense; and that one can also observe numerous structural elements of the popular devotion in the Breviary". [225] The invitatory, hymn (song),

---

[221] Guiver 111.
[222] Guiver 118f.

[223] Cf. Neunheuser, Stundengebet und Volksfrömmigkeit 181f.
[224] Cf. ibidem 187
[225] Schnitzler, Stundengebet und Volksandacht 71

versicle, the prayer and finally the Our Father and Hail Mary can be mentioned as such elements, besides certain other richer and more varied secondary elements. [226] Schnitzler also considers, against the historical background of the German prayerbook literature, that "a widespread type of devotion is closely related in form to the structure of one of the Little Hours, these for their part are related to the commemorations, actually votive offices added to the main Office, something very common in the Middle Ages. The Rosary which followed could take the place of the psalms... It is an essential characteristic of a devotional service that it is the Office of the laity, or their Day Hours in honour of a saint or praise of a sacred mystery. A Devotion might be considered as an attempt to make the treasures of the Divine Office accessible to layfolk; in this respect Evensong for the people may not perhaps be quite in accordance with rubrics, but is certainly more understandable." [227] The Salve Devotion and Benediction with the Blessed Sacrament remind one clearly of the Liturgy of the Hours. The first stems from a custom, first found in the 13th cent., "at the end of the evening Office of singing the Salve Regina with versicle and concluding prayer", and at the same time going in procession to the Lady Altar; in time an independent devotion gradually developed from the custom. Benediction with the Blessed Sacrament arose from a "customary exposition of the Sacrament after (Thursday) Mass. With time the exposition was transferred or even prolonged to the evening and ended with Benediction. In the 16th cent. this popular devotional exercise was joined to the Salve prayer on certain days." [228]

The Divine Office is not the only root of popular Devotions, there is another, that which we can term edifying literature. From this source a special kind of Devotion came into being, the "meditation type", as distinct from the "divine office type". Because of its catechetical element this type of devotion was furthered intensively during the Counter Reformation. As well as prayer there was also an instruction, even the prayers became prayed catechetical instruction. The meditation type as an instruction in Christian Doctrine and at the same time, with the help of prayer-books, as contemplation and prayer, became very common as a parish devotion during the Counter-Reformation and Enlightenment Age, and often ended with Benediction with the Blessed Sacrament. [229] Here there is also a bond with the Office: at the morning Office in cathedrals instruction was given in the readings and homilies, we easily perceive a strong underlining of proclamation of the faith. During the Middle Ages this kerygmatic tradition was continued in the preaching at the services. There was again a revival in the Lenten sermons and catechism lessons of the Counter-Reformation, in the sermons during the parish missions and even in numerous Services of the Word in our own time. [230]

"The lesson from history as well as from our present day situation is clear: in the area of extra-sacramental church services freedom as well as a great variety of form is possible, and all this should most certainly be upheld and furthered. In this respect we should never forget that all human and church life, with the fullness of its hopes and aspects, must find in these areas an appropiate field of expression, something which

---

[226] Jungmann names the elements, that is, readings from Scripture, singing, popular prayers and the priest's prayer as belonging to the structures of a devotional exercise and joins them to the Liturgy of the Hours, Cf. Jungmann, Sonntagsandacht 57-60.

[227] Schnitzler, Meßopfer und Nachmittagsandacht 358f.

[228] Meyer, Andachten 159

[229] Cf. Schnitzler, Meßopfer und Nachmittagsandacht 360-362; Andachten 160.

[230] Cf. Meyer, Andachten 161-163.

is beyond the possibilities of a sacramental service." Meyer says this in face of something which is a possible danger, that is, a danger that the Mass might become in many places the only possible liturgical celebration. We cannot forget that "penance and reconciliation, praise, thanksgiving, petition, adoration, devotion can never be offered full satisfaction in the celebration of the Eucharist, it is obviously too short, there must be another possibility and another place where all these aspects can come to full flowering and expression, where they can be put into practice and deepened." [231]

5.5.2. EXAMPLES OF POPULAR DEVOTIONS

A. *Devotions with the Blessed Sacrament*

Benediction with the Blessed Sacrament is closely related to the eucharistic piety of the Middle Ages and to the feast of Corpus Christi. On this feastday the Blessed Sacrament was not taken to the tabernacle immediately after the procession, but was left exposed on the altar during Mass. Then the custom arose of exposing the Sacrament immediately before morning prayer in choir, it was placed on that altar from which the procession was to set out; later there was exposition during the whole office in choir on the feastday itself and in its octave. [232] Besides that "there then arose a special kind of exposition in votive Masses de corpore Christi, these were celebrated on Thursday and became one of the most popular devotions in Germany and Austria during the later Middle Ages". [233] Nevertheless the link between the Divine Office and Exposition of the Sacrament and the afternoon devotions accompanying it existed: Exposition took place during Divine Office, the monstrance was therefore placed on the altar, without eucharistic hymns being sung at the same time. The host was to be seen in the monstrance and the passionate longing of people simply to gaze at it was so fully satisfied. The evolution to Benediction began when the procession with the Sacred Host to the Altar was ritually expanded, in that at the end of the Office antiphons and responsories were sung and a short procession through the church was held. [234] Such processions were then also held outside Corpus Christi time, again joined to daily liturgy.

In places where there was no Divine Office in choir devotions were held at the time of Vespers or Compline. "From the second half of the 13th cent. hymns were sung or litanies recited in honour of the Crucified or his mother in churches or chapels. The Salve Regina was very often sung at the end of Vespers and, where no choir office was held, it was sung 'about that time when the town gates were usually shut'. For that reason those devotions were simply named 'Salve Regina' in Germany and later in England, in Italy they were named 'laudi'." [235] Browe rejects however the view that Benediction issued from these Salve devotions; he holds the contrary opinion that it evolved from the exposition Masses and the Corpus Christi Day rites. Corpus Christi Confraternities were often in the forefront regarding its introduction, and the rubrics of the Corpus Christi feastday formed the background for the liturgical form. [236]

---

[231] Meyer, Andachten, 173.
[232] Cf. Browe, Verehrung 154.
[233] Browe, Verehrung 141.
[234] Cf. Browe, Verehrung 155
[235] Browe, Verehrung 157.
[236] Cf. Browe, Verehrung 159

Nevertheless we can speak of a relationship between Benediction and the Divine Office: exposition of the Sacrament during the Liturgy of the Hours on Corpus Christi and in the octave offered the faithful a welcome opportunity for participation in the liturgy, even if they did not take part in the Office itself, they could contemplate the eucharistic Christ. The fact that Benediction was held in the afternoon indicates to a certain extent a continuation of the clericalized Verspers, but without the Office liturgy which the faithful no longer understood; they were now free to concentrate on the eucharistic aspect.

This alienation of the faithful is now ended, the Liturgy of the Hours has been reformed so that the faithful can take part and it is even possible to establish again the bond between eucharistic Exposition and the Divine Office. The General Instruction on the Liturgy of the Hours does not mention a celebration of the Office before the exposed Sacrament, but the brochure in the Ritual "Taking Communion and Veneration of the Eucharist outside Mass", Number 96, lays down: "If the Sacrament is exposed on the altar during a longer period the office may be recited in its presence, especially the most important hours. The Praise and Thanksgiving which are offered to God in the Eucharist can be continued in the Office throughout the day." The Instruction "Eucharisticum mysterium" of May the 25th 1967 [237] prescribes that even short expositions of the Blessed Sacrament should be so arranged "that before the blessing with the Sacrament, there might also, if need be, a suitable time set aside for the reading of the Word of God, for hymns, prayers and periods of silent prayer". "Vespers might then be *one* possible time, besides others, for the reading of Scripture, singing, prayers, as well as for prayers in silence. In this instruction adoration of the Blessed Sacrament is understood as something of independent importance and priority, in which the Divine Office represents a possible form or variation." [238]

The following question can however be raised: is the importance and independent value of the Divine Office as sanctification of time, and that of eucharistic adoration as a factor preparing us for reception of the Eucharist diminished, when both are joined together?

B. The Stations of the Cross

The Way of the Cross as a Devotional Service originated where a Via dolorosa was erected. The custom of erecting stones in honour of the dead at crossroads was an old Germanic custom, in Christian times crosses were then put up instead of stones, this was one source for the crosses in memory of the Passion. Other sources were atonement crosses, or crosses which were erected at places where a procession made a halt when taking relics from one place to another. More important however were representations of places in Jerusalem (above all that of the Holy Sepulchre), which crusaders or pilgrims erected when they again reached home. Representations of the Passion, as for example, the Man of Sorrows (a figure of Christ bearing the crown of thorns), a Mount Calvary (a Calvary scene often erected upon a hill with Our Lady, Mary Magdalene and St John), or a Pieta (Our Lady with a figure of the dead Saviour lying on her

---

[237] Kaczynski 899-965. Number 66 / Kaczynski 964: "Etiam breves sanctissimi Sacramenti expositiones, iuxta normas iuris habendae, ita ordinandae sunt ut in eis, ante benedictionem cum sanctissimo Sacramento, pro opportunitate congruum tempus tribuatur lectionibus verbi Dei, canticis, precibus et orationi in silentio protractae."

[238] G. Fuchs, Singet Lob und Preis. Stundengebet mit der Gemeinde feiern, Regensburg 1993, 122.

knees, also named "vesper statue", because the scene took place "hora verspertina"). All these needed only a setting where they began, a town-gate, for example, representing Jerusalem, and at the end the Calvary, these two settings could then be joined together and, fundamentally at least, a Way of the Cross was complete. One could walk in meditation along this way, which the Franciscan Nicolas Wankel aptly named "The Lord's Path" in 1517. A book, the Stations of the Cross, by C. A. Cruys (Adrichomius) from the Netherlands exercised great influence. The Spanish General of the Franciscans, A. Daza, gave instructions for the Stations of the Cross Devotion in his book "Exercitia Spiritualia" in 1626, these then became the final form for the Stations as a devotional service. In 1750 the Stations of the Cross in the Roman Colosseum were blessed, and from here the devotion spread throughout the whole world. Even in our day the Stations of the Cross Devotion is a well-beloved meditation during Lent. One must recommend however that the Lord's Passion be not separated from the Easter Message – as was the case in medieval Passiontide piety – we recommend for that reason – even in Lent – the introduction of a last station, that of the "empty sepulchre", in view of the wonder of Easter. [239]

C. Services the Word and Devotions in honour of the Virgin Mary

a. May Devotion: In order to counteract the after-effects of heathen cult forms (fertility cults) in May, the month of re-awakening life in nature, the medieval church promoted devotion to Christ's Passion, even if May always belongs, at least in part, to Eastertide. At the same time, however, a pronounced Marian piety developed, which became more and more identified with May. The May Devotion itself grew up and flowered in the Italian Baroque. Italian Jesuits published books with instructions and ideas for family devotional prayers in May. [240] The May Devotion however was already being celebrated by the Church, publically and officially; it consisted of meditations, prayers, the Litany of Loreto and was concluded by Benediction with the Blessed Sacrament. From Italy the May Devotion spread into France, and it was French nuns who held the first "classical" May Devotion in Germany, that was in Munich in 1841. The dogmatic definition of the Immaculate Conception of the Virgin Mary in 1854 was something which in no small way furthered everywhere the popularity of the devotion. Küppers also sees in the lightening-like spread an aspect of the Restoration Period. In times of general threat and uncertainty the Devotion reached – as also the whole Marian piety – high points of popularity. [241] Pope Paul VI mentions the same aspect in his Encyclica "Mense maio" of April the 29th 1965. The Pope speaks of "a dear custom of our predecessors", "in that they chose the month of Mary in order to invite Christian people to public prayer, as often as the difficulties of the Church or a threatening world danger demanded this". [242] The demand of the 2nd Vatican Council that both liturgical times and also concordance with the sacred liturgy be granted due and fitting consideration is also valid for the May Devotion, this Devotion must at the same time flow out from the liturgy and lead people back to it. (cf. SC 13). In other words: the mystery of Christ must ever be in the

---

[239] Cf. E. Kramer, Kreuzweg und Kalvarienberg. Historische und baugeschichtliche Untersuchungen, Kehl-Straßburg 1957 (Studien zur deutschen Kunstgeschichte 313).

[240] The Book of Devotions brought out by Alfonso Muzzarelli (1749-1813) had special influence: Il mese di Maria ossia il mese di Maggio consagrato a Maria santissima, Ferrara 1786.

[241] Cf. Küppers 250

[242] AAS 57 (1965) 353-358. 354.

foreground during a May Devotion, the Virgin Mary is joined to this mystery "by an unbreakable bond". "In the Blessed Virgin the Church admires and praises the sublimest fruit of Redemption. As in a chrystal-clear image and with great joy the Church sees in her that which it wishes and hopes fully to beome" (SC 103). Küppers sees in these words the "canon for present-day veneration of the Blessed Virgin" laid down by the 2nd Vatican Council. [243]

b. Rosary prayer and Rosary Devotion / "Angelus".Christians in the West and East are familiar with continuous repetition of a prayer or of a short sentence as one of the accepted prayer practices. The numbers 50 or 150 recalling the biblical psalter played a special role even in the time of ancient Irish monasticism. The putting together of three "fifties", that is, the Our Father and the Hail Mary said after each other fifty times was a penance given to those who could neither read nor write as a substitute, instead of reciting the whole psalter. At the same time independently of that the relationship of the number 150 to the psalter expressed a popular wish to imitate the Divine Office, in which the psalms were an important part and which had now long become the prayer of clerics. For this reason the kinship between rosary and Divine Office is according to Schnitzler obvious: "the kinship lies however less with the manner the Office was moulded into the canonical hours and rather more with the material which the hours were made of: the psalter." [244] Other forerunners of the rosary were medieval repetitive prayers which portrayed the life and passion of Jesus and which were combined, especially among Cistercians, with the Hail Mary. The Cistercian nuns of St Thomas near Trier thus combined 100 Aves with 100 brief accounts of mysteries of the Faith. [245] Besides Carthusians and Benedictines it was above all Dominicans who promulgated the rosary. The marian psalter of Alan of Rupe OP (d. 1457) consisted of 15 Our Fathers, 150 Hail Marys with 150 mysteries of the life of Jesus from the Annunciation to his Return in Glory. This prayer of the cloister developed into a genuine prayer of layfolk through the founding of rosary confraternities, it became so rooted in popular piety that it withstood all attacks of the reformers. In fact the rosary also became, through the promotion of marian piety (in the form of marian congregations and other confraternities), a strength of the Catholic Reform. Fuchs sees in the custom, which in many place is still observed, of saying the rosary in common before an evening Mass a connection with Vespers, even if we are less aware of the connection. [246] In his Apostolic Letter "Marialis Cultus" of February the 2nd 1974 Pope Paul stresses the rosary as marian meditation on Christ. [247] The month of October as rosary month has its historical background in the victory of the Christian fleet over the Turkish at Lepanto on the 7th of October 1571, the victory was held to be an answer to the rosary prayers of the faithful. Pius V ordered that the anniversary of the victory be held as an ecclesiastical feastday and named "Beatae Mariae Virginis de victoria", something which was quite in accordance with the old and deeply rooted tradition of praying the rosary.

---

[243]   Cf. Küppers 322f.

[244]   Schnitzler, Stundengebet und Volksandacht 71.

[245]   Cf. A. Heinz, Die Zisterzienser und die Anfänge des Rosenkranzes. Das bisher unveröffentlichte älteste Zeugnis für den Leben-Jesu-Rosenkranz aus St Thomas a. d. Kyll (um 1300), Analecta Cisterciensia 33 (1977) 262-309; R. Scherschel, Der Rosenkranz – das Jesusgebet des Westens, Freiburg-Basel-Vienna 1979 (FThSt 116).

[246]   C. Fuchs 131.

[247]   Cf. Number 44 – Kaczynski 3266: "Est igitur Rosarium evangelica prex."

A parallel form to the rosary was the prayer "The Angel of the Lord" ("Angelus") said three times daily when church bells were rung in the morning, at midday and in the evening. "Since the prayer was regularly recited, morning, midday and evening, it was likened to the Office and contributed to the sanctification of the day. One can compare the rosary with the meditative Office of Readings, and the angelus with the Hours said at fixed and fitting times." [248] The three Aves and between them the two scripture quotations Lk 1:38 and John 1:14 is a form first accounted for in a catechism which appeared in Venice in 1560. "After this form had been approved by Pius V in 1571 for the newly brought out Officium Parvum BMV its dissemination was certain." [249]

Bibliography

P. Browe, Die Verehrung der Eucharistie im Mittelalter, München 1933, Reprint Sinzig 1990.

F. Courth: Marianische Gebetsformen: W. Beinert / H. Petri (eds.): Handbuch der Marienkunde, Regensburg 1984, 363 – 403.

J. A. Jungmann, Die Sonntagsandacht – ihr Ursprung und ihre Elemente, Lebendige Seelsorge 4 (1953) 54 – 60.

B. Kleinheyer, Maria in der Liturgie: W. Beinert / H. Petri (eds.): Handbuch der Marienkunde, Regensburg 1984, 404 – 439.

K. Küppers, Marienfrömmigkeit zwischen Barock und Industriezeitalter, St. Ottilien 1987 (MThSt 27).

H. B. Meyer, Andachten und Wortgottesdienste. Zwei Grundtypen nicht-sakramentaler Liturgie? LJ 24 (1974) 157-175.

B. Neunheuser, Stundengebet und Volksfrömmigkeit: M. Klöckener / H. Rennings (eds.), Lebendiges Stundengebet. Vertiefung und Hilfe (FS Brinkhoff), Freiburg-Basel – Wien 1989, 181 – 196.

Th. Schnitzler, Meßopferfeier und Nachmittagsandacht: F.X. Arnold / B. Fischer (eds.): Die Messe in der Glaubensverkündigung, Freiburg i. Br. 2nd edn. 1953, 353- 363.

Th. Schnitzler, Stundengebet und Volksandacht: J. A. Jungmann (Hg.): Brevierstudien. Referate aus der Studientagung von Assisi 14.-17. September 1956, Trier 1958, 71 – 84.

---

[248] G. Langgärtner, Der "Engel des Herrn" und sein heutiger Sinn: Liturgie konkret 8/1981, 1-4. 3.
[249] A. Heinz: "Der Engel des Herrn". Erlösungsgedächtnis als Volksgebet, HID HD? 33 (1979) 51-58. 52.

Part VI

The Hallowing of Time 2:
Celebrating the Year of the Lord

6.1. THE YEAR OF THE LORD: THE ANNUAL CELEBRATION OF CHRIST'S SAVING MYSTERIES

The sanctification of time is concerned not only with that of the twenty-four hours of the day by means of the Liturgy of the Hours, but also of the yearly cycle in which the Church "unfolds the whole mystery of Christ from the Incarnation and Nativity to the Ascension, to the day of Pentecost and the joyful hope of the coming of the Lord" (SC 102). The commencement of the Year of the Lord in the Latin Rite with the first Sunday of Advent through the course of its festive seasons and feasts from the Nativity via the celebration of the Death and Resurrection, the Ascension and the sending of the Holy Spirit and through the period called Ordinary Time, the last Sundays of which by proclaiming the second coming of the Lord, seem to prepare once more for Advent, create the impression that the Year of the Lord – at least in the period between Advent and Pentecost – is concerned with following every year the course of Jesus's life and, if one counts the Sundays of Ordinary Time, the life of the Church until Christ comes again. But the celebration of the Year of the Lord is not a chronological attempt at an historical remembrance of the life of Jesus. All feasts and commemorations in the Year of the Lord celebrate man's salvation through the one great saving deed of the incarnate, crucified, risen and glorified Son of God, under the aspect in which it appeared in the events celebrated on the days commemorated and is made present in the liturgical celebration.[1] Thus the constantly recurring annual cycle is already an image of the timeless superabundance of divine life while lies behind the course of time. The content of the annual cycle of celebration is the mystery of Christ with his Church, "i.e. it is concerned with the celebration of the saving deeds of the Lord in the today of this world and of the Church. Thus, the Church's year does indeed contain much taken from the life of the earthly Jesus. But the Jesus of history is one with the glorified Jesus (the Jesus of faith). For this reason the Church's year is not a mere recalling of individual incidents of Jesus's earthly life, but the celebration of the whole mystery of Christ." In all of this, though, Odo Casel's understanding of "remembrance" as "memory of the mystery" (*Anamnesis*) and with this memory the presence of the mystery – as presented in the first part of this work – must not be forgotten.[2]

The task of the Church, according to the Constitution on the Liturgy of the Second Vatican Council, is "to celebrate in sacred remembrance on particular days throughout the year the work of salvation of her divine bridegroom" (SC 102). This memorial celebration is *anamnesis*,, "and with this any attenuation to a purely psychological recalling is excluded. The Council does not rule out a pedagogical or educational function of the Church's year, but this function is expressly indicated as secondary (cf.105). The content of the memorial celebration is the Redeemer's work of salvation. The focus is not the person of Christ so much as his work of redemption. Even if in this context it

---

[1]   Cf. Berger, Ostern und Weihnachten 17: "When one make a point of saying that Good Friday and Easter are celebrating the same thing, then one could say, taking into account the kernel of all feasts, that Christmas and Easter celebrate the same thing. Underlying both days is the same basic idea – the glorification of the Lord."

[2]   Auf der Maur, Feiern im Rhythmus der Zeit I,225.

speaks only of the saving deeds of Christ, the Constitution understands as implied all of salvation history."[3]

General Presentations and wider Bibliography:

A. Adam, Das Kirchenjahr mitfeiern. Seine Geschichte und seine Bedeutung nach der Liturgiere-form. Freiburg-Basel-Vienna 5th edn. 1991.

H. Auf der Maur, Feiern im Rhythmus der Zeit I: Herrenfeste in Woche und Jahr. Gottesdienst der Kirche. Handbuch der Liturgiewissenschaft. Edn. by H. B. Meyer, H. Auf der Maur, B. Fischer, A. A. Häußling, B. Kleinheyer. Vol.5, Regensburg 1983.

J. Baumgartner, Das Kirchenjahr. Feiern christlicher Feste, Fribourg-Mödling 1978.

K. H. Bieritz, Das Kirchenjahr. Feste, Gedenk – und Feiertage in Geschichte und Gegen-wart, München 2nd edn. 1994.

P. Guéranger, Das Kirchenjahr. Translated and edn. by J. B. Heinrich, 14 vols., Mainz 1874 (1) – 1898 (14).

P. Jounel, La dimanche et la semaine; l'Année: Martimort IV: La liturgie et le temps. Paris 1983, 23-168.

S. Marsili and others, L'anno liturgico. Anamnesis VI, Torino 1988.

D. R. Moser, Bräuche und Feste im christlichen Jahreslauf, Graz-Vienna-Köln 1993.

P. Parsch, Das Jahr des Heils. 3 vols., Klosterneuburg 14th edn. 1952-1953.

J. Pascher, Das liturgische Jahr, München 1963.

J. Pinsk, Gedanken zum Herrenjahr, edn. by Th. Schnitzler, Mainz 1963.

F. Reckinger, Gott begegnen in der Zeit. Unser Kirchenjahr, Paderborn 1986.

M.Righetti, Manuale di storia liturgica II: L'Anno Liturgico – Il Breviario, Milan 1955.

E.Sauser, Heilige und Engel im Kirchenjahr, Regensburg 1979.

6.1.1. THE YEARLY CELEBRATION AS SUCH

Specifically avoiding any attempt to historicize, the new division of the Year of the Lord takes as its starting-point the Easter Triduum and determines seven periods: I. The sa-cred triduum from Holy Thursday to Easter Sunday, II. Eastertide (from Easter Sunday to Pentecost Sunday), III. Lent (from Ash Wednesday to midday on Holy Thursday), IV. Christmastide, V. Advent, VI. Ordinary Time, VII. Rogation and Ember Days.[4] This means that there are three great coherent periods: a) The Easter Cycle (Lent or Quadra-gesima, the Sacred Triduum, the fifty days of Eastertide or Pentecost), b) The Christmas Cycle (Advent and Christmastide) and c) Ordinary Time. The latter includes thirty-three or thirty-four Sundays which do not have a specific character and lasts from the feast of the Baptism of the Lord, i.e. the Sunday after the 6th January, until the feast of Christ the King, i.e. the last Sunday before Advent. Ordinary Time is interrupted by the great block of the Easter Cycle. This means that Sundays in Ordinary Time are resumed on the first Sunday after Pentecost, the feast of the Holy Trinity, and so calculated that the feast of Christ the King is always the thirty-fourth Sunday in Ordinary Time. In addition to the major solemnities of the Christmas Cycle, feasts of the Lord such as the Presen-

[3]   Auf der Maur, Feiern im Rhythmus der Zeit I,226f.
[4]   Cf. NUALC 18-47 – Kaczynski 1289-1318.

tation, the Annunciation, the Transfiguration and the Feast of the Holy Cross have a fixed day in the calendar (2nd February, 25th March, 6th August and 14th September respectively); the dates of other feasts depends on the date of Easter.

The Breviary of 1568 and the Missal of 1570 divided the feasts of the Lord according to a complicated system similar to systems employed in medieval times.[5] A distinction was made between the "major Sundays" (*Dominicae maiores*) of the First Class (Sunday 1 of Advent, all Sundays of Lent, Easter Sunday, Low Sunday, Pentecost Sunday) and of the Second Class (Sunday 2-4 of Advent and the former Sundays before Lent) and all the other Sundays of the year called "ordinary Sundays" (or *Dominicae minores*). Weekdays were divided into "higher major ferials" (themselves divided into "privileged" and "unprivileged" and "ordinary, minor ferials". In addition there were the following classes of feast: "Double of the First Class", Double of the Second Class", "Major Double" "Double", "Semidouble", "Simple". Many doubles had octaves, which in turn were divided into privileged octaves (further divided into 1st, 2nd and 3rd orders), ordinary octaves and simple octaves. Thus, Easter Sunday was classified as a "Double of the First Class with a privileged Octave of the 1st Order" while Christmas was a "Double of the First Class with a privileged Octave of the 3rd Order".[6] The term "double" stemmed from the practice on major feasts of celebrating a double night office, that of the vigil at the beginning of the night and that of the feast after midnight. "Even if this actual arrangement disappeared, the term *duplex* (i.e. double office) remained and from now on was used in describing the rank of feasts on which there was never a double office."[7] This complicated system affected above all the question of precedence of a feast to be celebrated ahead of another liturgical day and the commemorations to be made at Mass and in the Liturgy of the Hours. Many attempts were made to simplify this system but it was not until "The General Norms for the Liturgical Year and the New General Roman Calendar" of 1969,[8] which had been requested by the Liturgy Constitution of the Second Vatican Council,[9] that a real reform was effected. "Celebrations are divided according to their importance in Solemnities, Feasts and Memorias,"[10] "Memorials are either obligatory or optional. They are celebrated on the appropriate weekdays according to the regulations laid down in the general introductions to the Missal and to the Liturgy of the Hours."[11]

The arrangement of the Sundays and weekdays of Ordinary Time was also subjected to a radical reform by the General Instruction on the Church's Year and the new liturgical books. The system of reckoning used in the Missal of 1570 stems form the eighth century; Sundays were counted with reference to important feasts. There were four Sundays after Epiphany and twenty-four after Pentecost, whereby depending on the date of Easter (and with it the beginning of Lent) the extra Sundays after Epiphany (Sundays 3 to 6 after Epiphany) were made up by inserting them between the twenty-third and twenty-fourth Sundays after Pentecost. In the reformed system the division into time after Epiphany and time after Pentecost is abandoned in favour of a general

---

[5]   Cf. Eisenhofer I, 589, where e.g. the ordinary of the Dominican Order of 1267 is mentioned.
[6]   Cf.Adam, Kirchenjahr 31.
[7]   Eisenhofer I, 589.
[8]   Cf. Kaczynski 1268-1332.
[9]   Cf. SC 107.
[10]   NUALC 10 - Kaczynski 1281.
[11]   NUALC 14 – Kaczynski 1285.

"Ordinary Time" of "Time Throughout the Year". This term comes from the 1960 Code of Rubrics. [12]

Even though the so-called "Ordinary Time" is spoken of as not having a particular stamp, nevertheless it is marked by the Sunday celebration of the Easter mystery as the weekly Pasch: "The Paschal Mystery, death and resurrection, is the real kernel of Christ's redeeming work. This is celebrated in the weekly cycle on Sunday and in the yearly cycle at Easter. For this reason Sunday and the yearly Easter are the centre of the liturgical shaping of the year. [13] It is precisely this paschal stamping of the yearly cycle which make it clear that neither here, nor at Easter itself, nor on the other feasts, are we dealing with an historicizing commemoration, but with the actual making present of salvation in a celebration which is subject to the changes of time. The Christian faith shares this understanding of the feast with the children of Israel.

6.1.2. THE JEWISH FESTAL CALENDAR

The Jewish festal calendar is also a yearly celebration. Along with the weekly Sabbath, this celebration is marked by various festivals, all of which have the saving presence of Jahweh as their theme and in the light of his saving deeds in the history of his people, celebrate God's actual presence and his fidelity to his covenant. At the time of Jesus, three of these feasts were still pilgrimage feasts (*regalim* from regal / foot, pilgrimage made on foot): The Passover (or in Hebrew *Pesach*), the Feast of Weeks (*Shavuoth*) and the Feast of Tabernacles (*Succoth*). Every Jew who had completed his twelfth year was obliged to make the pilgrimage to Jerusalem every year on one of these feasts. On the Passover the focus of the celebration was on the exodus of the people of Israel from bondage in Egypt. A sacrificial feast of nomadic origin (with the motif of the slaughtered lamb) and a harvest festival of agricultural stamp (the feast of unleavened bread – *matzoth* – at the beginning of the barley harvest) were fused and by means of the motif of the exodus from Egypt combined with the religion of Jahweh. The Feast of Weeks (*Shavuoth*) is the fiftieth day after *Matzoth*, a thanksgiving festival for the wheat harvest. This agricultural feast came to be connected historically with the Jahweh cult as a memorial of the giving of the Covenant on Sinai. Similarly, the seven-day-long Feast of Tabernacles during which the faithful live in lightly-built huts made of branches, is of agricultural origin, being a thanksgiving for the wine harvest. Again, this celebration is grounded in salvation history by linking it with the exodus from Egypt (Lev 23.42f.). In the early medieval period the final day of the Feast of Tabernacles was interwoven with the Feast of the Torah (*Simcath Thora*), the day on which the continuous reading of the Torah ends and begins immediately again. [14]

Between the three pilgrimage festivals, each of which has its own festal scroll (i.e. readings for the feast – The Song of Songs for the Passover, the Book of Ruth for *Shavuoth* and Koheleth at *Succoth*), lie the feast of New Year and the Day of Atonement. Under Babylonian influence, New Year (*Rosh Hashana*) which was originally placed at the new moon following the autumn equinox was transferred to new moon after the spring equinox. At the centre of the liturgy is the blowing of the ram's horn, the shofar, which recalls Abraham's sacrifice of Isaac, prevented by God himself. According to

---

[12]   Cf. Auf der Maur, Feiern im Rhythmus der Zeit I, 43-46.
[13]   Auf der Maur, Feiern im Rhythmus der Zeit I, 227.
[14]   Cf. Ben-Chorin 159f.

Ben-Chorin, the Israelites, during the period of Babylonian exile, learned about the throne-festival of *Marduk*. This was also New Year's Day. Integrated into the religion of Jahweh, the New Year became the day on which the God of judgement ascended his throne.

The Feast of Atonement (*Yom Kippur*) is celebrated in the first autumn moon. On this day only was the High Priest permitted to enter behind the curtain into the Holy of Holies to sprinkle the cover of the Ark of the Covenant with the blood of a steer he had just sacrificed for his own sins and those of the other priests. Inside the Holy of Holies he made an offering of incense. Then one of two goats was chosen and sacrificed for the sins of the people; its blood was poured out behind and in front of the curtain of the Holy of Holies. By a laying on of hands the second goat was symbolically burdened with the sins of the people and driven into the desert. After the destruction of the Temple the Feast of Atonement became a strict day of penance with an atonement liturgy in the synagogue which was prepared for by ten days penance. [15]

The feast of the Dedication of the Temple (*Chanukka*) recalls the re-consecration of the desecrated Temple by Judas in 164 BC as related in 1 Maccabees. This is on the 25th of the month of *Kislev*, which always falls in the Christian season of Advent. In the week of *Chanukka* the seven-branched *Chanukka* lamp is central. On each day of the feast a new flame is lighted. The background to the festival of *Purim* in the last month of the Jewish year is found in the experience of exceptional rescue from persecution during the Persian diaspora as reflected in the Book of Esther which is read at the liturgy in the synagogue on this feast. Three of the five fast days are associated with the destruction of Jerusalem, as is the day of mourning on the tenth day of *Teveth*, though the latter has become a general day of mourning for all Jewish victims of persecution. The day of mourning in summer on the ninth day of *Av*, which is the strictest of fast days and on which the Book of Jeremiah is read, is for all the catastrophes in the history of the Jewish people. [16]

According to Ben-Chorin, Christian theology and in particular the dialectical theology of Karl Barth, has not infrequently considered earthly-human history and divine salvation history as separated from each other, as if they happened on two different levels. "Distinctions of this kind are unbiblical and therefore also un-Jewish. Jewish feast are historical feasts which proclaim God as the Lord of history. This is evidenced in the newest of our feasts, the *Yom Ha-azmauth*, Israel's Independence Day which recalls the establishment of the Israeli state on 14th May, 1948." [17]

6.1.3. TERMS FOR THE CHRISTIAN FESTAL YEAR

The first known example of a special term encompassing all feasts and seasons of the year is the *Postilla* of Johannes Pomarius, a Lutheran preacher at Magdeburg, which appeared in that city in 1585. He choses the term "Church's Year" and in doing so distinguished the year beginning in the Church with the first Sunday of Advent from the

---

[15]   Cf. Ben-Chorin 160f.
[16]   Cf. Ben-Chorin 161-163.
[17]   Ben-Chorin 164.

year outside the Church.[18] In the ensuing period the term was adopted by both Protestants and Catholics. Kranemann sees in the term "Church's Year" an expression of a "constantly growing difference between the Church's time and that of the merchants", already beginning in the thirteenth and fourteenth centuries, long before the Reformation; this amounts to a divergence between the *festa chori* celebrated in church and the *festa fori*, the real festivals celebrated by the people. The increasingly complex organisational structures (particularly those of an ever-expanding organised commerce) demanded a more exact division of time, as was being made possible by the erection of tower-clocks. The market calendar no longer corresponded with the Church calendar. "In future, the time of believing merchant's business life is different from the time of his religious life. Finally, Renaissance man of the fifteenth and sixteenth centuries, sees himself as fully the master of his own time. Apparently it is in this period that the term 'Church's Year' arises."[19] The bustle of the world and the liturgical action of the Church have become two distinct entities and the former must concede a niche as it were in the diary to the latter. Thus the term "Church's Year" expresses the anabatic dimension precisely from a negative perspective: man is active, he accepts the invitation to communication with God in the liturgy when the calendar permits it – but these are special dates over against the rest of the run of life. Nevertheless, the term "Church's Year" is still frequently used, among others by Karl Rahner.[20]

Other terms include *Année chrétienne* or "Christian Year", *Année spirituelle* or "Year of Salvation" (*Jahr des Heiles* - P. Parsch). Official documents like to use the term "Liturgical Year" (*annus liturgicus*, *année liturgique*), thus SC 107; similarly Guéranger whose German translator, though, substituted the term *Kirchenjahr*.[21] "Year of the Lord" (*Herrenjahr*) emphasises the primarily katabatic dimension of the yearly cycle. Thus the year of the Lord with the annual Easter at its centre is analogous to Sunday, the "Day of the Lord" (*dies dominica, kyriake*) as the weekly Easter. All feasts and seasons of the year of the Lord celebrate under different aspects of the one mystery of Christ his liturgical coming among and saving presence in the celebrating community.

As well as the general Roman calendar, which is the foundation of the year of the Lord, local calendars contain "feasts confined to particular churches and religious orders which feasts are generally linked to the yearly cycle. It is entirely fitting that particular churches and religious orders should honour in a special way the saints with whom they are particularly connected. Local calendars will be compiled by the responsible authorities and approved by the Apostolic See."[22]

6.1.4. FEASTS CELEBRATING EVENTS AND IDEAS

The difficult division of feasts of the year of the Lord into those that celebrate events and those that celebrate ideas arises precisely in the context of the one saving presence of Christ in the various commemorations of the facts of salvation.

---

[18] Cf. B. Kranemann: Zu Geschichte und Bedeutung des deutschen Begriffs "Kirchenjahr". In: Alw 33 (1991) 35-42.37, which, however, is based on the possibility that Pomarius himself could have taken the term from elsewhere.

[19] Kranemann 41.

[20] Cf. K. Rahner: Das große Kirchenjahr. Geistliche Texte. 2nd edn. Freiburg-Basel-Vienna 1998.

[21] Cf. Auf der Maur, Feiern im Rhythmus der Zeit I, 211f.

[22] NUALC 49. Cf. on all of this Adam, Kirchenjahr 171f.

Jungmann identifies the primitive pattern of a feast as existing, "when a significant event forms its object". [23] The event being celebrated presses for the inclusion of the religious, the final reality of God and with it demands worship, as Jungmann, appealing to Pieper's definition of a festival, [24] rightly says. Feasts that have become institutions should be distinguished from this primitive type: permanent values ought to be brought to renewed consciousness form time to time; these may be values of the natural order (e.g. harvest festivals) or cultural values (e.g. a state's national day). But the value being celebrated must have a weight of its own if a feast is to be established. One example would be the anniversary of the foundation of an association on which one can meditate on the principles underlying the association. "The feasts of the Church's year belong to this category – and yet at the same time have a nature of their own." [25]

The essence of the Church festival lies in *anamnesis*. The latter is more than an individual growth in awareness of a Redemption that has been effected. In human celebration that which is celebrated becomes present through divine action: "The work of Redemption itself becomes present and effective in a new way: *opus redemptionis exercetur*; it becomes effective in the manner which we try to apprehend by using the opaque term "mystery"." [26] This fundamental theme is, however, broken up. Firstly, the single passage through death to resurrection commemorated at Easter is split into what Augustine [27] called the *triduum crucifixi* (Good Friday), *sepulti* (Holy Saturday) and *suscitati* (Easter Sunday). The overall theme is further divided into Ascension and Pentecost. The theme of the entry of the Saviour into the world which clusters around Epiphany and Christmas constantly presents new partial aspects of the single theme of Redemption. This is even true of the feasts of the saints; the Redemption which became event in Christ is evidenced in the life and death of the saints.

But the more the single Christ-event is opened out in the various feasts, the more the event that underlies a particular feast recedes, the more the feast itself disappears. The celebrating people is absent, feasts become *festa chori* and no longer *festa fori*, the influence on the ritual form of the Mass of the day or on the Liturgy of the Hours diminishes constantly. How do things stand, though, with the feast based on an idea, a feast which scarcely has any foundation in an historical event?

Jungmann addresses Baumstark's thesis that all the great Christian feasts are not commemorations of events in salvation history but are intended, rather, to express the great religious ideas. Botte has disagreed with this: "Easter, Epiphany, Christmas are not *fêtes d'idées*. They are not concerned with eternal truths but facts of salvation history." For Jungmann these positions are not contradictory: "The great feasts are based on the fundamental saving events", however the feasts do not celebrate the events themselves, but the salvation that lies behind them and that they mediate. "But salvation and redemption are abstract concepts, 'ideas', through which the object of a given feast is appropriately expressed. Thus is articulated the notion that in these ancient feasts the main interest was not in a making present of the historical details, but in their salvific

---

[23]   Jungmann, Das kirchliche Fest 165.

[24]   Cf. J. Pieper, Muße und Kult, München 1955; Ibid.: Zustimmung zur Welt. Eine Theorie des Festes, München 2nd edn. 1964.

[25]   Jungmann, Das kirchliche Fest 166.

[26]   Jungmann, Das kirchliche Fest 167f.

[27]   Augustine, Ep. 55.24 – CSEL 34/2, 195. Ambrose already speaks in similar fashion of "triduum illud sacrum, intra quod triduum et passus est et quievit et resurrexit", Ep. 23,13 – PL 16, 1030.

significance, in the ongoing mystery of Christ."[28] In an event the triune God's unchanging will to save is "embodied", as this will was effectively proclaimed in the particular details of the economy of salvation in Christ, once upon a time in salvation history, and is now proclaimed actually once more in the celebration of these events.

Real "feasts of an idea" have to be distinguished from those just described. Feasts that celebrate an idea lack the anamnetic element – e.g. the feast of the Holy Trinity as a late product of the struggle with Arianism. "Here we are indeed faced with one of the 'eternal truths' which are valid independently of the salvation-event."[29] More strongly rooted in events of salvation are the feasts of the Body and Blood of Christ, the Sacred Heart of Jesus and Christ the King, but even in these it is no longer the event itself (institution of the Eucharist, acceptance of the Cross, admission of kingship before Pilate) that forms the object of the feast, but salvation in the form of an "idea". The interpenetration of idea and person is particularly apposite in the case of the cult of a saint divorced from the place of that saint's burial. In these instances the saint is celebrated less as a person than as an "programme" or agenda – as an example and ideal of a Christian life. With this, the idea can be distinguished from the person, the latter serving now merely as the bearer of the former; Jungmann gives as an example the feast of St Joseph the Worker as an attempt by the Church to christianise the 1st May, the secular (and socialistically tinged) festival of work.[30]

6.1.5. DATES OF FEASTS AS AN ECUMENICAL PROBLEM

The Christian calendar represents a combination of the Jewish-Babylonian lunar year and the solar year usual among the Egyptians and Romans. Fixed days of the year are reckoned according to the Roman solar year, "whereby the so-called months are divorced from the actual lunar cycle and simply serve as an artificial division of the solar year. Over against this, the feast of Easter and all feasts depending on it stem from the Jewish lunar-solar year." Determination of the year goes back to the so-called "Julian Calendar" introduced by Julius Caesar in 44 B.C, which in its precision "represented the first successful attempt to reconcile the calculation of time with astronomical realities, to the extent that it remained unaltered in all of the Christian world until the year 1582".[31]

Nevertheless the Julian Calendar was inaccurate to the extent of eleven minutes and fourteen seconds every year. In the course of 128 years this amounted to a whole day so that by the sixteenth century the discrepancy between astronomical time and calendar time had grown to ten days. Both the spring and autumn equinoxes occurred ten days earlier than calculated. In 1582, Pope Gregory XIII's (1572-1585) reform of the calendar corrected this discrepancy by declaring the day following 4th October 1582 to be 15th October. A further drifting apart of the astronomical and calendar year was prevented by a precision of the rule for leap-years: years ending a century were not longer to be reckoned leap-years unless they could be divided by four.

---

[28] Jungmann, Das kirchliche Fest 171f.
[29] Jungmann, Das kirchliche Fest 173. Attention should be drawn to the inherent consistency of a feast of an idea: thus, to misunderstand Pentecost as a feast of the Holy Spirit divorced from the event of salvation or, as in the eighteenth century, to wish to introduce a feast of the Heavenly Father.
[30] Cf. Jungmann, Das kirchliche Fest 176.
[31] Plank, Zeitrechnung and Festdatierung 183.

Because of the divisions which had arisen between Christians, the introduction of this "Gregorian" calendar was extremely difficult. It was not adopted by German Protestants until 1700 and by the English until 1752. The Orthodox and old Eastern Churches held fast to the Julian calendar. The discrepancy between the Gregorian and Julian calendars remained the same only until 1700. A revision of the Gregorian rule for leap-years increased the gap to 13 days. This affects the calculation of the date of Easter because there was not unity in the method of determining the equinoxes. The Julian and Gregorian methods of calculating the date of Easter differ, firstly, in that the spring equinox (21st March) falls thirteen days later according to the older reckoning than under the newer calendar. In addition, Gregory XIII's correction of inaccuracies in the calculation of the months has added a further four days to dates calculated according to the older style. "The Gregorian date of Easter frequently irritates Orthodox Christians because it can coincide with or even anticipate the date of the Jewish Passover. Accordingly, the date of the Jewish Passover is often marked in Orthodox calendars and great care is taken that their own Easter is celebrated later than this. Should, according to usual reckoning, Easter coincide with the Jewish feast, then the Orthodox Passover is postponed by a week."[32] Because of its greater accuracy the secularised states introduced the Gregorian calendar into Orthodox countries in the twentieth century; for example into the Soviet Union in 1923. But the Orthodox Church refused to accept this a clung to the Julian calendar, thereby separating itself completely from the secular year.[33] An initiative of the Ecumenical Patriarch Melitos IV. Metataxes, led to the introduction in Greece in 1924 of the calendar called after him known as the "Melitianic Mixed Calendar". According to this all fixed feasts are calculated according to the Gregorian calendar while Easter and all feasts dependent on it are calculated according to the Julian calendar. Despite the disagreements that resulted from its introduction to Greece – leading even to schisms ("Old Calendar-Palaioimerologites") – this mixed calendar is very widespread in the Orthodox world.[34]

6.1.6. CELEBRATING THE YEAR IN THE BYZANTINE RITE

In the Byzantine Rite as in the West the Easter Cycle with the preceding *Quadragesima* or Lent (*Tessarakoste*) and the following fifty days, the *Pentakoste* naturally stands out in the run of the liturgical year. The celebration of the death and resurrection of the Lord stamps the theology, spirituality and liturgy of the Byzantine Church so persistently[35]

---

[32] Plank, Zeitrechnung und Festdatierung 188.
[33] The same applies to the Greek-Catholic Ukranian Church – and this in the middle of the diaspora in the West!
[34] The calendar is in force in the Patriarchates of Constantinople, Alexandria, Antioch, Georgia, Rumania and Bulgaria, as well as in the Churches of Cyprus, Greece, Albania, (former) Czechoslovakia, Poland and America. The Patriarchates of Moscow and of Serbia as well as the Russian Orthodox Church in Exile and the monks of Athos retain the pure Julian calendar. The Orthodox Church of Finland and parts of the Orthodox diaspora follow the pure Gregorian calendar. Cf. Plank, Zeitrechnung und Festdatierung 190.
[35] Cf. e.g. J. Tyciak, Die Liturgie als Quelle östlicher Frömmigkeit, Freiburg i.Br. 1937 (Ecclesia Orans 20): Ch.1: Vom Auferstehungsgeist der Ostkirche: 1-22; H. J. Schulz, Der österliche Zug im Erscheinungsbild byzantinischer Theologie: B. Fischer / J. Wagner (eds.), Paschatis Sollemnia. Studien zu Osterfeier und Osterfrömmigkeit, Freiburg-Basel-Vienna 1959, 239-246.

that as well as the individual Sunday[36] the whole celebration of the year is marked by it: "Outside the season of Pentecost every Sunday in the mature Byzantine Rite is textually so marked by the resurrection of the Lord that a cycle of eight Sundays respectively imitates Pentecost exactly, and from the first to the eighth Sunday celebrates a continuous cycle of resurrection offices, in accordance with the Church's eight singing-tones. The liturgical book that contains these offices is called *Oktoëchos* and is attributed to St John Damascene."[37] The book which contains the full texts, including the Liturgy of the Hours, changing according to the liturgical singing-tones, for the week following the Sunday is called *Paraklitike* or "Greater *Oktoëchos*". The proper texts for the feasts of the year of the Lord are contained in the 12 volumes of the so-called "Monthly Books" (*Menäen*); these are divided into several classes of feast, different according to Slavic or Greek traditions. The liturgical year begins on 1st September and ends on 31st August.

Feasts of the first class are the twelve Solemnities which, when they fall on a Sunday displace the resurrection office provided in the *Oktoëchos*. Apart from Easter, and Pentecost, which in any case always fall on a Sunday, these feasts are: The Birth of the Virgin (8th September); The Exaltation of the Holy Cross (14th September); The Presentation of the Virgin (21st November); The Nativity of Our Lord (25th December); The Epiphany (6th January); *Hypapante* (Presentation of Our Lord in the Temple, 2nd February); The Annunciation (25th March); Saints Peter and Paul (29th June); The Transfiguration (6th August) and The Dormition of the Virgin (15th August). On the days following these feasts occur the so-called *synaxes* or accompanying feasts dedicated to a person or persons who played a particular role in the event just celebrated. These are Saints Joachim and Anne (9th September); The Mother of God (26th December), St John the Baptist (7th January), Saints Simeon and Hanna (3rd February); The Archangel Gabriel (26th March) and the *synaxis* of all the twelve Apostles (30th June). Feasts of the second class are combined with the Sunday but do not displace it. Under no circumstances do feasts of the third to the fifth class (all of them feasts of saints) displace a Sunday. The classification of these feasts is regulated according to the proportion of proper texts in the Divine Liturgy and the Liturgy of the Hours.[38]

6.1.7. THE LITURGICAL YEAR IN THE CHURCHES OF THE REFORMATION

The Reformed Churches stand naturally in the tradition of the West as it developed up to the time of the Reformation. The Catholic inheritance is preserved to a greater or less degree in the various denominations. The so-called "devotional feasts" or "feasts of ideas" from the Middle Ages were not retained, nor were new feasts accepted.

For Luther and the other Reformers, festive days and seasons have a merely pedagogical value; "We can be sure of salvation without Easter and Pentecost and, as Paul

---

[36] Cf. P. Plank, Der Sonntag in den östlichen Kirchen. Österliches Erleben im Erhoffen, Hören und Schauen. In: A. M. Altermatt / T. A. Schnitker / W. Heim (eds.): Der Sonntag. Anspruch – Wirklichkeit – Gestalt (FS Jakob Baumgartner), Würzburg – Fribourg 1986, 175-186.

[37] Schulz, Liturgie, Tagzeiten und Kirchenjahr 73.

[38] Cf. the classification of feasts and the various quantities of liturgical texts in Edelby, Liturgikon 563-569; Schulz, Liturgie, Tagzeiten und Kirchenjahr 75f.

teaches, we cannot be damned because of Easter, Pentecost, Sunday or Friday".[39] All feasts for which no scriptural warrant can be found are to be abolished; but the feasts commemorating Christ are to be retained, even when these feasts were, according to contemporary understanding Marian feasts such as the Presentation (*Mariä Lichtmeß*) and the Annunciation of the Lord (*Annuntiationis Mariae*).

In a visitation charter drawn up by Luther and Melanchthon in 1528 the list of feasts comprises "apart from the Sundays the following feasts of Christ: Christmas Day, The Circumcision, Epiphany, Easter, Ascension, and Pentecost. Further, the three Marian days, Purification, Annunciation and Visitation along with St John, St Michael, Apostles days and St Mary Magdalene, to the extent to which they had not already fallen into disuse".[40] This list became the canon not only for the Lutheran Churches of the sixteenth century, but also influenced the calendar in the book of Common Prayer of 1549 which added the Holy Innocents and All Saints. Schulz suggests[41] the influence of the Roman Ember Days in the Reformed Swiss celebration of the Lord Supper once in each of the four seasons. The greater retention of elements of the traditional Church year in the Lutheran reform is connected with the fact that "Luther, who at first argued for preaching based on a continuous reading of Scripture, decided to base this preaching on the traditional pericopes already provided. Since the gospel at Mass was read and commented on in the vernacular, the gospel pericopes attained a particular importance as the dominating element proper to each Sunday and feast."[42]

The purpose of a Reformed Sanctoral was to illustrate the Gospel as lived out in the lives of martyrs and saints; the actual liturgical celebration, however, very quickly gave way to a transfer to the private, pedagogical and historical spheres so that from then on the currency of lives of saints and martyrs – "purified" for a Protestant audience and including Protestant martyrs of the Reformation era – was as edifying Bibliography. This no longer influenced the form of the liturgy. The Anglican Church alone possessed a Sanctoral. It was only in the nineteenth century that a Protestant calendar of saints was once more compiled in German-speaking regions.[43] In this the Prussian Agenda of 1822 marked the resumption of the Reformed tradition of the sixteenth century. Other feasts, however, had been added such as Reformation Day (31st October) and "Eternity Sunday" (*Ewigkeitssonntag*), introduced in 1816 by the king of Prussia on the Sunday before the first Sunday of Advent as a day of remembrance of the dead. In addition there was the Day of Penance and Prayer (*Buß- und Bettag*) on the Wednesday before "Eternity Sunday", introduced to Germany only in the nineteenth century.

Bibliography

S. Ben-Chorin, Die Feste des jüdischen Jahres, ThPQ 125 (1977) 158-164.

R. Berger, Ostern und Weihnachten. Zum Grundgefüge des Kirchenjahres, Alw 8 (1963) 1-20.

R. Berger, Jahr der Kirche – Jahr des Herrn, Gottesdienst 10 (1976) 164f.

K. F. Ginzel, Handbuch der Chronologie. 2 vols., Leipzig 1906/1914, Reprint Leipzig 1958.

---

[39]   Luther, writing in his tract "Von den Konziliis und Kirchen" of 1539, WA 50, 559, 6-9 quoted from Schulz, Ordnung 4.
[40]   Schulz, Ordnung 7.
[41]   Cf. Schulz, Ordnung 9-11: "The Four Seasons Rhythm"
[42]   Schulz, Ordnung 12.
[43]   Cf. Schulz, Ordnung 14-18.

Ph. Harnoncourt, Der Kalendar: Gottesdienst der Kirche 6,1. Feiern im Rhythmus der Zeit II/1, Regensburg 1994, 9-63.

J. A. Jungmann, Das kirchliche Fest nach Idee und Grenze: Th. Filthaut / J. A. Jungmann (eds.), Verkündigung und Glaube (FS F. X. Arnold), Freiburg i. Br. 1958, 164-184.

G. Kunze, Die gottesdienstliche Zeit: K. Müller / W. Blankenburg, Leiturgia. Handbuch des evangelischen Gottesdienstes I, Kassel 1954, 437-534.

P. Plank, Zeitrechnung und Festdatierung als ökumenisches Problem: HOK II, Düsseldorf 1989, 182-191.

F. Schulz, Die Ordnung der liturgischen Zeit in den Kirchen der Reformation, LJ 32 (1982) 1-14.

H. J. Schulz, Liturgie, Tagzeiten und Kirchenjahr des byzantinischen Ritus: HOK II, Düsseldorf 1989, 30-100.

6.2. SUNDAY AS THE WEEKLY PASSOVER, THE CHRISTIAN WEEK AND EMBER DAYS

6.2.1. SUNDAY

According to the Constitution on the Liturgy, Sunday is the original feast-day of the Church received from apostolic tradition and the kernel of the whole liturgical year. [44]

On Sunday the weekly remembrance of Christ's resurrection is celebrated. Sunday is the "Lord's Day". The dignity of Sunday is derived completely from the Paschal mystery: "Easter is, in fact, from the beginning only Sunday writ large". [45]

A. The Week

The weekly celebration of the memorial of the resurrection presupposes the existence of the week as a division of time. While the day is marked by the cycle of light and darkness, the month by the lunar cycle and the year by the changing seasons, these are natural divisions of time unlike the week which is a purely social invention and as such differently organised in different cultures. The Mesopotamian and Jewish weeks – and, following these, the Christian week – were of seven days, while the Roman week had eight, the Chinese ten and other cultures from Africa, to Southeast Asia and Central America, weeks of from three to six days. The weekly rhythm is determined either by the repetition of certain activities, e.g. market days, or by the return in a regular cycle of a day marked by a religious accent. In Israel the Sabbath determines the weekly cycle of seven days. [46] According to Müller "the seven-day week with a weekly return of a day of rest is the very particular gift of the people of Israel to the human race, even if a Graeco-Roman planetary week made its reception easier". [47]

Weekdays in the Greek cultural sphere were named after five planets – plus the sun and the moon – which in Babylonian astrology were already adored as gods, thus

---

[44] Cf. SC 106.
[45] J.A. Jungmann, Das kirchliche fest nach Idee und Grenze: Th. Filthaut / J.A. Jungmann (eds.), Verkündigung und Glaube (FS F.X. Arnold), Freiburg i.Br. 1958, 164-184. 167.
[46] Cf. Auf der Maur, Feiern im Rhythmus der Zeit I, 19f.
[47] A. Müller, Sonntagstheologie von unten. Der Sonntag im Beziehungsfeld zwischen Anthropologie, Soziologie und Theologie: A. M. Altermatt / T. A. Schnitker / W. Heim (eds.), Der Sonntag. Anspruch – Wirklichkeit – Gestalt (FS J.Baumgartner), Würzburg-Fribourg 1986, 236-247.237.

establishing the seven-day scheme still evident in the European names: Saturn (Saturday) – Sun (Sunday) – Moon (Monday, *Lundi, Montag*) – Mars (*Mardi, Martedi*) – Mercury (*Mercredi, Mercoledi*) – Jupiter (*Jeudi, Giovedi*) – Venus (*Vendredi, Venerdi*). This planetary week is clearly discernible only in the first century after Christ, which leads Rordorf to the opinion that, since no other seven-day cycle was known before then, the Graeco-Roman planetary week developed from the Jewish seven-day week. [48] Before the Christian mission had introduced them to the legacy of Jewish theology and spirituality of the Sabbath, the Gentile-Christian communities had already come into contact with the Jewish seven-day week by way of the planetary week.

B. The Sabbath

The Sabbath [49], the origins of which lie so far back in Israel's history that they can no longer be clearly reconstructed, underwent a thematic change during the Babylonian Exile: up to then it was primarily a day of rest and as such a social institution (cf. Ex 23.12; 34.21). With the Exile however, the Sabbath and Sabbath rest were primarily referred to Jahweh, without the abandonment of the anthropological-social dimension. Since he himself had rested on the seventh day (Ex 20.8-11), God had established the day of rest as part of the order of Creation; observance of the Sabbath rest is an expression of faithfulness to the Covenant (Ex 31.12-17) and there are hints of the commemoration of the great deeds of God which is to be observed on the Sabbath (Dt 5.12-15). Since the time of Jesus the Sabbath is also an expression of the eschatological hope connected to the coming of the Messiah. Since the Exile the Sabbath is marked by the coming together of the liturgical assembly. Flavius Josephus called the synagogue the *sabbataion,* indeed the Sabbath possibly contributed to the emergence of the synagogue itself.

Until the final break with Judaism the Jewish-Christian communities observed the Sabbath, though this was never the case among the Gentile-Christian communities. With the third or fourth centuries came a new appreciation of the Sabbath, particularly in the East: fasting was forbidden on that day and, by means of a liturgical assembly, it had a special character as a day of commemoration of the Creation, alongside the commemoration on Sunday of the day of Redemption through the Cross and Resurrection of Christ. [50] The Sabbath had a connection with the Paschal events. It was, of course, the day on which Christ's body rested in the tomb, but his soul was in the underworld, announcing his resurrection to those waiting there. [51] Thus, Saturday is Sunday's brother and shares in the joy of the resurrection. [52] This particularly Eastern form of veneration of Saturday never became part of Western piety but, rather, in the context of the question of fasting became a strongly contested point of controversy between East and West, since the latter – as demonstrated as early as Innocent I – fasted on Saturday. Fasting on Saturday was a weekly recapitulation of Holy Saturday and with it an extension of

---

[48]   Cf. Rordorf, Der Sonntag 36f.

[49]   On the Sabbath cf. Auf der Maur, Feiern im Rhythmus der Zeit I, 28-35.

[50]   Today, this appreciation of the Sabbath is most marked in the Ethiopian Church. Cf. E. Hammerschmidt, Stellung und Bedeutung des Sabbats in Äthiopien, Stuttgart 1963.

[51]   Cf. the priest's prayer at the Great Entry in the Liturgy of St John Chrysostom, Kallis 104: "With the body you were in the tomb, with the soul as God in the realm of the dead, in paradise with the thief and enthroned as Christ, with the Father and the Spirit, fulfilling all, O Thou immeasurable One."

[52]   Cf. G. Schreiber: Die Wochentage im Erleben der Ostkirche und des christlichen Abendlandes. Köln – Opladen 1959, esp. 219f.

the Good Friday fast which lasted until the Easter Vigil.[53] Rordorf explains the lack of an observance of the Sabbath and of Sabbath piety in the West by suggesting that in the post-Constantinian era Sunday itself had become the actual Christian "Sabbath".[54]

C. The Names for Sunday

The oldest references to Sunday are found in the New Testament itself.[55] However varied the origins "of this specifically Christian institution" may be, it can be said with certainty that "the celebration of Sunday is anchored in the Paschal event to the extent that later, in very different communities and at different times, it was inspired by the resurrection or the appearance of the risen Lord on the first day after the Sabbath".[56]

The oldest name for Sunday is "the first day after the Sabbath". This term links the resurrection of Christ with the first day of Creation, the primeval creation of light with the beginning of the light of Christ in the resurrection. In the tradition of Syria and Asia Minor the term "Lord's Day" (kyriaké heméra, dies dominica) emerged, a term in which the linguistic proximity to "The Lord's Supper" (kyriakón deipnon) is palpable. "The Lord whose name is borne by the day is not the Father or the Triune God: it is Christ, the crucified and risen Son of God. The Lord's Day means nothing other than Christ's Day."[57] This reference is still found in many European languages, thus in the kyriaki of New Greek, in the French dimanche, the Italian domenica and the Spanish domingo. One term which hardly impinges on modern consciousness is the "eighth day" which has an eschatological ring: the eighth day, the last Day of the Lord which has no evening is still to come; it will come when the world's time has run out, the world whose week is begun again and again by the Lord's Day. That these Lord's days which will follow one another until the Lord comes again are stamped by the resurrection is evidenced by the use of the term "Resurrection Day" (anastasimos heméra) by many Greek theologians and which has survived down to the present day in the Russian word for Sunday Voskresseniye, literally, the resurrection. The German and English words, Sonntag and Sunday go back to the name used in the Graeco-Roman planetary week, but were referred to Christ as the "Sun of Justice" (cf. Mal 3:20).[58] This reference allowed even the Fathers of the Church to adopt without scruple the pagan term for the day of the sun.[59]

D. The Sunday Eucharist

It is not possible to describe the earliest celebrations of Sunday with any accuracy. However, Paul's great esteem for the Lord's Supper, as reflected in 1Cor 11.17-34, may have influenced how Christians celebrated. It "is scarcely to be doubted that he had Sunday in mind, when in the A.D. 112, Pliny the Younger, governor of the province of Bithynia, reported to the Emperor Trajan that it was the practice of Christians to assemble for

---

[53] Cf. Jungmann. Beginnt der Woche mit Sonntag? 227.
[54] Cf. Rordorf, Der Sonntag 151.
[55] Cf. Auf der Maur, Feiern im Rhythmus der Zeit I, 36-38.
[56] Auf der Maur, Feiern im Rhythmus der Zeit I, 39.
[57] A. Heinz, Der Tag den der Herr gemacht hat. Gedanken zur Spiritualität des Sonntags: ThGl 68 (1978) 40-61. 41.
[58] Cf. Adam, Kirchenjahr 38-42; Auf der Maur, Feiern im Rhythmus der Zeit I 46f.
[59] Cf. Heinz, Der Tag 43f. Heinz quotes St Jerome: "If the Lord's Day is called the Day of the Sun by the pagans we are glad to accept this name: for today [Jerome is speaking of Easter] the Light of the World has risen, today the Sun of Justice has risen, under whose wings is salvation."

worship on a fixed day".[60] The *Didache* explicitly attests to the Eucharist on Sunday: "Gather on the Lord's Day, break the bread and give thanks, having confessed your sins beforehand so that your sacrifice may be pure."[61] The Eucharist is also clearly assigned to Sunday by Justin Martyr and by Hippolytus of Rome.

The ideal of a single eucharistic assembly of the local Church on Sunday was current until the later Middle Ages; here the whole Church gathered round its Lord was visibly presented, in keeping with a prescription of the *Didaskalia* from the third century: "Instruct the people by rules and by exhortations to attend the assembly regularly and never to be absent. They ought always to be present so that the Church may not be diminished by their absence and the body of Christ deprived of none of it members."[62]

This unity was protected in the Middle Ages by the strict obligation to attend the parish Mass in one's own parish church, an obligation which was not relaxed until the year 1517 by Pope Leo X following agitation by the mendicant orders. From then on it was possible to fulfil one's Sunday obligation outside one's own parish community, namely by attending Mass in a Franciscan or Dominican church. The obligation to take part in Mass on Sunday was no longer ordered towards the representation of the ecclesial reality as the eucharistic assembly gathered around the altar, no longer the coming together of the community for the Supper of the Lord, but the fulfilment of a command to worship God (*religio*) laid down in natural law and anchored in the Ten Commandments. "But the ancient pattern of the parish Mass long continued to be influential. The prohibition of bination on Sundays which was consistently maintained for a long time is partly explained by the desire not to fragment into several Masses, the single liturgical assembly of the parish community around the altar of the mother church."[63] Nevertheless the ideal of single Sunday parish Mass was lost in a modern pastoral practice geared towards the salvation of the individual. The command of the ancient Church to take part in the eucharistic assembly so that the (local) Church could display its true image, was changed to an obligation to "attend" just any Mass on a Sunday. "Sunday Masses were multiplied to offer all the most convenient opportunity of fulfilling their 'Sunday obligation'. Participation at the Sunday liturgy was widely understood individualistically as the weekly occasion for every person "to attend on God and to his soul".[64] The shortage of priests can be fruitful to the extent that the multiplicity of Sunday Masses will have to be reduced to a single Mass set in the "framework" of the Liturgy of the Hours. Indeed this reduction can appeal to the Constitution on the Liturgy: "One goal is to aim for a growth in the sense of community in the parish by means of the communal celebration of the Sunday Mass" (SC 42).

What do we know about the time of the Sunday assembly? John's placing of Easter (John 20:19-29) can be taken as an indication, "that the Johannine communities of Asia Minor gathered on the evening of the first or the eighth day to celebrate the eucharistic meal". The two times for assembly mentioned in Pliny's letter, one in the morning during which a song (*carmen*) was sung to Christ as God, and one in the evening, at which one came together for a common meal, are not clearly identifiable as the Lord's

---

[60]   Heinz, Der Tag 48.
[61]   Didache 14,1 – Wengst (ed.) 86f.
[62]   Didaskalia II,59, quoted from Heinz, Der Tag 51.
[63]   Heinz, Der Tag 52.
[64]   Heinz, Der Tag 50.

Supper, as agape or as morning praise. Against this, Justin in his description of the Eucharist, seems to place it in the morning of Sunday - a day not yet a day of rest – when he says that the reading from the Scriptures should continue for as long as the time allows. Hipploytus also indicates Sunday morning as the time for the liturgy. Finally, the morning celebration of the Eucharist and Vespers in the evening are "the two great constants which stamped Sunday worship in the Churches of East and West from the third or fourth centuries". [65] It is the "third hour" which was mentioned about the year 530 in Rome and spreading out from there in Gaul increasingly as an express regulation. [66] Later the time of Mass was tied up with the times for the shorter offices of the Liturgy of the Hours. Towards the end of the Middle Ages the tendency was to celebrate Mass later than at the third hour, but an attempt was made to remain true to tradition by celebrating Mass after the office of None on fast days and on ordinary days after Sext. The "anticipation" of the small hours by their transfer to the morning enabled the morning celebration of Mass to take place at a later hour. Johannes Burchard's rules of 1502 which were incorporated in the Missal of 1570, provided that Mass on Sundays and feastdays should follow Terce, on lesser feasts and weekdays, Sext and on penitential days should follow None. Since the midday and afternoon offices had by now been transferred to the morning, the effect of this was that Mass was always in the morning. [67] With the modern era came a greater liberalisation of the timing of Mass a development connected with the fact that "now the boundaries between a public and private Mass is becoming increasingly blurred". [68] In particular, the upheavals in society in the nineteenth and twentieth centuries reinforced this liberalisation and made pastoral considerations uppermost in the timing of Masses. The Code of Canon Law of 1917 still instructed that Mass could only be celebrated in the morning, [69] but against the background of the Second World War evening Mass was permitted. The timing of Mass is not longer prescribed nor is its celebration linked to any of the offices of the Liturgy of the Hours. [70]

E. The Obligation to Participate in the Sunday Liturgy

Attendance at the Sunday liturgy was taken for granted by the first Christians; on the other hand the Letter to the Hebrews (10:25) is already warning those who stay away. In the ancient Church the spectrum ranged from New Testament warnings to absentees to the zeal of the North African martyrs at Abitinae who at the beginning of the fourth century and in the face of dangers of every kind confessed themselves unable to live without the *dominicum*, the Lord's Supper on Sunday. [71] In the beginning there was no "Sunday obligation" any more than Sunday was a day of rest; both were parallel developments.

---

[65]   Cf. Auf der Maur, Feiern im Rhythmus der Zeit I, 39f.
[66]   Cf. Jungmann MSI, 323. The practice on fast days was different. Ambrose is already familiar with evening Masses on these days, and "in Carolingian times the Mass at the ninth hour just as much an established practice as that at the third hour on other days", op. cit. supra 324f.
[67]   Cf. Jungmann MS I, 324f.; Meyer, Eucharistie 514.
[68]   Jungmann MS I, 325.
[69]   Can.821§1 states that Mass may not be celebrated earlier than one hour before sunrise and not later than 1 p.m. in the afternoooon.
[70]   Cf. Jungmann MS I, 372f.; Meyer, Eucharistie 515.
[71]   Cf. Adam, Kirchenjahr 37.

In 321 A.D. the Emperor Constantine ordered judges, town-dwellers and all the gainfully employed, with the exception of farmer, to abstain from work on Sundays. In 337 attendance at the liturgy was made obligatory in law for all Christian soldiers. This meant that soldiers were excused duty to attend the liturgy while pagan soldiers were obliged at the same time to pray together to their own gods, in other words to worship on Sunday as the day of Christian observance. Abstinence from, servile work analogous to the Jewish Sabbath rest did not yet play any role, so that the granting of freedom from work was more likely based on social and political grounds – religious peace in the Empire. [72]

Despite all warnings and instructions, absenteeism remained the problem. The provincial Council of Elvira in Spain, about the year 300, decreed that any person living in a town who did not come to church for three Sundays, should be temporarily excommunicated, to make it clear that he had been disciplined. Many later synods imitated this rule, for example those of the Gallo-frankish Church, which also emphasised the importance of attending the whole Mass and this in one's own parish church. From the sixth century on the sanctification of Sunday by abstinence from work played an increasing role. In 538 the provincial Council of Orelans was the first official Church body to demand this. Despite all alleged distancing from Jewish Sabbath legislation, "there is a growing impression of Sunday as an extension of the Old Testament Sabbath laws, which the ancient church had so vehemently resisted". [73]

All of these obligations were still, however, disciplinary in character and were not yet understood as binding under pain of sin in the sense of a later moral theology. This began to change in the period of High Scholasticism when, with reference to the Third Commandment, emphasis was placed on the sanctification of Sunday as man's religious obligation. But still, the Sunday obligation in the modern understanding of a duty, under pain of mortal sin, to attend Sunday Mass, was unknown... "It is the doubtful achievement of the post-Scholastic period from the middle of the fifteenth century, to have furthered attendance at the liturgy on Sundays and on feasts by means of a general commandment of the Church, binding under pain of mortal sin." [74] The first to press this view was the Dominican archbishop, Antoninus of Florence (d. 1459). In the sixteenth century it became a generally accepted opinion that missing Sunday Mass was a serious sin. In the era of the Counterreformation this notion was reinforced by Peter Canisius when in his *Catechismus minimus* he placed the commandments of the Church on a par with the Commandments of God. Nevertheless, it should not be overlooked that in the formal legal sense, the Sunday obligation was not introduced until 1917 with Canon 1248 of the Code of Canon Law. [75]

F. The Overshadowing of the Easter Character of Sunday

In contrast to the "once more clearly recognised Easter character of Sunday, its celebration for a thousand years was stamped more by the mystery of the Trinity. Up to the recent past, the model or quintessential Sunday in popular imagination was not Easter

---

[72]   Cf. Auf der Maur, Feiern im Rhythmus der Zeit I, 41.43. Rordorf, Der Sonntag 160-165, suggests that the imperial decrees are to be understood not just in terms of the Christian Sunday, but also of the cult of the sun which was widespread in the Roman Empire and for which Sunday was also the weekly feast.
[73]   Adam, Kirchenjahr 43.
[74]   Auf der Maur, Feiern im Rhythmus der Zeit I, 42.
[75]   Cf. Auf der Maur, Feiern im Rhythmus der Zeit I, 41-43.

Sunday, but Trinity Sunday."[76] In this development the Preface of the Holy Trinity, which Clement XIII prescribed in 1759 as the regular preface for Advent and for all of the time after Pentecost, played a key role. It had emerged in Spain in the sixth or seventh century when the residual hostility of Germanic Arianism made it necessary to provide in the celebration of Mass an expression of true Trinitarain belief. Originally intended for the first Sunday after Pentecost, which was first introduced for the whole Church in 1334 by John XXII, as Trinity Sunday, the preface of this feast was sung on the Sundays after Pentecost since these Sundays did not have proper prefaces.[77] No less influential was the weekly Mass-series of Alcuin (d. 803), Charlemagne's court theologian, which assigned the votive Mass *in honorem s. Trinitatis* complete with the preface of the Holy Trinity, to Sunday. The Mass of the Trinity became the regular Mass formulary between Pentecost and Advent. It is reported that Bishop Ulrich of Augsburg (d. 973) celebrated an early Mass *de ss. Trinitate* on Easter Day and only then celebrated the main Mass as that of Easter. Even Protestant orders of communion from the time of the Reformation attest that the Mass of the Trinity continued to be the usual formulary for the Sunday liturgy *per annum*. Long after the Council of Trent the custom – still usual in Protestantism – continued of naming the Sundays "after Trinity" (*post Trinitatis*).[78]

But it was not only Trinitarian piety that clouded the vision of the Easter dimension of Sunday. The further development of the liturgical year, for example by the introduction of feasts celebrating a theological idea, as well as the constantly growing number of feasts of saint, endangered the Easter character of the Sunday celebration; indeed Sunday as the weekly Passover vanished completely when these feasts fell on a Sunday. In the allocation of feasts in the Missal of 1570 a large number of Sundays throughout the year could be dropped in favour of the saints' days, for example the minor Sundays (*dominicae minores*) i.e. all Sundays except those of Advent, of the four weeks before Lent and of Lent itself. In the past, until the revised Code of Rubrics of 1960, Sunday could be displaced, so that there was a danger that the vision of Sunday as the weekly commemoration of Christ's Easter victory could be lost from view.[79]

G. Sunday in the Renewed Liturgy

Sunday as the weekly Passover is the day on which the whole community celebrates the Eucharist. According to No.106 of the Constitution on the Liturgy all who believe in Christ are obliged to assemble (*in unum convenire debent*) for the Eucharist on this primal feastday (*primordialis dies festus*), an obligation correctly understood by Hollerweger as more moral that juridical.[80] More, the obligation is an "ontological assertion" and is included as such in the form of the Sunday obligation in the Code of Canon Law of 1983: it is a self-evident feature of being a Christian that the Passover of the Lord should be celebrated with other believers in order to find there the source of one's life.

---

[76] A.Heinz, Trinitarische und österliche Aspekte in der Sonntagsfrömmigkeit des Mittlealters. Zeugnisse aus Liturgie und volksfrommen Beten: A. M. Altermatt / T. A. Schnitker / W. Heim (eds.), Der Sonntag. Anspruch-Wirklichkeit-Gestalt (FS J. Baumgartner), Würzburg-Fribourg 1986, 82-98.82.

[77] Cf. op. cit.supra 83f.

[78] Cf. op. cit.infra 84-86.

[79] Cf. H. Hollerweger, Der Sonntag in der vom II.Vatikanum erneuerten Liturgie. Das Zeugnis der Dokumente: A. M. Altermatt / T. A. Schnitker / W. Heim (eds.), Der Sonntag. Anspruch – Wirklichkeit – Gestalt (FS J. Baumgartner), Würzburg-Fribourg 1986, 99-112.101.

[80] Cf. Hollerweger, Der Sonntag 102/

Without this coming-together the individual Christian suffers as does the community as a whole. The day of the Eucharist is the day of the weekly Passover, Sunday, and for this reason it has an ecclesiological and soteriological significance which can hardly be exaggerated. Believers must commemorate (anamnetically) the death and resurrection of the Lord in order to be able to live from his saving deeds. This commemoration happens pre-eminently in the Sunday assembly, "on that day of the week on which the Lord rose from the dead on which, according to apostolic tradition, the Easter mystery is celebrated in a special way in the Eucharist". [81] Because of their connection with the Passover, the yearly Easter, but also Sunday as the weekly Passover, are the preferred season and days for the celebration of Baptism. [82] This Easter character of Sunday, the final retrieval of which was based on the Constitution on the Liturgy, has led to the overcoming of the pre-conciliar Trinitarian accent especially of the Sundays outside the great liturgical seasons. [83]

For this reason, the Constitution on the Liturgy decreed that no other feast could displace Sunday "unless this feast was of the highest importance; for the Lord's Day is the foundation and kernel of the whole liturgical year" (SC 106). Because of the particular significance of Sunday, only a solemnity or feast of the Lord can replace it, "but the Sundays of Advent, Lent and Easter rank before all feasts of the Lord and before all solemnities. Solemnities that fall on one of these Sundays are to be anticipated on the previous Saturday." [84] There are four exceptions to this principle that a feast may not replace the Sunday: the Sunday in the Octave of Christmas, i.e. the Feast of the Holy Family; the Sunday after 6th January, the Feast of the Baptism of the Lord; the Sunday after Pentecost as the Feast of the Holy Trinity, and then the last Sunday of the year, the Solemnity of Christ the King. [85]

Sunday today is less endangered by the Church's Calendar of feasts than it is by its exploitation – for however well-meaning motives – to highlight certain themes or causes [usually connected with a collection]: "If there is no longer any great threat from feasts of ideas or of saints, the so-called 'thematic Sundays' are filling what is perceived as a lacuna". [86] Von Arx names a frightening list of such Sundays in the German-speaking countries alone, stretching from the "World Day of Peace" through the "World Day of Religious Vocations", "Caritas Sunday" to "Adveniat Sunday" in Advent. To suit these various themes and intentions, liturgical texts are prepared by official and semi-official Church sources, which are appropriate for the topic in question but which displace the Sunday celebration. "The Missal itself began the process of replacing the Sunday texts with its own thematic Mass formulas. Thus, it instructs that the Mass for the Spread of the Gospel, 'is to be used on Mission Sunday'." [87] Von Arx recommends that to keep at least the Mass free from such themes, thus enabling it to preserve its own proper theme which is the death and resurrection of the Lord, these themes and intentions should be

---

[81]   The Instruction "Eucharisticum Mysterium" of 25th May 1967 no. 25. - Kaczynski 923.
[82]   Cf. Ordo Baptismi parvulorum, Praenot. 9 – Kaczynski 1820.
[83]   Cf. Hollerweger, Der Sonntag 103.
[84]   NUALC 5 – Kaczynski 1276.
[85]   Cf. NUALC 6 – Kaczynski 1277.
[86]   Cf. W. v. Arx, Der Sonntag und die Zwecksonntage. Die Verbindung aktueller Anliegen mit der Sonntagsliturgie: A. M. Altermatt / T. A. Schnitker / W. Heim (eds.), Der Sonntag. Anspruch – Wirklichkeit – Gestalt (FS J. Baumgartner), Würzburg-Fribourg 1986, 127-138.127.
[87]   Ibid. 129.

transferred to other liturgical contexts such as Liturgies of the Word, Devotions etc.[88] But does this thematization of Sunday destroy it as the *day* of the Lord? Must every intention of the Church, however justified, legitimate and even necessary, find a liturgical expression? Would it not suffice simply to announce the purpose of the collection at the offertory at Sunday Mass?

But with this a further set of problems is mentioned, the virtual monopoly of the Sunday liturgy by the Eucharist. To enable the faithful to fulfil their Sunday obligation or to make this as convenient as possible the original single Sunday Mass was multiplied.[89] The (re-)introduction of evening Mass and the Vigil Mass[90] led to such a plethora of Masses that neither the time nor the energy remained for the full celebration of the other services of the liturgy, in particular of the Liturgy of the Hours. The result, for the greater part, was a eucharistic monoculture of many Masses, which made virtually impossible the ecclesiologically highly relevant but also experientially not inconsiderable ancient Christian ideal of the single eucharistic "general assembly of the people of God"[91] in the parish. This eucharistic monoculture must be seriously questioned if a theologically and pastorally convincing liturgical culture of Sunday is to be retrieved.

6.2.2. THE WEEK

The weekdays are sanctified by the Liturgy of the Hours. The *Didache* already attests to the marking of Wednesdays and Friday by fasting,[92] which was the general custom until the fourth century.[93] Except in Egypt and Rome the weekday fast ended with a celebration of the Eucharist; this was also celebrated in Antioch on the Christian Sabbath. Augustine is a witness for daily Mass in Africa at the end of the fourth and beginning of the fifth centuries, Chrysostomos the same for Constantinople, and there are witnesses for the practice in Gaul for the sixth century. For a long time Rome preserved the non-eucharistic character of the weekdays and it is only from the eighth century that daily Mass became usual there.

The marking of Wednesday and Friday by fasting is the beginning of an Easter thematization of the days of the week: Wednesday is the day of betrayal, Friday the day of crucifixion, Sunday the day of resurrection. Innocent I explained the custom in the West of fasting on Saturday by linking it also with Christ's sufferings: in contrast to the East where Saturday has an Easter character the emphasis here is on the sorrow of the Apostles In Rome there were no formularies for weekday Masses except for those on

---

[88] Cf. ibid. 134.

[89] Cf. Meyer, Eucharistie 507f. A second reason mentioned by Meyer which was particularly imporatnt in the nineteenth and twentieth centuries – though never a legal obligation – was the notion that daily celebration of Mass was part of priestly piety.

[90] Daily evening Mass was permitted by Pius XII on 19th March 1957 in the Motuproprio "Sacram communionen". Cf. AAS 49 (1957) 177f. On the Vigil Mass, cf. the Instruction "Eucharisticum Mysterium" of 25th May 1967, no.28 – in Kraczynski 926. Though opposed to the Vigil Mass, an article by G. May contains valuable references to Bibliography concerning it: G.May, Die Erfüllung der Feiertagspflicht des Meßbesuchs am Vorabend der Sonn – und Feiertage: ThPQ 116 (1968) 148-165.

[91] Thus F. Kohlschein, Bewußte, tätige und fruchtbringende Teilnahme. Das Leitmotiv der Gottesdienstreform als bleibender Maßstab: Th. Maas-Ewerd (ed.): Lebt unser Gottesdienst? 54.

[92] Didache 8,1 – ed. Wengst 78/79: Your fastdays ought to have nothing in common with those of the hypocrites! They fast on Monday and Thursaday; but you should fast on Wednesday and Friday."

[93] Cf. Jungmann, Beginnt die christliche Woche mit Sonntag? 24-226.

Ember days and Lent. Alcuin (d. 803) composed 21 formularies for ferial days without assigning them to any fixed day of the week, but this happened soon afterwards. But in this process, it was only on Friday that the salvation-history perspective was evident. In the twelfth century Honorius of Autun in his *Gemma animae* offered a salvation-history view of the week. Other series were inspired by different themes such as the "subjective appropriation of salvation" or "the whole Christian scheme of salvation". The Missal of 1570 offered a series of votive Masses, but it was not until 1920 that these were assigned to specific days of the week. [94]

The notion in the East of Saturday as the "brother" of Sunday, which was based on a piety of Easter, was reflected slightly in the West by the Marian character of Saturday. The most important justification for regarding Saturday as Mary's day is found in Caesarius of Heisterbach (d.1240) and states: "In the universal hopelessness of Holy Saturday when Christ lay dead in the tomb, Mary alone clung to belief in her son's resurrection. The Marian devotion of Saturday can be understood only in the light of Sunday, the commemoration of the resurrection." [95]

For a long time, apart from Lent, Ember days and the later votive Masses, the Roman liturgy had no specific formularies for weekday Masses. If there were no feast and if one did not want to celebrate a votive Mass, then the formulary of the previous Sunday was used. This is still basically the case with the Missal of 1970, though this offers more possibilities for variation. [96] Missals in the various countries provide their own formularies for Masses on weekdays in ordinary time; the German Missal has four series each containing six ferial Masses, the second and fourth series being thematically arranged. [97] The Byzantine rite also has a weekly cycle, "that links every day of the week with the commemoration of a particular mystery, a saint or group of saints. Thus Sunday is dedicated to the commemoration of the Resurrection, Monday to the Holy Angels, Tuesday to St John the Baptist, Wednesday to the mystery of the Cross, Thursday to the Apostles, wonder-workers and bishops – especially St Nicholas. On Saturday are commemorated, confessors, martyrs, all the saints and all the dead." The Mother of God "is commemorated every day at every liturgy, in particular on Sunday, Wednesday and Friday because of her role in the mystery of the Redemption." [98]

6.2.3. QUARTERTENSE

Ember Days were peculiar to the Roman liturgy and spread with it. These are celebrations of the city of Rome whose origins cannot be clearly ascertained: they probably

---

[94] Incarnation (Sunday), Baptism (Monday), Nativity (Tuesday), Betrayal (Wednesday), Eucharist and Arrest (Thursday), Cross (Friday), Burial (Saturday), Resurrection (Sunday), Gemma animae 2,67 - PL 172, 640ff.; on all of this cf. Auf der Maur, Feiern im Rhythmus der Zeit I, 52f.

[95] Heinz, Der Tag 55f. Cf. also on this Jungmann, Beginnt die christliche Woche mit Sonntag? 230.

[96] Cf. GIRM 323: "On weekdays in ordinary time one may replace the prayers of the previous Sunday with those of another Sunday in ordinary time. The prayers in the Missal in the formularies of Masses for special intentions may also be chosen. It is always possible to use only the collect from one of these formularies."

[97] The themes of Week 2 are: The Church (Monday), Unity (Tuesday), Conversion and Healing (Wednesday), The Lord's Table (Thursday), The Sufferings of Christ (Friday), God's Eternal Covenant (Saturday); the themes of Week 4 are: Eternal Consummation (Monday), The Spread of the Gospel (Tuesday), Love of Neighbour (Wednesday), The Holy Spirit (Thursday), Redemption (Friday), Mary (Saturday).

[98] Edelby, Liturgikon 40.

go back to pagan sowing – and harvest-festivals.[99] They coincide roughly with the start of each of the four seasons and were commemorated by fasting and special liturgies on Wednesday, Friday and in the vigil of Saturday to Sunday. The 25 Quartertense sermons of Leo I (d. 461) show that the celebration of these days was an established custom in Rome in his time. A note in the sixth-century *Liber Pontificalis* says, indeed, that Callixtus I (217-222) had already ordered a fast on three Saturdays at the time of the wheat-, wine- and oil-harvests.[100] In the West, Quartertense consisted essentially in fasting on the Wednesday and Friday with a Mass on these days – unusal for Rome as these were weekdays – and with the celebration of the vigil of Saturday to Sunday. In the sixth century, Ember days in March were added to the existing days in Summer, September and December. The exact dating of all of these days was not finally fixed until a Roman synod under Gregory VII: the first week of Lent, the octave of Pentecost, and the weeks after the feast of the Exaltation of the Cross (14th September), and the feast of St Lucy (13th December). Since the fifth century the Ember days have been the preferred times for ordinations. On the Wednesdays and Fridays candidates were presented and examined, the actual ordination took place at the vigil Mass before the Sunday.[101] From the eighth century on the name *quattuor tempora* became normal and entered many European language, thus in French *Quatre-Temps* or the English Quarter-day/Quartertense or Ember-days.

The reform of the liturgical year has basically retained Quartertense. Bishops' conferences are responsible for "determining dates and the nature of the celebration", so that Ember-days "are actually appropriate to local and human realities".[102] The penitential character of the Quartertense liturgy is retained, though this should also be conscious of responsibility for one's neighbour and for the problems of the world.[103]

Bibliography

A. M. Altermatt / T. A. Schnitker/ W. Heim (edd), Der Sonntag. Anspruch-Wirklichkeit-Gestalt (FS Jakob Baumgartner), Würzburg-Fribourg 1986.

H. Auf der Maur, Feiern im Rhythmus der Zeit I: Herrenfeste in Woche und Jahr. GdK V, Regensburg 1983.

I. H. Dalmais, Le dimanche dans la liturgie byzantine, MD 46 (1956) 60-66.

P. Grelot, Du sabbat juif au dimanche chrétien 1. Enquête sur le sabbat juif, MD 123 (1975) 79-107.

P. Jounel, Le dimanche et la semaine: Martimort IV, Paris 1983, 23-41.

J. A. Jungmann, Beginnt die christliche Woche mit Sonntag? Ibid.: Gewordene Liturgie. Studien und Durchblicke, Innsbruck-Leipzig 1941, 206-231.

---

[99] Thus Auf der Maur, Feiern im Rhythmus der Zeit I, 54 citing G.Morin: L'Origine des Quatre-Temps. In: RBen 14 (1897) 337-346. The individual festivals are mentioned – the *feriae messis* – wheat-harvest (June/August), *feriae vindemiales* – wine-harvest (September) and the *feriae semantinae* – sowing (December). Cf. also Adam, Kirchenjahr 154-159.
[100] Cf. Adam, Kirchenjahr 155. Adam considers this note in the pontifical to be reliable.
[101] Cf. op.cit.supra, 153.
[102] NUALC 46 – Kaczynski 1317.
[103] Cf. Adam, Kirchenjahr 156-158 on the various suggestions from the German-speaking bishops' conferences for a renewed Quartertense liturgy.

J. A. Jungmann, Der liturgische Wochenzyklus. Ibid.: Liturgisches Erbe und pastorale Gegenwart. Studien und Vorträge, Innsbruck-Vienna-München 1960, 332-365.

G. Langgärtner, Erneuerung der Quatember. Anliegen. Modelle, Aktionen, Würzburg 1976.

M. Righetti, Manuale di storia liturgica II: "Anno Liturgico – Il Breviario. Milano 1955, 17-37: Il Ciclo settimanale.

W. Rordorf, Der Sonntag. Geschichte des Ruhe – und Gottesdiensttages im ältesten Christentum, Zürich 1962 (AThANT 43).

6.3. THE EASTER FESTIVE CYCLE

There are two "plateaux" in the liturgical year, the Easter and the Christmas cycles, each of which surrounds a central feast-day. "Christians and Easter celebrate the same thing. The same basic vision underlies both days: the glorification of the Lord". [104] At the same time, each of the cycles has its own specific meaning: "Obviously our attention will continue to focus above all on the Nativity at Christmas and on the Resurrection at Easter, but "above all" should not become "only". Accordingly, the liturgical year in its basic structure is nothing other than the constantly recurring celebration of the coming of the glorified Lord to his people." [105] This is confirmed by the fact that the feasts and seasons grew little by little, and that their origin is contained in the weekly commemoration of the Christ event in all its nuances and aspects in the celebration of Sunday as the weekly Passover: according to Jungmann, "From the beginning Easter is but Sunday writ large". [106]

6.3.1. JEWISH PASSOVER AND CHRISTIAN EASTER

The roots of the Hebrew word *pesach*, in Aramaic *pascha*, are obscure; the Greek translation of the Old Testament confirms the translation of the Hebrew verb *psh* as "(preserving) passing over", or "passing through". Thus *psh* is interpreted on the one hand as God's preserving passing over of the first-born of Israel in the last of the plagues of Egypt and on the other as the passage of the chosen people through the Red Sea. *Pesach* as the feast of deliverance from Egyptian slavery has a long pre-history: a pre-Israelite, nomad Spring festival with animal sacrifice and blood rites was "historicized", anchored in the religious history of Israel and transformed into a celebration of salvation history. Independently of the Pesach there existed the feast of Unleavened Bread (feast of *Mazzoth*); this was of agricultural origin and was celebrated at the beginning of the barley harvest. Israel adopted this feast when they took possession of the land, and transformed it, like the *Pesach*, into a celebration of the deliverance from Egypt, becoming an element of that commemoration. From the time of the reform of the cult under Hezekiah and Josiah, the laws governing the *Pesach* were regarded as an integral part of the Torah. Worship was centralised in the Temple at Jerusalem, thereby making the *Pesach* a pilgrimage festival of the whole people. After the Exile only the slaughter of animals took place in the Temple, the *Peasch* meal taking place in the family circle. At the time of Jesus the *Pesach* consisted in four elements: a) the clearing out of all

---

[104] Berger, Ostern und Weihnachten 17.
[105] op.cit.infra, 19.
[106] J.A.Jungmann, Das kirchliche Fest nach Idee und Grenze: Th.Filhaut / J.A.Jungmann (eds.), Verkündigung und Glaube (FS F.X. Arnold), Freiburg i. Br. 1958.

remaining leavened bread – this had to be completed by midday of 14th *Nisan*; b) the Temple sacrifice – at about three o'clock in the afternoon the lambs were slaughtered in the Temple; c) *Pesach* meal with the family or other group – the festive meal was rich in ritual, following ritually prescribed questions and answers concerning the meaning of the action the story of the Exodus (*Haggada*) was recounted, there were several blessings (*Berakoth*) and the praise psalms (Ps 113-118 & 136); d) on 15th *Nisan* the Feast of Unleavened Bread began; probably in Jesus's time only the first of the seven days was a festival on which the eating of the unleavened bread was obligatory. [107]

The New Testament makes a close connection between Christ's resurrection and the Israel's *Pesach* festival. The *Pesach* of the old covenant finds its fulfilment in Christ's Pasch as a passage through death and hell to glory. The deep-rootedness of the Christian Easter in the Jewish *Pesach* is indicated by the use of the slightly altered term "Pascha" for this feast in all European languages except German and English. [108] "Even if we do not possess any direct witness from the earliest times, it can be taken with virtual certainty that the apostolic Church was familiar with the feast of Easter." Reasons for this are: the early community continued to take part in the Jewish liturgy, thus also in the *Pesach*. The Synoptics present the Last Supper as a *Pesach* meal as well as Jesus's death on the cross at the hour of the slaughter of the lambs in the Temple in the context of the *Pesach*. The re-interpretation is obvious: the Christian *Pesach haggada* is the story of the suffering, death and resurrection of the Lord, the passage is now the Christ's *transitus* from heaven to earth, yes down to Hell (*descensus ad inferos*) and his return in the glory of the Father; liberation is the Redemption effected by Christ. In Christ is fulfilled what was foreshadowed mysteriously in the *Pesach* feast of the people of the old covenant. [109]

6.3.2. THE HISTORY OF THE CHRISTIAN CELEBRATION OF EASTER

The rooting of the Christian Easter in the Jewish *Pesach* is shown by the dispute over Easter in the second century, [110] which also casts a light on Sunday as the weekly Pasch.

Every week the commemoration of the resurrection was celebrated on the first day of the week; the question was should one celebrate the yearly Pasch on a day other than this holy day? Towards the end of the second century, the communities of Asia Minor – the so-called "Quartodecimans" – celebrated the Pasch to co-incide with the date of the Jewish *Pesach* on 14th *Nisan*, the day of the full moon of the first month of the Hebrew Spring, regardless of on what day of the week fell. Most Churches, however, celebrated the Pasch on the Sunday after the 14th *Nisan*. This dispute was settled by the Council of Nicea, at which the Sunday after the first full moon of Spring was prescribed for the universal Church. The practice of the Quartodecimans is distinguished from that of the rest of the Church also in that the former emphasises more the redeeming death,

---

[107] Cf. Auf der Maur, Feiern im Rhythmus der Zeit I, 56-63.

[108] As early as Bede the Venerable (d.735) there is a derivation of the terms "Ostern" or "Easter" from a putative Spring goddess Ostara. The truth is, though, that "Ostern" and "Easter" come from a mistranslation of "hebdomada in albis"; "in albis" was mistakenly read as a plural of "alba" to mean "red dawn", in Old High German, "eostarun". Cf. D.R.Moser, Bräuche und Feste im christlichen Jahreslauf, Graz-Vienna-Köln 1993, 211-216.

[109] Cf. Auf der Maur, Feiern im Rhythmus der Zeit I, 69.

[110] This is reported by Eusebius of Caesarea, Hist. Eccl. V.23-25 – SChr 41, 66-72.

the latter the resurrection and glorification of the Lord. [111] The separation of the date of the Christian from the Jewish Pasch was encouraged by new systems of reckoning the occurrence of 14th *Nisan*, such as in Rome and in Alexandria. Plank mentions in particular the chronological works of Bishop Anatolios of Laodicea (d.282), a native of Alexandria, according to whom the Christian Easter should always be celebrated after the Spring Equinox; this increased the difference in date from the Jewish Pasch. [112] Completely independently of a difference centred around dates, Talley sees, both the Quartodeciman and the Sunday Easter celebration essentially characterised by agreement on the content of the feast: the commemoration of the passion, resurrection and the expectation of the the coming again of the Lord. [113]

The celebration of this commemoration consisted in a single liturgy of a full vigil concluding with the Lord's Supper. Odo Casel interprets the Easter celebration as a commemoration of a *transitus* of the passing over of Christ from the realm of death into the realm of the fullness of God's life. The night watch was still completely marked by fasting and sadness, both of which were overcome in the joy of the Eucharist. The Easter celebration contained both sadness and joy, and was thus a re-living of the Resurrection as a passing over from death to life. For the catechumens, buried with Christ and rising with him in the Easter rites of initiation, the Easter celebration meant the sacramental re-living of this *transitus* (cf. Rom 6:1-14). It is not known when the rite of initiation became part of the Easter Vigil but it is already mentioned by Tertullian and by Hippolytus. [114] On the other hand it is suggested that it was only in the early fourth century that the Easter Vigil had become the annual night for baptism, although in the context of the *transitus* this connection was established from the beginning. [115]

According to Casel, the Easter celebration which is now stamped only by the joy of the Resurrection, is based on an historicizing re-living of the whole passion of Christ, which suggested itself most strongly and could develop in the pilgrimage centre that was Jerusalem. There, were also celebrated – as it were "on location" – Palm Sunday, Holy Thursday and, of course, Good Friday. The Easter celebration itself must have been influenced by these preceding celebrations: "It was not possible for this night still to be filled with the memory of the Lord's sufferings, with the mourning and sadness of the faithful, as was the case in the first three centuries. For the preceding days had so occupied them with memories of the Passion and swept them up into a re-living of this, that from now on Easter night could be dedicated almost exclusively to the commemoration of the Resurrection." [116]

The account by Egeria [117] shows particularly clearly how precisely in Jerusalem the commemoration "on location" led to the elaboration of a single Easter celebration encompassing all aspects of salvation, into the remembrance on the days preceding the main festival of the events on these days reported by the gospels. But elsewhere, too,

---

[111] Thus B. Lohse, Das Passafest der Quartadecimaner, Gütersloh 1953.

[112] Cf. Plank, Zeitrechnung und Festdatierung 186. Reference is made to the Ecclesiastical History of Eusebius of Caesarea (Hist.eccl. VII,32 – SChr 41, 225-227).

[113] Cf. Th. J. Talley: Liturgische Zeit in der Alten Kirche. Der Forschungsstand, LJ 32 (1982) 25-45.28

[114] Cf. B. Kleinheyer, Sakramentliche Feieren I. Die Feiern der eingliederung in die Kirche: GdK 7,1, Regensburg 1989, 42.

[115] Cf. Auf der Maur, Feiern im Rhythmus der Zeit I, 72f.

[116] O. Casel: Art und Sinn der ältesten christlichen Osterfeier. In: JLw 14 (1938) 1-78.78.

[117] Cf. Auf der Maur's tabular summary of Holy Week in Jerusalem in Feiern im Rhythmus der Zeit I, 78.

by the end of the fourth century the Easter Vigil had been expanded into the Sacred Triduum, to the three paschal days of Good Friday, Holy Saturday and Easter Sunday devoted to the Passion, Death and Resurrection. As already witnessed by the *Didascalia* and Tertullian, there had been an earlier Easter fast on Good Friday and Easter Saturday leading up to the celebration of the Easter Vigil. Jungmann even speaks of a *biduum* of penance inside the Paschal Triduum, forming a threshold to the joy of Easter Day. [118] The fast was justified by the notion of the Lord's sleeping in the tomb, but liturgically these days were not particularly marked. Ambrose and Augustine, though, speak already of a sacred triduum of the Crucified, Buried and Risen One, [119] although for them the actual "Pasch" was the Easter Vigil, which Augustine describes as *mater omnium vigilarum*. [120]

Out of the three days of Easter grew the "Great Week", which by the time of Egeria began on the Sunday before Easter with the commemoration of Jesus's entry into Jerusalem. This development led to the elaboration of special liturgical celebrations. Thus Augustine is familiar with a Good Friday liturgy at which the story of the Lord's Passion "is solemnly read". Auf der Maur suggests that Psalm 21 (22) was also part of this liturgy. [121]

Tertullian and the fasting regulations of Hippolytus show that the Pasch flows over into a fifty-day season of joy, into Pentecost. [122] While initially the exaltation of Christ as a whole was the object of the Easter celebration as of the following festive season, there later developed here too specific emphases during certain sections of Pentecost and an "historicizing" unfolding of the one mystery of salvation. The Easter Octave is known since the third century. During this week the mystogogical cathechesis of the newly-baptised took place, a liturgical instruction about what they had experienced at the Easter Vigil. Pentecost, the "fiftieth day" was originally the solemn close of the fifty-day season of joy, the days of which according to Ambrose "must be celebrated like those of Easter", since they "are like a single Sunday". [123] The whole Easter mystery is still expressed when, in Egeria as in Jerome, the "contents" of the feast on the fiftieth day are said to be, along with the sending of the Holy Spirit, the Ascension of Christ: this was before the fortieth day was reserved for the "historical" remembrance of the Ascension alone, which itself, just like the sending of the Holy Spirit, was taken out of the totality of the Paschal event. The fiftieth day eventually was celebrated only as the day of the sending of the Holy Spirit and with that the Easter character of the feast was completely forgotten, the day becoming a feast of the Holy Spirit with its own octave. [124]

If the Easter Vigil had once lasted from Saturday evening to Sunday morning, Jerome was protesting as early as 390 against tendencies to shorten the vigil whereby

---

[118] Cf. J.A. Jungmann: Beginnt die christliche Woche mit Sonntag? 227f.
[119] Ambrose, Ep.23,13 – PL 16,1030: "Triduum illud ssacrum "intra quod triduum et passus est et quievit et resurrexit." Augustine, Ep. 55,24 – CSEL 34/2, 195: "Sacratissimum triduum crucifixi, sepulti et suscitati."
[120] Sermo 219 – PL 38, 1088.
[121] Cf. Auf der Maur, Feiern im Rhythmus der Zeit I, 77. Cf. W. Roetzer: Des hl. Augustinus Schriften als liturgiegeschichtliche Quelle. München 1930, 36-38.
[122] Tertullian, De Oratione 23,2 – CSEL 20, 196f.; Hippolytus, TradAp.33 – Geerlings (ed.) 288-290.
[123] Exp. Luc. 8,25 – PL 15, 1722f.: "Ergo per hos quinquaginta dies jejunium nescit Ecclesia, sicut Dominica qua Dominus resurrexit, et sunt omnes dies quamquam Dominica."
[124] Cf. Auf der Maur, Feiern im Rhythmus der Zeit I, 79-83.

it was already over before midnight. [125] In Rome in the sixth century, the celebration of the Eucharist with which formerly the vigil ended on Sunday morning, was counted as belonging to Holy Saturday, so that Gregory the Great speaks of a second Mass on Easter Sunday morning which was attended by the whole community. [126] The constant advancement of the hour of the Vigil brought it by the ninth century to the afternoon of Holy Saturday, to the time of the office of None, where since the end of the primitive period, the "fasting Masses" had been celebrated. In the succeeding period, the Vigil was treated like a "fasting Mass" and being treated the same way, was moved even to the morning of Holy Saturday when the custom grew of anticipating in the morning the office of None prescribed to be said before the "fasting Mass". [127] The Sacred Triduum itself also underwent a change: In the North in the ninth century, the cessation of work for the Easter octave "which is to be celebrated as a single Sunday" [128] was restricted to the days from Easter Monday to Wednesday, thereby creating a second "Easter Triduum" following the actual Paschal Triduum. But this was set for after Easter Sunday which was reckoned, very correctly, to the original triduum of the Crucifixion, Burial and Resurrection. But matter did not remain there. At the end of the Middle Ages the group of six days of the double triduum was moved forward by a day, giving both triduums a new character. Now there was Passion Triduum from Holy Thursday to Easter Saturday and an Easter Triduum from Easter Sunday to Easter Tuesday. What can be superficially illustrated by the reduction of feast-days at the time of the Reformation is the loss in the late Gothic period of the overview of the death and resurrection of Christ and the contemplation in isolation of both aspects of salvation events which actually belong to each other. [129]

The reform of the Roman celebration of Easter began in 1946, when Pius XII gave the Congregation of Rites the task of investigating the possibility of a liturgical reform. The first step towards renewal was in 1951 with the promulgation of a decree of the congregation *ad experimentum* for one year, but renewed in 1952 for a further three years. [130] According to the decree the Easter Vigil was no longer an anticipation of the celebration of Easter but was the main celebration, and was fixed on the night between Holy Saturday and Easter Sunday. A further step in the reform was taken with the *Ordo Hebdomadae Sanctae instauratus* of 1956 [131] (with the *Instructio* of 16th November 1955 [132]), which includes the renewed order for the celebration of Easter night from 1951-52. [133] All these reforms were taken up into the renewed liturgy.

[125] In Mt 25,6 – CChr SL 77,237: "Ut in die vigilarum Paschae ant noctis dimidium populus dimittere non liceat."

[126] Gregory the Great, Dialogues 4,32 – PL 77,372. Cf. J.A.Jungmann: die Vorverlegung der Ostervigil seit dem christlichen Altertum. In: LJ 1 (1951) 48-54.50f.

[127] Cf. on this Jungmann op.cit.supra. 53.

[128] This still in Durandus in his "Rationale divinorum officiorum" VI,89,2.

[129] On this cf. B. Fischer, Von einen Pascha-Triduum zum Doppel-Triduum der heutigen Rubriken (1959): Ibid., Redemptionis Mysterium 84-94.

[130] Dominicae resurrectionis vigilium. Decretum de solemni vigilia instauranda. Rubricae Sabbato sancto servandae si Vigilia paschalis instaurata peragatur. In: AAS 43 (1951) 128-137. "Instaurata vigilia paschalis." Decree and "Rubricae Sabbato sancto servandae si vigilia paschalis instaurata peragitur cum variationibus per decretum diei 11 Ianuarii 1952 approbatis." In: AAS 44 (1952) 48-63.

[131] Ordo Hebdomadae Sanctae instauratus. Editio typica. Romae 1956.

[132] AAS 47 (1955) 842-847.

[133] Cf. Auf der Maur, Feiern im Rhythmus der Zeit I, 128-132; H.E. Jung: Die Vorarbeiten zu einer Liturgiereform unter Pius XII. In: LJ 26)1976) 165-182.

6.3.3. THE LITURGY OF HOLY WEEK AND OF THE THREE DAYS OF EASTER

A. Palm Sunday

"Holy Week is a commemoration of the Passion of Christ, which begins with his messianic entry into Jerusalem" [134] This corresponds to the old Roman celebration of Palm Sunday which was stamped completely by the Passion. The custom of reading the Passion according to Matthew goes back to the time of Pope Leo I. Under the influence of the liturgy at Jerusalem, however, the other Western liturgies concentrated on Jesus's entry into Jerusalem. According to Egeria's report of about the year 400, the commemoration of this entrance had already taken dramatic form. Christians gathered in the afternoon for a liturgy of the Word on the Mount of Olives from where, with palm – and olive-branches in hand, they processed into the city of Jerusalem. [135] The name "Palm Sunday" existed in Spain and Gaul by about the year 600, but there was as yet no procession with palms. In these regions, on the sixth Sunday of Lent, the *traditio Symboli* to the catechumens, along with their anointing, took place. At this ceremony the gospel of the anointing of Jesus at Bethany (John 12:1-11) was read, followed immediately by the reading of verses 12 to 16, which report the entry into Jerusalem. From the end of the eighth century, though, the number of reports of actual processions with palms begins to multiply. In the course of time these processions begin to incorporate ever more playful-dramatic forms, such as, for example, the use of a carved figure of Christ seated on a donkey fitted with wheels. The Roman-German pontifical of the ninth century linked the Roman tradition of the Passion with the Jerusalem palm procession and this linking stamped further developments until they were fixed by the Missal of 1570 in the form of a *statio* with liturgy of the Word and blessing of palms, procession to the church where the Mass of the Passion was celebrated. [136] Nevertheless, "the commemoration of the entry and the celebration of the Passion remained side-by-side as two independent entities. The only connection between them consisted in the carrying of palms throughout the ceremonies; the thematic connection was not successful." [137] This criticism holds in principle for the renewed liturgy, because the proclamation of the Passion – from the relevant Synoptic Gospel depending on the lectionary year – is still the focal point of the Mass, following the reading of the third song of the suffering servant from the book of Isaiah (50:4-7) and the hymn from the Letter to the Philippians (2:6-11) on Christ's obedience unto death. Only the opening section of the Mass is stamped by the entry into Jerusalem.

B. Holy Thursday

Egeria reports that in Jerusalem two Masses were celebrated, one in the afternoon to conclude Lent, then a further Mass, at which all communicated, to commemorate the institution of the Eucharist. [138] At the end of the fourth century many Churches were familiar with this double celebration of the Eucharist, as in Gaul where the evening Mass had the special name of *Natale Calicis.* [139] Originally at the centre of the Roman cele-

---

[134] NUALC 31 – Kaczynski 1302.
[135] Egeria, Peregranatio 31 – SChr 296, 272-274.
[136] Cf. Adam, Kirchenjahr 95-97; Auf der Maur, Feiern im Rhythmus der Zeit I, 99-101.
[137] Auf der Maur, Feiern im Rhythmus der Zeit I, 101.
[138] Cf. Egeria, Peregrinatio 35 – SChr 296, 278-281.
[139] Cf. Jounel 60f.

bration of Holy Thursday was the reconciliation of penitents, as witnessed by Innocent I in 416. Auf der Maur links this reconciliation with the name of the day, while the titles in the modern German missal make it clear that the Chrism Mass in the morning still belongs to Holy Week, whereas the evening Mass of the Lord's Supper is already part of the Sacred Triduum. A complicated historical development [140] led finally to the adoption by the Missal of Pius V of a single Mass on Holy Thursday morning at which, in the cathedral church, the holy oils were blessed.

A particular feature of the liturgy of Holy Thursday is the washing of the feet. In the West, outside of Rome, it counted since the fifth century as part of the rite of initiation. [141] The seventeenth Council of Toledo (694) urged very emphatically that the washing of feet on Holy Thursday was performed in imitation of Christ. The ceremony came to Rome in the twelfth century via the Romano-Germanic pontifical and finally into the Missal of 1570. While the latter "placed this washing of feet at the end of the Mass, the renewed order of Holy Week of 1955 placed it after the gospel and homily. It has retained this position in the Missal of 1970. While before the reform of 1955 the ceremony was prescribed for cathedrals and abbey-churches, the new order includes all churches, 'so long as pastoral conditions suggest its advisability'." [142] Further elements of the celebration were the particular method of reserving the Blessed Sacrament for the communion at the liturgy of Good Friday. This was done by means of an (anticipated!) "sacred tomb", or Easter Sepulchre, with which were associated the special decoration of this tomb, eucharistic adoration during the night of Holy Thursday and the ritual stripping of the altars. Irenaeus and Augustine record a forty-hour fast to correspond with the approximate length of time Christ spent in the tomb. This is the basis for the forty hours of adoration of the sacrament exposed behind a curtain in the Easter Sepulchre, frequently along with a crucifix or with a corpus taken from a crucifix. With the anticipation of the Easter Vigil the forty hours of adoration began already on the evening of Holy Thursday [143] and acquired the character of a watching with Christ in his fear unto death. The stripping of the altars was originally a purely practical affair which happened every day, but following changes in the adornment of altars, became a special event associated with this liturgically highly important day and eventually come to be interpreted allegorically as a sign of Jesus's abandonment and his being stripped of his garments. The stripping of the altars is still mentioned but no longer in a ritual form. The transfer of the Blessed Sacrament to a special place of reservation is also provided for, along with the recommendation of adoration during the night.

In keeping with tradition, the Chrism Mass is to take place in the morning of Holy Thursday, but, according to the ordo for the blessing of the oils of 1970, can take place on another day as close as possible to Easter. [144] The bishop concelebrates this Mass with his presbyters in the cathedral church. The unity of the priesthood of the local Church is also expressed in the oils blessed at this Mass, because when in the sacraments of Baptism and the Anointing of the Sick a priest uses the oils consecrated by the bishop, the latter's ministry of leadership in all the congregations of his diocese is made present.

---

[140] Cf. Auf der Maur, Feiern im Rhythmus der Zeit I, 103f.
[141] Cf. Kleinheyer, Initiation 74-76.
[142] Adam, Kirchenjahr 60.
[143] Cf. Adam, Kirchenjahr 61f.
[144] Cf. *Ordo benedicendi olea et conficiendi chrisma* of 3rd December 1970, Nos 9-10: De die benedictionis, Kaczynski 240, 2241.

In accordance with Western tradition, the consecration of the Oil of the Sick takes place before the final doxology of the Eucharistic Prayer, the consecration of the other oils after the final prayer of the Mass. A "Renewal of Consecration to the Priestly Life" may form part of the Chrism Mass. [145]

C. Good Friday

The first traces of a Good Friday liturgy are found in the reports of Egeria's pilgrimage. About the year 400, the Christians of Jerusalem gathered on the morning of Good Friday to venerate the cross, and at midday for a liturgy of the Word which concluded at about three in the afternoon. [146] This liturgy of the Word in which the reading of the Passion played a major role, but during which psalms referring to the sufferings of Christ were also sung, began to spread. The veneration of the cross could only develop where relics of the Cross were available, as in Rome where such a relic had been presented by the Empress Helena. According to one seventh-century source, the Pope processed with this relic from the Lateran Basilica to the church of the Holy Cross of Jerusalem, which had been built by Helena. There the relic was venerated by the clergy and the people during which time two lessons were read from the Old Testament along with the Passion according to John. This liturgy concluded with solemn Prayers of the Faithful. As early as the seventh the combination of veneration of the Cross with the communion of the faithful was introduced. When the Frankish Church adopted this liturgy in the eighth century, further developments followed, in particular the elaboration of the simple communion-service into the Mass of the Pre-sanctified. [147] In the 11th century the liturgy of the Good Friday was finished in the known structure, readings, intercessions, veneration of the cross and communion. [148] It is precisely here that Baumstark's law of the "preservation of the most ancient in the times of greatest liturgical importance" [149] is confirmed.

The celebration begins with the silent prostration by the celebrant and his assistants. This gesture is retained in the liturgy only on this day and at ordinations. After the opening prayer, introduced only in 1956, the three readings follow – an Old Testament reading of the suffering servant (Is 52:13-53:12), a reading form the Letter to the Hebrews (Heb 4:14-16; 5:7-9) and the Passion according to John. The homily is followed by the Solemn Prayers, the ancient Roman intercessions, though with the alterations of the 1970 Missal in respect of the prayers for the Jews and for the unity of the church. The veneration of the Cross then begins, either with an unveiling of, or the display of an unveiled Cross. Connected with the first form the custom is retained, which grew up in the north of France in the ninth century, of carrying the veiled cross through the church, gradually unveiling it during the singing of the antiphon *Ecce lignum crucis*. This found its way into the Missal of 1570. [150] The veneration of the

---

[145] Cf. Adam, Kirchenjahr 100f.; Jounel 89: "Le pape Paul VI a voulu, en effet, que la Messe chrismale soit une fête du sacerdoce, dans laquelle les prêtres pourraient renouveler en présence de leur évêque les engagements qu'ils ont pris lors de leur ordination."

[146] Cf. Römer 39.

[147] This followed the form of the Mass but without a Eucharistic Prayer. It is not to be confused with the "Liturgy with pre-sanctified gifts" which is usual during Lent in the Byzantine rite, since that liturgy is really Vespers to which a communion-service is added.

[148] Cf. Römer 42.

[149] A. Baumstark, Das Gesetz der Erhaltung des Alten in liturgisch hochwertiger Zeit, JLw 7 (1927) 1-23.

[150] Cf. Auf der Maur, Feiern im Rhythmus der Zeit I, 110.

Cross originally took place in silence but with time was accompanied by chants, of which the *Improperia*, the so-called "reproaches" of our Lord on the cross, linked since the fifteenth century with the *Trisagion* [151] sung in Geek, are the most important. The communion-service was retained. The practice of infrequent Communion during the Middle Ages led to the priest alone communicating on Good Friday and this became a regulation in the Missal of 1570. It was not until the reform of 1956 that Communion for the faithful was re-introduced. [152] Another correction was the fixing of the time of the celebration at the ninth hour, three o'clock in the afternoon. This, mentioned from earliest times, is in accordance with the hour of Lord's death as reported in Mt 27:46. Like the Easter Vigil the liturgy of Good Friday had taken place early in the morning, the rule of the "ninth hour" being applied to the time of the office of None which was already anticipated in the morning. [153] The Missal of 1970 retained this correction already made in 1956. The Byzantine liturgy of Good Friday does not have a veneration of the Cross. [154] This may perhaps have vanished from the rite with the sack of Jerusalem by the Persians in 614, when the relics of the Cross were stolen. When the relics were brought back after the victory of Heraclius the rite was not restored. In its place the veneration was transferred completely to the Exaltation of the Cross, or to the third Sunday of Lent. The Byzantine Good Friday is marked by the carrying of the *epitaphion*, an embroidered icon of the laying of Christ in the tomb, with which during Vespers the burial of Christ is symbolically imitated. [155]

D. The Celebration of Easter Night.

Easter night is the centre of the Paschal Triduum. [156] On the this night, "the mother of all vigils". "the Church watches in vigil for the Resurrection of the Lord and celebrates it in sacred symbols. For this reason, the whole vigil is to be held at night, that is, may not begin until darkness has fallen and must end before dawn on Sunday." [157] The liturgy of Easter night consists in four elements, the Liturgy of Light, the Liturgy of the Word, Celebration of Baptism and Celebration of the Eucharist.

The Liturgy of Light begins with the blessing of the Easter fire. This was unknown in the old Roman liturgy and was taken later into the Roman Easter vigil from the pagan Spring fires of the Celtic north, Gaul and Ireland. [158] This is followed by the – now optional – decoration of the Paschal candle with Cross, Alpha and Omega, the figures of the year – In question and the grains of incense. Unlike the fire, the lighting of the candle is one of the original elements of the vigil, as attested to by the Easter homilies of Asterios Sophistes. The evening service of thanksgiving for the light as handed down by Hippolytus, [159] as well as the *lucernarium* at the normal congregational Vespers provide

---

[151] On the chants for the veneration of the Cross and on the Reproaches cf. Auf der Maur, Feiern im Rhythmus der Zeit I, 110f.

[152] Cf. Auf der Maur, Feiern im Rhythmus der Zeit I, 132.

[153] Cf. Auf der Maur, Feiern im Rhythmus der Zeit I, 108.

[154] One element of such a veneration can be seen in the erection of a cross painted with an icon of the corpus in the centre of the church during the Good Friday service. Cf. Schulz, Liturgie, Tagzeiten und Kirchenjahr 81.

[155] Cf. Edelby, Liturgikon 140-141, 601-603. On the third Sunday of Lent, 98f., cf. also Schulz, Liturgie, Tagzeiten und Kirchenjahr 81.

[156] Cf. NUALC 19 – Kaczynski 1290.

[157] NUALC 21 – Kaczynski 1292.

[158] Cf. Auf der Maur, I,89.

[159] Cf. TradAp. 25, Geerllings 275-277.

further examples and parallels. In any case, since light as a motif of "enlightenment" is part of initiation, there is are internal connections between the celebration of Initiation on Easter night and the Paschal theme of transition from darkness to light [160]

The lighted Paschal candle is carried into the darkened church by the deacon [161] who lifts it up three times with the cry *Lumen Christi* [162] – *Deo Gratias*. The candles of the faithful are lighted from the Paschal candle and when the latter has been place in its special candle-stick the solemn Easter proclamation -*praeconium paschale* – is begun, a berakah over the light of the candle (sometimres called for this reason the *benedictio cerei*), also known as the *Exsultet*, from its opening words. [163] The *Exsultet* used today is one of several which developed differently in different regions from the fifth to the tenth centuries. Its text can be traced to the about the year 700, but "goes back with the greatest probability to the end of the fourth century. Even if St Ambrose cannot be accepted as the author, all the indications are that the text comes from northern Italy or southern Gaul and that its compiler was influenced by Ambrose." [164] It was not until the twelfth or thirteenth centuries that the *benecictio cerei*, with the text of the *Exsultet* was included in the liturgical books of the Roman curia, there having been great reservations in Rome it its regard during the first millennium, [165] Although the Liturgy of the Word belongs to the original elements of the Easter vigil, the full Roman version of this liturgy is not evident in the sources until the sixth or seventh centuries. Here is present already the basic structure provided for today, i.e. Reading – (Responsorial) Chant – Prayer. [166] In the modern Easter vigil nine lessons from the Bible are read, seven [167] from the Old Testament and two from the New Testament, the "epistle" and "gospel", which follow the *Gloria* during which all lights and candles in the church are lit. It is desirable that in the Liturgy of Baptism which follows the homily, the sacrament of Baptism be actually administered. In the Missal of 1970, the structure of the Liturgy of Baptism from the renewed vigil of 1951 was retained: litany, blessing of the baptismal water, baptism, renunciation of Satan and renewal of baptismal promises by the whole congregation followed by sprinkling with the baptismal water. If there is to be no baptism or the blessing of water for baptisms in the Easter season, then, leaving out the litany and the

---

[160] Cf. Auf der Maur, Feiern im Rhythmus der Zeit I, 74.

[161] This too is an indication of the connections with the evening thanksgiving for the light, because, according to Plank, the deacon assumes the function of the housewife in the Jewish celebration of Sabbath Eve, of which a liturgy of light is a part. In Judaism the family or house group could be replaced by a community of disciples around a Rabbi. Cf. Gerhards, Benedicam 30, note 33.

[162] Auf der Maur, – in Feiern im Rhythmus der Zeit I, 91 - says that the "Lumen Christ" was already known in the fifth century in Western domestic evening devotions as an acclamation accompanying the lighting of lights, "in the eighth century we find this greeting of the light at supper in monasteries".

[163] On the Exsultet cf. G. Fuchs / M. Weikmann, Das Exsultet. Geschichte, Theologie und Gestaltung der österlichen Lichtdanksagung, Regensburg 1992.

[164] Auf der Maur, Feiern im Rhythmus der Zeit I, 90.

[165] Cf. Fuchs-Weikmann 17: In a letter to a deacon, Praesidius of Piacenza, in 384, Jerome refuses his request to write a hymn of praise to the Easter candle, "since in my opinion neither the exaggerated praise of meadows, flowers and bees, nor the use of wax candles at all, are fitting for the celebration of the Pasch. Instead he tells him to be a (true) monk."

[166] Cf. Auf der Maur, Feiern im Rhythmus der Zeit I,91.

[167] The rubrics allow the number of Old Testament readings to be reduced to three, for pastoral reasons and, indeed, "in cases of urgency" even to two. In all cases the reading about the crossing of the Red Sea (Ex 14) may never be omitted. On the history of the pericopes used in the Easter vigil cf. Auf der Maur, Feiern im Rhythmus der Zeit I, 92f.

solemn blessing of the water, there is a simple blessing of water which is used for the renewal of baptismal promises. [168]

Today the Mass begins with the preparation of the gifts. Formerly it started with the prayers at the foot of the altar, thus clearly marking it off from what had gone before. Auf der Maur states that many sources speak of a new entrance from the sacristy during which the Kyrie litany was sung as an entrance chant, followed by the Gloria and opening prayer, which survived as the oldest Roman entry rite down to the Missal of Pius V. The office of Vespers which, because of the anticipation of the vigil had formerly followed it, has been dropped. In the Missal of 1570 this consisted in Psalm 117 (116) with alleluia, *Magnificat* with the antiphon *Vespere autem sabbati* and a collect. [169] The return to the correct timing of the vigil rendered Vespers meaningless, for which reason the reform of 1951 substituted a form of Lauds made up of Psalm 117 (116) with *Benedictus* and the antiphon *Et valde mane*. This office was not included in the Missal of 1970. [170]

The elements of Liturgy of Light, Liturgy of the Word, Baptismal Liturgy and two celebrations of the Eucharist were also formerly part of the Byzantine all-night Easter vigil. This single vigil has developed into two separate services. The liturgy of the "Great Saturday" consists in the combination of Vespers of fifteen Old Testament readings with the Liturgy of St Basil, which these days is celebrated in the morning of Holy Saturday. What is now regarded as the actual Easter vigil is made up of a celebration of light, a shortened *Orthros*, i.e. Matins and Lauds and the Liturgy of St John Chrysostom. The Liturgy of Baptism has fallen into disuse. [171]

E. Easter Sunday

Because the Easter vigil lasted until the early morning and ended with the celebration of the Eucharist, there was originally no proper liturgy celebrated in the morning of Easter Sunday. But Egeria and Augustine already mention a further Eucharistic celebration in the morning. [172] With the displacement of the Easter vigil to the morning of Easter Saturday, this Mass on Easter Sunday morning became increasingly a festive Easter High Mass in its own right. At least in German-speaking regions in the Middle Ages there developed a so-called "Celebration of the Resurrection", with dramatic elements, which was foreign to the Roman rite. [173] This was made up of the *elevatio*, a representation of the Resurrection in which the Cross or the Blessed Sacrament was taken out of the "Sacred Grave", as well as a dramatisation of the visit of the women to the tomb to anoint the body – *visitatio sepulchri*. There also developed in the late Middle Ages the custom of the *tollite portas* rite, taken into the celebration from the Palm Sunday liturgy or the rite of consecrating a church. This was a dramatisation of Christ's triumph over the Devil by the harrowing of Hell. [174] The restoration of the Easter vigil has meant that

---

[168] Cf. Auf der Maur. Feiern im Rhythmus der Zeit I, 135.
[169] Cf. Auf der Maur. Feiern im Rhythmus der Zeit I, 96f.
[170] Cf. Auf der Maur. Feiern im Rhythmus der Zeit I, 131.
[171] Cf. Schulz, Liturgie, Tagzeitengebet und Kirchenjahr 83-87; Edelby, Liturgikon 142-145.
[172] Egeria, Peregrinatio 39,2 – SChr 296, 292; Augustinus Sermo 224-228 – PL 38, 1039-1102.
[173] Cf. B. Fischer, Die Auferstehungsfeier am Ostermorgen. Altchristliches Gedankengut in mittelalterlicher Fassung (1943): Ibid., Redemptionis mysterium. Studien zur Osterfeier und zur christlichen Initiation. A. Gerhards / A. Heinz (eds.), Paderborn-München-Vienna-Zurich 1992, 13-27. There is already something similar in Eisenhofer I, 548.
[174] Cf. Fischer, op.cit.supra 17-23.

these celebrations have lost their meaning, but as early as 1953, Fischer suggested the value of combining with the vigil valuable elements from these old Resurrection celebrations which were popular among the faithful. [175] Vespers of Easter Sunday is marked by commemoration of baptism and played an important role in Roman baptismal Vespers, which since the Middle Ages were celebrated throughout the whole Easter octave, a practice which spread outwards from Rome. [176]

6.3.4. LENT – THE EASTER PENITENTIAL SEASON

The Latin name, Quadragesima, [177] mentioned by Jerome about the year 384 with regard to Rome, refers to the symbolic number 40, which is used in the Scriptures as an expression of the length of time needed for penance and preparation before a saving event or a divine revelation. [178] Apart from the fast on Friday and Saturday before Easter there is little that can be said about the earliest period. The first mention of a forty-day fast is in an Easter letter of Athanasius of Alexandria in 334. At the end of the fourth century Egeria reports such a fast in Jerusalem. [179] Jerome mentions the fast in Rome about the year 384 and Ambrose reports it in Milan. [180] Quadragesima was generally known by the end of the fourth and the beginning of the fifth centuries and was connected with the elaboration of the Easter vigil into the great baptismal feast of the year as well as the institutionalisation of the cathechumenate, or the *photizomenate*, the forty days of immediate preparation for the reception of Baptism at the vigil in Easter night. Since the fifth century the reconciliation of public penitents was concentrated at the end of Lent, in Rome, for example, on Holy Thursday. This explains the emphasis on the practice of penance during Lent. The two groups most immediately affected by Lent, the catechumens and the penitents were joined by the community in general, who through penance, fasting, spiritual exercises and liturgical celebrations, prepared themselves for Easter. Though there is no doubting the influence of the preparation of cathechumens and the liturgical peculiarities associated with this preparation on the season of Lent, Auf der Maur is equally sure that it is not certain that the penitential character of Lent can be exclusively explained by the preparation for Easter. [181]

The length of Lent varied according to its end and the way in which it was reckoned; for example, on whether or not Saturdays were to be counted as fast-days. At the end of the fourth century Lent began on the sixth Sunday before Easter and included forty days of preparation – which were not fast-days in the strict sense – which ended with the beginning of the Sacred Triduum on the evening of Holy Thursday when the reconciliation of penitents took place. At the turn from the fifth to the sixth century, in order to arrive at forty full days of fasting, Good Friday and Holy Saturday were reckoned

---

[175] Cf. B. Fischer, Osternachtfeier am frühen Ostermorgen. Ein Desideratum zur wiederhergestellten Oster-liturgie (1953): Ibid., Redemptionis mysterium 48-56.

[176] Cf. B. Fischer, Formen gemeinschaftlicher Tauferinnerung im Abendland: Ibid., Redemptionis mysterium. Studien zur Osterfeier und zur christlichen Initiation. A. Gerhards / A. Heinz (eds.), Paderborn-München-Vienna-Zurich 1992, 141-150.

[177] The term entered the Romance langauges as, "Quaresima", "Carême", while the English "Lent" refers to the lengthening days of Spring and the German"Fastenzeit" isolates one aspect of the season.

[178] E.g.: Forty days of the Flood, Gen 7:4ff.; Israel's forty years in the desert; Jesus fasts forty days in the desert, Mk 1:13 par.

[179] Cf. Easter Letter no.6 of AD 344, 6.13 – PG 26, 1386. 1389: Egeria, Peregrinatio 27,1 – SChr 296, 256.

[180] Jerome, Ep.24,4 – PL 22,428; Ambrose, Exp. in Ps 40,37 – PL 14, 1087.

[181] Cf. Auf der Maur, Feiern im Rhythmus der Zeit I, 144f.

as fast-days and four extra days were added before the first Sunday of Lent. Lent then began with Ash Wednesday as the *caput quadragesimae* or *caput ieunii* (the "head" of the forty days or of the fast). The distribution of ashes, from which Ash Wednesday gets its name, was already in Scripture a sign of penance and was part of public penance.[182] At the end of the first Millennium the signing with ashes on the Wednesday before the first Sunday of Lent was still confined to the by then very rare public penitents. By the end of the eleventh century however, the giving of ashes had spread to all the faithful and this was included in the Missal of 1570. In the Missal of 1970 the celebration of Ash Wednesday was so altered that the distribution of ashes no longer took place before Mass but after the liturgy of the Word.[183]

Up until the reform of 1969 Ash Wednesday was preceded by a "pre-Lent" with the Sundays of Quinquagesima, Sexagesima and Septuagesima, giving round figures for the time left before Easter Sunday. The development of this "pre-Lent" is attributed by some to Gallican or Byzantine influences.[184] On the other hand, the war-torn situation at the time of the Great Migrations of the Goths and Lombards, emphasized as early as Grisar, encouraged the emergence of a particular enthusiasm for prayer and penance. In any case, fasting was not particularly a part of "pre-Lent", but the use of violet vestments, the dropping of the *Alleluia*, *Gloria* and *Te Deum*, gave the season its unambiguously penitential character.[185]

Because there was no fast on Saturday, the "brother of Sunday, the Church of Jerusalem and its heirs in the Byzantine Church, "needed", practically, eight weeks of fasting to reach the number of forty. But at a later stage, Holy Week along with Palm Sunday and the Saturday before it – the "Saturday of the Raising of Lazarus" – were excluded from the forty days in the narrower sense. To make up for this, the Sundays and Saturdays of the six weeks up to Lazarus Saturday, were re-incorporated into the forty days. Further, before Lent itself a three-week "pre-Lent" was inserted, beginning with the "Sunday of the Pharisees and Publicans" (Gospel: Lk 18:10-14), followed by the "Sunday of the Prodigal Son" (Gospel: Lk 15:11-32), the Sunday of "Abstinence from Meat" or Carnival, and the Sunday of *Tyrophage* or "Eating of cheese".[186] In the week of *Tyrophage* it is still permitted to eat egg – and milk-based foods, while in the "pure" fasting-weeks these foods are also excluded. Among the Sundays of the fast, the first and the third are of particular importance: the first as the "Sunday of Orthodoxy" on which the final victory over the Iconoclasts in 843 is commemorated, the third as the "Sunday of the Veneration of the Holy and Life-giving Cross".[187] This might lead to the mistaken conclusion that the Sunday of the Veneration of the Cross has the same roots as the former Passion Sunday in the Latin Lent as it existed until the reform of the liturgy. Edelby suggests that a possible background to the commemoration is the translation of a particular relic of the Cross to Constantinople.[188]

---

[182] Cf. R.Meßner, Feiern der Umkehr und Versöhnung: GdK 7,2, Regensburg 1992, 90, 117,125f.

[183] Cf. Auf der Maur, Feiern im Rhythmus der Zeit I, 151-153.

[184] Cf. Auf der Maur, Feiern im Rhythmus der Zeit I, 147.

[185] Cf. Adam, Kirchenjahr 81f. Cf. on this Grisar, Das Missale im Lichte römischer Stadtgeschichte 10f. This is explicitly dealt with in Ch.10, pp.54-58: Die Vorfastenstationen in geschichtlicher Beleuchtung.

[186] Cf. Schulz, Liturgie, Tagzeiten und Kirchenjahr 68; Edelby, Liturgikon 62-68. On Byzantine reckoning of fast-days and on "pre-Lent" cf. Edelby, Liturgikon 58-60.

[187] Cf. Schulz, Liturgie, Tagzeiten und Kirchenjahr 69; Edelby, Liturgikon 98.

[188] Cf. Edelby, Liturgikon 98.

According to ancient discipline, days of penance were aliturgical days. However, to give the faithful the opportunity of receiving Communion, in the Byzantine Church today the Liturgy of the Pre-Sanctified is celebrated on the Wednesdays and Fridays of Lent as well as on the Monday, Tuesday and Wednesday of Holy Week. This takes the form of Vespers with the distribution of Holy Communion. [189] In Rome, though, since the sixth century the Eucharist was also celebrated on weekdays.

There was a caesura on the fifth Sunday of Lent, called by the Missal of 1570, borrowing from an older tradition, *Dominica in passione Domini*. The transfer of the scrutinies connected with the initiation of adults to the weekdays meant that new texts had to be composed for the Sundays. The texts of the Passion fell on the fifth Sunday of Lent, thus making it a kind of threshold to Holy Week, which begins on the following Sunday with the commemoration of the Entry of Jesus into Jerusalem. This caesura was underlined by the covering of crosses and images in the church – a play on the passage John 8:59b from the gospel of the day, allegorically interpreted by Durandus – which goes back to the notion of the "hunger-blanket" or "fasting-veil" as a sign of "fasting" of the eyes. This covering did not become official until the seventeenth century when it was included in the *Caeremoniale Episcoporum*. [190] In the reform of the liturgy the former caesura inside of Lent vanished with Passion Sunday. The Missal of 1970 provides for the retention of the covering of crosses and images if Bishops' Conferences are in favour. [191]

According to SC 109, Lent has a double function: preparation for Baptism and a reminder of the baptized of their Baptism with their preparation through penance for the celebration of Easter. This is the purpose of the special baptismal and penitential references in the Lenten liturgy. SC 110 also indicates the social and external dimensions of penance. "Lent lasts from Ash Wednesday to the start of the Mass of the Lords Supper on Holy Thursday. The *Alleluia* is not sung from Ash Wednesday to the night of Holy Saturday." [192] With the latter provision, the reform of the liturgy follows the Western tradition which gives the *Alleluia* a particularly Easter character and so does not sing it during Lent. [193]

6.3.5. QUINQUAGESIMA / PENTECOST – THE EASTER FESTIVE SEASON

"The fifty days from the Sunday of the Resurrection to Pentecost Sunday is celebrated as a single feast-day, as 'the great day of the Lord'. During these days in particular the *Alleluia* is sung." [194] For, "the fifty days of Easter joy, the Pentecost, celebrate the one event, the glorification of the Lord. Different stages of this glorification can, indeed, be

---

[189] Cf. Edelby, Liturgikon 61.
[190] Cf. Auf der Maur, Feiern im Rhythmus der Zeit I, 148-151.
[191] Cf. Adam, Kirchenjahr 94f. A further special day within Lent, marked out from the rest of Lent, at least in some places, by the wearing of rose-coloured vestment, is the fourth Sunday of Lent, known as "Laetare" Sunday from the entrance-chant. The happier character of this Sunday is possibly explained by the "Opening of the Ears", the Ephata rite, for catechumens, and certainly by the custom in which the Pope on this day, in accordance with a Roman folk-custom marking the end of Winter, presented a golden rose to an important personage. Cf. Adam op. cit. infra, 92.
[192] NUALC 28 – Kaczynski 1299.
[193] Cf. Jungmann MS I 544f. On the various medieval rites for "burying" the *Alleluia*, cf. Eisenhofer I, 492f.
[194] NUALC 22 – Kaczynski 1293.

distinguished – the New Testament speaks of Resurrection, Ascension, Enthronement at God's right hand, Sending of the Holy Spirit, Second Coming. We celebrate each of these individual stages on a day of its own, but in reality they are all commemorated together in every celebration. The Gospel of John very clearly describes all of these events of the glorification as happening together on Easter Day." [195]

The Church had a model for a fifty-day festival in the Jewish Festival of Weeks, particularly since the outpouring of the Holy Spirit is dated by Rev 2.1ff. to the fiftieth day. Since the seventeenth century, (in German-speaking regions) the common First Communion of children takes place on the octave day of Easter, *Dominica in Albis*. This date, close to Easter Sunday, the main day for baptisms, is chosen as a reminder that First Communion is actually a Baptismal Eucharist and one of the sacraments of initiation. Since the seventh century, on the Monday after the octave, so long as the Easter Vigil was still the regular occasion for Baptism, the *Pascha annotinum*, the annual communal commemoration of Baptism took place. This fell into disuse when Baptism at the Easter Vigil was abandoned and the practice of baptising children immediately after birth became the norm. [196] Unlike the Missal of 1570, the Sundays in Eastertide are no longer designated Sundays *after* Easter, but Sundays *of* Easter itself, of which the first is the third day of the Paschal Triduum. The reason for this is the greater emphasis on the unity of Eastertide as a single feast-day.

Nevertheless, two feast-days stand out from the fifty, Ascension and Pentecost. The term "Pentecost" was less and less applied to the whole season and increasingly to its last day on which, in Jerusalem, both the sending of the Holy Spirit and the Ascension were commemorated, the former in the morning, the latter in the afternoon. [197] Since the fourth century the sending of the Holy Spirit became more and more the focus of the day. In the course of the historicizing elaboration of the single paschal theme, the feast of the Ascension came to be attributed to the fortieth day after Easter. This development, mentioned by John Chrysostom as one of the earliest witnesses, was received in Rome under Leo I. [198] The number forty had a negative effect to the extent that the forty days of Lent were seen to be mirrored in the forty days after Easter and the Ascension came to be regarded as an end of the Easter season. Several dramatic elements underlined this perception, such as theatrical representations of the Ascension itself, but particularly the custom the extinguishing of the Paschal Candle after the gospel, a practice retained by the Missal of 1570, all the more so since the feast had had its own vigil from the seventh century and an octave since the eleventh. [199] The feast of the Ascension, however, cannot be about an historicizing "taking leave" of his disciples by Jesus, nor can its themes be the "glorification" of the Lord – the Lord's glorification being inseparably part of the whole Easter event. The idea behind this feast is that, with the glorification of the Lord, some part of us, our human nature, which the Lord shares with every human being since the Incarnation and for all eternity, has been introduced into the glory of God. The Lord's glorification is the beginning and pledge of man's glorification. [200]

---

[195] Berger, Ostern und Weihnachten 4.
[196] Cf. B. Fischer: Formen gemeinschaftlicher Tauferinnerung im Abendland. In: Redemptionis mysterium 141-150; 145f.: Pascha annotinum.
[197] Egeria, Peregrinatio 43 – SChr 296, 298-302.
[198] Cf. Auf der Maur, Feiern im Rhythmus der Zeit I, 81f.
[199] Cf. Auf der Maur, Feiern im Rhythmus der Zeit I, 120f.
[200] Cf. the collect in the Missal for Ascension Day: "quia Christi Filii tui ascensio est nostra provectio."

The transformation of the feast of the Ascension into an historicizing commemoration of the Lord's glorification, was accompanied by the same change to the feast of Pentecost. Less and less was it seen as the conclusion of the fifty days of Eastertide, but became, rather, a feast on its own, acquiring its own octave in the seventh century. For a long time yet the sending of the Holy Spirit continued to be seen as being connected with the Ascension, but not any more with the death and resurrection of the Lord. The texts added in the Middle Ages – a second *Alleluia* and the Sequence – address the Holy Spirit directly. This is not just a general alteration of the addressee of liturgical prayer, but also a sign that Pentecost had become a feast of the Holy Spirit. [201]

The octave of the Ascension was abolished in 1956. The new ordering of 1969 abolished the "Time after the Ascension" which had not been added to the *Codex Rubricarum* until 1960, but the new ordering was inconsistent to the extent that a Pentecost novena, which marked the weekday Masses between the Ascension and Pentecost was inserted. "The weekdays after the Ascension to the Saturday before Pentecost are a preparation for the Descent of the Holy Spirit." [202] Over against that, with the abolition of the vigil and octave of Pentecost it has become clear once more that this day marks the end of the fifty days of Easter.

The Byzantine Church had always retained this view of the feast of Pentecost. At Vespers on the feast, a visible sign of the end of Eastertide is the reintroduction of kneeling for prayer. [203] During Eastertide prayer is permitted only while standing. The Byzantine Church gives a strong Trinitarian accent to the feast of Pentecost, but not one that can be compared to that of Trinity Sunday in the West. Thus, unlike in the West, the liturgy does not contain "dogmatic teaching texts, and the theology of the Trinity is completely oriented towards salvation-history. At Pentecost the revelation of the triune God in the economy of salvation, through the Son in the Holy Spirit, is completed, both Persons effecting salvation in the world to divinize man by assuming him into the inner-Trinitarian communion. The solemnity of the Holy Spirit is not celebrated until Pentecost Monday, the first day after Pentecost. [204]

In the Easter season there had developed a penitential and petitionary element, the major and minor litanies, which are combined in the German term *Bittage* or days of intercession, in English, rogation days. The major litany (*litania major*) has its origin in a procession traditionally held in pagan Rome on 25th April in honour of the goddess Robigo – hence the term *Robigalia*. This procession was to ward off mildew from the seed. This pagan custom was christianized in Rome, spread with its inclusion in the Roman liturgy and was included in the Missal of Pius V. It is not possible to make a connection between this practice and the feast of Mark the Evangelist which falls on the 25th April. The minor litanies (*litania minores*) began in Vienne in Southern Gaul, where in 469 the bishop, Mamertus, ordered them with an accompanying fast on the three days before the feast of the Ascension on account of the visitation of the town by failure of the harvest and earthquakes. Other dioceses of Southern Gaul adopted the custom, Rome finally doing so at the start of the ninth century. [205] The reordering of

[201] Cf. Auf der Maur, Feiern im Rhythmus der Zeit I, 122-124.
[202] NUALC 26 -Kaczynski 1297.
[203] Cf. M. Arranz, Les Prières de la Gonyklisia ou de la Génuflexion du jour de la Pentecôte dans l'ancien Euchologie byzantin, OrChrPer 48 (1982) 92-123.
[204] Cf. Edelby, Liturgikon 212-221.
[205] Cf. Auf der Maur, Feiern im Rhythmus der Zeit I, 121f. Adam, Kirchenjahr 159f.

1969 retains the rogation days along with ember days. [206] "The adaptations of the time and manner of observance of rogation days to various regions and the different needs of the people should be determined by episcopal conferences. The competent authority should set up norms for the extent of these celebrations over one or several days for their repetition during the year, as local needs dictate." [207] With this, the rogation days are no longer, at least in principle, tied to the fifty days of Easter, within which they form a foreign element.

Bibliography

R. Berger, Ostern und Weihnachten. Zum Grundgefüge des Kirchenjahres, ALw 8 (1963) 1-20.

O. Casel, Art und Sinn der ältesten christlichen Osterfeier, JLw 14 (1938) 1-78.

A. Chavasse, La structure de Carême et les lectures des messes quadragésimales dans la liturgie romaine, MD 31 (1952) 76-119.

B. Fischer / J. Wagner (eds.), Paschatis Sollemnia. Studien zu Osterfeier und Osterfrömmigkeit (FS J. A. Jungmann), Freiburg-Basel-Vienna 1959.

B. Fischer, Redemptionis mysterium. Studien zur Osterfeier und zur christlichen Initiation, A. Gerhards / A. Heinz (eds.), Paderborn-München-Vienna-Zurich 1992.

P. Plank, Zeitrechnung und Festdatierung als ökum. Problem: HOK II, Düsseldorf 182-191.

M. Righetti, Manuale di storia liturgica II: L'Anno Liturgico – Il Breviario. Milano 1955, 95-246.

G. Römer, Die Liturgie des Karfreitags, ZKTh 77 (1955) 39-93.

H. J. Schulz, Liturgie, Tagzeiten und Kirchenjahr des byzantinischen Ritus: HOK II. Düsseldorf 1989, 30-100.

H. Schürmann, Die Anfänge der christlichen Osterfeier, ThQ 131 (1951) 414-425.

6.4. THE CHRISTMAS CYCLE

The historicizing of Christmas as the feast of the birth of the Lord is, "a later development exactly the same as that of the individual days of the celebration of Easter. At its core and origin, the Christmas cycle celebrates the same fundamental process, the same complete saving event as Easter". [208]

6.4.1. ADVENT

Advent originated in the liturgies of Gaul and Spain in the fourth century. The feast of the Epiphany was preceded by three weeks of intensifying religious activity. Shortly after Gallican sources attest to a period of fasting which began on the feast of St Martin, 11th November, the *Quadragesima sancti Martini*. This period of fasting did not end with Christmas but with the older feast of the Epiphany. Counting between the feast of St Martin and Epiphany according to the Eastern model, i.e. counting only the actual fast-days, thus eliminating from these eight weeks not only the Sundays but also the Saturdays which in the East were not fast-days, then the result is forty fast-days between 11th November and 6th January. [209] The feast of Epiphany was, at least from region to

---

[206] Cf. NUALC 45 – Kaczynski 1316.
[207] NUALC 46 – Kaczynski 1317.
[208] Berger, Ostern und Weihnachten 6.
[209] Cf. Jungmann, Advent und Voradvent 242f.

region, more important than Christmas, particularly as a date for baptism which required a forty-day period of preparation. [210] The penitential preaching of Irish missionaries which proclaimed the Christ who was to come again primarily as an eschatological judge, led to the development of Advent – dedicated to the expectation of the one who is to come again – as a period of penance and fasting. [211] The rapid development of the feast of Christmas, however, which spread from Rome stood in the way of the full development of the pre-Epiphany "Lent". "A Lent which was interrupted in the middle by a solemnity, itself possibly even followed by a further feast, was no longer a proper Lent." But to allow the *Quadragesima sancti Martini* to end on 25th December meant the loss of the full forty days fast. The length of the Advent fast varied greatly. Its beginning could range from 15th November to as far back as September. [212] The liturgy corresponded largely to that of the forty days before Easter. Its focus was the coming of Christ, not, however, with a view to his coming in the flesh at Christmas, but his return as a strict judge at the end of time, a return which demanded penance and conversion. [213]

The situation was completely different in Rome, where there is a complete absence of ancient witnesses for an Advent season. In December there was the Ember week before Christmas but its content was no different from the other Ember weeks throughout the year. The development of Advent in Rome can be dated to the sixth century. The Rule of Saint Benedict does not yet know of Advent and the Advent homilies of Gregory the Great date from the end of the sixth century. "While in the Gallican region the sources indicate first an ascetical observance of Advent and only much later a liturgical celebration, the first and relatively early witnesses for the region of Rome show evidence only of a liturgical celebration of the season." [214] Roman Advent swung between five and four Sundays. This as well as the absence of fasting show that here there were no parallels to the pre-Easter Lent.

The mixing of Roman Advent and the Gallican pre-Advent "Lent" was the result of the adoption of the Roman liturgy in the Frankish empire. It was from here that the mixed form returned to Rome under German influence, to become the norm for all of Western Christendom. The north took over the four Sundays of Advent – originally until the 11th century five Sundays – as well as the texts of the Roman liturgy of Advent. "For the rest, though, the north with its lenten view of Advent remained victorious". [215] This is true in the matter of fasting [216] but also for the liturgy. The *Gloria* of the Mass was omitted from the turn of the second millennium, as was the *Te Deum* at Matins. The violet and sometimes black of the vestments corresponded with Lenten practice. Nevertheless, these facts ought not to blind one to the fact that, "All of these penitential elements of the liturgy of Advent were more on the surface. Fasting was not able to impose itself in the long term. On a deeper level the Advent liturgy itself remained strongly different from that of Lent. The basic thrust is a hopeful expectation of the

---

[210] Cf. op.cit.supra. 246f. Jungmann mentions an instruction of Gregory the Great according to which baptisms other than at Easter had to happen "paenitentia ac abstinentia quadraginta diebus indicta", Ep.8, 23 – PL 77, 925 A.

[211] Cf. Croce 290f.

[212] Cf. Jungmann, Advent und Voradvent 250-259.

[213] Cf. op.cit.supra, 260f.

[214] Op. cit. supra, 265.

[215] Op. cit. supra, 268f.

[216] Cf. op. cit. Supra, 269-272.

one who is to come. Thus, the development remained stuck between both poles. The Gallican element had changed the external appearance of the Roman Advent liturgy only slightly." [217] The Gallican Advent survived primarily in the readings for the last Sundays after Pentecost, for which Jungmann, analogously to the term "Pre-Lent" used the designation "Pre-Advent". [218]. The reform of the rubrics of 1955 and the Codex Rubricarum of 1960 raised the rank of the four Sundays of Advent, but it was with the Second Vatican Council that the real reform came. "Advent begins with first Vespers of the Sunday that falls on or nearest to the 30th November. It ends before first Vespers of the Nativity. [219] "The season of Advent has a double character. On the one hand it is a time of preparation for the great feasts of Christmas with their commemoration of the first coming of the Son of God among men. On the other hand Advent directs hearts by means of these thoughts to the expectation of the second coming of Christ at the end of the ages. Under both aspects, the season of Advent is a time of devoted and joyful expectation." [220] Both aspects follow one another: from the first Sunday until the 16th December the second coming of the Lord is the focus of the liturgy, while "the weekdays from the 17th to the 24th December are directed immediately to the preparation for Christmas". [221] This second phase is marked by the singing of the O-Antiphons at Vespers on these days. [222]

In the calendar of the Byzantine Church, on 15th November, the day after the feast of the Apostle Phillip, the Christmas fast begins. [223] The earliest reference to this "Phillip's Fast" is from the Byzantine Patriarch Nicephoros (806-815). The fast lasts for forty days until Christmas Eve. [224] Any further Advent character is lacking in the time that follows. At the most there is a trace of this in the "Sunday of the Lord's Ancestors" which is celebrated between the 11th and 17th December. Through the celebration of the "holy ancestors of the Lord in the flesh" as well as of the Old Testament prophets who foretold the coming of Christ, this represents a sort of Advent preparation for the Nativity. [225] This Sunday is repeated on the "Sunday of the Fathers", the last Sunday before Christmas. [226]

6.4.2. CHRISTMAS DAY (25th DECEMBER)

The earliest reference to Christmas Day on 25th December is found in a Roman chronography of the year 354. The data presented there allow one to conclude that Christmas was already being celebrated about the years 335 to 337. [227] The religion-

---

[217] Op. cit. Supra, 276.

[218] Cf. op. cit. Supra, 286-294.

[219] NUALC 40 – Kaczynski 1311.

[220] NUALC 39 – Kaczynski 1310.

[221] NUALC 42 – Kaczynski 1313.

[222] Cf. on this, Th. Schnitzler, Die O-Antiphonen, HlD 29 (1975) 145-154.

[223] Cf. Edelby, Liturgikon 678f. 15th November is also the memoria of the martyrs Gurias, Samonas and Habib. This day does not have a special character as the start of the Christmas fast, even if the readings, Eph 6:10-17 and Lk 20:46-21.4, can be related to it.

[224] Cf. Jungmann, Advent und Voradvent 250.

[225] Cf. Edelby, Liturgikon 713.

[226] Edelby, Liturgikon 720: "This feast is a prolongation of the feast of the Ancestors of the Lord. This time the Church honours all who before the time of Christ were 'pleasing to God'. Thus the feast is an immediate preparation of the feast of Christmas."

[227] Thus Auf der Maur, Feiern im Rhythmus der Zeit I, 166.

history thesis has, however, succeeded in asserting itself over this hypothesis based on date reckoning. The thesis states that this feast of the birth of Christ the true sun, is a christianization of the pagan feast of the birth of the unconquered sun, which was fixed by the Emperor Aurelian for this day in the year 275. Again, the celebration of the Nativity on 25th December is mentioned at the head of the list of "depositions" which is concerned with annual festivals. According to Berger this is of considerable significance for the early Roman theology of the feast of Christmas. In this list of the feasts of the martyrs, the primary concern is not with the day of death of the individual martyr. The focus is rather on the date as that on which the community comes together to honour the saint now living in the glory of God. As with the feasts of the martyrs, so at Christmas the actual birth of Christ from Mary is "only the starting-point, the calendar date of the celebration, the content of which, beyond doubt, surpasses it. One considers the event of the birth but one celebrates what followed from it. One celebrates the one who was born as he is today." [228] For this reason the feast was not at first called *in nativitate Domini*, but "very simply *natale Domini* and similarly eight days later *octava Domini* and not *octava natalis Domini*. For the celebration does not celebrate simply the moment of the birth, but celebrates the one born as the present Lord. Therefore it is not so strange that the texts of the old Roman Christmas Mass, our Mass during the day, is little concerned with the events at Bethlehem", but focuses far more on the fact that the eternal Logos of the Father has assumed our flesh. Similarly at the centre of the Byzantine liturgy is the adoration by the Magi – the *proskynesis* – of the one who has become man. The events of the birth itself are the theme of the vigil. [229]

Form Rome the feast first spread to Africa and Northern Italy. In Spain it is mentioned by the Synod of Saragossa in 380, while it seems to have been known in Gaul only at the end of the fifth century. In the East, too, the 25th December spread quickly until the middle of the sixth century. [230]

According to the homilies of Leo I, the content of the feast in Rome was the Incarnation of Christ, which in line with the theology of the feast as presented by Berger, embraced the events from the Annunciation to the Nativity, while the Adoration of the Magi and the Slaughter of the Holy Innocents already belong to Epiphany. In North Africa, though, both of these motifs were still aspects of the feast of Christmas, for reasons similar to those Berger gives for the Roman theology of the feast. The three Masses of Christmas are of Roman origin, the Masses celebrated at night, *in nocte*, at dawn, *in aurora*, and in the day, *in die*, as reported by Gregory the Great. [231] The oldest of these Christmas Masses is the – originally only – Pope's Mass in the day. Very likely in imitation of the Church of Jerusalem of the fourth and fifth centuries, which on Christmas Night - then, however, the night to the 6th January – went to Bethlehem, a midnight Eucharist was celebrated in Santa Maria Maggiore, in the crypt of which there was a

---

[228] Berger. Ostern und Weihnachten 7f. On this, Berger quotes from a Christmas sermon of Leo I, (Sermon 26,2 – PL 54, 213 AB): "The child that the Son of God did not disdain to become, despite his glory, has in the meantime grown to be a man; with time the triumphant progress of his suffering and resurrection has been completed and thus all the deeds of his self-lowering undertaken for our sake are finished; but our festive celebration to-day renews for us the sacred beginnings of Jesus, as he was born of the Virgin Mary."

[229] Cf. Berger op. cit. Supra, 8-10.

[230] Cf. Auf der Maur, Feiern im Rhythmus der Zeit I, 166-168.

[231] Hom. 8,1 – PL 76, 1103f.

representation of the grotto of Christ's birth at Bethlehem and which for this reason was known as *Sancta Maria ad praesepe*. The latest of the three Masses of Christmas is the Mass at dawn. Its development and title can be explained by its stational church on the Palatine Hill, St Anastasia, a martyr much revered in the Byzantine East and celebrated on 25th December. In the early morning on the way back from Santa Maria Maggiore to St Peter's, the Pope passed by this church and, "possibly as a gesture of friendship towards the Byzantine officials on the Palatine" celebrated the Eucharist there. It is not known. "if there was ever a complete Mass of St Anastasia on this morning. In any case, the surviving formulae have a Christmas character and only the commemoration of the saint is confined to the prayers of the day." [232] The three Masses were included in the Sacramentary and spread via the Roman liturgy all over the West, without at first making the three separate stations obligatory. Medieval mysticism referred the three Christmas Masses to a threefold birth of the Lord. Thus Tauler distinguishes the birth of the Logos from the Father before all time, celebrated at night, from the Birth of the Son from the Virgin, celebrated at dawn, and from the constantly occurring birth of God in the soul of the believer, celebrated in the day. [233]

The three Masses are retained by the Missal of 1970, but these are now optional, not obligatory. The Mass at night is marked by the Gospel of the Birth of the Lord, Lk 2:1-14. The Dawn Mass continues this narrative, Lk 2:15-20; in this gospel the symbolism of light in stronger than in the extract read at the first Mass. [234] The prologue to the Gospel of John, Jn 1:1-18, determines the mood of the third Mass of Christmas, raising the feast in its significance for man's salvation far above a romanticization which can be problematic and from a consumerism which falsifies its very core. The Vigil Mass also belongs to the Christmas liturgy. This is a Mass in the evening of 24th December which has as its gospel, unchanging in every year of the lectionary, the genealogy of Jesus, Mt 1:1-25). This Mass is a problem in parishes where it is celebrated as the last Mass of Advent. It really belongs to Christmas, contains a Gloria and insertions in the Eucharistic Prayer, and ought to be celebrated after first Vespers of the feast and not as previously on the morning of 24th December. Matters are further complicated by the growing tendency to celebrate Christmas Night Mass - "Midnight Mass" – as a vigil Mass.

Despite a frequently expressed opinion to the contrary, the Byzantine celebration of Christmas takes place, naturally, since the adoption of 25th December in the East towards the end of the fourth century, [235] on this day. However, because of the time differences between the Gregorian and Julian calendars, the 25th December in the Julian reckoning ("old style") coincides with the 7th January of the "new style", i.e. of the Gregorian calendar. Throughout the whole of the nineteenth century the Julian 25th December coincided with the Gregorian 6th January, which encouraged the mistaken belief that Orthodoxy, or the Byzantine Church had no Christmas feast of its own. [236] The vigil liturgy of Christmas on the evening of 24th December is a combination of the

---

[232] Auf der Maur 170.

[233] Cf. Adam, Kirchenjahr 105.

[234] Cf. Adam, Kirchenjahr 107.

[235] Auf der Maur says very rightly in, Feiern im Rhythmus der Zeit I, 168: "It must be clearly borne in mind that the transfer of a feast from West to East, as happened in the case of Christmas, is an extremely rare phenomenon in the history of the liturgy."

[236] Cf. Plank, Zeitrechnung und Festdatierung als ökumenisches Problem 185.

first part of Vespers with the Liturgy of St Basil, or of St John Chrysostom if the day is a Saturday or Sunday. At this celebration the gospel of the Birth of the Lord, Lk 2:1-20, is proclaimed. On Christmas Day itself, which is entitled "The Birth of our Lord, God and Saviour Jesus Christ according to the Flesh", to distinguish it from the birth from the Father before all time, the Liturgy of St John Chrysostom is celebrated with the gospel of the Adoration of the Magi, Mt 2:1-12.[237]

6.4.3. THE CHRISTMAS OCTAVE

In the renewed liturgy, only Christmas and Easter have octaves. The Octave day itself coincides with New Year's Day, which, since Julius Caesar's reform of the calendar in 46 BC, has been on 1st January. Already the name of the month refers to the double-faced Roman god Janus, who was celebrated with superstitious practices on New Year's Day. Individual Fathers of the Church and synods countered the excesses of the pagans with the penance and fasting of Christians. The Roman Church made 1st January a feast of Mary, in the Commemoration (*Natale*) of the Mother of God. There is possibly Byzantine influence behind this, it being common in Byzantium to celebrate immediately after a feast or in the octave of greater feasts, so-called "Accompanying Feasts", or *synaxes*, which were dedicated to person who were in a special way connected to the main person or played a special role in the event just celebrated. In the case of the birth of the Lord, this would be his mother, Mary, whose feast in the Byzantine calendar is on 26th December.[238] This is indeed the oldest Marian feast and its roots reach back to the era before the Council of Ephesus.[239]

In the seventh century as further Marian feasts were brought to Rome – again from the Byzantine East – the feast of Mary on the eighth day after the Nativity was overshadowed once more and made way for a specific celebration of the octave. In Spain and Gaul, however, a feast of the Circumcision of the Lord had established itself, which led to the duplication in the title which was still present in the Missal of 1570, *In circumcisione Domini et octava Nativitatis*. Since the renewal of the liturgy, the 1st January is once more celebrated as a Marian feast, *In Octava Nativitatis Domini – Sollemnitas sanctae Dei genetricis Mariae*.[240] Adam regrets with reason that the liturgy on the first day of the year does not, or does not sufficiently, take into consideration, the expectations and feelings of people today.[241]

The Feast of the Holy Family falls on the Sunday within the Christmas Octave. This feast was taken into the universal calendar by Pope Benedict XV in 1921 and placed on the first Sunday after Epiphany. In 1893, Pope Leo XIII had acceded to the request of certain dioceses and religious orders and permitted its celebration, placing it on the third Sunday after Epiphany. This is a feast of devotion or of an idea which had its roots in the Baroque devotion to the Holy Family and which, starting in Canada according to Adam, experienced a world-wide upsurge in the nineteenth century.[242] In Auf

---

[237] Cf. Edelby, Liturgikon 727-737.
[238] Cf. Edelby, Liturgikon, 737: "Synaxe der allheiligen Mutter Gottes". In addition, the 26th December is the memoria of St Euthymios of Sardes, Bishop and Martyr.
[239] Cf. Adam, Kirchenjahr 129.
[240] With the qualification in NUALC 35f, "Memoria of the day on which the Saviour received the name Jesus".
[241] Cf. Adam, Kirchenjahr 118f.
[242] Cf. Adam. Kirchenjahr 121.

der Maur's critical opinion, which is well worthy of consideration, the reform of the liturgy, "did not have the courage to eliminate this bourgeois-romantic idyll", and on top of that added it to the Octave of Christmas. [243] Even before the Christmas Octave had taken shape, there was already a series of feasts of saints which was celebrated in the week after Christmas. The Middle Ages called these saints, the "Companions (*comites*) of Jesus". [244] These were the Protomartyr St Stephen on 26th December, the Holy Innocents as victims of the slaughter at Bethlehem, 28th December, as well as the optional memorials of the martyr St Thomas Becket, murdered at Canterbury in 1170, on 29th December and Pope St Sylvester I on 31st December. [245] The veneration of St Stephen received a strong impetus from the discovery of his relics in Jerusalem in the year 415, but the reason for celebrating his feast on 26th December remains unexplained. The feast of St John the Apostle was originally also the feast of his brother James the Greater. This feast was established in Rome since the first half of the sixth century. It is only since the reform of the rubrics in 1960 that the feast of the Holy Innocents has been put on the same footing as the other feasts of martyrs. Previously it had a mourning stamp with violet vestments and the absence of the *Gloria*. It appears, according to Adam, "to have developed in the West. It is first mentioned in the calendar of the North African city of Carthage in 505, many Fathers of the Church having previously praised the martyrdom of these children." [246]

6.4.4. EPIPHANY (6th JANUARY) AND THE BAPTISM OF THE LORD.

The origins of the Feast of the Epiphany – or the Feast of the Theophany; "The Appearance of the Lord" or the "Appearance of the Divinity of the Lord [247] – lie in Egypt. Clement of Alexandria (d. 215) reports that the Gnostic community of the Basilidians celebrated a night vigil on the 6th January at which they commemorated the baptism of Jesus. [248] At the Baptism, according to Gnostic understanding, the Logos took possession of the man Jesus and thus appeared on earth. There are two further motifs connected with the baptism of Jesus in the Jordan: it is at once the begetting and birth of the perfect aeon and of the light as well as the sacred marriage in which are joined the human nature of Jesus and the divine Logos. Nikolasch considers that the Church's feast of the Epiphany developed as a reaction to this feast of the Basilidians. [249] But there are two further layers of sources of the feast of the Epiphany underlying the date of the feast of this gnostic group. In Egypt in the night from the 5th to 6th January, as reported by Epiphanius of Salamis (d.403), the birth of the Sun-god Aion from the virgin Kore was celebrated. [250] The same witness reports a cult of the Nile on 6th January during which water is drawn from the river; in this cult a role was played by the notion that on

[243]   Cf. Auf der Maur, Feiern im Rhythmus der Zeit I, 164.
[244]   Thus, e.g. Durandus, Rationale div. Off. VII, 42, 1.
[245]   Cf. NUALC 35 – Kaczynski 1306. In 35e, the 29th, 30th and 31st December are described as "days within the Octave".
[246]   Cf. Adam, Kirchenjahr 119f.
[247]   Cf. J. A. Jungmann, Der Gottesdienst der Kirche auf dem Hintergrund seiner Geschichte, Innsbruck-Vienna-München 1955, 231f.: At Epiphany the gaze is directed more at the divine aspect of the Child. At Christmas the condescension of the Son of God is more in the foreground.
[248]   Stromata I,147,1 – PG 8, 887f.
[249]   Cf. F. Nikolasch: Zum Ursprung des Epiphaniefestes. In: EL 82 (1968) 393-429.428.
[250]   Panarion haeresion 51,22 – K. Holl (ed.) II. Leipzig 1922, 285f. This passage is not contained in PG.

this night wine rather than water flowed from certain springs. [251] In any case, Epiphanius reports about the year 375 that the Egyptian Church celebrated the birth of the Lord on 6th January simultaneously with his first miracle at Cana. [252] This supports the thesis that the Church used the same elements of celebration to put an orthodox interpretation on a Gnostic feast. This feast spread everywhere from Egypt.

The birth at Bethlehem along with the visit of the Magi, baptism in the Jordan and the miracle at Cana eventually formed complex of content for the celebration of the Epiphany that arose with the emergence of the feast of the Nativity on 25th December. In Jerusalem, according to Egeria's report, only the birth of Jesus was celebrated on 6th January. For this reason, the community went to Bethlehem for the night liturgy. [253] It was only when at the end of the fifth century Jerusalem had adopted 25th December that the Baptism of Jesus became the focus of the feast on 6th January. The same is true for Antioch and Syria, Constantinople and Cappadocia. In Gaul, too the baptism in the Jordan remained the theme of the feast after the birth of Jesus had become the focus of 25th December. But along with the baptism were the Adoration of the Magi and the miracle at Cana. The same was the case in Spain and Northern Italy. [254]

According to the homilies of Leo I (440-461) the Adoration of the Magi was the sole theme of the feast in Rome. This was able to assert itself when the Roman liturgy was adopted by the Frankish Empire, but still the *tria miracula*, the Magi, Baptism and Cana, reflecting the eastern influences on the traditions of the Gallican liturgy, were mentioned in the antiphons of the Benedictus and Magnificat in the Liturgy of the Hours. Since the translation of the their putative relics from Milan to Cologne, the "Three Kings" became so much part of the celebration of the Epiphany in German-speaking regions that there was a danger that the 6th January would be mistaken for their feastday. [255]

In the Byzantine rite the Baptism of the Lord is the determining festal content of 6th January. The feast has a vigil (*paramonia*) in the theme of the Mass texts (the *troparion* and the gospel, Lk 3:1-18) is the baptism by John. The gospel of the feast itself tells the story of the baptism of Jesus by John, but the emphasis is not in the baptism itself but on the voice of the Father confirming the divinity of the Son. Thus, the Baptism of the Lord according to the festal *troparion*, is the revelation, the "epiphany", of the presence of the Son of God in the flesh and of the Holy Trinity. [256] This day is specially marked by the great blessing of water in remembrance of the baptism in the Jordan. At this blessing a cross tied to a rope is plunged into a lake, a river or harbour basin. The 6th January also has a *synaxis* or accompanying feast dedicated to a person close to Christ in the salvation event. In this case it is John the Baptist who is celebrated on 7th January. [257]

---

[251] Panarion haeresion 51,30 -PG 41, 941 A.

[252] Panarion haeresion 51,16 -PG 41, 920 B-C; 51,29 - PG 41, 940 A-B.

[253] Egeria, Peregrinatio 25, in which, however, the folio on the ceremonies in Bethlehem is missing, but which can be supplemented, according to the editor Maraval, by the Armenian lectionary. On this, cf. Maraval's remarks S. 250f., note 2.

[254] Cf. Auf der Maur, Feiern im Rhythmus der Zeit I, 158f.

[255] Cf. Adam, Kirchenjahr 123.

[256] Cf. Edelby, Liturgikon 761-770. The festal troparion (Edelby 768) runs: "By your Baptism in the Jordan, Lord, the adorable Trinity was revealed. For the voice of the Father witnessed to you, naming you the beloved Son, and the Holy Spirit in the form of a dove confirmed the certainty of the word. Christ, God, who appeared and lighted up the world, Glory to you!".

[257] Cf. Edelby, Liturgikon 770-773.

With the confining of the content of the feast in the West to the adoration of the Magi, the Baptism of the Lord was transferred to the octave day of the Epiphany. It is likely that the coincidence of the strong Gallican tradition – Baptism of Jesus, Adoration of the Magi, Miracle at Cana – with the Roman tradition of the Adoration of the Magi that led to the separation of the theme of the feast: Adoration of the Magi on 6th January, Baptism in the Jordan on the octave. In this context can be seen the gospel of the Miracle at Cana which is read on the second Sunday after Epiphany, now the second Sunday of Ordinary Time, Year C.[258] The reform of the liturgical year placed the feast of the Baptism of the Lord even closer to the 6th January, by assigning it to the Sunday immediately following this day.[259]

Since the reduction in the number of holidays, a development adumbrated in the eighteenth century and continued unabated since then, the Epiphany became more and more a solemnity celebrated on a normal working day. This is taken into account in the regulation, "when this solemnity is not a holy day of obligation, it is transferred to the Sunday between 2nd and 8th January."[260]

6.4.5. THE PRESENTATION OF THE LORD (2nd FEBRUARY)

Egeria reports this feast as the *dies quadragesima de epiphania*,[261] which took place on the fortieth day after the birth of the Lord. Since in Egeria's time the latter was commemorated in Jerusalem on 6th January, the Presentation was, accordingly, on 14th February. The present date of 2nd February is the fortieth day after 25th December. In the East, the feast is known as the *hypapante*, from the meeting of the Lord with Simeon and Anna as the representatives of the people of the covenant who were waiting for him. The Missal of 1570 took over the term "The Purification of Mary – *In Purificatione B.M.V.*' which stems from Roman tradition but one easily misunderstood. The Missal of 1970 decided on the designation "Presentation of the Lord – *In Presentatione Domini*" to underline that this is a feast of the Lord and not a Marian feast. From the characteristic procession with lights, referring to the "Light that Enlightens the Gentiles" in the Canticle of Simeon, Lk 2.32, the feast is variously know in European languages as *Lichtmeß, Candlemas, Candelore, Chandeleur*. The procession with lights was already known in the middle of the fifth century and replaced in Rome a pagan expiatory procession which took place every five years at the beginning of February as a city procession (*amburbale*). The Missal of 1970 provides two forms of procession. The first starts with a *statio* and the blessing of candles followed by a procession to the church for the celebration of the eucharist. The second foresees an solemn entry for a Mass into which the blessing of candles is incorporated.[262] The Byzantine feast of the Hypapante on 2nd February has a vigil and is followed a day later by the "synaxis in honour of the holy and righteous Simeon, called Theodochos, and the holy prophetess Anna".[263]

---

[258] Cf. Auf der Maur, Feiern im Rhythmus der Zeit I, 169.
[259] Cf. NUALC 38 – Kaczynski 1309.
[260] Cf. NUALC 37 – Kaczynski 1308.
[261] Egeria, Peregrinatio 26 – Maraval (ed.) 254.
[262] Cf. Adam, Kirchenjahr 126-128; Auf der Maur, Feiern im Rhythmus der Zeit I, 176-179.
[263] Cf. Edelby, Liturgikon 802-811.

6.4.6. THE ANNUNCIATION OF THE LORD (25ᵗʰ MARCH)

In the new ordering of the Church's year, the season of Christmas ends on the Sunday
after the Epiphany of the Lord. [264] Because of the relevance of its content to the feast of
Christmas, the feast of the Annunciation of the Lord which has always been outside the
Christmas cycle, will be discussed here. The feast developed in Constantinople in the
middle of the sixth century and spread first to the East. In the Byzantine calendar it has
a vigil and on the following day an accompanying feast, the *synaxis* of the Archangel
Gabriel. [265] There is evidence of the feast in Rome and Spain in the seventh century,
though it is not contained in the liturgies of Milan or Gaul at this period, while in
the latter the actual content of the feast is contained completely in the context of the
preparation for Christmas. The feast was first adopted in Gaul in the eighth century.
After Spain had adopted the Roman liturgy around the end of the first millennium, the
feast was celebrated in the whole of the West on 25ᵗʰ March. Before this in Spain,
since the Synod of Toledo about the year 656, the Annunciation of the Lord had been
celebrated on 18ᵗʰ December.

In all likelihood the 25ᵗʰ March is probably the oldest date of the feast, since the
day, immediately close to the Spring equinox, is referred to variously in the bible as the
first day of creation, the day of the conception of Christ, the day of his birth and the
day of his death on the cross. "The reasons why this day, on which according to various
traditions several events in Christ's life took place, should finally become that on which
the Annunciation is celebrated, remain unexplained. Since the feast of Christmas on
25ᵗʰ December is older, one can surmise that in the course of a growing historicization,
the feast of the Annunciation was assigned to the day which not only lay exactly nine
months before but, moreover, in terms of calendar reckoning, among other things contained the event of the conception of Christ." [266] The Missal of 1570 provided a Marian
preface for the Mass of the day. This was usual since the eleventh century and points to
the shifting of emphasis from a feast of the Lord to one of Our Lady. [267] The renewed
Missal once more gives the feast its oldest title, "The Annunciation of the Lord" and
a new set of texts with a proper preface. The reference to Christmas is expressed by
the rubric which directs the congregation to kneel at the words *et incarnatus est* of the
Creed, as at Christmas. But it is precisely the remaining reference to Christmas as well
as the proximity to Holy Week and Easter which, according to Adam, have prevented
the further development of this feast. [268]

---

[264] NUALC 33 - Kaczynski 1304: "The season of Christmas reaches from first Vespers of the Nativity to the
Sunday after Epiphany or the Sunday after the 6ᵗʰ January inclusive."

[265] Cf. Edelby, Liturgikon 848-856.

[266] Auf der Maur, Feiern im Rhythmus der Zeit I, 93.

[267] Thus, too, the title of the feast in the Missal of Pius V: In festo Annuntiationis B.M.V. This has entered modern languages as "Mariä Verkündigung, Maria Boodschap, Annunciation of the Blessed Virgin
Mary". This shift surely has its origins in the earliest term used in the East, "Euangelismos tes Theotokou"
in the sixth century in Constantinople. Today it is known in the East as the "Annunciation of our most
holy Godbearer and ever-Virgin Mary", cf. Edelby, Liturgikon 849.

[268] Adam, Kirchenjahr 104: "The original content of the feast of Christmas is the incarnation of the God-
man, his "appearing in the flesh", thus, conception as well as birth. For this reason it is understandable
that the feast of the Annunciation of the Lord on 25ᵗʰ March, which was added in the seventh century,
did not become a holy day of obligation, standing morover as it does in the shadow of the approaching
feast of Easter and Holy Week."

Bibliography

W. Croce, Die Adventsliturgie im Lichte der geschichtlichen Entwicklung, ZKTh 76 (1954) 257-292, 440-472.

P. Jounel, Le temps de Noël: Martimort IV. Paris 1983, 91-111.

J. A. Jungmann, Advent und Voradvent. Überreste des gallischen Advents in der römischen Liturgie: Ibid., Gewordene Liturgie. Studien und Durchblicke. Innsbruck-Leipzig 1941, 232-294.

F. Nikolasch, Zum Ursprung des Epiphaniefestes, EL 82 (1968) 393-429.

M. Righetti, Manuale di storia liturgica II: L'Anno Liturgico – Il Breviario. Milano 1955, 37-95: Il Ciclo liturgico natalizio.

A. H. M. Scheer, Aux origines de la fête de l'Annonciation, QL 58 (1977) 97-169.

6.5. FEASTS OF THE LORD THROUGHOUT THE YEAR

Individual aspects of salvation are expressed in different feasts of the Lord throughout the year. The total context of the single economy of salvation ought not, however, to be overlooked. The individual feasts of the Lord, regardless of whether they commemorate an event or an idea, regardless of when and under what circumstances they came into being, have as their theme the one who became man, was crucified and rose again.

6.5.1. CORPUS CHRISTI (SECOND THURSDAY AFTER PENTECOST)

The development of the feast of Corpus Christi cannot be explained outside the context of the specifically Western piety of the High Middle Ages, with its concentration on gazing at the Eucharistic bread. The request for a feast devoted specially to the Eucharist was expressed by the circle around Juliana of Liege, strengthened by a vision which she had in the year 1209. She saw the full moon with a stain on it which she interpreted as the lack of a feast of the Eucharist. She told her confessor, Jacob Pantaleon, the later Pope Urban IV, of this vision. In the year 1247, the bishop of Liege instituted a feast for his diocese. In 1264, Urban IV – encouraged by the miracle of the Host at Bolsena – extended the feast to the whole Church. But, apart from the Lower Rhine, in Translyvania, Hungary and certain regions of France, the reception of the feast was so tepid that the Council of Vienne, 1311-1312, had to promulgate it anew, but once more without any lasting success. It remains "to be investigated whether or not the Corpus Christi procession, which developed just towards the end of the thirteenth century, made a decisive contribution towards the popularity and final reception from below of the prescribed feast". [269] The original title of the feast was, *Festum sanctissimi corporis Domini nostri Iesu Christi*, which appeared in the Missal of 1570 as, *In festo corporis Christi*. [270] The name of the feast itself is a sign of an attenuated Eucharistic piety, completely concentrated on the visible form of bread, while the Eucharistic wine – as in the general development of Communion under the species of bread alone – was completely

---

[269] Auf der Maur. Feiern im Rhythmus der Zeit I, 201.

[270] This either remained so in modern languages - e.g. *Corpus Domini* or *Corpus Christi* in Italy and England - or received a vernacular variant such as the German *Fronleichnam*, the Lord's body, from *"fron"/"lord"* and *"lichnam"/"body"*, while in French the feast was simply called *Fête-Dieu*, or in Dutch *Sacramentsdag*. Cf. Auf der Maur, Feiern im Rhythmus der Zeit I, 200.

neglected. Even the former feast of the Precious Blood on 1ˢᵗ July, omitted from the new calendar, did not compensate for this narrow view of the Eucharist. In any case, it was connected with the veneration of the relic of the Precious Blood, for example at Reichenau and Bruges. It was only in the seventeenth and eighteenth centuries that the feast was celebrated apart from the veneration of a relic, and then with great regional differences. In 1849, under Pope Pius IX, the feast was introduced to the general calendar in thanksgiving for his return from exile in Gaeta. Pope Pius XI raised the feast to a solemnity in 1933 as part of the celebration of 1900 years of the Redemption. The feast never had an element of the veneration of the Eucharistic blood analogous to that of the Eucharistic bread at Corpus Christi. [271] The one Eucharist under both species gives its title to the latter feast in the Missal of 1970, *Sanctissimi corporis et sanguinis Christi sollemnitas*.

The Corpus Christi prayers of the Missal of 1570 were adopted by the Missal of 1970. It is likely that these were composed by St Thomas Aquinas; at least the author is very close to Aquinas's thought, so that one can speak at least of his "theological authorship". [272] The former preface, that of Christmas, which might inspire notions of a renewed "Incarnation" in the Eucharist, [273] was replaced by a proper preface of the Eucharist. The sequence, *Lauda Sion Salvatorem*, was retained. In all probability it too goes back to St Thomas Aquinas. At its centre is a presentation in verse of the dogma of Christ's real presence in the Eucharistic elements.

The most striking element of the celebration has always been the procession of the Blessed Sacrament. This is not mentioned in the earliest sources but without it the feast would not have been received "from below". The original form, i.e. a procession punctuated by stops at particular places, completed by Benediction, was particularly easily related in the fifteenth century to the type of rogation procession typical of German-speaking regions. In this, a town or village, including its fields, were traversed, the procession making a halt or station at each of the four directions of the compass where a blessing for good weather was given. Part of the rite was the custom of reading at these stations the beginnings of the four Gospels as blessings. [274] This was complemented by the addition of a blessing with the Host at each of the four stations, followed by a fifth blessing to complete the procession. Both types of procession were constantly being enriched by elements, even to the presentation of talbeaux or Eucharistic plays at the stations, which became "phenotypically determining elements of Corpus Christi", despite the fact that the procession was not officially included in the *Caeremoniale Episcoporum* until the year 1600 and in the *Rituale Romanum* until 1614 (XI,1,1). In the post-Tridentine period the splendid elaboration of the feast of Corpus Christi and its procession was intended to serve the self-representation of the Catholic Church, which

---

[271] Cf. Auf der Maur, Feiern im Rhythmus der Zeit I, 194f.

[272] Adam speaks in Kirchenjahr 141 of a "theological authorship".P.M. Gy defends Aquinas's direct authorship, cf. L'office du Corpus Christi et S.Thomas d'Aquin. État d'une recherche. In: Revue des sciences philosophiques et théologiques 64 (1980) 491-507.

[273] Cf. Jungmann, Christusgeheimnis 309: "Corpus Christi has the appearance of a new version of the solemnities of Christmas, inspired by the spirit of the new age, which saw it as the feast of feasts – to this day still in French, *la fête-Dieu*."

[274] This led to the reading of the prologue to the Gospel of John as a blessing-formula at the end of Mass, cf. Jungmann MSII, 554-559.

self-representation was itself intended to attract those of other denominations. [275] The purpose of the procession of the Blessed Sacrament at Corpus Christi is to express publicly belief in the Eucharistic presence and is far removed from any triumphalism.

"It is for the local Ordinary to decide whether and in what form the Corpus Christi or any other Eucharistic processions are to be held, or if they are to be replaced by another public liturgy. For this reason, bishops and bishops' conferences have issued appropriate regulations, particularly for Corpus Christi processions. A basic form is, Mass – possibly followed by a longer period of exposition and adoration –; procession, with or without stations; benediction and reposition." [276] Following the Second Vatican Council the Corpus Christi was discontinued in many places or was replaced by a Mass in a public place. In other places the procession was given new life, to the extent that Auf der Maur's radical questioning of the contemporary significance of the feast [277] needs to be assessed in the light of many positive pastoral experiences. [278]

6.5.2. THE FEAST OF THE SACRED HEART OF JESUS (THE THIRD FRIDAY AFTER PENTECOST)

The origins of the veneration of the heart of Jesus pierced with the lance, are found in the devotion to the Passion of Christ in the High Middle Ages. This also developed a particular piety surrounding the sacred head crowned with thorns and of the five wounds. In the sixteenth century in France the Jesuits in particular encouraged devotion to the Sacred Heart of Jesus, forming a counter-balance to the rigorist Augustinianism of the Jansenists with their emphasis on predestination. In the seventeenth century the French Oratorians, Cardinal Pierre Bérulle and Jean Eudes (d. 1680) the greatest protagonists of the devotion. From 1672, Eudes celebrated, with his community and with episcopal permission, a feast of the Sacred Heart. The spread of the feast was helped by, "a vision experienced in 1675 by the mystic Margaret Mary Alacoque (d. 1690), in which Jesus, pointing to his heart on his battered body, ordered a special feast for the Friday after the octave of Corpus Christi". [279] It was, however, only in 1856 that Pope Pius IX extended it to the whole Church, Pope Clement XIII having permitted it as a local feast to the Bishops of Poland and to the Roman Archconfraternity of the Sacred Heart in 1765. In 1899, Pope Leo XIII raised it in rank as did Pius XI again in 1928, putting it on a par with the feast of Christmas! In 1956 Pope Pius XII issued the encyclical *Haurietis aquas*, to commemorate the centenary of the extension of the feast to the whole Church by Pius IX.

In order to emphasize the connection with Good Friday, the feast of the Sacred Heart has, since it began, fallen on the third Friday after Pentecost, the first free Friday after the former octave of Corpus Christi. The Missal of 1970 adopted for the feast "for the most part, the texts which Pope Pius XI commissioned the Benedictine abbot H.Quentin

[275] Cf. Auf der Maur, Feiern im Rhythmus der Zeit I, 203.
[276] Meyer, Eucharistie 595.
[277] Cf. Auf der Maur, Feiern im Rhythmus der Zeit I, 206f.: Is the procession now simply a piece of folklore? What significance can a public procession of the Blessed Sacrament have in completely Catholic regions today? Is the feast, which developed from medieval Eucharistic piety, not now "redundant", with the restoration of a biblical and early Christian Eucharistic piety more in keeping with that of the first millennium?
[278] Cf. Adam, Kirchenjahr 143f.
[279] Aud der Maur, Feiern im Rhythmus der Zeit I, 208.

to assemble, with his personal co-operation. While earlier texts had been stamped by the Passion and the mysticism of the Song of Songs, Pius XI placed greater emphasis on the notion of reparation."[280] This feast poses a problem for Auf der Maur in that it is a typical devotional feast of a particular group within the Church with a very specific spirituality which has been extended to the universal Church. Moreover, the feast is one of an idea containing a typical tendency to isolate a single aspect of the mystery of salvation. The idea is the Saviour's love, not the event of salvation itself, and vicarious reparation, both concentrated on the motif of the opened heart. The feast of the Sacred Heart, "has and retains its meaning when devotion to the Sacred Heart is rooted in the people and its celebration is a living expression of this devotion. It runs into difficulty when this is not, or no longer, the case, or, as for example in the young Churches of Asia, appears scarcely possible for cultural reasons."[281]

6.5.3. CHRIST THE KING (THE LAST SUNDAY OF THE CHURCH'S YEAR)

This most recent of the feasts celebrating an idea was established by Pope Pius XI, who in his encyclical *Quas primas*[282] of 11th December 1925 promoted the recognition of the kingship of Christ as a cure against the destructive forces of the times. This recognition was to be effected by the institution of a special feast. An external impulse was provided in 1925 by the 1600th anniversary of the Council of Nicea (AD 325) with its definition of the divinity of Christ and the reason and foundation of all discourse concerning his universal, indeed cosmic, kingship. Originally the feast was celebrated on the last Sunday of October. This was in order to create a connection with the feast of All Saints which followed immediately: In his saints, Christ triumphs as king.[283]

But the praise of Christ as glorified *Kyrios* and Lord over creation is surely the theme of the whole of the Church's year. "Every Sunday, by its very name *dominica, kyriake*, is designated as a day of Christ the King. The commemoration of the kingship of Christ permeates the whole Church's year. Basically the reminder of the notion of Christ's kingship "is nothing other than the Easter quality which permeates and must permeate our liturgy from beginning to end."[284] Jungmann wrote these critical sentences in 1941, in the middle of the Second World War and under the National Socialist regime. The institution of the feast, only a few years after the Bolshevik October Revolution and at a period when Europe was replete with fascism and dictatorships, cannot, in fact, be separated from the uncertainties following the collapse of the monarchical system in the First World War and can be understood against this contemporary historical background. But is this feast needed outside the context of this time of upheaval?

The Missal of 1970 included this feast but transferred it to the last Sunday of the liturgical year in order better to express its eschatological dimension. This is reflected in the title of the feast in the Latin Missal, "Solemnity of Our Lord Jesus Christ, King of the Universe". The Mass texts were only slightly altered, but the enhanced biblical

---

[280] Adam, Kirchenjahr 145. Cf. on this H. A. Reinhold, Zur Geschichte und Bedeutung des neuen Herz – Jesu-Officiums, JLw 8 (1928) 246-249.
[281] Auf der Maur, Feiern im Rhythmus der Zeit I, 209f.
[282] AAS 17 (1925) 593-610.
[283] Cf. Adam, Kirchenjahr 147.
[284] Jungmann, Christusgeheimnis 317f.

proclamation of the three-year cycle presents a more rounded image of Christ. He is not presented as an idealised model king in contrast to concrete, earthly and therefore deficient forms of earthly government. The feast is a reminder that the glorified Lord is the goal of the Church year which is ending, the goal of all time and ages, the Lord who is the same yesterday, today and forever (Heb 13:8), the Alpha and Omega, the first the last, the beginning and the end (Rev 22:13). [285]

6.5.4. THE TRANSFIGURATION OF THE LORD (6th AUGUST)

The subject of this feast is the transfiguration of Christ on Mount Tabor as reported in the Synoptic Gospels, Mt 17:1-8; Mk 9:2-9; Lk 9:28b-36. The oldest reference to the feast is in East Syria at the beginning of the sixth century. Since the eighth century it was celebrated in West Syria and since about the year 900 in Byzantium under the title *Metamorphosis tou Sotéros.* "According to Baumstark's hypothesis, the roots of the feast probably lie in the commemoration of the consecration of the church on Mount Tabor." [286]

In the eleventh century the feast spread throughout all of the West but it was not until 1457 that it was extended by Pope Celestine III to the general calendar of the Latin Church with the title of *Transfiguratio*. This was done, though, as a special commemoration of the victory over the Turks led by Johannes von Capestrano and Johannes Hunyach on 22nd July 1456. The Missal of 1570 settled the date on 6th August. The texts of the Mass of the feast were included in the new Missal with a few small changes. The proper Preface, however, is new. [287]

That the 6th August ranks in the Byzantine calendar as a solemnity [288] reflects the fact that the biblical report of the Transfiguration on Mount Tabor are a key to the whole salvation-event and to the self-understanding of Byzantine theology. [289] According to Papandreou Orthodox theology and liturgy aim, despite all ascesis, not at the destruction of the world but its transfiguration. [290] On Tabor the real truth appears of the world taken up into salvation. [291]

6.5.5. EXALTATION OF THE CROSS (14th SEPTEMBER)

According to Egeria [292] the feast goes back to the dedication of the church of the Martyrdom – the church of the Holy Cross – on Golgotha on 13th September 335. In reporting this, Egeria mentions as if in passing the finding of the Holy Cross by the Empress Helena in the year 320 – the main emphasis of the festivities is completely on the dedication of the church. The same is true of the Armenian lectionary of Jerusalem. On 13th September the commemoration of the dedication of the Anastasis Basilica was

---

[285] Cf. Adam, Kirchenjahr 148; Jounel, in: Martimort IV, 122f.

[286] Auf der Maur, Feiern im Rhythmus der Zeit I, 189.

[287] Cf. ibid.; Adam, Kirchenjahr 148f.

[288] On the Byzantine texts of the feast cf. Edelby, Liturgikon 967-973.

[289] Cf. V.Lossky, La théologie mystique de l'Église d'Orient, Paris 1944, 145.

[290] Cf. D.Papandreou: die ökumenische und pneumatologische Dimension der orthodoxen Liturgie: K. Schlemmer (ed.), Gemeinsame Liturgie in getrennten Kirchen? Freiburg-Basel-Vienna 1991 (QD 132), 35-52, 41. Cf. J. D. Zizioulas, Die Welt in eucharistischer Schau und der Mensch von heute, US 25 (1970) 342-349, esp. 343ff.

[291] Cf. O. Clément, La beauté comme révélation: La Vie Spirituelle 637 (1980) 251-270. 264. M.Kunzler: Porta Orientalis 194-217.

[292] Cf. Egeria, Peregrinatio 48f. – SChr 296, 317-319.

celebrated; on the following day that of the church of the Martyrdom at which the relic of the Cross was displayed to the faithful. [293] The focus shifted from the celebration of the dedication to the solemn exhibiting of the relic of the Cross which was connected with its display on a raised place from which influenced the designation of the feast as *exaltatio crucis* or *hypsosis tou timiou kai zoopoiou staurou*. The feast spread rapidly in East and West and in the West in the seventh century adopted in double form, as the Finding of the Cross on 3rd May and the Exaltation of the Cross on 14th September.

It is suggested, in contrast to the older view [294], that the 3rd May is of Roman origin and even older than 14th September. According to the first recension of the "Pope's Book" (*Liber Pontificalis*) of about AD 530, there was a tradition in Rome that the Cross of Christ was discovered in the reign of Pope Eusebius on 3rd May 309. The solemn commemoration of this day is, however, not firmly established until the 7th century. In the eighth century the feast was adopted in Gaul and was included in the Roman Missal of 1570. [295] In Rome on 14th September the martyrs Cornelius and Cyprian were at first celebrated. Elements of the ritual veneration of the Cross developed only gradually; these were added to the original feast of the martyrs and eventually completely eclipsed it. While the Papal liturgy combined with the feast the exposition and veneration of a relic of the Cross, [296] already in the seventh/eighth centuries in the Roman titular churches the feast had become independent and was included in the liturgical calendar, while the veneration of a relic was replaced by the veneration of a representation of the Cross. The most tenacious survival was in of the use of "splinters" of the Cross in the imparting of blessings for protection from bad weather between 3rd May and 14th September. [297] Starting from Rome the 14th September was adopted by the other Western Churches. The *Codex Rubricarum* of 1960 abolished 3rd May as a feast and increased the rank of 14th September. In the Missal of 1970 the 14th September, the Exaltation of the Cross, is celebrated as a feast (*festum*). The new texts for the Mass – only the Preface of the old Mass with motif, tree of paradise / tree of the Cross, was retained – have as their theme the Redemption offered through the Cross. "Focussing on this central mystery of faith, the presider's prayers ask for a share in the fruits of Redemption (prayer of the day), forgiveness of sin (prayer over the offerings) and the glory of the Resurrection. Thus, the theme of the feast in basically the same as that of the liturgy of Good Friday." [298] In the Byzantine rite the Exaltation of the Cross is one of the solemnities which, in the form of a vigil, precede the commemoration of the dedication of the basilica at Jerusalem. [299] Further Byzantine feasts of the Cross are: 7th May, "Commemoration of the appearance of the venerable sign of the Cross in the heavens over Jerusalem during the reign of Constantius, the son of the great Constantine" on 7th May 351 – an event also reported by St Cyril of Jerusalem in his Catecheses. [300], also

---

[293] Cf. Auf der Maur, Feiern im Rhythmus der Zeit I, 186.

[294] Cf. Adam, Kirchenjahr 151: The 3rd May is of Gallican origin and is connected with the rescue of the relic of the Cross from the Persians by the emperor Heraclius in the year 628.

[295] Cf. Auf der Maur, Feiern im Rhythmus der Zeit I, 187.

[296] Cf. Jounel, Année 115: A Rome, la fête du 14 septembre fut longtemps marquée par une procession, qui partait de Sainte-Marie-Majeure pour aller au Latran vénérer la Croix avant que ne commence la messe."

[297] Cf. Auf de Maur, Feiern im Rhythmus der Zeit I, 188.

[298] Adam, Kirchenjahr 152.

[299] Cf. Edelby, Liturgikon 601-611.

[300] Cf.Edelby, Liturgikon 885, Auf der Maur, Feiern im Rhythmus der Zeit I, 188. On Cyril, cf. PG 33, 1179.

1st August. "Procession of the precious and life-giving Cross" – to ward off sickness and catastrophes, from the tenth century onwards, in the evening of the day before 1st August, the relic of the True Cross was carried from the imperial treasury and placed on the altar of Hagia Sophia where it remained until 15th August, the Dormition of the Virgin.[301]

6.5.6. THE FEAST OF THE DEDICATION OF A CHURCH

The feast of the dedication of a church is regarded as a feast of the Lord. The reason for this is that the quintessential Temple, not made by human hand and in which the fullness of the Godhead dwells, is the human nature of the second person of the Holy Trinity made man.[302] All Christians have entry to this temple, all participate in its life. Thus the church built of stone is always more than a necessary venue for the gatherings of a community; it is a concrete presentation of the foundational truth that all the faithful. as members of the mystical body, belong together under their head. As members of Christ's body, which is the true Temple, the many faithful make up a Church built of living stones. They come together in a visible temple made of real stone which is the perceptible expression of the invisible Temple, the Lord invisibly present in his Church, the Lord from whose glorified human nature as the source of divinity all salvation flows now as before, and this in the perceptible rites of the liturgy.

Natale, or *dies natalis* denotes not only the anniversary day of a martyr – the day of his or her death as their heavenly birthday - but also the anniversary of the election and consecration of a Pope, a bishop or also the dedication of a church. There were pagan models for the celebration of the anniversaries of temples, but more important was the annual celebration ordered by Judas Maccabeus for the re-dedication of the Temple at Jerusalem in the year BC 165, the so-called feast of *Chanukka*. About the year AD 400 Egeria described the celebration of the dedication of the basilica of the Resurrection and Martyrdom at Jerusalem.[303] From Rome the commemoration of the dedications of churches spread to all of the West. The dedications of the Lateran Basilica, of the basilicas of the Apostles Peter and Paul as well as the dedication of the Basilica of St Mary Major became significant beyond the bounds of the city itself.[304]

On 9th November is the feast of the dedication of the Lateran Basilica. The basilica, dedicated to the Saviour, built in AD 324 by the Emperor Constantine in the area of the imperial palace was further dedicated to St John the Baptist and St John the Evangelist at the beginning of the tenth century under Pope Sergius III. According to an inscription erected on the orders of Pope Clement XII (1730-1740), the basilica of St John in the Lateran is "Mother and Head of all Churches of the City and of the World". Through the Augustinian hermits the feast of its dedication spread beyond Rome and was included in the Missals of 1570 and 1970. The new Missal also includes, but as an optional memorial, the 18th November as the dedication of the basilicas of St Peter and St Paul Outside the Walls. The date of 18th November, witnessed as far back as the twelfth

---

[301] Cf. Edelby, Liturgikon 963; Auf der Maur, Feiern im Rhythmus der Zeit I, 188.
[302] Cf. Y. Congar, Das Mysterium des Tempels. Die Geschichte der Gegenwart Gottes von der Genesis bis zur Apokalypse, Salzburg 1969, esp. 53.129-133; J. Ratzinger, Auferbaut aus lebendigen Steinen: W. Seidel (ed.), Kirche aus lebendigen Steinen, Maniz 1975, 30-48. 37-42; M. Kunzler: Porta Orientalis esp. 627-629.
[303] Cf. Egeria 48f. Maraval (ed.) 317-319.
[304] On what follows cf. Adam, Kirchenjahr 152f.

century, was retained for the consecration of the new basilica of St Peter in 1626. The Constantinian basilica of St Paul Outside the Walls was destroyed by fire in 1823, was rebuilt and consecrated on 10th December 1854, but the old date of the dedication, 18th November was retained. The basilica of St Mary Major, first built in the fourth century under Pope Liberius (352-366), was dedicated by Pope Sixtus III to Our Lady on the 5th August in one of the years following the Council of Ephesus, a Council which had been so important for Marian piety. A Roman custom, whose meaning was later no longer understood, of scattering flowers on feasts of dedication, led to the legend of the miracle of a snowfall in Summer leading to the choice of site for the basilica. This was largely responsible for the spread of the feast as one of Our Lady, *Dedicatio B.M.V. ad nives*. [305] Its inclusion in the Missal and Breviary of Pius V was confirmed by the Missal of 1970, but as an optional memorial and without any mention of the legendary miracle of the snow. The celebration of the dedications of cathedral churches was more closely linked with the community in question and even more so the commemoration of the local parish church. The commemoration of the dedication of a cathedral is celebrated as a solemnity in the cathedral itself and as a proper feast of the diocese in the other churches of that diocese. Individual churches celebrate their dedication as a solemnity on the appropriate date, when that is known. A synod at Mainz in the year 813 ordered that the anniversary of the dedication was to be celebrated as a holy day of obligation, a practice continued to this day and associated with amusements and other enjoyments, known as *Kirmes* in German. Because of the excesses experienced at such feasts and because the real date of the dedication was not known in many places, there were demands as early as in the sixteenth century for the introduction of a single, common feast of dedication for all the churches of a region. The Missal of 1970 provides two sets of prayers for the anniversary of the dedication of a church. One is for the church whose actual dedication is being celebrated. The second is of the dedication of another church. Both have a wide choice of biblical readings. The prayers of both of these Masses refer to the church built of stone as in image of the community built of the living stones of the faithful as the temple of the Holy Spirit.

Bibliography

P. Browe, Die eucharistischen Flurprozessionen und Wettersegen, ThGl 21 (1929) 742-755.

P. Browe, Die Entstehung der Sakramentsprozessionen, Bonner Zeitschrift für Theologie und Seelsorge 8 (1931) 97-117.

P. Browe, Die Verehrung der Eucharistie im Mittelalter, München 1933, reprint Sinzig 1990.

S. Felbecker, Die Prozession. Historische und systematische Untersuchungen zu einer liturgischen Ausdruckshandlung, Altenberge 1995 (Münsteraner Theologische Abhandlungen 39).

P. Jounel, Le culte de la croix dans la liturgie romaine, MD 75 (1963) 68-91.

P. Jounel, Les fêtes du Seigneur au temps "per annum": Martimort IV, Paris 1983, 112-123.

J. A. Jungmann, Das Christusgeheimnis im Kirchenjahr. Eine geistesgeschichtliche Skizze: Ibid., Gewordene Liturgie. Studien und Durchblicke, Innsbruck-Leipzig 1941, 295-321.

K. Rahner, Einige Thesen zur Theologie des Herz-Jesu-Verehrung: Ibid., Schriften zur Theologie 3, Einsiedeln 1956, 391-415.

---

[305] Cf. H. Grisar, Das Missale in Lichte römischer Stadtgeschichte, Freiburg i. Br. 1925.

M. Righetti, Manuale di storia liturgica II: L'Anno Liturgico – Il Breviario, Milano 1955, 247-265.

E. Sauser, Herrenfeste im Kirchenjahr, Regensburg 1981.

6.6. FEASTS OF MARY AND OF THE SAINTS

Along with the mysteries of Christ, in the course of the liturgical year the Church also celebrates the saints, in particular the Mother of God. These feasts and commemorations are more than a way of honouring exemplary Christians of the past. Honour is not paid to the holy person, but rather to the power of grace, the turning of Holy Trinity towards man and the world through the Son and the Holy Spirit, as demonstrated in the saints. But since all grace comes through the Son, every feast of a saint, every commemoration, is an organic part of his year, the year of the Lord.

6.6.1. INTRODUCTION TO THE THEOLOGY OF THE VENERATION OF THE SAINTS

The history of the veneration of the saints starts in the era of the martyrs. Polycarp of Smyrna (d.c.155) "was probably the first martyr to receive a cultus from his community".[306] At first this veneration was confined to the burial place of the martyrs at which was celebrated the so-called *natale*, the day of death as the heavenly birthday. Among the martyrs the Apostles soon played a special role. It was only with the end of the persecutions that horizons were widened to include other kinds of holiness which were not indicated by martyrdom. This is true for "Confessors", saints in the widest sense who are not martyrs, as for the Mother of God, the veneration of whom is already evident in the early Church, but whose cultus only really developed fully after the Council of Ephesus in 431.[307]

This cultic veneration of a human being does not in any way diminish the sole mediatorship of Christ as Saviour, because it is divine grace which has not remained without effect, which has shown its power in human weakness and made that person a saint (cf. I Cor 15:10; 2 Cor 12:9). The honour paid to a saint is paid to the triune God who in turning towards a concrete human person in the form of uncreated grace, has saved that person, which salvation shows itself as holiness in the saint. God's power, that is God himself dwelling in the human person, shows its effectiveness in the saint, makes the saint capable of martyrdom, of witness, of heroic virtue or selfless dedication. For this reason Augustine considers it incorrect to pray for a saint as one might intercede for the deceased because God's grace which has shown its power in the saint raises him above every intercession of a human sinner, indeed the sinner must entrust himself to the intercession of the saint.[308]

---

[306] Adam, Kirchenjahr 167. Klauser, Märtyrerkult 37, points out that the roots of the Christian cult of martyrs lie "already in the esteem and private veneration of the just and of martyrs inherited from Judaism."

[307] Thus the venerable prayer, originating in the Christian East, "can, according to the latest research, be regarded as the oldest, extra-biblical, Marian prayer of all", the Greek text of which was discovered in Egypt in 1917 on a papyrus dating from the end of the third century. Cf. A. Heinz, Die marianischen Schlußantiphonen im Stundengebet: M. Klöckner / H. Rennings (eds.): Lebendiges Stundengebet, 342-367. 358f.

[308] "Inuria est enim pro martyre orare, cuius nos debemus orationibus commendari": Sermo 159,1 – PL 38, 868; In Joh tract. 84,1 – PL 35, 1847).

The nature of the saint is exemplified in Mary. This is also the teaching of late-Byzantine theology which will be looked at more closely here. [309] All the praiseworthy attributes of the Mother of God are based on the grace she has received from God. Gregory Palamas describes Mary as a "burning bush" and a "holy tongs" (Is 6), both of which contain the sacred flame without being burned, just as the human creature "contains" uncreated grace without losing his humanity. Mary's election and gift of grace, the birth of the Logos from her and her elevation over the angels are great acts of God for which the Church gives thanks in praise. The Logos who took flesh of her, saved, sanctified and divinized human nature. Thus Mary is "the borderline between created and uncreated nature". [310] This is true by analogy for all saints. Their "sanctity" is another way of expressing their having been "divinized", another word for God himself as uncreated grace with whom they are bound in the heavenly liturgy and the fullness of whose divine life they are privileged to enjoy. As the boundary between the uncreated and the created Mary's place in the history of salvation is indeed unique, but all saints as divinized human beings have reached that boundary. They are and they remain human beings, but through God's grace have entered the divine life, are divinized, have become "gods" by a grace-filled elevation. In Mary the eschatological goal of all people becomes visible, that of becoming saints.

Though perfected by participation in the liturgy of heaven, the saints are not separated from those living on earth. According to Nicholas Kabasilas it is not enough for them simply to offer the eternal sacrifice of praise, but they want to embrace angels, human beings and all created beings in their praise so that their blessedness which consists in praising God may be increased by a even greater number of those praising. Kabasilas finds a biblical example in the inclusion of the whole cosmos in the song of the Three Young Men in the furnace (Dan 3:57-88). "If already on earth the wish of the saints that God be praised is so great, how much more must it be when they are freed from their earthly bodies!" When one living on earth joins the heavenly praise of the saints – not only in words but also with sacrifices to God – then he prepares the greatest possible happiness for them. When in the Eucharist Christ returns the human gifts of bread and wine as his body and blood, in order to bind human beings to himself, then the joy of the saints is once again increased because their greatest happiness consists in the unity of all in Christ. [311] And Symeon of Thessaloniki, from the same late-Byzantine era as Kabasilas, also underlines the uninterrupted connection between the angels and saints in heaven with the Church on earth. The perfected remain in contact with the Church's cares and needs since the progress of the Church on earth brings with it an increase of heavenly beatitude. [312]

Just as little as the veneration of the saints does not diminish the glory of Christ, so petition for the intercession of the saints does not betray a lack of trust in God. In both is reflected the unity of the Church, which encompasses that living, or better, "fighting",

---

[309] Cf. on what follows M. Kunzler, Porta Orientalis 249-255; Ibid., Insbesondere für unsere allheilige Herrin. Der Axion-estin-Hymnus als Zugang zum Verständnis des prospherein hyper im Heiligengedächtnis der byzantinischen Chrysostomos-Anaphora: Andreas Heinz / Heinrich Rennings (eds.): Gratias agamus, 227-240.

[310] Cf. Hom. 37 in Dormitione Deiparae - PG 151, 472 B.

[311] Cf. N. Kabasilas, Eis ten theian leitourgian 48,5-7 – SChr 4 b, 270-272.

[312] Cf. Dialogos 94 – PG 155, 280 D, where Symeon writes about the commemoration of the saints at the preparation of the gifts.

on earth as well as the triumphant Church of heaven. This unity is not simply a moral imperative but is based on God's turning to man and on the effect of uncreated grace, here and in heaven. Thus, it is the Paschal mystery, Christ himself, who has shown his power in the saints who have suffered with him and who are glorified with him. This Paschal mystery is proclaimed by the Church in the commemoration of the saints. (SC 104).

6.6.2. THE HISTORICAL DEVELOPMENT OF THE SANCTORAL

There was no explicit act of canonisation in the first millennium. The saints were included in calendars and martyrologies.[313] The fact that a special cultus developed around a martyr is shown by the homilies of the Fathers of the Church on his *natale*, his day of death seen as the day of his birth to heavenly glory. These days are indicated in calendars of which those contained in the "chronograph of the year 354"[314] were valid until the reform of the calendar in 1969! This chronography, a luxuriously illustrated almanach belonging to a rich Christian named Valentine, contains, among other information, two lists with anniversaries, the *depositiones episcoporum*, the dates of death of the popes who were not martyrs – from Lucius d.254 to Sylvester d.335 – and the *depositiones martyrum*, the list of martyrs celebrated in Rome. Also included are a calendar of the Church of Carthage from the sixth century, and from Gaul the "calendar tables of Polemius Silvius from the year 448 and the Gallican festal calendar reconstructed from the writings of Gregory of Tours (d. 594)."[315]

In contrast to the calendar, the Martyrology – which later became a liturgical book, the saint of the day being read from it every morning at the office of Prime – is a conflation of the names of various saints whose days of death fall on the same date. The *Martyrologium hieronymianum*, incorrectly attributed to St Jerome originated in Gaul in the fifth century and used as sources the Roman calendar of 354, continued until 420 and the calendar of Nicomedia which also contains the dates of Western martyrs, and an African calendar. While the *Martyrologium hieronymianum* provides only basic information such as place and date, the so-called "historical martyrologies" also provide biographical notes on the saints. These originated in the eighth and ninth centuries, the first author being Bede the Venerable (d. 735). Bede's work was complemented a century later by that of an anonymous cleric of Lyons. His work, in turn, was completed by the deacon Florus about the year 840. Confusion was caused by the work of Archbishop Ado of Vienne whose *Martyrologium Romanum parvum*, from about 860, based on Florus, was long regarded as the oldest Roman martyrology. The martyrology of Usuard of Saint-Germain-des-Prés, from about 865, built on Ado. In time this martyrology superseded all others and became the basis of the Roman martyrology.[316] Promulgated in 1584 by Pope Gregory XIII, it suffered from the unreliability of its sources but was continued until the last official edition of 1922.

Significant for the further development of the calendar was the transfer of canonization to the Holy See and the opening of the calendar to contemporary saints. In the

---

[313] On the following cf. Jounel, Année 135-143.
[314] The text of the chronograph is contained in the Liber Pontificalis, I,10-12.
[315] Eisenhofer I, 92.
[316] On the historical martyrologies and Ado's forgery, cf. H. Quentin, Les Martyrologes historiques du moyen-âge, Paris 1908.

tenth century the tendency began to appear to appeal to the authority of the Pope in the matter of canonization. This seems to have taken place for the first time in the case of Bishop Ulrich of Augsburg, d. 973, whose canonization was ratified in 993 by Pope John XV. A decretal of Pope Alexander II in the year 1171 stated that the elevation of a deceased person to the honours of the altar could only take place with the consent of the Roman Church. Since the Council of Trent canonization is the responsibility of the Roman Congregation of Rites. In 1634 beatification was added as a preparatory step to canonization. This permitted the cultus of the person in question for a particular region or for a particular religious order. The first to be beatified was Francis de Sales in 1665. [317] Since, at least since the Council of Trent, Rome had the sole competence for the regulation of the liturgy, and the sole competence in the matter of canonization, the feasts of saints and the accompanying liturgical texts and Mass formularies spread from this source. This centrally regulated practice is the exact opposite of the practice of the early Church where the commemorations of saints were celebrated only at their graves. Roman canonization also made more possible the inclusion in the list of saints Christians not long dead. The calendar issued with the Roman breviary in 1568 was valid until the reform of the rubrics in 1960 and, until the final reform of the calendar, experienced a veritable inflation of feasts of saints. [318]

It was not only the exaggerated veneration of the saints in the late Middle Ages, which drew the justified criticism of the Reformers that it obscured the sole mediatorship of Christ, it was also the efforts of many interest groups to have "their own" saint's day that led to a situation where the liturgical year was more and more being overlaid with feasts and commemorations of saints. There were constant appeals for reform of the calendar and associated with it a reduction in the number of saint's days. The introduction of a universally binding breviary in 1568 and the Missal of 1570 brought with them for the first time a universal calendar in which 156 ordinary day – "ferial days" – were accompanied by 158 saint's days. This already represented a significant reduction. But matters did not remain thus. By the beginning of the twentieth century the universal calendar had 230 feasts; many diocesan calendars had over 100 additional feasts. Despite the efforts of Pope Pius X to effect a new clearing of the calendar by year 1950m there were 71 ferial days as against 262 feasts of saints. Final reform came only with the Second Vatican Council. It was decreed that the liturgical year, the Lord's year, should have precedence over the feasts of saints, "so that the full cycle of the mysteries of salvation can be celebrated in a fitting manner" (SC 108). "Feasts of saints should not have a greater weight than those feasts which commemorate the actual mysteries of salvation. A considerable number of them can be left for celebration in local Churches in particular nations or religious orders and only those saints should be commemorated in the universal Church who are genuinely of universal significance" (SC 111).

However vague the criterion "universal significance", great worth was placed in the renewal of the universal calendar on the greatest possible universality. This was understood both with regard to time – by choosing saints from every century of the Church's history – and with regard to geography – by including saints, particularly

---

[317] Cf. Jounel, Année 138f.; W. Schulz, Das neue Seligsprechungsverfahren und Heiligsprechungsverfahren, Paderborn 1988.

[318] Jounel, Année 141: "entre la fin du XVIe siècle et le IIe concile du Vatican, le calendrier a connu une véritable inflation."

martyrs, from all parts of the world. It was also necessary to widen the horizons of sanctity, a priestly or monastic ideal needed to be expanded to accommodate in the Sanctoral every state of life, every expression of Christian existence. Historical truth was a deciding principle on which choices were based. Saints whose existence was legendary were not included in the new calendar. In principle the dates of feasts and commemorations continued to be based on the *natale*, on the day of death as the day of heavenly birth. Some dates were based on those of the translation of relics or on the anniversary of the dedication of churches associated with these saints. For many Eastern saints the date of their feast in the Eastern Church was adopted. Other changes in date were a consequence of the rule that in Lent and in the second part of Advent, i.e. from 17th to 24th December, no feasts of saint and no commemorations may be celebrated. At the celebration of Mass the rule is that on solemnities and feasts the proper texts, or those of the common, are to be used. On obligatory memorials the prayer of the day alone is compulsory. The same rules apply to the Liturgy of the Hours. [319]

6.6.3. SOLEMNITIES AND FEASTS OF THE MOTHER OF GOD

"In the celebration of this yearly cycle of the mysteries of Christ the Church honours with a special love Mary, the blessed mother of God, who is inextricably associated with the saving work of her son. In Mary the Church admires and praises the noble fruit of salvation. In her she sees with joy, as in a pure image, what she fully wishes and hopes to be." (SC 103). How close the link is between Mary and her son, is shown by the fact that two feasts of the Lord, the subjects of which concern Mary, but which are primarily about Christ himself, came in time to be considered in many places as Marian feasts. Thus, the Presentation of the Lord or *hypapante,* the meeting of the one who had appeared on earth with the people of the Old Covenant, became the Presentation of Our Lady. Similarly, the Annunciation of the Lord became the Annunciation of Mary. It must be a goal of liturgical renewal that the theological basis for the veneration of the Mother of God and the celebration of Marian feasts as presented in the Constitution on the Liturgy be translated into liturgical practice. As Pope Paul VI wrote in 1974 in his letter *Marialis Cultus*: The reform has to ensure in an organic way, and by emphasizing the link which unites them, the commemoration of the Mother of God within the annual celebration of the mysteries of her son. [320] Along with the special commemoration of the Mother of God in the context of the great feasts of the Lord, e.g. her feast on 1st January, the octave day of Christmas and the above mentioned feasts of the Annunciation and Presentation, are the feasts of the Dormition of the Virgin and Our Lady's Nativity, both of which go back to the early Church, while the feasts of the Immaculate Conception and the Visitation are later developments.

A. The Solemnity of the Immaculate Conception (8th December) [321]

On 9th December, nine months before the birth of Mary is commemorated, the Byzantine Church, since the eighth century, has celebrated the "Conception of Saint Anne, the mother of the God-bearer". [322] Jounel suggests that it was pilgrims returning from the Holy Land who in the eleventh century introduced the feast to England where it very

---

[319] Cf. Adam, Kirchenjahr 184-188.
[320] Cf. Marialis Cultus 2 – AAS 66 (1974) – Kaczynski 3224.
[321] On all of this cf. Jounel, Année 155f.; Adam, Kirchenjahr 173ff.
[322] Cf. Edelby, Liturgikon 710-712.

soon came to be called "The Conception of Mary". In his *Tractatus de Conceptione S.Mariae*, Eadmar, a pupil of St Anselm of Canterbury, promoted the theology of the Immaculate Conception along with the celebration on 8th December. The content of the feast, as defined in 1854 by Pope Pius IX, is that from the first instant of he conception in her mother's womb, Mary, by a unique privilege of divine grace and in view of the merits of Christ Jesus, the Saviour of Mankind, was preserved free from any stain of Original Sin. [323] The feast spread from England to Normandy and became very popular, became indeed the "feast of the Norman nation". It was brought by Norman students to Paris. But it was resisted by theologians. In 1140 Bernard of Clairvaux advised against the feast, since all men, including Mary, had to be rescued from Original Sin. [324] The feast and its content were, however, increasingly accepted. The Franciscans celebrated it from 1263 in Rome itself, where in 1477 a Franciscan Pope, Sixtus IV, confirmed the feast for the diocese, the way for the Immaculate Conception having been systematically prepared by theology since Duns Scotus. Clement XI extended the feast to the universal Church and it was further strengthened by the dogmatic definition of Pius IX on 8th December 1854. In 1863 the feast acquired proper texts for Mass and the Liturgy of the Hours. For the Mass the formularies composed by the private theologian of Sixtus IV, Leonardo Nogaroli, were revived, the Missal of Pius V having provided other texts since 1570. The Missal of 1970 adopted the 1863 for the most part, but introduced new readings, responsorial psalm, gospel acclamation and a proper preface.

B. The Visitation of the Blessed Virgin Mary (31st May / 2nd July) [325]

On 2nd July the Byzantine Church celebrates the "Deposition of the Precious Garment of Our Lady, the all-holy God-bearer, in the Blachernae Palace". This is the commemoration of the placing in the year 458 of a relic of the Virgin in the chapel of Our Lady in the Blachernae Palace at Constantinople. The gospel of the feast is that of the visit of Mary to Elizabeth which includes the *Magnificat* Lk 1:39-56. [326] The Franciscans adopted the feast in the year 1263 under Bonaventure, the master of the order, but transformed the content of the feast completely, emphasising Mary's visit to Elizabeth and the meeting of their unborn children, Jesus and John. Pope Urban VI confirmed the feast in 1389 but it was not until the Missal of 1570 included it in the general calendar that it became universally binding. The new calendar has assigned it to 31st May on the grounds that in this position between the Annunciation and the birth of John the Baptist the chronology of the feasts coincides better with the chronology of the Gospels. The German Missal, however, has retained the old date of 2nd July because of the deep roots the feast has among the faithful both in pilgrimages and in titles of churches. The new Mass-formulary is very different from its predecessor. [327]

---

[323] Cf. DH 2803.
[324] Cf. Ep. 174 – PL 182, 332-336.
[325] Cf. Jounel, Année 1554f.; Adam, Kirchenjahr 174f.
[326] Cf. Edelby, Liturgikon 935f.
[327] Cf. Adam, Kirchenjahr 174.

C. The Solemnity of the Assumption of the Blessed Virgin Mary into Heaven (15th August) [328]

The "Pope's Book", *Liber Pontificalis*, retains the Greek name for the feast on 15th August, *koimesis* – "falling asleep". A gospel-book of 740 designates it *Sollemnitas de pausatione sanctae Mariae*. The placing of the feast on this date does, in fact, appear to be connected with the dedication of a church of Our Lady which lay between Jerusalem and Bethlehem, which a Roman lady by the name of Icelia is said to have had built in memory of the *pausatio* – or *statio* -, the rest that Mary is believed to have taken on the way to Bethlehem to give birth to Jesus. [329] This generally celebrated feast changed subsequently into a *natale* or feast of the passing away, the falling asleep (*koimesis, dormitio*) of the Virgin. As such it was introduced into the Byzantine Empire by Emperor Mauricius (582-602). There is evidence in Rome since the seventh century of the *Natale sanctae Mariae,* while the sacramentary which Pope Hadrian I (772-795) sent to Charlemagne already contained the title "The Assumption of Mary". Pope Sergius I (687-701), a Syrian, added a procession to the basilica of St Mary Major to the celebration of the feast, but this was abolished in the sixteenth century under Pope Pius V. The procession took place at night when, accompanied by lights, the icon of Christ which was kept in Lateran was carried to the Forum and from there to St Mary Major where it was "received" by the icon of Mary *Salus populi Romani* and where the Pope celebrated the Eucharist. This feast acquired a new rank with the definition in 1950 of the dogma of the bodily assumption of Mary into heaven by Pope Pius XII. In the years 1950-51 the feast was given new texts for the Mass and the Liturgy of the Hours. The 1970 Missal retained most of the Mass-formulary of 1950, but the non-gospel readings and the proper preface are new. In an effort to supersede pagan folk-medicine, herbs were already being blessed at the end of the first millennium in German-speaking regions on the feast of the Assumption. This is connected on the one hand with the time of year when there were large quantities of herbs available, on the other hand, the language of symbol – Mary as lily, as mystical rose etc. – promoted the blessing of herbs on this day, a practice which has survived down to the present. Like no other feast of Our Lady, the 15th August shows what the veneration of Mary signifies in general and what it should bring about - to look with joy on the one who is assumed into heaven as on a pure image of what the Church itself fully wishes and hopes to be (SC 103).

D. The Birthday of the Blessed Virgin Mary (8th September) [330]

The feast originates in the dedication of the church of St Anne in Jerusalem which was built in the fifth century on the purported site of the house in which Mary was born. There is evidence of the feast in Constantinople in the sixth century and in Rome in the seventh. As with the 15th August, Pope Sergius I honoured this feast with a procession, but, according to Jounel, this did not manage to establish itself outside of monasteries. [331] The Mass of the feast celebrates Mary's birth in view of her motherhood of God and with it the birth of Christ. In the words of the prayer after communion, Mary is the

---

[328] Cf. Jounel, Année 151f.; Adam, Kirchenjahr 175-177.
[329] Cf. Edelby, Liturgikon 977.
[330] Cf. Adam, Kirchenjahr 177f.
[331] Cf. Jounel, Année 152.

"dawn of hope and salvation to the world. To an extent she shares this attribute with John the Baptist, whose birth is also commemorated by the Church.

E. Other Commemorations of Our Lady in the Course of the Year

From the seventeenth century on the number of Marian feasts and commemorations began to increase. Some of them had their roots in specific historical situations, others originated in the spirituality of different groups who, according to Jounel, were anxious to give greater authority to their goals by means of a general extension of their particular feast. [332]

The commemoration of Our Lady of Lourdes on 11th February goes back to the apparitions which took place from 11th February to 16th July 1858 and was instituted by Pope Pius X in 1907. In recognition of the theological character of private revelations, the title of the feast, "The Feast of the Appearance of the Immaculate Virgin Mary" was changed in the new Missal to "The Memorial of Our Lady", to show that the focus of the feast is the Mother of God herself and not the apparitions. [333] The memorial of Our Lady of Mount Carmel on 16th July was originally a feast of the Carmelite Order which was extended to the universal Church by Pope Benedict XIII in 1726. [334] The Missal of 1970 has retained as an optional memorial the Saturday after the Feast of the Sacred Heart of Jesus as the "Immaculate Heart of Mary". This memorial developed with devotion to the Sacred Heart but was not established until 1944 by Pope Pius XII, who had entrusted the human race to the "most gentle heart of Mary on 8th December 1942. [335] Similarly the commemoration of the Queenship of Mary is a product of the Marian piety of Pius XII who wanted to give the title, which is found far back in the Middle Ages, an official character. This is celebrated on 31st May, and on 22nd August according to the German regional calendar. The introduction of this memorial in 1954 took place to coincide with the hundredth anniversary of the definition of the dogma of the Immaculate Conception in 1854. [336] The commemoration of the Name of Mary on 12th September originates in the Spanish diocese of Cuenca. Following the liberation of Vienna from the Turkish threat by Jan Sobieski on 12th September 1683, Pope Innocent XI extended the feast to the whole Church. Pius X fixed the feast, formerly on the Sunday after Our Lady's Birthday, on 12th September. [337] The memorial of Our Lady of Sorrows on 15th September goes back to the veneration of the Mother of Sorrows, *Mater dolorosa*, which was widespread in the Middle Ages and finally focussed particularly on the "Seven Dolours". These were, the prophecy of Simeon; the Flight into Egypt; the Losing of the twelve-year-old Jesus in the Temple; the Meeting with Jesus on the way to Calvary; Standing under the Cross; Jesus in the Lap of his Mother; the Burial of Jesus. In 1721, Pope Benedict fixed the "Feast of the Seven Dolours of the Blessed Virgin Mary" for the Friday before Palm Sunday. Parallel to this in the Servite Order a similar feast developed on the third Sunday in September. In 1814, Pope Pius VII extended this to the universal Church in thanksgiving for his return from exile in France. Pius X transferred the feast to 15th September, the day following the Exalta-

---

[332] Cf. Jounel, Année 160.
[333] Cf. Jounel, Année 162; Adam, Kirchenjahr 178f.
[334] Cf. Jounel, Année 161; Adam, Kirchenjahr 179.
[335] Cf. Jounel, Année 162f.; Adam, Kirchenjahr 179.
[336] Cf. Jounel, Année 163.; Adam, Kirchenjahr 180.
[337] Cf. Jounel, Année 161.; Adam, Kirchenjahr 180.

tion of the Cross. The new calendar abolished the first commemoration before Palm Sunday and changed the name of the feast on 15th September to "Our Lady of Sorrows". This memorial has a sequence, the *Stabat mater*, whose author in today believed to be St Bonaventure. [338] The memorial of Our Lady of the Rosary on 7th October has its roots in the feast-days of the rosary confraternities of the later Middle Ages. The victory of the Christians under Don Juan of Austria over the Turkish fleet at the Battle of Lepanto on 7th October 1571 was attributed to the praying of the rosary. For this reason, Pope Pius V ordered that 7th October be observed as the feast of Our Lady of Victories, *festum B.M.V. de victoria*. His successor, Gregory XIII, conceded to all churches with an altar of the rosary a feast of the Holy rosary to be celebrated on the first Sunday of October. Following the victory of Prince Eugene of Savoy over the Turks near Peterwardein in 1716, Pope Clement XI extended the feast to the whole Church. Pius X transferred the feast once more to its original date of 7th October. [339] On the 21st November the memorial of Our Lady of Jerusalem is celebrated. The Latin title of this feast is the "Memorial of the Presentation of the Blessed Virgin Mary" and in the Byzantine calendar it is known as the "Entry of our all-holy Lady, the Mother of God and ever-Virgin Mary, to the Temple (The Offering of Mary)". [340] The origins of this feast lie in the consecration of the new church of Our Lady in Jerusalem on 21st November 543. This commemoration was linked to the legend in the apocryphal Gospel of James according to which Mary was brought to the Temple when three years old, to be raised by virgins of the Temple and to serve there. Despite its legendary content, the feast was accepted in Byzantium, its promoter in the fourteenth century being Philippe de Mézières who, along with the Greeks, wanted to undertake a new Crusade and on the basis of this "ecumenical" interest wished to introduce the feast to the West. The feast was already celebrated by on Cyprus by Latins influenced by Byzantium. While Sixtus IV introduced the feast to Rome in 1472, Pius V refused to include it in the new Missal and Breviary because of its legendary content. But in 1585, Pope Sixtus V prescribed it for the whole Church. [341] Certain reservations remain regarding the feast – precisely because the new calendar has included it. [342] "Whatever may lie behind this charming legend, the Church invites us above all to contemplate her [Mary's]inner preparation for her vocation as Mother of God." [343] Seen is this light, the memorial, separated from all legendary romanticism, can contemplate the workings of grace in Mary as a pattern for the workings of grace in the whole Church.

6.6.4. SOLEMNITIES AND FEASTS OF THE SAINTS

A. All Saints (1st November) and All Souls (2nd November)

The Byzantine Church celebrates the first Sunday after Pentecost as the Sunday of All Saints. The date itself is seen as an expression of the reality that all holiness is a fruit of

---

[338] Cf. Jounel, Année 162.; Adam, Kirchenjahr 180f.

[339] Cf. Jounel, Année 161.; Adam, Kirchenjahr 181.

[340] Cf. Edelby, Liturgikon 684.

[341] Cf. Jounel, Année 156.; Adam, Kirchenjahr 182.

[342] F. Mußner and B. Fischer have articulated this unease from the viewpoints of New Testament exegesis and of liturgy. In 1961, with a view to the expected reform of the calendar by the approaching Council, both unequivocally rejected the feast: F. Mußner / B. Fischer, Was wird bei einer Kalenderreform aus dem Fest Praesentatio B.M.V. (21.11), TThZ 70)1961) 170-181.

[343] Edelby, Liturgikon 684.

the Holy Spirit, who conveys the uncreated grace of the triune God to man and brings it to perfection in him. [344] While St John Chrysostom already knew this first Sunday after Pentecost as the feast of all martyrs, [345] there were in the East two others again; Ephraem the Syrian mentions the 13th May and the East Syrian has the Friday after Easter as the feast of all martyrs. There are traces of all three dates in Rome. Thus, on 13th May 609 or 610, Pope Boniface IV (608-615) consecrated the former temple of the Pantheon as a church in honour of the Virgin Mary and all martyrs. For this consecration the Pope ordered the transfer on 28 wagons of bones from the catacombs to the church. [346] The roots of a Roman feast of all the saints lie in the annual commemoration of this consecration at which traditionally only the martyrs were celebrated. A new appreciation of the non-martyrs is already evident in the consecration of an oratory in St Peter's by Pope Gregory III (731-741), "in honour of the Saviour, his holy Mother, all the Apostles, martyrs and all the perfected righteous ones who have died throughout the world". The idea of a feast of all the saints, already expressed in this dedication, did not become reality until Pope Gregory IV (827-844) urged Louis the Pious to introduce the feast throughout his empire. "Beleth suggests that the feast was transferred from May to the Autumn because the scarcity of food early in the year made it very difficult to feed the many pilgrims who streamed to Rome when the feast was held on 13th May." [347] In reality, it is more likely that Rome simply adopted the date for the feast of All Saints which had already established itself in England and Ireland since the middle of the eighth century, i.e. 1st November. The new proper preface provided by the Missal of 1970, illustrates a new aspect of the content of the feast. While in the eighth century the veneration of non-martyrs as saints was added, the proper preface makes clear, "that the feast includes not only canonized saints, but all the departed who have already reached perfection, including indeed deceased relative and friends". [348]

This points already to the inner connection with All Souls" Day, 2nd November. Pagan Rome has its days for remembering the dead, as in the *Parentalia* from 13th to 22nd February, during which the extended family remembered its deceased relatives. Christians initially retained the mortuary customs of the pagans to the extent to which they did not contradict the faith. But more and more they changed to specifically Christian customs, though these remained confined to the family circle. A common day for remembering the dead was foreign to the ancient Church. Such a day of remembrance of all the departed is first encountered in Isidore of Seville (d. 636) who required his monks on the day after Pentecost to celebrate Mass for the souls of all the dead. At the beginning of the ninth century, Eigil, the Abbot of Fulda ordered a commemoration of all the dead on 17th December, the anniversary of the death of St Sturmius, the monastery's founder. But the actual year of the establishment of All Souls Day is 998 [349], when Abbot Odilo of Cluny ordered a commemoration of all the dead on 2nd Novem-

---

[344] Cf. also Edelby, Liturgikon 225.

[345] Cf. the Enkómion eis tous hagíous pántas en hólô tô kósmô martyrésantes – PG 50, 706.

[346] Adam, Kirchenjahr 188.

[347] Eisenhofer I, 607.

[348] Adam, Kirchenjahr 189. Adam refers to the wording of the proper preface: "For today we see your holy city, our home, the heavenly Jerusalem. There the glorified members of the Church praise you for ever, our brothers and sisters who have already reached fulfillment. We also journey there in faith, encouraged by their intercession and their example, and walk with joy towards the promised goal."

[349] Eisenhofer I, 607, however, dates the *Statutum Odilionis pro defunctis* (PL 142, 1038) as late as 1030.

ber in every monastery under his jurisdiction. This was already the custom in Cluny itself under Odilo. Via the Cluniacs the feast spread rapidly north of the Alps but did not arrive in Rome until the thirteenth century. The custom of celebrating three Masses on All Souls" Day, as at Christmas, grew up among Spanish Dominicans at the end of the 15th century. [350] In 1748 Pope Benedict XIV confirmed the practice and extended it as a privilege to Spain, Portugal and Latin America. Pope Benedict XV extended the privilege to all priests of the Church in 1915. [351] The quantitive and cultic understanding of the sacrifice of the Mass which underlies this custom is as questionable as the fearful dreariness and lack of hope of the liturgy of the dead with its emphasis on the dreadful judgement and the guilt of man's sin as reflected since the Middle Ages in the sequence *Dies irae*. In contrast, all three Masses in the new Missal are marked by faith in the Easter mystery of Christ and by the confident petition to the Lord that the dead may share in his Easter victory.

B. Solemnity of St Joseph (19th March)

While Adam finds the first mention of a cultus of St Joseph – on 20th July – in Coptic calendars of the eighth and ninth centuries, Jounel cites martyrologies from northern France, composed about the year 800, one of which mentions for the modern date of 19th March, "The Feast of the Bridegroom of Mary the Mother of God". In the fifteenth century, under the influence of St Berdardine of Siena, the theologian Pierre d'Ailly and Jean Gerson, the Chancellot of Notre Dame in Paris, there developed a great blossoming of devotion to St Joseph. Gerson above all made great efforts to establish a special feast of the saint. Through his influence the feast of the Betrothal – or Marriage – of Joseph and Mary was first celebrated at Chartres, with liturgical texts composed by Gerson. In 1480 Pope Sixtus IV introduced the feast to the universal Church. Pope Gregory XV made it a holy day of obligation in 1621, while in 1870, Pius IX raised the feast in rank by declaring St Joseph patron of the Church. The feast was duplicated in 1847 when Pius IX extended a feast celebrated by French and Italian Carmelites, "The Feast of St Joseph Protector" to the whole Church and placed in on the third Sunday after Easter. Pope Pius X raised this second feast in rank but it was abolished by the Roman Congregation of Rites in 1956. Only a year earlier, though, another feast, a third, had been added when on 1st May 1955, Pope Pius XII instituted the "Solemnity of St Joseph the Worker, Spouse of the Blessed virgin Mary, Confessor and Patron of Workers". The choice of 1st May was an attempt to christianize or "church" the "Day of Work" which had at the very least socialist connotations; thus it was an ideological feast which in the final analysis simply used the foster-father of Jesus. The reformed general calendar retained the feast of St Joseph on 1st May as an optional memorial. The Mass for the feast on 19th March is new except for the proper preface which dates from 1920. [352]

---

[350] Cf. H. Kneller, Geschichtliches über die Messen am Allerseelentag, ZKTh 42 (1918) 74-113.

[351] According to Adam, Kirchenjahr 196f. "with the proviso that a celebrant was to accept a stipend for only one of the Masses. One of the other Masses was to be celebrated to compensate for foundation-Masses which for various reasons in the course of centuries had not been celebrated or had simply been forgotten. This rule still applies, but a priest is not obliged to avail himself of the privilege of celebrating the three Masses."

[352] Cf. Jounel, Année 159f.; Adam, Kirchenjahr 189-191.

C. Solemnity of "The Birth of John the Baptist" (24ᵗʰ June) and other Feasts of St John

While the Byzantine Church celebrates St John the Baptist as an accompanying feast or synaxis on the day after the Epiphany, 7ᵗʰ January, the 24ᵗʰ June is of Western origin and already mentioned by Augustine. The saying of the Baptist, "He must increase, I must decrease." (Jn 3:30) are referred by Augustine to the days which begin to grow shorter after the feast of St John, while after the birth of Christ they get longer. [353] With this the link with Christmas is established, the birth of the Baptist, as the Forerunner of Christ preceding the birth of Christ by six months. Eisenhofer suggests that 24ᵗʰ of June is the date of the feast and not 25ᵗʰ is explained by "the language of the Roman calendar: the eighth day of the calends of January, i.e. 25ᵗʰ December, corresponds to the eighth day of the Calends of July, i.e. 24ᵗʰ June". [354] Two further feasts of John the Baptist developed in the East. "The Conception of the holy and glorious Prophet John the Baptist" on 23ʳᵈ September and "The Beheading of John the Baptist" on 29ᵗʰ August. The first was not accepted in the West, [355] the second came via the Gallo-frankish liturgy into the Roman calendar. The 29ᵗʰ August is probably the anniversary of the consecration of the church of St John at Sebaste in Samaria, where the disciples of John are said to have buried his body. This date is regarded as the day of his death since the martyrology of Jerome.

D. Solemnity of the Apostles Peter and Paul (29ᵗʰ June) and other Feasts of The Apostles

On 30ᵗʰ June, the day after the solemnity, the Byzantine Church commemorates the "Synaxis of the Twelve Glorious and Illustrious Apostles". [356] This is possibly a relic of a feast dedicated to all twelve Apostles which once probably existed in the East. Usually, though, the veneration of an Apostle was associated with his grave. Naturally, in Rome it was the graves of the Princes of the Apostles – or *coryphei* as they are called in the Greek title of the feast – that influenced this veneration. The chronography of 354 already mentions 29ᵗʰ June as the date for the commemoration of the two Princes of the Apostles, a feast which was soon celebrated outside of Rome, as in Ambrose's Milan and in north Africa at the time of Augustine. The ancient Christian custom of celebrating the anniversary of the martyrs at their places of burial caused difficulties in Rome since the graves of Peter and Paul lay far distant from each another. [357] Thus developed the "Commemoration of the Apostle Paul" on 30ᵗʰ June which was celebrated in the basilica that lay outside the walls of the city on the road to Ostia. The new ordering of the liturgy has retained this feast only in the basilica itself. The Mass of the feast retains

---

[353] Cf. Sermo 287,4 – PL 38, 1302: "Natus est Johannes hodie: ab hodierno die mimuuntur dies. Natus est Christus octavo calendras januarias: ab illo die crescunt dies." Cf. Roetzer 45f.

[354] Eisenhofer I, 603, n.9.

[355] Edelby, Liturgikon 619, is of the opinion that the Latin Church, which appears in some Western martyrologies, suppressed the feast from the fifteenth century on, "probably to prevent the faithful linking it with the idea of freedom from Original Sin as the Western Church had done with regard to the feast of the Conception of the Mother of God since the [beginning of] the second millennium".

[356] Cf. Edelby, Liturgikon 933.

[357] Adam, Kirchenjahr 194, mentions liturgical celebrations at three different locations, all of which in the third century were held on 29ᵗʰ June. These were the commemoration of St Peter in the basilica called after him; that of St Paul far outside the walls and "finally a common celebration on the Via Appia 'ad catacumbas', near the present church of St Sebastian, where in the third century during the persecution of Valerian more than likely their bodies or at least their heads were temporarily kept".

the old readings, Acts 12:1-11; Mt 16:13-19, with the addition of 2 Tim 4:6-8.17f as a second reading, new presider's prayers and a new proper preface. The feast on 29th June focuses primarily on the sufferings of Peter and Paul. There are two further feasts whose themes are more their significance as apostles of the Church.

The feast of the Conversion of St Paul on 25th January comes from Gaul in the eighth century and was a parallel feast to that of the commemoration of the conferring of the primacy on St Peter celebrated a week earlier on 18th January. "Just as the subject of this feast was Peter's vocation to the headship of the Church, the subject of the other was Paul's summons to grace and his mission as apostle to the Gentiles." [358]

The feast of St Peter's Chair on 22nd February also refers to the conferring of the primacy. Its roots lie in the commemoration of the dead in pagan Rome, the so-called Parentalia, celebrated from 13th to 22nd of the month, at the end of which a family feast was held – *chari, charistia*, or *cara cognitio* – at which an chair was left empty for the deceased. Since St Peter's actual day of death is not known, he was commemorated on the general day of remembrance on 22nd February. The empty chair was later re-interpreted as the bishop's chair or *cathedra* and the feast referred to Peter's assumption of [leadership] of the Roman Church. The adoption of the Gallican feast of the office of St Peter on 18th January, led to a duplication of the feasts of Peter's chair, "which difficulty the compiler of the *Martyrologium Hieronymianum* tried to solve, by adding the words in Antiochia to the feast on 22nd February, thus turning the other feast on 18th January into that of 'St Peter's Chair in Rome' ". [359] Both commemorations were not prescribed for the universal Church until 1558 under Paul IV. In the reform of the rubrics in 1960 the feast on 18th January was abolished in favour of 22nd February, the older of the two feasts. This arrangement was adopted by the Missal of 1970. [360]

The feasts of the other Apostles and Evangelists [361] are fairly evenly spread throughout the year. The feast of St Matthias in the general calendar was transferred to the 14th May because the older date of 24th February always fell in Lent. This earlier date had been retained by the German regional calendar. St Mark the Evangelist is regarded as the first bishop of Alexandria. His veneration was promoted by the transfer in the eighth century of his relics to Venice, the city whose patron saint he became. First evidence of his cultus in Rome, however, dates from the tenth and eleventh centuries. The joint feast of the Apostles Philip and James the Less was originally on 1st May, the date of the re-consecration of the restored church of these apostles in Rome in the year 570. But, following the institution of the feast of St Joseph the Worker in 1955 and its placing on 1st May, Ss Philip and James were transferred to 11th May. In the reformed calendar their feast was placed on 3rd May, closer to the original date. The Apostle Thomas is said to have suffered martyrdom in India. Part of his relics were transferred to Edessa on 3rd July 384. Since the original date of his feast, 21st December, fell within the period of immediate preparation for Christmas, the day of the translation of his relics, 3rd July was chosen instead. St James the Greater, who along with Peter and John belonged to the narrower circle of Apostles, already suffered martyrdom under Herod and there was, early on, a church over his grave in Jerusalem. The discovery of

---

[358] Eisenhofer I, 605.
[359] Eisenhofer I, 605.
[360] Eisenhofer I, 605.
[361] On this cf. Adam, Kirchenjahr 199.

his relics in Compostella in Spain is as legendary as his evangelisation of Iberia, even though these legends were the cause of one of the greatest pilgrimage movements of the Middle Ages. Several sacramentaries of the eighth century give 25th July as the date of the feast. Veneration of St Bartholomew on 24th August is linked with the doubtful translation of his relics to Rome about the end of the first millennium. The same is true of the Apostle and Evangelist Matthew on 21st September. His relics are purported to have come from Ethiopia to Salerno in Italy, where in 1084 the exiled Pope Gregory VII consecrated the cathedral built over his grave. Veneration of the Evangelist Luke is shared with the East as is the date of his feast, 18th October. The joint feast of the Apostles Simon and Jude, 28th October, came late to Rome from Gaul, while the feast of St Andrew, 30th November, Peter's brother and the first of the Apostles to be summoned by Christ began early when Pope Simplicius, 468-483, caused a church to be built in his honour near St Mary Major. Andrew is wont to be promoted as the "apostolic founder" of the Church of Byzantium but this reference is more legendary than anything else and based on ecclesiastical politics. [362]

E. The Feast of the Archangels (29th September) and other Angels

The Byzantine Church celebrates, on 8th November, the "Synaxnis of the Angel Princes Michael and Gabriel of the other incorporeal Powers". [363] A church of St Michael built by Constantine close to the Bosphorus is early evidence of veneration of the Archangel. The date of 8th November, however, was determined by the consecration of the church of St Michael in the Baths of Arkadius at Constantinople. "Particularly in the case of the feasts of angels, the building of a church, where no other local memorial was present, was decisive for the start of a liturgical cultus, i.e. the feast of the dedication of the church in question automatically became the feastday of the Archangel, which was equally so in the East as in the West." [364] This is also the case of 29th September, the date of the consecration of the church of St Michael in Rome. According to Eisenhofer this is further the case for 8th May as the date of the dedication of the shrine of St Michael on Mount Gargano in Apulia. On the other hand, the 8th May 492 is regarded as the date on which the Archangel appeared at this site, which resulted in the development of the feast, *Apparitio S.Michaelis Archangelis*. Up to the reform of the rubrics in 1960 this feast existed side by side with that of 29th September. Before the reform, the title of the latter feast, "Feast of the dedication of the church of the Holy Archangel Michael", referred to the consecration of the Roman church. Gabriel and Raphael, the two other Archangels referred to in the Scriptures, were originally commemorated on separate days, but it was only in 1921, under Pope Benedcit XV, that their feast-days were included in the Roman calendar, Gabriel on 24th March and Raphael on 24th October. Both of these feasts were abolished as part of the re-ordering of the calendar and the commemoration of the Archangels Gabriel and Raphael were combined with that of St Michael on 29th September – just as originally on this day all other "incorporeal

---

[362] On Andrew as the apostolic founder of the Byzantine Church, cf. F. Dvornik, The Idea of Apostolicity in Byzantium and the Legend of the Apostle Andrew, Cambridge (Massachusetts) 1958; H. G. Beck, Kirche und theologische Literatur im byzantinischen Reich, 2nd edn. 1977, 34f.

[363] Cf. Edelby, Liturgikon 666-669. There is another lesser feast of the Archangel Michael on 6th September, the theme of which is a miracle of rescue attributed to him at Colossae (Chone), Cf. Edelby, Liturgikon 590f.

[364] Eisenhofer I, 602.

powers" along with the Archangel Michael had been commemorated. First traces of a specific feast of the Guardian Angels are found in the sixteenth century on France and in Spain, but the feast is not included in the Breviary of 1568. In 1582 the Holy See acceded to a request from the diocese of Valencia and permitted the celebration of the feast. In 1667, at the request of the Emperor Ferdinand II, Pope Clement IX extended the feast of the Guardian Angels to the Church in the Holy Roman Empire and assigned it to first Sunday in September. Pope Clement X assigned it to 2nd October and extended it to the universal Church. The new calendar has retained it as an obligatory memorial. [365]

A. Angenendt, Heilige und Reliquien. Die Geschichte ihres Kultes vom frühen Christentum bis zur Gegenwart, München 1994.

H. Auf der Maur, Feste und Gedenktage der Heiligen: GdK 6,1: Feiern im Rhythmus der Zeit II/1, Regensburg 1994, 665-357.

L. Heiser, Maria in der Christus-Verkündigung des orthodoxen Kirchenjahres, Trier 1981 (Sophia vol. 20).

P. Jounel, Le culte des saints: Martimort IV, Paris 1983, 124-145.

P. Jounel, Le culte de Marie: Martimort IV, Paris 1983, 46-166.

K. A. H. Kellner, Heortologie oder die geschichtliche Entwicklung des Kirchenjahres und der Heiligenfeste von den ältesten Zeiten bis zur Gegenwart, Freiburg. i. Breisgau, 3rd edn. 1911.

Th. Klauser, Christlicher Märtyrerkult, heidnischer Heroenkult und spätjüdische Heiligenverehrung, Köln-Opladen 1960.

B. Kleinheyer, Maria in der Liturgie: W. Beinert / H. Petri (eds.), Handbuch der Marienkunde, Regensburg 1984, 404-439.

M. Righetti: Manuale di storia liurgica II: L'Anno Liturgico – Il Breviario, Milano 1955, 265-303: Il culto e le feste di Maria SS; 304-360: Il culto e le feste dei Santi.

E. Sauser, Heilige und Engel im Kirchenjahr, Regensburg 1979.

---

[365] Cf. Adam, Kirchenjahr 204f.

Part VII

Appendices

7.1. SPECIFIED BIBLIOGRAPHY FOR THE ENGLISH EDITION

HANDBOOKS:

CHUPUNGCO, Anscar J. (Ed.): Handbook for Liturgical Studies.

Volume I: Introduction to the Liturgy. Collegeville/ Minnesota 1997.

Volume II: Fundamental Liturgy. Collegeville/ Minnesota 1998.

Volume III: The Eucharist. Collegeville/ Minnesota 1999.

Volume IV: Sacraments and Sacramentals. Collegeville/ Minnesota 2000.

Volume V: Liturgical Time and Space. Collegeville/ Minnesota 2000.

MARTIMORT, Aimé-Georges and others: The Church at Prayer. An Introduction to the Liturgy. 4 Vols. Collegeville, Minn., 1986-1987.

PART 1 CATABASIS: GOD'S DESCENT TO MAN

1.1. A "THEOLOGICAL TURNING-POINT" IN LITURGICAL SCHOLARSHIP?

BELL, C.: Ritual Theory, Ritual Practice. New York-Oxford, 1992.

ELIADE, M., ed.: The Encyclopedia of Religion. New York, 1995.

GEERTZ, C.: The Interpretation of Cultures: Selected Essays. London, 1975.

GRIMES, R. L.: Beginnings in Ritual Studies. Studies in Comparative Religion. Columbia, S. C., 1995.

GRIMES, R. L.: Research in Ritual Studies: A Programmatic Essays and Bibliography. Metuchen, N. J., 1985.

GRIMES, R. L.: Ritual Criticism: Case Studies in Its Theory. Columbia, S. C., 1990.

SCHRIJVER, G. de: Experiencing the Sacramental Character of Existence: Transitions from Premodernity to Modernity, Postmodernity, and the Rediscovery of the Cosmos. In: QL 75 (1994) 12-27.

Symbols and Society: Essays on Belief Systems in Aktion. Ed. C. E. HILL. Southern Anthropological Society Proceedings, no. 9. Athens, Ga., 1975.

TURNER, V.: The Anthropology of Performance. New York, 1986.

1.2. THE PROBLEMATICAL CONCEPT OF 'CULT' – OR: WHAT IS THE POINT OF WORSHIP AT ALL?

BELL, C.: Ritual Theory, Ritual Practice. New York-Oxford 1992.

ELIADE, M.: Images and Symbols. Studies in Religious Symbolism, trans. P. Mairet. New York 1961.

MALINOWSKI, B.: Magic, Science and Religion. New York 1957.

RAPPAPORT, R.: Ritual and Religion in the Making of Humanity. Cambridge 1999.

1.3. LITURGY – GOD'S WORK AND GOD'S SERVICE FOR THE MANY

BERGER, T.: Liturgy and Theology – an ongoing Dialogue. In: Studia Liturgica 19 (1989) 14-16.

CASEL, O.: The Mystery of the Christian Worship, ed. by B. Neunheuser. London 1962.

LACUGNA, C.: Can Liturgy ever again become a Source for Theology? In: Studia Liturgica 19 (1989) 1-13.

VAGGAGINI, C.: Theological Dimension of the Liturgy. Collegevill 1976.

1.4. THE VISIBLE WORLD AS THE PREREQUISITE FOR LITURGY

ADAM, A.: Foundations of Liturgy: An Introduction to Its History and Practice. Trans. M. J. O'Connell. Collegeville, Minn. 1992

BOUYER, L.: Rite and Man: Natural Sacredness and Christian Liturgy. Trans. M. J. Costelloe. Notre Dame, Ind., 1963.

CASSIRER, E.: the Philosophy of Symbolic Form. Trans. R. Manheim. 3 Vols. New Haven, Conn., 1953-1957.

FAGERBERG, W.: What Is Liturgical Theology? A Study in Methodology. Collegeville, Minn., 1992.

KAVANAGH, A.: On Liturgical Theology. New York 1984

LATHROP, G.: Holy Things: A Liturgical Theology. Minneapolis, 1993.

LEVESQUE, P. J.: A Symbolical Sacramental Methodology: An Application of the Thought of Louis Dupré. In: QL 76 (1995) 161-181.

POWER, D.: Unsearchable Riches: The Symbolic Nature of Liturgy. New York 1984.

RAHNER, K.: Meditations on the Sacraments. New York, 1977.

RAHNER, K.: The church and the Sacraments. Trans. W. J. O'Hara, Quaestiones disputatae 9. New York, 1963.

SCHMEMANN, A.: Introduction to Liturgical Theology. New York, 1986.

SHAUGHNESSY, J. D.: The Roots of Ritual. Michigan 1975.

SKELLEY, M.: The Liturgy of the World: Karl Rahner's Theology of Worship. Collegeville, Minn., 1991.

VAGAGGINI, C.: Theological Dimensions of the Liturgy. Collegeville, Minn. 1976. Trans. L.J. Doyle and W. A. Jurgens. Collegeville, Minn. 1976.

VERHEUL, A.: Introduction to the Litury: Towards a Theology of Worship. Trans. M. Clarke. Collegeville, Minn. 1968.

WAINWRIGHT, G.: Doxology: A Systematic Theology. New York 1980.

1.5. THE OLD TESTAMENT CATABASIS: THE DIVINE GIFT OF COMMU-NION

DANIÉLOU, J.: The Bible and the Liturgy. Notre Dame, Ind. 1956.

GAVIN, F.: The Jewish Antecedents of the Christian Sacraments. London 1928, Reprint New York 1968.

MOULE, C.F.D.: Worship in the New Testament. London 31964.

OESTERLY, W.O.E.: The Jewish Background of the Christian Liturgy. Oxford 1925.

SIGAL, P.: Early Christian and Rabbinic Liturgical Affinities: Exploring Liturgical Acculturation. In: New Testament Studies 30 (1984) 63-90.

1.6. THE LITURGY OF CHRIST THE HIGH PRIEST

BRASO, G.: Liturgy and Spirituality. Trans. L. J. Doyle. Collegeville, Minn., 1960.

CORBON, J.: The Wellspring of Worship. Trans. M. J. O'Connell. New York, 1988.

GUARDINI, R.: The Spirit of the Liturgy, trans. A. Lane. New York 1931.

IRWIN, K.: Liturgy, Prayer and Sprituality. New York, 1984.

NEUNER, J., and J. DUPUIS: The Christian Faith in the Doctrinal Documents of the Catholic Church, 413-428. Staten Island, N. Y., 1981.

VAGAGGINI, C.: Theological Dimensions of the Liturgy. Trans. L. J. Doyle and W. A. Jurgens. Collegeville, Minn., 1976.

1.7. THE SPIRIT, "TO BRING US THE FULLNESS OF GRACE" (EUCHARISTIC PRAYER IV)

MCKENNA, J. H.: Eucharist and Holy Spirit. The Eucharistic Epiclesis in 20th Century Theology. Great Wakering 1975.

MCKENNA, J. H.: Eucharistic Prayer: Epiclesis. In: Heinz, A. / Rennings, H. (Edd.): Gratias agamus. Studien zum eucharistischen Hochgebet (FS FISCHER). Freiburg-Basel-Wien: Herder, 1992, 283-291.

TAFT, R.: From logos to spirit: On the early history of the epiclesis. In: HEINZ, Andreas / RENNINGS, Heinrich (Hgg.): Gratias agamus. Studien zum eucharistischen Hochgebet (FS Fischer) Freiburg-Basel-Wien: Herder, 1992, 489-502.

1.8. CHURCH I: THE CHURCH AS THE PLACE AND BESTOWAL OF GRACE

HENDERSON, J. F.: Lay Ministry, Liturgical. In: The New Dictionary of Sacramental Worship. Ed. P. Fink, 670-73. Collegeville, Minn., 1990.

KAVANAGH, A.: On Liturgical Theology. New York, 1984.

LATHROP, G.: Holy Things: Foundations for Liturgical Theology. Minneapolis, 1993.

MARTIMORT, A.-G.: The Assembly: The Church at Prayer. Vol. 1, Principles of the Liturgy, 89-111. Collegeville, Minn., 1987.

POWER, D. N.: Unsearchable Riches: The Symbolic Nature of Liturgy. New York, 1984.

RAHNER, K.: The Church and the Sacraments. Trans. W. J. O'Hara. Westminster, Md., 1974.

SCHILLEBEECKX, E.: Christ: The Experience of Jesus as Lord. Trans. J. BOWDEN. New York, 1980.

SZAFRANKI, R. T.: The One Who Presides at Eucharist. In: Worship 63 (1989) 300-16.

1.9. ANAMNESIS: GOD'S DESCENT INTO TIME

BRANDON, S. G. F.: History, Time and Deity. A Historical and Comparative Study of the Conception of Time in Religious Thought and Practice. New York 1965.

GORMAN, B.S. / WESSMAN, A.E. (Edd.): The Personal Experience of Time. New York 1977.

KAVANAGH, A.: On liturgical theology. New York 1985.

SAGOVSKY, N.: Liturgy and Symbolism. (Grove Liturgical Study 16) Bramcote Notts 1978.

SCHMEMANN, A.: Introduction to liturgical theology. (The Library of Orthodox Theology 4). Portland 1966.

1.10. THEOSIS-THE DEIFICATION OF MAN AND OF THE WORLD AS THE PURPOSE OF THE DIVINE CATABASIS

AGHIORGOUSSIS, M.: Christian Existentalism of the Greek Fathers: Persons, Essence and Energies in God. In: GOTR 23 (1978) 15-41.

ALBERTINE, R.: 'Theosis' according to the Eastern Fathers, mirrored in the development of the Epiclesis. In: EphLit 105 (1991) 393-417.

CHRISTOU, P. C.: The Teaching of Gregory Palamas on Man. In: Diakonia (New York) 8 (1973) 231-241.

LOSSKIJ, V.: Darkness and light in the knowledge of God. In: ECQ 8 (1950) 460- 471.

MANTZARIDIS, G.: The Deification of Man. St. Gregory Palamas and the Orthodox Tradition (Contemporary Greek Theologians 2). Crestwood-New York 1984.

VASILEIOS, Archimandrit: Hymn of Entry. Liturgy and Life in the Orthodox Church (Contemporary Greek Theologians 1). Crestwood-Crestwood-New York 1984.

ZIZIOULAS, J. D.: Being as Communion. Studies in Personhood and the Church, with a foreword by J. Meyendorff (Contemporary Greek Theologians 4). Crestwood-New York 1985.

PART 2 ANABASIS: MAN'S ASCENT TO GOD

2.1. ANABASIS AND ITS VISIBLE FORM

BIEDERMANN, H.: Dictionary of Symbolism. Trans J. HULBERT. New York, 1992.

CAILLOIS, R.: Man, Play and Games. Trans. M. Barash, New York 1979.

CHARBONNEAU-LASSAY, L.: The Bestiary of Christ. New York, 1991.

CHEVALIER, J., and A. GHEERBRANT: A Dictionary of Symbols. Cambridge, Mass., 1994.

CRESPI, F.: Mediazione simbolica e societ. Milan, 1984.

DILLISTONE, F. W., ed.: Myth and Symbol. London, 1966.

DILLISTONE, F. W.: Traditional Symbols and the Contemporary World. London, 1973.

FAGERBERG, D. W.: What Is Liturgical Theology? A Study in Methodology. Collegeville, Minn., 1992.

HANDELMAN, D.: Play and Ritual: Complementary Frames of Meta-Communication. In: A.J.Chapman / H.c. Foot: It's a funny thing, humour. Oxford 1977, 185-192.

IRWIN, K.: Context and Text: Method in Liturgical Theology. Collegeville, Minn., 1994

SPERBER, D.: Rethinking Symbolism. Trans. A. MORTON. Cambridge Studies in Social Anthropology 11. Cambridge, 1975.

TODOROV, T., Symbolism and Interpretation. Trans C. PORTER. Ithaca, N. Y., 1982.

TURNER, V.: The Forest of Symbols. Ithaca, N. Y., 1970.

VAN DER LEEUW, G.: Religion in Essence and Manifestation. Trans. J. E. TURNER. Gloucester, 1967.

WAINWRIGHT, G.: Doxology: The Praise of God in Worship, Doctrine, and Life: A Systematic Theology. New York, 1984.

2.2. LITURGY AND CULTURE

The Inculturation of Liturgy

CHUPUNGCO, A.: Cultural Adaptation of the Liturgy. New York 1982.

CHUPUNGCO, A.: Liturgical Inculturation: Sacramentals, Religiosity, and Catechesis. Collegeville, Minn., 1992.

CHUPUNGCO, A.: Liturgies of the Future: The Process and Methods of Inculturation. New York 1989.

CHUPUNGCO, A.: Progress and Tradition. Washington 1995.

DUJARDIN, C.: Liturgy and Inculturation in the China Mission (1870-1940): in the Shackles of the Rites Controversy. In: QL 77 (1996) 96-108.

FRANCIS, M.: Liturgy in a Multicultural Community. Collegeville 1991

KAKKALLIL, J. M.: Liturgical Inculturation in India. In: QL 77 (1996) 109-116.

ROLL, S.: Liturgy in the Company of Women: The ESWTR Conference. In: QL 74 (1993) 231-234.

ROLL, S.: Traditional Elements in new Women's Liturgies. In: QL 72 (1991) 43-59.

SHORTER, A.: Towards a Theology of Inculturation. New York 1988.

WIJSEN, F.: All People See the Same Sun. Liturgy in Africa between Inculturation and Syncretism. In: QL 77 (1996) 77-95.

Catechesis and Liturgy

JOHN PAUL II.: On Catechesis in Our Time. Apostolic exhortation Catechesi tradendae. Washington, 1979.

KOCHUPARAMPIL, X.: Liturgy and Evangelization: An Eastern Orthodox Perspective. In: QL 74 (1993) 43-48.

KOCHUPARAMPIL, X.: The Liturgical Dimension of Evangelization. In: QL 72 (1991) 218-230.

PAUL VI.: On Evangelization in the Modern World. Apostolic exhortation Evangelii nuntiandi. Washington, 1976.

Sacred Congregation for the Clergy. General Catechetical Directory. Washington, 1971.

VAGAGGINI, C.: Catechism and Liturgy. In: Theological Dimensions of the Liturgy, 887-98. Trans. L. J. Doyle and W. A. Jurgens. Collegeville, Minn., 1976.

The Psychosociological Aspect of the Liturgy

BROWN, L. B., ed. Advances in the Psychology of Religion. Vol. 2. International Series in Experimental Social Psychology 11. Oxford, 1987.

FRIJDA, N. H.: The Emotions. Studies in Emotion and Social Interaction. Cambridge, 1987.

GODIN, A.: The Psychological Dynamics of Religious Experience. Birmingham, Ala., 1985.

JACOBI, J.: The Way of Individuation. Trans. R. F. C. Hull. New York, 1967.

JUNG, C. G.: Psychology and Religion. In: Psychology and Religion: West and East. 2nd ed. The Collected Works of C. G. Jung 11:3-105. Bollingen Series 20. Ed. H. Read, M. Fordham, G. Adler. Trans. R. F. C. Hull. Princeton 1969.

JUNG, C. G.: Symbols of Transformation: An Analysis of the Prelude to a Case of Schizophrenia. The Collected Works of C. G. Jung 5. Bollingen Series 20. . Ed. H. Read, M. Fordham, G. Adler. Trans. R. F. C. Hull. Princeton 1967.

JUNG, C. G.: Transformation Symbolism in the Mass. In: Psychology and Religion: West and East. The Collected Works of C. G. Jung 11: 201-296. 2nd ed. Bollingen Series 20. Ed. H. Read, M. Fordham, G. Adler. Trans. R. F. C. Hull. Princeton 1969.

JUNG, C. G.: Christ, A Symbol of the Self. In: Aion: Researches into Phenomenology of the Self. The Collected Works of C. G. Jung 9 / 2:36-71. 2nd ed. Bollingen Series 20. Ed. H. Read, M. Fordham, G. Adler. Trans. R. F. C. Hull. New York, 1959.

JUNG, C. G., and K. Kerényi: Essays on a Science of Mythology: The Myth of the Divine Child and the Divine Maiden. Trans. R. F. C. Hull. Princeton, N. J., 1969.

2.3. THE STUDY OF LITURGY AND ITS HISTORY

CAROLL, T.K.: Liturgical Practices in the Fathers. Wilmington, Del. 1988.

HAHN, F.: The Worship of the Early Church. Philadelphia 1973.

JUNGMANN, J.A.: Pastorale Care – Key to the History of the Liturgy. In: Pastoral Liturgy, London 1962.

The Liturgical History in the East

BAUMSTARK, A.: Comparative Liturgy. Rev. B. Botte. Trans. F. L. Cross. Westminster, Md., 1958.

BRIGHTMAN, F.: The Historia Mystagogica and Other Greek Commentaries on the Byzantine Liturgy. In: Journal of Theological Studies, London-Oxford 9 (1908) 392-393.

DALMAIS, I.-H.: Introduction to the Liturgy. Trans. R. Capel. Baltimore, 1961.

DALMAIS, I.H.: The Eastern Liturgical Families. In: The Church at Prayer. An Introduction to the Liturgy. Volume 1: Prinicples of the Liturgy, Collegeville/ Minnesota 1987, 27-43.

KING, A.A.: The Rites of the Eastern Churches. 2 Vols., Rome 1947-1948, reprinted under the title The Rites of Eastern Christendom, London 1950.

KOROLEVSKIJ, C.: Liturgical Publications of the Sacred Eastern Congregation. In: Eastern Churches Quarterly 6 (1945-1946) 87-96, 388-399.

MADEY, J.: The Eucharistic Liturgy in the Christian East. Kottayam 1982.

MEYENDORFF, J.: The Byzantin Legacy in the Orthodox Church. Crestwood-New York 1982.

MEYENDORFF, J.: Russia, Ritual and Reform. The Liturgical Reforms of Nikon. Crestwood-New York 1992.

NIN, M.: The Liturgical heritage of the Eastern Churches. In: Catholic Eastern Churches: Heritage and Identity. Rome, 1994.

SALAVILLE, S: An Introduction to the Study of Eastern Liturgies. Trans. J.M.T. Barton. London 1938.

SWAINSON, C.: The Greek Liturgies Chiefly from Original Authorities. Cambridge 1884, New York 1971.

SZÖVÉRFFY, J.: A Guide to Byzantine Hymnography: A Classified Bibliography of Texts and Studies. 2 vols. Medieval Classics: Texts and Studies 11-12. Brookline, Mass., and Leyden, 1978-1979.

TAFT, R.: The Byzantine Rite: A Short History. American Essays in Liturgy. Collegeville, Minn., 1992.

TAFT, R.: The Liturgy of the Hours in East and West: The Origins of the Divine Office and its Meaning for Today. 2nd rev. ed. Collegeville, Minn., 1993.

YOUSIF, P., ed.: A Classified Bibliography on the East Syrian Liturgy. Rome, 1990.

The Liturgical History in the West

ADAM, A.: Foundations of Liturgy: An Introduction to Its History and Practice. Trans. M. J. O'Connell. Collegeville, Minn., 1992.

BAUMSTARK, A.: Comparative Liturgy. Rev. B. Botte. Trans. F.L.Cross. Westminster, Md. 1958.

BRADSHAW, P.: The Search for the Origins of christian Worship. London, 1992.

BUGNINI, A: The Reform of the Liturgy (1948-1975). Collegeville. Minn., 1990.

CRICHTON, J. D.: Lights in the Darkness. Forerunners of the Liturgical Movement. Blackrock/Ireland: Columba Press, 1996.

DALMAIS, I.-H.: Introduction to the Liturgy. Trans. R. Capel. Baltimore, 1961.

DIX, G.: The Shape of the Liturgy. 2nd ed. Westminster, 1945. Reprint New York, 1982.

DUCHESNE, L.: Christian Worship: Its Origin and Evolution. Trans. M. L. McClure. London, 1956.

HOPE, D. M.: The Leonine Sacramentary: A Reassessment of its Nature and Purpose. Oxford, 1971.

JUNGMANN, J.: The Early Liturgy to the Time of Gregory the Great. Notre Dame, Ind., 1980.

KING, A. A.: Rites of Western Christendom. Vol. 4, Liturgies of the Past. Milwaukee, 1959.

KING, A.A.: Liturgies of the Primatial Sees. London 1957.

KLAUSER, Th.: A Short History of the Western Liturgy. Trans. J. Halliburton. 2nd ed. New York, 1979.

MORETON, B.: The Eighth-Century Gelasian Sacramentary: A Study in Tradition. Oxford Theological Monographs. London, 1976.

NIN, M.: The Liturgical heritage of the Eastern Churches. In: Catholic Eastern Churches: Heritage and Identity. Rome, 1994.

PORTER, W. S.: The Gallican Rite. Studies in Eucharistic Faith and Practice 4. London, 1958.

SALAVILLE, S.: An Introduction to the Study of Eastern Liturgies, London, 1938.

SEARLE, M.: New Tasks, New Methods: The Emergence of Pastoral Liturgical Studies. In: Worship 57 (1983) 291-308.

STRAWLEY, J.: The Early History of the Liturgy. 2nd rev ed. Cambridge, 1949.

VAN DIJK, S. and J. H. WALKER: The Origins of the Modern Roman Liturgy: The Liturgy of the Papal Court and the Franciscan Order in the Thirteenth Century. London, 1960.

VAN DIJK, S.: The Authentic Missal of the Papal Chapel. In: Scriptorium 14 (1960) 257-314.

VAN DIJK, S.: The Legend of the Missal of the Papal Chapel and the Fact of Cardinal Orsini's Reform. In: Sacris Eruditi 8 (1956) 76-142

VAN DIJK, S.: The Old-Roman Rite. Studia Patristica V: 185-205. TU 80, Berlin, 1962.

VAN DIJK, S.: The Lateran Missal. In: Sacris Eruditi 6 (1954) 125-179.

VAN DIJK, S.: The Ordinal of the Papal Court from Innocent III to Boniface VIII and Related Documents. Spicilegium Friburgense 22, Fribourg, 1975.

VOGEL, C.: Medieval Liturgy: An Introduction to the Sources, 257-265. Trans. and rev. W. Storey and N. Rasmussen. Washington, 1986.

WARREN, F.-E.: The Liturgy and Ritual of the Celtic Church. Oxford 1881.

WEGMAN, H.: Christian Worship in East and West: A Study Guide to Liturgical History. Trans. G. W. Lathrop. New York, 1985.

WHITE, J.: Roman Catholic Worship: Trent to Today. New York, 1995.

WILLIS, G. G.: History of Early Roman Liturgy to the Death of Pope Gregory the Great. London, 1994.

2.4. THE HUMAN BODY AS THE INSTRUMENT OF LITURGICAL ACTION

ARGYLE, M.: Bodily communication. 2nd ed. London, 1988.

BIRDWHISTELL, R. L.: Kinetics and Context: Essays on Body Motion Communication. Philadelphia, 1970.

DAVIS, M., and J. SKUPIEN, eds.: Body Movement and Nonverbal Communication: An Annotated Bibliography 1971-1981. Bloomington, Ind., 1982.

DAVIS, M.: Understanding Body Movement: An Annotated Bibliography. New York, 1972.

DUNLOP, C.: Processions. A Dissertation together with Practical Suggestions. Oxford 1932.

GOFFMAN, E.: Behavior in Public Places: Notes on the Social Organization of Gatherings. New York, 1966.

HINDE, R. A., ed.: Non-verbal Communication. Cambridge, 1972.

KEY, M. R.: Nonverbal Communication: A Research Guide and Bibliography. Metuchen, N. J., 1977.

LEVESQUE, P. J.: Eucharistic Prayer Position: From Standing to Kneeling. In: QL 74 (1993) 30-42.

MERLEAU-PONTY, M.: Phenomenology of Perception. Trans. C. Smith. New York, 1962.

MONTAGU, A.: Touching: The Human Significance of the Skin. New York, 1986.

SHIFF, W., and E. FOULKE, eds.: Tactual Perception. Cambridge, 1982.

2.5. SPEECH IN THE LITURGY

THISELTON, A. C.: Language, Liturgy and Meaning. Bramcote, 1975.

WAINWRIGHT, G.: The Language of Worship. In: The Study of Liturgy, ed. C. Jones, G. Wainwright, E. Yarnold, P. Bradshaw, 519-28. London-New York, 1992.2

BACH, K., and R. M. HARNISH: Linguistic Communication and Speech Acts. Cambridge-London, 1979.

BENVENISTE, E.: Problems in General Linguistics. Trans. M. E. Meek. Coral Gables, Fla., 1971.

DAUENHAUER, B. P.: Silence: The Phenomenon and Its Ontological Significance. Bloomington, Ind., 1980.

DOUGHERTY, I.: Silence in the Liturgy. In: Worship 69 (1995) 142-54.

DOWNEY, M.: Silence, Liturgical Role of. In The New Dictionary of Sacramental Worship. Ed. P. FINK. Collegeville, Minn., 1990.

DUCROT, O., and T. TODOROV: Encyclopedic Dictionary of the Sciences of Language. Baltimore, 1994.

EVANS, D. D.: The Logic of Self-Involvement: A Philosophical Study of Everyday Language with Special Reference to the Christian Use of Language About God as Creator. New York, 1969.

GRAINGER, R.: The Language of the Rite. London 1974

GREEN, G. M.: Pragmatics and Natural Language Understanding. Tutorial Essays in Cognitive Science. Mahwah, N. J., 1996.

HEIDEGGER, M.: On the Way to Language. Trans. P. HERTZ. San Francisco, 1982.

LADRIÈRE, J.: Language and Belief. Trans. G. BARDEN. Notre Dame, Ind., 1972.

LEIJSSEN, L.: Introduction: Liturgy and Language. In: QL 73 (1992) 5-14.

LUKKEN, G.: Per visibilia: Anthropological, Theological and Semiotic Studies on the Liturgy and the Sacraments. Ed. L. van TONGEREN and C. CASPERS. Liturgia condenda 2. Kampen, 1994.

REYNOLDS, L. D., ed.: Texts and Transmission: A Survey of the Latin Classic. Oxford, 1983.

RICOEUR, P.: The Conflict of Interpretations: Essays in Hermeneutics. Ed. D. Ihde. Nothwestern University Studies in Phenomenology and Existential Philosophy. Evanston, Ill., 1992.

RICOEUR, P.: The Rule of Metaphor: Multi-Disciplinary Studies of the Creation of Meaning in Language. Trans. R. CZERNY. University of Toronto Romance Series 37. Toronto, 1977.

SCHALLER, J. J.: Performative Language Theory: An Exercise in the Analysis of Ritual. In: Worship 62 (1988) 415-32.

SMITH, F., and G. A. MILLER, eds.: The Genesis of Language: A Psycholinguistic Approach. Cambridge, Mass., 1969.

TAFT, R.: The Structural Analysis of the Liturgical Units: An Essay in Methodology. In: Worship 52 (1978) 314-329.

WARE, J. H.: Not with Worships of Wisdom: Performative Language and Liturgy. Washington, 1981.

WHITE, J. F.: Liturgy and the Language of Faith. In: Worship 52 (1978) 57-66.

ZIMMERMANN, J. A.: Liturgy as Language of Faith: A Liturgical Methodology in the Mode of Paul Ricoeur's Textual Hermeneutics. New York-London, 1988.

2.6. MUSIC AND SONG IN THE LITURGY

CARDINE, E.: Gregorian Semiology. Sablé-sur-Sarthe, 1982.

CARROLL, J. R.: Compendium of Liturgical Musical Terms. Toledo, 1964.

DUCHESNEAU, C., and M. VEUTHEY: Music and Liturgy: The Universa Laus Document and Commentary. Washington, 1992.

The Early Middle Ages to 1300. Ed. R. CROCKER and D. HILEY. New Oxford History of Music 2. 2nd ed. Oxford-New York, 1990.

FELLERER, K. G., ed.: The History of Catholic Church Music. Trans. F. A. BRUNNER. Baltimore, 1961.

FOLEY, E.: Liturgical Music. In: A New Dictionary of Sacramental Worship. Ed. P. Fink, 854-70. Collegeville, Minn., 1990.

FOLEY, E.: Liturgical Music: A Bibliographic Introduction to the Field. In: Liturgical Ministry 3 (Fall 1994) 130-43.

GELINEAU, J.: Voices and Instruments in Christian Worship: Principles, Laws, Applications. Collegeville, Minn., 1964.

JONCAS, J. M.: Liturgical Musicology and Musical Semiotics: Theoretical Foundations and Analytic Techniques. In: Ecclesia Orans 8/2 (1991) 181-206.

JONCAS, J. M.: From Sacred Song to Ritual Music: Twentieth-Century Understandings of Roman Catholic Worship Music. Collegeville, Minn., 1996.

JONCAS, J. M.: Hymnum Tuae Gloriae Canimus. Toward an Analysis of the Vocal and Musical Expression of the Eucharistic Prayer in the Roman Rite: Tradition, Principles, Method. Rome 1991.

2.7. LITURGICAL DRESS

COPE. G.: Liturgical Colours. In: Studia Liturgica 7 (1970) 40-49.

DEARMER, P.: The Ornaments of the Ministers. London 1920.

NORRIS, H.: Church Vestments. Their Origins and Development. London 1940.

STUB, J.A.O.: Vestments and Liturgies. Minneapolis

2.8. THINGS: MATERIAL OBJECTS AS VEHICLES OF ANABATIC EXPRESSION

ADAMS, D.: Criteria in Styles of Visual Arts for Liturgy. In: Worship 54 (1980) 349-357.

ATCHLEY, E. G. / CUTHBERT, F.: A History of the Use of Incense in Divine Worship. London 1909.

AVGEROPOULOS, P. J.: The Holy Myron. An Historical, Liturgical and Theological Study. Crestwood (NY) 1987.

CLASSEN, C., D. HOWES, A. SYNNOTT: Aroma: The Cultural History of Smell. New York, 1994.

DENDY, D.R.: The Use of Lights in Christian Worship. Alcuin Club Collections 41, London 1959.

Environment and Art in Catholic Worship, ed. By Bishop's Committee on the Liturgy, National Conference of Catholic Bishops. Washington 1978.

Liturgical Books

CABROL, F.: The Books of the Latin Liturgy. Trans. Benedictines of Stanbrook. St. Louis, 1932.

SHEPPARD, L. C.: The Liturgical Books. New York, 1962.

FRERE, W. H.: Studies in Early Roman Liturgy. Vol. 2, The Roman Gospel-Lectionary. Alcuin Club Collections 30. Oxford, 1934.

FRERE, W. H.: Studies in Early Roman Liturgy. Vol. 3, The Roman Epistle-Lectionary. Alcuin Club Collections 32. Oxford, 1935.

ENGBERG, S. G.: The Greek Old Testament Lectionary as a Liturgical Book. In: Cahiers de l'Institut de Moyen Âge grec et latin 54 (1986) 39-48.

The Hymns of the Octoechus. Parts I-II. Monumenta Musicae Byzantinae, Transcripta 3 and 5. Copenhagen, 1940, 1949.

Images

GALADZA, P.: The Role of Icons in Byzantine Worship. In: Studia Liturgica 21 (1991) 113-135.

HERMERÉN, G.: Representation and Meaning in the Visual Arts: A Study in the Methodology of Iconography and Iconology. Stockholm 1969.

MITCHELL, W.J.T.: Iconology: Image, Text, Ideologiy. Chicago-London 1986.

PANOFSKY, E.: Studies in Iconology: Humanistic Themes in the Art of the Renaissance. New York 1972.

2.9. LITURGICAL SPACE

ADAMS, W.S.: An Apology for Variable Liturgical Space. In: Worship 61 (1987) 231-242.

BOUYER, L.: Liturgy and Architecture. Notre Dame, Ind., 1967.

CONGAR, Y.: The mystery of the Temple. Trans. R.F. Trevett. Westminster Md 1962.

DAVIES, J.G.: The Influence of Architecture upon Liturgical Change. In: Studia Liturgica 9 (1973) 230-240.

DEBUYST, F.: The Church: A Dwelling Place of Faith. Studia Liturgica 24 (1994) 29-44.

FRANKL, P.: Gothic Architecture. London 1962.

LUKKEN, G. / SEARLE, M.: Semiotics and Church: Architecture. Kempen 1993.

SCHWEBEL, H.: Liturgical Space and Human Experience. Exemplified by the Issue of the Multi-Purpose Church Builduing. In: Studia Liturgica 24 (1994) 12-28.

SMART, D. H.: Charles Borromeo's Instructiones fabricae et supellectilis ecclesiasticae: Liturgical Space and Renewed Ecclesiology after the Council of Trent. In: Studia Liturgica 27 (1997) 166-175.

STREZA, L.: The Mystagogy of Sacred Space according to Orthodox Theology. In: Studia Liturgica 24 (1994) 84-90.

WEBBER, R. E.: Church Buildings: Shapes of Worship. In: Christianity Today 25 (1981) 18-20.

WHITE, J. / WHITE, S.: Church Architecture. Nashville 1988.

WHITE, S.: Liturgical Architecture 1960-1990. A Select Bibliography. In: Studia Liturgica 20 (1990) 219-238.

2.10. THE CHURCH II: THE COMMUNITY AS ANABATIC REALITY

The Second Subject of Liturgical Action: the Gathered Community/ Participatio actuosa

Omnes Circumstantes: Contributions toward a History of the Role of the People in the Liturgy. Kampen 1990.

Structured Community in Celebration: Particular Liturgical Ministries

GALLEN, J.: Assembly. In: The New Dictionary of Sacramental Worship. Ed. P. FINK. Collegeville, Minn., 1990.

HENDERSON, J.F.: Lay Ministry, Liturgical. In: The New Dictionary of Sacramental Worship. Ed. P. FINK, Collegeville, Minn. 1990, 670-673.

HURD, B.: Liturgy and Empowerment: The Restoration of the Liturgical Assembly. In: That They Might Live: Power, Empowerment, and Leadership in the Church, ed. M. DOWNEY, 130-44. New York, 1991.

MARTIMORT, A.-G.: The Assembly. The Church at Prayer. Vol. 1, Principles of the Liturgy, 89-111. Collegeville, Minn., 1987.

Roles in the Liturgical Assembly. Papers of the Twenty-third Liturgical Converence at the Saint-Serge Institute in Paris, June 28 to July 1, 1976. Trans. M. J. O'Connell. New York, 1981.

VINCIE, C.: The Liturgical Assembly: Review and Reassessment. In: Worship 67 (1993) 123-44.

Liturgy and Law

HUELS, J. M.: Liturgical Law: An Introduction. Washington, D. C., 1987.

MARTIMORT, A.-G.: Structure and Laws of the Liturgical Celebration: MARTIMORT, ed., The Church at Prayer, 1:113-129. Collegeville, Minn., 1987.

MCMANUS, F. R.: Book IV: The Office of Sanctifying in the Church?cc. 834-1253?. The Code of Canon Law: A Text and Commentary, ed. J. A. Coriden et al., 593-642, 673-712, esp. 593-614. New York, 1985.

RICHSTATTER, T.: Liturgical Law: new Style, New Spirit. Chicago, 1977.

ROTELLE, J. E.: Liturgy and Authority. In: Worship 47 (1973) 514-526.

SEASOLTZ, R. K.: New Liturgy, New Laws. Collegeville, Minn., 1980.

Liturgy and Ecumenism

BÉKÉS, G. J. and VAJTA, V.: Unitatis redintegratio, 1964-1974: the Impact of the Decree on Ecumenism: SA 71, Rome 1977.

BEST, T.F. and HELLER, D. (Ed.): So We Believe, So We Pray: Towards Koinonia in Worship. DOP 171, Geneva 1995.

VERCRUYSSE, J. E.: Sacraments in an Ecumenical Prospective. In: QL 75 (1994) 70-83.

PART 3 THE CELEBRATION OF THE EUCHARIST

3.1. THE SACRAMENT OF SACRAMENTS

CABIÉ, R.: The Eucharist. Vol. 2 of The Church at Prayer, ed. A.G. Martimort. Trans. M.J. O'Connell. Collegeville 1986.

EMMINGHAUS, J.: The Eucharist: Essence, Form, Celebration. Rev. Ed. Collegeville 1992.

FINN, P. / SCHELLMAN, J. (Edd.): Shaping English Liturgy. Studies in Honor of Archbishop Denis Hurley. Washington 1990

JUNGMANN, J.A.: The Mass of the Roman Rite. Its Origins and Development. Trans. F. Brunner. Christian Classics. Westminster, Md 1986, Reprint 1002. Originally published in New York 1951-1955.

KILMARTIN, E.: The Catholic Tradition of Eucharistic Theology: Towards the Third Millenium. In: Theological Studies 55 (Woodstock 1994) 449-454.

KUCHAREK, C.: The Byzantine-Slav Liturgy of St. John Chrysostom. Its Origin and Evolution. Allendale (USA) 1971.

MACY, G.: The Banquet's Wisdom: A Short History of the Theologies of the Lord's Supper. Mahwah NJ 1992.

POWER, D.: The Eucharistic Mystery: Revitalizing the Tradition. New York 1992.

POWER, D.: The Sacrifice We Offer: The Tridentine Dogma and Its Reinterpretation. New York 1987.

SCHULZ, H.J.: The Byzantine Liturgy: symbolic Structure and Faith Expression. New York 1986.

STENSVOLD, A.: Sacred Communication: An Analysis of the Structure of Communication in the Mass: QL 68 (1987) 167-174.

STEVENSON, K.: Eucharist and Offering. New York 1986.

3.2. A SKETCH OF THE HISTORY OF THE EUCHARISTIC CELEBRATION

ADAM, A.: Foundations of Liturgy: An Introduction to Its History and Practice. Trans. M. J. O'Connell. Collegeville, Minn., 1992.

ASHWORTH, H.: The New Patristic Lectionary. In: EphLit 85 (1971) 417-33.

AUDET, J. P.: Literary Forms and Contents of a Normal Eucharistia in the First Century. In: Studia Evangelica, ed. K. Aland and F.L.Cross, Texte und Untersuchungen zur Geschichte der altchristlichen Literatur 73 (5. Serie Bd. 18). Berlin 1959.

BALDOVIN, J. F.: The Urban Character of Christian Worship. The Origins, Development and Meaning of Stational Liturgy (OCA 228), Rome 1987.

BAUMSTARK, A.: Comparative Liturgy. Rev. B. Botte. Trans. F. L. Cross. Westminster, Md., 1958.

BOTTE, B. / BOBRINSKOY, B. / BORNET, R. (eds.): Eucharistie d'Orient et d'Occident. Paris 1970.

BRADSHAW, P.: The Search for the Origins of christian Worship. London, 1992.

BUGNINI, A: The Reform of the Liturgy (1948-1975). Collegeville. Minn., 1990.

CUMING, G.: Four very early Anaphoras. In: Worship 58 (1984) 168-172.

CUMING, G.: The Early Eucharistic Liturgies on Recent Research. In: The Sacrifice of Praise, Rme 1981, 65-69.

DALMAIS, I.-H.: Introduction to the Liturgy. Trans. R. Capel. Baltimore, 1961.

DIX, G.: The Shape of Liturgy. London 1964.

DIX, G.: The Shape of the Liturgy. 2nd ed. Westminster, 1945. Reprint New York, 1982.

DUCHESNE, L.: Christian Worship: Ist Origin and Evolution. Trans. M. L. McClure. London, 1956.

HARPER, J.: The forms and Orders of Western Liturgy from the Tenth to the Eighteenth Century. Oxford, 1991.

HOPE, D. M.: The Leonine Sacramentary: A Reassessment of ist Nature and Purpose. Oxford, 1971.

HUCULAK, Laurence Daniel: The Divine Liturgy of St. John Chrysostom in the Kievan Metropolitan Province during the Period of Union with Rome (1593-1839) (Analecta OSBM Series II, Sectio I, Bd. 47). Romae 1990.

JEREMIAS, J.: The Eucharistic Worships of Jesus. Trans. N. Perrin. Philadelphia 1990.

JUNGMANN, J.: The Early Liturgy to the time of Gregory the Great. Liturgical Studies 6. Notre Dame, Ind., 1959.

JUNGMANN, J.: The Early Liturgy to the Time of Gregory the Great. Notre Dame, Ind., 1980.

KENNEDY, C.: The Lateran Missal and Some allied Documents. In: Medieval Studies 14 (1952) 61-78.

KLAUSER, Th.: A Short History of the Western Liturgy. Trans. J. Halliburton. 2nd ed. New York, 1979.

MAZZA, E.: Mystagogy: A Theology of Liturgy in the Patristic Age. Trans. M. J. O'Connell. New York, 1989.

MAZZA, E.: The Origins of the Eucharistic Prayer. Trans. R. Lane. Collegeville 1995.

MORETON, B.: The Eighth-Century Gelasian Sacramentary: A Study in Tradition. Oxford Theological Monographs. London, 1976.

NIN, M.: The Liturgical heritage of the Eastern Churches. In: Catholic Eastern Churches: Heritage and Identity. Rome, 1994.

RIGHETTI, M.: Manuale di storia liturgica. Vol. 1, Introduzione generale. 3rd ed. Milan, 1964.

SALAVILLE, S.: An Introduction to the Study of Eastern Liturgies, London, 1938.

SHEPPARD, L.C.: Celtic Rite. In: New Catholic Encyclopedia III, Washington 1967, 384-385.

STRAWLEY, J.: The Early History of the Liturgy. 2nd rev ed. Cambridge, 1949.

TAFT, R.: Introduzione allo studio delle liturgie orientale: Bibliografia essenziale. (manuscript). Rome 1982.

TAFT, R.: The Byzantine Rite: A Short History. American Essays in Liturgy. Collegeville, Minn., 1992.

TALLEY, T.: Worship: Reforming Tradition. Washington 1990.

VAN DIJK, S. and J. H. WALKER: The origins of the Modern Roman Liturgy: The ordinals by Haymo of Faversham and Related Documents (1243-1307). 2 Vols. London, 1960.

VAN DIJK, S. and J. H. WALKER: The Origins of the Modern Roman Liturgy: The Liturgy of the Papal Court and the Franciscan Order in the Thirteenth Century. London, 1960.

VAN DIJK, S.: The Authentic Missal of the Papal Chapel. In: Scriptorium 14 (1960) 257-314.

VAN DIJK, S.: The Legend of the Missal of the Papal Chapel and the Fact of Cardinal Orsini's Reform. In: Sacris Erudiri 8 (1956) 76-142

VAN DIJK, S.: The Old-Roman Rite: Studia Patristica V: 185-205. TU 80, Berlin, 1962.

VAN DIJK, S.: Three Manuscripts of a Liturgical Reform by John Cajetan Orsini (Nicholas III). In: Scriptorium 6 (1952) 213-242.

VAN DIJK, S.: The Lateran Missal. In: Sacris Eruditi 6 (1954) 125-179.

VAN DIJK, S.: The Ordinal of the Papal Court from Innocent III to Boniface VIII and Related Documents. Spicilegium Friburgense 22, Fribourg, 1975.

VOGEL, C.: Medieval Liturgy: An Introduction to the Sources, 257-265. Trans. and rev. W. Storey and N. Rasmussen. Washington, 1986.

VOGEL, C.: Medieval Liturgy: An Introduction to the Sources. Trans. and rev. W. Storey and N. Rasmussen. Washington, 1986.

WEGMAN, H.: Christian Worship in East and West: A Study Guide to Liturgical History. Trans. G. W. Lathrop. New York, 1985.

WILLIS, G. G.: History of Early Roman Liturgy to the Death of Pope Gregory the Great. London, 1994.

3.3. THE VARIETY OF FORMS OF THE CELEBRATION OF MASS

BALDOVIN, J.: Reflections on the Frequency of Eucharistic Celebration. In: Worship 61 (1987) 2-15.

BRIANCHIANINOFF, G.: Concelebration of the holy eucharist in east and west. In: Eastern Churches Quarterly 10 (1953).

CHUPUNGCO, A: Toward a Ferial Order of Mass. In: Ecclesia Orans 10 (1993) 11-32.

GAMBER, K.: Concelebration in the Ancient Church. In: Christian Orient 2 (1981) 57-62.

KING, A. A.: Concelebration in the Christian Church, London 1966.

MATTHEWS, E.: Celebrating Mass with Children. New York, 1978.

MCGOWAN, J. C.: Concelebration. Sign of the Unity of the Church, New York 1964.

MCGOWAN, J. C.: Modes of concelebration and their relative value. In: North American Liturgical Week Preceedings 25 (1964), 101-112.

Sacred Congregation for Divine Worship. Directory for Masses with Children (November 1, 1973). Trans. International Committee on English in the Liturgy. Washington, 1974.

TAFT, R.: The Frequency of the Eucharist Throughout History. In: M. Collins / D. Power (Edd.): Can we always Celebrate the Eucharist. Concilium 152, New York 1982, 13-24.

TIHON, P.: Eucharistic Concelebration. In: Yearbook of Liturgical Studies 6 (1965) 3-32.

3.4. THE OPENING PARTS OF THE MASS

BALDOVIN, J.F.: Kyrie Eleison and the Entrance Rite of the Roman Eucharist. In: Worship 60 (1986) 334-347.

FRANCIS, M.: Uncluttering the Eucharistic Vestibule: the Entrance Rites Through Time. In: Liturgical Ministry 3 (Winter 1994) 1-12.

HANNON, K.: Gathering Rites. In: The new Dictionary of Sacramental Worship, ed. P. Fink, Collegeville 1990, 491-494.

KROSNICKI, T: Grace and Peace: Greeting the Assambly. In: Shaping English Liturgy, ed. P. Finn and J. Schellman, Washington 1990, 93-106.

SEARLE, M.: Semper Reformanda: The Opening and Closing Rites of The Mass. In: Shaping English Liturgy, ed. P. Finn and J. Schellman, Washington 1990, 53-92.

TAFT, R.: The Liturgy of the Great Church. An Initial Synthesis of Structure and Interpretation on the Eve of Iconoclasm. In: Dumbarton Oaks Papers 34/35 (1980/81) 45-75.

WITCZAK, M: The Introductory Rites; Threshold of the Sacred, Entry into Community or Pastoral Problem? In: Liturgical Ministry 3 (Winter 1994) 22-27.

3.5. THE LITURGY OF THE WORD

ASHWORTH, H.: The Prayer of the Faithful. In: Liturgy 37 (Winter 1994) 22-27.

BONNEAU, N.: The Synoptic Gospels in the Sunday Lectionary: Ordinary Time. In: QL 75 (1994) 154-169.

BRADSHAW, P. F.: The Use of the Bible in Liturgy: Some Historical Perspectives. In. Studia Liturgica 22 (1992) 35-52.

BURKE, J.: Witness to Faith: The Homily. In: American Ecclesiastical Review 163 (1970) 184-195; 270-281; 318-326.

KEIFER, R: To hear and Proclaim: Introduction to the Lectionary for Mass with Comemntary for Musicians and Priests. Washingteon 1983.

MELLOH, J.A.: The General Intercessions Revisited. In: Worship 61 (1987) 152-162.

VANLANDUYT, L.: The Psalms in the Catholic Sunday-Liturgy after the Reform of Vatican II: An Evaluation. In: QL 73 (1992) 146-160.

WIENER, C.: The Roman Catholic Eucharistic Lectionary. In: Studia Liturgica 21 (1991) 2-13.

ZIMMERMAN, J.: The General Intercessions: Yet Another Visit. In: Worship 65 (1991) 306-319.

3.6. THE PREPARATION OF THE GIFTS

KROSNICKI, T.: Mixtio aquae cum vino: A Case of Moral Unity. In: EphLit 104 (1990) 182-186.

KROSNICKI, T.: Preparing the Gifts: Clarifying the Rite. in: Worship 65 (1991) 149-159.

KEIFER, R: Preparation of the Altar and the Gifts or Offertory? In: Worship 48 (1974) 595-600.

MARCHAL, M: Peccatores ac Famuli: The Roman Preparation of the Gifts and Altar Reconsidered. In: Studia Liturgica 16 (1986-87) 73-92.

MCMANUS, F.R.: The Roman Order of Mass from 1964-1969: The Preparation of the Gifts. In: Shaping English Liturgy, ed. P. Finn and J. Schellman, Washington 1990, 107-138.

TAFT, R.: The Great Entrance. A History of the Transfer of Gifts and other Preanaphoral Rites of the Liturgy of St John Chrysostom. Orientalia Christiana Analecta 200, Rome 21978.

TAFT, R.: The Oblation and Hymn of the Chrysostom Anaphora. Ist Text and Antecedens. In: Miscellanea di studi di P. Marco Petta per il LXX compleanno vol. IV (= Bolletino della Badia Greca di Grottaferrata, n.s. 46 von 1992), published 1994, 319-345.

TAFT, R.: Towards the Origin of the Offertory Procession in the Syro-Byzantine East. In: OCP 36 (1970) 73-107.

3.7. THE GREAT EUCHARISTIC PRAYER

ALBERTINE, R.: The Epiclesis Problem: The Roman Canon /Canon I) in the Post-Vatican Liturgical Reform. In: PphLit 99 (1985) 337-348.

ALBERTINE, R: Problem of the (Double) Epiclesis in the New Roman Eucharistic Prayers. In: EphLit 91 (1977) 193-202.

DALLEN, J.: The Congregation's Share in the Eucharistic Prayer. In: Worship 52 (1978) 329-341.

GRANT, G. G.: The elevation of the Host: A Reaction to the twelfth Century Heresy. In: Theological Studies 1 (1940) 228-250.

JONCAS, M.: The Assembly's "Ownership" of the Eucharistic Prayer: Why and How. In: Today's Liturgy 16/3 (1994) 5-11.

KAVANAGH, A.: Thoughts on the New Eucharistic Prayers. In: Worship 43 (1969) 2-12.

KENNEDY, V.L.: The Moment of the Consecration and the Elevation of the Host. In: Medieval Studies 6 (1944) 121-150.

LAMBERTS, J.: The Elevation During the Eucharistic Celebration. Too Much of a Good Thing? In: QL 75 (1994) 135-153.

LEVESQUE, P.: Eucharistic Prayer Position: From Standing to Kneeling. In: QL 74 (1993) 30-42.

MAZZA, E.: The Eucharistic Prayers of the Roman Rite. New York, 1986.

MCKENNA, J.: The Epiclesis Revisited: A Look at Modern Eucharistic Prayers. In: ephLit 99 (1985) 314-336.

POWER, D.: The Sacrifice We Offer: The Tridentine Dogma and Its Reinterpretation. Edinburgh, 1987.

SCHNEIDERS, M.: Acclamations in their Eucharistic Prayer. In: Omnes Circumstantes: Contributions toward a History of the Role of the People in the Liturgy. Kampen 1990, 78-100.

SENN, F. (Ed.): New Eucharistic Prayers: An Ecumenical Study of Their Development and Structure. New York and Mahway NJ 1987.

SMOLARKSI, D.: Eucharistia: A Study of the Eucharistic Prayer. New York and Ramsey NJ 1982.

TAFT, R.: The Dialogue before the Anaphora in the Byzantine Eucharistic Liturgy II: The Sursum corda. In: OCP 54 (1988) 47-77.

TAFT, R.: The Interpolation of the Sanctus into the Anaphora: When and Where? A Review of the Dossier. In: OCP 57 (1991) 281-308; 58 (1992) 82-121.

VAGGAGINI, C.: The Canon of the Mass and the Liturgical Reform. Trans. P. Coughlin. Staten Island NY 1967.

WEGMAN, H.: The Rubrics of the Institution Narrative in the Roman Missal 1970. In: Liturgia, Opera Divina ed Umana, Bibliotheca Ephemerides Liturgicae Subsidia 28, Rome 1982, 319-328.

3.8. THE COMMUNION PART OF THE MASS

DANNEELS, G.: Communion under Both Kinds. In: The Church and the Liturgy, Concilium 2, Glen Rock NJ 1964, 153-158.

GALLAGHER, P.A.: The Communion Rite. In: Worship 63 (1989) 316-327.

KROSNICKI, T.: Ancient Patterns in Modern Prayer: Studies in Christian Antiquity 19, Washington 1973.

KROSNICKI, T.: New Blessings in the Missal of Paul VI. In: Worship 45 (1971) 199-205.

TAFT, R.: Receiving Communion – A Forgotten Symbol? In: Worship 57 (1983) 412-418.

TAFT, R.: The Fruits of Communion in the Anaphora of St. John Chrysostom. In: I. SCICOLONE (Hg.): Psallendum. Miscellanea di studi in onore del Prof. Jordi Pinelli Pons OSB (Analecta Liturgica 15 = Studia Anselmiana 105). Rom 1992, 275-302.

TAFT, R.: The Inclination Prayer Before Communion in the Byzantine Liturgy of St. John Chrysostom. A Study in Comparative Liturgy. In: Ecclesia Orans 3 (1986) 29-69.

TAFT, R.: The Litany following the Anaphora in the Byzantine Liturgy. In: NYSSEN, Wilhelm (Hg.): Simandron. Der Wachklopfer. Gedenkschrift für Klaus Gamber (1919-1989). Köln 1989, 233-256.

TAFT, R.: The Minister of the Holy Communion in the Eastern Traditions. In: G. KURUKA-PARAMPIL (Hg.): Tuvaik. Studies in Honour of Jacob Vellian (Syrian Churches Series 16). Kottayam 1995, 1-19.

TAFT, R.: Water into Wine. The Twice-mixed Chalice in the Byzantine Eucharist. In: Le Muséon 100 (1987) 323-342.

PART 4 THE SACRAMENTAL CELEBRATIONS OF THE CHURCH

4.1. ON THE SACRAMENTS AS SUCH AND THEIR RELATIONSHIP TO THE EUCHARIST AS FUNDAMENTAL SACRAMENT

GUZIE, T.: The Book of Sacramental Basics. New York 1981.

KELLEHER, M. M.: Liturgy as a Source for Sacramental Theology. In QL 72 (1991) 25-42.

KUCHAREK, C.: The Sacramental Mysteries. A Byzantine Approach. Allendale 1976.

MARTOS, J.: Doors to the Sacred: A Historical Introduction to Sacraments in the Christian Church. London 1981.

SCHILLEBEECKX, E.: Christ the Sacrament of Encounter with God. London 1963.

4.2. THE SACRAMENTS OF INITIATION

AUSTIN, G.: Anointing with the Spirit. The Rite of Confirmation. The Use of Oil and Chrism. New York 1985.

AUSTIN, G.: The essential Rite of Confirmation and Liturgical Tradition. In: EL 86 (1972) 214-224.

BALHOFF, M. J.: Age for Confirmation: Canonical Evidence. In: Jurist 45 (1985) 549-587.

BASTIAN, R.: The Effects of Confirmation in Recent Catholic Thought. Rom 1962.

BEDARD, W. M.: The Symbolism of the Baptismal Font. In Early Christian Thought. Washington 1951.

BEHRENS, J.: Confirmation, Sacrament of Grace. The theology, practice and law of the Roman Catholic Church and the Church of England. Herfordshire 1995.

BOHEN, B.: The Mystery of Confirmation. A Theology of the Sacrament. New York 1963.

BRAND, E. L.: New Rites of Initiation and Their Implications in the Lutheran Church. In: Studia Liturgica 12 (1977) 151-165.

BUCHANAN, C.: A Case for Infant Baptism. Bramcote Notts 1973.

BUCHANAN, C.: Baptismal Discipline. Bramcote Notts 1972 and 1974.

DIX, G.: Confirmation or the Laying on of Hands. London 1936.

DIX, G.: The Theology of Confirmation in Relation to Baptism. Westminster 31953.

FINN, Th. M.: The Liturgy of Baptism in the Baptismal Instuctions of John Chrysostom. Washington, 1967.

FISCHER, J. D. C.: Christian Initiation: The Reformation Period. London 1970.

FISCHER, J. D. C.: Confirmation then and now (ACC 60). London 1978.

FISCHER, J.D.C.: Christian Initiation. Baptism in the Medieval West. A Study in the Disintegration of the Primitive Rite of Initiation. Alcuin Club Collections 47. London 1965.

GENNEP, A. van: The Rites of Passasge, trans. M. Vizedom and G. Caffee, Chicago 1960.

GILLIS, I. R.: The Effect of the Sacrament of Confirmation. Washington 1940.

HARTMAN, L.: Into the Name of the Lord Jesus: Baptism in the Early Church. Studies of the New Testament and Its World. Edinbourgh 1997.

JEREMIAS, J.: Infant Baptism in the First Four Centuries. Philadelphia 1962.

JOHNSON, M. (Ed.): Living Water, Sealing Spirit. Readings on Christian Initiation. Collegeville 1995.

JOHNSON, M. E.: The Postchrismational Structure of Apostolic Tradition 21, the Witness of Ambrose of Milan, and a Trentative Hypothesis Regarding the Current Reform of Confirmation in the Roman Rite. In: Worship 70 (1996) 16-34.

KAVANAGH, A.: Confirmation: Origins and Reform. New York 1988.

KAVANAGH, A.: Initiation of Adults: The Rites. In: Worship 48 (1974) 318-335.

KAVANAGH, A.: On the Reform of Confirmation by Pope Paul VI in 1971 - Seminar. In: QL 70 (1989) 81-88.

KAVANAGH, A.: The Origins and Reform of Confirmation. In: QL 70 (1989) 69-80.

KAVANAGH, A.: The shape of baptism: The rite of christian initiation. New York 1974.

KLENTOS, J.: Rebaptizing Converts into the Orthodox Church. Old Perspectives on a New Problem. In: Studia Liturgica 29 (1999) 216-234.

LAMPE, G. W. H.: The Place of confirmation in the Baptismal Mystery. In: JThS 6 (1955) 110-116.

LAMPE, G. W. H.: The Seal of the Spirit. A Study in the Doctrine of Baptism and Confirmation in the New Testament and the Fathers. London 21967.

LEIJSSEN, L.: Confirmation. Status Quaestionis with an Overview of the Literature. In: QL 70 (1989) 1-28.

LEVADA, W. J.: Reflections on the age of confirmation. In: TS 57 (1996) 302-312.

LEVESQUE, J. L.: The Theology of the Postbaptismal Rites in the seventh and eighth century Gallican Church. In: EL 95 (1981) 3-43.

LOGAN, A. H. B.: Post-Baptismal Chrismation in Syria: the Evidence of Ignatius, the Didache and the Apostolic Constitutions. In: JThS 49 (1998) 92-108.

LYNCH, K.: The Sacramental Grace of Confirmation in Thirteenth-Century Theology. In: FrS 22 (1962) 32-149.172-300.

LYNCH, K.: The Sacrament of Confirmation in the Early-Middle Scholastic Period I. Texts. St. Bonaventure/New York u.a. 1957.

MARSH, Th.: A Study of Confirmation. In: IThQ 39 (1972) 149-163.319-336; 40 (1973) 125-147.

MARSH, Th.: Confirmation in Its Relation to Baptism. In: IThQ 27 (1960) 259-293.

MARSH, Th.: Gift of Community: Baptism and Confirmatio. Wilmington (Del.) 1984.

MARSH, Th.: The History and Significance of the Post-Baptismal Rites. In: IThQ 29 (1962) 175-206.

MASON, A. J.: The Relation of Confirmation to Baptism, as Taught in Holy Scripture and the Fathers. New York 1891.

MCDONNELL, K. / MONTAGUE, G.: Christian initiation and baptism in the Holy Spirit: evidence from the first eight centuries. Collegeville (Minn.) 1991.

MCDONNELL, K. / MONTAGUE, G.: Forum. A response to Paul Turner on "Christian Initiation and baptism in the Holy Spirit. In: Worship 71 (1997) 51-62.

MCKENZIE, T. / SAVELEVSKY, M. J.: Confirmation with First Communion? It Works! Chicago Catechumenate (May 1986) 16-23.

O'DOHERTY, M. K.: The Scholastic Teaching on the Sacrament of Confirmation. Washington 1949.

O'DONNELL, C.: The ecclesiastical dimension of Confirmation. A Study in Saint Thomas and in the revised rite. Rom 1990.

PETRAS, D. M.: Confirmation in the American Catholic Church: A Byzantine Perspective. Washington 1986.

POCKNEE, C. E.: Water and Spirit. A Study in the Relation of Baptism and Confirmation. London 1967.

QINN, F. F.: Confirmation Reconsidered: Rite and Meaning. In: Worship 59 (1985) 354-370).

RILEY, H. M.: Christian Initiation: A Comparative Study of the Interpretation of the Baptismal Liturgy in the Mystagogical Writings of Cyril of Jerusalem, John Chrysostom, Theodore of Mopsuestia and Ambrose of Milan. Washington, 1974.

Rite of christian Initiation of Adults. Prepared by the International Commission on English in the Liturgy and the Bishop's Committee on the Liturgy. Washington, 1988.

STEVENSON, K. W.: The Byzantine Liturgy of the Baptism. In: Studia Liturgica 17 (1987) 176-190.

SULLIVAN, F. A.: Baptism in the Holy Spirit: a Catholic interpretation of the Pentecostal Experience: Gr. 55 (1974) 49-68.

THORNTON, L. S.: Confirmation. Its Place in the Baptismal Mystery. Westminster 1954.

THURIAN, Max (Ed.): Churches Respond to Baptism, Eucharist, Ministry. Official responses to the 'Baptism, Eucharist and Ministry'. Text. Bd. I-VI (Faith and Order Paper 129, 132, 135, 137, 143, 144). Genf 1986-88.

THURIAN, Max (Ed.): Ecumenical Perspectives on Baptism, Eucharist and Ministry (Faith and Order Paper 116). Genève 1983.

TURNER, P.: Forum: Christian Initiation and Baptism in the Holy Spirit. In: Worship 70 (1996) 446-452.

TURNER, P.: Forum: confusion over confirmation. In: Worship 71 (1997) 537-545.

TURNER, P.: Sources of Confirmation. From the Fathers through the Reformers. Collegeville 1993.

TURNER, P.: The Meaning and Practice of Confirmation: Perspectives from a Sixteenth Century Controversy, New York u. a. 1987.

TURNER, P.: The Origins of Confirmation: An Analysis of Aidan Kavanagh's Hypothesis. In: Worship 65 (1991) 320-336.

WALSH, L. G.: The Sacraments of Initiation. London 1988.

WHITAKER, E.C.: Documents of the Baptismal Liturgy. 2nd ed, London 1970.

WHITAKER, E.C.: The History of the Baptismal Formula. In: The Journal of Ecclesiatical History 16 (1965) 1-12.

YSEBAERT, J.: Greek Baptismal Terminology. Its Origins and Early Development (GCP 1). Nijmegen 1962.

4.3. THE EUCHARIST AS SACRAMENT OUTSIDE OF MASS

COOKE, B.: Ministry to Word and Sacraments. History and Theology. Philadelphia 1976.

DANN, A.S.: Eucharistic Worship and Devotion outside Mass. Ed. By the Bishops' Commitee on the Liturgy (Study Text 11), Washington 1987.

GRABKA, G.: The Viaticum: A Study of Its Cultural Background.In: Traditio 9 (1953) 1-43.

HANNON, J.J.: Holy Viaticum: A Historical Synopsis and a Commentary. Washington 1951.

KING, A: Eucharistic Reservation in the Western Church. New York 1965.

MITCHELL, N.D.: Cult and Controversy: The Worship of the Eucharist Outside Mass. Studies in the Reformed Rites of the Catholic Church, vol. 4, New York 1982.

POWER, D.: The Eucharistic Mystery: Revitalizing the Tradition. New York 1992.

RUBIN, M: Corpus Christi: The Eucharist in Late Medieval Culture. Cambridge 1991.

4.4. THE SACRAMENT OF PENANCE

FINK, P.E.: History of the Sacrament of Reconciliation. In: Alternative Futures for Worship IV, Collegeville 1987, 43-72.

GY, P.M.: Penance and Reconciliation. In: Martimort, Church at Prayer III, 101-115.

POSCHMANN, B.: Penance and Anointing of the Sick. Trans. F. Courtney. New York 1964.

4.5. THE ANOINTING OF THE SICK

BOTTING, M.: Pastoral and Liturgical Ministry to the Sick. Bramcote Nottes 1978.

COLLINS, M. / POWER, D.: The Pastoral Care of the Sick. Concilium 234. Philadelphia 1991.

DUDLEY, M. / ROWELL, G. (Edd.): The Oil of Gladness: Anointing in the Christian Tradition. London-Collegeville 1993.

PORTER, H.B.: The Origin of the Medieval Rite for Anointing the Sick or Dying. In: Journal of Theological Studies 7 (London 1956) 211-225.

POSCHMANN, B.: Penance and Anointing of the Sick. Trans. F. Courtney. New York 1964.

ZIEGLER, J.: Let Them Anoint the Sick. Collegeville 1987.

4.6. THE SACRAMENT OF HOLY ORDERS

BARRETT, A.: The New Ordination Rite. In: Liturgy 15 (1990-1991) 121-131.

BOTTE, B.: Holy Orders in the Ordination Prayers. In: The Sacrament of Holy Orders. Collegeville 1962

BRADSHAW, P.F.: Ordination Rites of the Ancient Churches. New York 1990.

BRADSHAW, P.F.: The Participation of Other Bishops in the Ordination of a Bishop in the Apostolic Tradition of Hippolytus. In: Studia Patristica 18/2 (1989) 355ff.

BRADSHAW, P.F.: The Anglican Ordinal. Its History and Development from the Reformation to the Present Day. London 1971.

BUCHANAN, C.: Modern Anglican Ordination Rites. Bramcote 1987.

CUNNINGHAM, A.: The Bishop in the Church: Patristic Texts on the Role of the Episkopos. Theology and Life Series 13. Wilmington Del. 1985.

DIANICH, S.: The Ordained Ministry in Rites and Actions. In: Concilium 133 (1980) 59-65.

DIX, G.: The Ministry in thr Early Church. In: K.E. Kirk (Ed.): The Apostolic Ministry: Essays on the History and the Doctrine of Episcopacy. London1946, 183-303.

GY, P.M.: Notes on the Early Terminology of Christian Priesthood. In: The Sacrament of Holy Orders, Collegweville 1962, 98-115.

MARTIMORT, A.G.: Deaconesses: An Historical Study. San Francisco 1986.

POWER, D.: Appropriate Ordination Rites: A Historical Perspective. In: Alternative Futures for Worship VI, Collegeville 1987, 131-137.

WOOD, S.: The Sacramentality of Episcopal Consecration. In: Theological Studies 51 (Woodstock 1990) 479-496.

4.7. THE SACRAMENT OF MARRIAGE

CHARALAMBIDIS, S.: Marriage in the Orthodox Church. In: OiC (= One in Christ, London) 15 (1979) 204-223.

CHRYSSAVGIS, J.: The Sacrament of Marriage: An Orthodox Perspective. In: Asia Journal of Theology, 2 (Singapore 1988) 450-458.

EVDOKIMOV, P.: The Sacrament of Love. The nuptial mystery in the light of the orthodox tradition. New York 1985.

GOH, J. C. K.: Christian Marriage as a Realsymbol: Towards a Performative Understanding of the Sacrament. In: QL 76 (1995) 254-264.

MEYENDORFF, J.: Christian Marriage in Byzantium: The Canonical and Liturgical Tradition. In: Dumbarton Oaks Papers 44 (1990) 99-107.

PAYNGOT, C.: The Syro-Malabar Marriage. In: G. Farnedi (Ed.): La celebrazione cristiana del matrimonio, studi e testi. Atti del II. Congresso internazionale di Liturgia (Roma 1985) Roma 1986, 262-282.

SCHMEMANN, A.: The Mystery of Love. In: For the Life of the World. Sacraments and Orthodoxy, Crestwood-New York 2nd ed. 1973, 81-94.

SCHMEMANN, Alexandre: The Indissolubility of Marriage: The Theological Tradition of the East. In: W. Bassett (Ed.): The Bond of Marriage. An ecumenical and interdisciplinary study. Notre Dame-London 1968, 97-116.

SMIRENSKY, Alvian N.: The Evolution of the Present Rite of Matrimony and Parallel Canonical Developments. In: St. Vladimir's Seminary Quaterly 8 (New York 1964) 38-47.

SCHWERDTFEGER, A.: Ethnological Sources of the Christian Marriage Ceremony. Stockholm 1982.

STAVROPOULOS, A. M.: The Understanding of Marriage in the Orthodox Church. In: One in Christ 15 (London 1979) 57-64.

WARE, K.: The Sacrament of Love. The Orthodox Understanding of Marriage and its Breakdown. In: DR (= The downside review) 109 (1991) 79-93.

4.8. FURTHER SACRAMENTAL CELEBRATIONS OF THE CHURCH

BAUMSTARK, A.: Comparative Liturgy. Trans. F.L. Cross. Westminster, Md. 1958.

GY, P.M.: The Liturgy of Death – The Funeral Rite of the New Roman Ritual. In: The Way, Supplement No. 11 (Autumn 1970) 59-75.

MUNCEY, R.W.: A History of the Consecration of Churches and Churchyards. Cambridge 1930.

OWUSU, V.K.: The Roman Funeral Liturgy: History, Celebration and Theologie. Netteal 1993.

PEREZ, A.: Funerary Rituals and Inculturation: Can Cultural Practices for the Dead Enhance Our Funeral Celebrations? In: QL 77 (1996) 117-123.

ROWELL, G.: The Liturgy of Christian Burial: An Introductory Survey of the Historical Development of Christian Burial Rites. In: Alcuin Club Collections 59, London 1977, 31-56.

RUSH, A.: Death and Burial in Christian Antiquity. Washington 1941.

RUTHERFORD, R.: The Death of a Christian: The Order of Christian Funerals. Rev. Ed. Studies in the Reformed Rites of the Catholic Church VII, Colleville 1990.

PART 5 THE HALLOWING OF TIME 1: LITURGIA VERBI – LITURGY OF THE HOURS AND LITURGY OF THE WORD

5.1. THE HALLOWING OF TIME

DE VOGÜÉ, A.: The Rule of St. Benedict: A Doctrinal and Spiritual Commentary. In: Cistercian Studies 54, Kalamazoo Mich 1983, 127-172.

ROGUET, A.M.: The Liturgy of the Hours: The General Instruction with Commentary. Collegeville 1971.

TAFT, R.: Thanksgiving for the Light: Towards a Theology of Vespers. In: Diakonia 13 (1978) 27-50.

TAFT, R.: The Liturgy of the Hours in East and West: The Origins of the Divine Office and Its Meaning for Today. Collegeville 1986.

5.2. THE HISTORICAL DEVELOPMENT OF THE LITURGY OF THE HOURS

BAUDOT, J.: The Roman Breviary: its Sources and History. London, 1909.

BECKWITH, R. T.: The Daily and Weekly Worship of the Primitive Church in Relation to Its Jewish Antecedents. In: Evangelical Quarterly 56 (1984) 65-80.

BRADSHAW, P.F.: Daily Prayer in the Early Church: A Study of the Origin and Early Development of the Divine Office. New York 1982.

LEGG, J. W.: The Second Recension of the Quignon Breviary. Henry Bradshaw Society Vols. 35 and 42, London 1908, 1911.

MATEOS, J.: The Morning and Evening Office. In: Worship 42 (1968) 31-47.

SALMON, P.: The Breviary Through the Centuries. Trans. Sister David Mary. Collegeville, Minn., 1962.

5.3. THE RENEWED LITURGY OF THE HOURS AND ITS ELEMENTS

CAMPBELL, S.: From Breviary to Liturgy of Hours: The Structural Reform of the Roman Office 1964-1971. Collegeville 1995.

5.4. THE LITURGY OF THE HOURS IN THE CHURCHES OF THE EAST AND THE REFORMATION

GUIVER, G.: Company of voice. The society for Promoting Christian Knowledge 1988.

STRUNK, O.: The Byzantine Office at Hagia Sophia. In: Dumbarton Oaks Papers 9-10 (1955-1956) 175-202, esp. 200-201.

TAFT, R.: Selected Bibliography on the Byzantine Liturgy of the Hours. OCP 48 (1982) 358-404.

TAFT, R.: Mount Athos: A Late Chapter in the History of the Byzantine Rite. In: Dumbarton Oaks Papers 42 (1988) 179-194.

KARAY TRIPP, D.: Daily Prayer in the Reformed Tradition. An Initial Survey. In: Studia Liturgica 21 (1991) 76-107; 190-219.

5.5. SUNDAY WORSHIP IN THE ABSENCE OF A PRIEST

BARRAS, P.: Sunday Assemblies in the Absence of a Priest: The Situation and Trends in France. In: Studia Liturgica 26 (1996) 91-103.

BÜSSE, H: Worship Without a Priest. In: Studia Liturgica 26 (1996) 104-112.

HUGHES, K.: Sunday Celebrations in the Absence of Priest: Gift or Threat? In: Studia Liturgica 26 (1996) 113-118.

PART 6 THE HALLOWING OF TIME 2: CELEBRATING THE YEAR OF THE LORD

6.1. THE YEAR OF THE LORD: THE ANNUAL CELEBRATION OF CHRIST'S SAVING MYSTERIES

ADAM, A.: The Liturgical Year: Its History and Its Meaning after the Reform of the Liturgy. Trans. M. O'Connell. New York 1981; Collegeville 1990.

BUGNINI, A.: Rhe Reform of the Liturgy (1948-1975), chap. 21. Trans. M. J. O'Connell. Collegeville, Minn., 1990.

FRERE, W. H.: Studies in Early Roman Liturgy. Vol. 1, The Kalendar. Alcuin Club Collections 28. London, 1930.

TAFT, R.: The Liturgical Year: Studies, Prospects, Reflections. In: Worship 55 (1981) 2-23.

TALLEY, T.: The Origins of the Liturgical Year. New York 1986.

THURSTON, H.: Calendar: The Catholic Encyclopedia III, New York 1908, 158-166.

6.2. SUNDAY AS THE WEEKLY PASSOVER, THE CHRISTIAN WEEK AND EMBER DAYS

GARCÍA, J.: Contributions and Challanges to the Theology of Sunday. In: Worship 52 (1978) 369-374.

JACOBSON, B. S.: The Sabbath Service. An exposition and analysis of its structure, contents, language and ideas. Tel Aviv 1981.

PICKERING, W.: The Secularized Sabbath: formerly Sunday. Now the Weekend, in: SYRB 5. 1972, 33-47.

RORDORF, W.: Sunday. The History of the Day of Rest and Worship in the Earliest Centuries of the Christian Church. Trans. A.A.K. Graham. Philadelphias 1968.

TAFT, R.: Sunday in the Byzantine Tradition. In: Beyond East and West: Problems in Liturgical Understanding. Washington 1984, 31-48.

6.3. THE EASTER FESTIVE CYCLE

ANIKUZHIKATTIL, M.: The Formation and Structure of Eastern Penitential Liturgies. In: QL 72 (1991) 231-240. D 18,72

BERTONIERE, G.: The Historical Development of the Easter Vigil and Related Services in the Greek Church: Orientalia Christiana Analecta 193. Rome 1972.

CANTALAMESSA, R.: Easter in the Early Church. Trans. J. Quigley and L. Lienhard. Collegeville 1993.

CHUPUNGCO, A.: Shaping the Easter Feast. Washington 1992.

CHUPUNGCO, A.: The cosmic elements of Christian Passover (Analecta liturgica 3. Studia Anselmiana). Roma 1977.

POORTHUIS, Marcel: The Improperia and Judaism. In: QL 72 (1991) 1-24.

REGAN, P.: The Fifty Days and the Fiftieth Day. In: Worship 55 (1981) 194-218.

SENN, F.: Should Christians Celebrate the Passover? In: P. F. Bradshaw / L. A. Hoffman (Hgg.): Passover and Easter. The Symbolic Structuring of Sacred Seasons. Notre Dame, Indiana 1999.

STEVENSON, K.: The Ceremonies of Light: Their Shape and Function in the Paschal vigil Liturgy. In: EphLit 99 (1985) 170-185.

TAFT, R.: In the Bridegroom's Absence: The Paschal Triduum in the Byzantine Chruch. In: La celebrazione del Triduo Pasquale: Anamnesis e mimesis. Atti del III Congresso Internazionale di Liturgia Rome May 1988. Rome 1990, 71-97.

TAFT, R.: A Tale of Two Cities: The Byzantine Holy Week Triduum as a Paradigm of Liturgical History. In: J. Neil Alexander (Ed.): Time and Community: In Honor of Thomas Julian Talley. Washington 1990, 21-41.

VAN DIJK, S.J.P.: The Medieval Easter Vesper of the Roman Clergy. In: Sacris 19 (Steenbrugge 1969/1970) 261-363.

YUVAL, I. J.: Easter and Passover As Early Jewish-Christian Dialogue? In: P. F. Bradshaw / L. A. Hoffman (Hgg.): Passover and Easter. The Symbolic Structuring of Sacred Seasons. Notre Dame, Indiana 1999.

6.4. THE CHRISTMAS CYCLE

MERRAS, Merja: The Origins of the Celebration of the Christian Feast of Epiphany. An Ideological, Cultural and Historical Study. Joensuu/Suomi: Joensuu University Press, 1995.

ROLL, Susan: Botte Revisited: A Turning Point in the Research on the Origins of Christmas and Epiphany. In: QL 74 (1993) 153-170. D 18,74

STRITTMATTER, A.: Christmas and Epiphany: Origins and Antecedents: Theology 7 (1942) 600-626.

6.5. FEASTS OF THE LORD THROUGHOUT THE YEAR

BROOKS, N. C.: Processional Drama and Dramatic Processions in Germany in the Late Middle Ages. In: Jounral of English and Germanic Philology 32 (1933) 141-171.

FLETCHER, R.A.: Celebration at Jerusalem on March 25th in the sixth century. In: Studia Patristica V, Berlin 1962, 30-34.

GALLOP, R.: Corpus Christi in the Austrian Tyrol. In: Folk-Lore 45 (1935) 346-351.

HELLER, D.: A Common Date for Easter: A Reality in the New Millennium? In: Studia Liturgica 30 (2000) 239-248.

JOHNSTON, A.F.: The Guild of Corpus Christi and the Procession of Corpus Christi in York. In: Medieval Studies 38 (1976) 372-384.

NELSON, A.H.: The Medieval English Stage. Corpus Christi pageants and plays. Chicago 2nd ed. 1975.

RUBIN, M: Corpus Christi: The Eucharist in Late Medieval Culture. Cambridge 1991.

6.6. FEASTS OF MARY AND OF THE SAINTS

BROWN, P.: The Cult of the Saints. London 1981.

BROWN, P.: The Cult of the Saints, its Rise and Function in latin christianity. Chicago 1981.

CUNNINGHAM, L.: The Meaning of Saints. San Francisco 1980.

DONOVAN, K.: The Sanctoral. In: Ch. Jones (Ed.): The Study of Liturgy, London 1978, 419-431.

FISCHER, B.: Why is the Feast of the Visitation celebrated on July 2? In: J. Neil Alexander (Ed.): Time and Community: In Honor of Thomas Julian Talley. Washington 1990, 77-80.

KENNEDY, L.: The Saints of the Canon of the Mass. Citt del Vaticano 1938.

KISPAUGH, M.J.: The Feast of the Presentation of the Virgin Mary in the Temple. Washington 1941.

MORETON, B.: The Mass-Sets of the Sanctoral. In: The Eighth-Century Gelasian Sacramentary: A Study in Tradition. Oxford 1976, 102-159.

WARD, A.: Sancti Spiritus Luce repleta. The blessed Virgin of the Rotulus of Ravenna in Recent Latin Missals. In: Marianum 53 (1991) 221-252.

WHALEN, M.: Saints and Their Feasts: An Ecumencial Exploration. In: Worship 63 (1989) 194-209.

WILSON, S. (Ed.): Saints and Their Cults. Cambridge 1983.

7.2. INDEX OF NAMES AND TOPICS

A

C

D

E

G

I

N

W